WRITE MOVES

WRITE MOVES

[A CREATIVE WRITING GUIDE & ANTHOLOGY]

NANCY PAGH

broadview press

BROADVIEW PRESS – www.broadviewpress.com
Peterborough, Ontario, Canada

Founded in 1985, Broadview Press remains a wholly independent publishing house. Broadview's focus is on academic publishing; our titles are accessible to university and college students as well as scholars and general readers. With over 600 titles in print, Broadview has become a leading international publisher in the humanities, with world-wide distribution. Broadview is committed to environmentally responsible publishing and fair business practices.

Library and Archives Canada Cataloguing in Publication

Pagh, Nancy, 1963-, author
Write moves : a creative writing guide & anthology / Nancy Pagh.

Includes bibliographical references and index.
ISBN 978-1-55481-226-4 (paperback)

1. Authorship. 2. Creative writing. I. Title.

PN145.P34 2016 808'.02 C2016-902862-3

Broadview Press handles its own distribution in North America
PO Box 1243, Peterborough, Ontario K9J 7H5, Canada
555 Riverwalk Parkway, Tonawanda, NY 14150, USA
Tel: (705) 743-8990; Fax: (705) 743-8353
email: customerservice@broadviewpress.com

Distribution is handled by Eurospan Group in the UK, Europe, Central Asia, Middle East, Africa, India, Southeast Asia, Central America, South America, and the Caribbean. Distribution is handled by Footprint Books in Australia and New Zealand.

Broadview Press acknowledges the financial support of the Government of Canada through the Canada Book Fund for our publishing activities.

Canada

Edited by Karen Taylor

Book design by Chris Rowat Design

PRINTED IN CANADA

Table of Contents

("see also" means this text is quoted in full within the chapters)

Thanks

I'm grateful for the influence and support of so many people, among them

My parents, Sally and Richard Pagh, who read to me from the start and encouraged an early love of language and wordplay;

Many talented and caring teachers, especially Audrey Eyler, Melody Graulich, Anne McCracken, Donald Murray, Thelma Palmer-Lumina, and Laurie Ricou;

Julie Walchli, Tomi Eng, and Roberta Birks, and Brenda Miller and Suzanne Paola, whose textbooks *Landmarks: A Process Reader for Canadian Writers* and *Tell It Slant: Writing and Shaping Creative Nonfiction* were particularly inspiring as I set out to imagine my own;

Colleagues, peers, and friends who contributed ideas, reactions, and good vibes: Bruce Beasley, Kathy Chung, Sharon Damkaer, Janel Erchinger-Davis, Linda Flanagan, Margi Fox, Sam Green, Carol Guess, Jacqueline Howse, Iris Jones, Kristiana Kahakauwila, Judy Minks, Oliver de la Paz, Shannon Smythe, Kate Trueblood, June Walchli, Kami Westhoff, and Jeanne Yeasting;

Anonymous readers of drafts along the way; Austin VanKirk for a thorough look during revision; Karen Taylor for copyediting expertise; editor Marjorie Mather for saying "why don't you write it?" when I complained that the Broadview catalogue didn't have the textbook I was looking for;

All the students who patiently teach me how to teach; Brenna Adelman, Kim Bowman, Jessica Lee, Paul Rentko, and mic silverline for contributing ideas to the manuscript; Arlan Cashier, Carlos Mendoza, Madison Minder, Mallory Opel, Theresa Williams, and Bethany Yeager for sharing their writing in this book; and

Hali Laudermilk Cassels (1978–2015), who believed I was her mentor, but was mine.

Welcome

> Every moment, I am, without wanting or trying to, telling you to write like me. But I hope you learn to write like you. In a sense, I hope I don't teach you how to write but how to teach yourself to write. At all times keep your crap detector on. If I say one thing that helps, good. If what I say is of no help, let it go.
>
> —*Richard Hugo*[1]

Welcome Reader

I'm glad to meet you here on the page. You open this book for the same reason I imagined, drafted, and revised it: to learn more about how creative writing happens and how it moves us. I'm fascinated by the ways creative writing (and other forms of expression—photography, drawing, music, film, dance...) transports and changes people. I'm seduced by the possibilities and power of words—and committed to the notion that writing gets better when we invest in it, tend to it. For years I've collected and savored advice from favorite authors, artists, and educators. I composed this book for myself, to discover how the pieces fit together. And I wrote it as an extension of the work I do each day, trying to teach students in the caring and honest ways others have taught me.

The experts who astonished and shaped me most—Natalie Goldberg, Donald Murray, Richard Hugo (and my less known but no less appreciated high-school and university teachers)—all taught using their strong sense of personality and voice: they communicated as distinct, specific, *real* people. As a teacher, I noticed creative writing textbooks usually lack the vivacity that animated my own mentors and make literature itself so intense and pleasurable to read. Traditional textbooks tell us to write using "voice" but are themselves dry, voiceless. They offer tons of information about technique (useful, necessary stuff for the growing writer) but without the quirkiness, or—say it: FUN—of inspirational and aspirational "trade" books on writing. It seemed cold and strange to me that textbooks avoid mentioning the emotional experiences that cause us to write, that we experience as we *try* to write, that can happen as a result of having written.

In *Write Moves* I'm reaching out to you, not in the stiff exposition of a traditional textbook but as myself—an actual writer and woman, living in a certain time and place, with (for better and for worse) my own identity. My voice is most potent in the headnotes for each chapter after this introduction. If you find their informality irritating or less than useful, please skip those parts before starting the body of each chapter. I've woven the experienced voices of others into each chapter: you won't have just me as your companion in these pages; you'll have many writers and artists. From these examples and insights, glean what lights you up, what moves you forward, what helps you "learn to write like you."

Welcome Student

I've been thinking of you for more than twenty years now. About your bravery to sign up for a creative writing class when many of you—most—have had little experience with imaginative expression in school. You wonder: *How can creativity be graded? Where will I get ideas to write about? Do I have to write about personal things and show it to the class?* You love to read (or used to, before college assignments left too little time to devour stories) and you wish you could write something stunning like the books that inspired you. You hope so...but suspect it takes a gift, a special kind of person, to be a writer. Can creative writing be taught?

It can be taught and you can learn it. Just like someone who has never sketched before can learn to see and draw a tree or a boat, you'll discover the habits of attention and mind for writing. You'll learn craft—for the sketch artist, that's how to angle the pencil, how to create shadow and a sense of proportion, how to bring life to the line. For the writer, too, there is craft—image, sound, character, plot, and more to explore. You'll discover genre: what makes a poem a poem, or a story a story. You'll soon understand that creative writing isn't a competition about who's had the most outrageous life to confess or invent. Your ordinary life, ordinary self, is enough for the work ahead. Renowned photographer Sally Mann reassures us of this in her memoir *Hold Still*:

> Artists go out of their way to reinforce the perception that good art is made by singular people, people with an exceptional gift. But I don't believe I am that exceptional, so what is this that I'm making?
>
> Ordinary art is what I am making. I am a regular person doggedly making ordinary art. [...] Art is seldom the result of true genius; rather, it is the product of hard work and skills learned and tenaciously practiced by regular people.[2]

Welcome Teacher

You have great ideas about how to organize and teach your course. This book is amenable, flexible: assign it in whole or in part, in any order you choose. *Write Moves* serves as one text, combining an introduction to practice and process, a guide to matters of craft, a discussion of the genres most taught in introductory imaginative writing courses, and an anthology of diverse literary readings. You know best whether to begin with the lens of fiction, the craft of imagery, an invitation to journaling, a discussion of a poem, or a leap into a theme such as "writing about family." You know what bits your students don't need at their level and what's outside the scope of your course. Chapters are parsed into titled sections—you can assign or discuss *parts* of chapters easily with this shape. If your class is a workshop, this text supports it without assuming the format you'll adopt. Craft is presented in a cross-genre manner, useful whether your students are directed to write within, or free from, genre restrictions.

Each chapter concludes with prompts. Pick and choose, modify, rearrange, supplement, steal—they're enumerated just for your ease of reference communicating with students. You'll also find a list of suggested anthology readings near the conclusion of most chapters. *Write Moves* includes readings because good writers are also good readers; readings are presented separate from the chapters. Suggested texts pair well with their chapters (and prompts often reference them), but the tables of contents, arranged alphabetically by author, by genre, and by theme, make it simple for you to assign readings as *you* see fit, or to encourage your students to peruse and respond to works they select.

No anthology can include everyone's favorite instructional texts, and it isn't my goal to try. I've balanced canonical and noncanonical voices from Canadian, American, and global authors reflecting a range of styles, forms, themes, identities, and periods. With prose I've favored short texts, to model works of the lengths we often assign student writers. With poetry I've made sure to find unique work exhibiting (and bending) a range of forms.

For genre instruction, I present fiction and creative nonfiction in terms of story and personal essay because "Intro to" courses rarely cover the long forms (such as the novel, novella, memoir, new journalism). However, the definitions, traditions, and ethics of fiction and creative nonfiction are explicitly discussed in the story and essay chapters, and, for those teaching through the lens of fiction or nonfiction, those chapters and the alternate tables of contents support your choice. I've omitted drama because its teaching has largely migrated to departments of theater or drama; instructors who elect to include it will need a supplement to this text.

My own experience publishing creative writing is as a poet (although I've written a book of nonfiction too and some pieces for kids). Over the years, one of my beefs with multi-genre textbooks (usually penned by academics or novelists) has been their lack of attention to *sound* across genres. I've tried in particular to address this gap and also to help new writers understand *reflection* (which I've always found slippery to articulate and unaddressed in textbooks I've used). I found those chapters especially satisfying to work out.

I hope you'll discover useful and exciting material in *Write Moves*—resources that help you teach like yourself. I'd welcome and appreciate your feedback at Nancy.Pagh@wwu.edu.

Sincerely,
Nancy Pagh

Notes

1 Richard Hugo, *The Triggering Town: Lectures and Essays on Poetry and Writing* (New York: Norton, 1979), 3.

2 Sally Mann, *Hold Still: A Memoir with Photographs* (New York: Little, Brown and Company, 2015), 283.

PART I
PRACTICE

Why Write?

> I have written for many reasons: to feed my family and myself, to get ahead, to exercise power, to call attention to myself, to be published, to understand, to entertain, to make something that is my own, to find out what I have to say, and, above all, from need.... I can't explain it, but I must do it.
>
> —*Donald Murray*[1]

When I was thirteen years old, I would wake up in the middle of the night with voices in my head. Already you're thinking: the author of this book is crazy! But wait a minute—. I would wake up in my twin bed, in the soupy darkness that results when your parents cover your window with red curtains made from upholstery fabric, and I would hear words in a foreign language. I don't remember now what those words were, only that they seemed complicated, multisyllabic, and beautiful—the way that words can sound delicate, muscular, or crisp before we have any idea what they mean. For a while, I would lie there under the heavy cotton quilt, rolling its little knots and tassels of yarn between my fingers, trying to memorize the strange words. In the fall, I could hear the foghorn sounding its voice several miles off, down on the Guemes Channel, competing for my attention. Or maybe a slit of streetlight came in where the heavy curtains met—enough light to make out the face of the Six Million Dollar Man or the tartan-decked forms of the Bay City Rollers, pulled from Tiger Beat *fan magazine and arranged so carefully (I'm a Virgo) on my bedroom wall. Pretty soon I was thinking about band class, about Mr. Strickland throwing erasers at the boys in the trumpet section and he meant it, too, and the next thing you know it's morning and time for the big decision about trying to wear blue eye shadow or not. Where did those words go?*

I started to keep a notebook under my bed. Then when I woke up and heard the words, I could roll over, scrawl them down phonetically in the darkness, and trap them until the light of day. It surprised me to discover that those beautiful foreign words were in my own tongue—English. I looked them up in the Big Dictionary at school. Eulogistic. Unutterable. Infinitesimal. Tintinnabulation. Cinnabar. Assuage. Enigma. *What those words meant, I had never thought about before.*

> *But I wanted to. I felt as if my life might move beyond the boy band on the wall, beyond the eye shadow, the foghorn, the very tired band teacher, beyond thick red curtains—if I had the words to imagine it.*
>
> *Now that I look back, I see it wasn't crazy at all.*

Language That Is Our Own

Creative writers are sometimes stereotyped as sad and solitary figures, but writing is an expression of hope and connection. We need to communicate—to announce we're here, we exist, we matter. We wouldn't try to express ourselves if we felt hopeless about the possibility of connection. Even writing in private, just for ourselves, we hope to mean and understand something. No matter what subjects you choose to explore as you push your cursor across the field of the page, understand: as a new writer, you're not signing up to suffer or to isolate yourself. You're joining a community of people who write because we hope our words can add up to something that will surprise us, change us, *move* us and our readers.

The urge to write is a close relative to the urge a sculptor has to dig her hands in clay, the urge of a painter to stretch a canvas and move paint around, the urge of a composer to arrange silences between notes. We experience the urge to write for all sorts of different reasons and at different stages in life. Some of us are storytellers from the moment we can talk—we want to invent narratives before we can grip a yellow pencil. Some begin to write the first time we fall in love. New Mexico poet Jimmy Santiago Baca discovered writing poetry as an adult, in a maximum-security prison, as an alternative to violence. Emily Carr wrote in her journals to understand what she was trying to paint in the forests of British Columbia. Neurologist Oliver Sacks began writing at age fourteen: "My journals are not written for others, nor do I usually look at them myself, but they are a special, indispensable form of talking to myself."[2] My friend Paul started writing poems in his sixties, after his wife Susan died of cancer. Paul was a professor of philosophy, the author of many scholarly essays about medical ethics. But he felt he needed to say and discover something in his grief; although he'd never written a poem before, poetry was the shape his impressions had to make.

In Raymond Carver's story "A Small, Good Thing," a character named Ann experiences shock and grief over her young son. In a hospital, she shakes her head and tries to speak meaningfully with her husband and their doctor:

> "No, no," she said. "I can't leave him here, no." She heard herself say that and thought how unfair it was that the only words that came out were the sort of words used on TV shows where people were stunned by violent or sudden deaths. She wanted her words to be her own.[3]

How rare it is, and yet how necessary it sometimes feels, to have the ability to use authentic language that is our own. Words surround and interrupt us almost constantly, usually written with the intent to sell, manipulate, or distract us. We learn to tune them out—and when we *do* listen, it's with a healthy dose of skepticism. What we say, write, and even think tends to adopt the qualities of this bombarding, synthetic language. But when something *really matters* to us, we want to get outside the superficiality and sameness of that language, using words to dig someplace deep, explicit, and true. Although it is not "therapy," creative writing is (in Richard Hugo's words) "a slow, accumulative way of accepting one's life as valid."[4]

Chaos and Control

Creative writing, also called "imaginative writing," differs in purpose from other written communication. It exists to construct experiences for the reader—experiences we taste, touch, see, hear, and smell with our imagination. Other texts are designed to impart information clearly—and we are informed, but not emotionally *moved*. When we finish reading informative texts, their ideas may linger (we "get the gist" of them), but *the experience and expression* dissolves. We're used to seeing language function simply to convey information, and, as a result, we read by skimming. This relationship with language changes for the creative writer: we learn to read with great attention to the experience of language, and we learn to write with this same level of attention.

This difference between skimming and reading is part of the reason that, as readers, we can savor a favorite story over and over again and our enjoyment and understanding increase. All texts—office memos, résumés, bank statements, tweets, and the like—can be read repeatedly and analyzed for meanings beyond the surface. But creative writing is unique because it's composed with this purpose and experience in mind—not just for the reader, but also for the writer. The practice of imaginative writing is not about having an idea or point and effectively communicating it to your reader. Instead, creative writing begins with a scene, an image, a memory, a moment, a character, or even a sound or rhythm—and, as the words come, they trigger us to move and play, to discover what we didn't know we could mean. Rarely—so rarely!—do we know exactly what our story will reveal and then simply write it down. I've written scores of poems and for sure, *for sure*, the worst ones said what I meant when I first sat down to write them. The best grabbed me by the throat and shook me hard. They made me laugh out loud or nod my head and cry. They took me someplace I did not anticipate. We feel this sense of strangeness and transportation as we make creative writing, so that our readers will feel it too.

People who keep writing do it because we're open to this sensation of exploration, even though exploration carries risk and can make us uncomfortable. The practice of imaginative writing is a kind of courtship between the disorder of possibility and the order of language. As with any interesting courtship, there's some tension. The effort to express precisely and beautifully what might be said is, for a few authors, a kind of agony: the sentiment "I hate writing, but I love having written" has been attributed to authors as diverse as Robert Louis Stevenson, Dorothy Parker, Frank Norris, and George R.R. Martin.[5]

For many others, though, the experience of writing is a sweet dance, a shifting balance between chaos and control—we begin to write in one direction and then language leads us off into new possibilities and surprises. Chilean poet Pablo Neruda expresses how sensual the experience of writing is for him:

> I run after certain words... They are so beautiful that I want to fit them all into my poem... I catch them in mid-flight, as they buzz past, I trap them, clean them, peel them, I set myself in front of the dish, they have a crystalline texture to me, vibrant, ivory, vegetable, oily, like fruit, like algae, like agates, like olives... And then I stir them, I shake them, I drink them, I gulp them down, I mash them, I garnish them, I let them go... I leave them in my poem like stalactites, like slivers of polished wood, like coals, pickings from a shipwreck, gifts from the waves... Everything exists in the word... An idea goes through a complete change because one word shifted its place, or because another settled down like a spoiled little thing inside a phrase that was not expecting her but obeys her....[6]

"An idea goes through a complete change because one word shifted its place" Neruda points out. Can such openness to possibilities, can this delicious samba between what you intend and what the work itself seems to want, be taught? And even if it *can* be taught, why work to learn these moves unless you want to become a professional creative writer?

To Write as if We Matter

Poet Denise Levertov points out that when it comes to talent and genius, "You cannot will it to happen. But you can place yourself in a relationship to your art to be able to receive it if it should happen; this relationship is 'faithful attention.'"[7] *Write Moves* is a guide to help you cultivate a "faithful attention" to writing. Your work on the skills necessary for creative writing can lead to all sorts of side benefits. You'll become a better reader, able to perceive meaningful nuances and understand how writers create them. Like an architect who takes pleasure in visiting a beautifully designed house, for the rest of your life, you will walk through poems, essays, and stories, able to feel more keenly their effects because you understand the principles of design they adhere to carefully—or defy boldly. Your fluency with grammar and expression will grow; these abilities can be useful in all sorts of academic, corporate, and "real life" circumstances.

But those are the worthy side benefits. The power to define the world, *to define yourself in it*, is the essential benefit of any serious expedition into the practice and craft of creative writing. Gloria Anzaldúa answered the question "Why write?" this way:

> By writing I put order in the world, give it a handle so I can grasp it. I write because life does not appease my appetites and hunger. I write to record what others erase

> when I speak, to rewrite the stories others have miswritten about me, about you. To become more intimate with myself and you. To discover myself, to preserve myself, to make myself, to achieve self-autonomy.[8]

Whatever your own particular reason may be for writing now, and whether or not you're experiencing that special "urge" to write, consider this invitation: creative writing is an opportunity to discover how language defines and changes our understanding of the world and who we are in it. Don't worry that you need to live an uncommonly eventful life in order to write. Don't worry that you need to be born a genius. You need only hope that you can discover something about the experience of being alive by writing it in your own words.

Fiction writer Janet Burroway points out that all imaginative writing is in some sense autobiographical—no matter how inventive the story, all writing is drawn from our experience and our identity. We wear so many masks for our expected roles in this life, and so much of our time is spent in the classroom, on the job, watching television, surfing the Internet, updating our profiles, doing what we think we need to do to stay safe or to distract us from our feelings. What an opportunity—what a relief—to write as if we matter.

Suggested Reading from Our Anthology

Dorothy Allison, from *Two or Three Things I Know for Sure*
Sherwood Anderson, "Death in the Woods"
Samuel Green, "Some Reasons Why I Became a Poet"

Your Moves

1. Write about a memory of telling stories or singing songs in your childhood. When you think back on it now, what significance did these stories or songs have for you?
2. Write about one of the best things you ever read and how reading it made you feel. How did it make you feel this way? This reading need not come from a published book—it could be a text from a friend, a note your mom tucked into your lunch, a letter from a love or from grandpa.
3. Write about one of the best things you ever wrote—and one of the worst. How did writing each make you feel? Is it a "best thing" because it got a good grade, because it pushed you to write at a new level or in a new way, because it was read with respect, because you felt relief after "getting it out"? And was the "worst" related to a grade, your sense of commitment to the project, your discomfort with the audience, or something else? There are no wrong answers here—just listen to the experiences you've had with writing, the things you already know.

4. Read the "suggested readings" for this chapter (in the anthology) then create your own poem, personal essay, or story about why you write—or about why you don't.
5. Write about why you're reading this book or taking this class now. Why do you want or need to write? What are your reasons and what are your fears? What are your personal risks in trying to write, and what would a really good outcome be for you?
6. Make a list of a dozen "small noticings" in this moment: twelve tangible things you perceive with your five senses (the wind tossing a tree outside your window, a voice in the hallway, the steaming coffee in your favorite chipped mug). How many of these were you unconscious of until you searched for the materials nearby to describe?

Practicing Perception

> You cannot will it to happen. But you can place yourself in a relationship to your art to be able to receive it if it should happen; this relationship is faithful attention. —*Denise Levertov*[9]

> *It was foggy and we were delayed, ended up at Cypress Head. Saturday late afternoon went ashore and walked, first up a steepish, dusty rock-step then along a ridge trail. The light was incredible—suddenly like a new season altogether sparkling and clear. Maybe b/c of the fog, or maybe b/c I just don't see clear light so much on shore in Bellingham. The madronas were spectacular along the ridge, with the blue water of Rosario Strait dark behind them. So many more shades of deeper reds—mahogany and salmon, peach in speckles as the colors graduated toward that pale clean green in their trunks. A hot afternoon. Some trees had gone completely dead and gray, petrified, with striated cracks running down their trunks. I pressed my hand to one in the sun and the wood was warm, like a live animal. Then I went to a live tree in the sun, cupped it in my hand, and it was cold! Very cool, like touching a cool stream of water. It was moist, relative to the dead tree. Do cold-blooded animals feel like that? Such a reversal from expectation, from my own body.* (From Nancy's old writing notebook)

Showing Up

Writing as an experience, an ongoing practice, is different from what many of us associate with "being" a writer. "Being" a writer, in the world of fantasy, might mean signing copies of your latest hardback before an admiring crowd of fans, lunching at a stylish café with your publisher, fielding calls from your agent who recites the latest movie rights offers, languishing on a Caribbean beach beneath a palm tree with the latest-model laptop resting lightly upon your waxed thigh as you happily produce the next chapter in a thirty-three novel mystery series based entirely on the lyrics of songs by your favorite band (you're invited on tour with them next month).

"Writing practice" isn't drafting, revising, publishing, blogging, or promoting work: It's a habit we *do* as writers—beginning and experienced writers alike—to gain and maintain flexibility and skill. Practice makes us capable of writing our stories, poems, and essays the way a runner runs on many days to complete a half marathon a few times a year. It's "practice" in the sense that we do it with a sense of dedication—committing an hour first thing each morning for a year, ten minutes a day for a semester, once per day for as long as the toddler naps, two hours on Tuesdays, or for as long as it takes to wear the freshly sharpened lead off a #2 pencil each night before sleep. We practice regardless of mood or circumstance, much as one would commit to disciplined singing, golf, yoga, piano, weight lifting, meditation, sketching, swimming, knitting, fly fishing, rowing, or chess. Although there may be tangible outcomes down the road (singing in front of a live audience, hitting a hole in one, achieving the lotus position), practice is less about outcome and more about the human need to live as if our participation in life matters. Each kind of practice involves the honing of fundamentals through repetition, attention to form and detail, building and maintaining a level of dexterity, and saying (with the body, the fingertips, the heart or mind) "I've shown up." In a world that seems to compel us toward boredom, distraction, exhaustion, depression, cynicism, addiction, or apathy, *showing up* is a powerful action regardless of what we win, catch, or publish as its result.

Timed Practice

A plethora of terrific writers have published books about how to "do" writing practice, and my favorite remains Natalie Goldberg, whose *Writing Down the Bones* has supported millions of us as we've approached the blank page. Goldberg introduces the ten-minute form of daily practice: set a timer, open your notebook, and keep your pen moving across the page without caring a whit about spelling, grammar, or even margins. Just write. First thoughts, uncensored thoughts, thoughts that fly under the radar of our "internal editor"—these are the freshest, the richest. Express them with honesty and detail; no one is reading, and no one is judging if you sound brilliant, crazy, or sad. This stuff is not to be graded, not for posting on your blog.

This is "free writing," composed outside the bounds of audience expectation and outside the bounds of genre: here, you're not writing a novel, a play, a poem, a speech, a memoir, an essay, an article, a short story, or script. You're not keeping a diary, a coherent narrative of life story or a series of confessions. "So the point of my keeping a notebook," said novelist and memoirist Joan Didion, "has never been, nor is it now, to have an accurate factual record of what I have been doing or thinking."[10] Cartoonist Lynda Barry has her writing and drawing students write daily in their notebooks because this form of practice "makes us begin to notice when we notice something."[11] By expressing what we notice (not narrating what we have *done*—which is the terrain of the diary), we grow better able to understand *how* we notice. The individual way we each have of noticing the world is our bass line—our pulse or voice—as a creative writer. Even the fiction writer who trades in imagined characters and invented landscapes keeps a notebook—because fiction, too, is an invented expression of what an individual writer notices and finds true.

Writing in your journal or notebook you're loose, experimenting, cleansing what William Blake called the doors (in my imagination they are French doors—glass and many paned) of perception—because writing is a lens through which we bring perception on to the page, into consciousness. Here's a sample of painter Emily Carr's notebook writing (her spelling and grammar were corrected before it was printed in her posthumous book *Hundreds and Thousands: The Journals of Emily Carr*). In this entry, she pays attention to the forest undergrowth before her:

> [Excerpt from] September 29, 1935
>
> Down under the top greenery there is a mysterious space. From the eye-level of a camp stool you can peep in under. Once I went to some very beautiful children's exercises in a great open space. There was no grandstand. The ground was very level and it was most difficult to see. I took a camp stool and when my feet gave out I sat down. It was very queer down among the legs of the dense crowd—trouser legs, silk stockings, knickerbockers, bare legs, fat legs, lean ones—a forest of legs with no tops, restless feet, tired feet, small, big, lovely and ugly. It was more fun imagining the people that owned the legs than watching the show. Occasionally a child's face came level with yours down among the milling legs. Well, that is the way it feels looking through bracken stalks and sallal bushes. Their tops have rushed up agog to see the sun and the patient roots only get what they can suck down through those tough stems. Seems as if there is something most wonderful of all about a forest, especially one with deep, lush undergrowth.[12]

This degree of attention isn't unusual—it's necessary for artists. Musicians are always paying careful attention to sounds, painters to colors and shapes, carvers to wood grain, photographers to light, filmmakers to frames. Writers use language as our medium; we practice so that we may always be learning more about how to word our perspective of the world.

Prompts

Goldberg's books are filled with prompts to get the hand moving...and it is the *hand*, not the cursor, you might consider moving. Neuroscientists have found that handwriting, not keyboarding, is closely wired to our imaginative expression. So if you feel stuck when you compose using a screen and keyboard, try freehand for practice (screens are great, say those neuroscientists, for the brain that shapes and edits in revision). Aim to write continuously for ten minutes or until you fill one page minimum—no stopping to correct or edit. Use a timer so you need not worry about looking at a clock.

If you're ready to give it a try, here are a few of Goldberg's prompts and some of my own to get you started—use or modify them, as you wish:

Write something beginning with the words "I remember…" or "I am made of…."

Write about the best meal you ever ate.

Write about the first time you thought about sex or were intimate with someone.

Write about your home.

Write about ways of leaving.

Write about an outsider in your family, school, community, or team.

Write about sleeping, dreaming, or waking up.

Write about the hands of someone you know.

Write about something lost.

Write about starting over.

Write about looking up at the stars.

Write about someone who cuts your hair, drives your bus, cleans your office, or remembers how you like your coffee.

Write about your favorite childhood toy.

Write about an animal you have known.

Write about the smells of your summers.

Write about the moment you made a mistake.

Write about what someone said.

Write about a photograph or painting.

Write about the quality of light, or the textures in the room or space you inhabit right now.

Attention and Empathy

Although such prompts might seem slight or inconsequential—they don't say, "Write *War and Peace*" or "Write something to win a Nobel Prize"—in fact their consequences are vast because this kind of attention is radical. Most of the time, in school, at our jobs, in our opinions and ratings posted online, writing has the quality of a test: it's how our ignorance, competence, and taste are exposed for others to judge. In contrast, writing practice does not perform; it is the articulation of perception. The goal is understanding and accepting whatever we perceive. We live in a world where, today, real people are killed by drones, sold into slavery, left in communities without clean water or sanitation, mutilated, raped, bombed, bullied, forgotten. We may live in communities, extended families, networks of friends and colleagues, or households where such dramatic violations are not as obvious, yet many are addicted (to drugs, to food, to pornography, to our many games and distractions), depressed, or unsettled from lack of understanding, lack of acceptance.

These problems exist for many reasons but chief among them is that we are capable of growing desensitized to the humanity in ourselves and others. For protection—or more selfish reasons—we look away. We choose not to pay attention. Looking away or "tuning out" dilutes our capacity to feel, to be moved—even by simple, delicious, or beautiful experiences.

One of my favorite poems, "What I Saw" by Kathleen Flenniken, describes the sensation of beauty and empathy that can come simply by looking:

> Memory jumbles which I noticed first—
> the bicycle abandoned in the grass,
> discarded clothes, or sounds of splashing
> in the lake. She emerged from the weeds
>
> still wet, toweling dry, and must have seen me
> round the path, kicking through the leaves
> and morning frost, my sympathetic shiver,
> though she never met my eye. She turned
>
> her back but didn't wait to peel away
> her seal-black suit and what I saw
> was ampleness and white, the beauty
> of the world in late September.
>
> Sometimes when I think of it I stare.
> Sometimes she is me and I am her.

Paying attention like this, we are made vulnerable to what we see—the mundane, the beautiful, and the ugly impress themselves into us and cause us to feel and be connected.

Sitting With

Poet and essayist Lia Purpura writes about her urge to look away from ugly, painful things both small (chicken meat) and large (photos of torture victims published in the media). She reflects on a form of perception she calls "sitting with":

> To *sit with* you have to look into the gap in your understanding, not drive the conversation, not know where it's going. Not know beforehand at all where it's heading.... That's the space. That open field, where you're sitting with, and don't have to answer, but an atmosphere of response is forming.[13]

"Sitting with" is Purpura's alternative to looking away; it sustains her ability to notice and feel the marvelous parts of her life without denying that the miserable, bad, and unfair also exist.

Writing practice is "sitting with" the details of our lives; we attend, we cultivate an atmosphere in which we can respond to these details instead of looking away. The page is blank. We have no outline, no thesis, no plot, no reader. We write into the open field of the page with perhaps a prompt, a question, but without answers. One of my favorite teachers, Donald Murray (a barrel-chested, white-haired man who looked like Santa, if Santa had been a World War II paratrooper and won the Pulitzer Prize), describes the sensation:

> You may feel scared. Language may hold a mirror in which you fear to look; language may, like a dream, take you where you do not want to go. It may not. It may bring you peace, understanding, comfort, insight. Your words may be happy, sad, angry, funny; you may attack, construct, tear apart, connect; you may celebrate, explore, confirm, save. You do not know what you will discover. No writer does. Fear is part of the game.
>
> But this is a private game. You are writing to yourself. No one need see this draft; you take this adventure into the page alone. It takes courage, but in half a century of my own travels into myself and a quarter century as a guide to students of all ages who make this trip, I have seen none who have not found the trip worthwhile.[14]

The timer ticks, the details come, the response forms, the emptiness fills. We repeat the practice, "showing up" to witness the small and large details of a life lived, learning the words and rhythms to help us toward compassion and understanding. Caring about the details of our lives, we are perhaps led toward caring about the details of other lives. This is not moral superiority. It is simply practice: the squeegee applied regularly to the dirty glass doors of perception, preparing us for the stories and poems and personal essays to be seen ahead.

Procrastination and Perfectionism

Each day, each moment holds "reasons" (excuses) not to write. "I have long since decided," Margaret Atwood tells us, "if you wait for the perfect time to write, you'll never write. There is no time that isn't flawed somehow."[15] Procrastination and perfectionism are the great impediments to writing practice.

- **Procrastination** is something just about everyone is an expert at. I have a black belt in it myself. That creature called "will power"—deliberate control exerted to do something or restrain one's own impulses—is on the endangered species list. But most of us can work out what it takes to overcome our procrastination, at least in the short term, long enough to write. My favorite techniques include bribery ("if you write now, you can have chocolate later"), accountability (using software, a calendar, or collaboration with a friend to report progress), change of environment (going to a coffee shop, the attic, a park, or your desk expressly to write), and sensory deprivation (no music, no Facebook, no email, no feeds streams tweets or Tubes, no TV, no kitty, no book, snack, phone, comfy chair, or window—in short, make the physical environment *so boring* that it is a relief to write). My independent learning student Kim Bowman describes so wonderfully how she feels settling into her writing mind: "When I first sit down to write, I'm like a horse that is moving around so that the saddle can't be put on it, fidgeting, and then finally after the saddle is adjusted, the horse settles down and accepts that he is going to be ridden."

- **Perfectionism** asks us to wait until we have something "good enough" to write about or until we have the "right words" or the "right starting place" in mind. It gets us stuck in editing before we've even discovered what might be said. Remember that in writing practice, practice does *not* make perfect. Perfection isn't the point. Poet William Stafford, well known for rising early to write each morning, was asked how he managed to be so prolific. His answer? "I lower my standards."[16] Nineteenth-century writer and philanthropist John Ruskin embarked upon a project to teach basic drawing to working-class people; the purpose of drawing, he said, had little to do with drawing *well* or becoming an artist—it was about developing an ability to perceive. When we truly see beauty, Ruskin believed, we are able to understand it, hold on to it, and allow it weight in our lives. A student of mine had a lovely attitude about perfectionism: she called her notebook "little noticings" and wrote each day in its pages about at least one little thing she noticed. The modesty and humility of her practice freed her from the pressure of perfectionism. As a result, she wrote a great deal and later in the term she often mined these "little noticings" for the beginnings of essays that turned out to say some very big things.

Reading as Practice

In learning a craft—how to build cabinets or stone walls, how to sew quilts, carve canoes, design jewelry, write music, dance—you can learn enough to get started by researching online or perhaps through a special inclination or gift. But to flourish, most of us need to apprentice—spend time with masters, observing, copying, holding our tools as they do, pushing ourselves to meet standards we aren't ready to imagine alone. Analyzing how the masters bring about their work causes us to develop a higher level of perception about our own practice.

In our enthusiasm to make our mark on the page, we sometimes forget that reading literature is a necessary apprenticeship for every writer learning to create literature. Whether our goal is "mastery" or simply to become more articulate than we already are, we're likely to remain the sort of cabinet maker who builds a wonky project from a prefab kit or the sort of quilt maker who uses superglue instead of thread, if we don't practice our ability to read. To practice "close reading" of the texts in our anthology or elsewhere, do the following:

- Give the text your full attention; avoid multitasking as you read.
- Print (or obtain a print copy of) the text you're studying, because your brain isn't built to notice or retain details that appear on a screen.

- Reread to notice patterns and connections that unify the whole work.
- Attend not just to *what* is written but to *how* it is written on the level of the sentence.
- Look up all the words unfamiliar to you, and write their definitions in the margins.

If you're serious about developing perceptiveness as a reader, keep a reader's notebook—a spiral-bound notebook that you divide vertically down the center of each page (using a crease or a drawn line). Each time you begin a new reading, make a heading to identify the author and work. Then follow these steps:

- In the left column, quote (transcribe) the wording of your favorite passages—the ones that really move you, intrigue you, amaze and surprise you... or that appall you. Note the page number.
- In the left column, also summarize the plot points and aspects of the shape or form of that text that seem especially significant to you.
- In the right column, directly across the page from your transcriptions or notes, free write to express why you selected each passage (and made each note) and how it affects you. Record your perceptions about how this language and how these details accomplish what they do to you as a reader. Don't be concerned with summarizing or reporting—just focus on how this writer is creating effects that move you and have meaning for you. Because the purpose of literature is to move a reader, these are the moments to learn from as a close reader and as a writer.

Writing about what we've read helps us notice how literature works and what "moves" are available to borrow, modify, or try to outshine in our own writing. The practice also helps sear into our memory moments that we react to strongly—so we might respond to those moments in our own imaginative projects. My poem "After I Die" came about because I wrote in response to reading a passage in Muriel Blanchet's book *The Curve of Time*—a passage that I found moving, but that also bothered me. Blanchet describes a creepy feeling she had near a Native burial ground in the islands off the British Columbia coast. She uses the phrase "each moss-hung tree holding its grim burden against the evening sky" to describe the traditional practice of "tree burial" for the dead. I had been thinking about this wording, and thinking about a friend's fear of death—about how that fear seemed infectious, making *me* afraid of mortality too. I was also writing in my notebook about images I saw each day (creating entries like the passage about the arbutus/madrona trees in the headnote to this chapter). I drafted a poem, combining my reaction to what I had been reading, my "little noticings" of images around me, and my wish to comfort my friend and myself about death. Here is the poem, revised:

After I Die

My grandmother's pear or Italian plum
would be comfortable and sweet
but too domestic. I need
a wild tree. Cedar is my favorite trunk
but close-branched;
in cedar I can't see the sky.
Dreamy blossomed dogwood
are too slender for this purpose.
Douglas fir are tall enough and warm
in winter, but I have never felt at home
in a fir. After I die
take me to a madrona.

Choose one red-boled, round-hipped
and open at the shoulders.
Wear pants good for climbing and
bring a few lengths of cord.
Help each other help me
up through the branches,
through rubbery leaves or dry ones,
and tie me supine toward the sky:
I don't want to fall in the first wind.
There are laws against this sort of thing
so choose a place far enough out
that you can't find it again.

After I die the softest places
will come unstitched
and even bitter secrets I kept in my belly
will sound raucous
in the mouths of crows.
Curling red bark of madrona
pulls back from the limbs each summer
and I'll peel too, unwinding from bone.
In rainstorms, hard white pieces,
knuckles and ribs, will drop from branches
through wet green salal. The best part
is being allowed to scatter.

For Further Reading

Lynda Barry, *What It Is*

Natalie Goldberg, *Writing Down the Bones*

Francine Prose, *Reading Like a Writer: A Guide for People Who Love Books and for Those Who Want to Write Them*

Your Moves

1. Find a spiral notebook (cheap ones from the drugstore work great) to use as a writer's notebook, and get a comfortable pen. Set aside the first several pages just for listing your prompts—ideas for things to write about—or write these on the inside front and back covers. Go ahead and begin your list now, building from the list earlier in this chapter. Add to it every time you think of a new prompt idea.
2. Turn your writing notebook upside down and flip it over. You can write from the back, toward the center, to keep your reading journal. Go ahead and crease or draw a line down some of the pages now. When you've filled the two ends of the notebook so they meet near the middle, you're ready for another notebook.
3. Write a list of all the ways you procrastinate. Use this list later to stay mindful of the actions that delay your writing practice—and maybe also use it to draft a piece about procrastination.
4. Make one entry called "words that attract" and another entry called "words that repel." List all the words you can think of to put into these categories, according to which attract or repel you. Need a push? Begin with some of these: *pustular, creamy, vomit, serendipity, fizzy, bubbly, giggle, scrumptious, masticate, phlegm, wince, chimichanga, Zamboni, fletch, lucid, diarrhea.* Add your own words to these lists. Do you like having entries with titles? Continue the practice, or just use the date for the heading of each notebook entry.
5. Violinist Pinchas Zukerman said in an interview, "If you think you are god, if you think you know everything, forget about it: vulnerability is essential to art."[17] Write about what makes you vulnerable.
6. Peruse our anthology's table of contents by theme, and select one that interests you. What do *you* have to express on this theme?
7. "Ekphrastic" art means art that responds to other art—a song written in response to a sculpture, a painting in response to a ballet, glass designed in reaction to a story. Put on some music that inspires, haunts, or moves you (instrumental music often works best—soundtracks can be good). Free write to it without an agenda—just see how it sways your language. Experiment with changing the music every ten minutes—how does your writing change?
8. Carry your writer's notebook to a new setting—a library, park bench, busy lobby, beach, deli, the roof of your building. Write there. Start with what you notice; continue with what you will.
9. Write in public, eavesdropping on snatches of real conversation you overhear. Record the phrases accurately then write beyond them. Who are these people who say these things? Figure them out on the page.

10. Make an appointment with a friend to write together. Sit quietly and write in companionable silence for an agreed-upon amount of time (twenty minutes?). If you like, bring a "provocation"—a postcard, a song, a photograph, a handful of beads or feathers, a stone, a worn baseball, a shell.... Give one another the "provocations" as prompts.
11. Read Kathleen Flenniken's "What I Saw" and James Wright's "A Blessing"; then write about an unexpected sighting you had of a person or an animal. Make both the setting and character you witnessed vivid—even if your glimpse was actually fleeting. Reflect on why this sight has lingered in your mind.
12. Go online and look up your birthdate or the current day of the year on one of the "this date in history" sites. Use a factual detail from the entry as a writing prompt, weaving an historical event into your writing as my distance-learning student Carlos Mendoza does here in a short piece he titled "Young Don Juan":

    > It was the first bouquet of roses I had ever bought. Tonight was the big night. Although, at fifteen, every night was a big night. Tonight was Farah's birthday; Farah was going to have her fourteenth birthday party at her father's dance club. He owned a couple of businesses in Puerto Vallarta and arranged that the private room at the Mogambo be shut down so that thirty or so teenagers could celebrate his daughter's special day. I will never forget the summer of 1997, the same year Mike Tyson, the most devastating heavyweight boxer in history, bit off Evander Holyfield's ear. What a disgrace to the great sport of boxing. That summer I too chewed off more than I could handle.

Drafting

I do not write as I want to; I write as I can. —*Somerset Maugham* [18]

I've been drafting this chapter about drafting and revision for six or seven hours each day this week. I have a pretty good version of the first part—on drafting—but have nothing yet (but notes) on revision. Full of tangential ideas, I feel unsettled and nervous a lot of the time. It's a full marathon, and I'm at mile five.

The first two days on this chapter I wrote a whole different version of what I have now. Then I went to bed and my gut said, "I just don't like that tone. I sound too authoritative, negative, flippant, and boring. I sound like everything I hate about textbooks!" The next morning I had to start completely over—pushed everything down unseen below the lower margin on my monitor (unbearable to delete it yet!), then began the chapter again. After drafting for two more days (building four new double-spaced pages), I deleted everything I'd done in the first two days.

Each day now I begin by rereading everything drafted so far in the chapter. I fine-tune word choice (diction) and syntax (word order) for clarity, tone, and to sound good to my ear. I condense or cut the less necessary parts and reorganize what seems misplaced. Then I create today's new, rougher stuff. As I work, I'm surrounded by handwritten notes, and I keep rustling through them. Books I love and trust are near enough to reach out and touch, old friends I want to introduce you to. A yellow cat sleeps near me on this scratched red desk as I draft, try to find words for my instincts and thoughts, change my mind. (See the revision in the next chapter headnote.)

Running as Far as We Can

How writing happens, how something—a poem, a memoir, a play, a story, a song—is made in our minds and *becomes*, still seems a kind of magic. No matter how much we learn about the writing process, a sense of wonder about how it happens (and that it ever happens at all!) never dissolves. Perhaps wonder remains undiminished because generating new writing is a different journey for each writer, reinvented for each new project. No one can really teach us how and where to begin *this time*, but, as writers, we do have conversations about what conditions tend to foster creativity, how it feels during the generation process, and what habits tend to generate something viable in the drafting stage of creative writing.

Writers have discovered through these conversations that drafting is essentially a private experience that would look unproductive if observed by others. Fiction writer Lorrie Moore, for example, describes her drafting process this way:

> ... if a person were to watch me work—which I am grateful no one ever has—I suspect it might look like a lot of cutting and pasting of notes, stopping, starting, staring, intermittent flurries (as the weatherpeople say), sudden visitations (by invisible forces), the contemplation of the spines of various dictionaries and reference books stacked behind the computer, and much reheating of cold coffee (a metaphor and not a metaphor). But what it feels like is running as far as I can with a voice, a tuneful patch of a long, nagging idea.[19]

If you've had opportunities to write during class time and lifted your head to check out what other students are doing, you might have noticed something similar: the engaged students are each in an intimate bubble of personal space. Often their heads face something near (the back of another student, the surface of their own desk, the wall or board) but their eyes focus on some distant place. One might be jiggling a foot and another moving fingers to an internal rhythm she seems to hear. One poises a pen for whole minutes above a sheet of paper, perfectly still. It often looks like almost nothing productive is happening when we write! Yet, as Lorrie Moore said, it can feel like we're running as hard and far as we can.

Defusing Three Sources of Tension

Drafting is different from "writing practice" because now you have a project, an assignment, a deadline, an empty shape (maybe a sonnet or "55-word story") in mind to fill, or some specific content (a memory, a character in an interesting situation) to mold into a shape. But now suddenly you sit to write and nothing makes it onto the page. Or, no—you don't sit to write at all. You have to clean the sink! Change your shirt! Call mom! Make lunch! Update your profile! Wait until you *feel inspired*!

Most of us feel a tremendous *tension* when it's time to draft, and this tension can be debilitating. I think there are three main sources of this sense of anxiety:

1. **Drafting requires a form of silence and sustained attention that makes most humans deeply uncomfortable; silence and sustained attention are also hard to achieve in a practical way in our modern lives.** "The concentration of writing requires silence," says fiction writer Philip Roth, "... large blocks of silence. It's like hearing a faint Morse code—a faint signal is being given, and

I need quiet to pick it up."[20] Nonfiction author Rachel Carson agrees: "The discipline of the writer is to learn to be still and listen to what his subject has to tell him."[21] Some writers describe drafting as a personal violence to endure: "Writing is easy. You just open a vein and bleed" has been attributed to several (including Red Smith, Paul Gallico, and Ernest Hemingway). Although it's a myth that writers and artists must "suffer" to create, there's a shared sense that we all need *and yet resist* the difficult condition of silence necessary for new work—this tension is psychologically painful. "Before I write I must endure the silence, then the silence breaks out. In the beginning there was silence—no words. The word itself is a breaking out. The word itself is an act of violence; it breaks the silence" (Elie Wiesel).[22]

Accept that you may feel uneasy in this silent place, alone with the possibility of what might be thought, what might be written. But know that many have occupied this restless place before you (in fact, thousands of writers are probably sitting right now, in silence, just as you are). Our unease means we are human and engaged in the condition necessary for our writing. When you try to draft but find yourself cleaning your oven instead, here are some techniques to help transition into the silence:

- **Do ten minutes of writing practice**, just as you normally would, to clear your mind's chatter and calm yourself. Don't write about the project you'll draft; it's just routine practice now.
- **Engineer your environment:** wear earplugs (they work like headphones plugged into the voice inside). Eliminate all the visual noise and static of pop-ups and messages on your screen. Clear your desk, turn off the devices, write facing a wall: do whatever's necessary to free you from distraction and cultivate *your own* form of quietude. For some, that might mean building a cozy nest in the comforting mess or generating a safe wall of white noise.
- **If your body must, go ahead and clean the oven.** But turn off the TV and music; ask your roomies to leave the kitchen. Clean (or do something else physical and private—a walk, a swim, yoga) in nothing but the monotony of the refrigerator's hum or the traffic swishing by. Then go straight to your draft.
- **Allow significant amounts of time for drafting** (hours, not minutes), long enough that you can lose all sense of time passing and find the "zone" of sustained attention. Returning from this "zone," you realize you haven't heard or seen anything except the work—you've completely forgotten the clock. It's hard to find this zone when we're aware of time ticking away and our physical surroundings.

2. **Drafting has more tangible and defined goals than writing practice, which creates more tangible and defined risks and fears**, especially if you know you might show this writing to an audience. Some of us fear exposing something personal and private in the act of writing. Some of us believe the myth that great writing is inspired and arrives fully formed with very little effort: the writer is *a special person*. If we have a fantasy that writing can or will make us special, we experience terrible anxiety about losing that identity when we begin drafting and notice that our writing is not immediately awesome (writers, by the way, are not *special people*; writers are people who write). Some of us care so deeply about our material that we fear doing it an injustice by writing it badly. Fear of writing may never dissipate—even winners of the Nobel Prize in Literature, such as Gabriel García Márquez, claim fear animates their writing process: "All my life I've been frightened at the moment I sit down to write."[23] The natural response to fear is "fight or flight," and your sudden need to distract yourself from drafting is a form of flight. Here are some techniques to help you stay:

    - **Choose a tool that will be a companion in writing**—your favorite kind of pen with purple ink, the laptop plastered with stickers, the canary yellow writing pad. Don't get OCD about having conditions perfect, but do have a sensual and physical partner in your work and perhaps even a ritual (lighting a candle, tapping a bell, sharpening a row of pencils, walking before writing, or making a warm drink) to signal you've begun. The tool and ritual can reduce fear when you sit to write.

    - **Adopt Anne Lamott's philosophy of the "shitty first draft."** Erase your expectation for a perfect first draft—such drafts don't exist anyway! Just start badly, as Toni Morrison describes: "I don't mind writing badly for a couple of days because I know I can fix it—and fix it again and again and again, and it will be better."[24] It may also help to draft at a time of day when your mind is less critical, less apt to call everything you write "shitty"—for this reason, many writers draft early in the morning (nearer the state of unconsciousness and dreaming) and revise in the afternoon when the mind is more judgmental. If you're less a perfectionist late at night, that's a good time for you to draft.

    - **Try redefining fear as excitement or curiosity** about what might surprise you in your draft. ("The appeal of writing—of any kind of artistic activity—" says Joyce Carol Oates, "is primarily the investigation of mystery."[25])

    - **Invent ways to coach and reward yourself** for writing through fear. (What strategy worked to get you to leap off the high dive, to ask that "someone" to join you for coffee, to quit smoking, to touch a snake? Was the reward the experience itself, or something beyond the experience?)

- **Create a lockdown situation:** "Each morning I would thread my bathrobe sash through the spokes of the chair and tie myself in" (John McPhee).[26] Having an accountability partner helps. You can both work silently together at the library, at the kitchen table, or in separate locations for a set amount of time. No talking or messaging allowed—but sharing the results or a treat at the end of lockdown is a positive reward.

3. **We're often hyper conscious of a need to juggle many things *simultaneously* as we draft.** John Gardner's words from *The Art of Fiction: Notes on Craft for Young Writers* are enough to chill the blood: the writer "must shape simultaneously (in an expanding creative moment) his characters, plot, and setting, each inextricably connected to the others; he must make his whole world in a single, coherent gesture, as a potter makes a pot."[27] Awareness of the need to accomplish *so much at the same instant* can freeze us and arrest the drafting process as the mind scatters in a million directions at once. To thaw, try these strategies:

   - Remember that Gardner's advice is about how a revised and polished draft should *appear* to the reader—it's unlikely the whole world of a draft will be fabricated in "a single, coherent gesture." Rather, you prepare the clay and throw it many times—warping numerous pots along the way to the graceful yet sturdy vessel that makes it to the kiln for the fire. **See your early draft as clay to throw onto the potter's wheel:** get your fingers into it; learn the feel of it. It can be scraped off and thrown again without harm.

   - What do you think *unifies* your draft—what aspect holds everything together? What part is essential? Begin your draft there. If you feel yourself pulled in many directions as you write, return to the question of unity, and **release what's not part of *this* particular story, poem, or essay.**

   - **Use placeholders**—*blah blah blah*, ellipsis, or words that sound kind of like what you mean—to get you over the blocks or bumps in the road mid draft. (Paul McCartney composed the lyrics to "Yesterday" with the words "scrambled eggs" as a placeholder.) Move on after using placeholders to write what comes next.

   - Borrow a page from filmmakers: they almost never begin by filming the first scene that will appear in the edited movie. **Pick a modest part that feels less consequential as a place to start.** Novelist E.L. Doctorow said drafting is like driving at night: "You never see farther than your headlights, but you can make the whole trip that way."[28] But the really amazing thing is you don't even need to drive the trip in a particular order to create a draft. The arrangement may come at the revision stage.

- **Start at the start, despite having no plan.** Many writers, including Joan Didion, free-fall into a draft this way: "I don't have an outline or a logical sense of where to begin. I just start and hope things will fall into place. It kind of emerges as you go along. Maybe about a third of the way through I will begin to develop some general idea, probably nothing more specific than, say, three parts. Even this is open to change. This kind of inchoate groping seems to be the only way I can approach the thing."[29]

Habits of Hand, Habits of Mind

As you gain experience drafting, you'll discover the habits that work best for you. In the meanwhile, here are some habits I've developed that you can feel free to adopt, modify, question, or toss out:

- **Keep copies of work in progress.** Save work regularly using the "save as" function and renaming or numbering subsequent drafts (save handwritten or typed drafts in physical folders). Saving copies is important if you're a student because you're likely to be asked later to reflect on changes in your work, to "show" your drafting stages in a portfolio, or as proof of originality if there's any unfortunate question of plagiarism. Sometimes it's good to find material shed during the drafting and revising process—to recover a freshness lost or some material to use in another piece. Regularly back up all your writing on a flash drive or the cloud. Your computer is mortal.
- **Draft on a laptop, in longhand, with a typewriter—whatever way most pleases you.** Of course drafting on a screen saves paper and makes it easy to revise and reorganize, but a surprising number of current writers (even novelists) draft using longhand or an old typewriter; they usually prefer to transfer material to a computer at the revision stage. This "old school" preference exists partly because the old tools feel more tangibly connected to our bodies, making writing an intimate and significant feeling for some:

  > Writing in longhand has a special kind of magic to it for me. You are so engaged in the manual work of fashioning the word which flows out of the end of your hand as though it were a secretion from your own body, and you watch it being spilled on the page in a certain calligraphy, and it has an energy of its own that carries you along. (Richard Selzer)[30]

  There's also neurological evidence that doodling and forming letters by hand is more conducive to creative thinking and outside-the-box invention (the sort of mind we need for drafting) and that we see and read differently on the page than on the screen. The point isn't that one way is *better* but that you may find ease or pleasure by experimenting with a variety of composition tools. You'll also discover how equipment influences your work—the width of a screen or orientation of your page influences line lengths of your poems, MS Word capitalizes all your enjambed lines (changing tone) until you alter your program settings, and composing on unlined paper encourages free use of the visual field of the page.

- **Find a restriction.** We tend to think of art as an expression of freedom and individuality, *not* restriction. But the creator in us thrives on responding to restriction rather than to a vague invitation to "oh, just, do anything you like." Those of us who love food know that the centuries-long restriction of cooking with local ingredients has resulted in an astonishing range of culinary creativity. "I think that having some limitations can be very, very good," says chef Magnus Nilsson, who chooses to operate a restaurant in northern Sweden where it is winter six months of the year. Winter "naturally adds restrictions to the way we work," explains Nilsson, who chooses to use only locally sourced ingredients. "If you have everything all the time," Nilsson muses, "there's very little motivation, for most of us, to create something new and possibly better."[31] Film director Lars von Trier investigates this idea in his documentary *The Five Obstructions*. Wondering why *his* favorite director, Jørgen Leth, can't make a new film, von Trier challenges Leth to remake Leth's own 1967 film *The Perfect Human* in five different ways. Each way has a set of "obstructions" or restrictions. In one, the film must be made in Cuba and no shot can last more than twelve frames. In another, it must be animated. In another, it must be set in the "worst place on earth," but it cannot show the setting. These restrictions don't limit Leth; instead, they serve to inspire him toward innovation. The most interesting part of the documentary comes when it's revealed that one of the five "obstructions" is *no obstruction*. Leth can't make anything in response to this and requests a restriction for inspiration. And so it is for us as writers. We might select a "given" restriction (a rhyme scheme, a 700-word "flash fiction") or invent our own (an essay written entirely with the collective pronoun "we," a story in which three things are devoured). Restriction is to the creative writer what a silk handkerchief might be to bored lovers.

- **Work with or without an outline, as best suits your temperament or the nature of a project.** Projects that are narrative in nature do need what Raymond Carver calls a "scaffold"—a sense of the scope and plot of a short story—before the drafting stage. Lyrical projects accumulate as quilts or collages and are "sound-led": drafted with the ear, using riffs or runs of sound to determine what best attaches to what. The former benefits from a "prewriting" outline; the latter benefits from no outline.

- **Know your genre early—or don't.** Poems, stories, and essays each lend themselves to different drafting methods. For instance, if you know you're writing a poem, you'll jump right in and try line breaks. A story? Then you'll think about your character's desire and the plot early on. Essay? You'll be aware of "truth" and your pact of honesty throughout the drafting process. But sometimes it's okay to just begin and let the genre find you—or to refuse the idea of genre altogether. Writing that bends, combines, or resists genre is called a "hybrid text"; its author practices "hybridity." Prose poetry is a hybrid form: it combines the highly lyrical sounds and brevity associated with poetry with the prose (paragraph shape and lack of line breaks) and emphasis on character associated with fiction. Lorna Crozier's *small beneath the sky* is a memoir of growing up in the prairie city of Swift Current, Saskatchewan. It's about a small girl, a small city, gender, poverty, alcoholism, and love. But twelve parts—are they chapters? sections? poems?—of this text are not essay or story. Here's one:

> *first cause: light*
>
> You don't know what light feels or how its thinking goes. You do know this is where it's most at home. On the plains where you were born, there are no mountains to turn it back, no forest for it to shoulder through. A solitary tree marks its comings and goings like a pole sunk in the shore of the ocean to measure the tides. Here, light seems like another form of water, as clear but thinner, and it cannot be contained. When you touch it, it resists a little and leaves something like dampness on your skin. You feel it the way you feel a dog's tongue lick your cheek in the early morning. After an hour or two of walking, you are soaked in brightness. When you shake your head and shoulders, you see the spray. If you stay too long in the open, you could drown, its currents carrying you to its source, your body bobbing, then going under, your lungs full of lustre. Nowhere else in your travels will you see light so palpable and fierce. It is too huge for dreams, too persistent for solitude. All day long it touches you with the smallest of its million watery wings.

Is Lou Reed's "Walk on the Wild Side" a song, a spoken-word poem, a small anthology of stories—or all of these? One of my favorite performers is Ivan E. Coyote, a storyteller originally from Whitehorse whose work I've seen and heard in performance, in print books and journals, on CDs, online, and in short films. What's "told" there often has the cadence of spoken-word poetry, the conflict and arc of narrative fiction, and the sense of personal disclosure and searing honesty that comes when a transgender person says "this is who I am" in a personal essay. Not only have she/he pronouns shifted for describing Coyote on the book jackets over the years, but the fiction/nonfiction genre boundaries were crossed in marketing some of the books simply as "stories." Hybridity, I think, is an important way for writers to express identities and experiences that do not fit simply into given categories of literature or life.

When the long, hard run of drafting gets to you, remember the wise words of Robert Cormier: "The beautiful part of writing is that you don't have to get it right the first time, unlike, say, a brain surgeon."[32] Play, experiment, take a risk—kick up your heels or do a cartwheel if the run loses its meaning or pleasure. Nobody's watching.

For Further Reading

Kelli Russell Agodon and Martha Silano, *The Daily Poet: Day-by-Day Prompts for Your Writing Practice*

Anne Lamott, *Bird by Bird: Some Instructions on Writing and Life*

Tara L. Masih (ed.), *The Rose Metal Press Field Guide to Writing Flash Fiction*

Brenda Miller and Holly J. Hughes, *The Pen and the Bell: Mindful Writing in a Busy World*

Your Moves

1. Start with your notebook, flipping through your accumulated writing to find a passage dominated by your attention to imagery and the way your language sounds. You were trying to word something *just so*—or perhaps being playful, even nonsensical—and the articulation of this imagery became interesting. Perhaps it's just a list of interesting words. Transfer it onto a page and begin making a poem from this skeleton.
2. Start with your notebook, flipping through your accumulated writing to find a record of a memory: a scene from your past that, for some reason, you still remember. Transfer this scene onto your screen, adding more detail. Reflect. Why do you remember it, still? What power does it carry? You have started a personal essay. Continue.
3. Start with your notebook, flipping through your accumulated writing to find a line of dialogue overheard or a description of a person. Begin a file with the words "What if ...," posing a question about that person or about that line of dialogue. Begin drafting from the tension of this query: write a story to reveal your answer.
4. Start with your response to literature you've read. Writers are reading all the time, thinking, reacting to it. The world's literature is a long and amazing conversation with writers "writing back" to one another—even if they're not alive in the same generation. I've just visited a display of Japanese hanging scrolls showing the poetry of Fujiwara no Sadayori, who lived from 995 to 1045. His work consciously responds to a poem composed by another Japanese poet in the year 905. You might do something similar by writing on the theme of a work you admire or resist, or by choosing a minor character of a story to become the main character (a richer and dif-

ferently understood character) in your own. Jean Rhys created *The Wide Sargasso Sea* in this way from *Jane Eyre*; Joyce Carol Oates invented her short story "The Lady with the Pet Dog" as a modern reaction to "The Lady with the Dog" by Anton Chekhov; Kamel Daoud built *The Meursault Investigation* through his resistance to the treatment of a minor character in *The Stranger* by Albert Camus.

5. Start with a speaking voice you can hear in your mind. Give this voice rein; let it speak on your page. Your story needs a narrator, your poem needs a speaker, and often your essay needs to sketch people and their dialogue. Let this received "character" tell your draft. You may later find this voice is one angle or side of yourself, a parent or family member, a figure from your community or childhood. But, at the drafting stage, just listen and write what this voice whispers or shouts.
6. Start with a photograph or a news story, then write your way to an understanding of these characters, the situation they face, their desires, actions, and perspectives. A family photo or picture you've saved for a long time can provide an entrance to a draft.
7. Start with an idea for writing that you've been saving "for later." Start with your best material. Don't worry about "using it up" early in your writing life—more ideas will come to you, and you can always revisit this great concept again later.
8. Start with a list: a list of words you associate with your favorite vacation spot, a list of hairstyles you have worn. List recipes you know by heart, people who lived in your apartment building when you were fifteen, all the species of trees you can identify, spices you have tasted, states and provinces or cities you have visited, ice cream flavors you have licked. List your allergies, phobias, and scars. Choose something from a list as a source of authority, a "way in" to your draft. Or make the list itself your structure for a "list poem" or collage-shaped piece of prose.
9. Start with a cliché or an example of idiom. My colleague Kami Westhoff gives students in her fiction class a list of clichés to select from; they must use one *literally* to create a fictional story. Try one of these: A loose cannon, cry your eyes out, bark up the wrong tree, have a bone to pick, a fly on the wall, egg on your face, one fry short of a Happy Meal, cool as a cucumber, go to the dogs, hold your horses, stop on a dime, see the light, made my blood boil, put two and two together, roll with the punches, brokenhearted, turn over a new leaf, a little bird told me, roll over in the grave, an albatross around the neck, hightail it out of here. Read Samuel Green's poem "Some Reasons Why I Became a Poet," and see how he twists nine such phrases to give each a new meaning.

10. Start with a dream. Lift some image, figure, or fear out of it to explore in a draft. Will you shape it into something surreal or explore the unconscious with your draft?
11. Start with some art that intrigues you. It could be a carving, a photograph, a painting, a song, a piece of blown glass, a necklace. Begin by describing what you notice; then see where the project might carry you—into a poem, a story, a personal essay. Poet Rainer Maria Rilke's poem "Archaic Torso of Apollo" is "ekphrastic"—art inspired by art: the poem's speaker describes viewing a sculpture of the god Apollo, which leads him to a new understanding about his own life.
12. Start with a pet—if you've known animals. Animals are complicated beings in their own ways, with concerns and personalities. My cat Bo is timid; he hides under the bed any time the doorbell rings. He has a pointy face like a ferret, and his head is disproportionately small for his silver-gray body. He mutters all day long. He is in love—totally, helplessly in love—with my other cat, Simon. Simon is Zen, pale as apricots and interested in everyone. He comes to the door when the bell rings, and nothing makes him happier than workmen reeking of tobacco, than lying on the floor with one to fix the stove together. Bo's greatest pleasure is to throw himself into Simon, to bury his nose in Simon's silken fur and sleep there. I imagine they are people—perhaps having dinner together at the Pepper Sisters restaurant downtown, in a red booth. How do they each react to their waitperson? Do they go clubbing after their meal? What human desire and conflict, what human resolution can I imagine extending from the personalities and yearnings I witness in my pets?
13. Start with an assignment or challenge devised by a peer. Writers dare, coerce, and cajole one another into projects. Mary Shelly's *Frankenstein* exists because a group of friends competed with each other to write the most frightening story. She won.
14. Start with collaboration. My friends Jim Bertolino and Anita Boyle have written three chapbooks of collaborative poems (the first called *Pub Proceedings*) by writing lines in turn as they enjoy their microbrews.[33] I love to generate "exquisite corpse" poems in a circle in class: each person writes a first line of a poem then passes it to the right. Everyone writes the second line to the draft just received, folding the paper between the two lines so that only the last line is visible to the next writer. Repeat this all the way around the circle, everyone continuing to see and write "just one line." Each line must include imagery and use sound in a playful way, and lines can enjamb. Reading the surreal results aloud is surprising and fun—and then each of us takes home the collaboration our first line started to revise into a personal draft.

We sometimes forget how productive collaboration can be for artists of all sorts—especially collaboration between people who don't think or work alike. One of my favorite films is the noir *Double Indemnity* (best last scene!), coscripted by Billy Wilder and Raymond Chandler...who didn't get along. Wilder later reflected that discord, artistic tug-of-war, is necessary for collaboration: "If two people think alike, it's like two men pulling at one end of a rope. If you are going to collaborate, you need an opponent to bounce things off of."[34]

Revision

I have rewritten—often several times—every word I have ever published.

—*Vladimir Nabokov*[35]

It's late July and my fingernails are stained dark purple. I bought fifteen pounds of dead-ripe black cherries today and have been washing them, removing their pits with a paperclip, and freezing them for smoothies to enjoy later. As I nudge the bent metal into each cherry, hook its pit and gently tug, I think about this manuscript. I've been writing this chapter about drafting and revision for six or seven hours each day for a week. I've created several pages of prose but the rest is a skeleton of notes and quotes. Tangential ideas pop into my head in clusters of inspiration or procrastination. I feel unsettled, nervous—I'm trying to grab something I can't quite reach or even see.

The first two days on this chapter I wrote something completely different from what exists now. But my gut said, "I just don't like that tone. I sound too authoritative, negative, boring—like everything I hate about textbooks!" *The next morning I started over completely—pushed everything down unseen below the lower margin on my monitor (unbearable to delete it yet!) and then began again. After drafting for two more days, building four new double-spaced pages, I deleted everything I'd done in the first two days. It felt good to let the useless part fall away and discover I need to break this material into two chapters.*

Each day now I reread everything drafted for the "Drafting" chapter. I fine-tune what's on the page for clarity and for sound. I condense or cut the unnecessary parts, reorganize what seems misplaced. Then I branch from the trunk of this reworked material and create today's new, rougher stuff. Every two hours or so—if I don't completely forget the time—I stretch, go to the kitchen, and pit a few more pounds of luscious fruit as my mind goes on writing. It's incremental work, for sweetness. (Compare this revised headnote to an earlier draft, the version printed as a headnote for the "Drafting" chapter.)

Writing Is Rewriting

New and practiced writers are "on the same page" emotionally when we draft: feeling tension and fear, we launch into a new project and squeeze out a draft. You might expect this anxiety to chase you all the way through the writing process. But, if you listen to the voices of experienced writers, you may be surprised (and relieved) to discover that revision is something authors enjoy. Pulitzer Prize–winning novelist Toni Morrison calls revision "the best part" of her work:

> Because the best part of all, the absolutely most delicious part, is finishing it and then doing it over. That's the thrill of a lifetime for me: if I can just get done with that first phase and then have infinite time to fix it and change it. I rewrite a lot, over and over again, so that it looks like I never did. I try to make it look like I never touched it, and that takes a lot of time and a lot of sweat.[36]

As Morrison points out, terrific writing carries *the illusion* that it arrived in the world perfectly formed, the result of spontaneity and genius. Experienced writers have lived our way to understanding the truth:

> All writers write badly—at first. Nobel Prize winners, Pulitzer Prize winners, writers of blockbuster movies, writers with distinguished academic reputations, writers who influence and persuade, instruct and inspire, comfort and anger and amuse and inform, all write badly. Writers who write novels, speeches, news stories, screenplays, corporate memos, textbooks, plays, poems, history books, scientific reports, legal briefs, grant applications, TV scripts, songs—all write badly—at first.
>
> Then they rewrite. Revision is not the end of the writing process but the beginning. First emptiness, then terror, at last one word, then a few words, a paragraph, a page, finally a draft that can be revised. (Donald Murray)[37]

The delight and satisfaction published writers express about rewriting might seem suspicious to you now—wrung out from your experience of producing a draft. You may feel vulnerable about sharing your draft with a teacher, mentor, or peers, and protective or defensive about continuing to work with the material. Whether you feel proud or embarrassed of this draft, you may associate revision with failure, with punishment. Revision is not an anticipated delight for the novice writer.

If you're reading this book—whether for a class or on your own—you've made a decision to take writing seriously, to engage professionally in the art writers create. One of the most significant transformations you're likely to make as you take on the habits of a working writer is to fall in love with revision—or, at the very least, to learn to trust your capacity to rewrite.

The initial steps in revision are to gain distance from your draft (not look at it for a day or more) and then to adopt a new stance toward the draft: become its reader. This shift from "writer" to "reader" is an essential and imaginative task. Becoming an outsider to the text, you grow objective: you can recognize passages to cut and now the cutting doesn't seem to draw blood as it did when the draft felt like it was part of *you*. In revision, you see the material is trying to have a life without you—it does not exist to *say what you meant*. You spend hours helping the draft become the best possible version of its self for the strangers it will meet. Now that this work is no longer *you*, it no longer hurts to change it.

The Transition from Author to Reader

We edit language and rearrange text as we draft. In ye olden days of the twentieth century (or now, if you use a typewriter or pen to draft), a writer would reach a point when it became necessary to hand copy or retype a "rough draft" for legibility. From edited pieces physically taped together and from pages with arrows indicating where to move stuff, the writer made one new script of the full project. Crossed-out chunks of text were shed. This act marked the movement from "drafting" to "revising." The writer read this clean new script from start to end, marking changes throughout (reading it many times in this way), and then copied or typed *again* a new, improved version. That's one "revision." The writer read this revision through again from start to finish, marked changes throughout, and copied or typed it *again*. How many times? Raymond Carver did "as many as twenty or thirty drafts of a story" and at least "ten or twelve drafts."[38] I drafted the page you're reading now on a computer, read through it and changed it substantially about fifteen times over the course of a year, and then printed out the book manuscript and began to revise on paper (later transferring the results into the file and revising more). On page 51 is a scan of my first time through the printed draft with a pencil.

There's no correct number of revisions—but think days and weeks for short pieces, not minutes or hours (months and years for book-length projects).

Now that most of us write in a paperless environment, it's harder to tell when we've shifted from drafting to revising. But we still need to make the shift consciously, even if we aren't physically hand copying, retyping, or printing drafts. Otherwise, we're trapped in what Steven Pinker calls the writer's "curse of knowledge": we know *what we know* about our draft, so, reading it as ourselves, we are unable to know *what our reader does not know* and needs to know for the piece to work. We can't see, for instance, that our reader can't hear our character, visualize our scene, or perceive the symbolism perfectly obvious to us. Familiarity with our own work incapacitates us from revising it. When we transition from knowing our work as its author, to knowing it as a reader, our focus alters from "what I want to say," to "how does this material work as a piece of art?" It's an active choice to lift "the curse of knowledge"—and it's wonderful because we no longer waste energy defending the choices we made while drafting and no longer feel wounded about big or little alterations.

Try adopting physical changes to mark and enforce the transition into the act of revision. If you've been drafting on a screen, print your draft and revise on paper (if you've drafted by hand or typewriter, now switch to a screen). If you draft wearing a

[45]

The initial steps in revision are to gain distance from your draft (not look at it for a day or more) and then to adopt a new stance toward the draft: you become its reader. This shift from "writer" to "reader" is essential. Imagine yourself someone else, a stranger to the draft, experiencing it over and over "for the first time." As an outsider to this text, you can see possibilities you never intended. You can be objective: you can recognize passages to cut and now the cutting doesn't seem to draw blood as it did when the draft felt like it was part of *you*. In revision you recognize the material is trying to have a life without you—it does not exist to *say what you meant.* The draft is trying to tell you what it needs, what it can be, how it can astonish you. You spend hours with this draft, helping it become the best possible version of itself for the strangers it will meet, for the readers who want to be moved by encountering it. And in this way, your story or poem or essay is no longer *you*. It no longer hurts to change and improve it. This work is so different from drafting. As you grow proficient, more confident, perhaps rewriting becomes a pleasure.

The Transition from Author to Reader

Writers often edit language and re-arrange as they draft. In the olden days (or today, if you use a typewriter or hand write your drafts), a writer would reach a point when she would recopy by hand, or type, a "rough draft": make one continuous script of the full project instead of pieces physically taped together or pages with arrows indicating where to move stuff and with large chunks crossed out. This would be the moment to move from "drafting" to "revising." The writer reads this draft from start to end, marking changes throughout (perhaps reading it several times in this way), then recopies or types *again* a new, improved draft. That's one "revision." The author reads this revision through again from start to finish, marks changes throughout, then

T-shirt and slouched on the sofa, enforce the new role by wearing an ironed shirt, a jacket, or a hat—or by working now at a library, café, or different room in your home.

Exceeding Your Initial Expectations

When revision begins, everything is up for negotiation and the draft is about to exceed your first expectations. How?

- **Let go of the trigger.** Drafts begin with what Richard Hugo called a "trigger": your assumption about what started or caused your draft to be written. Revision is the time to let go of that assumption and explore what the draft can "really" be about—which is different and often greater or deeper than your original intent. In this sense, re-*vision* is re-*seeing* the possibilities of the project and letting go of what limits it: "I revise because it gradually takes me into the heart of what the story is *about*. I have to keep trying to see if I can find that out," explained Raymond Carver.[39] "I'm happy when the revisions are big," said Saul Bellow. "I'm not speaking of stylistic revisions, but revisions in my own understanding."[40]

  It feels both exciting and humbling to see your draft change into something "it" seems to want, to take on a meaning and heft that surprises you, its author: "No surprise for the writer, no surprise for the reader," Robert Frost famously spoke.[41] Could your poem about your grandfather's deathbed *really* be about the power of memory to lock us into a false identity? Could your story about a car trip *really* be about the care strangers give one another? Could your essay about your mom *really* be about our capacity to love?

- **Open to figurative possibilities.** When drafting, we usually wrestle to write in a manner that is clear and literal. But the revision stage allows us to open up to the possibilities of using images to find figurative meaning. The draft may have random metaphors or similes throughout, but revision enables us to group and shape these figures of speech to work together toward meaning. Yesterday, for example, I spent all afternoon drafting the note at the start of this chapter—and all evening revising it (and I will continue to revise it for months). I began with the intention to talk about some experience of my own with drafting; my purpose was to ground this description of drafting in my real life. I mentioned cherries just because that's literally true: I did buy fifteen pounds of cherries yesterday, did work on pitting them in stages throughout the day (and today, too!). But, as I revised, I began to see figurative connections between picking cherries and drafting, pitting cherries and revising. The phrases "I nudge the bent metal into each cherry, hook its pit and gently tug," "ideas pop into my head in clusters," "I branch from the trunk of this reworked material," and "it's incremental work, for sweetness" were all added in revision. These are the parts that most satisfy me now, and I did not originally intend them.

- **Cut deep.** The power to remove is equal to the power to write, and nothing belongs in your draft just because it happens to be there *now.* "I believe more in the scissors than I do in the pencil," said Truman Capote.[42] The first pages of a story or essay, passages of exposition, unnecessary scenes, clichés and vague words, instances of "passive voice" (using the verbs "is, am, was, were, are, be"), and unneeded articles and adjectives are the most likely candidates for excision in your first trip through your project with a knife. This cutting requires great patience and bravery. As Deborah Eisenberg writes, "For me, most writing consists of siphoning out useless pre-story matter, cutting and cutting and cutting, what seems to be endless rewriting, and what is entailed in all that is patience, and waiting, and false starts, and dead ends, and really, in a way, nerve."[43] Hemingway aimed to cut every word, letter, and punctuation mark not *absolutely* necessary. This kind of cutting strengthens by condensing language:

  > A sentence should contain no unnecessary words, a paragraph no unnecessary sentences, for the same reason that a drawing should have no unnecessary lines and a machine no unnecessary parts. This requires not that the writer make all his sentences short, or that he avoid all detail and treat his subjects only in outline, but that every word tell. (William Strunk, Jr.)[44]

  Having trouble revising an unwieldy paragraph or project? It sometimes helps to write it again without peeking at the original; we tend to forget the filler and recall the essentials.

- **Experiment with shape and perspective.** A draft can find a whole new life through a different arrangement. Take a story out of its present chronological order. Change a block-shaped poem into tercets or into lines of varied lengths. Transform a sonnet into free verse. Try a braided essay for a personal essay stuck in narration. To experiment with perspective, change a present-tense poem to past tense, make the minor character in a story its narrator, or try second-person point of view for your essay. In revision, think about how different structures and perspectives can alter your work's relationship with the reader and change or deepen its present meaning. By adopting the epistolary shape of a series of thank-you letters to the men in her life, Mary-Louise Parker transforms her memoir *Dear Mr. You* into a book about gratitude; it moves beyond a simple account of her experiences with men. Sometimes we don't discover a meaningful shape until the revision stage.

- **Tighten beginnings and endings.** Arguably the most important—certainly the most judged and remembered—bits of any project will be the first and last passages. Work particularly on the cadence, word choice, imagery, and tone of these moments. A good lead doesn't just present your reader with information;

it seduces us into continuing and contains the kernel or seed that will bloom to make the ending satisfying to reach. Endings, agree writers of all genres, should feel both inevitable and surprising. Unlike academic papers—which often start and conclude predictably with versions of a thesis—creative writing demands the unexpected, delivered in original language:

> HEMINGWAY: "... I wrote the ending to *Farewell to Arms*, the last page of it, thirty-nine times before I was satisfied."
> INTERVIEWER: "Was there some technical problem there? What was it that had you stumped?"
> HEMINGWAY: "Getting the words right."[45]

Novice poets and prose writers often add a moral, summation, or restatement of their *point* at the draft's end; it's usually better to delete such abstractions.

- **Play with your title.** If you haven't yet drafted or are ambivalent about the title, it's a sign that you haven't known or committed to what your draft is really about yet. So try on some titles—the attempt could reshape your whole understanding of your project. A title that refers to something literal in the draft ("Simple Recipes") tends to lift it into figurative possibility (directions not just for cooking, but for living). Imagery ("Father Holding Baby") makes a memorable and inviting title. Puns are often put to good use in titles ("Out on Main Street" refers to being outside walking on a street but also to being outed as queer and made to feel a cultural outsider in public). Clichés or worn phrases also work when they're delivered with a wink or a twist (*Cloudy with a Chance of Meatballs*). Titles can succinctly explain an expository context ("Car Crash while Hitchhiking") or offer an abstract idea ("Power") without interrupting the narrative or structure of the draft itself. A title can establish a mood ("Eulogy"), identify the main character or speaker ("The Cinnamon Peeler"), or cite song lyrics or other art relevant to your work (*Go Tell It on the Mountain*). Titles can tease and intrigue ("The Day I Sat with Jesus on the Sundeck and a Wind Came up and Blew My Kimono Open and He Saw My Breasts"), pose a question (*Do Androids Dream of Electric Sheep?*), or use irony (*A Heartbreaking Work of Staggering Genius* seems to ironically reference overzealous book blurbs). Compressed as a line of poetry, titles often play with sound (alliteration in *Smilla's Sense of Snow*) and cadence (iambic tetrameter in *Tequila Makes Her Clothes Fall Off*).

Feedback and Workshop

Many writers prefer the creativity and discovery of revision over the drudgery of drafting:

> I like to mess around with my stories. I'd rather tinker with a story after writing it, and then tinker some more, changing this, changing that, than have to write the story in

> the first place.... Maybe I revise because it gradually takes me to the heart of what the story is *about*. I have to keep trying to see if I can find that out. (Raymond Carver)[46]

"Workshop" is collaboration during the revision process; it means giving and getting feedback within a community of writers, then returning to your draft individually to choose which feedback to use and how to apply it. If you take a creative writing class, your teacher may design a workshop or series of workshops so peers can read one another's drafts and learn how to offer constructive criticism (if you're writing without a classroom, you might want to create a local or virtual group of people interested in responding to one another's writing).

There are many styles of workshop, including

- Distributing and reading work in advance to prepare, or reading and responding "cold"
- Working in small groups, or having a whole class look together at one draft
- Reading and responding anonymously, or openly
- Allowing the writer to explain and question, or asking the writer to remain silent and listen
- Meeting in a classroom, leaving the class to workshop in a less formal space, or meeting online

Regardless of the workshop format, here are a few notes that may help you make the most of these experiences:

PREPARING FOR WORKSHOP

- **Ready your draft for engagement.** Double space all work, and use a large enough (12 point) easily readable (such as Times New Roman) font. Readers inevitably (if unconsciously) give single-spaced text and writing with obvious sloppiness less consideration. Use page numbers—necessary during discussion of your work.
- **Be considerate of others' time.** If the group agreed to exchange one poem or four pages of prose, don't bring more. If you've set a deadline for an online exchange, don't post your contribution late. If you're assigned to read each other's drafts in advance, set aside plenty of time (and not *just before* the meeting). If you're bringing printed copies, don't leave the task until the last minute and arrive late.
- **Commit your reactions to paper.** Make brief notes as you read (before or during workshop). Be sure to share this thinking in workshop, even if a charismatic peer has a totally different response than your own. Notes are to remind *you* of your honest response—not corrections to pass on to the author.

DURING WORKSHOP

- **Convey your experience as a reader.** Indicate where you engage and disengage from the draft and point out the sources—the moments in the draft itself—that inspire those reactions. Use the vocabulary of craft to be explicit and professional. It can help the writer if readers summarize their perceptions of "what the work is about" and then tell which parts of the draft led to these understandings.
- **Don't explain or defend your work.** The goal of workshop is to help each writer lift the creator's "curse of knowledge" and identify how the draft is functioning now *from the point of view of readers.* Explaining your draft (sharing the context or "what you meant") infects your readers with your own "curse of knowledge." Defending your draft disables you from hearing your reader's full response; it's a defense mechanism to defer receiving feedback. Just listen. Later, transfer the urge to explain and defend into energy for revision: let the revised work speak for itself.
- **Resist the urge to advise or overshare.** Describe what you notice as a reader, what the draft does accomplish, what seems incomplete or unfinished. But try not to tell any writer what the draft *should* do. You aren't in workshop to build a draft by committee! If a draft reminds you of a personal experience, resist the urge to share your story. It will take away from time meant for giving feedback and will suggest your critique is personal rather than about the text itself.
- **Avoid saying "I like it," "I can relate."** The use of "like" is rampant due to Facebook, and we have a natural and kind urge to put one another at ease during workshop by saying we "like" something. Peers sometimes react to content in drafts by saying they've had a similar experience and can "relate." These phrases lead away from considering the draft itself. Minimize your judgment (liking or not liking) and remember: writing that engages and moves us even though we *cannot relate* (that is, we don't have personal experience with this subject matter) is really terrific writing.
- **Try not to suggest change just for the sake of change.** "No passion in the world is equal to the passion to alter someone else's draft," wrote H.G. Wells.[47] Resist the urge to make a draft *your* draft, to suggest adopting your style. Also resist the urge to copyedit or proofread for correctness (called "line editing") until the draft has already been revised many times and is about to be submitted for a final grade or publication.
- **Remember it isn't a competition.** "A good workshop continually signals that we are all in this together, teacher too," says teacher and poet Marvin Bell.[48] Understand that we're all participating in workshops to grow as writers, to learn more about our craft. Compassion, tact, honesty, and a sense of humor

are all strengths here. Pointing out that you appreciate or notice a *risk* a writer has taken with a draft is perhaps the most valuable move to make in workshop.

After Workshop

- **Note and assess the feedback you received.** While feedback is still fresh in your mind, write about what you heard and what ideas come to mind and excite you now (you might do this as a brainstorm or as notes on your draft). Useful details from workshop will quickly dissolve from your memory! It's likely you'll have received several *contradictory* critiques. Rather than dismiss them as "cancelling out" one another, focus in particular on the aspects of your draft that caused disparate reactions: these are areas where your draft is sending mixed messages. Brainstorm to understand *why* readers perceived these cues in different ways. Doing so will lead you toward decisions about where and how to revise.
- **Take back the reins.** During workshop, discussion is out of your control. When you return to your draft afterwards, you're back in control and under no obligation to do what anyone suggested. You now understand how readers experience your work, and you can measure their responses against your goals for the project—and fine-tune those goals. In the revision stage of this textbook, four clever and caring teachers read it and gave detailed feedback. One said I should take out all the quotations by writers; another said the quotations were an asset and I should *add* quotations by other kinds of artists too. One said I should shrink or eliminate the "Practice" aspect and expand "Craft"; another said my attention to practice is what makes the textbook different from others and therefore unique and valuable. After receiving this contradictory feedback, I had to think about what my audience needs, what my purpose is, and what I can and want to mean with this book. *All* their feedback was ultimately helpful—even the suggestions I thoughtfully rejected—because these contradictory reactions forced me to better define what book I was writing. I made many revisions based on this new understanding of my own work.
- **Take stock of the feedback you gave.** Workshops aren't just to *get* feedback but to practice your skills at critique. Even if—worst case—you got no viable feedback from peers, your experience as a reader improves your ability to critique your own work. Given that the things that irk us in the drafts of others tend to be *the very things we ourselves have some trouble with as writers*, apply the feedback you gave others to your own draft.

Line Editing and Polishing

Revision is "complete" when the content and structure of your revision is set. Now you turn your full attention to line editing and polishing before submitting your work for credit or for publication.

- **Line Editing** is examining your text slowly, line by line, for grammar, spelling, and punctuation correctness. You're reading only on the level of the sentence: is each sentence complete, comma and semicolon used correctly, dash formatted right, word spelled correctly? Is that fiancé or fiancée—blond or blonde? Should dialogue be indented there? Some writers read their draft backward—last sentence to first—to stay focused on the level of the sentence and not slip into revising (for content) or editing (for clarity and style). When examining a poem, check whether it uses sentences (if so, all should be grammatically correct; if not, then there should be *no* periods, no sentences).
- **Polishing** is making certain the formatting and visual aspects are consistent throughout the work. Here you are working to fulfill the practical submission requirements of the assignment and to use professional standards (page numbering, double spacing, one-inch margins, consistent indentation format for paragraphs). Check that nothing superficial can distract the reader. Has the printer run low on ink, causing light pages, blank spots, odd colors, or bars across the page? Should page breaks be inserted to eliminate widow and orphan lines (a first or last line of a paragraph or quotation stranded as the first or last line of a page) or to reunite poems with their titles? Save work as a PDF and check it before printing; writing can look different on the page than it appeared on screen. Check work on the page a final time before submitting it in print or online.

When you line edit and polish, *you're not actually reading for content at all*: it's impossible to pay close attention to these nitpicky but crucial details when you're also thinking about what the text says. If you're considering the topic of your essay or the imagery in your poem as you line edit and polish, you have slipped back into revising. This recursive approach is normal—nobody does all the revising, then all the line editing and polishing. But it's important to *end* with line editing and polishing so as to eliminate errors introduced in revision and ensure your final piece is as strong as possible. This last push has the effect of making your grammar, spelling, and formatting invisible—they will recede, so the real work of your creative writing can impress and touch the reader. Every instance of writing "peaked" when you meant "piqued" bursts the bubble of illusion and wrenches your reader out of the world of imagination and into the world of correction. Each tiny oversight dilutes the artistic and emotional effect of your work; line edit and polish so your creative writing is as potent and engrossing as you want it to be.

Many writers need support with line editing and polishing—it's almost impossible to see the errors we've made, because we tend to read what we *meant to write* rather than what is actually there in black and white. Try this:

- **Exchange drafts with peers** in class for a line editing and polishing workshop—don't discuss revision or content at all, just correct the revised draft before a due date.
- **Rely on a trusted reader** (a roomie, parent, classmate, friend, mentor) to play this role and mark up the errors on your draft. As you make these corrections in the file, be sure to ask for explanation of fixes you don't understand.
- **Use your campus writing center** for support. Your reader there will not line edit your manuscript for you but can help you find *patterns* of errors and explain them. Seek and repair each instance of these errors, knowing how to avoid them next time. You may be asked to read your draft aloud; the support staff member can help point out where you have verbally corrected yourself and not read what's actually in print, and then can help you get your real message into your written work.
- **Search online for "common sentence errors"**; you'll find a multitude of university resources to help you identify and correct mistakes at the sentence level. Lists such as the "20 most common sentence errors" are useful.
- **Attend to those colorful squiggles** in Microsoft Word—they can draw your attention to flubs you don't notice. But be sure you do not accept these suggested revisions without investigating whether they are actually useful corrections.
- Long term, **take a course in grammar and editing**, or brush up on the topic using a text such as *The Blue Book of Grammar and Punctuation*. Your effort will pay off when you self-publish or submit work to editors for their consideration.

For Further Reading
Claire Kehrwald Cook, *Line by Line: How to Edit Your Own Writing*
Donald M. Murray, *The Craft of Revision*
William Strunk, Jr. and E.B. White, *The Elements of Style*

Your Moves

1. Give your draft a yellow highlighter test: highlight every word and phrase that can be imagined using the five senses (seen, heard, smelled, tasted, touched). The passages marked are "showing"; passages unmarked are "telling." All creative writing is predominantly showing. Reduce the telling.
2. Remove nonessential passages, whether telling or showing. Much of what's written at the drafting stage is necessary to find traction and momentum but unneeded in the final work; these parts dilute and weaken the project. In an essay, remove what you've included "just because it happened"; in a

story, cut the exposition before the action and the narrative unrelated to the story's meaning; in a poem, delete the abstractions and concluding "thesis."

3. Divide your entire draft into segments (usually paragraphs—but segments can be stanzas, sentences, or lines for poems). Rearrange these parts and notice how the emphasis and meaning of the project changes with each new shape. Set aside leftover parts. Note in the spaces between parts where new writing is needed.
4. Track the arc of your main character, narrator, poem's speaker, or essay's "I" by making an outline of what that person experiences. Revise so that your human figure experiences a conflict, question, or desire early, and experiences change or discovery by the end. Revise minor characters beyond "types" or stereotypes.
5. Eliminate "poor me" complaints and mean-spirited passages written with a "poison pen"; both are signals to a reader that you haven't gained mature or artistic perspective on your material.
6. Experiment with point of view and perspective. Try rewriting with a secondary character as narrator in your story; try second or third person instead of first person in your poem; try past tense instead of present for an essay (this creates a "now" from which to look back on experience). Consider how these shifts change what your project is about and can make it deeper or more original.
7. Play with alternate forms and structures. Plot your story in a new order; change a poem from a visual block into couplets; change a narrative essay into a lyric essay. Open yourself to a new or more complicated understanding of your material that may emerge.
8. Be ruthless in your elimination of every cliché and each instance of tired wording. Cut every phrase you've seen before in someone else's writing.
9. Decrease or eliminate adjectives (the *pretty*, *fluffy*, *happy*, *dark*, *foreboding*, and *ominous* clouds). Increase figurative language that adds to atmosphere and mood: for instance, "Midwestern clouds like great grey brains" (Denis Johnson, "Car Crash while Hitchhiking") or "the clouds open their white blouses" (James Bertolino, "The Blouses").
10. ~~Passive sentences are in need of revision~~. Revise passive sentences into active sentences. (Find passive sentences by looking for the verb "to be"—*is*, *am*, *are*, *was*, *were*, *be*—coupled with another verb and sometimes with "by." Passive: The boy was bitten (by the dog). Active: The dog bit the boy.)
11. Count. Count the number of words in each sentence. Do you get 10, 10, 11, 9, 9, 10? Monotony is deadly in prose; better results are 10, 23, 5, 12, 2 (or any variation of your choice). Try counting stressed and unstressed syllables (usually in poetry, but it's helpful in prose too). If you find three or

more consecutive unstressed syllables, you've found a patch of dry, "prosaic" language. Interrupt this effect by rearranging the syntax, altering the diction, and cutting unnecessary syllables.

12. While you are counting words in sentences, look at how sentences are structured. Do most follow a subject-verb-object order? Are there questions, exclamations, commands? Varying sentence structure also helps avoid dull prose.
13. "Kill your darlings" has been attributed to Ginsberg, Faulkner, Wilde, Welty, Plath, and other authors who quoted and believed Arthur Quiller-Couch (who first said "murder your darlings" in the early twentieth century). The advice is sound, regardless of debate over its source: delete your pet, precious, and self-indulgent passages for the greater good of this work (or save them in a file called "Darlings" for another day).
14. Brainstorm a list of at least twenty alternate titles for your piece. Notice how each title shades and contextualizes the work in a different way. Find a title you love, and revise the project to suit this new direction.

Notes

1 Donald Morison Murray, *Shoptalk: Learning to Write with Writers* (Portsmouth, NH: Boynton/Cook, 1990), 4.

2 Oliver Sacks, *On the Move: A Life* (Toronto: Alfred A. Knopf, 2015), 383.

3 Raymond Carver, "A Small, Good Thing," in *Where I'm Calling From: New and Selected Stories*, ed. Tess Gallagher, 308–32 (New York: Atlantic Monthly P, 1991), 325.

4 Richard Hugo, *The Triggering Town: Lectures and Essays on Poetry and Writing* (New York: Norton, 1979), 72.

5 "Don't Like to Write, But Like Having Written," *Quote Investigator: Exploring the Origins of Quotations*, http://quoteinvestigator.com/2014/10/18/on-writing/.

6 Pablo Neruda, *Memoirs*, trans. Hardie St. Martin (New York: Farrar, Straus and Giroux, 1977), 53–54.

7 Denise Levertov, *Conversations with Denise Levertov*, ed. Jewel Spears Brooker (Jackson, MS: UP of Mississippi, 1998), 96.

8 Gloria Anzaldúa, "Speaking in Tongues," in *This Bridge Called My Back: Writings by Radical Women of Color*, 4th edition, ed. Cherrie Moraga and Gloria Anzaldúa, 161–71 (Albany, NY: SUNY P, 2015), 167.

9 Levertov, *Conversations*, 96.

10 Joan Didion, "On Keeping a Notebook," in *Slouching Towards Bethlehem: Essays*, 131–41 (1968; repr. New York: Farrar, Straus and Giroux, 2008), 133.

11 Lynda Barry, *Syllabus: Notes from an Accidental Professor* (Montreal, PQ: Drawn & Quarterly, 2014), 182.

12 Emily Carr, *Hundreds and Thousands: The Journals of Emily Carr* (Toronto: Clarke, Irwin and Company, 1978), 200.

13 Lia Purpura, "On Looking Away: A Panorama," in *On Looking: Essays*, 123–36 (Louisville, KY: Sarabande Books, 2006), 128–29.

14 Donald Morison Murray, *Shoptalk: Learning to Write with Writers* (Portsmouth, NH: Boynton/Cook, 1990), 2.

15 Margaret Atwood, quoted in Murray, *Shoptalk*, 47.

16 William Stafford, quoted in Mary Rose O'Reilley, *Radical Presence: Teaching as Contemplative Practice* (Portsmouth, NH: Boynton/Cook, 1998), 47.

17 Paul Kennedy, "Playing Mozart with Pinchas Zukerman," *Ideas*, CBC, Tuesday, January 14, 2014.

18 Somerset Maugham, *The Summing Up* (London: Vintage, 2001), 40.

19 Lorrie Moore, "The Art of Fiction No. 167 [interview by Elizabeth Gaffney]," *The Paris Review* 158 (Spring–Summer 2001), http://www.theparisreview.org/interviews/510/the-art-of-fiction-no-167-lorrie-moore.

20 Michiko Kakutani, "Is Roth Really Writing about Roth?" *The New York Times*, May 11, 1981, https://www.nytimes.com/books/98/10/11/specials/roth-really.html.

21 Rachel Carson, letter written in 1956, quoted in Geoffrey W. Chase, *Critical Reading and Writing in the University Community: The Environment* (New York: Harcourt Brace, 1993), 110.

22 Elie Wiesel, quoted in H.A. Walker, "How and Why I Write: An Interview with Elie Wiesel," *Journal of Education* 162, no. 2 (Spring 1980): 57–63.

23 Quoted in Marlise Simons "Love and Age: A Talk with García Márquez," in *Conversations with Gabriel García Márquez*, ed. Gene H. Bell-Villada, 141–47 (Jackson: UP of Mississippi, 2005), 147.

24 Toni Morrison, "The Site of Memory," in *What Moves at the Margin: Selected Nonfiction*, ed. Carolyn C. Denard, 65–80 (Jackson: UP of Mississippi, 2008), 79.

25 Quoted in Michael Schumacher, "Joyce Carol Oates and the Hardest Part of Writing," in *Conversations with Joyce Carol Oates*, ed. Lee Milazzo, 135–46 (Jackson: UP of Mississippi, 1989), 139–40.

26 Quoted in Murray, *Shoptalk*, 58.

27 John Gardner, *The Art of Fiction: Notes on Craft for Young Writers* (New York: Vintage Books, 1991), 46.

28 E.L. Doctorow, "The Art of Fiction No. 94 [interview by George Plimpton]," *The Paris Review* 101 (Winter 1986), http://www.theparisreview.org/interviews/2718/the-art-of-fiction-no-94-e-l-doctorow.

29 Quoted in Murray, *Shoptalk*, 150.

30 Quoted in Murray, *Shoptalk*, 61.

31 PBS, "Winter," *The Mind of a Chef*, season 3 episode 9, October 21, 2014.

32 Quoted in Yvonne N. Bui, *How to Write a Master's Thesis* (Los Angeles: Sage, 2014), 94.

33 James Bertolino and Anita K. Boyle, *Pub Proceedings* (Egress Studio P, 2001). Note: The second and third chapbooks of poetry from these collaborators are *Bar Exams* (2004) and *Lit-Wads* (2013).

34 John Gregory Dunne, "The Old Pornographer: Billy Wilder," *New Yorker*, November 8, 1990, 90.

35 Vladimir Nabokov, "Interviews: Anonymous (1962)," in *Strong Opinions* (New York: Vintage International, 1990), 2.

36 Toni Morrison, "The Site of Memory," 79.

37 Donald Murray, *The Craft of Revision*, Anniversary edition (Boston: Wadsworth Cengage Learning, 2013), 1.

38 Raymond Carver, "Raymond Carver [interview]: Mona Simpson and Lewis Buzbee/1983," in *Conversations with Raymond Carver*, ed. Marshall Bruce Gentry and William L. Stull, 31–52 (Jackson: UP of Mississippi, 1990), 43.

39 Raymond Carver, *No Heroics, Please: Uncollected Writings* (London: Collins-Harvill, 1991), 109.

40 Maggie Simmons, "Free to Feel: Conversation with Saul Bellow," in *Conversations with Saul Bellow*, ed. Gloria L. Cronin and Ben Siegel, 161–70 (Jackson: UP of Mississippi, 1994), 165.

41 Robert Frost, "The Figure a Poem Makes (1939)," in *The Collected Prose of Robert Frost*, ed. Mark Richardson, 131–33 (Cambridge, MA: Belknap P of Harvard UP, 2007), 132.

42 Quoted in Murray, *Shoptalk: Learning to Write with Writers*, 181.

43 Mervyn Rothstein, "An Ex-waitress's Writing Success," *The New York Times*, April 22, 1986, http://www.nytimes.com/1986/04/22/theater/an-ex-waitress-s-writing-success.html.

44 William Strunk, Jr. and E.B. White, *Elements of Style*, 3rd edition (London: Collier Macmillan, 1979), 23.

45 Ernest Hemingway, "The Art of Fiction No. 21 [interview by George Plimpton]," *The Paris Review* 18 (Spring 1958), http://www.theparisreview.org/interviews/4825/the-art-of-fiction-no-21-ernest-hemingway.

46 Raymond Carver, *No Heroics, Please*, 108–09.

47 Quoted in Murray, *The Craft of Revision*, 34.

48 Marvin Bell, "32 Statements about Writing Poetry," in *We Wanted to Be Writers: Life, Love, and Literature at the Iowa Writers' Workshop*, by Eric Olsen and Glenn Schaeffer, 87–88 (New York: Skyhorse, 2011), 88.

PART II
CRAFT

Image, Detail, and Figurative Language

> We are important and our lives are important, magnificent really, and their details are worthy to be recorded. This is how writers must think, this is how we must sit down with pen in hand. We were here; we are human beings; this is how we lived. Let it be known, the earth passed before us. Our details are important. Otherwise, if they are not, we can drop a bomb and it doesn't matter. —*Natalie Goldberg*[1]

Two small memories of being a little kid. One: We're in a huge warehouse down on the waterfront; machines stand silent around us. Distant relatives have come and we're touring the plywood mill where Dad labors as a sheet turner. I look around but don't see the desk or table, the pots of ink, crayons or pencils, the stacks of paper. This can't be the true place Dad goes to cut wallet-size pieces of paper, to draw the head of the president, to color each one green. When I've asked what Dad does at work, I've been told "he makes money." Two: My mother, grandmother, and I pick ripe raspberries into white enamel kettles. We'll have some on shortcake tonight, but most will get sugared and preserved. Grandma's root cellar is filled with shining glass jars of canned peaches, green beans, cherries, and pickles. Up the row I hear them speaking in quiet voices about a man my family knows. "He got canned at work," one says. I picture the huge glass jar, the man lowered carefully through its opening. He is sealed up, stored on some shelf in the warehouse. I understand from their voices that my mother and grandmother think this development was inevitable and shameful. I do not yet understand—because as children, we don't—that adults speak figuratively. The images their words cause in my child mind are vivid because language is still new and fresh.

Creating an Experience

If somehow you had to forget everything else you had learned about creative writing, the one friend to lock in an embrace and keep as your companion in writing forever is imagery. Imagery is the specific language of *concrete detail* that causes us to imagine: it's the foundation of all imaginative writing. The creation of images that can pass between humans and connect us to one another is what *all* art strives to do: "How do images move and transfer?" writes cartoonist Lynda Barry. "Something inside one person takes external form—contained by a poem, story, picture, melody, play, *etc.*—and through a certain kind of engagement, is transferred to the inside of someone else. Art as a transit system for images."[2]

In the art of writing, squiggles on a page or screen are translated into sounds and words in our mind, and *only* the signals that speak to our five senses can make us imagine, make us feel, and sometimes make us moved. I mean physically moved: we get goose bumps, widen our eyes, feel the hairs rise on our neck or arms, suck in our breath, shake our head, or read aloud with a trembling voice, even cry. These are outward signs we're moved internally. We read literature to feel; we write literature to feel. Here is a tremendous distinction: other kinds of writing try to explain, inform, or persuade; creative writing *moves* us through images.

Writing that offers abstraction can inform, but it does not move us. "War is terrible." "Sacrifice is honorable." "Love changes us." "Our true nature never really changes." We might resist or agree with such generalizations, but we don't feel them in our body unless the abstract can be made tangible through imagery, unless they speak the language of the five senses that most humans share in common:

- **Sight**

  And the shirts,
  all the starch gone out of them,
  clearly depressed,
  hang limply in the closet,
  wire question marks
  at their necks. (Lana Hechtman Ayers, "He's Gone")[3]

- **Sound**

  There was an old man who sold potatoes from a dory in the harbor. His voice was like sand. He talked to me every day.

  Potatoes from the earth, potatoes from the cellar! You can still taste the summer! You can still taste the summer!

  Later I would think of his voice when reading of trolls under bridges. (Steven Kuusisto, "Harbor Songs")[4]

- **Smell**

  What I remember of childhood, of being frightened at night and coming into my parents' bedroom, is the molasses smell of people breathing all night in a closed room. (Kathleen Dean Moore, "Muskgrass Chara")[5]

- **Taste**

  ...I ease one [cherry tomato]
  loose from its siblings,

from its clear plastic coffin,
place it on my tongue.

Just to try. The smooth
surface resists, resists,
and erupts in my mouth:
seeds, juice, acid, blood

of a perfect household. (Sandra Beasley, "Cherry Tomatoes")[6]

- **Touch**

  He was afraid of being lost, so he repeated trail marks to himself: this is my mouth tasting the salt of her brown breasts; this is my voice calling out to her. He eased himself deeper within her and felt the warmth close around him like river sand, softly giving way under foot, then closing firmly around the ankle in cloudy warm water. (Leslie Marmon Silko, *Ceremony*)[7]

- **and, rarely, sensory abilities that seem to go beyond these five:**

  The travelling salesman had fed me pills that made the linings of my veins feel scraped out. My jaw ached. I knew every raindrop by its name. (Denis Johnson, "Car Crash while Hitchhiking")[8]

Underline each word and phrase of imagery in Brian Turner's poem "Eulogy" (below), and you'll notice that nearly the whole poem is underscored as something we can smell, taste, touch, see, or hear with our imagination. Underline each word and phrase of imagery in James Dao's 2009 *New York Times* article (below) on the same topic, and notice almost nothing is underlined. It's not that the poem is "better" but that creative writing and expository writing (writing that informs) have different purposes—so they use different techniques to accomplish those purposes. Both require careful attention to detail, but journalism uses detailed information (fact) where creative writing uses sensory detail (image). There's no correct "ratio" of imagery for any story, essay, or poem you write, but you'll discover imagery must be prevalent in any project that succeeds at moving your reader. How many different senses do you notice deployed in Turner's short poem? How do his images make you feel?

Eulogy

It happens on a Monday, at 11:20 A.M.,
as <u>tower guards eat sandwiches</u>
<u>and seagulls drift by on the Tigris River.</u>
<u>Prisoners tilt their heads to the west</u>
<u>though burlap sacks and duct tape blind them.</u>
<u>The sound reverberates down concertina coils</u>
<u>the way piano wire thrums when given slack.</u>
And it happens like this, on <u>a blue day of sun</u>,
when <u>Private Miller pulls the trigger</u>

to take brass and fire into his mouth:
the sound lifts the birds up off the water,
a mongoose pauses under the orange trees,
and nothing can stop it now, no matter what
blur of motion surrounds him, no matter what voices
crackle over the radio in static confusion,
because if only for this moment the earth is stilled,
and Private Miller has found what low hush there is
down in the eucalyptus shade, there by the river.

PFC B. Miller
(1980–March 22, 2004)[9]

Families of Military Suicides Seek White House Condolences

Since at least the time of Abraham Lincoln, presidents have sent letters of condolence to the families of service members killed in action, whether the deaths came by hostile fire or in an accident.

So after his son killed himself in Iraq in June, Gregg Keesling expected that his family would receive a letter from President Obama. What it got instead was a call from an Army official telling family members that they were not eligible because their son had committed suicide.

"We were shocked," said Mr. Keesling, 52, of Indianapolis.

Under an unwritten policy that has existed at least since the Clinton administration, presidents have not sent letters to survivors of troops who took their own lives, even if it was at the war front, officials say. The roots of that policy, which has been passed from administration to administration via White House protocol officers, are murky and probably based in the view that suicide is not an honorable way to die, administration and military officials say.

But at a time when the Pentagon is trying to destigmatize mental health care in hopes of stemming a near epidemic of suicide among service members, the question of whether the survivors of military suicides deserve presidential recognition has taken on new significance.[10]

Turner served seven years in the US Army, in both Bosnia-Herzegovina and Iraq. Perhaps more than many of us, he has something to say—some opinion, idea—about war. But his poem demonstrates the understanding all artists must have: art isn't journalism, opinion, or lecture. Art *creates an experience* by using concrete sensory details, inviting and trusting us to decide what that experience can mean. Maxine Kumin calls such work "a terrible specificity of detail" and "by terrible I mean unflinching. Honest and sometimes compassionate." The creative writer, she explains, "names and particularizes and thus holds for a moment in time"[11] whatever she or he is drawn to explore. In this way, our writing may be apolitical (without conscious political agenda) or political (choosing to fill in the sensory human details often left out of history, reportage, and official records, details necessary for human understanding). Renée Sarojini Saklikar's *children of air india* helps us imagine the palpable and particular lives of the eighty-two children murdered on Air India Flight 182, Canada's worst mass murder, heavily reported but poorly understood. Her poems about these lives and their contexts are political, but without the clichés, vague promises, and abstract answers so common in politics.

Using Specific Details

We write not with wisdom or opinion but with an attachment to something in the world that intrigues or compels us: a moment and the true way the body can take that moment in through our mouths, eyes, ears, nose, and the receptors of our skin. Our work describes a series of material moments, and, whether they are remembered or invented moments, our reader must imagine them to feel them.

Novice creative writers often resist using specific details. They aim to generalize, thinking readers would prefer to fill in the details with memories from their own lives. These writers assume "blankness" will make their writing universal and better—or will at least not alienate the reader. This resistance to specific detail is a mistake in two important ways:

- First, incongruous as it may sound, "**the more particular, the more specific you are, the more universal you are**" (Nancy Hale).[12] Your reader will respond to your writing (first physically, then emotionally) by experiencing the details you put in it. For example, my father was Danish, humorous, and humble. Never could I have imagined the visual detail James Baldwin uses to characterize his proud and chilling Harlem father in "Notes of a Native Son" who "looked to me, as I grew older, like pictures I had seen of African tribal chieftains: he really should have been naked, with war-paint on and barbaric mementos, standing among spears."[13] Had Baldwin simply generalized "my father was proud," I could not have experienced the feelings Baldwin sought to pass to me.

  I've never owned a dog or flushed a pheasant from an English field, but because Jeanette Winterson uses specific detail in "The 24-Hour Dog," I can feel this narrator's sensual admiration of a new puppy and feel her apprehension:

  > He was soft as rainwater. On that first night I took him across a field mined with pheasants that flew up in our faces when we fused them out. The vertical explosion of a trod pheasant is shock enough when you know it. I knew it and it still skitters me.[14]

- Second, **the way you present specific details shapes what and how those details can mean.** It's not only the concrete details themselves but your particular way of expressing and arranging them that brings power to your writing. In the first paragraph of Winterson's story about the dog, the words "mined," "fused," "explosion," and "shock" would be absent had she generalized and written instead "The first night I got the puppy I walked him in a field and we saw birds." The way she wrote it, this passage implies her story will explore some kind of risk, danger, violence, or battle because her imagery connotes landmines, lit fuses, detonation, and perhaps even post-traumatic stress.

The images we use are *always choices*, always selected for their denotation (literal meaning), connotation (implied meanings), and sound. Listen to Tim Seibles as he chooses comic, self-deprecating images to show us his speaker's effort to begin another day:

Treatise

Those mornings when your body refuses the call
for posture, and your blood shines through your veins
like a great slug on its one sticky foot,
you might think about the stupid things we have to do
in trying simply to touch—how the body
always understands, while the mind is so stuffed
with half-luck and cold gravy
that often you talk to no one but yourself.

Who hasn't known that long conversation
in which nothing is said, but everything is meant,
where the first-date-clumsy silence
is really hope for a slow stroke on the arm
or a sweet invitation of eyes, but for some reason
you just keep talking then go home
wearing a glum smile like a third shoe and mumbling
what you might've said—the *abracadabra*
that would've changed the night into a sloppy kiss.

Can your body be blamed as it lies there knowing
each day will probably be like the rest:
you will see someone you want to touch, but you won't.
You won't because the mind always goes back
to the goofy routine—just as your eyes come to her
laced in the soft haze of a sexual dream,
your mind puts on its big shoe
and twirls the little cane: you walk by
like a duck while she does the same. When
you should've said, *Let's do it standing up*
before age can deface us. Let's cook it good'n'slow
before life's dumb mistakes can erase us.

Sometimes I feel my penis,
like a prisoner in solitary confinement,

raking his rusty cup against the hard bars
of this life pleading for a woman
whose name I don't even know—a genuine pleading
as though for the secret to a secret
that's been kept ever since the first sperm serenaded
the pinkness of the womb and coaxed an egg
to come out and play.

Don't you have to wonder who thought up the steps
for this grumpy parade? Because this world
shouldn't be ridiculous. What remains buried in dreams
and under these wonderful clothes, the blood
can never forget. So, those low mornings when light sags
and your lungs seem broken, remember: the good kiss
is always better than the rest of the date—
the tongue itself, far superior
to the words it shapes. Get up.[15]

Figuring the Figurative

In "Treatise," the poet's astonishing description of a penis as "a prisoner in solitary confinement, / raking his rusty cup against the hard bars / of this life pleading for a woman" shows another powerful use for imagery. "Figurative language" is concrete, literal imagery that also makes a comparison. In a surprising and memorable way, Seibles compares a penis to a prisoner to show us that humans can feel deprived of humanity without the possibility of sexual connection or touch. Making imagery comparative is how creative writers express abstract ideas compactly, gracefully, and memorably. This is how—as Janet Burroway put it—literature is able to "mean more than it says."[16] When we're drafting a project, we often don't know what we "mean"—we simply choose imagery that "feels right" or "sounds right" instinctively. Figurative language is a toolbox full of ways to make our images richer, deeper, and more original:

- A **simile** makes a comparison between two things using the words *like* or *as* (and, infrequently, *so*, *resembling*, or other comparative words). Simile makes a speaker or narrator seem slightly self-conscious, drawing attention to the act of comparison. Here, Faulkner's narrator compares a character's body to a pale and bloated corpse, her eyes to coal:

  > She looked bloated, like a body long submerged in motionless water, and of that pallid hue. Her eyes, lost in the fatty ridges of her face, looked like two small pieces of coal pressed into a lump of dough as they moved from one face to another while the visitors stated their errand. (William Faulkner, "A Rose for Emily")[17]

- A **metaphor** states a comparison without acknowledging the comparison is consciously made—it just *is*. It's simpler, a slightly more authoritative device than simile. Here, Page's garden has become green lace:

The snails have made a garden of green lace:
broderie anglaise from the cabbages,
chantilly from the choux-fleurs, tiny veils— (P.K. Page, "After Rain")[18]

- An **analogy** makes a comparison that is more elaborate than one made in a metaphor or simile. It likens an unfamiliar or complicated *situation or idea* to something simpler or more familiar that readers can imagine. An analogy is often a form of explanation, critique, or consciousness-raising:

The Dance

All of us dance
on a cent's edge.

The poor—because they are poor—
lose their step,
and fall

and everyone else
falls on top. (Humberto Ak'Abal)

- A **conceit** or extended metaphor occurs when a writer sustains and develops a figurative comparison beyond its initial mention:

The yellow smoke that rubs its muzzle on the window-panes
Licked its tongue into the corners of the evening,
Lingered upon the pools that stand in drains,
Let fall upon its back the soot that falls from chimneys,
Slipped by the terrace, made a sudden leap,
And seeing that it was a soft October night,
Curled once about the house, and fell asleep. (T.S. Eliot, "The Love Song of J. Alfred Prufrock")[19]

- An **allusion** is a brief reference to an external context—a person, place, or thing of literary, historical, or cultural significance. The writer expects the reader to have enough knowledge to spot the allusion and understand its comparison to the topic at hand—or to look it up. In his poem about the sacredness of fatherhood, Hayes makes two allusions to figures from the Hebrew bible: Noah, the patriarch who saved all the animals in his ark, and Joseph, a man sold into slavery who rose to prominence and adopted two sons.

    But to rescue a soul is as close
as anyone comes to God.
    Think of Noah lifting a small black bird
from its nest. Think of Joseph,
    raising a son that wasn't his. (Terrance Hayes, "The Same City")[20]

- A **symbol** is something that stands for something else: a flag, a logo, a trademark are symbols suggesting their country, organization, or product. A skull and crossbones suggests pirates; the Mr. Yuck face suggests poison; the image of a red hand on a signal at an intersection means "don't cross now." Symbols aren't universal—they depend on context. A star might mean one thing on an actor's dressing room door, another on a student's exam, still another thing to a Jew, and something else to an astrologer. Alexie uses two symbols in his poem about faith in marriage: a Christian symbol of resurrection (the empty tomb vacated by Jesus) and a Spokane Indian symbol of regeneration (the returning salmon):

  Look. I don't know what
  would help me believe
  that we have become sacred.

  Sweetheart, are we the stone
  rolling from the mouth
  of the tomb that cannot keep him?

  Sweetheart, are we the salmon
  rising from the mouth
  of the river that cannot keep them? (Sherman Alexie, "Rise")[21]

- **Personification** bestows human characteristics on anything nonhuman or represents an abstract quality in human form:

  The wind blows through [Wyoming] most every day unchoreographed with the spontaneous inelegance of a brawl. (Mark Spragg, "In Wyoming")

- **Punning** is a form of word play that suggests two or more meanings from the same word. A pun exploits multiple meanings of words or of similar-sounding words, as Dionne Brand does here with the word "develop":

  On looking at "the photograph of Mammy Prater an ex-slave,
  115 years old when her photograph was taken"

  she waited for her century to turn
  she waited until she was one hundred and fifteen
  years old to take a photograph
  to take a photograph and to put those eyes in it
  she waited until the technique of photography was
  suitably developed
  to make sure the picture would be clear (Dionne Brand, "Blues Spiritual for Mammy Prater")[22]

- **Metonymy** is a figure of speech in which a concept, person, or thing is called not by its own name but by the name of something associated in meaning. Vermette uses it to compare a missing brother to aspects of the music he loved:

    her brother is
    heavy metal ballads
    a thin ripple bass line
    a long
    slow current
    of guitar
    a smooth wave of lyrics

    you always
    remember (Katherena Vermette, "heavy metal ballads")[23]

- **Synecdoche**, like metonymy, is a kind of substitution; the writer uses a part of something to represent the whole. We use this figure of speech quite a lot when we swear, referring to a whole person by naming one body part (such as "asshole"). Eliot's speaker uses synecdoche to compare himself to a crab—the crab's claws stand for the whole:

    I should have been a pair of ragged claws
    Scuttling across the floors of silent seas (T.S. Eliot, "The Love Song of J. Alfred Prufrock")

- **Sense switching**, or literary synesthesia, is a form of comparison that simulates for the reader a feeling of synesthesia (a neurological condition in which one form of sensory stimulation evokes the sensation of another—for instance, when hearing a particular sound produces the visualization of a color). This vivid, layering effect on the senses is created by switching from one sensory organ to another while describing the same thing. Emily Dickinson uses this move when she switches from "blue" (sight imagery) to "buzz" (sound imagery): "There interposed a Fly— / With Blue—uncertain— / stumbling Buzz— / Between the light—and me—." The anonymous writer of this haiku cross stimulates sight and taste:

    home-grown lettuce
    the taste of well-water
    green[24]

In conversation, people often mistakenly use the word *literally* simply for emphasis, when speaking figuratively: "I literally cried my eyes out!" means one's eyeballs did in fact pop from their sockets and dangle by their optic nerves due to the force of tears (a statement more likely to amuse or distract than to elicit the desired sympathy). Such nonsense is spoken when figurative phrases become so overused, so cliché, that we're disabled from recognizing the imagery once so unique and powerful in them. Writers reinvent the world—refresh how to perceive the world—when we describe it in our own words.

Suggested Reading from Our Anthology
Kelli Russell Agodon, "Geography"
Stephanie Bolster, "Many Have Written Poems about Blackberries"
Ann Choi, "The Shower"
Langston Hughes, "Harlem (2)"
Stephen Kuusisto, "Horse"
Patrick Lane, "The Far Field"
Alistair MacLeod, "The Boat"
Madison Minder, "Green"
Simon Ortiz, "My Father's Song"
Richard Selzer, "The Knife"
Richard Siken, "Scheherazade"
Madeleine Thien, "Simple Recipes"

Your Moves

1. Practice using specific detail: choose one item from a group of similar objects, and then describe it in your notebook so that your chosen object could be recognized from among the group. I do this in class sometimes by bringing a box of rocks or leaves. Is your rock three inches in circumference or two, smooth or lumpy, flecked with colors you can name, scented, dusty, or ringed?
2. Move from literal description into figurative: that rock you're still holding, is it like a pumice for softening feet? Is it ringed with white lines like a planet, or smooth and speckled as a robin's egg? Could it be a lost filling from a giant's tooth—or perhaps the period that ends the sentence of a love note spelled out in boulders on a sandy beach?
3. Write in your notebook about a memory you have gratitude for. Focus on what you could see, smell, taste, hear, and touch in this scene. Even a little scene will do, like listening from your bed while your older sister made coffee ... describe how the sounds, then scent, reached you. Read "My Father's Song" by Simon Ortiz and notice how important the sensation of touch is to his gratitude poem.
4. Write to uncover a difficult or traumatic memory, looking to Patrick Lane's poem, "The Far Field" for example. Focus on imagery and the meaning that surfaces, not on judgment or "poor me."
5. Writers tend to overuse sight imagery and underuse all other forms of imagery. Read Stephen Kuusisto's "Horse" and notice how rich this imagery

is, none written from sight. Create an extended description of a setting you know well, using all forms of imagery *except* the visual.

6. Read Richard Siken's "Scheherazade" and Madison Minder's "Green" then write a passage in your notebook with your own dreamlike and surreal imagery.
7. Write about a tool or instrument you can use with precision (your liquid eyeliner, the office copy machine, a lathe, fish hook, hockey stick, or pooper-scooper). Write a collage of instructions, memories, associations, and reflections as Richard Selzer does with his essay "The Knife."
8. Read Stephanie Bolster's poem "Many Have Written Poems about Blackberries" then write about something in your environment that you think people have written about before, but never in the way *you* can. Roses, the ocean, skyscrapers, traffic, the moon, streetlights, falling leaves, the tracks of a Ski-Doo... what's your pleasure? Follow Bolster's lead by using inventive figurative comparisons.
9. Try some haiku: compressed and succinct image-based poems that gained distinction in seventeenth-century Japan. Haiku often suggest a mood or season, imply a comparison, and connote far more than they say. In English, haiku often follow the 5-7-5 syllable restriction. They can have titles, or not. Here are a few examples:

Untitled

Taking morning tea,
the monk remains in silence—
chrysanthemums bloom (Matsuo Bashō)

Sleepless at Crown Point

All night, this headland
Lunges into the rumpling
Capework of the wind.
(Richard Wilbur)

Untitled

winter and summer solstice	冬と夏の至日
two women apart	離ればなれの二人の女は
share the same sensation	同じ感覚を分かち合う (Yasuko Kurono)

10. Choose an object in your daily life and personify it, as though this object had a consciousness and could perceive the world around it. What does this object see, touch, smell, taste, and hear—and what new form of knowing is revealed as a result? Use Sylvia Plath's poem "Mirror" as a model.
11. Read "Harlem (2)" by Langston Hughes, noticing how simple and concrete the poem appears even though it is about the complex issue of racism. Try writing about a social or political issue that matters deeply to you—but using image and analogy, not opinion or argument, as your source of power.

12. Write about a change you have noticed in your lifetime, but write only about the things that embody or illustrate this change. It might be a change you have noticed in a friendship, in the body of a loved one, in your hometown, or—? Read Ann Choi's poem "The Shower" to see how delicately, yet effectively, this can be done.
13. Notice how vividly Madeleine Thien's story "Simple Recipes" captures the domestic life of her narrator's family—especially in her description of washing rice and preparing meals. Write to describe how you do something with your hands at home—how you prepare a meal, change a diaper, put groceries away, groom your dog, take your bath....
14. We often tack on a moral or thesis at the end of a draft when, in fact, imagery is a much more powerful form of conclusion. Trust your reader to "get it." Begin a new project with a vision of the image that will act as your conclusion—then write your way to this ending. Or revise a lackluster project by creating a new, image-rich ending. Read "The Boat" by Alistair MacLeod to see how a master concludes with unforgettable imagery.

Sound

I write a single sentence at a time, and then I read it aloud. It's like the old Perrine textbook, *Sound and Sense*. Like any writer of fiction, I need to give information, but I try to relay it in a creative and sound-conscious way. Prose needs to aspire to something more than declarative sentences. I hesitate to say that it should express itself in a beautiful manner because that might seem pompous, but that's the general idea. —*Alistair MacLeod*[25]

I've been writing in my notebook at night, before bed, cursoring across my day and choosing moments and details to describe. This writing, on lined pages of a cheap notebook, is a kind of sketchwork—language in strokes, stipples. Describing something (a dead loon I saw washed up against the breakwater this afternoon; the letters P O E T inked across the fingers of my student's right hand), I begin, add, murmur toward words that feel accurate but unusual. I smudge the literal into the figurative—what the loon's body was like, reminds me of. These word sketches help me see little moments in isolation, turning them in my mind to discover their facets like a jeweler meeting a diamond. These are not poems, stories. They're nothing to show anyone. But another day I'm at the gym, on the elliptical, and someone's body near me reminds me of the gothic letters staining my student's fingers, brings to mind the best phrases from my notebook and a sudden new word. Or I'm walking in the park and the creek running through it brings to mind the loon's floating shape, a term I found to describe her curved throat. The notebook images, phrases, and sounds resurface—I focus, really, on nothing else—and now I feel a rhythm and a sense of something to follow... some question, some curiosity. This rhythm I feel (it often comes when I am moving: exercising, cleaning, doing physical work) isn't music but a pace—a shaping of time that helps me fit words together in a new order. This is how my poems usually begin: imagery and language together find a sonic pulse that compels me forward. Finding the sound and shape of one line, I'm pushed over the edge of it into the next, and the next.

Sound Like You Mean It

The sounds language makes begin communicating to us even before we have time to take in the meanings of words and sentences. Anger, fear, tenderness: we hear them immediately—then the sense of the words adds another layer of meaning. We learn as children to listen not just to *what* people say but to *how* they say—because we know sounds have something important to tell. Have you ever felt as if the sounds a person was making were at odds with what that person was telling you, that *how* you were being told was opposed to *what* you were being told? Maybe your boss was speaking in a warm and encouraging voice but telling you that you were being laid off. Perhaps a friend was using a light, teasing voice to say something deeply critical about you. Have you heard a wildly enthusiastic person selling a juicer, cosmetics, or absorbent towels on an infomercial and had the gut knowledge that you were being manipulated? When sounds seem out of step with the real meaning of conversation, it's human to react with confusion or suspicion. In those instances, the spell of belief is broken: we laugh at the infomercial, wonder what sort of agenda our friend has suddenly developed, and doubt that our boss appreciates our economic reality.

But when sound and sense combine forces, it's a powerfully moving thing. Consider the opening of Vladimir Nabokov's *Lolita*. This novel's narrator might have said, "I desired Lolita," and we would be informed of, but unmoved by, his experience. He gives us this opening instead: "Lolita, light of my life, fire of my loins. My sin, my soul. Lo-lee-ta: the tip of the tongue taking a trip of three steps down the palate to tap, at three, on the teeth. Lo. Lee. Ta."[26] This passage sounds sensuous, obsessive, and filled with longing. How it sounds matters to what it means.

It's important to write like you (or your story's narrator, your poem's speaker) mean what you say. Stories, poems, and essays move us by using sound in ways that feel authentic to the experiences explored on the page. An exuberant and joyful poem *sounds* exuberant and joyful; an intimate and sad essay *sounds* like a human being having that experience. If, as a writer, I depend only on the meanings of words to communicate with you, my work is likely to come across as bland, flat, and—even worse—inauthentic or phony.

We learn to *write like we mean* by listening. Listen carefully to how you and others complain, brag, comfort, plead, threaten, and woo. Notice the ways that speech from different geographies, social classes, genders, generations, and eras can make the "same" language bend and sing differently. How we use words with "f" and "t" and "c" and "k" sounds when we're hurt or mad as hell. How "awww" and "ooooo" sounds erupt from sane adults when puppies or babies join us. What's happening when a sentence has a lot of "p" and "b" sounds close together or when the sibilant "sssss" sneaks into a description? Notice your girlfriend, her hands clenched into fists. She's talking. In. Short. Fragments. Or maybe it's late at night, your heads together on the pillow, and her voice is soft and dreamy as a run-on sentence, telling you about this place she went on vacation every summer when she was a kid in

New Brunswick and there was this waterfall.... Listen. Let these patterns of sounds intuit their way into your writing. Write by ear.

The Mind's Ear

Using imagery to describe the world's sounds, we bring our reader's imagination into that world. But language itself is a sonic world, made tangible when heard aloud or heard silently in our "mind's ear" as readers. In creative writing, it's essential to write not just *about* sound but *with* sound. When I listen to Peggy Shumaker's essay "Moving Water, Tucson," it communicates to me not just with its imagery of a summer storm and flash flood in a desert arroyo; I experience this information as a sensual flood because Shumaker's words are sonically arranged and repeated to create that effect. Listen:

> Under sheet lightning cracking the sky, somebody's teenage brother decided to ride the flash flood. He stood on wood in the bottom of the ditch, straddling the puny stream. "Get out, it's coming," the kids yelled. "GET OUT," we yelled. The kid bent his knees, held out his arms.
>
> Land turned liquid, that fast, water yanked our feet, stole our thongs, pulled in the edges of the arroyo, dragged whole trees, root wads and all, along, battering rams thrust downstream, anything you left there gone, anything you meant to go back and get history, water so high you couldn't touch bottom, water so fast you couldn't get out of it, water so huge the earth couldn't take it, water... We couldn't step back. We had to be there, to see for ourselves. Water in a place where water's always holy. Water remaking the world.

Shumaker's passage builds and rushes like the floodwater; when you read it out loud, the effect is even more pronounced (and you should read *your* work out loud as you draft and revise it, to hear it the better). Marilyn Dumont builds a completely different sonic landscape for her poem "Still Unsaved Soul"; clear and palpable anger communicates itself with grit and force:

> If I hear one more word
> about your Christian God
> I'm gonna howl
> I'm gonna crawl outta my "heathen"
> skin and trick you
> into believing I am the Virgin
> Mary and take you to bed.
>
> If I hear one more line
> about your white church
> I'm gonna start singing and dancing
> with all my "false gods"
> in a giveaway dance and honour
> you with all the "unclean" sheets from my bed.

If I hear one more blessed thought
or witness one more holy act
I'm gonna throw-up
35 years of communion hosts
from this *still unsaved soul.*

Generated from the contexts of colonialism, genocide, the missionary schools that indigenous and Métis peoples were subjected to, and negative stereotypes against Native women ("squaws"), Dumont's poem sounds tense, wounded, but also declarative and strong: it speaks with the voice of a woman who has decided, "No more!" It announces her decision in no uncertain words. Listen to the terse, staccato burst of the first line—each word a single syllable and the phrase itself a conditional, high-pitched threat ("If—"). If this writer chose the formal sound of "going to" instead of the colloquial "gonna," the poem would have a different speaker and a different tone. Using our innate understanding that people repeat ("If I hear one more..." and "I'm gonna") to pointedly instruct, scold, and emphasize, Dumont takes a huge risk. She makes her speaker sound angry—for certainly, some readers will turn away from that anger. But as a writer, she has valued and shaped the raw authentic sound of that truth.

Cultivating a Sound Garden

Because poetry has existed longer than the written word, it's the literary form that makes the most use of sound (and meaningful silence). Humans used sound to aid memorization so that long family and tribal histories could be memorized, recited, and passed on as poems. This was happening for centuries before written texts existed; but because humans retain a sense of pleasure and meaningfulness in the sounds of language, both prose writers and poets continue to use these resources. Listen to this short paragraph from surgeon Richard Selzer's essay "The Knife," describing his experience of surgery:

> A stillness settles in my heart and is carried to my hand. It is the quietude of resolve layered over fear. And it is this resolve that lowers us, my knife and me, deeper and deeper into the person beneath. It is an entry into the body that is nothing like a caress; still, it is among the gentlest of acts. Then stroke and stroke again, and we are joined by other instruments, hemostats and forceps, until the wound blooms with strange flowers whose looped handles fall to the sides in a steely array.

Selzer describes something frightening (splitting another person open in surgery), yet the pleasing quality of his diction (word choice) arrests us; it alerts us to his care and tenderness during this act. This "pleasing quality" of his language is not by chance. It happens when words share similar sounds (not always *letters*) in the same neighborhood (not necessarily in the same sentence or line, but heard within a few seconds of one another). These effects cause us to savor language, to slow down, and to pay attention. We have many more tools available to help cultivate a sound garden:

- **Assonance** is the repetition of vowel sounds ("d*ee*per and d*ee*per into the person ben*ea*th"; "the w*ou*nd bl*oo*ms with strange flowers wh*o*se l*oo*ped").
- **Consonance** is the recurrence of consonant sounds ("in*st*rumen*ts*, hemo-*stats*"; "*l*ooped hand*l*es fa*ll*").
- **Alliteration** is the repetition of *initial* consonant sounds ("A *s*tillness *s*ettles"; "*h*eart and is carried to my *h*and").
- **Onomatopoeia** refers to words that sound like what they mean (the *snuffle* and *gargle* of the suction machine).
- **Repetition** is the reuse of whole words or phrases ("*It is* the quietude of *resolve* layered over fear. And *it is* this *resolve* that lowers us..."; "*stroke* and *stroke* again").

We can work with sonic effects not just in our diction but also in our structure (in lines and in sentences). We can use **meter** (see the poetry chapter) and the following:

- **Anaphora** refers to a repeated word or phrase at the start of concurrent lines in a poem. Irena Klepfisz uses anaphora in her long poem "Bashert":

  These words are dedicated to those who survived
  because life is a wilderness and they were savage
  because life is an awakening and they were alert
  because life is a flowering and they blossomed
  because life is a struggle and they struggled
  because life is a gift and they were free to accept it[27]

  This effect also happens in prose by starting a series of sentences with the same word or phrase.

  In the above-mentioned paragraph from "The Knife," concurrent sentences begin with "*It is* the..." and "And *it is* this..." and "*It is* an...." Speech and sermon writers (think of Martin Luther King, Jr.'s "I Have a Dream" speech) and spoken-word poets use this sonic device often; it creates a rhythm that brings structure, urgency, and weight to their words.

- **Cacophony** is a sonic effect used to enhance the reader's feeling of unpleasantness when distasteful situations or dreadful things are described. Dissonant, harsh, inharmonious—this language is stressful to pronounce (achieved often with consonants p, b, d, g, k, ch, sh) and can seem relatively loud. (Elsewhere in "The Knife" Selzer uses cacophony: "Within the belly a tumor squats, toadish, fungoid. A gray mother and her brood. The only thing it does not do is croak. It too is hacked from its bed....")
- **Euphony** means "sweet voiced" (from the Greek) and is soft, soothing language arranged in a harmonious way to create a pleasant, peaceful feeling.

Vowels (a, e, i, o, u) and easily pronounced and enunciated consonants (l, m, n, r, y) characterize its languid and lovely nature. ("And if the surgeon is like a poet, then the scars you have made on countless bodies are like verses into the fashioning of which you have poured your soul. I think that if years later I were to see the trace from an old incision of mine, I should know it at once, as one recognizes his pet expressions." —"The Knife")

- **Cadence** refers to the pace and velocity of language (its speed) and to the arrangement of stressed and unstressed syllables in patterns (its rhythm). My students often call this "flow"—an intentional quality to how lines or sentences move along through time and relate to one another. Play with cadence using these techniques:

    - **Count words.** Sometimes sentences in a paragraph all have the same number of words. It can be boring that every sentence is about the same length. It can get monotonous to have very little variation in sentence length. How dull it sounds when every sentence has twelve words like this. Yikes! When sentences tick along with the unchanging beat of a metronome, boredom prevails. Richard Siken's speaker in his prose poem "You Are Jeff" is not bored; his sentences vary widely until the end, when the last four are so short they seem like ellipses aimed at an approaching hairpin turn:

        > There are two twins on motorbikes but one is farther up the road, beyond the hairpin turn, or just before it, depending on which twin you are in love with at the time. Do not choose sides yet. It is still to your advantage to remain impartial. Both motorbikes are shiny red and both boys have perfect teeth, dark hair, soft hands. The one in front will want to take you apart, and slowly. His deft and stubby fingers searching every shank and lock for weaknesses. You could love this boy with all your heart. The other brother only wants to stitch you back together. The sun shines down. It's a beautiful day. Consider the hairpin turn. Do not choose sides yet.[28]

    - **Vary sentences.** Unvarying sentence structure can make your language sound monotonous too. Shake it up! Here's a quick guide to sentence structures:

        Simple: Hubert invited Esperanza to a party. She did not want to go.
        Compound: Hubert invited Esperanza to a party, but she did not want to go.
        Complex: Although Hubert invited Esperanza to a party, she did not want to go.
        Loose (having the main point at the beginning):Esperanza stayed at home and painted her toenails a vibrant shade of electric purple because she knew that, if she went to the party, it would be dull.
        Periodic (having the main point at the end): Because she knew the party would be dull, Esperanza painted her toenails a vibrant shade of electric purple and stayed at home.

- **Scan syllables.** My students often enjoy T.S. Eliot's "The Love Song of J. Alfred Prufrock" for its cadence. Here's how the poem begins:

  Let us go then, you and I,
  When the evening is spread out against the sky
  Like a patient etherized upon a table;
  Let us go, through certain half-deserted streets,
  The muttering retreats
  Of restless nights in one-night cheap hotels
  And sawdust restaurants with oyster-shells:
  Streets that follow like a tedious argument
  Of insidious intent
  To lead you to an overwhelming question...
  Oh, do not as, "What is it?"
  Let us go and make our visit.

  A lot is happening with sound there, but the cadence underpins it all, created by Eliot's arrangement of **stressed and unstressed syllables**. Isn't that just a matter of how you personally pronounce or emphasize words? No, it's really not. If you say a sentence and want your voice inflection to carry meaning, you can emphasize certain words. For example, compare the different meanings of the following sentences if they were spoken:

  I *went* to the store. (I've already been there)
  I went to the *store*. (I didn't go somewhere else)
  I went to the store. (I'm the one who went to the store)

  To indicate that kind of inflection on paper, you have to italicize it—because you aren't physically there to read the phrase out loud to your audience.

  Cadence isn't about using emphasis for drama, irony, or clarification; it's a sonic measurement independent of sentence structure or line breaks, created by hearing the beat of each word and surrounding that word with an arrangement of syllables composed for their "flow" together. Sometimes you have to use a dictionary to hear the sound of a word; it's important to use a paper or electronic dictionary that shows pronunciation (not just the definition). Using a dictionary is a normal and everyday occurrence in the life of a writer: we're always learning more words, learning more about words.

  When you look up a word in the dictionary, you can see how many syllables it has, which syllable has the primary or "hardest" stress (sometimes called the "beat") and whether there are one or more secondary stresses in that word. You'll be surprised by how many words you "mishear" in your head. As you draft and revise, look words up not just to be certain of their meanings but also to know how readers hear them. For example:

cal-cu-la-tion: ,kal – kye – ‘la – shen.

The “ , ” before the first syllable means that this syllable has a secondary accent or secondary stress (different dictionaries use different symbols; there is a key to understand the code at the front of each kind of dictionary). The “ ‘ ” before the third syllable means that this syllable carries the main beat, accent, or stress of the word: calcu***LA***tion. We say the word with a soft accent on the first syllable, an unaccented second syllable, a stressed third syllable, and then a last unaccented syllable. You could write “calculation” musically this way: “BEAT rest BEAT rest,” or you could use the following symbols to scan it: “ / ˘ / ˘ .”

If you look at nonliterary prose (an office memo or email, a news article, the catalogue description of an item, or instructions) and attempt to scan it for cadence, you’ll get muddled pretty quickly. You’ll find runs of single-syllable articles, prepositions, and pronouns (such as *to, it, the, an, or, by, if, they*) that you can’t tell whether to stress or not, and then maybe three or four seemingly accented syllables together in a row, and so on. It never really falls into a pattern or has any sense of “flow”—it’s not musical, nor was it intended to be.

“The Love Song of J. Alfred Prufrock” isn’t locked into one consistent rhythm pattern; it’s not written entirely in meter (see the poetry chapter regarding meter), but it does often fall into a cadence that lasts for several lines at a time. Eliot alternates an unstressed syllable, then a stressed one, then unstressed, stressed, and so on. This pattern has a name (it’s called “iambic pentameter”; you’ve made its acquaintance if you’ve read Shakespeare), but the name is not so important—what is important is simply the fact that there is a repeated pattern; you could scan it like this:

˘ / ˘ / ˘ / ˘ / ˘ /
Of restless nights in one-night cheap hotels

˘ / ˘ / ˘ / ˘ / ˘ /
And sawdust restaurants with oyster-shells:

If this doesn’t quite make sense to you, read the lines out loud and emphasize each accented syllable as indicated above. Then read it aloud again and emphasize the ***un***accented syllables: it would sound weirdly offbeat, like this:

OF rest-LESS nights IN one-NIGHT cheap HO-tels

AND sawDUST restAUrants WITH oySTER-shells.

Much of “The Love Song of J. Alfred Prufrock” falls into a graceful rhythm of alternating unstressed/stressed syllables—but not all of the poem does that. The exceptions help the poem feel more modern and natural than metered verse or nursery rhyme.

Richard Selzer's "The Knife" is affective—it causes the reader to feel—because it weds terrific content with prose that attends to our human need for meaningful sounds. Although the essay is prose (not poetry), it is crafted at times with the same rhythm Eliot uses, alternating between unstressed and stressed syllables for much of the essay. Again, here is an example from the paragraph we looked at earlier:

a STILLness SETtles IN my HEART
is CARried TO my HAND
it IS the QUIeTUDE
LAYered Over FEAR
reSOLVE that LOWers US, my KNIFE and ME.

Use the Gas and Use the Brakes

When language is sped up it sounds more intuitive, playful, or witty; when slowed, it gives the impression of thoughtfulness, intellect, sorrow, or weight. In a short piece of writing, you might sustain a very fast or slow pace for effect; in a longer work, it's often necessary to vary the pace in accordance with the changing moods or temperament of your narrator or speaker.

- **Slow your pace** by maximizing unstressed syllables and using adjectives, multisyllabic words, technical or formal diction, inverted syntax, complex sentences with many clauses, and—in poems—short lines, end-stopped lines, aeration (white space within lines, between words), dropped lines, and end rhymes. Here is Henry James forcing us to absorb action slowly in his story "The Beast in the Jungle":

> He had been standing by the chimney-piece, fireless and sparely adorned, a small perfect old French clock and two morsels of rosy Dresden constituting all its furniture; and her hand grasped the shelf while she kept him waiting, grasped it a little as for support and encouragement. She only kept him waiting, however; that is he only waited. It had become suddenly, from her movement and attitude, beautiful and vivid to him that she had something more to give him; her wasted face delicately shone with it—it glittered almost as with the white lustre of silver in her expression.[29]

Notice that James is describing a man who is *waiting*; the almost unendurably long sentences cause us to linger for a long time on these few seconds, creating a feeling of tension or stress in *us* that mimics the tension of the moment. Slow doesn't mean dull. Jacqueline Marcus makes her poem "Hanalei Bay" sound slower by inserting white space into the field of her poem; this gives it the weight of contemplation:

Maybe we're here, just once, to remember these dazzling pines,
and the hush of waters,
                                and the low blue clouds

just barely touching the sea?

Maybe there is no final enlightenment,
                                no promise of heaven—

only the moon,
a sailboat skirting the harbor, the flurry of birds

in the sure ease of the heart.[30]

- **You can "sound fast"** by using contractions, run-on sentences (repeatedly using the conjunction "and"), sentence fragments, and rapid-fire alliteration; by including lists; by placing stressed syllables right next to each other (rather than separated by repeated unstressed syllables); and with simple repetition. In poems, longer lines, enjambment, the absence of end rhyme, and stripping away most or all punctuation also increase speed. Barbara Hamby's "Ode to My 1977 Toyota" uses many of these techniques in her zooming poem that begins like this:

  Engine like a Singer sewing machine, where have you
      not carried me—to dance class, grocery shopping,
  into the heart of darkness and back again? O the fruit
      you've transported—cherries, peaches, blueberries,
  watermelons, thousands of Fuji apples—books,
      and all my dark thoughts, the giddy ones, too,
  like bottles of champagne popped at the wedding of two people
      who will pass each other on the street as strangers
  in twenty years. Ronald Reagan was president when I walked...

Creative writing that is lyrical (concerned with rendering the interior life and intimate emotions of a speaker or narrator) makes more use of cadence and sound than do works that are conversational (like realistic conversation) or prosaic (like "regular" or nonliterary prose). An early twentieth-century experimenter with the notion of lyric writing, Gertrude Stein shocked her readers over a hundred years ago by emphasizing music more than sense in her portraits collected as *Tender Buttons*. Here is a taste of her "Roastbeef":

> In the inside there is sleeping, in the outside there is reddening, in the morning there is meaning, in the evening there is feeling. In the evening there is feeling. In feeling anything is resting, in feeling anything is mounting, in feeling there is resignation, in feeling there is recognition, in feeling there is recurrence and entirely mistaken there is pinching. All the standards have steamers and all the curtains have bed linen and all the yellow has discrimination and all the circle has circling. This makes sand.

> Very well. Certainly the length is thinner and the rest, the round rest has a longer summer. To shine, why not shine, to shine, to station, to enlarge, to hurry the measure all this means nothing if there is singing, if there is singing then there is the resumption.[31]

Stein is experimenting with extremes—you may not want to flex your work this far toward the significance of sound. But whether you're crafting poetry or prose, remember that creative writing is a sensual experience; the pleasure we feel as readers is not based only—or even *mostly*—on the sense or meanings of words. Our first pleasure is in the sounds language makes. Challenge yourself to write something with language so compelling and purposeful-sounding that someone on the other side of a wall could "overhear" it—without recognizing any of the actual words—and still find the language moving.

Suggested Reading from Our Anthology

Sandra Cisneros, "My Wicked Wicked Ways"
Jim Crace, untitled flash fiction from *The Devil's Larder*
T.S. Eliot, "The Love Song of J. Alfred Prufrock"
David Foster Wallace, "Incarnations of Burned Children"
Kathleen Halme, "A Study in *O*"
Maria Hummel, "I'm This Many"
Nancy Pagh, "Love Song: After T.S. Eliot"
Sina Queyras, "On the Scent, #14"
Peggy Shumaker, "Moving Water, Tucson"
Lawrence Sutin, "Father Holding Baby"
Bethany Yeager, "Divorce"

Your Moves

1. Do a YouTube search and watch and hear the spoken word of Shane Koyczan, ("To This Day"), Patricia Smith ("Skinhead"), Robert Lashley ("Blues for Big Mama"), Kate Tempest ("Lonely Daze"), and Jack McCarthy ("Drunks"). Begin a spoken-word piece with a goal to perform it out loud eventually. Attend to cadence, use rhyme to aid your memorization, and perhaps experiment by composing through voice recording.
2. Find a poem written in a language you do not know but written in letters you are able to pronounce. Read it aloud several times and examine the patterns you see on the page. Write a line-by-line "translation," based only on the meaning you glean from the sounds in the poem, the shape you see on the page, and the content your imagination can provide. Do NOT check a translation to see what the poem is about until you are done.

3. Make a list of silly words. Make a list of ugly words. Make a list of beautiful words. What do you notice about the sounds of the words in each category? Write a piece that uses most of the words from one list.
4. Write about something beautiful (like a baby) using cacophony (ugly sounds) and then write about something dreadful (like murder) using euphony (sweet sounds). To what degree do the results create suspicion, revulsion, or humor? Do you like these effects?
5. Do you have a favorite letter or sound? Read Kathleen Halme's "A Study in *O*" and then write your own study (it doesn't have to be a poem) exploring all the possibilities of your favorite—or just of a letter or sound that intrigues or challenges you.
6. Compose a monologue from the point of view of an angry character. Try to convey anger on the page through word choice and sentence structure—go easy on the exclamation points, and no italics or bold is allowed. Now write a second monologue, about the *same* topic or experience, through the perspective of a character in a totally different mood. These characters are not allowed to tell us their emotional state—it must be evident from how they sound.
7. Read Sina Queyras's "On the Scent, #14" and then brainstorm a list of slang and colloquialisms used by a social group or clique *you* know well. Write to capture the essential character of that group through the sounds they make to one another.
8. Read the full text of T.S. Eliot's poem "The Love Song of J. Alfred Prufrock"; then read Nancy Pagh's riff on it called "Love Song: After T.S. Eliot." Choose any poem in the anthology that attracts you with its use of sound then write your own riff on it, paying particular attention to cadence.
9. Remember a place you associate with your childhood. Remember the terrain of the landscape, the beat of the city. Remember the people who populated this place and the sounds of their voices; what rhythm and patterns do you hear? Write to capture the sound of one person from your childhood in conversation. Or imagine the voice of the land itself, the town or the city speaking.
10. After reading Lawrence Sutin's brief essay "Father Holding Baby," write your own frank confession that also uses a repeated phrase ("Baby kept crying" in Sutin) appropriate to your own experience.
11. Read Bethany Yeager's "Divorce" and Bhanu Kapil's "Three Voices" then write a lyrical (sound-led and image-rich) prose exploration about a time in your life when you experienced intense emotion. Revise it into a piece readers could "overhear" as literature meant for us all.
12. Read Maria Hummel's "I'm This Many" then write to capture the sound of a child speaking. Revise it into a draft meant for adult readers, but retain the energy of a child's voice.

13. Read Jim Crace's untitled flash fiction from *The Devil's Larder* and mark the text for stressed and unstressed syllables. What pattern do you notice? Take a passage from your notebook or a piece you have drafted and rewrite it into iambics: arrange the stressed and unstressed syllables into a "rest BEAT rest BEAT" pattern throughout. Will you have to delete some words entirely? Find synonyms? Change syntax? How do these revisions for sound influence your meaning—and are you pleased with the results? Keep the parts you love.
14. Take material from your notebook and experiment with arranging it into very short lines (like Sandra Cisneros does in "My Wicked Wicked Ways"). Then experiment with revising this material into run-on prose sentences (as David Foster Wallace does with "Incarnations of Burned Children"). Which effects inspire you to keep working with the material or show you something new about it?
15. Return to a story you've been working on. Choose a moment when you want the action to slow suddenly, a moment that needs to carry weight and attention (perhaps the climax?). Revise this passage into slow, rich, quiet language. Revise the sound of the passages immediately before and after it to contrast in pace.
16. Consider the concept of prayer and then write in the voice of a character praying, or as yourself praying. Is this a prayer of thanks, a prayer for forgiveness, a prayer for help? What unique sounds do prayers make? Is it possible or good to write about something nonreligious using the cadence of prayer? Here is an example from Flannery O'Connor's prayer journal, written when she was a student:

    > Dear God, tonight it is not disappointing because you have given me a story. Don't let me ever think, dear God, that I was anything but the instrument for Your story—just like the typewriter was mine. Please let the story, dear God, in its revisions, be made too clear for any false & low interpretation because in it, I am not trying to disparage anybody's religion although when it was coming out, I didn't know exactly what I was trying to do or what it was going to mean.[32]

Character and Setting

> A first meeting. A meeting in the desert, a meeting at sea, meeting in the city, meeting at night, meeting at a grave, meeting in the sunshine beside the forest, beside water. Human beings meet, yet meetings are not the same. Meeting partakes in its very essence not only of the persons but of the places of meeting. And that essence of place remains, and colors, faintly, the association, perhaps, forever. —*Ethel Wilson*[33]

I live in Bellingham, Washington. If you've never been here, this information means almost nothing. If you live in my region, you might associate this place—and me—with rain, marijuana, cross-border shopping, or snowboarding a nearby snow-capped mountain. I read online that apparently most Bellingham men wear woolen hats, toques, much of the year. Broad associations don't help you imagine my Bellingham in any meaningful way. I need to write how my Bellingham radiates from a center that is Whatcom Falls Park—where my drinking water licks whorls into sandstone as it falls through a creek toward the saltwater bay. My town glows with frontier brick in sunlight and rainlight, built on west-facing hills rising from that bay. Around me are fishers, hipsters, students, painters, addicts, clerks, baristas, and farm-machinery salespeople walking the tree-lined streets, browsing the kale and roasted hazelnuts at the farmer's market this Saturday morning. My Bellingham smells like three-day-old hot-dog water left on the back of a stove—an association lingering from the pulp mill where my grandfather worked; the mill left town years ago. My Bellingham is bounded to the northwest by the semipermeable membrane marking the Lummi reservation, a place I take students on field trips. A place I read about, knowing almost no one there. How complicated, the "my," the "I," the "us" of any place called home.

A Symbiotic Relationship

Character and setting are involved in a deeply symbiotic relationship, making it hard to tear one apart from the other. The story of *who we are* (our "nature") entangles with every imaginable element of *where we've been* ("nurture"). We're all individuals with an essential self or character that has been shaped, tested, and made tangible and real to others through a vast network of contexts. These include the social contexts of family and of our work, recreation, and friendship communities; the historical contexts of our era, generation, and ethnic communities; the geographical contexts of our region and town; and the political and economic contexts that daily surround us and measure our boundaries. Fashion—what we wear on our bodies—plays a role in discovering and expressing our character, even if we think we make no conscious decisions about style. All of these are "setting."

Setting is intrinsic to the understanding and expression of character—and setting comes to the reader filtered *through* or *for* the development of character. Novice creative writers sometimes assume characters are active and interesting whereas setting is inactive, static, and relatively unimportant—just a backdrop. The drafts that result from this misapprehension are populated by generic, wooden, featureless "nobodies" whose fault is that they exist "nowhere" in particular.

Somebody Somewhere

Creating individual and moving "somebodies" in animated and specific "somewheres" is the work of creative writers in all genres. Getting beyond "flat" characters, beyond the "cardboard backdrop" of shallow setting, brings authenticity and depth to stories, essays, and poems. Whether you are writing about real or invented characters and settings, it's equally important to create them in your reader's imagination. Your audience encompasses readers beyond the other students in class, beyond folks you know; because of digital technologies, more than ever before, as a writer you must anticipate access to global audiences. So detail is crucial. Give us your mother standing at the bleached-oak kitchen cabinet fiddling with the plastic black basket of the electric coffeemaker; give us her shag haircut, floral apron, habit of poking out the tip of her tongue while she thinks, and her liberal use of the phrase "got it" and Dior's "Poison."

When our characters inhabit Calgary in the 1930s or the planet Zorlon in the 2080s, we know we'll have to bring that setting alive by describing the technology, fashion, furnishings, phrases, currencies, and sights and sounds of the era. But we often forget that our *own* setting is historical; this forgetting blinds us from noticing and using the tangibles that characterize *now.* Your audience may read your project ten, fifty, or a hundred and fifty years from now, unable to assume details about people and culture that you take for granted. Understand that your reader seeks concrete touchstones to place your writing in a setting and to show us who that character really is. Understand all writing is historical.

"Write what you know" is a truism meant, of course, to be stretched and tested. But setting your writing in places you've actually experienced, inhabited by characters based on aspects of people you know, brings a level of truth to your work that's usually missing if you make your main character a fashion photographer (a job you know practically nothing about) in New York City (where you've never lived) in the seventies (before you were alive). Value the specific suburb, reservation, small town, island, inner-city neighborhood, valley, or prairie you know intimately. Value the old women who work in your church, the big-bellied men your father fishes with, the geek boys in your Scout troop, the fellow selling sunglasses and umbrellas near your bus stop every day.

Places and people you came of age with are *gold* for you now, as a writer, because you innately understand what is luminous and real about them. Poet Linda Gregg calls these our "resonant sources": the concrete details from youth, embedded in our way of knowing. Writing from these sources, we can choose "the two or three particulars that create a whole landscape, which manifest a city street with its early morning rain."[34] When we write places and people far away from our own understanding, we often write as a tourist: we're enthusiastic, but on a predictable and packaged tour.

Desire and Change

Literary fiction is built on the foundation of individual characters we can connect and empathize with, even if they're up to things we don't approve of. Nonfiction and poetry need character too, although we sometimes forget this is so. Virginia Woolf puts her finger on the requirement for a "who":

> Here I come to one of the memoir writer's difficulties—one of the reasons why, though I read so many, so many are failures. They leave out the person to whom things happened. The reason is that it is so difficult to describe any human being. So they say: "This is what happened"; but they do not say what the person was like to whom it happened. And the events mean very little unless we know first to whom they happened.[35]

The personal essay's "I" and the poem's speaker (unless one is writing a "persona poem"—and arguable even then) are each *a shaped version* of the writer's self. This self is a character. Whether writing a fictional character or a shaped version of the self, the writer must understand the character at hand—the character who inhabits that particular poem, essay, or story—and must also understand what all *written* characters do: all characters in literature *desire* and *change*. Let me elaborate.

A character is essentially a desire or yearning, represented as a specific person; the "arc" or journey a character makes and the reader's satisfaction with the conclusion of that journey rest on the character's ability to act in expression of her or his desire. The actions that characters take because of desire cause tension or trouble (or add *more* trouble to a problem dropped on their doorstep). Unless you're a drama queen, you hate trouble in real life. But in your writing, this form of tension is necessary because there's no movement or energy on the page without it. Desiring revenge, Ahab sets off in the wake of Moby Dick. Desiring passion, Madame Bovary chases her romantic fantasy. Desiring wisdom, Doctor Faustus makes a deal with the devil.

Desire (an abstraction) is made tangible through the settings that characters find themselves in and the actions they take. In stories, desire is often revealed slowly. Pud, the narrator of "Out on Main Street," yearns for a simple yet authentic identity (abstraction); her desire is made manifest to the reader through the tensions she experiences when she and her partner go to Vancouver's Little India district for sweets. In poems and essays—especially lyrical, nonnarrative pieces—desire is revealed through imagery and the sound of language. The tension of a poem or essay is usually a question (spoken or implied) about how an image can mean. You can see this desire illustrated in the way Mary Oliver's poem "The Summer Day" shows us an "I" closely attending to the details of watching and wording one grasshopper on her palm. "Who made the world?" her poem begins; the speakers of all poems and personal essays, in their myriad ways, are chasing a similar desire, asking, by paying attention to the details, "What can I know and speak about life?"

Passive figures who have no desire are called "flat" characters (appearing briefly to move a scene forward, they have no inner life or complexity the reader can access) or "stock" characters (they are an oversimplified "type" or stereotype, such as a gangsta or an absent-minded professor). Flat and stock characters lack the capacity for change. A story, essay, or poem with such inertia at its core will fail to engage a reader because it's boring to read about predictable automatons who do or think exactly what we expect and don't seek meaning: the ability to gain insight and to change is a moving human quality that we all admire and hope for. We come to the page, come to literature, wanting to experience a change with a character or speaker.

Characters must be capable of change. The nature of the change varies among stories, essays, and poems:

- **In stories, desire can relate to any theme and the resulting change can be external** (expressed as an action) **or internal** (expressed as thought or reflection). The capacity for change applies both to the protagonist (the main character, with whom we are meant to mainly identify) and to the antagonist (or villain). The less appealing a character is, the more necessary the *possibility* of change and redemption, to sustain tension and interest. For instance, as chilling an antagonist as I've ever encountered is The Mistfit in Flannery O'Connor's story "A Good Man Is Hard to Find." While The Misfit, an escaped prisoner, holds a gun to grandmother (the protagonist) and her vacationing family, he remembers his effort to reach an understanding about his criminal past:

> "Turn to the right, it was a wall," The Misfit said, looking up again at the cloudless sky. "Turn to the left, it was a wall. Look up it was a ceiling, look down it was a floor. I forget what I done, lady. I set there and set there, trying to remember what it was I done and I ain't recalled it to this day. Oncet in a while, I would think it was coming to me, but it never come."[36]

The slim possibility that The Misfit will understand what started his cycle of violence and change his mind about the unfolding crime intensifies the tension. This backstory also makes The Misfit more complex, so that we're better able to understand *his* desire for freedom now at any cost.

- **In personal essays and memoirs, a desire is always for the speaker—the "I"—to better understand and make new meaning in the present from past experience.** The "I" is the main character; that character's action is the quest to find meaning by composing the essay itself ("what happened" in the past is not the main action of an essay). Change is made tangible in an essay by reflection or by any other means to communicate that a discovery has been made (for example, by the transformation of imagery from a past experience into figurative meaning in the present rendition of it).

  Essays usually include characters in addition to the "I." Susan Lester's "Belongings" braids together characterization of her adopted son with imaginings of the boy's Korean birth mother; Lester, the main character of her personal essay, desires a wider understanding of mothering—ways mothers claim and release their children. She begins her quest by creating her son as a tangible character:

  > At twenty, he has square feet and wide bones and thick coarse hair; a smile that, while slow, is generous.
  >
  > You want to pet him. From all the bulk and fur of him you wouldn't expect his hands, magician hands. Quick. He draws caricatures in charcoal, plays Bach on guitar, juggles beanbags and folds colored papers into deer and mice, cuts perfect stars with a scissors in one snip, hiding, always hiding the effort.
  >
  > "Ancient Oriental secret," he tells you when you ask. Understand that he drills himself in skills, wrests them painfully from nothingness, trains his hands as if they are wild animals.

- **In poems, the speaker is the main character; the speaker's desire is to word feelings, experiences, or states of mind that seem "beyond" normal language.** Change happens in a poem when the speaker moves from considering the poem's initial or "apparent" topic (the literal imagery that is the poem's tangible setting) to the realization or suggestion of something else. Language carries the speaker to this shift; the wording up to that point in the poem has built a platform from which to leap into another knowing, another plane of perception. In formal poems, the change can happen at a prescribed place. For example, in a traditional fourteen-line sonnet, the shift (called the "volta") occurs as the poem moves from the octave (first eight lines) to sestet (last six lines). At the volta of Edna St. Vincent Millay's sonnet "[What Lips My Lips Have Kissed, and Where, and Why]," the speaker turns her attention away from memories of young lovers and toward acceptance of age and solitude. Line nine begins, "Thus in winter," signaling this shift.

In lyric poems, such as Janice Mirikitani's "Recipe," change is often communicated by a leap. Mirikitani's speaker changes focus from the application of eyeliner onto Asian eyes (to make them appear more "round" and Western), to realizing a terrible angst and sadness about body image and racism. James Wright's "A Blessing" makes a bold leap from scene to spiritual reflection at its conclusion. For lyrical speakers, such as Mirikitani and Wright, the desire is to notice and word the details around them, searching for understanding and meaning through this act of perception.

Because a narrative poem tells a story, its "I" expresses desire and change much as a character would in fiction. In "Power" by Corrinne Hales, the speaker is a young girl attracted to the idea of forcing a train to come to a stop by pretending a body is lying on the tracks. She and her brother stuff old clothes to look like a body and then watch as the train indeed stops. But their power to halt the train is no longer the speaker's focus by the end of the poem:

> I tried to remember which of us
> That red shirt had belonged to,
> But morning seemed too long ago, and the man
> Was falling, sobbing, to his knees.
> I couldn't stop watching.
> My brother lay next to me,
> His hands covering his ears,
> His face pressed tight to the ground.

The speaker's desire for one kind of power has been transformed into her discovery of the power to frighten and hurt people. The observation that now "morning seemed too long ago" signals her change, and her distance, from the child the speaker was just hours before.

Poems can contain vivid characters. "The Colonel," a prose poem by Carolyn Forché, gives us an unforgettable one:

> What you have heard is true. I was in his house. His wife carried a tray of coffee and sugar. His daughter filed her nails, his son went out for the night. There were daily papers, pet dogs, a pistol on the cushion beside him. The moon swung bare on its black cord over the house. On the television was a cop show. It was in English. Broken bottles were embedded in the walls around the house to scoop the kneecaps from a man's legs or cut his hands to lace. On the windows there were gratings like those in liquor stores. We had dinner, rack of lamb, good wine, a gold bell was on the table for calling the maid. The maid brought green mangoes, salt, a type of bread. I was asked how I enjoyed the country. There was a brief commercial in Spanish. His wife took everything away. There was some talk then of how difficult it had become to govern. The parrot said hello on the terrace. The colonel told it to shut up, and pushed himself from the table. My friend said to me with his eyes: say nothing. The colonel returned with a sack used to bring groceries home. He spilled many human ears on the table. They

were like dried peach halves. There is no other way to say this. He took one of them in his hands, shook it in our faces, dropped it into a water glass. It came alive there. I am tired of fooling around he said. As for the rights of anyone, tell your people they can go fuck themselves. He swept the ears to the floor with his arm and held the last of his wine in the air. Something for your poetry, no? he said. Some of the ears on the floor caught this scrap of his voice. Some of the ears on the floor were pressed to the ground.

Notice that the "I" in Forché's poem remains the main character, despite the overwhelming presence of the colonel. It is the "I" with whom we empathize; the speaker's desire is her search for the way to word—and thereby "speak back" to—the colonel's unspeakable cruelty ("There is no other way to say this.").

Creating Memorable Characters

Characters can be brought to life on the page using a combination of moves:

- **Dialogue.** New writers are shy about putting words into the mouths of characters, but we need to *hear* a character to *know* a character. Joan Didion says dialogue "reveals the character to the writer and, ultimately to the reader. I don't have a very clear idea of who the characters are until they start talking."[37] Resist the urge to sanitize and correct your characters' dialogue; we all have an "accent" and voice, which good dialogue reflects. What's important is that dialogue feels authentic and natural, and that it's clear who's speaking (identifying the speaker is called "tagging"). Do use dialogue for scenes in personal essays, and make it representative of what your character *could* have said; we understand you weren't taking notes or recording at the time. Dialogue in this type of personal nonfiction is meant to be essentially, not factually, accurate. Even poems benefit from speaking characters; notice how the colonel in Forché's poem above comes sharply into focus when he says, "I am tired of fooling around.... As for the rights of anyone, tell your people they can go fuck themselves."

- **Indirect characterization.** Direct characterization occurs when the text offers a generalization or judgment about a character. Carolyn Forché might have used direct characterization in her prose poem above by telling us the colonel was a murderer, a psychopath, or a terrorist. She does not, however. Forché understands readers are informed but not moved by character summations—because, if the character has already been assessed, there's no active work left for the reader to do. She uses indirect characterization instead, showing us the way the colonel expects his wife and maid to move everything around him, the way he swears at an animal, waves the dried ears in his visitors' faces, dramatically sweeps the ears to the floor, raises his own glass of wine for effect, and then declares his performance something suitable for the poet to immortalize. His arrogance and violence are palpable through the more tangible gestures of indirect characterization.

- **Character observation.** Characters—like real people—constantly notice and react to their environment. Seeing what characters do and don't notice, we have a stronger sense of who they are. "The more you have them [characters] observe things, the more you get to know them," says Dan Chaon.[38] Here's Dina, an incoming freshman during orientation at Yale, in ZZ Packer's story "Drinking Coffee Elsewhere." A counselor asks everyone to play Trust, the game that has a player fall back into the arms of others:

> "No way," I said. The white boys were waiting for me to fall, holding their arms out for me, sincerely, gallantly. "No fucking way."
>
> "It's all cool, it's all cool," the counselor said. Her hair was a shade of blond I'd seen only on *Playboy* covers, and she raised her hands as though backing away from a growling dog. "Sister," she said, in an I'm-down-with-the-struggle voice, "you don't have to play this game. As a person of color, you shouldn't have to fit into any white, patriarchal system."
>
> I said, "It's a bit too late for that."
>
> In the next game, all I had to do was wait in a circle until it was my turn to say what inanimate object I wanted to be. One guy said he'd like to be a gadfly, like Socrates. "Stop me if I wax Platonic," he said. I didn't bother mentioning that gadflies weren't inanimate—it didn't seem to make a difference.[39]

Dina's observations show us she's African American, smarter than most of the people around her at Yale, sarcastic, highly conscious of status, suspicious of the motives and abilities of others, and doubtful of her own ability to make a difference. Dina tells us none of these things; all are communicated in the passage by how Dina observes her setting.

- **Unconscious action.** It's human nature to give more credit to *un*conscious action than to deliberate or conscious action. If someone tells us we look nice today (conscious action) but their brow is furrowed and they're distractedly staring at our shabby runners (unconscious action), we believe their true opinion is that we *don't* look nice today. Characters can't notice their own unconscious actions, but they can notice the results (for instance, the ragged fingernails and reddened cuticles caused by unconscious nail biting) or how other characters react to them. The unconscious gestures of your characters make them human; readers look to these clues about their real or deeper nature. A great deal is communicated about the character Wes, and the narrator (Edna) who loves him, through indirect action in Raymond Carver's story "Chef's House":

> Wes had this look about him. I knew that look. He kept touching his lips with his tongue.

When we read this passage, we know without being told that Wes is on the verge of returning to alcoholism, and we know Edna knows this too.

Many Uses for Setting

"Place is character," Richard Russo has said, and "to know the rhythms, the textures, the feel of a place is to know more deeply and truly its people."[40] There are many ways to understand setting and its relationship with character:

- **Setting as the revelation of a character.** Nobel-prize winner Alice Munro is among the best at writing intimately of character through setting. Known especially for fiction about the girls and women who inhabit Canada's small towns, Munro introduces us here to Del:

  > We spent days along the Wawanash River, helping Uncle Benny fish. We caught the frogs for him. We chased them, stalked them, crept up on them, along the muddy riverbank under the willow trees and in marshy hollows full of rattails and sword grass that left the most delicate, at first invisible, cuts on our bare legs. Old frogs knew enough to stay out of our way, but we did not want them; it was the slim young green ones, the juicy adolescents, that we were after, cool and slimy; we squished them tenderly in our hands, then plopped them in a honey pail and put the lid on. There they stayed until Uncle Benny was ready to put them on the hook.[41]

  Dropping in to this riverbank we see Del in her element—confidant, clever, not yet socialized as a girl to be squeamish about frogs or afraid of the grass that would slice her exposed legs. She knows the ways of these frogs; she kills the young ones with her bare hands, "tenderly," perhaps with compassion for their sacrifice. The frogs themselves suggest a second use of setting:

- **Setting as a metaphor or symbol.** As readers, we're moved by literature that is rich and complex in ways we often don't consciously perceive the first time we read it. This is why a second—or fifth—reading continues to engage and move us. Having read Munro's *Lives of Girls and Women* before, I know its theme is the painful journey from "green" and "young" childhood through female adolescence in a patriarchal community. So the fate of the squished young frogs—soon to be on Uncle Benny's hook—feels figuratively relevant for the trials Del will face ahead. In Forché's "The Colonel," the setting "The moon swung bare on its black cord over the house" gives us a metaphor connoting interrogation or torture beneath a bare light bulb.

- **Setting as ambiance.** "Atmosphere" is the emotional aura of a piece, created by the setting and the objects in it. "Mood" is the attitude created in the reader by the combination of setting, theme (topic), and diction (word choice). Note that "mood" is distinct from "tone": the attitude of the author or narrator. You could merge atmosphere and mood together and refer to the "ambiance" of setting—the color or feeling setting contributes. Weather and time (a stormy night, a sunny day) are often used to create ambiance. When your character's internal emotional state is *the same* as the ambience or external setting (happy on a sunny day), the atmosphere is bland and static; your story hasn't started. When your character and setting are at odds (grumpy on a sunny day), the atmosphere is charged and the necessary tension has begun.

- **Setting as foreshadowing.** Foreshadowing is an advance signal or warning of what's to come. Its purpose is to arouse the reader, creating more tension. In O'Connor's "A Good Man Is Hard to Find," a family is stranded after an accident lands the family car in the ditch:

  > The road was about ten feet above and they could see only the tops of the trees on the other side of it. Behind the ditch they were sitting in there were more woods, tall and dark and deep. In a few minutes they saw a car some distance away on top of a hill, coming slowly as if the occupants were watching them. The grandmother stood up and waved both arms dramatically to attract their attention. The car continued to come on slowly, disappeared around a bend and appeared again, moving even slower, on top of the hill they had gone over. It was a big black battered hearse-like automobile.

  The "tall and dark and deep" woods of this setting are ominous enough (and O'Connor will continue to mention them as the plot unfolds), but the way the HEARSE moves slowly, like a funeral procession across the landscape, until it stops before the family occupying a grave-like ditch, is a clear foreshadowing that someone or something is going to die.

- **Setting as a character.** As the genres of travel writing and nature writing testify, setting is among the most popular of characters in literature. Henry David Thoreau's *Walden* is perhaps the ultimate example. A naturalist, land surveyor, scholar, poet, and resident, Thoreau lived at Walden Pond for two years, taking its measure scientifically, aesthetically, and philosophically from day to day, season to season. "Of all the characters I have known, perhaps Walden wears [lasts] best."[42] Walden is figurative: "It is earth's eye; looking into which the beholder measures the depth of his own nature. The fluviatile trees next the shore are the slender eyelashes which fringe it, and the wooded hills and cliffs around are its overhanging brows."[43] And Walden is a specific and literal place where, in the early spring of 1846, using a compass, a chain, "a cod-line and a stone weighing about a pound and a half," Thoreau sized it up: "The greatest depth was exactly one hundred and two feet; to which may be added the five feet which it has risen since, making one hundred and seven."[44] The book's title, simply *Walden*, alludes to the pond's significance as a central character—much like *Jane Eyre*, *Moby Dick*, or *Anna Karenina*—a character so particular that Thoreau, meeting it face to face, "can almost say, Walden, is it you?"[45]

Suggested Reading from Our Anthology

Reinaldo Arenas, "The Downpour"
Raymond Carver, "Chef's House"
Michael Crummey, "Bread"
Corrinne Hales, "Power"
Kristiana Kahakauwila, "Thirty-Nine Rules for Making a Hawaiian Funeral into a Drinking Game"
John Marshall, from *Taken With* series, #22
Janice Mirikitani, "Recipe"
Howard Norman, from *I Hate to Leave This Beautiful Place*
Flannery O'Connor, "A Good Man Is Hard to Find"
Elise Partridge, "Edwin Partridge"
Mark Spragg, "In Wyoming"

Your Moves

1. Create a list or catalogue of your "resonant sources" in your notebook—the textures, sights, tastes, sounds, and smells ingrained in your earliest memories. Perhaps begin this entry by writing "I am made of...."
2. Read Mark Spragg's "In Wyoming"; then write in your notebook about the place you know most intimately. It need not be a state or province or a place outdoors. Who are the collective "we" that populate this place, and how does setting shape them?
3. Read "Edwin Partridge" by Elise Partridge; then write in your notebook to capture the essential qualities of a family member by showing this character in settings she or he has inhabited. Focus on how this person interacts with, notices, or responds to the details of the world.
4. Think about a "black sheep"—a person who stood apart from a group you belonged to—in your family, your school, your community, your team, wherever. Experiment with using "showing" to explore this character in the setting as you remember it. Does this writing lead to insight about this character's "desire" or relationship with the group?
5. Write about a character in the wrong setting—an environment unsuitable to who that character really is. This character might be a narrator or someone with whom a narrator interacts and comes to understand. It could be you.
6. Write about someone entirely at home, capable, and attuned to setting—perhaps a setting you know well. If you write a story, a *change* to this setting is the main conflict. If you work toward a poem or essay, write using imagery to discover something you didn't already know about the relationship between people and our environments.

7. Write about a character who believes a change of setting (a different apartment, a move across town, changing from a city life to a rural life, leaving the country) will change everything. Does it?
8. Read about Howard Norman's encounter with a shaman in the excerpt from his memoir *I Hate to Leave This Beautiful Place*; write about a conflict or clash between two characters over a territory or space. Make this setting and the characterization vivid. Choose your literal ground: a city, an armrest between seats on a plane, a top bunk, or office? Figure out what they are *really* fighting over.
9. Read Kristiana Kahakauwila's "Thirty-Nine Rules for Making a Hawaiian Funeral into a Drinking Game"; then write about yourself or a fictional character attending a regional or local event that is imbued with the culture and history of its setting. Dialogue must be present and reflect the local dialect.
10. Read Emily Carr's "The Cow Yard" and then write a story, poem, or essay about a place that was magical to you as a child. Work to avoid sentimentality. Make this experience tangible for a reader fifty years in the future, when the world will have changed.
11. A driver's license lists your name, birthday, address, height, weight, sex, and eye color. Draft a descriptive sketch about a character (a fictional character or someone you know) without using any of this information (including the revelation of gender through third-person pronouns). What other characterizations reveal who this character is?
12. Write about a feature of a setting as if it were a character (personified). Rain on your roof, litter on Euclid Street, eelgrass in the cove, the footpath behind the school, the stove in your kitchen.... What does it desire? What is its conflict? How does it change? Read Richard Shelton's "The Stones"; is your exploration the start of a magical realism story like his?
13. Read "Moving Water, Tucson" by Peggy Shumaker and "The Downpour" by Reinaldo Arenas. Notice how their language captures the energy of a dramatically changing setting. Write about a setting in flux, changing. Create active, living language—not the dry passivity of boring old nature documentaries.
14. Michael Crummey's poems and stories often explore the history of his family and community in rural Newfoundland. Read "Bread" and then write a brief story or narrative poem telling an event that occurred a generation or more ago in your family or home community. You may need to interview a family member or look online to find an old newspaper story. Write to capture the essence of the place, how it shaped the characters you are imagining now.

15. Revise a poem or essay that seems flat: signal a change in your character or speaker by having that person pose a question (in dialogue or internal reflection) at or near the conclusion. Does it work best to answer the question or let it hang? See John Marshall's poem "#22" from his *Taken With* series for an example of this move.
16. Revise a story by expanding your use of setting and including foreshadowing. See Raymond Carver's "Chef's House" and Flannery O'Connor's "A Good Man Is Hard to Find" for examples of this move.

Scene, Exposition, and Reflection

Don't say the old lady screamed—bring her on and let her scream.
—*Mark Twain*[46]

We write to taste life twice, in the moment, and in retrospection. —*Anais Nin*[47]

Once, my father parked our Ford Galaxy on the shoulder of a two-lane highway then walked back to pull quills from a dead porcupine using a set of pliers he kept in the trunk. When we got home he taped five quills to a square of cardboard he cut for this purpose with his pocketknife. The quills were larger than my mother's sewing needles, black, with sharp ivory-colored tips. They looked like a miniature arrangement of spears, perhaps for a diorama. This road kill artifact was for "show and tell." Did you have show and tell in elementary school? We did, and often. This meant we were always on the hunt for some object to bring to class. During show and tell a child would show, then pass around the room, some found object. Everyone could touch it, smell it, rattle it, turn it upside down. Once, a Filipino classmate brought pieces of real sugarcane and we could bite and suck on them. But showing was only half the assignment: you had to tell the story of your object ("We were driving down highway 20 and there was this PORCUPINE!") and you had to explain what you knew about it ("Porcupines are nocturnal rodents that eat plants and climb trees and if a dog attacks a porcupine it will get a face full of these quills!"). Show and tell. Creative writing in a nutshell.

Three Modes to Direct

Stories, essays, and poems are shaped by scene, exposition, and reflection. Knowing how to distinguish and choose between these three modes puts you into both the writer's and the director's chair: you decide what scenes to shoot, what contextual information to convey by shorter and simpler means, what characters' thoughts get expressed through action or through voice-over as though they're speaking their mind. Most of us are pretty savvy viewers of film, television, and advertising; it's not hard to see that our work as writers shares creative strategies with the art of directing film: we decide the form that will reach our reader's imagination.

Scene reaches the imagination tangibly. Imagery is set in place, and the director says "Action!" Characters begin to move, gesture, speak with each other, and interact with the world around them. Action can be as forceful as an explosion at a fireworks factory or as subtle as a lover's eye contact shifting slightly away. In visual media, action is filmed (and often recorded, too); in creative writing, it's described and narrated. Scene creates the impression we're there, experiencing what happens through our senses. This is "showing."

The maxim "show don't tell" is common in creative writing classrooms—not because telling is forbidden but because showing is so crucial and is frequently pushed aside by vast amounts of unnecessary exposition. Exposition is the most common form of telling, and it means conveying information or summarizing events to *inform us of them* rather than to *show them happening.* Overused, exposition is boring and causes the reader to disengage; it seems a lot like some arrogant person blabbing on and on about information relevant to that person but not to us. When readers can imagine and feel we're experiencing a scene, it feels like "our own"—more relevant and interesting to us than exposition.

Reflection is another form of telling, but I rarely see it overused in drafts—perhaps because reflection can be so personal and make the writer feel vulnerable. It works much like looking into the reflecting surface of a mirror and perceiving oneself: we are (or our character is) somehow "apart," looking across at the self from some distance and assessing it. Reflection is a perception or understanding about being and living, expressed so readers feel that they are perceiving it too, thinking it with you. It is an intimacy to allow another person inside a self, to see how one mind works in its rare and deep moments of reflection.

Causing Scenes

Like imagery, scene moves the reader with description using the five senses. We might see the silhouette of a pine tree "write a Chinese poem on the moon" (Malcolm Lowry), hear a boy make "great, flatulent noises by pressing my lips to my forearm" (Stephen Kuusisto), "smell mullets / roasting in a glaze of brown bean paste / and sprinkled with novas of sea salt" (Garrett Hongo), taste "mechouia, the spicy mixture of charcoal-roasted chiles and tomatoes" (Ruth Reichl), and touch—knowing "the difference between a kiss and a *kiss* is the tongue. Inside one's own mouth, there is precious little space for the intruder. Yet in it comes, tenderly or with bravado" (Madeleine Thien).[48]

Unlike imagery, scene orchestrates action through time—beginning with "Action!" and ending with "Cut!" The "Action!" is signaled when readers are made aware we're in a specific setting, a particular moment, and the action moves forward through time. The "cut" is signaled with a transition into exposition or reflection, with white space on the page indicating a **jump cut** or shift to a different scene (different time, setting, point of view, or mood) without transition, or when the piece ends. This lyric poem by Mary Oliver uses scene for its center; notice when the action begins and when the cut occurs:

The Summer Day

Who made the world?
Who made the swan, and the black bear?
Who made the grasshopper?
This grasshopper, I mean—
the one who has flung herself out of the grass,
<u>the one who is eating sugar out of my hand,</u>
<u>who is moving her jaws back and forth instead of up and down—</u>
<u>who is gazing around with her enormous and complicated eyes.</u>
<u>Now she lifts her pale forearms and thoroughly washes her face.</u>
<u>Now she snaps her wings open, and floats away.</u>
I don't know exactly what a prayer is.
I do know how to pay attention, how to fall down
into the grass, how to kneel down in the grass,
how to be idle and blessed, how to stroll through the fields,
which is what I have been doing all day.
Tell me, what else should I have done?
Doesn't everything die at last, and too soon?
Tell me, what is it you plan to do
with your one wild and precious life?

A **tableau** is an arrangement, an image of a moment in a scene where all motion has been stopped and frozen—for instance, Leonardo da Vinci's painted mural *The Last Supper* depicts arrested figures in the act of eating. **Narrative** is an account of connected events, animated through time—like pressing "play" on a tableau and suddenly setting it into forward motion. Narrative poems are mostly scene. Look at "Power," by Corrinne Hales. Only line one is exposition; everything else in the poem carries us through the stages of one event.

As the director of your scenes you get to choose where to place the camera relative to the set and actors. The poems by Hales and Oliver use "close up." Hales places the speaker right next to the brother, his face and hands filling our field of vision in our imagination as the poem ends. The grasshopper washing her face and gazing with her "enormous and complicated eyes" is also written so that we see her large; she fills our mind's full screen. These are choices each writer has made, saying, "Look very closely at this part right here; it really matters to what my poem is about!" If you write every scene *all* in close up, you'll have a claustrophobic, obsessive sort of project—as though the narrator has no perspective or ability to see the "big picture." But if you write scenes with no close up, the narrator seems withdrawn and disconnected, unable to observe the nuances of the world; then readers don't know where the focus of attention lies.

Ernest Hemingway is famous for fiction written almost entirely in scene, using no reflection and *very* little exposition. In "Hills Like White Elephants," the scene telescopes back and forth between the "long shot" (or panorama) of hills in the distance, the "middle shot" of the train station, and the "two shot" (a close-up of two characters), which focuses on just the couple as they argue. We imagine the opening of this story as if it is shot with a moving camera, able to pan and change focus: our eye is directed logically (not randomly) from the far panorama of the hills to the nearer train station, and then finally it settles on the two shot of the couple. The motion and energy of narrative begins with our mind's eye made to move across the tableau of setting; the scene begins when the girl speaks:

> The hills across the valley of the Ebro were long and white. On this side there was no shade and no trees and the station was between two lines of rails in the sun. Close against the side of the station there was the warm shadow of the building and a curtain, made of strings of bamboo beads, hung across the open door into the bar, to keep out flies. The American and the girl with him sat at a table in the shade, outside the building. It was very hot and the express from Barcelona would come in forty minutes. It stopped at this junction for two minutes and went to Madrid.
>
> "What should we drink?" the girl asked. She had taken off her hat and put it on the table.
>
> "It's pretty hot," the man said.
>
> "Let's drink beer."
>
> "Dos cervezas," the man said into the curtain.
>
> "Big ones?" a woman asked from the doorway.
>
> "Yes. Two big ones."
>
> The woman brought two glasses of beer and two felt pads. She put the felt pads and the beer glassed on the table and looked at the man and the girl. The girl was looking off at the line of hills. They were white in the sun and the country was brown and dry.
>
> "They look like white elephants," she said.
>
> "I've never seen one," the man drank his beer.
>
> "No, you wouldn't have."
>
> "I might have," the man said. "Just because you say I wouldn't have doesn't prove anything."

Hemingway's fiction demonstrates another truth about writing scene: "One line of dialogue is worth paragraphs of description" (Leslie Epstein).[49] The female character in this excerpt, named Jig, communicates volumes about her anger, disillusion, and distance from her partner with her words "No, you wouldn't have." Hemingway's restraint in not giving us their backstory or even offering a tag with her lines (such as "she said with a pout" or "the redhead retorted" or "she sobbed") invites and trusts us to witness, conjecture, and credit the cues about the cause for Jig's remark and the reaction it gets from the man.

Perhaps because we associate the word "essay" with academic writing, it's easy to forget that personal essays and creative nonfiction always rely on scene as well. "Almost all creative nonfiction, essays or books, are, fundamentally, collections of small stories—or scenes—that together make one big story," writes Lee Gutkind. He assigns his students a "yellow highlighter test": leaf through a memoir or personal essay you love and, with a highlighter, color in all the scenes. "I promise: You will find you have highlighted a major portion of the text." Gutkind adds:

> Notice—and this is critical—that something happens, no matter how trivial, in each scene.... The beginning engages a reader, makes a promise. The end of the scene fulfills the promise and makes the audience want to know what will happen next, moving the action forward, ideally to another scene, another block of yellow, until the whole story is told and your point is established.[50]

Gutkind encourages each of us to test our personal essays: are the scenes present, does each make a promise, does each cause the reader to wonder what will happen next—and long to understand why? Try the test with this passage from Amy Tan's short personal essay about memory, "Confessions." Careful: you won't highlight it all if you pay attention!

> She had pushed me into the small bedroom we shared, and as she slapped me about the head, I backed into a corner, by a window that looked out on the lake, the Alps, the beautiful outside world. My mother was furious because I had a boyfriend. She was shouting that he was a drug addict, a bad man who would use me for sex and throw me away like leftover garbage.
>
> "Stop seeing him!" she ordered.
>
> I shook my head. The more she beat me, the more implacable I became, and this in turn fueled her outrage.
>
> "You didn't love you daddy or Peter! When they die you not even sad."
>
> I kept my face to the window, unmoved. What does she know about sad?
>
> She sobbed and beat her chest. "I rather kill myself before see you destroy you life!"
>
> Suicide. How many times had she threatened that before?
>
> "I wish you the one die! Not Peter, not Daddy."
>
> She had just confirmed what I had always suspected. Now she flew at me with her fists.
>
> "I rather kill you! I rather see you die!"

"We all tend to use too little scene in creative nonfiction," write Brenda Miller and Suzanne Paola, authors of *Tell It Slant: Writing and Shaping Creative Nonfiction*. "We especially forget the possibilities of representative scene."[51] A **representative scene** makes use of all the tools of scene but offers a sense of *the typical* rather than of one particular scene. Perhaps you want to show your family's dynamic by writing a breakfast scene. But you can't remember any one *specific* morning: what your mother wore and said, your little brother's gesture with a spoon or what brand of cereal he was eating, the clothes you had picked to wear that day, whether your packed lunch contained a peanut-butter sandwich cut on the diagonal or straight across. That's okay; do your best to research, remember, and imagine the details authentic to the historical period and honest in the essentials about people you're exploring—and give us a scene. It's a good idea to "tag" or signal to the reader that this scene is representative. Instead of starting your scene with "One time Chris and I were longboarding down Taylor Street" or "That day Chris and I longboarded down Taylor Street," you might begin "All that summer, Chris and I longboarded down Taylor Street" or "Chris and I would longboard down Taylor Street." After any of these four beginnings, your next sentence could be dialogue or narration, and we're into a scene. But with the last two beginnings, the reader understands the scene represents the kind of boarding you did and your relationship with Chris, not one specific incident.

Malcolm Lowry's "The Forest Path to the Spring," about a period in his life when he and his wife Marjorie lived in a squatter's shack on Burrard Inlet while he tried to write and cope with his alcoholism, begins with a representative scene: "At dusk, every evening, I used to go through the forest to the spring for water. The way that led to the spring from our cabin was a path wandering along the bank of the inlet through snowberry and thimbleberry and shallon bushes, with the sea below you on the right...."[52] This scene of walking along the path begins to fill our imagination, yet we understand that it's many scenes combined into one walk down the path. The sensation continues, even as Lowry introduces characters and dialogue:

> There was another lonely man from the Yorkshire moors, who lived quite alone down beyond the lighthouse, and though he seldom came up to our little bay we saw him, from time to time, when we walked down to the point. It was his joy to make sure that the automatic lighthouse was working, he told us, and in fact he would start to talk, as if half to himself, as soon as he saw us approaching.
>
> "They heagles, how they fly in great circles! Nature is one of the most beautiful things I ever saw in my life. Have you seen the heagle yesterday?"
>
> "Yes, we did, Sam—"
>
> "Why the heagle went round to get his bearings, to look over the country. Two miles wide, hin great circles... Pretty soon you'll see crabs under these stones, and then it will be spring. They're some crabs in spring no bigger than a fly. Now have you ever seen how an elephant was constroocted? And where did those old Romans get them shields but from the rooster's wings?"
>
> "Roosters, Sam?"

Had Lowry only told us he met strange and wonderful people who lived very close to nature, we wouldn't feel we've had a little taste of those meetings, or sensed his compassion for and interest in such outsiders.

In the twenty-first century, we're faced with a particular challenge in the writing of scene. So much living now happens online; unless we want to set all our writing in the past, or write about characters strangely unaware of technology, we need to invent lively and compelling ways of inscribing this network reality. From the outside, all network life looks much the same: that scene is of a character fixated on a device, with little tangible action for the reader to experience sensually. From the inside, network life is limited to a set of environments, programs, and jargon undergoing rapid change—it will have changed by the time most readers access our writing. Details about the network world of the present time are likely to seem quaint or parodic for readers twenty, ten, or even five years in the future. Add to this the fact that many of our readers *are reading* as a deliberate choice to engage in a medium that's not the network; the last thing this audience wants to imagine in detail is the network. As a digital immigrant, I'm vastly curious how you—the digital natives coming of age as creative writers now—will transform the writing of scene, as each generation does. Scene will remain, if changed (for instance, splicing in text messages represented in alternate font). Despite the ever-evolving platforms, programs, and apps, our humanity and our reliance on words remain fixtures in both our network and nonnetwork lives.

Going on an Exposition

Exposition explains or summarizes to condense information or experience, distilling what would take many sentences or paragraphs to show through scene. It sacrifices detailed sensory experience in order to communicate backstory, context, and plot. If you read Amy Tan's passage above carefully, you noticed that the following is actually not scene—it's exposition: "My mother was furious because I had a boyfriend. She was shouting that he was a drug addict, a bad man who would use me for sex and throw me away like leftover garbage." Tan's next sentence ("Stop seeing him!" she ordered) is scene; Tan isn't summarizing the dialogue in the second instance, she is making it speak on the page. Judiciously using exposition, Tan focuses on the violent energy in the present, but we know more about the past that led to this scene and the desire of the characters in it.

Because exposition is summary rather than a sensory creation of experience on the page or screen, readers and viewers alike feel impatient and disconnected if exposition goes on much longer than a few sentences. It feels like we're being lectured at, not engaged, when exposition comes at us. **Information dump** is the term for large chunks of exposition not carefully interwoven into a narrative. **Idiot lecture** is dialogue that exists for purely expository reasons—the sitcom character's roommate repeating the events of the last episode to the main character (for the viewers who missed last week's show) or the villain explaining his sinister plot to our hero while the hero is temporarily immobilized. Science fiction author Jo Walton is credited with the term **incluing**: "the process of scattering information seamlessly through the text, as opposed to stopping the story to impart the information."[53] This talent is especially needed in science fiction, which must invent entire worlds using vast amounts of contextual information.

Here are a couple of useful rules when it comes to exposition.

- First, expect to draft a lot of it and cut most of it. You needed to draft it to understand the contexts and plot of your project, to have these passages as placeholders—but your reader doesn't want or need most of the exposition after you've decided what to reveal through scene, and delivered with those scenes.
- Second, when exposition *is* necessary, remember to express it not as neutral information but with a sense of your narrator's voice and using everything you know about good writing. For example, here's an expository passage to help establish the setting early in Eden Robinson's novel, *Monkey Beach*. Active verbs and an imperative tone show us something about this narrator's character as we absorb the information itself:

> Find a map of British Columbia. Point to the middle of the coast. Beneath Alaska, find the Queen Charlotte Islands. Drag your finger across the map, across Hecate Strait to the coast and you should be able to see a large island hugging the coast. This is Princess Royal Island, famous for its kermode bears, which are black bears that are usually white.[54]

Thought, Distance, Reflection

In the physical world, "reflection" literally means a change in the direction of a wave front (waves of sound, water, light...) between two different media (such as yourself and a rock cliff), so that the wave front (waves of sound) returns to the media from which it originated (returns to you, in the form of an echo). Look into a mirror: waves of light travel from your face to the surface of the mirror and back to you, so you see your face reflected. The word "reflect" comes from Latin, meaning "bent back." Figuratively, we use the term "reflection" to mean the mind bending back to consider our experience or what we know—it's serious thought, rumination, deliberation, pondering. A rare and extreme form of reflection is **epiphany**: a sudden realization that can follow a period of reflection about a problem. Isaac Newton's observation of a falling apple is said to have given him an epiphany—a sudden understanding of gravity.

In literature, reflection is a way of *writing about thinking* that causes us to feel we're in the mind of a narrator whose conscious energy goes out then bends back to reach an understanding. It's usually not as extreme as an epiphany—although sometimes a character, like the narrator of James Joyce's "Araby," does have an epiphany ("I saw myself a creature driven and derided by vanity; and my eyes burned with anguish and anger") as the climax of a story.[55] Nor is reflection often written in forms as extreme as **stream of consciousness** (long passages or entire projects written to replicate the flow of consciousness and everything the mind notices). Reflection is a mode—like exposition and scene—particularly useful for showing a character's *internal change* and for widening your scope of meaning beyond the self or a single character.

Reflection requires distance—a space for the waves of thought to go outward, bend, and return. In her novel *Ravensong*, Lee Maracle's character Stacey confronts a white character's cultural assumptions about sexual purity. The confrontation causes Stacey to look at her own cultural experience in juxtaposition with his; she reflects through internal monologue:

> "She had a miserable home life," Steve continued, recounting the violence in Polly's family home. "No girl who is loved at home would go out and look for sex." Stacey laughed.
>
> "What's so funny?"
>
> She realized he was not kidding. One thing white people say about us is true, Stacey told herself: we have no illusions that virginal behavior is virtuous. People love, laugh and have babies. Half the women on the reserve had no piece of paper to prove their husband's devotion or to legitimize their right to mother children, but no one dared to refer to them as anything but so-and-so's wife or somebody's mother. Where do you begin telling someone their world is not the only one?[56]

In Alexander MacLeod's story "Adult Beginner I," Stace's distance comes from being in an extreme state—distant from her normal action and thought. In this excerpt, the first paragraph is scene, the second reflection:

> It is time to go. Stace releases the rope, pushes out into the water as hard as she can. Near the sides, in the shelter of the pilings, the current is almost still, but it picks up quickly as she moves outward and pulls her away in a long diagonal. She can barely breathe, but she calls out his name, forces her face in, swings her arms and kicks. Something vegetal and slimy brushes up against her thigh and lets go. Her stroke is short and tight and she feels heavy, already exhausted. It's hard to stay up and difficult to go on. Every thirty seconds she has to stop and lift her head, get her breathing back and look for bearings. She searches above and below and yells again. His name, the word Brad, sounds pitiful and small.
>
> We are made most specifically by the things we cannot bear to do. She realizes it now, feels it in the powerful movement of this different water. The old discomforts coming home: a familiar tightening in her diaphragm, the intimate constriction of her larynx, sticky weight in her arms and legs, the scurrying in her brain. Fear is our most private possession.[57]

First-person reflection is often expressed in present tense, even when the surrounding narrative is written in past tense. After narrating a scene in past tense, Ruth, the narrator of Marilynne Robinson's *Housekeeping*, reflects in a present-tense voice grown older, wiser:

> To crave and to have are as like as a thing and its shadow. For when does a berry break upon the tongue as sweetly as when one longs to taste it, and when is the taste refracted into so many hues and savors of ripeness and earth, and when do our senses know any thing so utterly as when we lack it? And here again is a foreshadowing—the world will

> be made whole. For to wish for a hand on one's hair is all but to feel it. So whatever we may lose, very craving gives it back to us again. Though we dream and hardly know it, longing, like an angel, fosters us, smooths our hair, and brings us wild strawberries.[58]

Notice that in all three examples above, the reflecting character moves from the world of the "I" or self into thinking about the world of "we," "people," "you," "us," and "our"—because reflection leads to an understanding or questioning that is bigger and wider than the individual.

Fiction writers employ reflection sparingly on the page. Using scene and figurative language instead, they invite the *reader* to do most of the work of reflection (thinking about what the scene has come to signify). If a story is all literal, with no use of figurative language, it leaves the reader unsatisfied because there's no reflection for us to do; without the implied reflection of figurative language, the reader is passive and unmoved. Even the minimalist Hemingway invites us to reflect with the simile posed by his title "Hills Like White Elephants."

Poets also minimize reflection, expressing the world through imagery (both literal and figurative) and sound rather than in any form of "telling." Where a story or essay might "turn" or change modes into reflection, a poem is more likely to offer unusual imagery for the reader to reflect on. Consider the leap made at the conclusion of James Wright's poem "A Blessing." It takes us to the verge of realization then refuses to tell us what it means: we ourselves are compelled to reflect:

> Suddenly I realize
> That if I stepped out of my body I would break
> Into blossom.

Creative nonfiction, a genre that aims to both "show" and "tell," embraces reflection. In fiction, reflection can sometimes feel like authorial intrusion. But in personal essay or memoir, the author is expected to step in and speak their mind.[i] It's no intrusion at all; it's the purpose of this form of writing. Here's Patrick Lane, stepping in and out of reflection in his memoir *What the Stones Remember*. He recalls a scene from his boyhood, hiking alone, standing "on a crest in a frothing meadow of glacier lilies and anemones." Then he continues:

> Grasses, their stalks flattened and flung by the winter snow, lay like fallen hair upon the earth, and their new green spears caught the wind with frail hands. A mountain meadow and a boy in the long-ago of the last century. Did I know then it was a garden I looked out upon? Had I been asked I would not have understood the question. Garden? Wilderness? I gave the meadow no thought. Had someone asked me if what I saw was beautiful I would not have known what he meant. A boy is a boy and he is the place he inhabits. He is what surrounds him and the boy I was remains with me in the image of yellow lilies and creamy anemones among the grasses and scattered stones.[59]

---

i Note that this textbook occasionally uses a plural pronoun such as "their" rather than singular alternative pronouns such as "his or her" to refer to a singular entity (in this case "the author"). Some writers do this consciously to avoid gender-specific pronouns.

Lane's reflection that "a boy is a boy and he is the place he inhabits" is not only about his *own* childhood self; it is Lane's understanding now, as an adult in the present moment of writing, about the nature of boyhood.

Time is often the source of reflective distance in creative nonfiction: the "I" perceives or understands "now," in the present moment of writing, something about memory or "self" that our essay explores. For this reason, childhood is rich subject matter for personal essays: we have lived our way to a perspective about our own childhood—and perhaps about childhood more generally as a state of existence. It's hard to write this way about love when we've recently fallen deeply in love for the first time or to write about addiction, college, or our recent surgery if we haven't had time to live beyond it and reflect "back" on it.

Mundane, common, or normal moments can provide surprisingly rich opportunities for reflection. Written entirely in second-person "you" and describing waking in bed with a lover and suddenly discovering a sense of discomfort, Brenda Miller's "Getting Yourself Home" uses reflection delicately, yet so powerfully:

> You shut your eyes, take a deep breath. You try to remember what your meditation teacher told you about the breath: how you enter your true home with each inhalation, each exhalation, a cadence old and plain as those worn-out concepts of love, of compassion. So you try it: you breathe in, you breathe out, but there's a glitch in your throat, a mass in your chest, and your body feels nothing like home, more like a room in a foreign hotel, the windows greasy, the outlets reversed, the noise of the street rising like soot. The body's no longer an easy abode, not in this bed, not with two strangers lying in the dark and waiting—breath held—for morning finally to arrive.

Miller's passage moves from scene (breathing), to figurative language (her body becoming, through simile, "like a room in a foreign hotel"), to reflection: "The body"—our bodies, the human experience of being embodied—is not an easy place to live sometimes. These shifts feel subtle, but they lift her essay to a "universal" plane that speaks directly to us about something intimate that we all have in common: living in our bodies.

Reflection is a mind in conversation with itself about the experience of trying to live. It's very hard to narrate a past event in the present tense and achieve reflection because when the event occurred, we didn't yet have the distance necessary to reflect on it: we gain that ability "now," in the present moment of writing. We have to stretch, to reach, in order to word the "larger" meaning that goes beyond the "I" and includes the "we" and "us." What gives us the right, the authority, to reflect? Every human being has the right to reflect on what our being means. Some believe it's not just a right but a moral responsibility for all humans ("The unexamined life is not worth living," said Socrates).[60] But a passage of reflection standing alone is only a philosophical maxim or phrase. In creative writing, we *earn* reflection by connecting it to scene and image. We dramatize the understanding of human life by grounding it in one concrete and specific life.

Suggested Reading from Our Anthology

Taiaiake Alfred, "What I Think of When I Think of Skin"
Barbara Bloom, "Making Things Right"
T. Alan Broughton, "Song for Sampson"
Terrance Hayes, "The Same City"
Ernest Hemingway, "Hills Like White Elephants"
David Ignatow, "The Bagel"
Brenda Miller, "Getting Yourself Home"
Amy Tan, "Confessions"
Walt Whitman, "When I Heard the Learn'd Astronomer"
Jeanette Winterson, "The Three Friends"
James Wright, "A Blessing"

Your Moves

1. Start with one vivid memory and write it first as a scene or representative scene (one paragraph to one page in length, not a word of exposition or reflection included). Then write a couple of sentences of exposition about that scene, contextualizing it or giving background information. Last, write a paragraph of reflection: What do you understand now, from a distance, about yourself then? What do you understand now about that era, or about a theme you recognize in your scene, that you could not have understood or worded while you were living it?

   Give these three pieces of writing to a peer or mentor and ask for feedback: Does your writing show that you understand the distinction between scene, exposition, and reflection? Do you have questions about these three modes to discuss together?
2. Read Terrance Hayes, "The Same City"; then reflect on "one thing I will remember all my life." What is *your* one true thing? Write in your notebook to name this truth and to capture details from a scene in your life that brought you to this way of knowing.
3. Evelyn Lau's "An Insatiable Emptiness" and Amy Tan's "Confessions" focus on the mother-daughter relationship and the daughter's struggle for separation and empowerment. Write a collage of small scenes in your notebook, exploring your own struggle or effort to separate from a parent or from a controlling person. Have you lived your way to a perspective from which you can also reflect on this experience or period in your life?
4. An "elegy" is a goodbye to a loved one who has died. It is a respectful form of remembering what was unique about someone, an attempt to say what that person meant to the writer. Barbara Bloom's "Making Things Right," Elise Partridge's "Edwin Partridge," and T. Alan Broughton's "Song for

Sampson" are elegies. Read these and then draft a poem or prose elegy to someone you have lost. Focus your attention on scene and on cutting the exposition as much as possible.

5. Using as a model Taiaiake Alfred's essay "What I Think of When I Think of Skin," write your own collage of scenes leading to reflection on a unifying theme. Call yours "What I Think of When I Think of ________," using "Skin" or another word in its place in your own title.
6. Read Jeanette Winterson's story "The Three Friends," which is an allegory—a representation of abstract meaning in concrete form. Create your own fictional allegory about an "-ism" (such as racism, sexism, heterosexism, sizeism, ageism, commercialism, hedonism, perfectionism, pessimism, stoicism, nihilism). Use scene and specific detail (never exposition or opinion) to discover and convey your understanding about this abstraction.
7. Use second-person point of view ("you") and only one scene, as Brenda Miller does in "Getting Yourself Home," to write about a moment or experience that prompted you to think and assess. In your conclusion, switch from "you" to the "we" or "us" pronoun as you reflect on a condition that is human and shared.
8. David Ignatow's "The Bagel" expresses emotional truth through a surreal or absurd scene. Create your own poem or flash fiction story using this technique.
9. Read James Wright's poem "A Blessing"; then try your own poem that describes one memorable scene and concludes with an understanding or realization—one that you made at the time or one that your poem's speaker makes in the present "now" of the poem. A restriction: this concluding reflection must be expressed using figurative language (as demonstrated in Wright's poem).
10. In "When I Heard the Learn'd Astronomer," Walt Whitman gives us a scene in which the poem's speaker leaves a university classroom to learn something more important. Write about learning something in an unconventional or unexpected way. Revise this writing into a poem, story, or essay using the "yellow marker test" to identify and eliminate the exposition.
11. Take a story you've drafted that seems unfocussed. Decide what its theme is: what is the unstated idea or purpose at the heart of this project? Cut away every word that does not contribute to the theme and then create a substantial scene that shows the theme without telling it.
12. Transform an autobiographical story into a personal essay. Retain the essentials of the story at the core in the form of one scene, but put a reflective "frame" around it: speak from your "now" perspective at the beginning and ending to reflect on why this memory comes to your mind at present and what it has come to mean.

Voice and Perspective

> When you are writing you must assume that the next thing you put down belongs not for reasons of logic, good sense, or narrative development, but because you put it there. You, the same person who said that, also said this. The adhesive force is your way of writing, not sensible connection.
>
> —*Richard Hugo*[61]

How many names have you had in your lifetime so far? Nicknames, pet names, fake ID names, second-language names, derogatory or hurtful names? When I was a young writer, I wanted to write about beautiful things—my love of language was (still is) deeply connected to my love of all the sensual things that touched me physically and emotionally. But at some point I needed to write about ugly things. I needed to write fierce and angry. I needed to write brave. I decided I needed a new name to write with a new voice. I called her Semolina Pelchard (yes, a variation on a Beatles song), and she helped me voice the things "I" couldn't, or didn't, say with creative writing. Semolina could be cranky and outraged and weird and witty on the page, and I grew to really like her. In fact, she started writing all my best stuff! Over time I stopped writing as Semolina (I never published under that name; it's just who I imagined I was as I wrote). I stopped thinking of her as "she"; although I had imagined that Semolina was another, different voice, she had been me all along. She was part of what made me real and alive, but I only felt comfortable writing from a narrow part of my voice until I made her up. Years later, when I wrote a series of poems about my obesity and wrote poems about an abuser, I put my name to them. My voice.

An Animated Presence

Writing that conveys "voice" means writing animated with the presence of a specific person. Writing with and without voice is a little like the difference between a bear and a bear rug. A bear rug has fur and claws and a head—but there's something dead about the glass eyes, plastic tongue, and *flatness* of the thing on the floor. I know this is true because my dad shot a little cinnamon-colored bear who ripped in through the roof of a tent one November when dad was hunting elk. We ate the bear meat. The bear rug occupied our living room for many years. It was pretty, and interesting, but also absent in a way that made it furniture, not bear. Bears cause more emotional and palpable reactions than bear rugs because their aliveness speaks to our own. Creative writing—unlike writing that seeks to inform—exists so that the aliveness of one person can meet the aliveness of another through the page, even if writer and reader live in different places and times.

Donald Murray teaches us that "voice is the quality in writing, more than any other, that makes the reader read on, that makes the reader interested in what is being said and makes the reader trust the person who is saying it."[62] Knowing how crucial voice is to imaginative writing, some courses used to promise that novice writers would "find their voice" by enrolling—as though voices had been "lost" or students needed to fabricate or invent a voice. If you're an alive person, you don't need to be taught how to be or how to invent an animated presence. You are one; you have one. The trick is to resist the urge to write as a formulaic or so-called "universal" version of a person—a "nobody in particular." The qualities that make you particular, weird, rare, and utterly yourself are much more thrilling to readers than the qualities that make you correct, normal, nice, and expected. Readers trust you and "let themselves go" into your written world if they sense you trust them enough to show yourself in your language, in your manner of expression.

Sometimes we use the word "voice" in a wider and important way—not as a matter of artistic style but as a matter of personal or political power. To "have a voice" in this sense means to be articulate as an individual or to belong to a community or group with the power to make itself widely heard. Those of us born into families, cultures, or classes that do not express openly using language; those with less educational opportunity; those identified as outliers who should be silent and listen to the majority or "normal" view can be "voiceless" in this sense. The practice of creative writing is only one of many routes toward achieving *this* kind of "voice"—yet it's among the best. The study and practice of creative expression is perhaps the least expensive and most attainable route toward this kind of wider "voice." Its cultivation demands our time and commitment but not the backing of any political party, approval of family or community, or donations from judging patrons.

Literary voice is a form of exposure—the intimacy of self embedded within artistry. Wright Morris says voice is the presence "of what is most personal to the writer" and "through voice, the writer is invisibly omnipresent."[63] This sense of a "someone" rather than an "anyone" behind the language is often what distinguishes poetry from verse, an essay from anecdote, and "literary fiction" from "genre fiction." Voice isn't worn like a mask or persona; it's not cultivated or controlled. Rather, "The voice is the element over which you have no control: it's the sound of the person behind the work" (John Hersey).[64] Writing with voice is achieved *by not thinking about voice*, not trying to manufacture, cover up, or standardize what is innately your own unique sound, style, and manner on the page.

Painter Emily Carr (whose writing would later win Canada's highest literary honor) struggled mightily over this issue of voice when she began to write. Her first readers (her sisters, her summer-school writing teacher) encouraged her to strip voice from her prose and make her writing conform to simple plots; they wanted her to sound just like writers they read in popular magazines of the time. But *nothing* about Emily Carr conformed to popularity! She reflected often in her journals about the struggle to write in her own way, in her own unusual voice, which she "went down deep into [her]self and dug up":[65]

> It had no plot. (Of course it had no plot but it had something else; it had life.)...I do know my mechanics are poor. I realize that when I read good literature, but I know lots of excellently written stuff that says nothing. Is it better to say *nothing* politely or to say *something* poorly? I suppose only if one says something ultra-honest, ultra-true, some deep realizing of life, can it make the grade.[66]

Carr eventually found Ira Dilworth, a friend and editor who helped with the spelling and mechanics of her prose but preserved what became Carr's unique, "ultra-honest" and recognizable voice.

After years of work, our voice may become widely recognized. Raymond Carver (who has one of the most known voices in fiction) describes this effect:

> I think that a writer's signature should be on his work, just like a composer's signature should be on his work. If you hear a few bars of Mozart, you don't need to hear too much to know who wrote that music, and I'd like to think that you could pick up a story by me and read a few sentences or a paragraph, without seeing the name, and know it was my story.[67]

But Lorrie Moore, whose work is also imbued with a very strong sense of voice, suggests we shouldn't worry or scheme about this "signature" as young or apprenticing writers:

> A writer who thought a lot or articulately about the evolution of his or her own voice and work would be a little doomed, I think. For purposes of artistic sanity one should probably not be standing outside one's own oeuvre looking in like that—or at least not very often.[68]

If you need a little help getting out of your own way for your voice to thrive, remember that years and years of experience as a writer in the academic setting of school has trained you to mistrust and eliminate voice in order to succeed in scholarly writing. Give yourself permission to let your natural humor, cadence, vocabulary, and forms of intelligence show as forms of your personal authority in creative writing. Your voice is informed by a myriad of factors—the region where you grew up; the language of your family, ethnicity, community, and class; your gender; your extrovert loquaciousness or introvert precision and quiet. To journey toward *sounding like who you are*, know and accept yourself:

- Ask friends, people you trust, to describe your speaking manner—especially when you're relaxed and sharing stories about your life. What are you like as a talker? Read your work aloud to see where you could add more of the elements they noticed and named.
- Have no fear of influence—devour and imitate the styles of other writers. Students often say to me, "I don't read, because I'm afraid of being *influenced* as a writer." Ridiculous! Would someone who wants to cook say, "I don't taste any food except the meatballs, tossed salad, and Jell-O I eat every day because I don't want my cooking to be influenced"? The instantly recognizable guitar voice of George Harrison was influenced by the rockabilly of Carl Perkins and the sitar virtuosity of Ravi Shankar (among others). Artists are influenced; people are influenced. We are not static but are learning and growing due to influence. Our voices thrive on such encounters as we transition from apprentice to master. Emulate the minimalism of Ernest Hemingway one week, the hyperbolic humor of David Sedaris the next, and the proud and forthright cadences of Maya Angelou the week after that. The "moves" that are right for you will stick and the others will fall away without harm.
- Consider the collective "voice of your own generation" and ask yourself whether a form of peer pressure is at work, making you sound like everyone else in your age group. How is your personality distinct? Where are your own greatest pleasures in language? Embrace the verbal moves that make you different from others of your cohort: these signatures are assets, setting your voice apart.

Many Points of View

Voice brings the reader toward a sense of the writer's presence; you'll notice and understand voice better when you read several different works by an author and appreciate the sense of an essential "creator" these works have in common, despite their various themes and characters. Point of view and perspective are also aspects of "presence" on the page, but they change with each writing task. Perspective and point of view are choices you make for every written project; these choices shape *the amount of distance the reader senses* within each work:

- **Point of view** is the distance between the reader and the narrator or speaker.
- **Perspective** is the distance between the narrator or speaker and the action.

With each project you begin, you choose a point of view and a perspective that, together, create the amount of distance you feel is necessary for that particular essay, story, or poem to work. One of the most common revisions any creative writer makes to a draft is to alter the point of view or perspective to increase or decrease the effects of this sensation of distance. As you experiment with point of view (POV), your choices include:

First-person POV ("I")

- A **central point of view** comes from the main character. In poetry, a *speaker*; in fiction, a *narrator*; or in the personal essay, an *I* or a *speaker* is the self who experiences the conflict and change your project explores. First-person central is a common point of view in literature. Edwidge Danticat uses it in her story "Children of the Sea," which begins,

  > They say behind the mountains are more mountains. Now I know it's true. I also know there are timeless waters, endless seas, and lots of people in this world whose names don't matter to anyone but themselves. I look up at the sky and I see you there. I see you crying like a crushed snail, the way you cried when I helped you pull out your first loose tooth. Yes, I did love you then.[69]

- A central but **unreliable narrator** throws a twist into projects. Again, this individual experiences the conflict and change your project explores, but clues signal to the reader that this narrator is so biased or unstable that his or her point of view can't be trusted. Humbert, the obsessed narrator of *Lolita*, is famously unreliable.

- A **peripheral POV** comes through a minor character who observes and understands more than the main character. Nick Carraway in *The Great Gatsby*, for instance, can understand and tell Gatsby's story better than Gatsby could himself. The peripheral point of view can allow for reflection and a tone unavailable to the main character. And, of course, this point of view can carry a narrative to a point in time beyond the main character's demise.

Second-person POV ("you")

- This point of view is indicated with the pronoun "you" and can mean the narrator or speaker is addressing the reader, is addressing another character, or is addressing herself in her own mind as the reader "overhears." Brenda Miller sustains second-person POV throughout her personal essay "Getting Yourself Home":

  > You're in the bed of a stranger. Well, not a stranger, really—he's your boyfriend, after all, you agreed to this designation just the other day, both of you content from an afternoon of careful courtship, the binoculars passed from hand to hand as you watched the trumpeter swans and the snow geese sharing a field in the Skagit River plains. But now his face, when you glimpse it sidelong, looks so rigid, the mouth shut tight, the head tilted up and away. Even those creases around his ear, those lines you once found endearing, now seem a deformation.

Third-person POV ("she," "he," "it," or the character's name or, more rarely, "they" and "them" as singular pronouns in gender-neutral narratives)

- Third-person **limited** (also called "limited omniscient") POV allows us to see a character's interior world and the exterior setting around her as she experiences it. It is "limited" in the sense that, once established, we can't pop into a different character's perspective or into fully omniscient voice: we stay limited within this character's frame of perception. See it in James Joyce's "Eveline."
- **Omniscient** POV speaks from an all-knowing perspective that understands the past, present, and future and is free to tell readers anything, even what the characters themselves may not know. Gabriel García Márquez uses it in "The Handsomest Drowned Man in the World."
- **Objective** POV knows no more than a person observing the scene would witness—just what's present to the senses, not the interiors of characters. It's an eyewitness or "fly on the wall" stance, and Ernest Hemingway's point of view in "Hills Like White Elephants" serves as an example.

Collective group POV ("we" or "they")

- The collective pronoun "we" is used rarely but effectively to explore the united perspective of a whole community, clique, or group; it emphasizes the closeness of a group that seems to think and speak in one voice. Gwendolyn Brooks employs it famously in her poem "We Real Cool." Kristiana Kahakauwila uses it in her story "This Is Paradise":

> Midmorning the lifeguards fan across the beach and push signposts into the sand. The same picture is on all of them: a stick figure, its arms aloft, its circle head drowning in a set of triangle waves. CAUTION, the signs read. DANGEROUS UNDERTOW.
>
> We ignore it. We've gone out at Mākaha and Makapu'u before. We've felt Yokes pull us under. We are not afraid of the beaches and breaks here in Waikīkī. We are careless, in fact, brazen. So when we see her studying the warning, chewing the right side of her lip, we laugh. *Jus' like da kine, scared of da water. Haoles, yeah.*[70]

In *The Art of Fiction*, John Gardner uses the term "psychic distance" to speak about how closely and intimately the narrator (and therefore the reader) might stand relative to a character—or how far apart they might be kept from one another. Gardner offered the following example, which shows how psychic distance can be whittled or expanded—from wide (#1) to narrow (#5):

1. It was winter of the year 1853. A large man stepped out of a doorway.
2. Henry J. Warburton had never much cared for snowstorms.

3. Henry hated snowstorms.
4. God how he hated these damn snowstorms.
5. Snow. Under your collar, down inside your shoes, freezing and plugging up your miserable soul....[71]

POV choices let the writer control the degree of distance and, therefore, intimacy. Once you find the right POV for a project, consider it a kind of "contract" to sustain with the reader—it will be difficult and awkward to change the POV within a text unless there is a natural and important reason for breaking it.

The Lens of Perspective

Perspective includes not just *who* tells and *how* but also *when*—conveyed through verb tense. Verb tense might seem a casual decision, but each option conveys its own degree of distance between the narrator or speaker and the action. Present tense communicates immediacy, nearness; past tense suggests having lived to the point of gained understanding about the past; future tense feels magical or fatalistic:

- **Present tense:** "You stand around. You smoke. You spit. You are wearing your two shirts, two pants, two underpants. Jesús says, if they chase you throw that bag down" (Richard Rodriguez).[72]
- **Past tense:** "Sundays too my father got up early / and put his clothes on in the blueblack cold" (Robert Hayden).[73]
- **Future tense:** "I will die in Paris, on a rainy day" (César Vallejo).[74]

You can get tangled in "verbs with helpers" or other complicated verb forms in early drafts; it's often a smart choice to eliminate the awkwardness of the following tenses by revising into a simpler past or present tense:

- Present continuous action (present progressive): *They are walking*
- Past continuous action (past progressive): *They were walking*
- Recent past (present perfect): *They have walked*
- Distant past (past perfect): *They had walked*
- Future (future perfect): *They will have walked*

Perspective shapes every piece of creative writing, and, once established in the opening lines, it *usually* stays consistent (or risks irritating and confusing the reader). But you can switch perspective or point of view *if the switch is done both meaningfully and convincingly.* Sometimes a story's narrator switches from past tense into present tense as action becomes immediate. Flannery O'Connor's "A Good Man Is Hard to Find" is told in third-person limited point of view but switches to omniscient POV to create the denouement or "falling away" after the story's climax. Lyric poems use first-person point of view but sometimes switch to second-person "you" near the end when the speaker is simultaneously addressing herself and the reader (as Mary Oliver does in "The Summer Day"). Braided essays weave together jump-cut sections, each establishing then sustaining its own point of view and verb tense.

Other elements of craft connected to perspective include use of colloquial language, tone, authorial intrusion, and irony:

- **Colloquial voice** is writing crafted to sound more like authentic speech than like formal, written English. Using words, phrases, and the rhythms of spoken language, we can limit colloquial voice to dialogue or employ it throughout a piece to give the effect of a monologue or conversation the narrator or speaker is having with the reader. Class, ethnicity, region, gender, and other markers of identity can be signaled in this way. Here's the colloquial voice of narrator Gracie Mae, from Alice Walker's story "Nineteen Fifty-Five":

  > He's gitting fat for sure, but he's still slim compared to me. I'll never see three hundred pounds again and I've just about said (excuse me) fuck it. I got to thinking about it one day an' I thought: aside from the fact that they say it's unhealthy, my fat ain't never been no trouble. Mens always have loved me. My kids ain't never complained. Plus they's fat. And fat like I is I looks distinguished. You see me coming and know somebody's *there*.[75]

  Rarer examples of colloquial voice are written in **pidgin**, which means a simplified version of a language developed as a means of communication between two or more groups that don't have a language in common. A pidgin isn't a native language; it's often a hybrid of two or more languages and is learned as a second language, allowing people or groups to communicate with each other without having a shared native tongue. (It usually developed in trade situations, under colonialism.) Because pidgins usually have low prestige, literature presented in pidgin often carries the perspective of a cultural outsider or vulnerable character. Shani Mootoo's "Out on Main Street" is composed in pidgin because this voice is integral to the narrator's identity. Mootoo's other stories and novels aren't written in pidgin; students often mistakenly assume that this colloquial approach is the only way Mootoo "could" write, when in fact it's a perspective choice for one story.

- **Tone** is, in general, the quality of sound produced by a voice or instrument. In conversation, our tone is the feeling conveyed by our physical voice, inflection, and word choice. In creative writing, tone has a more explicit meaning: it's the *attitude* of an author or narrator/speaker toward a subject or audience, as revealed by language. Tone may be bitter or sentimental, serious or ironic, casual or formal, or it may convey any other attitude that humans experience.

The angry tone of the speaker in Marilyn Dumont's "Still Unsaved Soul" is discussed in the chapter about sound. Students often tell me that they find writing in iambic pentameter leads them toward a nostalgic or gentle tone. Patricia Lockwood's poem "Rape Joke" is fascinating for its alternating tone, which reflects the speaker's complicated attitude not about rape but about our willingness to read a poem about rape culture.

- **Authorial intrusion** occurs when the point of view of the author "breaks the wall" of the narrating point of view already established—it interrupts the readers' relationship with the narrating POV and makes us suddenly aware we're in an artificial story. Ethel Wilson uses authorial intrusion in her 1954 novel *Swamp Angel* in two ways:

  1. As an aside (parenthetical). Here, Euro-Canadian character Maggie visits Vancouver's Chinatown. Two times Wilson interjects to speak directly to the reader, telling us that the Chinese faces were secret *from Maggie's perspective*, but not secretive *in fact*, and that Maggie is mistaken in her belief that she can easily interpret the faces of people of her own race:

     > She paused, too, at a live-poultry market. Quite secret—from her—were the faces of those who bought and those who sold. She considered these enigma faces but, although she thought that she could read easily the faces of her own race (but she could not), these others were sealed from her.[76]

  2. As the author's (not character's) insight. Here, a dull-minded character named Vera fails to perceive her husband Haldar's desires. It's the author, not Vera, who concludes that none of us knows another person before marriage:

     > It never entered [Vera's] mind that anyone—certainly not Haldar who came from the prairies—would ever wish to leave a town and go and live in the backwoods. She had not reckoned with Haldar.
     >
     > We never really know each other before marriage, do we.[77]

- **Irony** is a contradiction between the way things appear and the way they really are. Conversationally, we often refer to **cosmic irony** (the notion that fate or the gods are toying with us for their own sick amusement). In literature, irony can be a plot device that has the audience's knowledge of events or characters surpassing that of the characters themselves (**dramatic irony**). Or it can be a figure of speech in which words are used so that their intended meaning is different from their actual meaning (**verbal irony**). **Sarcasm** is a form of verbal irony calculated to judge or hurt someone—through, for example, false praise ("Love your hat!").

Another's Voice

Some writing tasks compel us to imagine and project voices distinctly different from our own. Writing in "persona" is the most common of these. A persona is a mask donned in first-person POV. Persona poetry is written from the perspectives of mythological figures, fabled or historical figures, or cultural icons. The purpose of persona is never simply to retell or dramatize the story the reader already knows; instead, persona seeks new meaning. Julianna Baggott's persona poem "Monica Lewinsky Thinks of Bill Clinton While Standing Naked in Front of a Hotel Mirror" was published after US President Clinton's affair with White-House intern Lewinsky; it demanded an empathy and way of seeing not at all present in media coverage of the time:

> You are someone who knew me before
> I was the world's collective joke
>
> about cigars, thongs, stained dresses,
> when I was a girl named Monica.
>
> I miss her much more than I miss you.[78]

Identities are borrowed and reframed in projects related to persona. Nick Carbó explores immigration with the Filipino figure Ang Tunay na Lalaki in his poetry collection *Secret Asian Man*. Fiction writer Angela Carter distills and recontextualizes fairytales in her story collection *The Bloody Chamber*. Susan Lester's essay "Belongings" imagines beyond characterization and nearer the terrain of persona to explore a silent figure in her family.

Students are often attracted to the notion of writing in a child's voice, from the point of view of childhood—perhaps because childhood is one theme all young writers have the expertise and authority to write about. Unless you're taking a course explicitly on writing *for* children, remember that your audience is adult; your project about childhood needs to offer an adult understanding about childhood, as Emma Donoghue does so skillfully with her novel *Room*. Narrated in the first-person POV of a five-year-old boy, *Room* is a fictional story about a young woman who was abducted and held as a sex slave; Jack, the child narrator, results from this situation. He has lived his entire life in a small room, loved and protected by his mother, sheltered from understanding their situation:

> I count one hundred cereal and waterfall the milk that's nearly the same white as the bowls, no splashing, we thank Baby Jesus. I choose Meltedy Spoon with the white all blobby on his handle when he leaned on the pan of boiling pasta by accident. Ma doesn't like Meltedy Spoon but he's my favorite because he's not the same.[79]

This narrative is about their escape from the room and Jack's journey to meet the world beyond it; the POV choice shapes our experience, so we focus on the innocence, creativity, and spirit of the boy and on his relationship with his mother, not on the abuse or abuser. It takes intricate and subtle writing to deliver adult artfulness and meaning through a child's POV like this, particularly in the present tense. Executed without skill, such work can be saccharine and irritatingly "cute." Framing the child's point of view within a "now" perspective as an adult speaker or narrator can provide a solution for a draft that lacks content meaningful for the adult reader.

More rarely, students will stretch to imagine and write from what's called an Other point of view. The Other refers to a minority perspective; explicitly, it means writing as a relative "majority" or privileged author through an imagined minority identity that is not your own. A straight person writes from a queer character's point of view. A man writes from a woman's point of view. A white woman writes from a Métis man's point of view. A middle-class author writes from the POV of an impoverished person. An able civilian writes as a disabled veteran. In the late twentieth century many critics were up in arms about any writer "appropriating" a minority perspective that she or he had not actually lived—even in fiction. What gives you the right to imagine and represent a perspective and experience wholly unlike your own?

Creative writing gives you the right *to try*. Understand that you are likely to get a great deal wrong, that you will have to do more than imagine—you will have to research, ask, listen, and learn. Stereotype and caricature will cause real pain, and you must take ethical responsibility for the mistakes in your draft. But try. Isn't this the point of literature—to show us there are more voices than our own?

Suggested Reading from Our Anthology

Emily Carr, "The Cow Yard"
Josh Lefkowitz, "Saturday Salutation"
Susan Lester, "Belongings"
Patricia Lockwood, "Rape Joke"
Marty McConnell, "Frida Kahlo to Marty McConnell"
Shani Mootoo, "Out on Main Street"
Michael Ondaatje, "The Cinnamon Peeler"
Sylvia Plath, "Mirror"
Simon Rich, "Unprotected"
David Sedaris, "The Drama Bug"
Richard Shelton, "The Stones"
Priscila Uppal, "Sorry, I Forgot to Clean Up After Myself"

For Further Reading

Nisi Shawl and Cynthia Ward, *Writing the Other*

Your Moves

1. Read Simon Rich's "Unprotected," Richard Shelton's "The Stones," and Sylvia Plath's "Mirror"; then choose an inanimate object in your immediate surroundings and write in your notebook from its point of view (as if it were a character in your particular setting). What are the needs and conflicts your character faces in this setting?
2. Write in your notebook in persona, speaking from the first-person POV you imagine for a mythological, fairytale, fable, historical, cultural, or pop-culture figure. But don't just tell the story we associate with this figure—drop your persona into an unexpected context and cause the reader to empathize with the (unexpected) humanity of this perspective: Persephone at the grocery store, Spiderman buys a used car, Bruce Lee waits on tables, David Suzuki at the dentist, Barbie does yoga, Sir John A. Macdonald orders a macchiato, Wayne Gretzky flies coach.
3. Read Josh Lefkowitz's "Saturday Salutation" and notice how he uses a formal, "high" tone to create humor through exaggeration. Try writing a passage of elevated exaggeration in your notebook—what effects can you create? Or look up the poem "Song of Myself" by Walt Whitman (online) and see how Lefkowitz is emulating the last part. Choose a writer whose voice *you* can exaggerate and play with in your notebook.
4. Read Patricia Lockwood's "Rape Joke" and Priscila Uppal's "Sorry, I Forgot to Clean Up After Myself." Write about a personal experience you had or a social experience your generation is sharing now. Choose one that is absolutely serious and important to you, and write using dark humor, irony, or edgy comedy to approach this topic "sideways," as Lockwood and Uppal do.
5. Read the stories by Kristiana Kahakauwila and Shani Mootoo; then write in your notebook to play with the possibilities of colloquial language. Are you beginning to discover a fiction or nonfiction character here? Or are you exploring the colloquial aspects of your *own* voice?
6. Read "Frida Kahlo to Marty McConnell" and then write a letter of advice to yourself from the point of view of someone who is a real hero to you. This is a persona poem: emulate or invent a strong voice for your hero, as Marty McConnell has done in her poem. Title your draft in the same manner, with both names.
7. Write a story about something you did, but imagine and tell it from the point of view of someone who witnessed what you did. Or narrate this story in the voice of someone you know (a parent, grandparent, friend, lover), telling the tale as if that person *had* witnessed your action. What other shades of meaning can your imagined narrator imbue with this particular voice?

8. Write a flash fiction story or narrative poem using the collective noun "we" as the narrating point of view. Who is this group, community, tribe, or gang that speaks in a collective voice? Or try a braided personal essay, using the collective noun in one "strand" of your draft to voice the perspective of a group to which you belonged.
9. Draft an "If I were..." poem from the perspective of an "ordinary" person (*not* a mythological, historical, or cultural figure) who lives in a different historical time or geographical region than you do. Michael Ondaatje wrote "The Cinnamon Peeler" after traveling to Sri Lanka to research. Perhaps your poem will be grounded in what you learned from travel or historical research?
10. Read Susan Lester's "Belongings," noticing how she repeatedly uses the tag "maybe..." to allow herself permission to imagine and adopt a perspective that is fictional inside her nonfiction essay. Try it: draft a nonfiction personal essay using tags such as "maybe," "what if," "perhaps," "I might," "I wonder," or others that signal where you enter the realm of imagination rather than factual experience.
11. Read Brenda Miller's personal essay "Getting Yourself Home," written in the second-person ("you") point of view. Then draft your own second-person essay, using enough candor that the reader knows the "you" is *you*.
12. Draft a first-person story or narrative poem in monologue, from the perspective of an "unreliable narrator"—a character whom the reader can tell is lying, one who lacks credibility and yet whose voice makes your audience want to hear this story and understand its truth.
13. Read Emily Carr's "The Cow Yard," noticing what a strong and particular voice she has. Draft an essay about your childhood identity in *your* voice, avoiding the cute or sentimental language so tempting to those of us who appreciate and value a childhood experience.
14. Read "The Drama Bug" by David Sedaris, noticing what a distinct voice he has. Write in *your* voice to tell a true coming-of-age story.
15. Interview a person you know well but whose identity is in some way markedly different from your own, someone whose age, race, height, weight, social class, ethnicity, physical or mental disability, religion, first language, or other characteristic marks them as Other. Ask your interviewee to tell you about an experience that illustrates what it's like living in this identity day to day. Be very careful just to *listen* (and take notes); don't say "I know" or fill the silences with your own story or assumptions (this interview is not about you). Ask your interviewee what they wish other people to understand about this experience. With their permission, after the interview, draft a poem, story, or personal essay based upon what you heard and learned. As with any good creative writing, focus on image, scene, and

"showing," not abstraction. Show the draft to your interviewee for discussion and feedback, and then revise.

16. Revise a story to tell it from a different (minor) character's point of view. Or use the same character's point of view but at a different point in his or her life, and revise the narrative to use a different verb tense. What new tensions and possibilities arise from this shift? Read Raymond Carver's "Chef's House," paying close attention to the effects of peripheral point of view and past tense.

Notes

1 Natalie Goldberg, *Writing Down the Bones: Freeing the Writer Within* (Boston: Shambhala, 2010), 55–56.

2 Lynda Barry, *Syllabus: Notes from an Accidental Professor* (Montreal: Drawn & Quarterly, 2014), 9.

3 Lana Hechtman Ayers, *Dance from Inside My Bones* (Valdosta, GA: Snake Nation P, 2007), 50.

4 Stephen Kuusisto, "Harbor Songs," in *Eavesdropping: A Memoir of Blindness and Listening*, 3–6 (New York: W.W. Norton & Company, 2006), 4.

5 Kathleen Dean Moore, *The Pine Island Paradox* (Minneapolis: Milkweed Editions, 2004), 167.

6 Sandra Beasley, "Cherry Tomatoes," in *Theories of Falling* (Kalamazoo, MI: New Issues/ Western Michigan University, 2008), 9.

7 Leslie Marmon Silko, *Ceremony* (New York: Penguin, 2006), 168.

8 Denis Johnson, "Car Crash while Hitchhiking," *Jesus' Son: Stories*, 3–10 (New York: Picador, 2009), 3.

9 Brian Turner, *Here, Bullet* (New York: Alice James Books, 2014), 20.

10 James Dao, "Families of Military Suicides Seek White House Condolences," *The New York Times*, November 25, 2009.

11 Quoted in Donald Morison Murray, *Shoptalk: Learning to Write with Writers* (Portsmouth, NH: Boynton/Cook, 1990), 133.

12 Quoted in Murray, *Shoptalk*, 133.

13 James Baldwin, "Notes of a Native Son," in *Collected Essays*, 63–84 (New York: Penguin Books, 1998), 72.

14 Jeanette Winterson, "The 24-Hour Dog," in *The Book Lover*, ed. Ali Smith, 247–55 (New York: Anchor Books, 2008), 247.

15 Tim Seibles, "Treatise," in *Hurdy-Gurdy* (Cleveland, OH: Cleveland State University Poetry Center, 1992), 19–20.

16 Janet Burroway, *Imaginative Writing: The Elements of Craft*, 4th ed. (London: Pearson, 2014).

17 William Faulkner, "A Rose for Emily," in *The Broadview Anthology of Short Fiction*, 2nd ed., ed. Julia Gaunce, Suzette Mayr, Don LePan, Marjorie Mather, and Bryanne Miller, 154–62 (Peterborough, ON: Broadview P, 2012), 156.

18 P.K. Page, "After Rain," *Canadian Poetry Online*, University of Toronto Libraries, http://canpoetry.library.utoronto.ca/page/poem1.htm.

19 T.S. Eliot, "The Love Song of J. Alfred Prufrock," in *The Broadview Anthology of Poetry*, ed. Amanda Goldrick-Jones and Herbert Rosengarten (Peterborough, ON: Broadview P, 1993), 474.

20 Terrance Hayes, "The Same City," *Hip Logic* (New York: Penguin Books, 2002), 89.

21 Sherman Alexie, "Rise," *One Stick Song* (Brooklyn, NY: Hanging Loose P, 2000), 81.

22 Dionne Brand, "Blues Spiritual for Mammy Prater," *No Language Is Neutral* (Toronto: McClelland & Stewart, 1998), 17.

23 Katherena Vermette, "heavy metal ballads," *North End Love Songs* (Winnipeg: Muses' Co., 2012), 91.

24 Jane Reichhold, "Haiku Techniques," *Frogpond: Journal of the Haiku Society of America* 23, no. 3 (Autumn 2000): 63–74 and online at http://www.ahapoetry.com/haiartjr.htm.

25 William Baer, "A Lesson in the Art of Storytelling: An Interview with Alistair MacLeod," *Michigan Quarterly Review* 44, no. 2 (Spring 2005), http://hdl.handle.net/2027/spo.act2080.0044.217.

26 Vladimir Nabokov, *Lolita* (New York: Vintage Books, 2010), 9.

27 Irena Klepfisz, "Bashert," in *Blood to Remember: American Poets on the Holocaust*, ed. Charles Adés Fishman (St. Louis, MO: Time Being Books, 2007), 239–41.

28 Richard Siken, "You Are Jeff," *Crush* (New Haven, CT: Yale UP, 2005), 50–58, see page 50.

29 Henry James, "The Beast in the Jungle," in *The Turn of the Screw and Others Stories*, ed. Kimberly C. Reed, 83–122 (Peterborough, ON: Broadview P, 2010), 110.

30 Jacqueline Marcus, "Hanalei Bay," in *Close to the Shore: Poems*, 63–64 (East Lansing: Michigan State UP, 2002).

31 Gertrude Stein, "Roastbeef," in *Tender Buttons: Objects, Food, Rooms*, 21–25 (Mineola, NY: Dover, 1997), 21.

32 Flannery O'Connor, *A Prayer Journal* (New York: Farrar, Straus, and Giroux, 2013), 9.

33 Ethel Wilson, *Swamp Angel* (Toronto: Macmillan of Canada, 1990), 95.

34 Linda Gregg, "The Art of Finding," *Texts*, October 25, 2006, https://www.poets.org/poetsorg/text/art-finding.

35 Virginia Woolf, "Sketch of the Past," in *Moments of Being: Autobiographical Writings*, 78–160 (London, UK: Pimlico, 2002), 79.

36 Flannery O'Connor, "A Good Man Is Hard to Find," *A Good Man Is Hard to Find*, ed. Frederick Asals, 31–54 (New Brunswick: Rutgers UP, 1993), 48.

37 Joan Didion, "The Art of Fiction No. 71 [interview by Linda Kuehl]," *The Paris Review* 74 (Fall-Winter 1978), http://www.theparisreview.org/interviews/3439/the-art-of-fiction-no-71-joan-didion.

38 Dan Chaon, "A Conversation with Dan Chaon," in *Story Matters: Contemporary Short Story Writers Share the Creative Process*, ed. Margaret-Love Denman and Barbara Shoup, 144–55 (Boston: Houghton Mifflin, 2006), 149.

39 ZZ Packer, "Drinking Coffee Elsewhere," in *Drinking Coffee Elsewhere: Stories* (New York: Riverhead Books, 2003), 105.

40 Richard Russo, "Location, Location, Location: Depicting Character through Place," in *The Complete Handbook of Novel Writing*, ed. Meg Leder and Jack Heffron, 160–76 (Cincinnati: Writer's Digest, 2002), 167.

41 Alice Munro, "The Flats Road," *Lives of Girls and Women* (Toronto: McGraw-Hill Ryerson, 1971), 1.

42 Henry David Thoreau, "Walden," in *Thoreau: Walden and Other Writings*, ed. Joseph Wood Krutch, 105–351 (Toronto: Bantam Books, 1962), 248.

43 Thoreau, "Walden," 243.

44 Thoreau, "Walden," 316.

45 Thoreau, "Walden," 249.

46 Quoted in Murray, *Shoptalk*, 155.

47 Anaïs Nin, *The Diary of Anaïs Nin, 1947–1955* (San Diego: Harcourt, 1974), 149.

48 Quotations not in the anthology are taken from the following sources: Malcolm Lowry, "The Forest Path to the Spring," in *Hear Us O Lord from Heaven Thy Dwelling Place*, ed. Nicholas Bradley, 275–356 (Don Mills, ON: Oxford UP), 275; Garrett Kaoru Hongo, "Who Among You Knows the Essence of Garlic?" *Yellow Light: Poems*, 42–43 (Middletown CT: Wesleyan UP, 1982), 42; Ruth Reichl, *Tender at the Bone: Growing Up at the Table* (New York: Random House, 2010), 162; Madeleine Thien, "The Tongue, from Childhood to Dotage," in *In the Flesh: Twenty Writers Explore the Body*, ed. Lynne Van Luven and Kathy Page, 27–32 (Victoria, BC: Brindle and Glass, 2012), 30.

49 Quoted in Murray, *Shoptalk*, 151.

50 All quotations in this section taken from Lee Gutkind, "The Yellow Test," *The New York Times*, August 27, 2012, http://opinionator.blogs.nytimes.com/2012/08/27/the-yellow-test/?_r=0.

51 Brenda Miller and Suzanne Paola, *Tell It Slant: Creating, Refining, and Publishing Creative Nonfiction*, 2nd edition (New York: McGraw-Hill, 2012), 167.

52 Lowry, "The Forest Path," 275.

53 Jo Walton, "Thud: Half a Crown & Incluing," *LiveJournal*, May, 16, 2007, http://papersky.livejournal.com/324603.html?page=1.

54 Eden Robinson, *Monkey Beach* (Toronto: Vintage, 2000), 4.

55 James Joyce, "Araby," in *The Dead and Other Stories: A Broadview Anthology of British Literature edition*, ed. Joseph Black and Melissa Free, 27–33 (Peterborough, ON: Broadview P, 2014), 32.

56 Lee Maracle, *Ravensong* (Vancouver: Press Gang, 1993), 71–72.

57 Alexander MacLeod, "Adult Beginner I," *Light Lifting* (Windsor, ON: Biblioasis, 2010), 134.

58 Marilynne Robinson, *Housekeeping* (New York: Farrar Straus Giroux, 1980), 152–53.

59 Patrick Lane, *What the Stones Remember: A Life Rediscovered* (Boston: Trumpeter, 2004), 2–3.

60 Plato, "Apology," in *The Broadview Anthology of Social and Political Thought: From Plato to Nietzsche*, ed. Andrew Bailey, 17–29 (Peterborough, ON: Broadview, 2008), 27.
61 Richard Hugo, "Writing Off the Subject," in *Triggering Town: Lectures and Essays on Poetry and Writing*, 3–10 (New York: W.W. Norton, 1979), 5.
62 Donald Murray, *The Craft of Revision: Anniversary Edition* (Boston, MA: Wadsworth Cengage Learning, 2013), 195.
63 Wright Morris, *About Fiction: Reverent Reflections on the Nature of Fiction with Irreverent Observations on Writers, Readers & Other Abuses* (New York: Harper & Row, 1975), 127.
64 John Hersey, "The Art of Fiction No. 92 [interview by Jonathan Dee]," *The Paris Review* 100 (Summer-Fall 1986), http://www.theparisreview.org/interviews/2756/the-art-of-fiction-no-92-john-hersey.
65 Emily Carr, *Hundreds and Thousands: The Journals of Emily Carr* (Vancouver: Douglas & McIntyre, 2006), 189.
66 Carr, *Hundreds and Thousands*, 18.
67 Raymond Carver, *Conversations with Raymond Carver*, ed. Marshall Bruce Gentry and William L. Stull (Jackson, MI: UP of Mississippi, 1990), 132.
68 Lorrie Moore, "The Art of Fiction No. 167 [interview by Elizabeth Gaffney]," *The Paris Review* 158 (Spring-Summer 2001), http://www.theparisreview.org/interviews/510/the-art-of-fiction-no-167-lorrie-moore.
69 Edwidge Danticat, "Children of the Sea," in *Krik? Krak!*, 1–29 (New York: Vintage, 1996), 3.
70 Kristiana Kahakauwila, "This Is Paradise," *This Is Paradise: Stories*, 9–86 (New York: Hogarth, 2013), 9.
71 John Gardner, *The Art of Fiction: Notes on Craft for Young Writers* (New York: Vintage Books, 1991), 111.
72 Richard Rodriguez, "I Will Send For You or I Will Come Home Rich," in *Writing on the Edge: A Borderlands Reader*, ed. Tom Miller, 77–82 (Tucson: U of Arizona P, 2003), 77.
73 Robert Hayden, "Those Winter Sundays," in *Collected Poems of Robert Hayden*, ed. Frederick Glaysher (New York: Norton & Company, 1985), 41.
74 César Vallejo, "Black Stone Lying on a White Stone," *Neruda and Vallejo*, ed. Robert Bly, John Knoepfle, and James Arlington Wright (Boston: Beacon P, 1993), 249.
75 Alice Walker, "Nineteen Fifty-Five," in *You Can't Keep a Good Woman Down*, 3–20 (San Diego: Harcourt Brace Jovanovich, 1981), 12.
76 Ethel Wilson, *Swamp Angel* (Toronto: McClelland & Stewart, 2010), 18.
77 Wilson, *Swamp Angel*, 62.
78 Julianna Baggott, "Monica Lewinsky Thinks of Bill Clinton While Standing Naked in Front of a Hotel Mirror," in *Lizzie Borden in Love: Poems in Women's Voices*, 43–44 (Carbondale: Southern Illinois UP, 2006), 44.
79 Emma Donoghue, *Room* (New York: Little, Brown and Company, 2010), 6.

PART III
GENRE

Writing Poems

I am overwhelmed by the beautiful disorder of poetry, the eternal virginity of words.
—*Theodore Roethke*[1]

My writer friends go away to retreats—cabins, shared houses, rustic hotels where their everyday habits and distractions are distant, suspended, silenced. There they can't procrastinate by doing the dishes, running errands. They have written proposals, applied and paid for stays somewhere to write. I can't afford a writing retreat, so this summer, for three weeks, I go on retreat at home. I turn down other work, stock up my freezer, pay my bills in advance. I pack the material I might need for drafting poems. I take it to the spare bedroom and I sleep there and pretend I am far away from home. No computer. No phone. I'm here to draft a poem each day. I wake up in a strange room and each morning I write. I'm giving imagery and sound my full attention. And I'm trying a new technique: I choose a book of poems, randomly flip it open, slap down my finger, and whatever line it lands on I read. I read the line and not the next line—instead, I compose what I would write as the next line. Don't overthink. What could follow? I do this twenty times, maybe more, creating a list of twenty+ random lines. Then I begin to work these lines into a draft, changing their order, deleting, adding, seeing the possibility of a poem emerge. Time passes, light shifts; I'm unaware of it. I'm an unwashed lady in pajamas, forgetting to make breakfast, desk tumbled with books. I cut an unromantic figure, my hair standing up on one side. But my mind feels loose, limber. It's half asleep when I begin writing in the morning, like a body slipping out to jog on a misty morning, before the brain can stop it. When I'm drafting poems I don't plan them. But I plan a space in my life for them, running out into each day until I find one.

The Eternal Virginity of Words

"Prose" means ordinary language, arranged into sentences and paragraphs. This is prose that you're reading right now. "Poetry," distinct from prose, is more challenging to define—but many have tried. Poetry is "language at its most distilled and most powerful" (Rita Dove), "the spontaneous overflow of powerful feelings" (William Wordsworth), "emotion put into measure" (Thomas Hardy), "nearer to vital truth than history" (Plato), and "the best words in the best order" (Samuel Taylor Coleridge).[2] According to Marvin Bell, "What they say 'there are no words for'—that's what poetry is for. Poetry uses words to go beyond words."[3]

Poetry goes "beyond words" through its density. Using many aspects of language at the same time, a poem *means* in several ways at once. Poems are more about language—about what language can do, how the human finds expression in language—than they are about any subject or theme. In this way, poetry is a lot like jazz—jazz is not so much about a particular song as it is about how that song can be played. Jazz players apprentice and become proficient at their instruments until their ability to play becomes part of their nature. A jazz performer is exquisitely well prepared yet feels loose while playing—not consciously planning or thinking about what notes come next, not reading sheet music or performing a memorized song, but *reaching* for some new musical possibility of expression by riffing on the song's structure.

When we write poems, we don't faithfully relate a story that happened to us or an idea we have, because that just isn't what poems exist to do. Poems *reach from* experience or observation to explore and play with language. That's why it's important never to assume a poem is autobiographical; although it might begin with a life experience, the real energy and power of the poem is its exploration of language. A poem is a *made version* of experience, a crafted sequence of sounds, details, and perceptions. It is an autobiography of the writer's relationship with language, not of the writer's life. If you find yourself forcing personal experience or ideas you've already formulated into your poem draft, you'll experience struggle, frustration, and even a sense of futility. When you shift your purpose, let go of the notion that a poem is about relating some event or explaining an idea, then you can enter that looser zone of the jazz musician—playing, riffing, moving beyond the original subject of your poem to find new music. Good poems move us outside the ways of knowing that are logical, rational, or "normal." For many, poetry "heals the wounds inflicted by reason" (Novalis)[4] by using language in these uncommon ways.

Maybe because poetry has mattered so deeply and to so many people for centuries, new writers are sometimes intimidated to join this tradition of language experimentation. But it's important to remember that forms of poetry are all around us in song, in spiritual practices, in playful talk, teasing, the timing of comedians, the voices of our grandparents, the books we read to our children, and in the particular rhythms of our cultures and homes. The poet's job is to show that language is never all used up, never "done," never spoiled: words remain eternally "virgin" (as Roethke says), and, by putting them into new relations with one another, we discover fresh ways of knowing and feeling. If, in your writing notebook, you find yourself creating passages with particular attention to sounds, to strange or delicious word combinations, to compressed language or fragments, to images that figuratively suggest feelings or ideas, then you may be already on your way to drafting poetry. Poets tend to

- emphasize sound over sense,
- use density rather than verbosity,
- arrange language into lines and stanzas rather than paragraphs,
- combine the attitudes of play and intensity,
- respect silence, and
- value feeling or intuition over rationality.

Lines and Rhymes

All the elements of craft outlined in this book (sound, image, figurative language, character, setting, voice, perspective, scene, narration) can be used in poetry, and poets have additional, specialized tools. The most significant of these "extra" tools are lines and forms—ways to sculpt the visual field or "look" of the poem on the page and shape the sonic or "heard" experience it creates.

The "I" or narrating voice of a poem is called the "speaker" because poems are meant to be heard aurally. If a poem uses visual devices that cannot be heard (and is meant to be read on a screen or page rather than performed), we still hear its language in our "mind's ear." So poets are deeply attentive both to the look and sound of a poem. We read it aloud over and over as we draft and revise, line by line.

In Latin, lines were known as *versus*, which translates as "turns." The modern English term "verse" comes from this word—so a poem, or a verse, is a series of turns. Breaking prose into lines doesn't *cause* poetry, but it is a poet's cherished tool for creating density and rich meaning. A **line "breaks"** when you press "enter,"
as I just did. Here, the reader has to turn
back to the left margin and the start of the next line.
This creates a sense of "flow" that is independent
from the way the grammar of a sentence
proceeds along as you read. It's called **enjambment**
when you break a line like this, where there
isn't a period, comma, colon, or semicolon at the end.
The line above and this one is **end stopped**,
because it ends with a period, comma, or semicolon,
which causes us to wait longer before reading on. So
you have a kind of tension between what the sentence
wants and what the line wants. You have *two*
energies to work with simultaneously, when you break
lines.

Lines can be used in many ways:

- They **can help a poem slow down** (short lines) **or speed up** (longer lines):

  I want to be doused
  in cheese

  & fried. I want
  to wander

  the aisles, my heart's
  supermarket stocked high

  as cholesterol. I want to die
  wearing a sweatsuit—

  I want to live
  forever in a Christmas sweater,... (Kevin Young, "Ode to the Midwest")[5]

  Compare the poetic fragment above, which is the way Young wrote it, to the one below.

  I want to be doused in cheese & fried. I want to wander the aisles, my heart's supermarket stocked high as cholesterol. I want to die wearing a sweatsuit—I want to live forever in a Christmas sweater,... (Young's poem with altered line breaks)

- **Lines can be used to indicate breath**. A spoken-word poet might create lines as a memory devise. Although the poem is never published or seen on a page, the poet memorizes the work in units of breath, line by line. Allen Ginsberg, engaged by the powers of meditation and chant, wrote lines to the length of his full breath. To read his poems aloud you must take deep breaths and sustain a careful exhalation; here are the first *three* lines of his poem "Sunflower Sutra":

  I walked on the banks of the tincan banana dock and sat down under the huge shade of a Southern Pacific locomotive to look at the sunset over the box house hills and cry.
  Jack Kerouac sat beside me on a busted rusty iron pole, companion, we thought the same thoughts of the soul, bleak and blue and sad-eyed, surrounded by the gnarled steel roots of trees of machinery.
  The oily water on the river mirrored the red sky, sun sank on top of final Frisco peaks, no fish in that stream, no hermit in those mounts, just ourselves rheumy-eyed and hung-over like old bums on the riverbank, tired and wily.[6]

- **Lines can provide tension through enjambment**. Enjambment puts extra emphasis on the words poised at the ends and beginnings of lines because it creates a slight gap, both visually and in time, between these words. This additional weight on the last word of a line can create additional layers of meaning; we think the poet means one thing, and then the next line "corrects" that meaning—so we have two or more meanings from the same word caused by the line-break choice. Consider the effects of enjambment in this poem about a father who punishes a son, the poem's speaker, by whipping him with a tree limb:

> I rose a last time, my father dropping
> the last limb of the tree beside me.
> I stood there in my bones wanting it not to be
> over, wanting what had happened to continue, to go
> on and on forever, my father's hands on me. (Patrick Lane, "The Far Field")

By dividing the line "wanting it not to be / over," Lane invites us to assume (in the time before we reach the next line) that this speaker wishes the beating had never been, had never happened. We're surprised when the word "over" radically changes this meaning. We experience the speaker's realization that he longed so deeply for his father's distant love that any attention (even abuse) was cherished. The active experience of realizing this with Lane—instead of being flatly told—is how this poem moves us, and the effect would be lost without enjambment. We are moved by any line that seems to lead in one direction but then surprises with another:

> It is dusk. The birds sweep low to the lake and then dive
> up. The wind picks a few leaves off the ground (Roo Borson, "Ten Thousand")[7]

- **Lines can create a sculptured sense of structure** by looking visually "**regular**" (all approximately the same length) or "**irregular**" (varying in length). They can even visually complement the subject of the poem (for example, a poem about a tree in which the words are arranged into the shape of a tree. This type of arrangement creates what is called a "concrete" poem.). "**Dropped**" **lines** begin horizontally and then step down to the next line without returning to the left margin. "**Aeration**" is inserting white space between lines or even between words to orchestrate visually a sense of space and silence (see Siken's "Scheherazade"). A "**stanza**" is a unit of lines with white space above and below, creating a hesitation slightly stronger than a single line break. Stanzas can be "regular" (for example, each stanza of a poem having two lines [couplets], three lines [tercets], or four [quatrains]) or "irregular" (stanzas of varying lengths).

- **Lines can measure sound into increments**, much like song—by controlling the number and pattern of beats in a line (**meter**) and by arranging rhymed words at the end of lines into a structure (**rhyme scheme**).

As a new writer, you don't have to and *won't* understand all the rules and possibilities of rhyme and meter (called **prosody**) as you begin. John Lennon, remember, didn't even know his guitar was supposed to have six strings when he began to write songs on four strings. But it's valuable to understand some basics for measuring lines with prosody; if you keep writing poetry, your curiosity about these options will grow.

Rhyme can occur at the ends of lines (**end rhyme**) and within lines (**internal rhyme**). To map the **rhyme scheme** (pattern of rhyme) of a poem, assign letters as shorthand. For example, a poem in which lines one and two rhyme and lines three and four rhyme could be mapped this way: AABB. If lines one and three rhyme and two and four rhyme, the rhyme scheme is ABAB. And so on. Mapping or scanning the rhyme, and marking the stressed (/) and unstressed (˘) syllables using symbols (explained in the chapter on sound), is called **scansion**.

- **Perfect rhyme** (also called exact rhyme or true rhyme) has identical stressed vowel sounds and any sounds following the stressed syllable are also identical; the consonants before the stressed vowels differ (true/blue/hue/do/pew, great/hate/mate). Poems tend to sound comical or hackneyed if most of the rhymes are perfect—particularly if the lines are also end stopped; if you want a poem to sound sincere and natural, venture into other forms of rhyme (or venture into free verse) and use enjambment. Beginning poets often assume a poem must have clear and obvious rhymes or else it's not *a real poem*. That's just not been true for more than a hundred years.

- **Imperfect rhyme** (slant rhyme, off rhyme, half rhyme, near rhyme) is created using words that are sonically similar but not identical rhymes. Usually the accented vowels are different and the following consonant sounds are identical (four/hair, have/give). Assonance (cold/home, leap/green) can be used as imperfect rhyme. I think a delicious form of imperfect rhyme also happens when consonants in different words are formed using the tongue, lips, and breath in nearly the same position (pro*p*/bi*b*, fro*m*/whe*n*, sin*k*/bu*g*), but not everyone would agree that this is actually "rhyme."

- **Visual rhyme** (sight rhyme, eye rhyme) happens when words are spelled as if they would rhyme, but the pronounced sounds do not rhyme. For example, I live in a part of the world where we often see and hear the word "slough"; it's pronounced "slew" and means a sluggish channel of water. I could visually rhyme "slough" with "enough" or "cough," although they sound nothing like "slough." Visual rhyme isn't cheating or failed rhyme; it provides a rest or witty wink that diverts a rhyme scheme from monotony. Some visual rhyme is heard in performance as imperfect rhyme or consonance (move/dove, laughter/daughter), even if the visual kinship between words goes unnoticed.

Measuring Meter

In the chapter on sound, you read about rhythm, cadence, and stressed and unstressed syllables. With rhythm, you feel invited to tap your foot to the beat; with meter, you break the lines every so many taps, and you're counting, keeping track. This is a move only poets make—not prose writers. We use the term **foot** to mean the unit of measurement—the unit that's repeated over and over, causing the beat. A foot is usually made up of one stressed syllable plus one or two unstressed syllables; here are some of the names of feet:

- An **iamb** (˘ /) has one unstressed syllable followed by one stressed syllable: a*bout*. Iambic meter is the most frequently used meter in the English language. Iambic lines tend to create a gentle, smooth song. A*bout* a*bout* a*bout*.
- A **trochee** (/ ˘) is the reverse of an iamb: a stressed syllable followed by an unstressed syllable: *mur*der. This meter tends to sound forceful or hard. *Mur*der *mur*der *mur*der.
- An **anapest** (˘ ˘ /) has two unstressed syllables followed by a stress (sounding like a galloping horse): come a*gain*. This measure tends to sound breezy, casual, and light when repeated. Come a*gain* come a*gain* come a*gain*.
- The **dactyl** (/ ˘ ˘) begins with a stressed syllable, which is followed by two unstressed syllables (sounding like a waltz): *Con*template. This measure sounds forceful but graceful in repetition. *Con*template *con*template *con*template.
- A **spondee** (/ /) is a foot composed of two stresses: *hard core*. It is used in an iambic or trochaic line sometimes to substitute for the regular two-syllable foot, when you want to call particular attention to what's being said at that moment. It brings a sense of closure to the end of a line, as in this iambic one: I *gig*gled; Ru*pert frowned*. That *dude* is *hard core*.
- A **pyrrhic** (˘ ˘) foot—two unstressed syllables—is the opposite of the spondee. It creates a hesitant first foot in this trochaic line: in a *mur*der *some*one *gets* an *aw*ful *whack*ing.

Feet can be arranged into lines long or short—line lengths are determined by the number of beats per line. So, for example, lines in the rest-*beat* (iamb) pattern with five beats per line are called iambic pentameter. Here are some of the names for measured line lengths, followed by an example written in iambics:

monometer = one foot: If *you*

dimeter = two feet: If *you* should *care*

trimeter = three feet: If *you* should *care* e*nough*

tetrameter = four feet: If *you* should *care* e*nough* to *run*

pentameter = five feet: If *you* should *care enough* to *run away*
hexameter = six feet: If *you* should *care enough* to *run away* with *me*
heptameter = seven feet: If *you* should *care enough* to *run away* with *me*, come *on*
octameter = eight feet: If *you* should *care enough* to *run away* with *me*, come *on* and *run*

Poems in meter often have regular line lengths (all the same length), but it's possible to adopt other patterns, such as alternating tetrameter, trimeter, tetrameter, trimeter, etc.

- **Accentual** meter, accentual verse, is a bit different: here, only the stress/beat is counted—the number of unstressed syllables can vary. Rap lyrics use an accentual meter.
- **Syllabic** verse is a form of measure in which all the syllables (not just stressed syllables) are counted to determine line length. Haiku is one of the most known forms of syllabic verse.

Samuel Green's poem "Stroke"—a poem published in 2014 and written in memory of his grandmother—is good to spend a little time with. Look at the end of the lines. Is there a rhyme scheme? Are you sure? How about meter? What's happening there? Does it matter that the lines are end-stopped and quite long at first and then become short as the poem signals it is ending? How is the shape of this poem, visually and sonically, important to your experience of what it means?

Stroke

Where is the axe, says the ice in the trough, left in the field for the cows.
    Here, says the file on the bench in the shed, stuck in a hole by the vise.
Where is the cup with a chip in its rim, says the sink with its saucer & spoon.
    Here, says the kitchen linoleum square, in fragments the color of bone.
Where is the milk, says the pail on the porch, scalded & shining & worn.
    Here, say the bells of the shuffling heifers, stalled at the door of the barn.
Where is the cream for the cinnamon cat, says the tuna can under the stairs.
    Here, says a shelf in the cold-box, with the butter & leftover pears.
Where is the heat for the dinner, say the skillet & pans on the range.
    Here, say the split chunks of alder & fir, carefully dried & arranged.
Where is the ball made of leftover twine, says the unfinished rug on the stool.
    Here, says the awkward crochet hook, made from an old-fashioned nail.
Where is the woman who lives in this house, says the work coat still hung on a chair.
    Here, says the wind through the grass of the field,
    here say the waves on the bay past the bluff,
    here says the breath in the air.
Not here, say the cows, *not here,* says the cat, *not here,* say the boots by the door.
Not here, says the stove, *not here,* says the coat, *not here,* says the shape on the floor.[8]

Shapes for Our Singing

Poetry isn't an emotional morass or a chaotic rant; calling our writing "poetry" doesn't excuse us from the drafting and revision process writers use to bring shape and form to literary work. We're singing, not screaming. The shapes that our poems can sing in are many; here are some to try:

- **Free verse** poems were first called "free" because they broke out of the bindings of strict meter and predictable, end-stopped rhyme patterns, which some thought made nineteenth-century poetry lugubrious, predictable, and boring. By the late nineteenth century, poets began to value cadences and structures sounding more like natural speech than did the artificial-sounding meter and rhyme schemes previously in common use. When rhyme and meter stopped being crucial to poetry in the twentieth century, emphasis shifted to the power of imagery, diction (word choice), and more nuanced and varied rhythms and sounds. Because free verse is written to fit no *predetermined* shape, it can produce a poem that impresses us as spontaneous and unique; but every free verse poem must make its own shape.
- **Formal or fixed-form poems** are crafted with the understanding that restriction can lead to exciting discoveries: forced to navigate a "given" shape, we have to compromise what we intend to say. These compromises—if we work *with* instead of against them—often lead to drafts that delight us and teach us what's possible in our work. In this way, the form "triggers" the poem. Restrictions usually include a set poem length (a predetermined number of lines—such as a sonnet having fourteen or a sestina having thirty-nine), line length (a number of beats, or syllables, per line), rhyme scheme, or use of a refrain (lines or words repeated in prescribed positions within the poem). A poet who can meet all the restrictions of a fixed form, yet do it in a way that feels fresh, charms us. "Broken" or "shattered" forms are written by poets who select just *some* of the restrictions of a fixed form. They tip their hats to an inherited form, while reinventing it.
- **Prose poems** remind me of the eternal question: Is a burrito a sandwich? A prose poem has no sliced lines; a burrito has no sliced bread; but both "wrap around" quite effectively and delightfully. A prose poem is built from one long line that appears on the page as a block or paragraph (looking like prose); its margins are usually both left and right justified to signal that it's a poem and not a lost paragraph in search of a story or essay. A prose poem will appear as wide or narrow as the margins of a page allow (it changes shape when reprinted in different size formats); the author gives no signal about where lines should be broken. This choice not to break the poem into lines has an important effect: prose poems tend to go fast. They use all the sonic elements and density of

poetry, and they often have a run-on quality that makes them somewhat surreal or manic. Prose poems tend to feature speakers who experience or reflect on dramatic or heightened emotional states using a lyrical style, but there is no hard rule about content or expression.

- **Spoken-word** poetry is meant to be performed and heard, not read on a page. The voice—sometimes the whole body—replaces the field of the page as the site for this poem. You'll find spoken-word poems on YouTube, author sites, and at other net addresses, but the best place to experience them is live, at an open mic at a local coffee shop, library, book store, house party, or at a "poetry slam" (performance competition). Poetry has been memorized and recited for much longer than poetic texts have existed, so the roots of spoken word sink deep. But the term "spoken word" refers specifically to a modern oral cultural movement. Individuals or collaborative teams perform frank stories, commentaries, or monologues using a strong cadence based in the rhythms used by blues singers and beatniks of earlier eras. Spoken-word poetry uses verbal acrobatics layered over a beat that sounds akin to hip-hop. And much like hip-hop (which began as a grassroots art outside the record industry and traditional performance venues), spoken-word poetry grew outside of academic institutions and publishing firms that determined what poems would be taught and made available. Spoken-word poetry can be confessional, political, streetwise, hard-edged, slangy, and passionate. It's often rhymed, as both a value and a memory device.

- **Found poems** are made by borrowing, arranging, and imagining new contexts and meanings for language that you find in ordinary texts (e.g., magazines, signs, posters, brochures, menus, directions, labels, packaging, handbooks, field guides, advertising, recipes) or in literary texts. Noticing that a different or more complex meaning—unintended in the original source or sources—could arise by playing with the "found" text is the starting point for composing a found poem. Although found poems tend to be relatively voiceless, they're a great way to practice relaxing your critical muscle that wants to tense up and make your poems logical and "normal."

  In addition to selecting and juxtaposing found parts to make a poem (which is a bit like making a collage—yes, you can "smudge" to make verb tense or the pronouns consistent), be sure to create an original title for a found poem. Write your found poem title from scratch, to unify and contextualize the work—to give it a new meaning. Offer the source of your found material between the title and the body of your poem or in a footnote. Annie Dillard's "Signals at Sea" sources a book about maritime navigation and the use of semaphore (how sailors on ships would raise lettered flags [pennants] to signal meaning to other passing ships before radio transmission or during times of radio silence). Dillard arranges excerpts from the book into an order that speaks about communication not just between ships but between people.

The varieties of found poems are marvelous. Blackout poems, erasure poems, and cut-up poems can be viewed online with a search. Visual art can add to found poetry; poet and textile artist J.I. Kleinberg (chocolateisaverb.wordpress.com) carefully rips phrases from magazine headlines, arranges them into haiku-like collages, and photographs the results. The rips and arrangements, as much as the fragments of language, are part of her poetry's beauty.

When you find your poem's shape, you find its force and energy. Drafting becomes a matter of riding that force, seeing where its language can carry you. On that journey, you will likely encounter two issues. The first is sentimentality. Sentiment means feeling, and certainly feeling belongs not only in poetry but in all art. We read poems in order to feel and be moved; we write poems for the same reason. But sentimentality means *nostalgia for feeling*—not the feeling itself, but wallowing in the memory of having felt. Substituting *nostalgia about a feeling* for *the experience that generated the feeling in the first place* is the fastest way to lose energy in a poem's draft...and lose your reader. You'll notice yourself slipping into sentimentality when you write in abstractions *about* feeling rather than writing with imagery to cause your reader to feel.

And finally, after you've found your poem's shape and energy, how do you stop it? When you draft and you're riffing and experimenting with language, how can a poem reach a conclusion? It's commonly said that a poem satisfies us best when the ending feels "both inevitable and surprising"—when the body of the poem creates an expectation in us that's met or realized at the end and when that realization simultaneously avoids seeming predictable. Endings tend either toward "closing" and narrowing to give a sense of completeness or toward "opening" and stretching to signal we've reached a position from which the reader must leap. Some possibilities include:

Closed endings

- Repeat or reference a phrase from the beginning of the poem, which can now be understood in a new context or as having a new meaning.
- Repeat or reference a strong image from earlier in the poem, which can now be understood in a figurative context.
- Return to a pattern established in the body of the poem, after briefly departing from it near the end.
- Use a short, emphatic sentence as your last line. This strategy is especially effective if you've been using enjambment and longer sentences throughout the body of your poem.

- Come to a hard, full stop in the last line, using as few unaccented syllables as possible and spondees for the last foot or two.
- Repeat the same meter in the final two lines of a poem that is otherwise written in free verse.
- Rhyme the last two lines of an otherwise unrhymed poem, making a couplet.

Open endings

- Introduce a new speech act. For instance, if the poem has been expressed as a series of statements, end with a question, an apology, a request, a command, or a promise. Or, if the poem has been a series of questions, end with an answer.
- Show a dramatic change in the speaker's attitude or understanding through a change in tone.
- Shift from first-person "I" to second-person "you" or collective "we" at the end, signaling a widening understanding of the poem's theme and addressee.
- Introduce a new image that comes as a surprise but has a subtle connection to the rest of the poem.
- Break out of any kind of regularity or pattern that was established in the body of the poem.

Trust your reader enough to avoid "summing up" at your poem's conclusion—that sort of ending works well for academic papers but not for poetry. Your poem's ending is the last bite of a delicious meal, the parting glance at a love, the final note of a song. Make it language to savor.

Suggested Reading from Our Anthology
Sherman Alexie, from *Totem Sonnets,* "One" and "Seven"
Elizabeth Bachinsky, "For the Pageant Girls"
James Crews, "Lover Boys"
Natalie Diaz, "My Brother at 3 A.M."
Annie Dillard, "Signals at Sea"
Barbara Hamby, "Ode to My 1977 Toyota"
Paul Martínez Pompa, "Exclamation Point"
Edna St. Vincent Millay, "[What lips my lips have kissed…]"
Mallory Opel, "Among the Blossoms"
Tom Sleigh, "Aubade"
Patricia Smith, "Hip-Hop Ghazal"
James Tyner, "At a Barbecue for R.C. One Week after He Is Out of Iraq"
Theresa Williams, "Urgent Note for My Son Langston"

For Further Reading
Alfred Corn, *The Poem's Heartbeat: A Manual of Prosody*
Steve Kowit, *In the Palm of Your Hand: The Poet's Portable Workshop*

Your Moves

1. It takes perseverance and skill to write what Steve Kowit calls a "Purposefully Awful Poem": a poem that fails simultaneously on many levels. Have fun drafting a truly bad poem, a real stinker, using the means listed below. Label each of the ways your poem achieves its awful purpose, connecting the label to the highlighted or circled infraction:
   - abstraction substituting for imagery
   - cliché instead of your own fresh language
   - pointlessly formal or antique language ("thou, O, thus, whence")
   - inverted word order (unnatural for modern language: "if sleep I well, I'm rested")
   - obvious rhyme ("June/moon")
   - overuse of adjectives ("the creepy old dusty brick mansion")
   - purposeless line breaks
   - senseless punctuation (using periods, commas, and the like, but not writing actual sentences)
   - prosaic (having many unstressed syllables and lacking compression)
   - MS: letting Microsoft decide what words/lines get capitalized, where margins are
   - sentimentality (self-pitying or self-involved declarations of nostalgic emotion)
   - misuse of allusion or symbol (references to Greek gods, to Shakespeare, to the flag, to a medicine wheel, or to the occult, for example, when these allusions serve no purpose or have no meaning in the context of the poem)
   - hipsterism (obsessed with seeming cool at any cost)
   - titular fail: no title, a pompous title, or a title that spoils the poem's surprise

2. The limerick (sometimes capitalized because that's also a city in Ireland) is a very short poem written in meter and rhyme. The form causes the limerick to be comedic, ironic, and often bawdy. In fact, it's hard to write a serious, sincere, gentle limerick. After you've heard a few limericks, you'll recognize from the first line what's coming: you're being set up for a twist or "groaner" in the last line (a bit like a knock-knock joke). Here's an old one:

   There was an old man of Nantucket,
   Who kept all his cash in a bucket;
   But his daughter, named Nan,
   Ran away with a man—
   And as far as the bucket, Nantucket.[9]

   Lines 1, 2, and 5 rhyme and follow the same meter: / ˘ ˘ / ˘ ˘ / with one, two, or no unaccented syllables before or after this base (˘ / ˘ ˘ / ˘ ˘ / ˘ as the poem above does, or ˘ ˘ / ˘ ˘ / ˘ ˘ / ˘ is fine too). Lines 3 and 4 are shorter, rhyme just with each other, and use the same "beat rest rest beat" pattern: / ˘ ˘ /, or ˘ / ˘ ˘ /, or ˘ ˘ / ˘ ˘ /. Try two (or more) of your own. Does this poem's form indeed entice you toward the silly, ironic, or naughty?
3. Read "Signals at Sea" by Annie Dillard; then go online and read some erasure and blackout poems. Create a found erasure, or blackout poem all your own. Be sure to invent the title yourself and credit your sources.
4. Read "My Wicked Wicked Ways" by Sandra Cisneros and then write a poem about what you see when you look at a family picture taken in your childhood. Include both present and future tense to describe the photo and to suggest what would come next for your family or yourself. Or read "Among the Blossoms" by Mallory Opel and try this advanced move: write about a family photograph and make use of at least four vocabulary words from the field of photography (Opel uses "expose," "viewer," "focus," and "composition"), but use these terms figuratively to describe the subject of the photograph.
5. There's a reason people need to write love poems! Read James Crews's "Lover Boys" and Michael Ondaatje's "The Cinnamon Peeler," and then write a love poem to make your reader swoon with you.
6. Traditionally, an aubade is a poem of "sweet sorrow" as lovers part at daybreak. But it can also be a poem about parting under other circumstances. Read Tom Sleigh's "Aubade"; then write your own poem with the same title about a parting or loss.
7. Write a *brief* yet vivid poem in the form of an instruction (see "Recipe" by Janice Mirikitani) or a definition (see "Exclamation Point" by Paul Martínez Pompa). What is your poem's subject matter beyond the literal instruction or definition?

8. Read Samuel Green's "Some Reasons Why I Became a Poet" and Barbara Hamby's "Ode to My 1977 Toyota" and then create a list poem—a poem that accumulates by cataloguing details.
9. Have you ever written a prose poem? Read the examples by Carolyn Forché, Sina Queyras, Paul Martínez Pompa, and James Crews; then try your own. Focus on density, compression, and sound.
10. Write a poem of praise, celebration, or honor in the form of an ode (see Barbara Hamby's "Ode to My 1977 Toyota"). Or write a toast in the form of a poem (see James Bertolino's "Wedding Toast," kerouac.english.www.edu/~bertolino/JamesPoetryWeddingToast.htm). Note that the ode and the toast both use elevated or "formal" speech. For a twist, focus on something specific that is not normally praised or much noticed.
11. Write a political poem or a poem of social conscience. Create an emotional and intellectual response by *avoiding political speech entirely.* Read these examples from our anthology: Theresa Williams, "Urgent Note for My Son Langston"; James Tyner, "At a Barbecue for R.C. One Week after He Is Out of Iraq"; Patricia Lockwood, "Rape Joke"; Paul Martínez Pompa, "Exclamation Point."
12. Create a "field of the page" poem that does not look like a strip on the page. See Richard Siken's "Scheherazade" for inspiration, noticing his use of aeration and dropped lines.
13. Try a translation poem. Find online or at the library a poem written in a language you don't know (it's important that you not know the language at all!). Line by line, recreate the *sounds* and *shape* of that poem using English. You won't be translating the poem's literal meaning but rather the effects of its language. Notice where a word gets repeated; repeat your equivalent in the same space. Replicate long or short lines, patterns of rhyme and stanzas, and punctuation. Don't worry about making sense in your rough draft—just aim to use plenty of imagery, nouns and verbs, and sonic equivalents. Once you reach the end of the draft, revise it toward the best poem it can be from the bones you've got now. If a translation of the source poem is available to you, don't read it until your revision is done—it will arrest your creativity.
14. Many poets feel fourteen lines is the perfect length for a poem. That's long enough to use specific imagery and detail, to develop a sense of the speaker's rhythm and character, and to have the speaker experience a change or understanding. But it's short enough to require density and brevity—every word must count. Plus, if your lines are all medium length, the resulting poem is a little box—a satisfying square on the page—because the poem is as wide as it is long. Try a fourteen-line poem (I call these "14ers"). If you are inclined, try a traditional sonnet (using all the conventions listed

below) or try a "broken sonnet" (selecting just *some* of these conventions). Read the following 14ers from our anthology to see a range of styles and possibilities: Edna St. Vincent Millay, "[What lips my lips have kissed...]"; Rainer Maria Rilke, "Archaic Torso of Apollo"; Maria Hummel, "I'm This Many"; Richard Siken, "Scheherazade"; John Marshall, *Taken With* series, #22; Kathleen Halme, "A Study in O"; Kathleen Flenniken, "What I Saw" (in the chapter on practicing perception); and Sherman Alexie's two poems from *Totem Sonnets*.

Traditional sonnet conventions include the following:

- Writing all lines in iambic pentameter (˘ / ˘ / ˘ / ˘ / ˘ /)
- Using a rhyme scheme (try ABAB CDCD EFEFGG or ABBA CDDC EFGEFG)
- Creating a shift or change as the poem transitions between lines 8 and 9 (called the "volta")—The shift might be between describing a specific incident or person and then stating an understanding or question about it; beginning with something personal and then expressing a wider context; contradicting a tone or belief explored in the first eight lines with the theme or manner of the final six; or starting with a proposition and juxtaposing it with an explicit experience expressed in the last six lines
- And often, writing on the theme of love

15. Write a poem in a traditional form that makes use of refrain (a villanelle, pantoum, or ghazal). The technique of refrain (a repeating phrase or line) is well used in poems about time passing, obsession, memory, consciousness, dreaming, grieving, ritual, repetitive experiences, and unusual states of mind. The meaning of the repeated segment of your poem should expand and transform as it is placed in each new context (otherwise, the poem will feel mechanical or comic). Look online for specific guidelines and read the anthology examples for the villanelle (Elizabeth Bachinsky, "For the Pageant Girls"), pantoum (Natalie Diaz, "My Brother at 3 A.M."), and ghazal (Patricia Smith, "Hip-Hop Ghazal") forms.
16. Poems can bore if they just describe. Write or revise one poem so that it uses at least five different speech acts. See Sylvia Plath's "Mirror" for example—it's optional to have your poem personify an object, as Plath's does. There are *many* speech acts (look online), but here are a few to consider: address, apology, boast, claim, command, confession, contradiction, declaration, dialogue, exclamation, hypothesis, invitation, lament, oath, plea, prayer, protest, question, rebuttal, reproach, request, revelation, vow.

17. Read Samuel Green's "Stroke," noticing the effects of meter. Revise a free-verse draft into any meter, seeing what new phrasings and energy might come about. Revise again: do you keep some, all, or none of the metered passages?
18. Read Tom Sleigh's "Aubade," noticing the effects of regular stanzas. Revise a poem draft by breaking it into regular stanzas, seeing what new tensions might result. Sleigh uses quatrains (four-line stanzas); you might try quatrains, tercets (three-line stanzas), or couplets (two-line stanzas).

Writing Stories

You have the sheet of blank paper, the pencil, and the obligation to invent truer than things can be true. You have to take what is not palpable and make it completely palpable and also have it seem normal so that it can become a part of the experience of the person who reads it. —*Ernest Hemingway*[10]

Like all children, I loved stories—picture-book stories of rabbits stealing carrots from a garden, children's stories of baby dragons that fly. As a young adult, I devoured book-length stories about girls on the frontier of the Great Plains, boys tempted into gang life, the journey of a prophet. I listened to stories every day at the supper table, at Sunday school, on the playground, on the news, in the lyrics of songs. I needed to write poems from the time I was ten or eleven, and I even published some, so when I enrolled in creative writing in college I assumed I could write stories. I wrote terrible stories! In all my stories, the only thing that happened was a random accident (a car crash, an earthquake, a fall) in the first paragraph; then the narrator would pass out and wake up and pass out again and wake up again. This loss and regaining of consciousness would continue until the story reached its assigned length. I wrote stories like I wrote my lyric poems: plotless evocations of mood in lovely language. Nice language was not enough. I didn't know what a story does.

Later, I wrote a story about a woman named Nora who worked at the Seattle aquarium and chopped herring to feed the mammals. No serious accident befell Nora in the opening paragraph. Instead, her conflict was her passivity, seen by the reader in Nora's relationships with other characters. At the end of the story, Nora gets into a huge tank at the aquarium where, day after day, all the fish swim around clockwise. She swims against their current and suddenly all the fish turn and swim as a school counterclockwise with Nora. Okay—not brilliant. But I was starting to learn what a story does.

How Stories Move

Stories frame almost everything we know and do, creating a sense of purpose and meaning. History, we're told, is a version of the human story written by winners, who make current society and the way we live in it seem inevitable. Before history was written, oral myths and origin stories began the narratives of how people arrived in this world, the mistakes we made and the lessons we learned in order to survive with one another. Adam and Eve. Raven and the clamshell. Vishnu asleep on a sea that trembles with the sound Ommm. *Long time ago. In the beginning. Once upon a time.* For millennia, peoples all across the earth sat around fires telling stories that allowed them to shape the world as a meaningful place. Today, we gather around the flickering lights of the movie screen, television, or stage or we come in solitude to the e-book or page to hear a story, not simply for entertainment or to pass time. "The reason we tell stories," writes Barry Lopez,

> is to keep each other from being afraid. We tell stories and write poems, historically, to keep awe and aspiration and comprehension and other components of hopeful lives bright in each other's hearts. Storytelling is how we're moved to take care of each other when we recognize how extremely thin the veneer of civilization we cherish is, and how very hard it is to keep that veneer from shredding in the wind.[11]

We each understand our own life as a story, told finally in obituary. Attracted to someone, we may wonder, "Is this the start of a story we'll tell our children?" Waking from a dream, we try to hold it a few moments more—believing, perhaps, it's a story our unconscious has whispered to our conscious mind. Even seeing an old penny in the street, we might bend to pick it up with the hope that this day's story might change course, veering toward luck. In our most bitter or anguished moments (when we divorce, lose a job, lose a child, lose our way), we are in shock: "This is not how my story goes." Evidence suggests an effective treatment for post-traumatic stress includes shaping the chaos of pain into the story of its cause, then telling and retelling this story in a safe environment. "Truth and reconciliation," a social process to work toward healing after war and other massive atrocities, allows witnesses and even perpetrators to tell their stories publicly without fear of prosecution. Among our greatest fears, Alzheimer's disease: if we forget our stories, can we know who we are or how to exist?

Stories help us understand our truth, personally and culturally. Joan Didion famously wrote, "We tell ourselves stories in order to live."[12] We all want our lives to matter, to be relevant; stories help us attach our small existence to a larger narrative and to larger meanings. But stories can cage and limit us in grave ways, too. Visit any serious news site and see who's killing today because our stories (about religion, about borders, about who started it) lock us in hate. Visit any not-serious news site and see the celebrity gossip—stories to shame, to ridicule, to make us feel superior to the model who can't keep it together, the star in trouble again, the actress who left the house *in those pants.* How many of us feel trapped at some point by our life's narrative, ours the story of the last one picked for the team, the loner, mom's favorite, the martyr to her kids, the "smart" sister, the passed-over employee, the cut-up, the fuck-up, the geek, the strong one, the one who stays, the one who leaves. Although I would wish Alzheimer's disease on no one, several of my students have written about grandparents with the disease who reach a point at which they seem no longer anxious or sad. Their narrative and sensation of time gone, these grandparents live in each moment without anger, disappointment, or anything but delight in this "new" person—their grandchild—with them now in a fresh and amazing world. It's a passing stage of the disease, teaching us about the freedom that might come from forgetting or rewriting the scripts of our lives. Fiction, a mirror built of stories into which we can gaze and possibly recognize ourselves, lets us practice letting go of *our* story, so we can return to it, perhaps changed by our empathy with whomever we discover in that mirror.

The Story Arc

You already know how to hear and tell a story verbally. When I invite students to tell stories about something funny or frightening that happened to them, they're quickly able to tap into a reserve of personal stories they've told before. They know stories begin by placing a character in a scene at a particular time ("Okay, so last summer I was out at Lake Padden with two friends and it was after midnight"). They soon introduce a problem: a source of tension or conflict for the character to overcome ("but *some*body had to drive us all home!"). Then, as the tension rises, the tellers bring details alive with their voices, often quoting dialogue and speaking faster just at the climax or peak of the action. Finally, to signal the story has reached an end, they take a little leap sideways or ahead to throw a new light on the events ("the cop had thought I was my twin sister!") or to signal their attitude now in summing up the experience ("well, whatever—at least I got a stuffed opossum out of it"). Instinctively, most of us grasp the basic "arc" or structure of Western storytelling, which can be mapped like this:

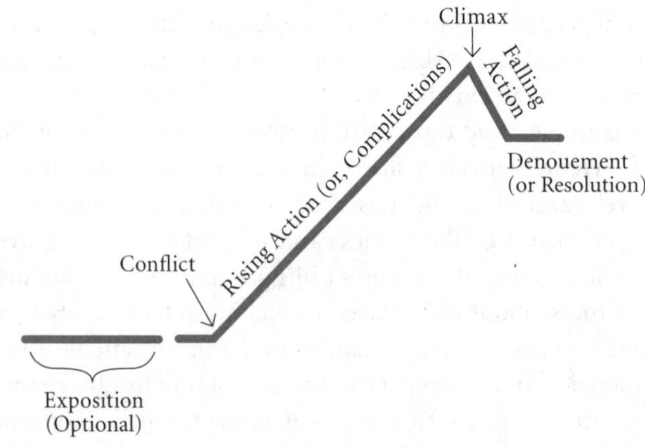

Here are some ways to activate that story arc:

- A novel or long story might begin in **exposition** (briefly establishing the "normal" life of the character), but very soon a **conflict** is introduced: a source of tension or trouble that will cause the main character to change. In short stories, the sense of conflict is often shown or implied immediately in the lead (opening sentences):

  > The Grandmother didn't want to go to Florida. (Flannery O'Connor, "A Good Man Is Hard to Find")

  > A man stood upon a railroad bridge in northern Alabama, looking down into the swift water twenty feet below. The man's hands were behind his back, the wrists bound with a cord. A rope closely encircled his neck. It was attached to a stout cross-timber above his head and the slack fell to the level of his knees. Some loose boards laid upon the ties supporting the rails of the railway supplied a footing for him and his executioners—two private soldiers of the Federal army, directed by a sergeant who in civil life may have been a deputy sheriff. (Ambrose Bierce, "An Occurrence at Owl Creek Bridge")

- Introducing us to a character in conflict, the story's lead makes a pact with the reader: we will journey together through the meaningful complications (**rising action**) of this conflict until we reach its highest or most intense point (**climax**), which causes the character to change (**resolution**). The journey may continue just a bit longer (**denouement**), to show the effects of this change after the conflict has ended. Flannery O'Conner's lead makes a pact with the reader: Grandma is going to Florida and will experience meaningful complications and change as a result. Placing a bound man in a noose, Bierce immediately shows us the conflict: a man is about to be hanged. But without the complications and resolution that follow, we won't have a satisfying short story about the condemned man.

When creative writing students begin to *write* stories, their verbal storytelling instinct often goes haywire. Instead of a short story, we get a stock character (a common social or literary stereotype) moving through a series of events; each event carries equal weight and is presented chronologically and ploddingly over the scope of one day. It usually begins with an alarm clock (or any timekeeping device popular in the present moment) going off. Even though the story's truth has nothing to do with *time*, the novice writer's story begins with the alarm. I've *never* heard a student tell aloud the story of his encounter with a skunk, her week spent volunteering after the hurricane, his doomed relationship with an outrageous roommate, or her cross-country trip on a Greyhound bus and begin "That morning I couldn't believe the alarm clock could be so loud and infuriating!" But many begin *writing* a story this way, with the misunderstanding that a storyteller's purpose is to describe some stuff that happens to a character one day. Not understating plot, this writer becomes trapped in gluey, interminable pages of description and narration and fails either to hook the reader or deliver a satisfying story.

You have the option to draft many pages of character exploration in search of a plot, but the process will demand *many* hours of rewrites before your draft is ready for your first workshop, your first reader's eyes—and there's no guarantee a plot will ever reveal itself. Few of us have a *real* talent, a gift, for lying: for inventing situations and details that are absolutely convincing and carry the listener to an intended purpose. Most fiction writers rely on conflict *rooted in real-life situations they know and understand*. You can too, by coloring and reimagining your experiences through the perspectives of characters you create. When you have the sense of an interesting character and an interesting conflict, the next move is usually to work out the scaffold or outline for your story and plot before drafting.

Plotting Time

In literature, we use the term "story" more explicitly than the layperson does to mean *a series of events in their chronological order*. "Plot" means a series of events *purposefully arranged* into the order that best reveals the story's meaning or subtext. "What happens" is not the meaning of any story; meaning is tied to the emotional significance, the weight of feeling and understanding created in the reader. As a fiction writer, you'll work out in your imagination a series of events that are all part of the story; however, if you express your short story as that list—even with a few juicy details thrown in here and there—your reader will remain unmoved and unsatisfied because a list of events lacks a sense of causal relationships between events.

Your short story must have both "story" and "plot" to create the sensation that the parts are related to a meaningful whole. To save yourself fruitless wandering in prose, map your story and plot before you draft. Working with a vertical (list) or horizontal (time line) outline form, chronologically list all the actions and interactions of your characters so you can conceive of them unfolding through passing days, hours, and minutes. This outline is "story." Many fiction writers discover story when a sense of an ending comes first to mind: they imagine a moment in a scene that could serve as a climax, and then they invent what could lead up to and create that moment (John Irving said this was how his novel *A Prayer for Owen Meany* began to form in his mind). You don't need to *think up* story in chronological order, but you do need to chart it chronologically to understand the story's scope and to make sure it's watertight temporally. (I know writers who also draw the physical space of their story's setting: sketching the floor plan, arranging the streets and locales of the city, they map the story spatially as well as temporally.)

Next, make a separate plot outline that reflects the following choices:

- **Which parts of the story will I dramatize (show through scene), include as exposition, and leave out entirely?** A crucial decision before drafting is perspective. Where is your narrator *in time* as she or he tells this story? What parts of the story are past, present, and future? It's likely that much of the story is "past"—context, background—and therefore unneeded dramatically to show your character's experience of change. It's also likely that part of the story is "future" and not part of the short story you're writing now. Trust your reader's emotional intelligence: give us your character's journey and change through *only* the crucial scenes, leaving out as much explanation as possible to keep the momentum flowing. Ambrose Bierce might have started "An Occurrence at Owl Creek Bridge" with details about the main character, Peyton Farquhar, with Farquhar's childhood in Alabama or with his courtship of his wife. Or he could have begun earlier that same day before the noose was tightened around Farquhar's throat. Bierce did not because these elements are not, ultimately, crucial to the version of the story he wants to tell. Bierce does, however, include many paragraphs about the main character's flight in the river and through the woods—an experience that takes only *seconds* in the story. This plot choice controls the reader's emotional experience and ability of make meaning from it; it reflects a decision Bierce has made about why he is telling us this story. You, too, must decide why you are telling a particular version of the story you have outlined.
- **What arrangement or order will you use to disclose the necessary elements of the story?** Chronology may seem like the "default" structure to you now only because your story was mapped first in this manner. As you shape your project for your reader to encounter it, you have many tools to edit and arrange the plot to emphasize certain moments, particular meanings. Remember the Quentin Tarantino/Roger Avary film *Pulp Fiction*? The end of the story occurs about three quarters through the film when Bruce Willis and Maria de Medeiros flee LA on a chopper. But the end of the plot is the scene at the diner, when John Travolta and Samuel L. Jackson have an intense conversation about redemption (the film's resolution) then leave the diner with the briefcase (the film's denouement). Such plot decisions transform the raw material of story into art.

Plotting time is an effort to communicate with the reader about what the story means; where you choose to begin, where you choose to end, and where you direct our attention to linger—these are key moves. Here are some ways to shape the reader's experience of time:

- **Expand and contract our perception of time:** write the most important aspect of your story as detailed scene and delete unnecessary scenes (many great short stories take place in just one scene); use exposition only for *essential* contextual information (keep it succinct).

- **Experiment with *in medias res*** (Latin for "in the midst of things"), the technique of beginning your story in the middle of the action rather than with exposition or the "alarm clock" long before the real gist of your story. Most short story drafts get the critique that "the story doesn't really start" until page two or three. So jump right in and avoid that reaction. Here's one of my favorite examples of *in medias res*, the opening lines of Ernest Hemingway's "The Short Happy Life of Francis Macomber":

  > It was now lunch time and they were all sitting under the double green fly of the dining tent pretending that nothing had happened.[13]

  With this lead we're plopped into a scene in which it's clear *something* embarrassing or shameful has already happened, and we're dying to know what.

- **Flash back and flash forward** to fill in backstory, which you may need to do if you use *in medias res*, or to jump ahead in time and avoid plodding chronology. To flash back, signal to your reader that the narrative is shifting back in time. Wayson Choy uses the technique in *The Jade Peony.* A narrator admires the deft fingers of her grandmother, skilled at weaving fibers. Jook-Liang (the narrator) is eight years old as the passage begins:

  > Poh-Poh refused to teach me any of her knots. Once she did try, when I was six, but I seemed too clumsy, too awkward, not fearful enough of failure. My six-year-old fingers slipped; I clutched at Grandmother's body, glimpsed her hand raised above me, ready to slap. Then she froze, her hand in mid-strike, held back; tears welled up in her eyes. "No, no, *no*!" Furious, she shook me off. "No more teach!" [....]
  >
  > Now I was almost nine, swallowing, knowing nothing.[14]

  The word "Once" signals the shift back in time; then "Now" signals we've caught up again to the original time frame. It's important to let the reader know when the flashback has ended; do this with a "catch-up" word such as "now," or insert a section break after the flashback and resume a new section in the present time of the narrative.

  Choy's scene continues using the flash-forward technique:

  > And there was no other way to learn. No one could ever follow her quick-moving fingers. She would later teach Baby Brother some juggling, tell him paperfolding stories, even show him how to make simple toys, like paper cranes, toss rings—or windchimes when he grew old enough. But all her womanly skills she would keep away from me, keep to herself until she died....

  Here, "she would later" moves us years and years ahead.

- **Play with jump cuts.** Cut your story into sections (one or a few paragraphs each) and arrange them as a collage out of chronological order. Put extra white space between the sections to indicate they are not intended to be read chronologically or that there is a gap or "jump" in time between them (each section begins "flush left," with subsequent paragraphs within the section indented). Arrange them for juxtaposition—placing them near one another to suggest patterns or relationships other than chronological time. Madeleine Thien's "Simple Recipes" demonstrates this technique.

- **Try embedding the end in the beginning.** You might do this as a "frame" (starting the story with the final scene, flashing back then narrating to bring us again to that point, and then concluding the final scene). But you can also underscore meaning in a beautiful way by embedding the *language* of the ending in the story's lead. The reader is usually moved and satisfied by the conclusion of such a piece without consciously knowing why (until rereading the story). David Foster Wallace does this in "Incarnations of Burned Children." Here is his lead: "The Daddy was around the side of the house hanging a door for the tenant when he heard the child's screams and the Mommy's voice gone high between them." When Foster Wallace writes in the conclusion "the child's body expanded and walked about and drew pay and lived its life untenanted," his figurative use of the unhung, dangling door and the untenanted, empty child come together to create a sense of an ending. This effect is underscored by Foster Wallace using another shaping method, motif.
- **For an artful insinuation of meaning, venture into motif.** A motif is any recurring element that has figurative significance. It could be a scene in flashbacks, a repeated image, or even a repeated word. The tenant's door, left swaying, recurs several times in "Incarnations of Burned Children." This recurrence lifts the image beyond the literal to figurative meaning and lends shape to an explosive small narrative. We're all quite used to visual motif in film. For instance, director Sean Penn uses an airplane contrail and a human form with outstretched arms as motifs in his film *Into the Wild*. The repeated contrail images suggest that technology or the main character's father (an aerospace engineer) follow him into wild spaces; the "arms" motif makes a Christ-figure association with the main character. Motif creates a sense of meaningful order outside of chronology.

Plotting Trouble

Every story needs a character in trouble. Janet Burroway points out that, in fiction, unlike in real life, "only trouble is interesting."[15] Without the early introduction of an internal or external conflict for the main character to face (or flee), there is no story. In real life, some people seem able to live happily without trouble bearing down on each moment; in fiction and autobiography, there's no story without it.

But trouble need not be as extreme as a noose around your character's neck in the lead. Here's the more subtle way Denis Johnson uses trouble to begin "Steady Hands at Seattle General":

> Inside of two days I was shaving myself, and I even shaved a couple of new arrivals, because the drugs they injected me with had an amazing effect. I call it amazing because only hours before they'd wheeled me through corridors in which I hallucinated a soft, summery rain. In the hospital rooms on either side, objects—vases, ashtrays, beds—had looked wet and scary, hardly bothering to cover up their true meanings.
>
> They ran a few syringesful into me, and I felt like I'd turned from a light, Styrofoam thing into a person. I held up my hands before my eyes. The hands were as still as a sculpture's.
>
> I shaved my roommate, Bill. "Don't get tricky with my moustache," he said.
>
> "Okay so far?"
>
> "So far."
>
> "I'll do the other side."
>
> "That would make sense, partner."

Although this narrator sounds content and calm, two conflicts immediately energize Johnson's story: the narrator is a drug addict facing rehabilitation (*will he be okay?*) and his interaction with Bill the roommate is marked by tension, which is signaled in Bill's sarcastic remark "That would make sense, partner." The journey we make to understand the source of this tension between the young narrator and Bill (Bill understands something about addiction that the more romantic young narrator does not) lifts this writing beyond medical report or anecdote and into the terrain of short story. It seems simple: two guys have a conversation in rehab, and the one with steady hands shaves the other. But the plot choice *not* to begin with the alarm clock on the day the narrator will overdose, the order in which the two characters reveal parts of their pasts and their attitudes about addiction to one another, and the final action create a deliberate structure that shapes what "Steady Hands at Seattle General" means. The story would mean differently if plotted differently: if it began in the narrator's childhood or on his wedding day many years after rehab or if it ended with his overdose and death or with a flashback to his first high, this whole short story would be about something else.

Novelist E.M. Forster famously pointed out that "The king died and the queen died" is story, whereas "The king died and then the queen died of grief" is plot because the latter shows us a causal relationship within the trouble. Trouble invites our attention (who can look away from an accident occurring before our eyes?); stories turn the attention and tension of trouble into meaning. This is what humans ask from stories: What does our trouble mean? What are the truths that guide our lives? The ordering decisions you make with plot reflect not only who you are as a writer but also what meaning *you* make of this world. If this sounds serious, it is:

storytelling demands you risk showing readers what you know about and care about. But you need not know about and care about everything at once. V.S. Pritchett puts it this way: "the short story tells us only one thing, and that, intensely."[16]

There are many approaches to the intensity of "trouble" in fiction. Two contrasting forms of arrangement to try are the action plot and the "inner-life" plot:

- **The action plot** concentrates on tension mounting or elevating due to a succession of incidents related to each other by a causal factor. Each event in the plot causes the next; every action is a reaction to or extension of the action before it. The journey a character makes in the action plot is through a progression of external circumstances culminating in a climax. The character in an action plot is not without an inner life, but the resolution of this plot is *a perception or understanding the character reaches about the way the world is* (rather than a revelation of identity or true self). The resolution might be indicated by internal monologue or physical reaction in the climax or denouement. Shani Mootoo's "Out on Main Street," David Sedaris's "The Drama Bug," and Sherwood Anderson's "Death in the Woods" are examples of the action plot. Luisa Valenzuela's "Vision Out of the Corner of One Eye" demonstrates a "twist" action plot: the causal factor for the action is not what the reader is led to assume it is. In a "twist," the resolution reveals a surprise.
- **The "inner-life" plot** concentrates on the main character's internal landscape. The primary journey in this plot arrangement is one of emotion or consciousness, climaxing and then resolving with *an extended moment of emotion that reveals something to or about the character regarding that character's identity or true self.* The narrator in Lewis Nordan's "Owls" lives in the external world and has tangible experiences, but the real journey he makes and the change he realizes by the short story's ending are internal. "Inner-life" stories can be light on external action, but they are gripping nonetheless because of this internal drama and change, which sometimes even includes epiphany. Kate Chopin's "The Story of an Hour," James Joyce's "Eveline," and Madeleine Thien's "Simple Recipes" demonstrate ways that plot choice can shift the focus from external action to a character's inner life and emotional change.

Do extroverts have a taste for the action plot and introverts for the inner-life plot? How can a writer plot a story for mixed introvert and extrovert audiences? Stretching to understand how plot matters, we're pulled to appreciate the various ways people remember and tell their own stories—and the meanings emphasized or shed through these choices.

Plot is a special challenge for the writer creating an autobiographical narrative. Often, an autobiographical rough draft will be dull, and, when faced with critique, the writer defensively exclaims, "But it really happened that way!" This is no valid excuse: as a story writer, you control the plot in both fiction and creative nonfiction. Things that "really happened" must be left out, emphasized, and arranged into an order for the purpose of bringing your reader to an understanding of your story's truth.

Truth and Fiction

I was lucky enough to hear Tim O'Brien, author of *The Things They Carried*, speak a few years ago in Toronto. He read "On the Rainy River," a first-person narrative about a young American facing the Vietnam War draft who drives north to the Canadian border and considers crossing it to escape the war. As O'Brien read us his story, no one in the quiet room could doubt the young narrator was O'Brien himself. "On the Rainy River" begins this way:

> This is one story I've never told before. Not to anyone. Not to my parents, not to my brother or sister, not even to my wife. To go into it, I've always thought, would only cause embarrassment for all of us, a sudden need to be elsewhere, which is the natural response to a confession. Even now, I'll admit, the story makes me squirm. For more than twenty years I've had to live with it, feeling the shame, trying to push it away, and so by this act of remembrance, by putting the facts down on paper, I'm hoping to relieve at least some of the pressure on my dreams. Still, it's a hard story to tell. All of us, I suppose, like to believe that in a moral emergency we will behave like the heroes of our youth, bravely and forthrightly, without thought of personal loss or discredit. Certainly that was my conviction back in the summer of 1968. Tim O'Brien: a secret hero.

O'Brien finished reading his story—a story, notice, in which he names the main character "Tim O'Brien," then he told us it was a lie. He said *fiction is a lie that tells the truth*. Distinguishing between "story-truth" and "happening-truth," he asked us to understand the necessity for lies that give shape to and help us understand truth. Whether *author* O'Brien actually drove to that river is not our business or care as readers of his fiction. His story is honest because it does what a good story must do: it makes us feel and understand the concrete experience of the river, of the era, of the decision about whether to cross, and of the conflict veterans face over whether to tell their stories when these diverge from our expectation for a hero's story. This version of war is true, whether autobiographical to O'Brien or not. Without moralizing or judging, "On the Rainy River" lifts us out of our own shoes and puts us in those of another person who has sprung authentically to life on the page. Ethically, O'Brien has permission to do this because the word "fiction" is printed in small letters on the jacket of his book. Calling his story "fiction," he has made a pact with us: he will lie to tell us the truth.

Stories can be autobiographically true. "Creative nonfiction" stories are akin to fiction and distinct from essays by their shape: structured into the narrative arc of a story, their truth is revealed mainly through plot rather than reflection. David Sedaris is a master of both the autobiographical story and the comic personal essay.

In his sarcastic, hyperbolic, comedic voice (recognizably the same voice in his stories and essays), he regales us with tales based often upon his North Carolina childhood. One of my favorites, "The Drama Bug," begins like this:

> The man was sent to our class to inspire us, and personally speaking, I thought he did an excellent job. After introducing himself in a relaxed and genial manner, he started toward the back of the room, only to be stopped midway by what we came to know as "the invisible wall," that transparent barrier realized only by psychotics, drug fiends, and other members of the show business community.

Despite the phrase "personally speaking," which signals a conversational tone rather than intimate disclosure, we've landed in a story: the guest actor visited a class, Sedaris was bitten by the drama "bug" and began to torment his family by adopting exaggerated mannerisms and Elizabethan English, he and his friend Lois joined a community theater group led by the visiting actor, Sedaris saw the visiting actor for the hack he actually was, and, with mom's help, Sedaris gained new insight into the relationship between "acting" and "lying." The "action plot" structure is built on external conflict (this happens, then this, then this) leading to a resolution (seeing the world of acting in a new light) and denouement (thanks, mom). The plot is structured to carry us from a glimpse at a theatrical form of lying (in the lead) to a recognition that we all can act or perform, in loving ways, in our nontheatrical lives.

Whether the "I" of this (or any) story is autobiographical cannot be determined by the writing itself but rather from the pact Sedaris makes with us in calling his work creative nonfiction. J.D. Salinger's *Catcher in the Rye* uses a similar conversational tone, but we know it is fiction because Salinger presents it to us as a novel (not a memoir), which begins

> If you really want to hear about it, the first thing you'll probably want to know is where I was born, and what my lousy childhood was like, and how my parents were occupied and all before they had me, and all that David Copperfield kind of crap, but I don't feel like going into it, if you want to know the truth.[17]

In a class or workshop, your teacher and peers can tell whether what you've written functions as a story. But unless they research you the way a reporter might if you write a bestseller, they have to take your word for it as to whether that story is fiction or creative nonfiction. This is an ethical pact you keep with the community of your class.

A few published writers elect not to label their stories fiction or nonfiction—calling them simply "stories" ("short stories" means fiction). Their resistance creates a bit of a nightmare for librarians, book marketers, compilers of "best seller" lists, and other cataloguers of media. It's likely to focus attention on the author's refusal to join the fiction or nonfiction camp rather than on the work itself. But perhaps it's also a way to shift the ethical weight onto the reader: Does this story ring true to *you*?

Literary Fiction and Genre Fiction

A few words about a source of frustration and sadness in many teacher-student relationships: I'm talking about conflict over "genre fiction." The frustration begins in communicating what "genre fiction" means. Fiction is a genre (a category) of creative writing; poetry, creative nonfiction, and drama are other genres. Within the larger umbrella of the fiction genre, some stories fall into the (confusedly named) subcategory called "genre fiction." The kind of fiction generally taught in creative writing classes—the kind included in this textbook—is called "literary fiction." Teachers often believe students should learn to write "literary fiction" not "genre fiction" for class, but sometimes students aren't told what genre fiction is, why they can't write it for class, or why their teacher is so *against* it.

"Genre fiction" is entertaining storytelling that uses stock or stereotypical characters in formulaic and predictable narratives that we recognize as a type. The zombie story, the vampire story, the horror story, the detective story, the spy story, the cowboy western, "chick-lit," the action/thriller, the romance, the bodice ripper (romance set in ye olden days in which the heroine is subjected to violence), the "after surviving the apocalypse" story, science fiction, and speculative fiction are among the vast catalogues of "genre fiction." Here's the case against and for writing genre fiction in a creative writing class.

First, the prosecution: Writing genre fiction is like baking brownies from a box mix. You provide the bowl, the pan, and the oven, but everything else is packaged in the box. Your teacher thinks she is teaching you to cook. She's excited to show you how to sharpen your knives and handle them, how to dice and scald and braise and caramelize. Maybe even flambé! Your teacher wants you to throw open the cupboards of your own experience, dive into the vegetable crisper of your own imagination, concoct something tasty and satisfying using the rudiments every cook learns: how to boil, how to simmer, how to combine, how to toss. Teachers often think genre writing will limit or thwart your effort to learn the craft of good writing because attempting genre fiction generally results in what's called "empty writing"—writing without meaning beyond clichéd emotion or thought. Empty calories. Also, as foodies or chefs themselves (that is, as readers and authors of literary fiction), teachers just don't enjoy brownie-mix concoctions (and must sometimes consume and respond to twenty or thirty of these in one night!). Indeed, most people don't like reading genre fiction unless they are *really into* that specific genre. People who are *really into* zombies like a zombie story, and the rest don't, unless the genre is "elevated" beyond its formula by an especially talented and risk-taking writer. As apprentices, writing students aren't usually equipped to elevate a genre.

The defense: Who doesn't love the heady combination of sugar, fat, salt, and chocolate known as the brownie, whether it comes from a box or not? There are most certainly times when a brownie-mix treat satisfies and an exquisitely and originally composed salad does not. The *students* in class seem to enjoy them even if the teacher doesn't. "Doesn't our taste count?" they say. Don't our values matter too? Or students offer these explanations. I didn't realize I was writing genre fiction; because that wasn't my intention, it can't *be* genre fiction. Genre fiction sells; if I want to support myself financially as a writer, why shouldn't I write it? Some very important literature has been written as "genre": for instance, early feminists and minority writers used and continue to use the sci-fi genre to invite readers to imagine more ethical societies (on other planets). These writers moved our society (on this planet) forward using this form of storytelling. No longer the pariah in academic settings, genre fiction is now studied and written in MFA graduate writing programs at accredited universities. It's legit.

If, in your notebook or journal, you find yourself imagining characters—what they say, how they react, what they reveal, what they keep secret, why they are who they are—or describing your own life as a pattern with "chapters" you'd like to understand, then you're already on your way to drafting stories. If you're writing outside a classroom, then *you* can make the decision about embracing or banning genre fiction. If you're in a creative writing course, it's good to have a frank conversation about expectations and evaluation as they relate to genre fiction.

Suggested Reading from Our Anthology

Ambrose Bierce, "An Occurrence at Owl Creek Bridge"
Kate Chopin, "The Story of an Hour"
Gabriel García Márquez, "The Handsomest Drowned Man in the World"
Denis Johnson, "Steady Hands at Seattle General"
James Joyce, "Eveline"
Rachel Knudsen, "How to Enter the Ocean"
Paul Lisicky, "Snapshot, Harvey Cedars: 1948"
Aimee Nezhukumatathil, "The Witching Hour"
Lewis Nordan, "Owls"
B.J. Novak, "Julie & the Warlord"
Luisa Valenzuela, "Vision Out of the Corner of One Eye"
Thomas S. Whitecloud III, "Blue Winds Dancing"

For Further Reading

Janet Burroway, *Writing Fiction: A Guide to Narrative Craft*
Robert Olen Butler, *From Where You Dream: The Process of Writing Fiction*

Your Moves

1. Dip your toe into story structure by writing a "55-word story," a fiction narrative exactly ten sentences long. The first sentence must have precisely ten words, the second sentence nine words, the third sentence eight words, and so on until the final sentence composed of a single word. All acronyms

and digits must be spelled out ("28" is "twenty-eight," which counts as two words). The 55-word story must include a setting, a character in conflict, and a resolution (or sense of "ending"). To compose, write the numbers 10 through 1 (the number of words allowed in each sentence) down the left side of your page. Draft the story first as a list of sentences then transcribe your draft into prose format (see the example below). Notice that each time a new character speaks, the story is indented. Here's a 55-word story called "Wax and Wane" I've written as an example:

> "Say that again," she whispered, tickling fingers through his hair.
>
> "God you're beautiful," he gasped, watching moonlight ignite her.
>
> "Say it again, Duane," she whispered, fervently ablaze.
>
> "You're beautiful, beautiful, beautiful, beautiful, Diana—Beautiful!" The bed seemed to float transcendentally.
>
> "Say it again," she whispered. Duane shifted the comforter. The moon waned.
>
> "You're beautiful."
>
> "Really?"

2. Write a "postcard story" using Rachel Knudsen's "How to Enter the Ocean" and Paul Lisicky's "Snapshot, Harvey Cedars: 1948" as examples of the form. Start with an image on a postcard (junk and antique shops are great places to find old postcards—boxes of them!); then imagine a story inspired by the image, but not too literally. The story must fit onto the back of the postcard in a readable font (short!).
3. Invent a flash fiction story (fiction imagined for a two-page space, under 750 words). It must have a vivid "action plot twist" or surprise ending, as does Luisa Valenzuela's "Vision Out of the Corner of One Eye."
4. Read B.J. Novak's dialogue story "Julie & the Warlord," and then listen to the NPR *This American Life* podcast dramatizing it as a voice play. Write your own single-scene, five-minute dialogue story. If you're in a class, perform these together as five-minute plays for workshop (using the draft as the script).
5. All stories are about a journey of one kind or another. Write a story titled "The Journey" that features a physical, external journey (by bus, train, sled, boat, camel, Mazda, plane, foot, gondola, cable car, ice skates, or whatever). BUT use an "inner life plot." What is the internal tension your character faces? Conclude with an expanded moment of arrival that reveals your character's identity or a truth. This story might be autobiographical (like Thomas S. Whitecloud III's "Blue Winds Dancing") or fiction set in an era when that form of transportation was used.
6. Read Aimee Nezhukumatathil's "The Witching Hour" and David Sedaris's "The Drama Bug" and then write your own story about a conflict you

faced as a child or young adult. Do not write your story as literature for children. Shape the conflict you experienced and its resolution into the arc pattern of a literary story without fictionalizing it; make the truth an adult form of knowing.

7. Write a story focused on expanding a moment in time—giving this moment weight and meaning. It will take much longer to *read* the moment than that moment would actually take "in real life." See James Joyce's "Eveline" and Ambrose Bierce's "An Occurrence at Owl Creek Bridge" as examples of this technique.
8. Kate Chopin's "The Story of an Hour" does indeed focus on one hour—particularly the time the main character spends alone thinking about what has just transpired. Write your own "story of an hour" fiction: focus on one character who receives shocking news in a scene. Your character must reflect and look back as a result of this news and be changed. Plot your story so that the change is shown through action rather than exposition.
9. Magical realism is the use of an unrealistic element—typically the supernatural, magic, folklore, a dream—within a work of art that otherwise appears realistic. Some magical realist fiction respects traditional or indigenous "ways of knowing" and combines them with situations in modern or postcolonial life. Read "The Stones" by Richard Shelton and "The Handsomest Drowned Man in the World" by Gabriel García Márquez, and then write your own magical realist story.
10. Reimagine a commonly known myth, fable, or fairytale, and retell it as a story in a totally different setting and context, offering a competing or contrary truth. In this way, you will produce a story that has an original subtext about morals or commonly accepted beliefs. For instance, you might riff on Pandora, Odysseus, Rumpelstiltskin, the Frog Prince, "The Tortoise and the Hare," or "The Town Mouse and the Country Mouse." You might seek Angela Carter's collection of stories, *The Bloody Chamber*, as inspiration.
11. Write a story that uses a "how-to" structure, like Kristiana Kahakauwila's "Thirty-Nine Rules for Making a Hawaiian Funeral into A Drinking Game." As Kahakauwila does, make sure your story still retains the structure of a character, setting, conflict, rising action, and resolution even as it is presented within the device of the "how to." What does the "how to" add?
12. Write a story that brings a character "full circle," creating a suitable sense of an ending from the cloth of the story's beginning. See Lewis Nordan's "Owls" as an example of this shape.
13. "Metafiction" is a story about storytelling; it's written in a self-conscious manner, draws attention to the work's artificial or "made" nature, and asks

the reader to think about the relationship between reality and fiction. Read Sherwood Anderson's "Death in the Woods" again, noticing its elements of metafiction. Create your own metafiction—a story that dramatizes *your* belief about the relationship between fiction and reality.

14. Write a true story dedicated to someone you care about (put that person's name beneath your title, in dedication). Consider what purpose and truth your story is meant to have for the person to whom it is dedicated, for yourself, *and* for the reader of literature who seeks truth in art. Find a way for this story to satisfy all three.
15. Restrictive prompts can help the fiction writer begin to conceive a story. Here's one. Go to the Amazon.com website and find the product page for the movie *Saturday Night Fever.* Choose a review of this movie that intrigues you, and then click on the reviewer's name. If this person has reviewed twenty or more products other than movies, create a short story based on him or her as a fictionalized character. Through examining these products, work to understand this character's desire (not the person's desire for stuff but for something *this kind of stuff represents*). You must use at least ten of these products in your story (not as a parody or commercial but simply as tangible items in the setting), and your story's title must use the word "Saturday," "Night," or "Fever" (but not all three!). Be sure to change the reviewer's name into an invented character name (to avoid a lawsuit).
16. Revise a predictable or plodding "third-person" draft by disrupting the narrative and switching point of view. Break your draft into segments and rearrange these into a collage format, no longer in chronological order. Switch into first-person "I" point of view, and consider *why* this narrator needs to tell the story in a fragmented way. Reveal the "why" through new passages of reflection from the "I." Read Madeleine Thien's "Simple Recipes" as an example of the collage story.
17. Revise a "slice of life" or "fly on the wall" draft that lacks a sense of purpose or truth: add a motif—a literal and figurative image that recurs—contributing a sense of structure and meaning to the story.

Writing Personal Essays

More than a story, we want a voice speaking softly, urgently, in our ear. Which is to say, to our heart. —*Patricia Hampl*[18]

One summer, when I was about eleven, I went to stay with my grandparents for a week. They lived on twenty acres, a subsistence farm that stretched the salary my grandpa earned working nights at the pulp mill in town. There were cows in a barn, chickens in a hen house, an orchard of apple, plum, pear, cherry, and nut trees, a hayfield and pasture. Besides trying to catch feral kittens in the wood pile, my favorite thing to do was walk barefoot in the warm soil between blueberry bushes and raspberry canes, between rows of corn and beans, to the carrots. I would inspect the orange circles protruding from dirt then pull one up, rinse it in water from the pump house, and eat it. Even the dirt still clinging to carrots tasted wonderful. The air at the farm was fat, golden, slow, and heavy. At my parents' house fifty miles away, air was crisp and ocean-salty; even in summer you could feel something Arctic in it. Home seemed very far away.

One afternoon I walked to their mailbox out on the road and was surprised to discover a letter, addressed to me, from my dad. In his block lettering he described getting new tires on the car, giving our old refrigerator away, walking along the marina and meeting a friendly cat, and what the wind had been doing in our yard and on the channel. I've never forgotten the feeling of reading his simple but intimate letter, written for me. At the time, it said—in images of tires, an appliance, a cat, and the wind—"I am attentive to the fact you are away; I'm thinking of you." His letter comes to mind as I'm thinking about personal essays, which attend to the intimacies of our lives, inscribing them to be sent and received into the lives of others. The gesture: to sit, to select and shape the details noticed, to conjure one person's experience into the life of another. The Arctic tang materializing for you, so far away, who cannot be here.

The Umbrella of Nonfiction

"Personal essays" are intimately crafted pieces of creative writing. Each draws from the writer's own life and tries to neither inform nor persuade but to speak to the heart. Short as a prose poem or long as a novella, the personal essay is one of many kinds of writing together categorized as "creative nonfiction": literature rooted firmly in our real world—not in an invented or imagined world, as is the case with fiction. Like other forms of nonfiction (such as history, journalism, film criticism, travel writing, sports, and scholarly research), creative nonfiction is "true." But unlike history, criticism, journalism, and the like, creative nonfiction demands the use of the full range of tools we wield as creative writers: imagery and figurative language, scene, character, sound, voice, and perspective. We use these tools to bring our world vividly alive on the page and to "essay" (from the French verb *essayer*, "to try") to word its meaning.

As creative nonfiction writers, we have an important and complicated relationship with truth. Electing to write creative nonfiction—to sail it out eventually to an audience under that flag—we make a pact with ourselves and with our readers to tell the truth. Even if the truth is messy or painful, we promise *not to mislead or deceive* in creative nonfiction. This is a radically different challenge than the fiction writer's challenge, which is to say "what if…" and invent a convincing world before our eyes. The creative nonfiction writer attends to the ways *this world* matters and—to paraphrase Bret Lott—by essaying, we try to learn from what we've done, who we've known, what we've dreamed, and how we've failed, so that we might make order and meaning from our lives.

It's curious that, as readers, when we learn that a fiction—say, a novel—was actually based in fact, we're intrigued and delighted to know about this connection between the imagination and the real world. But when we read creative nonfiction and later learn the author deceived us, the natural human reaction is hurt, even ethical outrage. Take, for instance, the infamous case of James Frey, whose "memoir" *A Million Little Pieces* was discovered to be fabricated and exaggerated, or the hoax of Norma Khouri's fake memoir *Honor Lost*. Poetry and fiction maintain walls of artifice between the author and audience. Have you noticed that most works of fiction have a disclaimer on the copyright page? It usually says,

> This book is a work of fiction. Names, characters, places, and incidents are either the product of the author's imagination or are used fictitiously. Any resemblance to actual events or locales or persons, living or dead, is entirely coincidental.

Of course, fiction is *often* based on experiences and on the observations made in the writer's own life. So this disclaimer simply says "please read me in the spirit of imagination, not fact" (and "don't sue the publisher if you recognize someone"). This protective wall allows fiction writers to live without the burden of being *per-*

sonally intimate—on the page—with readers. Likewise, the poet always has the poem's "speaker" (an invented perspective) as a shield. It's not the reader's business to know—unless the poet gives an interview or otherwise signals, outside the poem itself—the veracity of personal experience represented in a poem. A *poem's* truth is not synonymous with its *author's* truth. The writer of personal essays and memoir chooses to lower this veil and own their truth. Such sincerity is an appeal for the reader's trust and, on the page—as in real life—trust should not be messed with.

Is it possible to be wholly honest, to tell "the whole truth and nothing but the truth" in writing? Just as it's impossible for a documentary film to tell the whole truth (a documentary is always shot, edited, shaped—it's a *version* of truth) or for even one photograph to tell the whole truth (the image is always taken from an angle, a perspective—it, too, is a *version*), the act of writing always mediates and changes experience. Words that describe an experience, no matter how carefully a writer chooses them, are not the experience itself but are one representation of it. In this way, creative nonfiction—like all writing—is art, which means it's artificial. The creative nonfiction writer decides it is possible to be sincere in art, even if language cannot tell *the whole* truth, and enters into an ethical pact with the reader. The essayist takes the risk of sincerity, believing there's more to life than sarcasm, fantasy, and masquerade. The essayist promises not to deceive.

Personal Truth

"Personal truth" is an understanding you privately hold about the way the world works; it's arrived at through your own experiences and reflections on them. It's not cliché, common wisdom, dogma, opinion, your taste, your style, your excuse, or the belief you've been handed fully formed. It's your own way of knowing, arrived at through living in and witnessing the world. A personal essay is your individual way of exploring your memories by representing them on the page through the moves of creative writing. As you draft your essay, you're making choices: what image to select, the order in which to disclose the events, which events to leave out, what word to pick, what rhythm to follow. As these choices accumulate, you're led toward a particular shape and meaning for your draft. "But is it honest? Is it meaningful to a wider audience than just myself?" you ask. You rearrange, reword, reflect, and resee the experience: by drafting a personal essay, you *make meaning* from experience. Personal truth is sometimes arrived at organically through the writing process—it can astonish the writer.

The sense of questing or groping for meaning is the energizing principle of the personal essay; it is the source of tension both for the writer and for the reader. Essayists write to chase not simply the ability to describe "what happened" but also a solution to the big mystery we all share in common: how to know what matters, and how to live a meaningful life. Because there's no single answer to such big questions, we are continually surprised and moved by the process of crafting personal essays. We can write many essays exploring the same memory, the same experience; because we're always growing and changing, we find new meaning, over and over, from the same material. We keep essaying, trying.

Questing is the energizing principle of the personal essay in another important way. Although our readers might be interested in "what happened" to us, the information or story we share is not our essay's source of intimacy or power. The peculiar, specific, unique ways our mind turns and shapes these events into our own private understanding—this is the real intimacy. How amazing, to let someone inside one's mind to see how it works! How vulnerable a writer is, to let the gears and the wheels, the rubber belts and grease of consciousness be exposed to readers. Unlike fiction writers, Patricia Hampl points out, essayists in this genre don't want to "tell a story":

> They want to tell it *all*—the all of personal experience, of consciousness itself. That includes a story, but also the whole expanding universe of sensation and thought that flows beyond the confines of narrative and proves every life to be not only an isolated story line but a bit of the cosmos, spinning and streaming into the great, ungraspable pattern of existence.[19]

As essayists, the triggers for our work—what sends us toward personal truth—are remembered scenes and moments, people we've watched with great tenderness or fear, objects we've touched, sounds and flavors that linger in our minds because they are part of the fabric of who we are. No need to dive with great white sharks, overdose on heroin, or sip from the Stanley Cup; often it's noticing the small but significant details in our everyday world that leads to powerful essay writing. For instance, here is Lia Purpura's brief personal essay "September 9"—in its entirety:

> Laid out perfectly where they fell in the tall grass, half sunk in the soft ground—the bones of a small cat. And how long did it take for the bones to clean, for the flesh to slip off and the eyes burn away? The shape the body made was placid-seeming, unlike the animals of prehistory, who, trapped in tar in the posture of shock, in half-light on a cave wall, are forever outrunning fire, weather, attack. In caves their broad, simple bodies are sketched in ochre flight: fear is the black cipher of an open mouth, the red oxide smudge on a flank. But I found these bones in the shape of sleep, of full and open expectancy, mid-stride in an airy leap. *Waiting for.* I learned it takes only days for a small animal's body to decompose at this time of year, to return itself to bone, to its simplest components—carbon, hydrogen, nitrogen, sulfur. To press its outline back into the soft earth, which is a welcoming, rich place still, late summer. A home receiving the body in, expecting it.[20]

With this essay, Purpura witnesses something simple and then follows her mind's journey to reach an understanding. To do this yourself, distinguish between your trigger (in her case, the bones of a small cat) and the real meaning or purpose your essay seeks (for Purpura, realizing that physical death is not to be feared). Philip Gerard refers to this distinction as having "an apparent subject and a deeper subject."[21] The excitement and wonder of essaying comes from the discovery of our deeper subject as we sit and write in the present moment, the "now" of the essay.

Although we might describe a scene that happened days or years ago, we're sifting memory through our "now" self who has perspective and the emotional distance necessary to translate raw experience into an essay. Purpura is not writing as she stands near the bones; time has passed. Her memory associates the bones with images she's seen of cave paintings (perhaps those of Lascaux and Altamira). She's researched how long it takes for decomposition in this climate; she's discovered the chemical components of bodies. She's chosen images and a shape for this thinking on the page. She's decided that a *very small* essay is the right size—perhaps because its trigger is the bones of a small cat? Yet she's given it weight, populated it with our shared and primal fear of dying, and written her way to a sense of ease and acceptance, inviting us to share this sensation.

The "I" of the Essay

Autobiography is a narrative of an interesting life (the politician, the mogul, the star, the hero). Memoir and personal essay are not so much about *interesting lives* as about *interesting ways of understanding* the details or moments of whatever life we've got. Readers of autobiography want to hear a story. Readers of memoir (long form) and personal essay (short form) want to overhear a mind in conversation with itself about the experience of trying to live.

This notion of "essaying" is a more recent invention than poetry or storytelling, but it has a history too. The roots of the personal essay sink at least as deep as the eleventh-century "court lady" Sei Shōnagon who served Empress Consort Teishi in Japan. *The Pillow Book*, written between the 990s and the early 1000s, is her collection of musings about court events and people, fragmented ideas, poetry, and lists—copious lists! "Rare Things," "Pleasing Things," and

> **Surprising and Distressing Things**
>
> While one is cleaning a decorative comb, something catches in the teeth and the comb breaks.
>
> A carriage overturns. One would have imagined that such a solid, bulky object would remain forever on its wheels. It all seems like a dream—astonishing and senseless.
>
> A child or grown-up blurts out something that is bound to make people uncomfortable.
>
> All night long one has been waiting for a man who one thought was sure to arrive. At dawn, just when one has forgotten about him for a moment and dozed off, a crow caws loudly. One wakes up with a start and sees that it is daytime—most astonishing.
>
> One of the bowmen in an archery contest stands trembling for a long time before shooting; when finally he does release his arrow, it goes in the wrong direction.[22]

Michel Eyquem de Montaigne (1533–92), a French winegrower and politician whose *Essais* never go out of print, is now often called "the father of the essay."

Writing in a manner we now call "stream of consciousness," he penned short pieces of nonfiction in which he did not record deeds, achievements, or stories, but small observations that explored his mind's individual flow: his way of paying attention. Here, for example, is an excerpt from "On Smells":

> Whatever the smell, it is wonderful how it clings to me and how my skin is simply made to drink it in. The person who complained that Nature left Man no means of bringing smells to his nose was in error: smells do it by themselves. But, in my particular case the job is done for me by my thick moustache: if I bring my glove or my handkerchief anywhere near it, the smell will linger there all day. It gives away where I have just come from. Those close smacking kisses of my youth, gluey and greedy, would stick to it and remain there for hours afterwards.[23]

The writings of Sei Shōnagon and Montaigne have in common a focus on the "I": their subject matter is the nature of individual perception. Autobiographies are often ghostwritten or written "with" a coauthor (it takes research, a few interviews, to come up with a life's chronology). Because personal essay is about the way an individual shapes or finds meaning in one's own life's details, it can't be ghostwritten. Only *you* can write about your moustache and the smells that linger in there.

The personal essay filters through the "I" of the self—but which self? Each of us has so many versions of self, all of them valid and true at least sometimes ("I" might simultaneously be a struggling student, a menace on the soccer pitch, a romantic with my sweetie, a strong soldier in the reserves, a quiet spirit with my elders, a cynic when someone's selling, and still my mama's own child).Usually the "I" of the essay is one of the "better" versions of self—a version that's contemplative, open-minded, and a bit more mature and articulate than the Friday-night-gaming-Dorito-smacking-expletive-shouting self. This "I" has a sense of reflective distance and perspective on the experience it describes. This "I" seeks to harm no one (it offers no "poison pen" rant about an ex-roomie, no "tell all" that pins its problems on dad's drinking). It seeks to bore no one (with a self-pitying "hot mess" of confused emotion), and it does not substitute another's experience for its own (a friend's drug habit, mom's enlightenment, sister's rotten marriage—these are *their* experiences, which this "I" does not get to tell in personal essay form).

The "I" of the personal essay is concerned with the private world of the self, distilled onto the page so that others, in reading about this world, might recognize a wider significance than singular experience. Phillip Lopate says essays are written and read with a faith that "there is a certain unity to human experience."[24] We look to the personal essays of others not for shock value or confession but to find this unity of shared human experience, made articulate. For example, reading Evelyn Lau's painfully intimate portrait of her eating disorder ("An Insatiable Emptiness"), any of us might recognize the human need to consume and purge (not just food) and the futility of it.

Form and Feeling

The personal essay is distinct from the impersonal five-paragraph, expository, persuasive, or research essays you might have been trained to write in high school and university. It has no single shape or form—a form must be invented each time you begin a new one. And if you try to write it as a rant or diary entry—full of feeling but without form—it will collapse under the weight of directionless emotion. Sincerity isn't enough; an essay requires a shape. "The true writer," says Jeanette Winterson, "knows that feeling must give way to form. It is through the form, not in spite of, or accidental to it, that the most powerful emotions are let loose over the greatest number of people."[25]

If you've been writing in your notebook as a witness to the details and experiences of your life, writing memories, writing about what memory means to you, recording and reflecting on your feelings, perhaps you've already begun some personal essays. As you move from your notebook to drafting, you may find you're naturally drawn into story rather than essaying. Remember that an essay can include story, but it also needs a perspective or frame of understanding in addition to the narrative. This perspective can be communicated through reflection, through juxtaposition (arrangement that suggests meaning through gaps and relationships, not narrative), or through figurative language.

Here are just some of the forms available to you with the personal essay:

- **An "expanded moment" essay** uses one scene as its core (like a story), but, unlike story, it does not depend on the conflict/action/climax/resolution structure of a story for its energy. Instead, it frames the scene with exposition and reflection, "expanding" on the scene by meditating on and wording its larger significance. Joy Harjo's "Suspended" is planted firmly in a scene: driving in the Creek Nation near Tulsa

  > ...the sun was boiling the asphalt, the car windows open for any breeze as I stood on tiptoes on the floorboard behind my father, a handsome god who smelled of Old Spice, whose slick black hair was always impeccably groomed, his clothes perfectly creased and ironed. The radio was on.

  The action that occurs in Harjo's essay is not the drive but rather her present-day quest to know and word why that moment is so memorable, still. Her work with the essay is to show how, on some atavistic level, she understood jazz "as a way to speak beyond the confines of ordinary language." Harjo could not have worded this meaning of the scene as she was actually living it, as a child. If you "expand a moment" from the distant or near past, be sure to word your present understanding, as Jean-Dominique Bauby does in "Bathtime."

- **A sketch or portrait essay** is an older and more traditional form focusing usually on a place (sketch) or person (portrait) or a combination of both. Using personal experience and close observation, the essayist moves from description of the surface to reflection on the essence of the person or place. Mark Spragg's "In Wyoming" and Susan Lester's "Belongings" are forms of sketch. Notice that the "I" is not absent from sketch and portrait (although it may be subsumed into a "we"). The writer's own relationship with and investment in the subject plays a significant role in this essay form.

- **An object essay** uses descriptions of a physical object around which to arrange scenes, reflections, and associations rather than telling a linear story. Richard Selzer's "The Knife" uses a scalpel as the "apparent subject" of each section of his essay about the awesome power he wields (with some discomfort) as a surgeon. Lia Purpura's "September 9" (earlier in this chapter) is a much shorter object essay, jutting off from her discovery of the bones of a cat to discuss mortality and fear. Your chosen object can be as mundane as Arlan Cashier's "Lost Sweater" and still work beautifully as your passport, your point of entry, to access a deeper and more complex theme.
- **A collage essay** works much like a visual collage: an assemblage of parts to suggest connections, relationships, and interesting contrasts. Individual segments or sections of the essay may be as short as a sentence or as long as several paragraphs. There are no transitions between sections; only white space (called "jump cuts") or sometimes symbols (the asterisk) or numerals mark its parts. The collage essay is connected by a theme, with the reader playing an active role in considering how the separate parts speak and matter to one another and to the theme. The essayist uses repeated words, images, or motifs to assure the reader of the unity of the various parts. Taiaiake Alfred's "What I Think of When I Think of Skin" and Jo Ann Beard's "The Fourth State of Matter" are examples of this form.
- **A braided essay** is similar to a collage, with the separate parts of the essay further divided and repeated; it weaves strands together, like braiding hair or rope. Strands can be narratives, scenes, reflections, lists, poems, or even "found" sources (ingredients, instructions, lyrics, researched facts, an obituary—working like extensions woven into hair). A braided essay accumulates slowly and purposefully, each strand interrupted by another and creating a series of juxtapositions all connected to a theme and to one another. Each strand can return once or many times—the pattern need not be regular. As with the collage, repeated words, images, and motifs assure the reader of the essay's unity. Use consistent verb tense and perspective within individual strands, so the reader quickly knows "we're back to that one" after a jump cut. Ivan E. Coyote's "This, That, and the Other Thing" is an example of a braided essay.

- **The hermit crab essay** got its name from Brenda Miller and Suzanne Paola, who described it in *Tell It Slant: Writing and Shaping Creative Nonfiction*. A hermit crab is a little tide-pool critter born without a protective shell; it backs into abandoned snail shells, wearing them like borrowed armor. The "shell" of your hermit crab essay is any ready-made written form: the menu, review, résumé, how-to guide, to-do list, horoscope, field guide, recipe, syllabus, quiz, Craigslist post, lost pet sign, word problem, contract, riddle... the possibilities are limitless. The hermit crab essay is a witty form because it always carries a slight tinge of parody. This outer edge of comedy can be your shield. As Miller and Paola write, "Think of the hermit crab and his soft, exposed abdomen. Think of the experiences you have that are too raw, too dangerous to write about. What if you found the right shell, the right armor? How could you be transformed?"[26] Consider these shells:

  A dating profile shell to contain an essay about your last relationship;

  A recipe shell to explore your relationship with your mother, the fabulous cook;

  A barber's catalogue of haircuts to write about your experience with chemo.

  The only restrictions are that this shell should be relevant to your topic and recognizable to your reader. Don't be fooled into thinking your how-to-dress-for-success essay is actually about *that*; it's about something much deeper and personal that you experienced at your workplace. The hermit crab's focus is quite serious beneath the carapace. Your personal experiences are required; *you* are the crab. Sonja Livingston's "The Ghetto Girls' Guide to Dating and Romance" (in the shell of an advice guide) and Arlan Cashier's "Lost Sweater" (in the shell of a "lost" poster one might staple to a telephone pole) are examples.

- **The lyric essay** is led by meaningful sound rather than narrative, logic, or rational thinking. This essay accumulates through association, intuition, patterns of rich imagery, and the flow of the unconscious. The territory of the lyric essay is the cadence of dream, fantasy, memory, desire, and emotion that we know in an elemental or sensual way. How to express that layer of self in words? By using language like a poet, employing assonance, alliteration, rhyme, word play, repetition, associations, gaps, silences, fragments, and juxtapositions to create essays that explore states of mind, moods, and questions rather than ideas, stories, opinions, or answers. A short lyric essay could easily be called a prose poem; the distinction is that prose poems are presented through the perspective of a "speaker," who may be fictional. With the lyric essay, you make a pact with your audience that the "I" is part of yourself. Bhanu Kapil does this with "Three Voices," Bethany Yeager with "Divorce."

- **A researched essay** involves investigation beyond or outside of personal experience but presents this material through an "I" whose main focus is not reportage but a human quest for what such facts can mean. *Any* personal essay might involve research, but this form requires a curiosity or need that compels you to visit the library, the archive, the newspaper reports, the witness statements and interviews, the science and figures. Your researched essay might begin with an event in your family history, which leads you to interview your parents and then to consult historical records. Or perhaps it starts with a news report you've never forgotten: go back and find out why. Your essay must bring the reader into the truth of this research, but your work is not to retell or report on the event in the manner of a journalist. Your focus is finding a deeper meaning within the authority and authenticity of researched details, using the full toolbox of the creative writer. Brian Doyle does this with the tragedy of 9/11 in his personal essay "Leap."

Sometimes it can seem like life is about dealing with one thing happening after another and another. The personal essay isn't about this *content* but about how we shape our understanding of it—about finding and expressing what Sandra Swinburne calls the "true things nestled within the small and familiar" details of our lives.[27]

Suggested Reading from Our Anthology

Jean-Dominique Bauby, "Bathtime"
Jo Ann Beard, "The Fourth State of Matter"
Arlan Cashier, "Lost Sweater"
Ivan E. Coyote, "This, That, and the Other Thing"
Brian Doyle, "Leap"
Patricia Hampl, "Red Sky in the Morning"
Joy Harjo, "Suspended"
Bhanu Kapil, "Three Voices"
Evelyn Lau, "An Insatiable Emptiness"
Sonja Livingston, "The Ghetto Girls' Guide to Dating and Romance"
Donald Murray, "War Stories Untold"
Brent Staples, "The Coroner's Photographs"

For Further Reading

Brenda Miller and Suzanne Paola, *Tell It Slant: Creating, Refining, and Publishing Creative Nonfiction*

Your Moves

1. Our families provide much of the rich material we explore in personal essays. You may decide later not to publish writing about your family, or to fictionalize it into story instead, or to share it with them privately before setting it loose in the world. But you always have the right to draft essays about your experiences within the family, as a way to understand yourself and the larger human theme of family. Dip into the readings about family in our anthology, and then begin your own essay.
2. Personal essays must be grounded in the sensual world—scenes and images we have experienced with our bodies through touch, sight, smell, taste, and sound. Look at some of the essays in the anthology that rely on the sensations of the body (essays by Taiaiake Alfred, Evelyn Lau, Jean-Dominique Bauby, and Stephen Kuusisto); then inscribe your own.
3. Patricia Hampl ("Red Sky in the Morning") says that in essays "we want a voice speaking softly, urgently, in our ear. Which is to say, to our heart."[28] Personal essays can be sites to share intimacies we would be too shy to speak aloud; they show us as readers how human it is to be vulnerable. Read the anthologized essays by Brent Staples, Brenda Miller, Bhanu Kapil, and Susan Lester. Write about something intimate you have never or rarely spoken about.
4. Borrow a move from Donald Murray ("War Stories Untold"): write about something that "seemed normal then." Show readers the normalcy of that period in your life, and show how different your "new normal" is today. Reflect on whether moments or habits from "then" penetrate the "now" and on the effects of this separation or relationship.
5. "Let me tell you a story..." Dorothy Allison begins in *Two or Three Things I Know for Sure.*[29] Write an essay about the stories you have told, using Allison's book and Donald Murray's "War Stories Untold" as your models. Or write an essay about how a story was invented about *you* by others (see Howard Norman, from *I Hate to Leave This Beautiful Place*).
6. Explore a sense of your place, neighborhood, or community in an essay, taking inspiration from the anthologized work of Mark Spragg, Reinaldo Arenas, Emily Carr, and Arlan Cashier. Be sure to include a vivid sense of setting and a strong sense of yourself as someone connected to it. Or write an essay about your time spent as an outsider in relation to a place or community, as Howard Norman does in *I Hate to Leave This Beautiful Place.*
7. Write a letter to someone you love, reminding that person of the details of the best time you both shared together. Tell your friend what this memory has come to mean to you now—how you look back and see it from your perspective today. In writing, consider what this epistle to your friend has

shown you about the nature of your memory. Include this understanding, and shape it and your letter into a portrait essay meant for readers of literary nonfiction. Variation: write the letter to a place you have loved, still using the direct address "you." Use this material (the letter and your reflection on memory) to create a sketch essay.

8. In your notebook, brainstorm a list of meaningful objects that might eventually lead toward an "object essay." Perhaps an object...
   that you frequently wear on your body;
   that you'd like to get rid of, but haven't;
   that you gave away;
   that was an unwanted, unwelcome, or insulting gift;
   that you can use or operate expertly;
   that you've ruined, spoiled, or destroyed;
   that was popular to own when you were a child or teenager;
   that is prominently displayed in your home;
   that you will literally take with you to the grave; or
   that carries or carried the scent of someone you have loved.

   When you hit on an object that seems like a passport into meditation or meaning, brainstorm associations, tangents, and small scenes that might later become part of your collage-shaped object essay.
9. Ekphrastic writing is created in response to the other arts. Begin an essay sparked by a reaction you have to a sculpture, drawing, painting, or photograph. You need not write about the art itself. What feelings and memories do you associate with it? What does it call up for you? Laurence Sutin ("Father Holding Baby") created *A Postcard Memoir*, a book made of many small essays (so small, each could fit on the back of a postcard); each essay is juxtaposed with the image of a postcard that inspired it. You can find old postcards at antique and junk stores to try this yourself. Museums such as the Metropolitan Museum of Art and the Art Gallery of Ontario have vast online catalogues of their holdings to peruse for inspiration.
10. Wording a "personal truth" is a significant gesture. Visit the website of This I Believe (thisibelieve.org), which makes available a long-running essay series heard on public broadcasting. Click on "explore" and then "browse by theme." Sample essays to see which cause you to reflect on your own beliefs. Draft a personal essay grounded in scene and experience (not opinion) that words what *your* belief is and how you came to hold it. Attend to the site instructions: this essay is not about religion and is not an argument for your belief. This kind of essay aims to be positive and personal. If you like the resulting draft, submit it to This I Believe.

11. In "Three Voices," Bhanu Kapil says, "I am not writing about myself as a rational human being. I'm writing about the substances of an animal and female life." Her lyric essay is grounded in sensations, textures, and intuitions. Write now in a way that tries to move away from logical, rational thinking. Stay close to the sensual, the emotional, the quest for inscribing that ephemeral "life beneath this life" that runs parallel to our surface consciousness. You can start over again and again—two voices, three voices, more. Begin with these words: "I am not writing about myself as a rational human being. I'm writing about...." After writing a few pages of this, reread. Try to understand the larger pattern or submerged meaning you did not intend. Revise toward a draft, retaining the beauty and shaping toward unity.
12. The sonically lyric essay infuses prose with poetic devices, spaces, and gaps. Begin to write toward the draft of a lyric essay by selecting one of the following fragments (or part of one) as an epigraph or as a repeated phrase. See where this poetic fragment can take you in mood and how it can help you discover potential moments and feelings from your own (fantasy?) life in a draft. Think about how you can use repetition, metaphor, white spaces, images, and sound as you build on this refrain. Credit the author of this fragment by writing "After Roo Borson"—or whomever's poem you quote—under your draft's title.

    Heavy tears are in this,
    not buried deeply, but just below the sand, where fish live
    with lowered heartbeats until the rains come.
    —"Summer Grass"
    by Roo Borson[30]

    Now that we're nothing, for example,
    we can be the rain. [....] Let us be fragile
    now that we're not the ocean. A form welcomes us.
    —"Now That We Are Nothing, For Example"
    by Eduardo Milan[31]

    I can lift out some curious detail
    that will carry me off to sleep—
    the watch that encircles his pale wrist,
    the expandable band,
    the tiny hands that keep pointing this way and that.
    — "Insomnia"
    by Billy Collins[32]

    I am beginning to understand
    my body as the little curtain closes.

The magician's assistant disappears—slips
through the trap door soundlessly....
— "The Surgical Theater as Spirit Cabinet"
by Oliver de la Paz[33]

We think by feeling. What is there to know?
I hear my being dance from ear to ear.
I wake to sleep, and take my waking slow.
— "The Waking"
by Theodore Roethke[34]

When there is no one left to cling to,
No one to fall on sobbing in mutual recognition
When it's over, maybe we cling to the world
That hurt us, seeing the face of someone
We loved in the face of someone we don't know
— "Decay"
by Karen Whalley[35]

13. Write a personal essay that speaks as an alternative understanding of a story reported on the news. To do this, write about your own personal experience of an event that was reported on the news (see Jo Ann Beard's "The Fourth State of Matter" as an example) or create a researched essay as Brian Doyle does with "Leap." Remember to stay in the genre of creative nonfiction: you are not writing as a journalist or editorialist.
14. Jo Ann Beard's longer essay, "The Fourth State of Matter," adopts a collage shape to describe and understand a period in her life that was a "perfect storm" of negative experience: her marriage breaking up, depression, a dying pet, tension, and tragedy at work. If you are ready to attempt a more complex essay, try the collage shape to find meaningful connections between the elements of a "perfect storm" period in your own life. What is the thread connecting Beard's essay; what is the thread in yours?
15. Revise a nonfiction story you wrote earlier into a braided essay. Proceed by adding new segments of reflection and perhaps "found" material and by compressing the narrative down to its essence—by inventing a whole new shape. How does this new work "mean differently"?
16. After drafting a personal essay, do a ten-minute freewrite on this topic: "What is the question this essay seeks to answer?" Elaborate on the nature of your essay's question, the ways you can approach it through the essay draft, and what is at stake for you personally in the attempt. Revise your draft based on what you learn from the exercise.

Notes

1 Theodore Roethke, *Straw for the Fire: From the Notebooks of Theodore Roethke, 1943–63*, ed. David Wagoner (Port Townsend, WA: Copper Canyon P, 2006), 256.

2 Rita Dove, "Rita Dove," *Lannan*, http://www.lannan.org/bios/rita-dove/; William Wordsworth, "Preface," *Lyrical Ballads, with Pastoral and Other Poems*, vol. 1, 4th ed. (London: R. Taylor and Co., 1805), x–xi; Thomas Hardy, *The Life and Work of Thomas Hardy*, ed. Michael Millgate (London: Macmillan, 1984), 322; Plato paraphrased in Ralph Waldo Emerson, "Nature (1836)," *Nature and Other Essays*, ed. Lisa Perniciaro, 1–34 (Mineola, NY: Dover, 2009), 30; Samuel Taylor Coleridge, *Table Talk of Samuel Taylor Coleridge*, ed. Henry Morley (London: George Routledge and Sons, 1884), 63.

3 Marvin Bell, "32 Statements about Writing Poetry," in *We Wanted to Be Writers: Life, Love, and Literature at the Iowa Writers' Workshop*, ed. Eric Olsen and Glenn Schaeffer (New York: Skyhorse, 2011), 87.

4 Novalis, "Fugitive Thoughts," in *Novalis: His Life, Thoughts, and Works*, ed. and trans. M.J. Hope (Chicago: A.C. McClurg & Co., 1891), 177. NB: The most common early translation is "Poetry heals the wounds given by reason" (as in this text) or "Poetry heals the wounds which the mind/the understanding/reason inflicts." Also, "Fugitive Thoughts" is often translated as "Detached Thoughts," and Novalis is a pseudonym for Friedrich von Hardenberg.

5 Kevin Young, "Ode to the Midwest," *Poetry* (July-August 2007): 264–65.

6 Allen Ginsberg, "Sunflower Sutra," in *Howl and Other Poems* (San Francisco: City Lights Pocket Bookshop, 1956), 35.

7 Roo Borson, "Ten Thousand," *Night Walk, Selected Poems* (Toronto: Oxford UP, 1994).

8 Sam Green, "Stroke," *All That Might Be Done* (Pittsburgh: Carnegie Mellon UP, 2014), 15.

9 According to *Wikipedia*, the earliest published version of this limerick appeared in the *Princeton Tiger*, November 1902, page 59.

10 Ernest Hemingway, "To Bernard Berenson, La Finca Vigia, 24 September 1954," in *Ernest Hemingway: Selected Letters, 1917–1961*, ed. Carlos Baker, 836–37 (New York: Simon and Schuster, 1981), 837.

11 Barry Lopez, "The Origins of Storytelling" *Poets & Writers* 44, no. 1 (Jan/Feb 2016): 48.

12 Joan Didion, "White Album," in *We Tell Ourselves Stories in Order to Live: The Collected Nonfiction*, ed. John Leonard, 179–342 (New York: Alfred A. Knopf, 2003), 179.

13 Ernest Hemingway, "The Short Happy Life of Francis Macomber," in *The Snows of Kilimanjaro and Other Stories*, 121–60 (New York: Scribner, 1995), 121.

14 Wayson Choy, *The Jade Peony* (Vancouver, BC: Douglas & McIntyre, 1995), 31–32.

15 Janet Burroway, *Writing Fiction: A Guide to Narrative Craft* (New York: HarperCollins, 1996), 31.

16 V.S. Pritchett, ed., "Introduction," *The Oxford Book of Short Stories*, xi–xiv (New York: Oxford UP, 1981), xi.

17 J.D. Salinger, *The Catcher in the Rye* (New York: Little, Brown, 1951), 3.

18 Patricia Hampl, "Red Sky in the Morning," in *I Could Tell You Stories*, 15–20 (New York: W.W. Norton, 2000), 19.
19 Hampl, "Red Sky in the Morning," 18.
20 Lia Purpura, *Increase* (Athens: U of Georgia P, 2000), 21.
21 Philip Gerard, *Creative Nonfiction: Researching and Crafting Stories of Real Life* (Cincinnati, OH: Story Press Books, 1996), 7.
22 Sei Shōnagon, *The Pillow Book*, trans. Ivan I. Morris (New York: Columbia UP, 1991), 117–18.
23 Michel de Montaigne, *The Essays of Michel de Montaigne*, trans. Michael Andrew Screech (London: Penguin, 1991), 353.
24 Phillip Lopate, "Introduction," in *The Art of the Personal Essay: An Anthology*, xxiii–lvi (New York: Random House, 1995), xxiii.
25 Jeanette Winterson, *Art Objects: Essays on Ecstasy and Effrontery* (Toronto: A.A. Knopf Canada, 1995), 105–06.
26 Brenda Miller and Suzanne Paola, *Tell It Slant: Writing and Shaping Creative Nonfiction* (New York: McGraw-Hill, 2005), 113.
27 Sandra Swinburne, "Essay, Dresses, and Fish," in Judith Kitchen (ed.), *Short Takes: Brief Encounters with Contemporary Nonfiction*, 354–58 (New York: W.W. Norton, 2005), 354.
28 Hampl, "Red Sky in the Morning," 19.
29 Dorothy Allison, *Two or Three Things I Know for Sure* (New York: Plume, 1996), 1.
30 Roo Borson, "Summer Grass," in *Short Journey Upriver Toward Ōishida* (Toronto: McClelland & Stewart, 2004), 11.
31 Eduardo Milán, "Now That We Are Nothing, For Example," *Reversible Monuments: Contemporary Mexican Poetry*, ed. Mónica De La Torre, Michael Wiegers, and Alastair Reid (Port Townsend, WA: Copper Canyon P, 2013), 415.
32 Billy Collins, "Insomnia," *Sailing Alone Around the Room: New and Selected Poems* (New York: Random House, 2002), 142–43, see page 143.
33 Oliver de la Paz, "The Surgical Theater as Spirit Cabinet," *Requiem for the Orchard* (Akron, OH: U of Akron P, 2010), 81–82.
34 Theodore Roethke, "The Waking," *The Collected Poems of Theodore Roethke* (Garden City, NY: Anchor P, 1975), 104.
35 Karen Whalley, "Decay," *The Rented Violin* (Keene, NY: Ausable P, 2003), 82–83.

PART IV
ANTHOLOGY

Alternate Tables of Contents

("see also" means this text is quoted in full within the chapters)

Contents by Genre and Form

Poetry

FREE VERSE

FORMAL POETRY

PROSE POETRY

Story

Essay

Fiction

SHORT STORY

FLASH FICTION

POSTCARD FICTION

Creative Nonfiction

Contents by Theme

ABUSE AND BULLIES

ANIMALS

THE ARTS AND ARTISTS

THE BODY

CHILDHOOD AND COMING OF AGE

DEATH AND DYING

FAMILY

FOOD

FRIENDSHIP

GRATITUDE

HUMOR IN MANY FORMS

IDENTITY

MARRIAGE AND COMMITMENT

MILITARY AND SERVICE

NATURE

SEX, ROMANCE, AND BREAKING UP

VIOLENCE AND TRAGEDY

WORK

Kelli Russell Agodon

Geography

I put my hand where my left breast used to be.

When she called, I didn't want to tell her
as if speaking the word over the telephone line
would confirm it, accept it, allow it
to keep growing.
Let us forget the unsettled lava bubbling beneath.

Instead, I said,
I am a map of the world.

The oceans and continents I carry
inside, the fragile imprint of the earth
I wear on my chest—
I am the mainland now, full of prairies
and hills, canyons and valleys
spread out across my land—
the unexplored mountain
has been replaced,
craters don't keep secrets.
I am reworking my topography.

We are all volcanoes.

I heard my mother crying
on the other side of the country; her tears
could flood the small cities I carry
above my ribcage. She whispered
to the phone, "What do you look like?"

I wanted to say,
I look like the moon, beautiful and complete.
I wanted to say,
I look like a gardenia leaf, solid and firm.
I wanted to say I am lovely.

Instead,
rivers flowed down the new terrain. [2003]

Sherman Alexie

from *Totem Sonnets*

One

Meryl Streep
Emily Dickinson
Dian Fossey
Flannery O'Connor
John Steinbeck
Helen Keller
Walt Whitman
Bruce Springsteen

Kareem Abdul-Jabbar
Zora Neale Hurston
Frida Kahlo
Pablo Neruda
Harriet Tubman
Muhammad Ali

Seven

Jesus Christ
Adam
Mary Magdalene
Eve

Jim Thorpe
Billy Mills
Billie Jean King
Ann Meyers

John Lennon
D.B. Cooper
Amelia Earhart
Martin Luther King, Jr.

Mother
Father

[1996]

Taiaiake Alfred

What I Think of When I Think of Skin

> When I stand before thee at the day's end, thou shalt see my scars and know that I had my wounds and also my healing. —Rabindranath Tagore, *Stray Birds*

What is skin? Anatomically, our skin is an organ comprising twenty square feet made up of three layers of constantly renewing cells that serve as the waterproof container of our physicality. But I'd be surprised if anyone thought that way about skin when they heard the word. Skin... Who can forget being touched? The skin ignites our passions, communicates our desires. Babies who are raised without skin touch—stroking, cuddling, and kissing—suffer for the neglect, making it nearly impossible for the adults they eventually become to have meaningful and caring attachments. That's how crucial a role our skin plays in the creation of love and affection and human bonds. It is protection for our other organs, and it's also the projection of our identities and emotions to others. The skin is both intimate and public. It is a thin membrane linking our inside life with our wider existence, and it's the pathway for our sensual experience of the world and our relationships with other people.

If I close my eyes and think "skin," the first thing that comes to mind is the feel of sun on my arms and back. With that thought comes a flood of memories of sunburned days as a young US Marine in tropical climes, when I just couldn't get enough of the smell of the sultry air and salty ocean mist, the feel of the hot sun on my face and my back. If I stay with the thought, I'm taken back to the fading light of a Carolina summer's day: I'm in the middle of a boisterous crowd of laughing teenaged girls and shirtless Marines. A girl reclines languidly in the sand, the late-afternoon wind blowing soft curls across her face, which is set in a distant look that makes her seem uninterested in any of the boys or the games we are playing. I am fascinated by, of all things, the sun-speckled skin of her cheeks, shoulders, and breasts. I manoeuvre to sit next to her, but once in position I just sit there, not saying a word, trying to think of the perfect phrase that will make her want to stay with me and not go off with someone else when the sun goes down. I am taken by surprise when she looks over at me, smiles sweetly, and reaches out to gently touch my shoulder. She studies my own skin as she slowly draws her finger all the way down my arm, lingering for a minute when her fingertip connects with mine. She looks up at me with her green eyes, then drops her gaze and finger into the sand. With an arch of her eyebrows, she writes her phone number in the sand, then throws her head back and laughs as she quickly sweeps away the words and the numbers she's written.

Skin is the conduit of pleasurable sensations, but we all know it's usually the point of first contact and one of the main receptors of pain as well. Thinking back to my youth, I also remember when the spell of that summer day was broken and I was reminded that not all obsessions with skin are so romantic.

A few weeks after I'd met that girl, I was invited to go meet her parents. When I showed up at their house and knocked on the front door, her mother opened it slowly and peered around to look at me standing there on her front porch. When she saw me, the hard stare she was wearing gave way to a look of shock. "Oh my, thank God you're not a nigger!" she blurted.

I didn't know what to say.

"When my daughter told us she'd met someone and he wasn't white, we naturally assumed..."

"No, ma'am, I am not black," I said cautiously.

"But you are dark, though. What are you?" she asked.

"I'm Mohawk," I replied. "A Native."

"You mean you're an Indian? Really?" After thinking about what I'd said for a couple of seconds, a smile came across her face. She took me by the arm and said, "Come on in, son."

A dreamy setting for memories of one's youth it surely is, but the American South in the twentieth century was definitely not a time and place to escape from the implications of one's melanin or suntan. I often wondered if there was any escape. Had there ever been a society that was blind to skin colour? There had to have been times in history when the colour of one's skin didn't mean much to people. Hadn't I read that the ancient Greeks didn't bother themselves too much over skin tone? But that's probably only because they made slaves of *everyone* they conquered, whether they were light-, medium- or dark-skinned. That's not exactly an enlightened perspective.

People seem to think that modern-day Canada is a post-racist society. But I don't believe it; that's not my experience. Maybe, like the ancient Greeks, the people who are dominant now in this land, white people, no longer have to organize their ideas and institutions around skin colour to maintain themselves in the privileged position they have inherited from their brutishly racist ancestors. After all, the original landlords of this continent are (thought to be) conquered; we've been relentlessly de-cultured, and our freedom to be ourselves has been deposited alongside all the masks, canoes, and ladles in the museum. We are no longer a threat, and to most people it must seem like we crave nothing more than mercy and to be finally allowed to conform. To the now-dominant newcomers to our lands, the primitive racism of their forebears, which was so obsessed with assigning a person's worth on the basis of gradations of skin colour, must seem so obnoxious; it is certainly obsolete.

The ideas and attitudes of the past have served their purpose but are no longer needed to keep us in our place now that any idea we original landlords had about evicting the overbearing tenants and securing our homeland is out of the question. Now that the return of even a portion of our homeland or reparations for what we've lost is regarded as a laughable suggestion, the white descendants of the newcomers are able to tolerate us original people and to see us as humans, to admire our resiliency, to laud our insights. Many even admire brown skin and want to feel the non-white aesthetic by touching that which not so long ago was the mark of a scary and despicable savage.

When I was a boy, growing up on an Indian reserve outside of Montreal, notions of savagism and civilization were still present and acknowledged as facts in this country; it was a time and place where the colour of your skin determined the quality of your existence. In the new multicultural Canada, a lot of people don't realize that, until very recently, if you were Native, the identification card you were issued by the government reported not only such usual information as name and date of birth, but also the complexion of your skin: light, medium, or dark. I've never delved into the historical reasons for this, but I'm fairly certain it has something to do with the government's notion that it was worth taking note of the lighter skinned mixed-race, and presumably assimilated, members of the band and to distinguish them from the ones who were medium in tone—marked as potentially civilizable—and especially from the tawny ones, who were thought to be still mired in dark savagism, generations away from being able to appreciate the glories of mayonnaise and smooth jazz.

The ideas behind this imagined caste system were utter nonsense, of course, and a total failure, it turns out. I grew up with some fierce savages who were whiter in skin tone than the Minister of Indian Affairs himself. Although my own status card flagged me as dark-complexioned, I've always been disappointed by my instinct for good behaviour. I ended up disease-free and graduated from high school. I went to college instead of jail. I still have all of my teeth and can even speak English without an accent when I want to. So much for the tawny curse of the uncivilized.

The racial attitudes behind the government's fantasy caste system have always held sway in most people's minds in this country, yet when you think about it, they really make no sense at all, socially or scientifically. Take the example of me and my sister: I've always been "dark" to the Department of Indian Affairs, but really just medium brown compared with most people in the world; my sister, who shares my parentage, which includes our English grandmother, is as fair and sun-burnable as a human being could be. Growing up in such an intensely governed place as an Indian reserve and in such a thoroughly racially mixed situation as the Mohawk Nation, we were, of course, hyper-aware of how our skins affected our lives and others' perception of us.

My favourite nickname for my sister was French Fry. Being a bratty brother, I would get a real kick out of holding up a fry next to my sister's face and saying, "Look, twins. They're both so skinny and white." Ha ha. But I was just teasing in the way kids do, and I never thought of my sister as any less of a Mohawk than myself. Though by that time it was the late 1970s, and in those revolutionary days being a light-skinned Native had lost its lustre, so to speak. It had gone from being a privilege to being a cultural liability. So maybe I was being a bit cruel after all. It's no wonder she keeps reminding me of that story, even thirty years later. Anyway, I had put up with my share of racialized nicknames from the reserve's fairer set. I remember that all of the darker kids on our reserve were called *Rahonsti*, which means Black, or else something silly, like Chic-chocolate, all the time.

Still, the government failed in its bid to divide us on the lines of skin colour—and a good thing too, because they had plenty of other divide-and-conquer strategies that did work. You know why I can confidently say that they failed? Because my sister, la French Fry herself, ended up living, working, and raising her kids in our Mohawk community. It was me, the brown-skinned, brown-haired, brown-eyed one, who left the reserve as soon as I was able to and made a life outside of our small community. Our skin colours turned out to be imperfect predictors of our future in this country, and very unreliable indicators of what kind of Mohawks we were, civilized or not. Skin colour is something we human beings naturally notice. But I learned early on in my life that it can never tell you anything meaningful about a person. Anyone reading these words who saw me on the street in Victoria would probably look at me and figure that I'm a Native, or at least the descendant of one, but that's as much as they'll know about me. And that's pretty useless information.

When I was a little boy, one of my chores was to help my father take his workboots off when he came home from his job. I looked forward to it. It was a son's act of devotion, sure, but also one of necessity. My father was an ironworker, and by the time he walked through the front door of our house late on a Friday night, he'd worked forty hours or more that week in the outdoors, thirty storeys up in the sky over New York City. Then he'd got in a car with a few other guys and driven the length of New York State, through the Adirondack Mountains, from the city to our reserve. On the way, he'd have drunk at least a six-pack of Schaefer beers. So he needed somebody to take off his boots.

If it was summertime, he'd have been working out in the sun without a shirt on, so I'd turn to my next job—which, now that I think of it, is probably responsible for my fascination with skin! He'd strip off his white T-shirt, and I'd climb up on the backrest of the couch, straddle his back, and start peeling skin off his shoulders and back. Every Friday night in the summer, I'd be peeling his back, the sunburned skin coming off in little strips and in big, saucersized patches. When he walked through the door of our house, he was a tough man with very dark skin, but after I was done, his back and shoulders would be a patchwork of pink and red and brown. He would sit on the couch and tell me to peel his back for him every time he came home, even though he'd flinch again and again as I peeled the skin to the flesh. This is what I would remember about him as he once again left on that journey across the great forest into the big city for another week of brutal work and hard sun thirty storeys up in the sky.

Scars are inscriptions, the work of others and ourselves, projected at the world. Fibroblast cells in our skin make collagen that we use to create the scar tissue that covers up the cuts and tears that have breached its multilayered integrity. In turn we generate reasons, excuses, and fantasies that coalesce into flesh as scars and become stories we present and defend in the world and before the mirror.

I was badly scarred when I was younger. When I was in Marine Corps boot camp, the rifle I was firing blew up when I pulled the trigger, sending gunpowder, shattered brass, and pieces of gun metal flying up into my face. I picked tiny pieces of brass out of my face for a few months after that and lived with the redness of the powder burns around my mouth and chin for a while longer. You can't see any powder burns or little puncture wounds on my face anymore; the skin has since healed. But I swear I can still feel them. I have to suppress a slight flinch each time I put a rifle up to my chin and squeeze the trigger.

Could we as humans have evolved the ability to scar as a form of story, as a reminder to ourselves and others not to do dangerous or dumb things? Well, we are intelligent creatures, even ironworkers and Marines. Tattoos are a form of scarring, and they tell a story about a person too. Unlike other scars though, tattoos, especially these days, are more fashion statement than healed-over wound—there's not much risk or pain involved in acquiring these kinds of scars. They are constructed evidences of what we want people to think about us.

I have a couple of tattoos myself. The one on my right bicep is a screaming eagle with my Mohawk name spelled out below it. On my other arm, there is an Asian dragon with the letters USMC inscribed underneath. What do these tattoos tell you about me? I could say that they are marks of pride I chose to put on my body to forever proclaim my dual warrior heritage as a Native and as one of the few and the proud, Uncle Sam's Misguided Children. But that is such a self-conscious telling of my story. Actually, I got the screaming eagle tattoo on a dare. My buddy Jake and I were on a three-day drinking binge, and he said he'd pay for it if I had the guts to get tattooed by the old biker in the dingy parlour we'd wandered into. I got the other one a couple of months later because I couldn't stand the asymmetry of having one arm tattooed and the other blank.

Accidental and instrumental scars are the same in one way, though. The lessons they represent always take a while to sink in; stories take time to develop, and the physical scarring process takes a while to heal the wound. A human being sheds a layer of skin every day; over the course of a month, we take on an entirely new skin. But it takes two years of collagen and blood vessels working together to make even superficial scars fade to where no one notices them—though every scar will always bear some faint visible witness to what has happened. Scars never do completely heal over, and they remain with us as remnants and reminders of the deepest cuts and most severe wounds we've suffered.

I had a dream about my skin being scarred by a bear. In this dream, I stand rooted in place as trees, clouds, earth, and wind spin around me. A grizzly bear appears—I don't know how I know she is a female—and enters the maelstrom, circling me many times, with her eyes locked on mine. The effect is a terrifying, paralyzing ferocity. Suddenly everything falls still. The bear is frozen in place in front of me. It's like I am alive in the middle of a diorama. She stares right at or through me. In an instant, she presses her face against mine. She holds me in an intimate embrace and her claws dig hard into the skin of my forearms. In an unspoken language of the spirit through her liquid black eyes, she says, "I am going to hurt you, but I will not kill you." Her stare intensifies, and she breaks the skin as she drags her claws all the way down, leaving thick lines of scars on my arms. As soon as the embrace ends, the wounds heal over and I am left standing alone, without fear or pain, feeling clean and strong. [2012]

Dorothy Allison

from *Two or Three Things I Know for Sure*

"Let me tell you a story," I used to whisper to my sisters, hiding with them behind the red-dirt bean hills and row on row of strawberries. My sisters' faces were thin and sharp, with high cheekbones and restless eyes, like my mama's face, my aunt Dot's, my own. Peasants, that's what we are and always have been. Call us the lower orders, the great unwashed, the working class, the poor, proletariat, trash, lowlife and scum. I can make a story out of it, out of us. Make it pretty or sad, laughable or haunting. Dress it up with legend and aura and romance.

"Let me tell you a story," I'd begin, and start another one. When we were small, I could catch my sisters the way they caught butterflies, capture their attention and almost make them believe that all I said was true. "Let me tell you about the women who ran away. All those legendary women who ran away." I'd tell about the witch queens who cooked their enemies in great open pots, the jewels that grow behind the tongues of water moccasins. After a while the deepest satisfaction was in the story itself, greater even than the terror in my sisters' faces, the laughter, and, God help us, the hope.

The constant query of my childhood was "Where you been?" The answer, "Nowhere." Neither my stepfather nor my mother believed me. But no punishment could discover another answer. The truth was that I did go nowhere—nowhere in particular and everywhere imaginable. I walked and told myself stories, walked out of our subdivision and into another, walked all the way to the shopping center and then back. The flush my mama suspected hid an afternoon of shoplifting or vandalism was simple embarrassment, because when I walked, I talked—story-talked, out loud—assuming identities I made up. Sometimes I was myself, arguing loudly as I could never do at home. Sometimes I became people I had seen on television or read about in books, went places I'd barely heard of, did things that no one I knew had ever done, particularly things that girls were not supposed to do. In the world as I remade it, nothing was forbidden; everything was possible.

I'll tell you a story and maybe you'll believe me.

There's a laboratory in the basement of the Greenville County General Hospital, I told my sisters. They take the babies down there. If you're poor—from the wrong family, the wrong color, the wrong side of town—they mess with you, alter your brain. That was what happened. That was it.

You believe me?

I'm a storyteller. I'll work to make you believe me. Throw in some real stuff, change a few details, add the certainty of outrage. I know the use of fiction in a world of hard truth, the way fiction can be a harder piece of truth. The story of what happened, or what did not happen but should have—that story can become a curtain drawn shut, a piece of insulation, a disguise, a razor, a tool that changes every time it is used and sometimes becomes something other than we intended.

The story becomes the thing needed.

Two or three things I know for sure and one of them is what it means to have no loved version of your life but the one you make.

Let me tell you a story. If I could convince myself, I can convince you. But you were not there when I began. You were not the one I was convincing. When I began there were just nightmares and need and stubborn determination.

When I began there was only the suspicion that making up the story as you went along was the way to survive. And if I know anything, I know how to survive, how to remake the world in story.

But where am I in the stories I tell? Not the storyteller but the woman in the story, the woman who believes in story. What is the truth about her? She was one of them, one of those legendary women who ran away. A witch queen, a warrior maiden, a mother with a canvas suitcase, a daughter with broken bones. Women run away because they must. I ran because if I had not, I would have died. No one told me that you take your world with you, that running becomes a habit, that the secret to running is to know why you run and where you are going—and to leave behind the reason you run.

My mama did not run away. My aunt Dot and aunt Grace and cousin Billie with her near dozen children—they did not run. They learned resilience and determination and the cost of hard compromises. None of them ever intended to lose their lives or their children's lives, to be trapped by those hard compromises and ground down until they no longer knew who they were, what they had first intended. But it happened. It happened over and over again.

Aunt Dot was the one who said it. She said, "Lord, girl, there's only two or three things I know for sure." She put her head back, grinned, and made a small impatient noise. Her eyes glittered as bright as sun reflecting off the scales of a cottonmouth's back. She spat once and shrugged. "Only two or three things. That's right," she said. "Of course it's never the same things, and I'm never as sure as I'd like to be." [1996]

Sherwood Anderson

Death in the Woods

She was an old woman and lived on a farm near the town in which I lived. All country and small-town people have seen such old women, but no one knows much about them. Such an old woman comes into town driving an old worn-out horse or she comes afoot carrying a basket. She may own a few hens and have eggs to sell. She brings them in a basket and takes them to a grocer. There she trades them in. She gets some salt pork and some beans. Then she gets a pound or two of sugar and some flour.

Afterwards she goes to the butcher's and asks for some dog-meat. She may spend ten or fifteen cents, but when she does she asks for something. Formerly the butchers gave liver to any one who wanted to carry it away. In our family we were always having it. Once one of my brothers got a whole cow's liver at the slaughter-house near the fairgrounds in our town. We had it until we were sick of it. It never cost a cent. I have hated the thought of it ever since.

The old farm woman got some liver and a soup-bone. She never visited with any one, and as soon as she got what she wanted she lit out for home. It made quite a load for such an old body. No one gave her a lift. People drive right down a road and never notice an old woman like that.

There was such an old woman who used to come into town past our house one Summer and Fall when I was a young boy and was sick with what was called inflammatory rheumatism. She went home later carrying a heavy pack on her back. Two or three large gaunt-looking dogs followed at her heels.

The old woman was nothing special. She was one of the nameless ones that hardly any one knows, but she got into my thoughts. I have just suddenly now, after all these years, remembered her and what happened. It is a story. Her name was Grimes, and she lived with her husband and son in a small unpainted house on the bank of a small creek four miles from town.

The husband and son were a tough lot. Although the son was but twenty-one, he had already served a term in jail. It was whispered about that the woman's husband stole horses and ran them off to some other county. Now and then, when a horse turned up missing, the man had also disappeared. No one ever caught him. Once, when I was loafing at Tom Whitehead's livery-barn, the man came there and sat on the bench in front. Two or three other men were there, but no one spoke to him. He sat for a few minutes and then got up and went away. When he was leaving he turned around and stared at the men. There was a look of defiance in his eyes. "Well, I have tried to be friendly. You don't want to talk to me. It has been so wherever I have gone in this town. If, some day, one of your fine horses turns up missing, well, then what?" He did not say anything actually. "I'd like to bust one of you on the jaw," was about what his eyes said. I remember how the look in his eyes made me shiver.

The old man belonged to a family that had had money once. His name was Jake Grimes. It all comes back clearly now. His father, John Grimes, had owned a sawmill when the country was new, and had made money. Then he got to drinking and running after women. When he died there wasn't much left.

Jake blew in the rest. Pretty soon there wasn't any more lumber to cut and his land was nearly all gone.

He got his wife off a German farmer, for whom he went to work one June day in the wheat harvest. She was a young thing then and scared to death. You see, the farmer was up to something with the girl—she was, I think, a bound girl and his wife had her suspicions. She took it out on the girl when the man wasn't around. Then, when the wife had to go off to town for supplies, the farmer got after her. She told young Jake that nothing really ever happened, but he didn't know whether to believe it or not.

He got her pretty easy himself, the first time he was out with her. He wouldn't have married her if the German farmer hadn't tried to tell him where to get off. He got her to go riding with him in his buggy one night when he was threshing on the place, and then he came for her the next Sunday night.

She managed to get out of the house without her employer's seeing, but when she was getting into the buggy he showed up. It was almost dark, and he just popped up suddenly at the horse's head. He grabbed the horse by the bridle and Jake got out his buggy-whip.

They had it out all right! The German was a tough one. Maybe he didn't care whether his wife knew or not. Jake hit him over the face and shoulders with the buggy-whip, but the horse got to acting up and he had to get out.

Then the two men went for it. The girl didn't see it. The horse started to run away and went nearly a mile down the road before the girl got him stopped. Then she managed to tie him to a tree beside the road. (I wonder how I know all this. It must have stuck in my mind from small-town tales when I was a boy.) Jake found her there after he got through with the German. She was huddled up in the buggy seat, crying, scared to death. She told Jake a lot of stuff, how the German had tried to get her, how he chased her once into the barn, how another time, when they happened to be alone in the house together, he tore her dress open clear down the front. The German, she said, might have got her that time if he hadn't heard his old woman drive in at the gate. She had been off to town for supplies. Well, she would be putting the horse in the barn. The German managed to sneak off to the fields without his wife seeing. He told the girl he would kill her if she told. What could she do? She told a lie about ripping her dress in the barn when she was feeding the stock. I remember now that she was a bound girl and did not know where her father and mother were. Maybe she did not have any father. You know what I mean.

Such bound children were often enough cruelly treated. They were children who had no parents, slaves really. There were very few orphan homes then. They were legally bound into some home. It was a matter of pure luck how it came out.

II

She married Jake and had a son and daughter, but the daughter died.

Then she settled down to feed stock. That was her job. At the German's place she had cooked the food for the German and his wife. The wife was a strong woman with big hips and worked most of the time in the fields with her husband. She fed them and fed the cows in the barn, fed the pigs, the horses and the chickens. Every moment of every day, as a young girl, was spent feeding something.

Then she married Jake Grimes and he had to be fed. She was a slight thing, and when she had been married for three or four years, and after the two children were born, her slender shoulders became stooped.

Jake always had a lot of big dogs around the house, that stood near the unused sawmill near the creek. He was always trading horses when he wasn't stealing something and had a lot of poor bony ones about. Also he kept three or four pigs and a cow. They were all pastured in the few acres left of the Grimes place and Jake did little enough work.

He went into debt for a threshing outfit and ran it for several years, but it did not pay. People did not trust him. They were afraid he would steal the grain at night. He had to go a long way off to get work and it cost too much to get there. In the Winter he hunted and cut a little firewood, to be sold in some nearby town. When the son grew up he was just like the father. They got drunk together. If there wasn't anything to eat in the house when they came home the old man gave his old woman a cut over the head. She had a few chickens of her own and had to kill one of them in a hurry. When they were all killed she wouldn't have any eggs to sell when she went to town, and then what would she do?

She had to scheme all her life about getting things fed, getting the pigs fed so they would grow fat and could be butchered in the Fall. When they were butchered her husband took most of the meat off to town and sold it. If he did not do it first the boy did. They fought sometimes and when they fought the old woman stood aside trembling.

She had got the habit of silence anyway—that was fixed. Sometimes, when she began to look old—she wasn't forty yet—and when the husband and son, were both off, trading horses or drinking or hunting or stealing, she went around the house and the barnyard muttering to herself.

How was she going to get everything fed?—that was her problem. The dogs had to be fed. There wasn't enough hay in the barn for the horses and the cow. If she didn't feed the chickens how could they lay eggs? Without eggs to sell how could she get things in town, things she had to have to keep the life of the farm going? Thank heaven, she did not have to feed her husband—in a certain way. That hadn't lasted long after their marriage and after the babies came. Where he went on his long trips she did not know. Sometimes he was gone from home for weeks, and after the boy grew up they went off together.

They left everything at home for her to manage and she had no money. She knew no one. No one ever talked to her in town. When it was Winter she had to gather sticks of wood for her fire, had to try to keep the stock fed with very little grain.

The stock in the barn cried to her hungrily, the dogs followed her about. In the Winter the hens laid few enough eggs. They huddled in the corners of the barn and she kept watching them. If a hen lays an egg in the barn in the Winter and you do not find it, it freezes and breaks.

One day in Winter the old woman went off to town with a few eggs and the dogs followed her. She did not get started until nearly three o'clock and the snow was heavy. She hadn't been feeling very well for several days and so she went muttering along, scantily clad, her shoulders stooped. She had an old grain bag in which she carried her eggs, tucked away down in the bottom. There weren't many of them, but in Winter the price of eggs is up. She would get a little meat in exchange for the eggs, some salt pork, a little sugar, and some coffee perhaps. It might be the butcher would give her a piece of liver.

When she had got to town and was trading in her eggs the dogs lay by the door outside. She did pretty well, got the things she needed, more than she had hoped. Then she went to the butcher and he gave her some liver and some dog-meat.

It was the first time any one had spoken to her in a friendly way for a long time. The butcher was alone in his shop when she came in and was annoyed by the thought of such a sick-looking old woman out on such a day. It was bitter cold and the snow, that had let up during the afternoon, was falling again. The butcher said something about her husband and her son, swore at them, and the old woman stared at him, a look of mild surprise in her eyes as he talked. He said that if either the husband or the son were going to get any of the liver or the heavy bones with scraps of meat hanging to them that he had put into the grain bag, he'd see him starve first.

Starve, eh? Well, things had to be fed. Men had to be fed, and the horses that weren't any good but maybe could be traded off, and the poor thin cow that hadn't given any milk for three months.

Horses, cows, pigs, dogs, men.

III

The old woman had to get back before darkness came if she could. The dogs followed at her heels, sniffing at the heavy grain bag she had fastened on her back. When she got to the edge of town she stopped by a fence and tied the bag on her back with a piece of rope she had carried in her dress-pocket for just that purpose. That was an easier way to carry it. Her arms ached. It was hard when she had to crawl over fences and once she fell over and landed in the snow. The dogs went frisking about. She had to struggle to get to her feet again, but she made it. The point of climbing over the fences was that there was a short cut over a hill and through a woods. She might have gone around by the road, but it was a mile farther that way. She was afraid she couldn't make it. And then, besides, the stock had to be fed. There was a little hay left and a little corn. Perhaps her husband and son would bring some home when they came. They had driven off in the only buggy the Grimes family had, a rickety thing, a rickety horse hitched to the buggy, two other rickety horses led by halters. They were going to trade horses, get a little money if they could. They might come home drunk. It would be well to have something in the house when they came back.

The son had an affair on with a woman at the county seat, fifteen miles away. She was a rough enough woman, a tough one. Once, in the Summer, the son had brought her to the house. Both she and the son had been drinking. Jake Grimes was away and the son and his woman ordered the old woman about like a servant. She didn't mind much; she was used to it. Whatever happened she never said anything. That was her way of getting along. She had managed that way when she was a young girl at the German's and ever since she had married Jake. That time her son brought his woman to the house they stayed all night, sleeping together just as though they were married. It hadn't shocked the old woman, not much. She had got past being shocked early in life.

With the pack on her back she went painfully along across an open field, wading in the deep snow, and got into the woods.

There was a path, but it was hard to follow. Just beyond the top of the hill, where the woods was thickest, there was a small clearing. Had some one once thought of building a house there? The clearing was as large as a building lot in town, large enough for a house and a garden. The path ran along the side of the clearing, and when she got there the old woman sat down to rest at the foot of a tree.

It was a foolish thing to do. When she got herself placed, the pack against the tree's trunk, it was nice, but what about getting up again? She worried about that for a moment and then quietly closed her eyes.

She must have slept for a time. When you are about so cold you can't get any colder. The afternoon grew a little warmer and the snow came thicker than ever. Then after a time the weather cleared. The moon even came out.

There were four Grimes dogs that had followed Mrs. Grimes into town, all tall gaunt fellows. Such men as Jake Grimes and his son always keep just such dogs. They kick and abuse them, but they stay. The Grimes dogs, in order to keep from starving, had to do a lot of foraging for themselves, and they had been at it while the old woman slept with her back to the tree at the side of the clearing. They had been chasing rabbits in the woods and in adjoining fields and in their ranging had picked up three other farm dogs.

After a time all the dogs came back to the clearing. They were excited about something. Such nights, cold and clear and with a moon, do things to dogs. It may be that some old instinct, come down from the time when they were wolves and ranged the woods in packs on Winter nights, comes back into them.

The dogs in the clearing, before the old woman, had caught two or three rabbits and their immediate hunger had been satisfied. They began to play, running in circles in the clearing. Round and round they ran, each dog's nose at the tail of the next dog. In the clearing, under the snow-laden trees and under the wintry moon they made a strange picture, running thus silently, in a circle their running had beaten in the soft snow. The dogs made no sound. They ran around and around in the circle.

It may have been that the old woman saw them doing that before she died. She may have awakened once or twice and looked at the strange sight with dim old eyes.

She wouldn't be very cold now, just drowsy. Life hangs on a long time. Perhaps the old woman was out of her head. She may have dreamed of her girlhood, at the German's, and before that, when she was a child and before her mother lit out and left her.

Her dreams couldn't have been very pleasant. Not many pleasant things had happened to her. Now and then one of the Grimes dogs left the running circle and came to stand before her. The dog thrust his face close to her face. His red tongue was hanging out.

The running of the dogs may have been a kind of death ceremony. It may have been that the primitive instinct of the wolf, having been aroused in the dogs by the night and the running, made them somehow afraid.

"Now we are no longer wolves. We are dogs, the servants of men. Keep alive, man! When man dies we becomes wolves again."

When one of the dogs came to where the old woman sat with her back against the tree and thrust his nose close to her face he seemed satisfied and went back to run with the pack. All the Grimes dogs did it at some time during the evening, before she died. I knew all about it afterward, when I grew to be a man, because once in a woods in Illinois, on another Winter night, I saw a pack of dogs act just like that. The dogs were waiting for me to die as they had waited for the old woman that night when I was a child, but when it happened to me I was a young man and had no intention whatever of dying.

The old woman died softly and quietly. When she was dead and when one of the Grimes dogs had come to her and had found her dead all the dogs stopped running.

They gathered about her.

Well, she was dead now. She had fed the Grimes dogs when she was alive, what about now?

There was the pack on her back, the grain bag containing the piece of salt pork, the liver the butcher had given her, the dog-meat, the soup bones. The butcher in town, having been suddenly overcome with a feeling of pity, had loaded her grain bag heavily. It had been a big haul for the old woman.

It was a big haul for the dogs now.

IV

One of the Grimes dogs sprang suddenly out from among the others and began worrying the pack on the old woman's back. Had the dogs really been wolves that one would have been the leader of the pack. What he did, all the others did.

All of them sank their teeth into the grain bag the old woman had fastened with ropes to her back.

They dragged the old woman's body out into the open clearing. The worn-out dress was quickly torn from her shoulders. When she was found, a day or two later, the dress had been torn from her body clear to the hips, but the dogs had not touched her body. They had got the meat out of the grain bag, that was all. Her body was frozen stiff when it was found, and the shoulders were so narrow and the body so slight that in death it looked like the body of some charming young girl.

Such things happened in towns of the Middle West, on farms near town, when I was a boy. A hunter out after rabbits found the old woman's body and did not touch it. Something, the beaten round path in the little snow-covered clearing, the silence of the place, the place where the dogs had worried the body trying to pull the grain bag away or tear it open—something startled the man and he hurried off to town.

I was in Main street with one of my brothers who was town newsboy and who was taking the afternoon papers to the stores. It was almost night.

The hunter came into a grocery and told his story. Then he went to a hardware-shop and into a drugstore. Men began to gather on the sidewalks. Then they started out along the road to the place in the woods.

My brother should have gone on about his business of distributing papers but he didn't. Every one was going to the woods. The undertaker went and the town marshal. Several men got on a dray and rode out to where the path left the road and went into the woods, but the horses weren't very sharply shod and slid about on the slippery roads. They made no better time than those of us who walked.

The town marshal was a large man whose leg had been injured in the Civil War. He carried a heavy cane and limped rapidly along the road. My brother and I followed at his heels, and as we went other men and boys joined the crowd.

It had grown dark by the time we got to where the old woman had left the road but the moon had come out. The marshal was thinking there might have been a murder. He kept asking the hunter questions. The hunter went along with his gun across his shoulders, a dog following at his heels. It isn't often a rabbit hunter has a chance to be so conspicuous. He was taking full advantage of it, leading the procession with the town marshal. "I didn't see any wounds. She was a beautiful young girl. Her face was buried in the snow. No, I didn't know her." As a matter of fact, the hunter had not looked closely at the body. He had been frightened. She might have been murdered and some one might spring out from behind a tree and murder him. In a woods, in the late afternoon, when the trees are all bare and there is white snow on the ground, when all is silent, something creepy steals over the mind and body. If something strange or uncanny has happened in the neighborhood all you think about is getting away from there as fast as you can.

The crowd of men and boys had got to where the old woman had crossed the field and went, following the marshal and the hunter, up the slight incline and into the woods.

My brother and I were silent. He had his bundle of papers in a bag slung across his shoulder. When he got back to town he would have to go on distributing his papers before he went home to supper. If I went along, as he had no doubt already determined I should, we would both be late. Either mother or our older sister would have to warm our supper.

Well, we would have something to tell. A boy did not get such a chance very often. It was lucky we just happened to go into the grocery when the hunter came in. The hunter was a country fellow. Neither of us had ever seen him before.

Now the crowd of men and boys had got to the clearing. Darkness comes quickly on such Winter nights, but the full moon made everything clear. My brother and I stood near the tree, beneath which the old woman had died.

She did not look old, lying there in that light, frozen and still. One of the men turned her over in the snow and I saw everything. My body trembled with some strange mystical feeling and so did my brother's. It might have been the cold.

Neither of us had ever seen a woman's body before. It may have been the snow, clinging to the frozen flesh, that made it look so white and lovely, so like marble. No woman had come with the party from town; but one of the men, he was the town blacksmith, took off his overcoat and spread it over her. Then he gathered her into his arms and started off to town, all the others following silently. At that time no one knew who she was.

V

I had seen everything, had seen the oval in the snow, like a miniature race-track, where the dogs had run, had seen how the men were mystified, had seen the white bare young-looking shoulders, had heard the whispered comments of the men.

The men were simply mystified. They took the body to the undertaker's, and when the blacksmith, the hunter, the marshal and several others had got inside they closed the door. If father had been there perhaps he could have got in, but we boys couldn't.

I went with my brother to distribute the rest of his papers and when we got home it was my brother who told the story.

I kept silent and went to bed early. It may have been I was not satisfied with the way he told it.

Later, in the town, I must have heard other fragments of the old woman's story. She was recognized the next day and there was an investigation.

The husband and son were found somewhere and brought to town and there was an attempt to connect them with the woman's death, but it did not work. They had perfect enough alibis.

However, the town was against them. They had to get out. Where they went I never heard.

I remember only the picture there in the forest, the men standing about, the naked girlish-looking figure, face down in the snow, the tracks made by the running dogs and the clear cold Winter sky above. White fragments of clouds were drifting across the sky. They went racing across the little open space among the trees.

The scene in the forest had become for me, without my knowing it, the foundation for the real story I am now trying to tell. The fragments, you see, had to be picked up slowly, long afterwards.

Things happened. When I was a young man I worked on the farm of a German. The hired-girl was afraid of her employer. The farmer's wife hated her.

I saw things at that place. Once later, I had a half-uncanny, mystical adventure with dogs in an Illinois forest on a clear, moon-lit Winter night. When I was a schoolboy, and on a Summer day, I went with a boy friend out along a creek some miles from town and came to the house where the old woman had lived. No one had lived in the house since her death. The doors were broken from the hinges; the window lights were all broken. As the boy and I stood in the road outside, two dogs, just roving farm dogs no doubt, came running around the corner of the house. The dogs were tall, gaunt fellows and came down to the fence and glared through at us, standing in the road.

The whole thing, the story of the old woman's death, was to me as I grew older like music heard from far off. The notes had to be picked up slowly one at a time. Something had to be understood.

The woman who died was one destined to feed animal life. Anyway, that is all she ever did. She was feeding animal life before she was born, as a child, as a young woman working on the farm of the German, after she married, when she grew old and when she died. She fed animal life in cows, in chickens, in pigs, in horses, in dogs, in men. Her daughter had died in childhood and with her one son she had no articulate relations. On the night when she died she was hurrying homeward, bearing on her body food for animal life.

She died in the clearing in the woods and even after her death continued feeding animal life.

You see it is likely that, when my brother told the story, that night when we got home and mother and sister sat listening, I did not think he got the point. He was too young and so was I. A thing so complete has its own beauty.

I shall not try to emphasize the point. I am only explaining why I was dissatisfied then and have been ever since. I speak of that only that you may understand why I have been impelled to try to tell the simple story over again. [1933]

Reinaldo Arenas

The Downpour

Perhaps the most extraordinary event I enjoyed during my childhood was one provided by the heavens: the heavy downpour. It was no ordinary rainfall. It was a tropical drenching, heralded by violent thunder in cosmic, orchestral bursts that resounded across the fields, while lightning traced the wildest designs on the sky, striking palm trees that suddenly burst into flames and then shriveled like burnt matches. And in no time the rain would come down strong and seem like a massive army marching across the trees. It would reverberate on the zinc roof of the passageway like gunfire; on the palm-frond thatch above the living room, it sounded like a million footsteps overhead. Water rushed down the gutters with the rumble of overflowing brooks and cascaded thundering into the barrels. And on the trees in the patio, from the uppermost leaves to the ground, the rain became a concert of drums with different registers and amazing rhythms; it was a fragrant resonance. I would run from one end of the passageway to the other and into the living room, look out the window, go to the kitchen and watch the pines in the patio, drenched and whistling out of control in the wind. Finally I would run outside, naked, and let the rain soak me through. I hugged the trees, rolled around in the grass, built small mud dams, behind which water would collect, and in those miniature ponds I would swim, plunge, and splash. I would go over to the well and watch water falling on water. I would look up at the sky and watch flocks of green *querequetés* also celebrating the torrential rains. I was not satisfied with rolling in the grass, I wanted to fly, to fly like those birds, alone in the downpour. I would go as far as the river, a river that roared under the spell of violence let loose. The power of the overflowing current would sweep away almost everything in its path: trees, stones, animals, houses. It was the mystery of the law of destruction, but also of the law of life. I did not know then where that river was headed, where that frenzied race would end, but something was calling me to go with it, saying that I too had to throw myself into those raging waters and lose myself, that only in that torrent, always on the move, would I find some peace. But I did not dare jump, I was always a coward. I would go as far as the riverbank, where the currents were roaring my name; another step, and the whirling waters would swallow me. How much trouble could have been avoided if I had done just that! Those waters were turbid and restless, powerful and lonely. It was all I had; only in those waters, in that river, had nature accepted me and now summoned me in its moment of greatest glory. Why not throw myself into those waters? Why not lose myself, vanish in them, find peace in that clamor that I loved? What joy to have done just that! But I returned home soaked; it was already dark. My grandmother was cooking dinner. It had stopped raining. I was shivering while my aunts and my mother set the table without paying much attention to me. I always thought that my family, including my mother, saw me as a weird creature, useless, confused, or crazy; a being outside the framework of their lives. They were probably right.

[1994]

Elizabeth Bachinsky

For the Pageant Girls: Miss Teen Motel 6 *et al.*

We met when we were young enough to know
each street, and side street, of our town by name.
That beauty changes us and why and how

becomes apparent when you live below
a mountain. What was its name again?
We met when we were young enough to know.

This is what we saw from our windows:
a parking lot, a dollar store, rain.
That beauty could change us and why and how

seemed unjust. Unfair! What did we know
but that our loves seemed dull and strange.
We met when we were young enough to know

we'd move to far-off places. We had hopes
to find ourselves on MTV, so certain
beauty could change us. Why and how

seemed unimportant, as long as we'd just go.
So some left, some didn't; all of us changed.
We met when we were young enough to know
that beauty could change us—not why or how. [2006]

Jean-Dominique Bauby

Bathtime

At eight-thirty the physical therapist arrives. Brigitte, a woman with an athletic figure and an imperial Roman profile, has come to exercise my stiffened arms and legs. They call the exercise "mobilization," a term whose martial connotations contrast ludicrously with the paltry forces thus summoned, for I've lost sixty-six pounds in just twenty weeks. When I began a diet a week before my stroke, I never dreamed of such a dramatic result. As she works, Brigitte checks for the smallest flicker of improvement. "Try to squeeze my hand," she asks. Since I sometimes have the illusion that I am moving my fingers, I focus my energy on crushing her knuckles, but nothing stirs and she replaces my inert hand on its foam pad. In fact, the only sign of change is in my neck. I can now turn my head ninety degrees, and my field of vision extends from the slate roof of the building next door to the curious tongue-lolling Mickey Mouse drawn by my son, Théophile, when I was still unable to open my mouth. Now, after regular exercise, we have reached the stage of slipping a lollipop into it. As the neurologist says, "We need to be very patient." The session with Brigitte ends with a facial massage. Her warm fingers travel all over my face, including the numb zone, which seems to me to have the texture of parchment, and the area that still has feeling, where I can manage the beginnings of a frown. Since the demarcation line runs across my mouth, I can only half-smile, which fairly faithfully reflects my ups and downs. A domestic event as commonplace as washing can trigger the most varied emotions.

One day, for example, I can find it amusing, in my forty-fifth year, to be cleaned up and turned over, to have my bottom wiped and swaddled like a newborn's. I even derive a guilty pleasure from this total lapse into infancy. But the next day, the same procedure seems to me unbearably sad, and a tear rolls down through the lather a nurse's aide spreads over my cheeks. And my weekly bath plunges me simultaneously into distress and happiness. The delectable moment when I sink into the tub is quickly followed by nostalgia for the protracted immersions that were the joy of my previous life. Armed with a cup of tea or a Scotch, a good book or a pile of newspapers, I would soak for hours, maneuvering the taps with my toes. Rarely do I feel my condition so cruelly as when I am recalling such pleasures. Luckily I have no time for gloomy thoughts. Already they are wheeling me back, shivering, to my room, on a gurney as comfortable as a bed of nails. I must be fully dressed by ten-thirty and ready to go to the rehabilitation center. Having turned down the hideous jogging suit provided by the hospital, I am now attired as I was in my student days. Like the bath, my old clothes could easily bring back poignant, painful memories. But I see in the clothing a symbol of continuing life. And proof that I still want to be myself. If I must drool, I may as well drool on cashmere. [1998]

Jo Ann Beard

The Fourth State of Matter

The collie wakes me up about three times a night, summoning me from a great distance as I row my boat through a dim, complicated dream. She's on the shoreline, barking. Wake up. She's staring at me with her head slightly tipped to the side, long nose, gazing eyes, toenails clenched to get a purchase on the wood floor. We used to call her the face of love.

She totters on her broomstick legs into the hallway and over the doorsill into the kitchen, makes a sharp left at the refrigerator—careful, almost went down—then a straightaway to the door. I sleep on my feet, in the cold of the doorway, waiting. Here she comes. Lift her down the two steps. She pees and then stands, Lassie in a ratty coat, gazing out at the yard.

In the porchlight the trees shiver, the squirrels turn over in their sleep. The Milky Way is a long smear on the sky, like something erased on a chalkboard. Over the neighbor's house Mars flashes white, then red, then white again. Jupiter is hidden among the anonymous blinks and glitterings. It has a moon with sulfur-spewing volcanoes and a beautiful name: Io. I learned it at work, from the group of men who surround me there. Space physicists, guys who spend days on end with their heads poked through the fabric of the sky, listening to the sounds of the universe. Guys whose own lives are ticking like alarm clocks getting ready to go off, although none of us is aware of it yet.

The collie turns and looks, waits to be carried up the two steps. Inside the house, she drops like a shoe onto her blanket, a thud, an adjustment. I've climbed back under my covers already but her leg's stuck underneath her, we can't get comfortable. I fix the leg, she rolls over and sleeps. Two hours later I wake up again and she's gazing at me in the darkness. The face of love. She wants to go out again. I give her a boost, balance her on her legs. Right on time: 3:40 a.m.

There are squirrels living in the spare bedroom upstairs. Three dogs also live in this house, but they were invited. I keep the door of the spare bedroom shut at all times, because of the squirrels and because that's where the vanished husband's belongings are stored. Two of the dogs—the smart little brown mutt and the Labrador—spend hours sitting patiently outside the door, waiting for it to be opened so they can dismantle the squirrels. The collie can no longer make it up the stairs, so she lies at the bottom and snores or stares in an interested manner at the furniture around her.

I can take almost anything at this point. For instance, that my vanished husband is neither here nor there; he's reduced himself to a troubled voice on the telephone three or four times a day.

Or that the dog at the bottom of the stairs keeps having mild strokes which cause her to tilt her head inquisitively and also to fall over. She drinks prodigious amounts of water and pees great volumes onto the folded blankets where she sleeps. Each time this happens I stand her up, dry her off, put fresh blankets underneath her, carry the peed-on blankets down to the basement, stuff them into the washer and then into the dryer. By the time I bring them back upstairs they are needed again. The first few times this happened I found the dog trying to stand up, gazing with frantic concern at her own rear. I praised her and patted her head and gave her treats until she settled down. Now I know whenever it happens because I hear her tail thumping against the floor in anticipation of reward. In retraining her I've somehow retrained myself, bustling cheerfully down to the basement, arms drenched in urine, the task of doing load after load of laundry strangely satisfying. She is Pavlov and I am her dog.

I'm fine about the vanished husband's boxes stored in the spare bedroom. For now the boxes and the phone calls persuade me that things could turn around at any moment. The boxes are filled with thirteen years of his pack-rattedness: statistics textbooks that still harbor an air of desperation, smarmy suitcoats from the Goodwill, various old Halloween masks and one giant black papier-mâché thing that was supposed to be Elvis's hair but didn't turn out. A collection of ancient Rolling Stones T-shirts. You know he's turning over a new leaf when he leaves the Rolling Stones behind.

What I can't take are the squirrels. They come alive at night throwing terrible parties in the spare bedroom, making thumps and crashes. Occasionally a high-pitched squeal is heard amid bumps and the sound of scrabbling toenails. I've taken to sleeping downstairs, on the blue vinyl dog couch, the sheets slipping off, my skin stuck to the cushions. This is an affront to two of the dogs, who know the couch belongs to them; as soon as I settle in they creep up and find their places between my knees and elbows.

I'm on the couch because the dog on the blanket gets worried at night. During the day she sleeps the catnappy sleep of the elderly, but when it gets dark her eyes open and she is agitated, trying to stand whenever I leave the room, settling down only when I'm next to her. We are in this together, the dying game, and I read for hours in the evening, one foot on her back, getting up only to open a new can of beer or take peed-on blankets to the basement.

At some point I stretch out on the vinyl couch and close my eyes, one hand hanging down, touching her side. By morning the dog-arm has become a nerveless club that doesn't come around until noon. My friends think I'm nuts.

One night, for hours, the dog won't lie down, stands braced on her rickety legs in the middle of the living room, looking at me and slowly wagging her tail. Each time I get her situated on her blankets and try to stretch out on the couch she stands up, looks at me, wags her tail. I call my office pal, Mary, and wake her up. "*I'm weary,*" I say, in italics.

Mary listens, sympathetic, on the other end. "Oh my God," she finally says, "*what* are you going to do?"

I calm down immediately. "Exactly what I'm doing," I tell her. The dog finally parks herself with a thump on the stack of damp blankets. She sets her nose down and tips her eyes up to watch me. We all sleep then, for a bit, while the squirrels sort through the boxes overhead and the dog on the blanket keeps nervous watch.

I've called in tired to work. It's midmorning and I'm shuffling around in my long underwear, smoking cigarettes and drinking coffee. The whole house is bathed in sunlight and the faint odor of used diapers. The collie is on her blanket, taking one of her vampirish daytime naps. The other two dogs are being mild-mannered and charming. I nudge the collie with my foot.

"Wake up and smell zee bacons," I say. She startles awake, lifts her nose groggily, and falls back asleep. I get ready for the office.

"I'm leaving and I'm never coming back," I say while putting on my coat. I use my mother's aggrieved, underappreciated tone. The little brown dog wags her tail, transferring her gaze from me to the table, which is the last place she remembers seeing toast. The collie continues her ghoulish sleep, eyes partially open, teeth exposed, while the Labrador, who understands English, begins howling miserably. She wins the toast sweepstakes and is chewing loudly when I leave, the little dog barking ferociously at her.

Work is its usual comforting green-corridored self. There are three blinks on the answering machine, the first from an author who speaks very slowly, like a kindergarten teacher, asking about reprints. "What am I, the village idiot?" I ask the room taking down his number in large backward characters. The second and third blinks are from my husband, the across-town apartment dweller.

The first makes my heart lurch in a hopeful way. "I have to talk to you right *now*," he says grimly. "Where *are* you? I can never find you."

"Try calling your own house," I say to the machine. In the second message he has composed himself.

"I'm *fine* now," he says firmly. "Disregard previous message and don't call me back, please; I have meetings." Click, dial tone, rewind.

I feel crestfallen, the leaping heart settles back into its hole in my chest. I say damn it out loud, just as Chris strides into the office.

"What?" he asks defensively. He tries to think if he's done anything wrong recently. He checks the table for work; none there. He's on top of it. We have a genial relationship these days, reading the paper together in the mornings, congratulating ourselves on each issue of the journal. It's a space physics quarterly and he's the editor and I'm the managing editor. I know nothing about the science part; my job is to shepherd the manuscripts through the review process and create a journal out of the acceptable ones.

Christoph Goertz. He's hip in a professorial kind of way, tall and lanky and white-haired, forty-seven years old, with an elegant trace of accent from his native Germany. He has a great dog, a giant black outlaw named Mica who runs through the streets of Iowa City at night, inspecting garbage. She's big and friendly but a bad judge of character and frequently runs right into the arms of the dog catcher. Chris is always bailing her out.

"They don't understand dogs," he says.

I spend more time with Chris than I ever did with my husband. The morning I told him I was being dumped he was genuinely perplexed.

"He's leaving *you*?" he asked.

Chris was drinking coffee, sitting at his table in front of the chalkboard. Behind his head was a chalk drawing of a hip, professorial man holding a coffee cup. It was a collaborative effort; I drew the man and Chris framed him, using brown chalk and a straightedge. The two-dimensional man and the three-dimensional man stared at me intently.

"He's leaving *you*?" And for an instant I saw myself from their vantage point across the room—Jo Ann—and a small bubble of self-esteem percolated up from the depths. Chris shrugged. "You'll do fine," he said.

During my current turmoils, I've come to think of work as my own kind of zen practice, the constant barrage of paper hypnotic and soothing. Chris lets me work an erratic, eccentric schedule, which gives me time to pursue my nonexistent writing career. In return I update his publications list for him and listen to stories about outer space.

Besides being an editor and a teacher, he's the head of a theoretical plasma physics team made up of graduate students and research scientists. During the summers he travels all over the world telling people about the magnetospheres of various planets, and when he comes back he brings me presents—a small bronze box from Africa with an alligator embossed on the top, a big piece of amber from Poland with the wings of flies preserved inside it, and, once, a set of delicate, horrifying bracelets made from the hide of an elephant.

Currently he is obsessed with the dust in the plasma of Saturn's rings. Plasma is the fourth state of matter. You've got your solid, your liquid, your gas, and then your plasma. In outer space there's the plasmasphere and the plasmapause. I like to avoid the math when I can and put a layperson's spin on these things.

"Plasma is blood," I told him.

"Exactly," he agreed, removing the comics page and handing it to me.

Mostly we have those kinds of conversations around the office, but today he's caught me at a weak moment, tucking my heart back inside my chest. I decide to be cavalier.

"I wish my *dog* was out tearing up the town and my *husband* was home peeing on a blanket," I say.

Chris thinks the dog thing has gone far enough. "Why are you letting this go on?" he asks solemnly.

"I'm not *letting* it, that's why," I tell him. There are stacks of manuscripts everywhere and he has all the pens over on his side of the room. "It just *is*, is all. Throw me a pen." He does, I miss it, stoop to pick it up, and when I straighten up again I might be crying.

You have control over this, he explains in his professor voice. You can decide how long she suffers.

This makes my heart pound. Absolutely not, I cannot do it. And then I weaken and say what I really want. For her to go to sleep and not wake up, just slip out of her skin and into the other world.

"Exactly," he says.

I have an ex-beauty queen coming over to get rid of the squirrels for me. She has long red hair and a smile that can stop trucks. I've seen her wrestle goats, scare off a giant snake, and express a dog's anal glands, all in one afternoon. I told her on the phone that a family of squirrels is living in the upstairs of my house and there's nothing I can do about it.

"They're making a monkey out of me," I said.

So Caroline climbs in her car and drives across half the state, pulls up in front of my house, and gets out carrying zucchinis, cigarettes, and a pair of big leather gloves. I'm sitting outside with my sweet old dog, who lurches to her feet, staggers three steps, sits down, and falls over. Caroline starts crying.

"Don't try to give me zucchini," I tell her.

We sit companionably on the front stoop for a while, staring at the dog and smoking cigarettes. One time I went to Caroline's house and she was nursing a dead cat that was still breathing. At some point that afternoon I saw her spoon baby food into its mouth and as soon as she turned away the whole pureed mess plopped back out. A day later she took it to the vet and had it euthanized. I remind her of this.

"You'll do it when you do it," she says firmly.

I pick the collie up like a fifty-pound bag of sticks and feathers, stagger inside, place her on the damp blankets, and put the other two nutcases in the backyard. From upstairs comes a crash and a shriek. Caroline stares up at the ceiling.

"It's like having the Wallendas stay at your house," I say cheerfully. All of a sudden I feel fond of the squirrels and fond of Caroline and fond of myself for heroically calling her to help me. The phone rings four times. It's the husband, and his voice over the answering machine sounds frantic. He pleads with whoever Jo Ann is to pick up the phone.

"Please? I think I might be freaking out," he says. "Am I ruining my life here, or what? Am I making a *mistake*? Jo?" He breathes raggedly and sniffs into the receiver for a moment then hangs up with a muffled clatter.

Caroline stares at the machine like it's a copperhead.

"Holy fuckoly," she says, shaking her head. "You're *living* with this crap?"

"He wants me to reassure him that he's strong enough to leave me," I tell her. "Else he won't have fun on his bike ride. And guess what; I'm too tired to." Except that now I can see him in his dank little apartment, wringing his hands and staring out the windows. He's wearing his Sunday hairdo with baseball cap trying to scrunch it down. In his rickety dresser is the new package of condoms he accidentally showed me last week.

Caroline lights another cigarette. The dog pees and thumps her tail.

I need to call him back because he's suffering.

"You call him back and I'm forced to kill you," Caroline says. She exhales smoke and points to the phone. "That is evil shit," she says.

I tend to agree. It's blanket time. I roll the collie off onto the floor and put the fresh ones down, roll her back. She stares at me with the face of love. I get her a treat, which she chews with gusto and then goes back to sleep. I carry the blankets down to the basement and stuff them into the machine, trudge back up the stairs. Caroline has finished smoking her medicine and is wearing the leather gloves which go all the way to her elbows. She's staring at the ceiling with determination.

The plan is that I'm supposed to separate one from the herd and get it in a corner. Caroline will take it from there. Unfortunately, my nerves are shot, and when I'm in the room with her and the squirrels are running around all I can do is scream. I'm not even afraid of them, but my screaming button is stuck on and the only way to turn it off is to leave the room.

"How are you doing?" I ask from the other side of the door. All I can hear is Caroline crashing around and swearing. Suddenly there is a high-pitched screech that doesn't end. The door opens and Caroline falls out into the hall, with a gray squirrel stuck to her glove. Brief pandemonium and then she clatters down the stairs and out the front door and returns looking triumphant.

The collie appears at the foot of the stairs with her head cocked and her ears up. She looks like a puppy for an instant, and then her feet start to slide. I run down and catch her and carry her upstairs so she can watch the show. They careen around the room, tearing the ancient wallpaper off the walls. The last one is a baby, so we keep it for a few minutes, looking at its little feet and its little tail. We show it to the collie, who stands up immediately and tries to get it.

Caroline patches the hole where they got in, cutting wood with a power saw down in the basement. She comes up wearing a toolbelt and lugging a ladder. I've seen a scrapbook of photos of her wearing evening gowns with a banner across her chest and a crown on her head. Curled hair, lipstick. She climbs down and puts the tools away. We eat nachos.

"I only make food that's boiled or melted these days," I tell her.

"I know," she replies.

We smoke cigarettes and think. The phone rings again but whoever it is hangs up.

"Is it him?" she asks. "Nope."

The collie sleeps on her blankets while the other two dogs sit next to Caroline on the couch. She's looking through their ears for mites. At some point she gestures to the sleeping dog on the blanket and remarks that it seems like just two days ago she was a puppy.

"She was never a puppy," I say. "She's always been older than me." When they say goodbye, she holds the collie's long nose in one hand and kisses her on the forehead; the collie stares back at her gravely. Caroline is crying when she leaves, a combination of squirrel adrenaline, and sadness. I cry, too, although I don't feel particularly bad about anything. I hand her the zucchini through the window and she pulls away from the curb.

The house is starting to get dark in that terrible early evening twilit way. I turn on lights, get a cigarette, and go upstairs to the former squirrel room. The black dog comes with me and circles the room, snorting loudly, nose to floor. There is a spot of turmoil in an open box—they made a nest in some old disco shirts from the seventies. I suspect that's where the baby one slept. The mean landlady has evicted them.

Downstairs, I turn the lights back off and let evening have its way with me. Waves of pre-nighttime nervousness are coming from the collie's blanket. I sit next to her in the dimness touching her ears, and listen for feet at the top of the stairs.

They're speaking in physics so I'm left out of the conversation. Chris apologetically erases one of the pictures I've drawn on the blackboard and replaces it with a curving blue arrow surrounded by radiating chalk waves of green.

"If it's plasma, make it in red," I suggest helpfully. We're all smoking illegally in the journal office with the door closed and the window open. We're having a plasma party.

"We aren't discussing *plasma*," Bob says condescendingly. He's smoking a horrendously smelly pipe. The longer he stays in here the more it feels like I'm breathing small daggers in through my nose. He and I don't get along; each of us thinks the other needs to be taken down a peg. Once we had a hissing match in the hallway which ended with him suggesting that I could be fired, which drove me to tell him he was *already* fired, and both of us stomped into our offices and slammed our doors.

"I had to fire Bob," I tell Chris later.

"I heard," he says noncommittally. Bob is his best friend. They spend at least half of each day standing in front of chalkboards, writing equations and arguing about outer space. Then they write theoretical papers about what they come up with. They're actually quite a big deal in the space physics community, but around here they're just two guys who keep erasing my pictures.

Someone knocks on the door and we put our cigarettes out. Bob hides his pipe in the palm of his hand and opens the door.

It's Gang Lu, one of their students. Everyone lights up again. Gang Lu stands stiffly talking to Chris while Bob holds a match to his pipe and puffs fiercely; nose daggers waft up and out, right in my direction. I give him a sugary smile and he gives me one back. Unimaginable, really, that less than two months from now one of his colleagues from abroad, a woman with delicate, birdlike features, will appear at the door to my office and identify herself as a friend of Bob's. When she asks, I take her down the hall to the room with the long table and then to his empty office. I do this without saying anything because there's nothing to say, and she takes it all in with small, serious nods until the moment she sees his blackboard covered with scribbles and arrows and equations. At that point her face loosens and she starts to cry in long ragged sobs. An hour later I go back and the office is empty. When I erase the blackboard finally, I can see where she laid her hands carefully, where the numbers are ghostly and blurred.

Bob blows his smoke discreetly in my direction and waits for Chris to finish talking to Gang Lu, who is answering questions in a monotone—yes or no, or I don't know. Another Chinese student named Shan lets himself in after knocking lightly. He nods and smiles at me and then stands at a respectful distance waiting to ask Chris a question.

It's like a physics conference in here. I wish they'd all leave so I could make my usual midafternoon spate of personal calls. I begin thumbing through papers in a businesslike way.

Bob pokes at his pipe with a bent paper clip. Shan yawns hugely and then looks embarrassed. Chris erases what he put on the blackboard and tries unsuccessfully to redraw my pecking parakeet. "I don't know how it goes," he says to me.

Gang Lu looks around the room idly with expressionless eyes. He's sick of physics and sick of the buffoons who practice it. The tall glacial German, Chris, who tells him what to do; the crass idiot Bob who talks to him like he is a dog; the student Shan whose ideas about plasma physics are treated with reverence and praised at every meeting. The woman who puts her feet on the desk and dismisses him with her eyes. Gang Lu no longer spends his evenings in the computer lab, running simulations and thinking about magnetic forces and invisible particles; he now spends them at the firing range, learning to hit a moving target with the gun he purchased last spring. He pictures himself holding the gun with both hands, arms straight out and steady; Clint Eastwood, only smarter. Clint Eastwood as a rocket scientist.

He stares at each person in turn, trying to gauge how much respect each of them has for him. One by one. Behind black-rimmed glasses, he counts with his eyes. In each case the verdict is clear: not enough.

The collie fell down the basement stairs. I don't know if she was disoriented and looking for me or what. But when I was at work she used her long nose like a lever and got the door to the basement open and tried to go down there except her legs wouldn't do it and she fell. I found her sleeping on the concrete floor in an unnatural position, one leg still awkwardly resting on the last step. I repositioned the leg and sat down next to her and petted her. We used to play a game called Maserati, where I'd grab her nose like a gearshift and put her through all the gears, first second third fourth, until we were going a hundred miles an hour through town. She thought it was funny.

Now I'm at work but this morning there's nothing to do, and every time I turn around I see her sprawled, eyes mute, leg bent upward. We're breaking each other's hearts. I draw a picture of her on the blackboard using brown chalk. I make *X*s where her eyes should be. Chris walks in with the morning paper and a cup of coffee. He looks around the clean office.

"Why are you here when there's no work to do?" he asks.

"I'm hiding from my life, what else," I tell him. This sounds perfectly reasonable to him. He gives me part of the paper.

His mother is visiting from Germany, a robust woman of eighty who is depressed and hoping to be cheered up. In the last year she has lost her one-hundred-year-old mother and her husband of sixty years. She mostly can't be cheered up, but she likes going to art galleries so Chris has been driving her around the Midwest, to our best cities, showing her what kind of art Americans like to look at.

"How's your mom?" I ask him.

He shrugs and makes a flat-handed so-so motion.

We read, smoke, drink coffee, and yawn. I decide to go home.

"Good idea," he says encouragingly.

It's November 1, 1991, the last day of the first part of my life. Before I leave I pick up the eraser and stand in front of the collie's picture on the blackboard, thinking. I can feel him watching me, drinking his coffee. He's wearing a gold shirt and blue jeans and a gray cardigan sweater. He is tall and lanky and white-haired, forty-seven years old. He has a wife named Ulrike, a daughter named Karein, and a son named Goran. A dog named Mica. A mother named Ursula. A friend named me.

I erase the *X*s.

Down the hall, Linhua Shan feeds numbers into a computer and watches as a graph is formed. The computer screen is brilliant blue, and the lines appear in red and yellow and green. Four keystrokes and the green becomes purple. More keystrokes and the blue background fades to the azure of a summer sky. The wave lines arc over it, crossing against one another. He asks the computer to print, and while it chugs along he pulls up a golf game on the screen and tees off.

One room over, at a desk, Gang Lu works on a letter to his sister in China. *The study of physics is more and more disappointing, he tells her. Modern physics is self-delusion and all my life I have been honest and straightforward, and I have most of all detested cunning, fawning sycophants and dishonest bureaucrats who think they are always right in everything.* Delicate Chinese characters all over a page. She was a kind and gentle sister, and he thanks her for that. He's going to kill himself. *You yourself should not be too sad about it, for at least I have found a few traveling companions to accompany me to the grave.* Inside the coat on the back of his chair are a .38-caliber handgun and a .22-caliber revolver. They're heavier than they look and weigh the pockets down. *My beloved elder sister, I take my eternal leave of you.*

The collie's eyes are almond-shaped; I draw them in with brown chalk and put a white bone next to her feet.

"That's better," Chris says kindly.

Before I leave the building I pass Gang Lu in the hallway and say hello. He has a letter in his hand and he's wearing his coat. He doesn't answer and I don't expect him to. At the end of the hallway are the double doors leading to the rest of my life. I push them open and walk through.

Friday afternoon seminar, everyone is glazed over, listening as someone explains something unexplainable at the head of the long table. Gang Lu stands up and leaves the room abruptly; goes down one floor to see if the chairman, Dwight, is sitting in his office. He is. The door is open. Gang Lu turns and walks back up the stairs and enters the meeting room again. Chris Goertz is sitting near the door and takes the first bullet in the back of the head. There is a loud popping sound and then blue smoke. Shan gets the second bullet in the forehead, the lenses of his glasses shatter. More smoke and the room rings with the popping. Bob Smith tries to crawl beneath the table. Gang Lu takes two steps, holds his arms straight out, and levels the gun with both hands. Bob looks up. The third bullet in the right hand, the fourth in the chest. Smoke. Elbows and legs, people trying to get out of the way and then out of the room.

Gang Lu walks quickly down the stairs, dispelling spent cartridges and loading new ones. From the doorway of Dwight's office: the fifth bullet in the head, the sixth strays, the seventh also in the head. A slumping. More smoke and ringing. Through the cloud an image comes forward—Bob Smith, hit in the chest, hit in the hand, still alive. Back up the stairs. Two scientists, young men, crouched over Bob, loosening his clothes, talking to him. From where he lies, Bob can see his best friend still sitting upright in a chair, head thrown back at an unnatural angle. Everything is broken and red. The two young scientists leave the room at gunpoint. Bob closes his eyes. The eighth and ninth bullets in his head. As Bob dies, Chris Goertz's body settles in his chair, a long sigh escapes his throat. Reload. Two more for Chris, one for Shan. Exit the building, cross two streets, run across the green, into building number two and upstairs.

The administrator, Anne Cleary, is summoned from her office by the receptionist. She speaks to him for a few seconds, he produces the gun and shoots her in the face. The receptionist, a young student working as a temp, is just beginning to stand when he shoots her in the mouth. He dispels the spent cartridges in the stairwell, loads new ones. Reaches the top of the steps, looks around. Is disoriented suddenly. The ringing and the smoke and the dissatisfaction of not checking all the names off the list. A slamming and a running sound, the shout of police. He walks into an empty classroom, takes off his coat, folds it carefully and puts it over the back of the chair. Checks his watch; twelve minutes since it began. Places the barrel against his right temple. Fires.

The first call comes at four o'clock. I'm reading on the bench in the kitchen, one foot on a sleeping dog's back. It's Mary, calling from work. There's been some kind of disturbance in the building, a rumor that Dwight was shot; cops are running through the halls carrying rifles. They're evacuating the building and she's coming over.

Dwight, a tall likable oddball who cut off his ponytail when they made him chair of the department. Greets everyone with a famous booming hello in the morning, studies plasma, just like Chris and Bob. Chris lives two and half blocks from the physics building; he'll be home by now if they've evacuated. I dial his house and his mother answers. She tells me that Chris won't be home until five o'clock, and then they're going to a play. Ulrike, her daughter-in-law, is coming back from a trip to Chicago and will join them. She wants to know why I'm looking for Chris; isn't he where I am?

No, I'm at home and I just had to ask him something. Could he please call me when he comes in.

She tells me that Chris showed her a drawing I made of him sitting at his desk behind a stack of manuscripts. She's so pleased to meet Chris's friends, and the Midwest is lovely, really, except it's very brown, isn't it?

It *is* very brown. We hang up.

The Midwest is very brown. The phone rings. It's a physicist. His wife, a friend of mine, is on the extension. Well, he's not sure, but it's possible that I should brace myself for bad news. I've already heard, I tell him, something happened to Dwight. There's a long pause and then his wife says, Jo Ann. It's possible that Chris was involved.

I think she means Chris shot Dwight. No, she says gently, killed too.

Mary is here. I tell them not to worry and hang up. I have two cigarettes going. Mary takes one and smokes it. She's not looking at me. I tell her about the phone call.

"They're out of it," I say. "They thought Chris was involved."

She repeats what they said: I think you should brace yourself for bad news. Pours whiskey in a coffee cup.

For a few minutes I can't sit down, I can't stand up. I can only smoke. The phone rings. Another physicist tells me there's some bad news. He mentions Chris and Bob and I tell him I don't want to talk right now. He says okay but to be prepared because it's going to be on the news any minute. It's 4:45.

"Now they're trying to stir Bob into the stew," I tell Mary. She nods; she's heard this, too. I have the distinct feeling there is something going on that I can either understand or not understand. There's a choice to be made.

"I don't understand," I tell Mary.

We sit in the darkening living room, smoking and sipping our cups of whiskey. Inside my head I keep thinking *Uh-oh*, over and over. I'm in a rattled condition; I can't calm down and figure this out.

"I think we should brace ourselves in case something bad has happened," I say to Mary. She nods. "Just in case. It won't hurt to be braced." She nods again. I realize that I don't know what *braced* means. You hear it all the time but that doesn't mean it makes sense. Whiskey is supposed to be bracing but what it is is awful. I want either tea or beer, no whiskey. Mary nods and heads into the kitchen.

Within an hour there are seven women in the dim living room, sitting. Switching back and forth between CNN and the special reports by the local news. There is something terrifying about the quality of the light and the way voices are echoing in the room. The phone never stops ringing, ever since the story hit the national news. Physics, University of Iowa, dead people. Names not yet released. Everyone I've ever known is checking in to see if I'm still alive. California calls, New York calls, Florida calls, Ohio calls twice. All the guests at a party my husband is having call, one after the other, to ask how I'm doing. Each time, fifty times, I think it might be Chris and then it isn't.

It occurs to me once that I could call his house and talk to him directly, find out exactly what happened. Fear that his mother would answer prevents me from doing it. By this time I am getting reconciled to the fact that Shan, Gang Lu, and Dwight were killed. Also an administrator and her office assistant. The Channel 9 newslady keeps saying there are six dead and two in critical condition. They're not saying who did the shooting. The names will be released at nine o'clock. Eventually I sacrifice all of them except Chris and Bob; they are the ones in critical condition, which is certainly not hopeless. At some point I go into the study to get away from the terrible dimness in the living room, all those eyes, all that calmness in the face of chaos. The collie tries to stand up but someone stops her with a handful of Fritos.

The study is small and cold after I shut the door, but more brightly lit than the living room. I can't remember what anything means. The phone rings and I pick up the extension and listen. My friend Michael is calling from Illinois for the second time. He asks Shirley if I'm holding up okay. Shirley says it's hard to tell. I go back into the living room.

The newslady breaks in at nine o'clock, and of course they drag it out as long as they can. I've already figured out that if they go in alphabetical order Chris will come first. Goertz, Lu, Nicholson, Shan, Smith. His name will come on first. She drones on, dead University of Iowa professors, lone gunman named Gang Lu.

Gang Lu. Lone gunman. Before I have a chance to absorb that she says, The dead are.

Chris's picture.

Oh no, oh God. I lean against Mary's chair and then leave the room abruptly. I have to stand in the bathroom for a while and look at myself in the mirror. I'm still Jo Ann, white face and dark hair. I have earrings on, tiny wrenches that hang from wires. In the living room she's pronouncing all the other names. The two critically wounded are the administrator and her assistant, Miya Sioson. The administrator is already dead for all practical purposes, although they won't disconnect the machines until the following afternoon. The student receptionist will survive but will never again be able to move more than her head. She was in Gang Lu's path and he shot her in the mouth and the bullet lodged in the top of her spine and not only will she never dance again, she'll never walk or write or spend a day alone. She got to keep her head but lost her body. The final victim is Chris's mother, who will weather it all with a dignified face and an erect spine, then return to Germany and kill herself without further words or fanfare.

I tell the white face in the mirror that Gang Lu did this, wrecked everything and killed all those people. It seems as ludicrous as everything else. I can't get my mind to work right, I'm still operating on yesterday's facts; today hasn't jelled yet. "It's a good thing none of this happened," I say to my face. A knock on the door and I open it.

The collie is swaying on her feet, toenails clenched to keep from sliding on the wood floor. Julene's hesitant face. "She wanted to come visit you," she tells me. I bring her in and close the door. We sit by the tub. She lifts her long nose to my face and I take her muzzle and we move through the gears slowly, first second third fourth, all the way through town, until what happened has happened and we know it has happened. We return to the living room. The second wave of calls is starting to come in, from those who just saw the faces on the news. Shirley screens. A knock comes on the door. Julene settles the dog down again on her blanket. It's the husband at the door, looking frantic. He hugs me hard but I'm made of cement, arms stuck in a down position.

The women immediately clear out, taking their leave, looking at the floor. Suddenly it's only me and him, sitting in our living room on a Friday night, just like always. I realize it took quite a bit of courage for him to come to the house when he did, facing all those women who think he's the Antichrist. The dogs are crowded against him on the couch and he's wearing a shirt I've never seen before. He's here to help me get through this. Me. He knows how awful this must be. Awful. He knows how I felt about Chris. Past tense. I have to put my hands over my face for a minute.

We sit silently in our living room. He watches the mute television screen and I watch him. The planes and ridges of his face are more familiar to me than my own. I understand that he wishes even more than I do that he still loved me. When he looks over at me, it's with an expression I've seen before. It's the way he looks at the dog on the blanket.

I get his coat and follow him out into the cold November night. There are stars and stars and stars. The sky is full of dead men, drifting in the blackness like helium balloons. My mother floats past in a hospital gown, trailing tubes. I go back inside where the heat is.

The house is empty and dim, full of dogs and cigarette butts. The collie has peed again. The television is flickering *Special Report* across the screen and I turn it off before the pictures appear. I bring blankets up, fresh and warm from the dryer.

After all the commotion the living room feels cavernous and dead. A branch scrapes against the house and for a brief instant I feel a surge of hope. They might have come back. And I stand at the foot of the stairs staring up into the darkness, listening for the sounds of their little squirrel feet. Silence. No matter how much you miss them. They never come back once they're gone.

I wake her up three times between midnight and dawn. She doesn't usually sleep this soundly but all the chaos and company in the house tonight have made her more tired than usual. The Lab wakes and drowsily begins licking her lower region. She stops and stares at me, trying to make out my face in the dark, then gives up and sleeps. The brown dog is flat on her back with her paws limp, wedged between me and the back of the couch.

I've propped myself so I'll be able to see when dawn starts to arrive. For now there are still planets and stars. Above the black branches of a maple is the dog star, Sirius, my personal favorite. The dusty rings of Saturn. Io, Jupiter's moon.

When I think I can't bear it for one more minute I reach down and nudge her gently with my dog-arm. She rises slowly, faltering, and stands over me in the darkness. My peer, my colleague. In a few hours the world will resume itself, but for now we're in a pocket of silence. We're in the plasmapause, a place of equilibrium, where the forces of the Earth meet the forces of the sun. I imagine it as a place of silence, where the particles of dust stop spinning and hang motionless in deep space.

Around my neck is the stone he brought me from Poland. I hold it out. *Like this?* I ask. Shards of fly wings, suspended in amber.

Exactly, he says. [1996]

Ambrose Bierce

An Occurrence at Owl Creek Bridge

A man stood upon a railroad bridge in northern Alabama, looking down into the swift water twenty feet below. The man's hands were behind his back, the wrists bound with a cord. A rope closely encircled his neck. It was attached to a stout cross-timber above his head and the slack fell to the level of his knees. Some loose boards laid upon the ties supporting the rails of the railway supplied a footing for him and his executioners—two private soldiers of the Federal army, directed by a sergeant who in civil life may have been a deputy sheriff. At a short remove upon the same temporary platform was an officer in the uniform of his rank, armed. He was a captain. A sentinel at each end of the bridge stood with his rifle in the position known as "support," that is to say, vertical in front of the left shoulder, the hammer resting on the forearm thrown straight across the chest—a formal and unnatural position, enforcing an erect carriage of the body. It did not appear to be the duty of these two men to know what was occurring at the center of the bridge; they merely blockaded the two ends of the foot planking that traversed it.

Beyond one of the sentinels nobody was in sight; the railroad ran straight away into a forest for a hundred yards, then, curving, was lost to view. Doubtless there was an outpost farther along. The other bank of the stream was open ground—a gentle slope topped with a stockade of vertical tree trunks, loopholed for rifles, with a single embrasure through which protruded the muzzle of a brass cannon commanding the bridge. Midway up the slope between the bridge and fort were the spectators—a single company of infantry in line, at "parade rest," the butts of their rifles on the ground, the barrels inclining slightly backward against the right shoulder, the hands crossed upon the stock. A lieutenant stood at the right of the line, the point of his sword upon the ground, his left hand resting upon his right. Excepting the group of four at the center of the bridge, not a man moved. The company faced the bridge, staring stonily, motionless. The sentinels, facing the banks of the stream, might have been statues to adorn the bridge. The captain stood with folded arms, silent, observing the work of his subordinates, but making no sign. Death is a dignitary who when he comes announced is to be received with formal manifestations of respect, even by those most familiar with him. In the code of military etiquette silence and fixity are forms of deference.

The man who was engaged in being hanged was apparently about thirty-five years of age. He was a civilian, if one might judge from his habit, which was that of a planter. His features were good—a straight nose, firm mouth, broad forehead, from which his long, dark hair was combed straight back, falling behind his ears to the collar of his well fitting frock coat. He wore a moustache and pointed beard, but no whiskers; his eyes were large and dark gray, and had a kindly expression which one would hardly have expected in one whose neck was in the hemp. Evidently this was no vulgar assassin. The liberal military code makes provision for hanging many kinds of persons, and gentlemen are not excluded.

The preparations being complete, the two private soldiers stepped aside and each drew away the plank upon which he had been standing. The sergeant turned to the captain, saluted and placed himself immediately behind that officer, who in turn moved apart one pace. These movements left the condemned man and the sergeant standing on the two ends of the same plank, which spanned three of the cross-ties of the bridge. The end upon which the civilian stood almost, but not quite, reached a fourth. This plank had been held in place by the weight of the captain; it was now held by that of the sergeant. At a signal from the former the latter would step aside, the plank would tilt and the condemned man go down between two ties. The arrangement commended itself to his judgement as simple and effective. His face had not been covered nor his eyes bandaged. He looked a moment at his "unsteadfast footing," then let his gaze wander to the swirling water of the stream racing madly beneath his feet. A piece of dancing driftwood caught his attention and his eyes followed it down the current. How slowly it appeared to move! What a sluggish stream!

He closed his eyes in order to fix his last thoughts upon his wife and children. The water, touched to gold by the early sun, the brooding mists under the banks at some distance down the stream, the fort, the soldiers, the piece of drift—all had distracted him. And now he became conscious of a new disturbance. Striking through the thought of his dear ones was a sound which he could neither ignore nor understand, a sharp, distinct, metallic percussion like the stroke of a blacksmith's hammer upon the anvil; it had the same ringing quality. He wondered what it was, and whether immeasurably distant or near by—it seemed both. Its recurrence was regular, but as slow as the tolling of a death knell. He awaited each new stroke with impatience and—he knew not why—apprehension. The intervals of silence grew progressively longer; the delays became maddening. With their greater infrequency the sounds increased in strength and sharpness. They hurt his ear like the thrust of a knife; he feared he would shriek. What he heard was the ticking of his watch.

He unclosed his eyes and saw again the water below him. "If I could free my hands," he thought, "I might throw off the noose and spring into the stream. By diving I could evade the bullets and, swimming vigorously, reach the bank, take to the woods and get away home. My home, thank God, is as yet outside their lines; my wife and little ones are still beyond the invader's farthest advance."

As these thoughts, which have here to be set down in words, were flashed into the doomed man's brain rather than evolved from it the captain nodded to the sergeant. The sergeant stepped aside.

II

Peyton Farquhar was a well to do planter, of an old and highly respected Alabama family. Being a slave owner and like other slave owners a politician, he was naturally an original secessionist and ardently devoted to the Southern cause. Circumstances of an imperious nature, which it is unnecessary to relate here, had prevented him from taking service with that gallant army which had fought the disastrous campaigns ending with the fall of Corinth, and he chafed under the inglorious restraint, longing for the release of his energies, the larger life of the soldier, the opportunity for distinction. That opportunity, he felt, would come, as it comes to all in wartime. Meanwhile he did what he could. No service was too humble for him to perform in the aid of the South, no adventure too perilous for him to undertake if consistent with the character of a civilian who was at heart a soldier, and who in good faith and without too much qualification assented to at least a part of the frankly villainous dictum that all is fair in love and war.

One evening while Farquhar and his wife were sitting on a rustic bench near the entrance to his grounds, a gray-clad soldier rode up to the gate and asked for a drink of water. Mrs. Farquhar was only too happy to serve him with her own white hands. While she was fetching the water her husband approached the dusty horseman and inquired eagerly for news from the front.

"The Yanks are repairing the railroads," said the man, "and are getting ready for another advance. They have reached the Owl Creek bridge, put it in order and built a stockade on the north bank. The commandant has issued an order, which is posted everywhere, declaring that any civilian caught interfering with the railroad, its bridges, tunnels, or trains will be summarily hanged. I saw the order."

"How far is it to the Owl Creek bridge?" Farquhar asked.

"About thirty miles."

"Is there no force on this side of the creek?"

"Only a picket post half a mile out, on the railroad, and a single sentinel at this end of the bridge."

"Suppose a man—a civilian and student of hanging—should elude the picket post and perhaps get the better of the sentinel," said Farquhar, smiling, "what could he accomplish?"

The soldier reflected. "I was there a month ago," he replied. "I observed that the flood of last winter had lodged a great quantity of driftwood against the wooden pier at this end of the bridge. It is now dry and would burn like tinder."

The lady had now brought the water, which the soldier drank. He thanked her ceremoniously, bowed to her husband and rode away. An hour later, after nightfall, he repassed the plantation, going northward in the direction from which he had come. He was a Federal scout.

III

As Peyton Farquhar fell straight downward through the bridge he lost consciousness and was as one already dead. From this state he was awakened—ages later, it seemed to him—by the pain of a sharp pressure upon his throat, followed by a sense of suffocation. Keen, poignant agonies seemed to shoot from his neck downward through every fiber of his body and limbs. These pains appeared to flash along well defined lines of ramification and to beat with an inconceivably rapid periodicity. They seemed like streams of pulsating fire heating him to an intolerable temperature. As to his head, he was conscious of nothing but a feeling of fullness—of congestion. These sensations were unaccompanied by thought. The intellectual part of his nature was already effaced; he had power only to feel, and feeling was torment. He was conscious of motion. Encompassed in a luminous cloud, of which he was now merely the fiery heart, without material substance, he swung through unthinkable arcs of oscillation, like a vast pendulum. Then all at once, with terrible suddenness, the light about him shot upward with the noise of a loud splash; a frightful roaring was in his ears, and all was cold and dark. The power of thought was restored; he knew that the rope had broken and he had fallen into the stream. There was no additional strangulation; the noose about his neck was already suffocating him and kept the water from his lungs. To die of hanging at the bottom of a river!—the idea seemed to him ludicrous. He opened his eyes in the darkness and saw above him a gleam of light, but how distant, how inaccessible! He was still sinking, for the light became fainter and fainter until it was a mere glimmer. Then it began to grow and brighten, and he knew that he was rising toward the surface—knew it with reluctance, for he was now very comfortable. "To be hanged and drowned," he thought, "that is not so bad; but I do not wish to be shot. No; I will not be shot; that is not fair."

He was not conscious of an effort, but a sharp pain in his wrist apprised him that he was trying to free his hands. He gave the struggle his attention, as an idler might observe the feat of a juggler, without interest in the outcome. What splendid effort!—what magnificent, what superhuman strength! Ah, that was a fine endeavor! Bravo! The cord fell away; his arms parted and floated upward, the hands dimly seen on each side in the growing light. He watched them with a new interest as first one and then the other pounced upon the noose at his neck. They tore it away and thrust it fiercely aside, its undulations resembling those of a water snake. "Put it back, put it back!" He thought he shouted these words to his hands, for the undoing of the noose had been succeeded by the direst pang that he had yet experienced. His neck ached horribly; his brain was on fire, his heart, which had been fluttering faintly, gave a great leap, trying to force itself out at his mouth. His whole body was racked and wrenched with an insupportable anguish! But his disobedient hands gave no heed to the command. They beat the water vigorously with quick, downward strokes, forcing him to the surface. He felt his head emerge; his eyes were blinded by the sunlight; his chest expanded convulsively, and with a supreme and crowning agony his lungs engulfed a great draught of air, which instantly he expelled in a shriek!

He was now in full possession of his physical senses. They were, indeed, preternaturally keen and alert. Something in the awful disturbance of his organic system had so exalted and refined them that they made record of things never before perceived. He felt the ripples upon his face and heard their separate sounds as they struck. He looked at the forest on the bank of the stream, saw the individual trees, the leaves and the veining of each leaf—he saw the very insects upon them: the locusts, the brilliant bodied flies, the gray spiders stretching their webs from twig to twig. He noted the prismatic colors in all the dewdrops upon a million blades of grass. The humming of the gnats that danced above the eddies of the stream, the beating of the dragon flies' wings, the strokes of the water spiders' legs, like oars which had lifted their boat—all these made audible music. A fish slid along beneath his eyes and he heard the rush of its body parting the water.

He had come to the surface facing down the stream; in a moment the visible world seemed to wheel slowly round, himself the pivotal point, and he saw the bridge, the fort, the soldiers upon the bridge, the captain, the sergeant, the two privates, his executioners. They were in silhouette against the blue sky. They shouted and gesticulated, pointing at him. The captain had drawn his pistol, but did not fire; the others were unarmed. Their movements were grotesque and horrible, their forms gigantic.

Suddenly he heard a sharp report and something struck the water smartly within a few inches of his head, spattering his face with spray. He heard a second report, and saw one of the sentinels with his rifle at his shoulder, a light cloud of blue smoke rising from the muzzle. The man in the water saw the eye of the man on the bridge gazing into his own through the sights of the rifle. He observed that it was a gray eye and remembered having read that gray eyes were keenest, and that all famous marksmen had them. Nevertheless, this one had missed.

A counter-swirl had caught Farquhar and turned him half round; he was again looking at the forest on the bank opposite the fort. The sound of a clear, high voice in a monotonous singsong now rang out behind him and came across the water with a distinctness that pierced and subdued all other sounds, even the beating of the ripples in his ears. Although no soldier, he had frequented camps enough to know the dread significance of that deliberate, drawling, aspirated chant; the lieutenant on shore was taking a part in the morning's work. How coldly and pitilessly—with what an even, calm intonation, presaging, and enforcing tranquility in the men—with what accurately measured interval fell those cruel words:

"Company!... Attention!... Shoulder arms!... Ready!... Aim!... Fire!"

Farquhar dived—dived as deeply as he could. The water roared in his ears like the voice of Niagara, yet he heard the dull thunder of the volley and, rising again toward the surface, met shining bits of metal, singularly flattened, oscillating slowly downward. Some of them touched him on the face and hands, then fell away, continuing their descent. One lodged between his collar and neck; it was uncomfortably warm and he snatched it out.

As he rose to the surface, gasping for breath, he saw that he had been a long time under water; he was perceptibly farther downstream—nearer to safety. The soldiers had almost finished reloading; the metal ramrods flashed all at once in the sunshine as they were drawn from the barrels, turned in the air, and thrust into their sockets. The two sentinels fired again, independently and ineffectually.

The hunted man saw all this over his shoulder; he was now swimming vigorously with the current. His brain was as energetic as his arms and legs; he thought with the rapidity of lightning:

"The officer," he reasoned, "will not make that martinet's error a second time. It is as easy to dodge a volley as a single shot. He has probably already given the command to fire at will. God help me, I cannot dodge them all!"

An appalling splash within two yards of him was followed by a loud, rushing sound, DIMINUENDO, which seemed to travel back through the air to the fort and died in an explosion which stirred the very river to its deeps! A rising sheet of water curved over him, fell down upon him, blinded him, strangled him! The cannon had taken an hand in the game. As he shook his head free from the commotion of the smitten water he heard the deflected shot humming through the air ahead, and in an instant it was cracking and smashing the branches in the forest beyond.

"They will not do that again," he thought; "the next time they will use a charge of grape. I must keep my eye upon the gun; the smoke will apprise me—the report arrives too late; it lags behind the missile. That is a good gun."

Suddenly he felt himself whirled round and round—spinning like a top. The water, the banks, the forests, the now distant bridge, fort and men, all were commingled and blurred. Objects were represented by their colors only; circular horizontal streaks of color—that was all he saw. He had been caught in a vortex and was being whirled on with a velocity of advance and gyration that made him giddy and sick. In a few moments he was flung upon the gravel at the foot of the left bank of the stream—the southern bank—and behind a projecting point which concealed him from his enemies. The sudden arrest of his motion, the abrasion of one of his hands on the gravel, restored him, and he wept with delight. He dug his fingers into the sand, threw it over himself in handfuls and audibly blessed it. It looked like diamonds, rubies, emeralds; he could think of nothing beautiful which it did not resemble. The trees upon the bank were giant garden plants; he noted a definite order in their arrangement, inhaled the fragrance of their blooms. A strange roseate light shone through the spaces among their trunks and the wind made in their branches the music of Æolian harps. He had not wish to perfect his escape—he was content to remain in that enchanting spot until retaken.

A whiz and a rattle of grapeshot among the branches high above his head roused him from his dream. The baffled cannoneer had fired him a random farewell. He sprang to his feet, rushed up the sloping bank, and plunged into the forest.

All that day he traveled, laying his course by the rounding sun. The forest seemed interminable; nowhere did he discover a break in it, not even a woodman's road. He had not known that he lived in so wild a region. There was something uncanny in the revelation.

By nightfall he was fatigued, footsore, famished. The thought of his wife and children urged him on. At last he found a road which led him in what he knew to be the right direction. It was as wide and straight as a city street, yet it seemed untraveled. No fields bordered it, no dwelling anywhere. Not so much as the barking of a dog suggested human habitation. The black bodies of the trees formed a straight wall on both sides, terminating on the horizon in a point, like a diagram in a lesson in perspective. Overhead, as he looked up through this rift in the wood, shone great golden stars looking unfamiliar and grouped in strange constellations. He was sure they were arranged in some order which had a secret and malign significance. The wood on either side was full of singular noises, among which—once, twice, and again—he distinctly heard whispers in an unknown tongue.

His neck was in pain and lifting his hand to it found it horribly swollen. He knew that it had a circle of black where the rope had bruised it. His eyes felt congested; he could no longer close them. His tongue was swollen with thirst; he relieved its fever by thrusting it forward from between his teeth into the cold air. How softly the turf had carpeted the untraveled avenue—he could no longer feel the roadway beneath his feet!

Doubtless, despite his suffering, he had fallen asleep while walking, for now he sees another scene—perhaps he has merely recovered from a delirium. He stands at the gate of his own home. All is as he left it, and all bright and beautiful in the morning sunshine. He must have traveled the entire night. As he pushes open the gate and passes up the wide white walk, he sees a flutter of female garments; his wife, looking fresh and cool and sweet, steps down from the veranda to meet him. At the bottom of the steps she stands waiting, with a smile of ineffable joy, an attitude of matchless grace and dignity. Ah, how beautiful she is! He springs forwards with extended arms. As he is about to clasp her he feels a stunning blow upon the back of the neck; a blinding white light blazes all about him with a sound like the shock of a cannon—then all is darkness and silence!

Peyton Farquhar was dead; his body, with a broken neck, swung gently from side to side beneath the timbers of the Owl Creek bridge. [1890]

Barbara Bloom

Making Things Right

for my father

Driving through the apple orchards
heavy with fruit,
I realize I have let the anniversary of your death
slip by—ten years already, or is it eleven?
It's a gray morning, and the clouds press down,
obscuring the sun.

I wonder if you knew
when you had to be helped on with your shoes
for the ride to the hospital
that you would never again
stroke your cat
or walk into your lab room
with its walls lined with antique instruments and books.

What I remember most from that time
is standing by your bed
as you grew smaller and smaller,
less and less of you
who had so frightened me as a child,
and looking down at you
lying there quietly
when it was too late to talk.

I just held your hand
and told you I loved you.
I don't know what you heard
or what you knew,
but those words were all that was left
that could matter
before you leapt off
from your bed
in that tiny white room
into something huge. [2007]

Stephanie Bolster

Many Have Written Poems about Blackberries

But few have gotten at the multiplicity of them, how each berry
composes itself of many dark notes, spherical,
swollen, fragile as a world. A blackberry is the colour of a painful
bruise on the upper arm, some internal organ
as yet unnamed. It is shaped to fit
the tip of the tongue, to be a thimble, a dunce cap
for a small mouse. Sometimes it is home to a secret green worm
seeking safety and the power of surprise. Sometimes it plunks
into a river and takes on water.
Fishes nibble it.

The bushes themselves ramble like a grandmother's sentences,
giving birth to their own sharpness. Picking the berries
must be a tactful conversation
of gloved hands. Otherwise your fingers will bleed
the berries' purple tongue; otherwise thorns
will pierce your own blank skin. Best to be on the safe side,
the outside of the bush. Inside might lurk
nests of yellow jackets; rabid bats; other,
larger hands on the same search.

The flavour is its own reward, like kissing the whole world
at once, rivers, willows, bugs and all, until your swollen
lips tingle. It's like waking up
to discover the language you used to speak
is gibberish, and you have never really
loved. But this does not matter because you have
married this fruit, mellifluous, brutal, and ripe. [1994]

T. Alan Broughton

Song for Sampson

What did we do for Sampson our cat?
For years we opened cans for him,
we spread out feast after feast
of golden-fleshed salmon, fine bits
of chicken in thick broth, and he ate
both morning and night. Each day
after he scratched his litter box
we emptied whatever he dropped.
Our laps spread like grassy plains,
and he alone was the pride, sunshine
flowing around the slats of the house
that was his cage, spreading over him
like honey, and his fur grew warm.
At night we gave him whatever place
on our bed was without the kicking feet
of our dreams, creatures he could not see
or smell. Often he lay on the rise and fall
of our breasts, the tide of breathing
and slow slap of heart as we rowed
toward morning. We took from him
all propagation and its will, left him
uncertain why faint odors of a passing female
made him stretch and sniff as if he sensed
his own life embalmed in air, a pharaoh's soul.
And this is why he pissed on our shoes—
not out of anger but to help us carry him
with us wherever we walked in the wide
world he could not enter, spreading musk
of Sampson over the surface of earth,
until he became immortal as the darkness
we eased him into, leaving us blessed. [2006]

Emily Carr

The Cow Yard

The Cow Yard was large. Not length and breadth alone determined its dimensions, it had height and depth also. Above it continually hovered the spirit of maternity. Its good earth floor, hardened by many feet, pulsed with rich growth wherever there was any protection from the perpetual movement over its surface.

Across the ample width of the Cow Yard, the Old Barn and the New Barn faced each other. Both were old, but one was very old; in it lodged the lesser creatures. The Cow alone occupied the New Barn.

But it was in the Cow Yard that you felt most strongly the warm life-giving existence of the great red-and-white, loose-knit Cow. When she walked, her great bag swung slowly from side to side. From one end of her large-hipped square body nodded a massive head, surmounted by long, pointed horns. From the other dangled her tail with its heavy curl and pendulum-like movement. As her cloven hoofs moved through the mud, they made a slow clinging squelch, all in tune with the bagging, sagging, nodding, leisureliness of the Cow's whole being.

Of the three little girls who played in the Cow Yard, Bigger tired of it soonest. Right through she was a pure, clean child, and had an enormous conscience. The garden rather than the Cow Yard suited her crisp frocks and tidy ways best, and she was a little afraid of the Cow.

Middle was a born mother, and had huge doll families. She liked equally the tidy garden and the free Cow Yard.

Small was wholly a Cow Yard child.

When the Cow's nose was deep in her bran mash, and her milk purring into the pail in long, even streams, first sounding tinny in the empty pail and then making a deeper and richer sound as the pail filled, Bong, sitting on his three-legged stool, sang to the Cow—a Chinese song in a falsetto voice. The Cow took her nose out of the mash bucket, threw back her great ears, and listened. She pulled a tuft of sweet hay from her rack, and stood quite still, chewing softly, her ears right about, so that she might not miss one bit of Bong's song.

One of the seven gates of the Cow Yard opened into the Pond Place. The Pond was round and deep, and the primroses and daffodils that grew on its bank leaned so far over to peep at themselves that some of them got drowned. Lilacs and pink and white may filled the air with sweetness in Spring. Birds nested there. The Cow walked on a wide walk paved with stones when she came to the Pond to drink. Hurdles of iron ran down each side of the walk and into the water, so that she should not go too far, and get mired. The three little girls who came to play used to roost on the hurdles and fish for tadpoles with an iron dipper that belonged to the hens' wheat-bin. From the brown surface of the water three upside-down little girls laughed up and mocked them, just as an upside-down Cow looked up from the water and mocked the Cow when she drank. Doubtless the tadpoles laughed, because down under the water where they darted back and forth no upside-down tadpoles mocked.

The overflow from the Pond meandered through the Cow Yard in a wide, rock-bordered ditch. There were two bridges across the ditch; one made of two planks for people to walk over, and the other made of logs, strong and wide enough for the Cow. The hens drank from the running water. Musk grew under the Cow's bridge; its yellow blossoms gleamed like cats' eyes in the cool dark.

Special things happened in the Cow Yard at each season of the year, but the most special things happened in Spring.

First came the bonfire. All winter the heap in the centre of the Cow Yard had mounted higher and higher with orchard prunings, branches that had blown down in the winter winds, old boxes and hens' nests, garbage, and now, on top of all, the spring-cleaning discards.

The three little girls sat on three upturned barrels. Even Bigger, her hands folded in a spotless lap, enjoyed this Cow Yard event. The Cow, safely off in the pasture, could not stamp and sway at her. Middle, hugging a doll, and Small, hugging a kitten, banged their heels on the sides of the hollow barrels, which made splendid noises like drums.

The man came from the barn with paper and matches, and off the bonfire blazed with a tremendous roar. It was so hot that the barrels had to be moved back. The hens ran helter-skelter. The rabbits wiggled their noses furiously as the whiffs of smoke reached their hutches. The ducks waddled off to the Pond to cool themselves. Soon there was nothing left of the bonfire but ashes and red embers. Then the barrels were rolled up close, and the three little girls roasted potatoes in the hot ashes.

Bigger told stories while the potatoes roasted. Her stories were grand and impossible, and when they soared beyond imagining, Small said, "Let's have some real ones now," and turned to Middle, "Will you marry?"

"Of course," came the prompt reply. "And I shall have a hundred children. Will you?"

Small considered. "Well, that depends. If I don't join a circus and ride a white horse through hoops of fire, I may marry a farmer, if he has plenty of creatures. That is, I wouldn't marry just a vegetable man."

"I am going to be a missionary," said Bigger, "and go out to the Heathen."

"Huh! if you're scared of our old cow, what will you be of cannibals?" said Small. "Why not marry a missionary, and send him out first, so they wouldn't be so hungry when you got there?"

"You are a foolish child," said Bigger. "The potatoes are cooked. You fish them out, Small, your hands and pinafore are dirty anyway."

The ashes of the bonfire were scarcely cold before Spring burst through the brown earth, and the ashes and everything. The Cow and the chickens kept the tender green shoots cropped down, but every night more pushed up and would not be kept under. The Cow watched the willow trees that grew beside the Pond. Just before the silky grey pussies burst their buds, she licked up as far as she could reach and ate them, blowing hard, upside-down sniffs—all puff-out and no pull-in—as though the bitter-sweet of the pussy-willows was very agreeable to her. She stood with half-closed eyes, chewing and rolling her jaws from side to side, with delighted slobbering.

About this time, the fussy old hens got fussier. After sticking their feathers on end, and clucking and squawking and being annoyed at everybody, they suddenly sat down on their nests, and refused to get up, staring into space as though their orange eyes saw something away off. Then they were moved into a quiet shed and put into clean boxes of hollowed-out hay, filled with eggs. They sat on top of the eggs for ages and ages. If you put your hand on them, they flattened their feathers to their bodies and their bodies down on their eggs and gave beaky growls. Then, when you had almost forgotten that they ever had legs and could walk, you went to the shed and put food and water before them. Fluffy chickens peeped out of every corner of the hen's feathers, till she looked as fat as seven hens. Then she strutted out into the yard, to brag before the other creatures, with all the chicks bobbing behind her.

One old hen was delighted with her chickens and went off, clucking to keep them close, and scratching up grubs and insects for them by the way, but when they came to the ditch her little ones jumped into the water and swam off. She felt that life had cheated her, and she sat down and sulked.

"How mad she must be, after sitting so long," said Bigger.

"As long as they are alive, I don't see why she should care," said Middle. "They'll come to her to be cuddled when they are tired and cold."

"Oh, girls," cried Small, bursting with a big idea, "if the hen hatched ducks, why couldn't the Cow have a colt? It would be so splendid to have a horse!"

Bigger got up from the stone where she was sitting. "Come on," she said to Middle, "she is such a foolish child. Let's play ladies in the garden, and leave her to mudpuddle in the Cow Yard."

The ducklings crept back to the old hen when they were tired, just as Middle had said they would. The old hen squatted down delightedly, loosening up her feathers, and the little ducks snuggled among them.

"Aren't they beastly wet and cold against your skin?" shouted Small across the ditch to the hen. "Gee, don't mothers love hard!"

She cast a look around the yard. Through the fence she saw the Cow in the pasture, chewing drowsily. Spring sunshine, new grass, daisies and buttercups filled the pasture. The Cow had not a trouble in the world.

Small nodded to the Cow. "All the same, old Cow; I do wish you could do something about a colt. Oh dear, I do want to learn to ride!"

Suddenly she sprang up, jumped the ditch, tiptoed to reach the iron hoop that kept the pasture-gate fast, and ran up to the Cow. "Be a sport, old girl," she whispered in the great hairy ear, and taking her by the horn she led the Cow up to the fence.

The Cow stood meek and still. Small climbed to the top rail of the fence, and jumped on the broad expanse of red back, far too wide for her short legs to grip. For one still moment, while the slow mind of the Cow surmounted her astonishment, Small sat in the wide valley between horns and hip-bones. Then it seemed as though the Cow fell apart, and as if every part of her shot in a different direction.

Small hurled through space and bumped hard. "Beast!" she gasped, when she had sorted herself from the mud and the stones. "Bong may call you the Old Lady, but I call you a mean, miserable old cow." And she shook her fist at the still-waving heels and tail at the other end of the pasture.

That night, when Small showed Middle the bruises, and explained how they had come, Middle said, "I expect you had better marry a farmer; maybe you're not exactly suited for a circus rider."

Spring had just about filled up the Cow Yard. The rabbits' secrets were all out now. They had bunged up the doors of their sleeping boxes with hay and stuff, and had pretended that there was nothing there at all. But if you went too close, they stamped their feet and wagged their ears, and made out that they were brave as lions. But now that it had got too stuffy in the boxes, the mother pulled down the barricade and all the fluffy babies scampered out, more than you could count.

One day when the Cow was standing under the loft, the loveliest baby pigeon fell plumb on her back. But there were so many young things around, all more or less foolish, that the Cow was not even surprised.

Then one morning the Father called the little girls into the Cow Yard, to see the pigmy image of the Old Cow herself, spot for spot, except that it had no wisdom. He had a foolish baby face and foolish legs; he seemed to wonder whose legs these were, and never dreamed that they were his own. But he was sure that he owned his tail, and flipped it joyously.

The Cow was terribly proud of him, and licked him and licked him till all his hair crinkled up.

Now, the Cow Yard was not Heaven, so of course bad things and sad things happened there too.

Close by the side of the ditch was a tree covered with ivy. The running water had washed some of the roots bare, and they stuck out. When the little girls sailed boats down the ditch, the roots tipped the boats and tried to drown the dolls.

It was not a very big tree, but the heavy bunch of ivy that hung about it made it look immense. The leaves of the ivy formed a dense dark surface about a foot away from the bole of the tree, for the leaves hung on long stems. The question was—what filled the mysterious space between the leaves and the tree? Away above the ivy, at the top, the bare branches of the tree waved skinny arms, as if they warned you that something terrible was there.

One day the children heard the Father say to the Mother, "The ivy has killed that tree."

It was strange that the ivy could kill anything. Small thought about it a lot, but she did not like to ask the older ones, who thought her questions silly. She would not have thrust her arm into that space for anything.

The pigeons flew over the tree, from the roof of one barn to the roof of the other, but they never lighted on it. Sometimes the noisy barn sparrows flew into the ivy; they were instantly silent, and you never saw them come out. Sometimes owls hoo-hoo-hooed in there. Once when Small was sitting on the chopping block, one flew out, perfectly silently, as though its business were very secret. Small crept home and up to bed, although it was not quite time, and drew the covers tight up over her head. To herself she called that tree "The Killing Tree."

Then one day she found a dead sparrow under the Killing Tree.

She picked it up. The bird was cold, its head flopped over her hand; the rest of it was stiff and its legs stuck up. Queer grey lids covered its eyes.

Small buried it in a little box filled with violets. A week later she dug it up, to see just what did happen to dead things. The bird's eyes were sunk away back in its head. There were some worms in the box, and it smelled horrid. Small buried the bird in the earth again quickly.

Winter came by and by and, looking out from their bedroom window, Middle said, "The Old Cow Yard tree is down." They dressed quickly and went to look.

The tree had broken the Cow's bridge and lay across the ditch; the forlorn top broken and pitiful. The heavy ivy, looking blacker than ever against the snow, still hid the mystery place.

"Mercy, it's good it did not fall on the Cow and kill her," said Small. "It's a beastly tree and I'm glad it is down!"

"Why should it fall on the Cow; and why was it a beastly tree?" asked Middle.

"Because and because," said Small, and pressed her lips together tight.

"You *are* silly," retorted Middle.

When they came back from school, the top branches were chopped up, and the ivy piled ready for burning. The little tawny roots of the ivy stuck out all over the bole like coarse hair. The Man was sawing the tree in lengths. He rolled one towards the children. "Here's a seat for you," he said. Middle sat down. Small came close to the Man.

"Mr. Jack, when you chopped the ivy off the tree did you find anything in there?"

"Why, I found the tree."

"I mean," said Small in a tense voice, "anything between the tree and the ivy?"

"There wasn't nothing in there that I saw," replied the Man. "Did you lose a ball or something maybe?"

"When are you going to burn the ivy?"

"Just waiting till you came home from school," and he struck a match.

Dense, acrid smoke blinded the children. When they could see again, long tongues of flame were licking the leaves, which hissed back like a hundred angry cats, before they parched, crackled, and finally burst into flames.

"Isn't it a splendid bonfire?" asked Middle. "Shall we cook potatoes?"

"No," said Small.

The next spring, when everyone had forgotten that there ever had been a Cow Yard tree, the Father bought a horse. The Cow Yard was filled with excitement; children shouted, hens ran, ducks waddled off quacking, but the Cow did not even look up. She went right on eating some greens from a pile thrown over the fence from the vegetable garden.

"I suppose we shall have to call it the Horse Yard now," said Small. "He's bigger and so much grander than the Cow."

Middle gave the horse an appraising look. "Higher, but not so thick," she said.

The horse saw the pile of greens. He held his head high, and there was confidence in the ring of his iron shoes as he crossed the bridge.

The Cow munched on, flapping the flies off her sides with a lazy tail. When she got a particularly juicy green, her tail forgot to flap, and lay curled across her back.

When the horse came close, the tail jumped off the Cow's back and swished across his nose. He snorted and pulled back, but still kept his eyes on the pile of greens. He left his four feet and the tips of his ears just where they had been, but the roots of his ears, and his neck and lips stretched forward towards the greens till he looked as if he would fall for crookedness. The Cow's head moved ever so little; she gave him a look, and pointed one horn right at his eye. His body shot back to where it should be, square above his legs, and he sighed and turned away, with his ears and tail pressed down tight.

"I guess it will be all right for us to call it the Cow Yard still," said Middle. [1942]

Raymond Carver

Chef's House

That summer Wes rented a furnished house north of Eureka from a recovered alcoholic named Chef. Then he called to ask me to forget what I had going and to move up there and live with him. He said he was on the wagon. I knew about that wagon. But he wouldn't take no for an answer. He called again and said, Edna, you can see the ocean from the front window. You can smell salt in the air. I listened to him talk. He didn't slur his words. I said, I'll think about it. And I did. A week later he called again and said, Are you coming? I said I was still thinking. He said, We'll start over. I said, If I come up there, I want you to do something for me. Name it, Wes said. I said, I want you to try and be the Wes I used to know. The old Wes. The Wes I married. Wes began to cry, but I took it as a sign of his good intentions. So I said, All right, I'll come up.

Wes had quit his girlfriend, or she'd quit him—I didn't know, didn't care. When I made up my mind to go with Wes, I had to say goodbye to my friend. My friend said, You're making a mistake. He said, Don't do this to me. What about us? he said. I said, I have to do it for Wes's sake. He's trying to stay sober. You remember what that's like. I remember, my friend said, but I don't want you to go. I said, I'll go for the summer. Then I'll see. I'll come back, I said. He said, What about me? What about *my* sake? Don't come back, he said.

We drank coffee, pop, and all kinds of fruit juice that summer. The whole summer, that's what we had to drink. I found myself wishing the summer wouldn't end. I knew better, but after a month of being with Wes in Chef's house, I put my wedding ring back on. I hadn't worn the ring in two years. Not since the night Wes was drunk and threw his ring into a peach orchard.

Wes had a little money, so I didn't have to work. And it turned out Chef was letting us have the house for almost nothing. We didn't have a telephone. We paid the gas and light and shopped for specials at the Safeway. One Sunday afternoon Wes went out to get a sprinkler and came back with something for me. He came back with a nice bunch of daisies and a straw hat. Tuesday evenings we'd go to a movie. Other nights Wes would go to what he called his Don't Drink meetings. Chef would pick him up in his car at the door and drive him home again afterward. Some days Wes and I would go fishing for trout in one of the freshwater lagoons nearby. We'd fish off the bank and take all day to catch a few little ones. They'll do fine, I'd say, and that night I'd fry them for supper. Sometimes I'd take off my hat and fall asleep on a blanket next to my fishing pole. The last thing I'd remember would be clouds passing overhead toward the central valley. At night, Wes would take me in his arms and ask me if I was still his girl.

Our kids kept their distance. Cheryl lived with some people on a farm in Oregon. She looked after a herd of goats and sold the milk. She kept bees and put up jars of honey. She had her own life, and I didn't blame her. She didn't care one way or the other about what her dad and I did so long as we didn't get her into it. Bobby was in Washington working in the hay. After the haying season, he planned to work in the apples. He had a girl and was saving his money. I wrote letters and signed them, "Love always."

One afternoon Wes was in the yard pulling weeds when Chef drove up in front of the house. I was working at the sink. I looked and saw Chef's big car pull in. I could see his car, the access road and the freeway, and, behind the freeway, the dunes and the ocean. Clouds hung over the water. Chef got out of his car and hitched his pants. I knew there was something. Wes stopped what he was doing and stood up. He was wearing his gloves and a canvas hat. He took off the hat and wiped his face with the back of his hand. Chef walked over and put his arm around Wes's shoulders. Wes took off one of his gloves. I went to the door. I heard Chef say to Wes God knows he was sorry but he was going to have to ask us to leave at the end of the month. Wes pulled off his other glove. Why's that, Chef? Chef said his daughter, Linda, the woman Wes used to call Fat Linda from the time of his drinking days, needed a place to live and this place was it. Chef told Wes that Linda's husband had taken his fishing boat out a few weeks back and nobody had heard from him since. She's my own blood, Chef said to Wes. She's lost her husband. She's lost her baby's father. I can help. I'm glad I'm in a position to help, Chef said. I'm sorry, Wes, but you'll have to look for another house. Then Chef hugged Wes again, hitched his pants, and got in his big car and drove away.

Wes came inside the house. He dropped his hat and gloves on the carpet and sat down in the big chair. Chef's chair, it occurred to me. Chef's carpet, even. Wes looked pale. I poured two cups of coffee and gave one to him.

It's all right, I said. Wes, don't worry about it, I said. I sat down on Chef's sofa with my coffee.

Fat Linda's going to live here now instead of us, Wes said. He held his cup, but he didn't drink from it.

Wes, don't get stirred up, I said.

Her man will turn up in Ketchikan, Wes said. Fat Linda's husband has simply pulled out on them. And who could blame him? Wes said. Wes said if it came to that, he'd go down with his ship, too, rather than live the rest of his days with Fat Linda and her kid. Then Wes put his cup down next to his gloves. This has been a happy house up to now, he said.

We'll get another house, I said.

Not like this one, Wes said. It wouldn't be the same, anyway. This house has been a good house for us. This house has good memories to it. Now Fat Linda and her kid will be in here, Wes said. He picked up his cup and tasted from it.

It's Chef's house, I said. He has to do what he has to do.

I know that, Wes said. But I don't have to like it.

Wes had this look about him. I knew that look. He kept touching his lips with his tongue. He kept thumbing his shirt under his waistband. He got up from the chair and went to window. He stood looking out at the ocean and at the clouds, which were building up. He patted his chin with his fingers like he was thinking about something. And he *was* thinking.

Go easy, Wes, I said.

She wants me to go easy, Wes said. He kept standing there.

But in a minute he came over and sat next to me on the sofa. He crossed one leg over the other and began fooling with the buttons on his shirt. I took his hand. I started to talk. I talked about the summer. But I caught myself talking like it was something that had happened in the past. Maybe years back. At any rate, like something that was over. Then I started talking about the kids. Wes said he wished he could do it over again and do it right this time.

They love you, I said.

No, they don't, he said.

I said, Someday, they'll understand things.

Maybe, Wes said. But it won't matter then.

You don't know, I said.

I know a few things, Wes said, and looked at me. I know I'm glad you came up here. I won't forget you did it, Wes said.

I'm glad, too, I said. I'm glad you found this house, I said.

Wes snorted. Then he laughed. We both laughed. That Chef, Wes said, and shook his head. He threw us a knuckleball, that son of a bitch. But I'm glad you wore your ring. I'm glad we had us this time together, Wes said.

Then I said something. I said, Suppose, just suppose, nothing had ever happened. Suppose this was for the first time. Just suppose. It doesn't hurt to suppose. Say none of the other had ever happened. You know what I mean? Then what? I said.

Wes fixed his eyes on me. He said, Then I suppose we'd have to be somebody else if that was the case. Somebody we're not. I don't have that kind of supposing left in me. We were born who we are. Don't you see what I'm saying?

I said I hadn't thrown away a good thing and come six hundred miles to hear him talk like this.

He said, I'm sorry, but I can't talk like somebody I'm not. I'm not somebody else. If I was somebody else, I sure as hell wouldn't be here. If I was somebody else, I wouldn't be me. But I'm who I am. Don't you see?

Wes, it's all right, I said. I brought his hand to my cheek. Then, I don't know, I remembered how he was when he was nineteen, the way he looked running across this field to where his dad sat on a tractor, hand over his eyes, watching Wes run toward him. We'd just driven up from California. I got out with Cheryl and Bobby and said, There's Grandpa. But they were just babies.

Wes sat next to me patting his chin, like he was trying to figure out the next thing. Wes's dad was gone and our kids were grown up. I looked at Wes and then I looked around Chef's living room at Chef's things, and I thought, We have to do something now and do it quick.

Hon, I said. Wes, listen to me.

What do you want? he said. But that's all he said. He seemed to have made up his mind. But, having made up his mind, he was in no hurry. He leaned back on the sofa, folded his hands in his lap, and closed his eyes. He didn't say anything else. He didn't have to.

I said his name to myself. It was an easy name to say, and I'd been used to saying it for a long time. Then I said it once more. This time I said it out loud. Wes, I said.

He opened his eyes. But he didn't look at me. He just sat where he was and looked toward the window. Fat Linda, he said. But I knew it wasn't her. She was nothing. Just a name. Wes got up and pulled the drapes and the ocean was gone just like that. I went in to start supper. We still had some fish in the icebox. There wasn't much else. We'll clean it up tonight, I thought, and that will be the end of it. [1988]

Arlan Cashier

Lost Sweater

The blue, size small Parks and Recreation Staff zip hoodie was last seen near a gas station in Grant's Pass, Oregon on a freezing morning in early January when, half-awake and wholly negligent, I removed it in a graffiti-decorated bathroom before a long drive up to Bellingham, Washington where I was to start school the following week. There is absolutely no other place on earth it could be. My current apartment has been scoured twice over and my parents back home have been phoned on numerous occasions with regard to the sweater's whereabouts.

The sweater is approximately three years old. It was given to me free of charge when I took a job as a Softball Field Monitor for the Sports Department of my local Parks and Recreation

District. I used to pull my hands into its fleecy sleeves on wintry California nights while watching slow-pitch softballers spill blood, sweat, and beer onto community playfields.

It has a pale white tint at the base of the sleeves from over a year of tearing open fifty-pound bags of calcium carbonate to replenish the supply of a leaky old field chalker with one broken wheel that would stick every so often while I marked the foul lines, causing a visible curve in the line that I'm positive players and umpires all noticed and laughed about behind my back.

If you look closely, you'll notice the cotton fabric is slightly worn and tattered from searching the thorny brush behind the diamond for wayward foul balls as burnt-out and boozed-up fathers with lips bulging from cheap tobacco fed me directions between dark brown spits. "Up a little. No, not that far. Now to the left. Down. Yeah, it landed somewhere around there."

From the sweater's neck hang two soft, thick blue strings with knots at the ends that I used to pull and tighten to close the hood around my red cheeks and forehead on bitter nights when I sat, no longer a Field Monitor but an awed spectator of dream teams with names like Masterbatters and Scared Hitless that were composed of local Little League coaches with middle-aged cannons for arms, reliving their glory days and high-school phenoms whose bright athletic futures were derailed by injury so now they work at their dad's local auto body shop and blast neon yellow softballs out of community parks every Wednesday night.

The sweater was last seen quite clean but there might still be light deposits of red field dirt in the bottoms of the front pockets where I would shelter my numb, clay-stained hands after returning the last of the dusty bases to the big green field storage box at the end of the night as the low gray fog began to creep in from the outfield. The grown men were all in their cars driving home to their families or single apartments where they would shower away the dirt and drink beer in front of an ESPN recap of the day's baseball action as I stood in my sweater, looking over the ball field, waiting for the lights to turn off.

PLEASE CALL (805) 405-3539 if found
(Reward possible)

[2016]

Ann Choi

The Shower

In the sixth grade
your hands were not much smaller
than they are now,
the reach between your thumb
and last finger not quite
an octave. You did not complain
and learned to choose
your music carefully.

Sharing noodles after school
in your house full of trophies,
we spoke of things expiring
without our knowledge. How time
quickens and wraps around us,
makes us women in bright clothes
caught by the permanence of the ring
around your finger.

I am your friend, accustomed
to your diligence.
Soon you will marry and fill
a house with sounds of dishes
and of children whose weight
you will gain and lose,
whose small fingers will separate
to play staccato,
one brief note after another. [1991]

Kate Chopin

The Story of an Hour

Knowing that Mrs. Mallard was afflicted with a heart trouble, great care was taken to break to her as gently as possible the news of her husband's death.

It was her sister Josephine who told her, in broken sentences; veiled hints that revealed in half concealing. Her husband's friend Richards was there, too, near her. It was he who had been in the newspaper office when intelligence of the railroad disaster was received, with Brently Mallard's name leading the list of "killed." He had only taken the time to assure himself of its truth by a second telegram, and had hastened to forestall any less careful, less tender friend in bearing the sad message.

She did not hear the story as many women have heard the same, with a paralyzed inability to accept its significance. She wept at once, with sudden, wild abandonment, in her sister's arms. When the storm of grief had spent itself she went away to her room alone. She would have no one follow her.

There stood, facing the open window, a comfortable, roomy armchair. Into this she sank, pressed down by a physical exhaustion that haunted her body and seemed to reach into her soul.

She could see in the open square before her house the tops of trees that were all aquiver with the new spring life. The delicious breath of rain was in the air. In the street below a peddler was crying his wares. The notes of a distant song which someone was singing reached her faintly, and countless sparrows were twittering in the eaves.

There were patches of blue sky showing here and there through the clouds that had met and piled one above the other in the west facing her window.

She sat with her head thrown back upon the cushion of the chair, quite motionless, except when a sob came up into her throat and shook her, as a child who has cried itself to sleep continues to sob in its dreams.

She was young, with a fair, calm face, whose lines bespoke repression and even a certain strength. But now there was a dull stare in her eyes, whose gaze was fixed away off yonder on one of those patches of blue sky. It was not a glance of reflection, but rather indicated a suspension of intelligent thought.

There was something coming to her and she was waiting for it, fearfully. What was it? She did not know; it was too subtle and elusive to name. But she felt it, creeping out of the sky, reaching toward her through the sounds, the scents, the color that filled the air.

Now her bosom rose and fell tumultuously. She was beginning to recognize this thing that was approaching to possess her, and she was striving to beat it back with her will—as powerless as her two white slender hands would have been.

When she abandoned herself a little whispered word escaped her slightly parted lips. She said it over and over under her breath: "free, free, free!" The vacant stare and the look of terror that had followed it went from her eyes. They stayed keen and bright. Her pulses beat fast, and the coursing blood warmed and relaxed every inch of her body.

She did not stop to ask if it were or were not a monstrous joy that held her. A clear and exalted perception enabled her to dismiss the suggestion as trivial.

She knew that she would weep again when she saw the kind, tender hands folded in death; the face that had never looked save with love upon her, fixed and gray and dead. But she saw beyond that bitter moment a long procession of years to come that would belong to her absolutely. And she opened and spread her arms out to them in welcome.

There would be no one to live for her during those coming years; she would live for herself. There would be no powerful will bending hers in that blind persistence with which men and women believe they have a right to impose a private will upon a fellow-creature. A kind intention or a cruel intention made the act seem no less a crime as she looked upon it in that brief moment of illumination.

And yet she had loved him—sometimes. Often she had not. What did it matter! What could love, the unsolved mystery, count for in the face of this possession of self-assertion which she suddenly recognized as the strongest impulse of her being!

"Free! Body and soul free!" she kept whispering.

Josephine was kneeling before the closed door with her lips to the keyhole, imploring for admission. "Louise, open the door! I beg; open the door—you will make yourself ill. What are you doing, Louise? For heaven's sake open the door."

"Go away. I am not making myself ill." No; she was drinking in a very elixir of life through that open window.

Her fancy was running riot along those days ahead of her. Spring days, and summer days, and all sorts of days that would be her own. She breathed a quick prayer that life might be long. It was only yesterday she had thought with a shudder that life might be long.

She arose at length and opened the door to her sister's importunities. There was a feverish triumph in her eyes, and she carried herself unwittingly like a goddess of Victory. She clasped her sister's waist, and together they descended the stairs. Richards stood waiting for them at the bottom.

Some one was opening the front door with a latchkey. It was Brently Mallard who entered, a little travel-stained, composedly carrying his grip-sack and umbrella. He had been far from the scene of accident, and did not even know there had been one. He stood amazed at Josephine's piercing cry; at Richards' quick motion to screen him from the view of his wife.

But Richards was too late.

When the doctors came they said she had died of heart disease—of joy that kills. [1894]

Sandra Cisneros

My Wicked Wicked Ways

This is my father.
See? He is young.
He looks like Errol Flynn.
He is wearing a hat
that tips over one eye,
a suit that fits him good,
and baggy pants.
He is also wearing
those awful shoes,
the two-toned ones
my mother hates.
Here is my mother.
She is not crying.
She cannot look into the lens
because the sun is bright.
The woman,
the one my father knows,
is not here.
She does not come till later.
My mother will get very mad.
Her face will turn red
and she will throw one shoe.
My father will say nothing.
After a while everyone
will forget it.
Years and years will pass.
My mother will stop mentioning it.
This is me she is carrying.
I am a baby.
She does not know
I will turn out bad. [1987]

Ivan E. Coyote

This, That, and the Other Thing

I don't have the recipe written down, so it tastes different every time. You need chipotle peppers, the smoked Mexican ones; I've seen them dried sometimes, but mostly I get the canned ones.

My friend Deanne Loubardious showed me how the first time, her striped shirtsleeves rolled up and over her tanned landscaper's forearms, and an unlit cigarette dangling in one corner of her mouth, as she chopped chicken into chunks with short, callused, dirt-worn-in fingers.

†

Step one:

First you boil the chicken in a stock pot with three or four peppers and about eight cups of water. Save the stock, let the chicken cool enough to take the bones out, and cut into bite-size pieces.

†

There is a feeling like none other that I know when I have a big batch cooling in the fridge, or simmering on the stove; it is a broad, back-turned-against-the-wolf-at-your-door kind of feeling, a you-don't-have-to-worry-about-hungry-company-showing-up-unexpected kind of feeling.

As I was about to feed my chosen family—feet planted firmly on the kitchen floor, toes staring down the dust bunnies cowering between the stove's legs—I thought, rather stereotypically, of my mother, which is odd really, because my father is the weekend gourmet, and I cooked for my sister and me on weekdays. My mother was usually out, either working late or taking night classes; I don't have any Mrs Cleaverish memories of her in the kitchen.

But my mother knew how to cook the standards: Sunday roast with Yorkshire pudding, turkey with all the trimmings, cream of turkey on toast for leftovers, boiled-carrots kind of stuff, passed on dutifully to her by her mother, my shrinking and pale grey grandmother.

Cooking made my mother nervous; she could have made prime time commercials for boil-in-the-bag corn and Royal City canned peas. I can even see her now, exclaiming over their convenience and home-cooked goodness, snipping open bags and pulling things from a spotless microwave with red and white checkered mitts on, smiling at the camera, and truly meaning every word of it.

Holiday meals were extravagant, yet conservative, served in heavy eighties handmade pottery bowls on matching woven placemats, cooked with great care but no love, cooked in reverence to obligation, not art.

†

Step two:

In a large, preferably cast iron pan (I'm a little old-fashioned in that way), make a roux, you know, from melted butter and flour; this will be the backbone of your cream sauce. Add a couple of cups of stock, tons of garlic, sautéed onion, and four or five more chipotles.

†

My father made Sunday breakfast for us all, crepes or waffles or buckwheat pancakes, fussed over sauces and served helpings all around with flourish and a showman's hand; he made too many dishes for what got done, ate too much, bloated, gloated over compliments from my mother's duly impressed girlfriends, and loved every last sliver of green onion of it all.

†

Step three:

While you're making the roux, boil eight or nine small potatoes in the stock, and when they are done, strain them out and chop them into bite-size pieces. If you are like me and have yet to purchase the entire Martha Stewart pot collection, you are now going to have to pour the stock into a large bowl to cool, so that you still have a big huge pot to keep on cooking in.

†

They divorced last summer, after twenty-seven years, and my mother has lost fifty pounds since. At first, she didn't eat at all.

When I went home in August, she was a carbon copy of her former self, picking at a bagel for breakfast and drinking only hot water with a squeeze of lemon.

Someone had to teach her how to cook for one.

So I took her to the Food Fair. She pushed the cart with resignation up and down the aisles, and I circled her like a babysitter, patiently extolling the virtues of couscous and Ichiban noodles.

"Purple cabbage," I explained, "is the bachelor's very best vegetable companion. Cheap cheap, and you can leave one of these fuckers in the crisper for two months and still make coleslaw, no problem, adds colour to a salad," etc., etc.

I'm not sure where exactly I had lost her, or even if she had heard anything I'd said at all, but I looked up from the plethora of produce suddenly and realized that she wasn't listening, that in fact her eyes were focused somewhere between the wheels of the cart and the permafrost always located about three feet under the concrete foundations of anything built in the place I come from, and she had begun to cry.

"I don't care anymore, that's why. That is why I can't eat. I don't care whether I live or die." She confessed this to me, as if no one was listening, and then she shook her head, as if someone else had spoken, and she couldn't quite agree with them.

†

Step four:

Pour the sauce base and onions into the large pot, add the chicken, the potatoes, a whole whack of sliced mushrooms, zucchinis, squash maybe sometimes, carrots, and a can of chick peas (I myself never have time to soak the little fuckers). Add a few more cups of stock and stir, like a cauldron, thinking always of your mother, even if she's not Mexican and doesn't like to cook really, and simmer, adding more stock as you boil it off.

†

My mother hired a moving company when the house was sold, and insured everything she owned. Two months before she could move into her new house on her own, the mover guy showed up, in tight Levi's and a big brass belt buckle with a front end loader on it, to drop off the boxes: special boxes, reinforced for dishes and collectibles, and long, flat boxes for pictures, and rolls and rolls of brown packing paper, tape, labels, pens, and detailed, photocopied instructions for wrapping everything.

"You have to wrap the bowls in four pieces each, four pieces, or it's not covered if anything gets broken, it says so right here. Four pieces each, or it's not covered."

She said this over and over to us all, like a mantra.

My father had conveniently left for Australia only days before, leaving her to sort, separate, itemize, wrap, box, label, or throw out everything they had collected together in the last twenty-seven years of marriage. We only moved once, six blocks down Twelfth Avenue, from Hemlock to Grove Street. My parents have had the same phone number all of my life.

I was kneeling on the carpet in the living room, packing up the cuckoo clock and an abstract stone carving of an owl, I think, listening to my mom giving orders to two of my almost uncountable cousins, Rachael and Lindsay, eleven and ten years old respectively, around the corner, in the kitchen.

"Four pieces each, remember, Rachael? Or else it's not covered, if anything gets broken."

"You throwing this out, Auntie Pat? Can I have it then?" one of them asked in her little girl falsetto.

"Lindsay," her mother, my aunt, interrupted, "what the fuck are you going to do with an hors d'oeuvres tray, you tell me? Just more junk to clutter up your room with. You can't see the floor in there as it is. Give it to the Sally Ann, Pat, it's still perfectly good," Roberta said, scrubbing the tops of the cupboards.

"Put it wherever you want it, just get rid of it," my mom said. "I don't want to see it again. I want to get rid of most of this stuff. How we ever collected so much stuff, I don't know. I don't even remember getting some of it, much less using most of it."

Their voices faded and mixed in the back of my head, as did the sound of dishes being wrapped in brown paper, and Fleetwood Mac on the tape deck. My dad had already taken the stereo and most of the CDs, and so, ironically and downright bittersweet at the time, we were forced to listen to sun-faded tapes from when I was a kid as we packed—I had scrubbed walls to America, vacuumed to Supertramp, sorted photos to Burton Cummings.

And now I was crying to "Lay Me Down in the Tall Grass." Tears obscured the cardboard box that I knelt in front of, and only the lump in my throat was keeping my heart from falling right out of my mouth and into the box.

I had been so busy packing and scrubbing, fending off the inevitable and largely looming family feud, making sure my mom ate enough, and my dad didn't drink too much, that I had forgotten to mourn. Mourn the dissolution of my family, and the passing on of the only house I really remember living in.

My mom walked in to the living room and noticed the tears before I could choke them off, and dropped to her knees beside me.

"I know this is hard. It's the hardest thing I've ever done. I don't think I can make it through this. I fucked everything up, didn't I? Everything is gone, everything, and it's all my fault. This is all my fault."

Her hands meant *this*, this home packed into boxes. She held her palms up, empty.

†

Webster's *Handy Pocket College Dictionary* defines pain in the following fashion:

> *1: n. as the suffering of body or mind. 2: pl. great care (as in taking pains to ensure...). 3: v. to cause suffering to.*

Also listed is painful, an adjective.

In reference also to pain, Leslie D. Weatherhead, the author of such illuminating reads as After Death, The Transforming Friendship, The Afterworld of the Poets, Jesus and Ourselves, and The Mastery of Sex Through Psychology and Religion, wrote in Psychology in Service of the Soul that without pain far back in the time of animal creation, we might never have come to be. We must allow a place for that minimum of pain which is how Nature warns us that something is wrong. The animal not warned by pain would have been destroyed. But there is evidence to show that when pain has given that warning, it ceases to be beneficial and becomes an evil thing.

And he cites as an example an experiment with two blisters inflicted by suggestion under hypnosis on a patient, one of which he suggested should be painful and the other non-painful, in which the painful one took twice as long to heal as the non-painful one. I think what he is saying is that whatever doesn't kill you makes you live.

Time takes the edge off of the unbearable, turns wounds into scars, agony becomes just an ache. What used to hurt all the time only bothers you when you move it just so.

Tragedy has a short shelf life.

This is how the world apologizes for being such a bitch sometimes. Eventually, crisis becomes just a circumstance, a situation that just must be dealt with.

So that's what happened. Time turned the gaping wound where my father had been into just an empty ache. Somewhere between her mouth and her chest and eventually minutes and then hours and then even days would pass between bouts of overwhelming lonely.

And this was a good thing.

†

Step five:

Right before you serve, take a cup of cooled stock and mix in five or six tablespoons of yogurt or mayonnaise, and blend until smooth. Pour this mess into the bigger mess and you have an awesome batch of spicy chipotle chicken in a light cream sauce to serve over brown rice or cous-cous. Make a salad, too, and you're set.

Feed yourself and three or four friends for at least three days, for about twenty-five bucks, if you have a big enough stock pot. Good for whatever ails you.

†

My mother has started to date the English chap she hired to paint her new guest bedroom. He is a creative and giving gourmet cook, and an amateur photographer. They hike a lot together.

She is taking tap dance lessons, and willow chair-making classes with a couple of girls from her office. They are all recently divorced, and just went in on a barbecue together, all having lost custody of their respective hibachis.

My father bought an airstream trailer, parked it behind his welding shop, and has not cut back on his drinking.

I look, and cook, just like my father, but I have my mother's teeth, and tits. [2000]

Jim Crace

from *The Devil's Larder*

17

Here is a question for your guests, next time you dine with new acquaintances at home. The coffee has been served. You sit, not quite at ease, confronted by the detritus of empty plates and by the awkwardness of strangers. You say, to break the ice, "Imagine it. You're on a raft, the two of you, three days from any land. Everybody else has drowned. The sea is calm; it's hardly bothering the raft. The four horizons offer you no hope of rescue. The skies are absolutely blue. Bad news. Blue skies provide no rain. The empty can you've found aboard the raft will not fill up with rain before eternity. You're bound to die of thirst within three days, before there's any chance of being washed up on a shore, unless you drink. You have to make a choice. What do you drink to save your lives? Sea water, or your own urine? Will you take piss or brine? Decide. You're caught between the devil and the salt blue sea. Don't hesitate to say."

I promise you, the woman always takes the devil. It does not bother her that piss contains her body waste, the excess, sterile toxins of her complicated life. She is at ease with body fluids; blemishes, has to be, she deals with them throughout her years. She finds salvation in herself, collects the urine in the can, and drinks.

The husband—again I promise you—selects the sea, invariably. He knows the dangers of the salt. They say it dries your blood and drives you mad. The water makes you thirstier, so you drink even more. But still a man can't face the poisons in his life. He'd rather die. He finds salvation in the seven tenths. He dips the can into the sea and drinks.

Which of the two survives, do you suppose? The woman, obviously. She must outlive the man. Her own bladder is soon empty, but the ocean is endless. Her husband's lips are white with salt, not thirst. She has a second chance through him. She makes her husband get his penis out and—despite his protests of disgust—fill the can for her. His water is quite clear. Not salty either. His kidneys have removed the salt. So long as he drinks sea, preferring universe to self, she will survive unscathed.

There are no shores. There are no rescue boats. No rain. [2001]

James Crews

Lover Boys

I showered with Ross this morning, worked lather into his skin until it was as pink as taffy. We got out, toweled each other off, my favorite part. He stepped onto the scale holding onto the wall for support and saying words to himself I'd think were prayers if I didn't know better. But I got on with him this time, our two wet bodies one weight, numbers going crazy until they stayed at 355. *We're fat*, I said.

He tried to keep down toast and eggs but that face: same as the night I'd stopped by the corner store on my way home for cheap Merlot and my favorite candy—which he hated—a bag of black licorice snaps. That face when I took out a piece, unwrapped the silver cellophane, but he opened his mouth anyway and I put it in. His eyes squinting, cheeks sucked in. *Here*, he said, drew me close and pushed the wet licorice into my mouth.

This evening when we finally made love again, it was so good I fell asleep after. I dreamed our blankets and sheets were an endless spill of licorice—355 pounds of it—falling from the wall, all I could eat. [2009]

Michael Crummey

Bread

I was twenty years younger than my husband, his first wife dead in childbirth. I agreed to marry him because he was a good fisherman, because he had his own house and he was willing to take in my mother and father when the time came. It was a practical decision and he wasn't expecting more than that. Two people should never say the word love before they've eaten a sack of flour together, he told me.

The night we married I hiked my night dress around my thighs and shut my eyes so tight I saw stars. Afterwards I went outside and I was sick, throwing up over the fence. He came out the door behind me and put his hand to the small of my back. It happens your first time, he said. It'll get better.

I got pregnant right away and then he left for the Labrador. I dug the garden, watched my belly swell like a seed in water. Baked bread, bottled bakeapples for the winter store, cut the meadow grass for hay. After a month alone I even started to miss him a little.

The baby came early, a few weeks after my husband arrived home in September. We had the minister up to the house for the baptism the next day, Angus Maclean we named him, and we buried him in the graveyard in the Burnt Woods a week later. I remember he started crying at the table the morning of the funeral and I held his face against my belly until he stopped, his head in my hands about the size of the child before it was born. I don't know why sharing a grief will make you love someone.

I was pregnant again by November. I baked a loaf of bread and brought it to the table, still steaming from the oven. Set it on his plate whole and stood there looking at him. That's the last of that bag of flour, I told him. And he smiled at me and didn't say anything for a minute. I'll pick up another today, he said finally.

And that's how we left it for a while. [1998]

Natalie Diaz

My Brother at 3 A.M.

He sat cross-legged, weeping on the steps
when Mom unlocked and opened the front door.
    O God, he said. O God.
        He wants to kill me, Mom.

When Mom unlocked and opened the front door
at 3 a.m., she was in her nightgown, Dad was asleep.
    He wants to kill me, he told her,
        looking over his shoulder.

3 a.m. and in her nightgown, Dad asleep,
What's going on? she asked. Who wants to kill you?
    He looked over his shoulder.
        The devil does. Look at him, over there.

She asked, What are you on? Who wants to kill you?
The sky wasn't black or blue but the green of a dying night.
    The devil, look at him, over there.
        He pointed to the corner house.

The sky wasn't black or blue but the dying green of night.
Stars had closed their eyes or sheathed their knives.
    My brother pointed to the corner house.
        His lips flickered with sores.

Stars had closed their eyes or sheathed their knives.
O God, I can see the tail, he said. O God, look.
    Mom winced at the sores on his lips.
        It's sticking out from behind the house.

O God, see the tail, he said. Look at the goddamned tail.
He sat cross-legged, weeping on the front steps.
    Mom finally saw it, a hellish vision, my brother.
        O God, O God, she said. [2012]

Emily Dickinson

I started Early – Took my Dog –

I started Early – Took my Dog –
And visited the Sea –
The Mermaids in the Basement
Came out to look at me –

And Frigates – in the Upper Floor
Extended Hempen Hands –
Presuming Me to be a Mouse –
Aground – opon the Sands –

But no Man moved Me – till the Tide
Went past my simple Shoe –
And past my Apron – and my Belt
And past my Boddice – too –

And made as He would eat me up –
As wholly as a Dew
Opon a Dandelion's Sleeve –
And then – I started – too –

And He – He followed – close behind –
I felt His Silver Heel
Opon my Ancle – Then My Shoes
Would overflow with Pearl –

Until We met the Solid Town –
No One He seemed to know –
And bowing – with a Mighty look –
At me – The Sea withdrew – [c. 1862]

Annie Dillard

Signals at Sea

(If the flags in A's hoist cannot be made out,
B keeps her answering pennant at the "Dip"
and hoists the signal "OWL" or "WCX.")

CXL Do not abandon me.
A I am undergoing a speed trial.
D Keep clear of me – I am maneuvering with difficulty.
F I am disabled. Communicate with me.
G I require a pilot.

P Your lights are out, or burning badly.
U You are standing into danger.
X Stop carrying out your intentions.
K You should stop your vessel instantly.
L You should stop. I have something important to communicate.

R You may feel your way past me. [1995]

Brian Doyle

Leap

A couple leaped from the south tower, hand in hand. They reached for each other and their hands met and they jumped.

Jennifer Brickhouse saw them falling, hand in hand.

Many people jumped. Perhaps hundreds. No one knows. They struck the pavement with such force that there was a pink mist in the air.

The mayor reported the mist.

A kindergarten boy who saw people falling in flames told his teacher that the birds were on fire. She ran with him on her shoulders out of the ashes.

Tiffany Keeling saw fireballs falling that she later realized were people. Jennifer Griffin saw people falling and wept as she told the story. Niko Winstral saw people free-falling backward with their hands out, like they were parachuting. Joe Duncan on his roof on Duane Street looked up and saw people jumping. Henry Weintraub saw people "leaping as they flew out." John Carson saw six people fall, "falling over themselves, falling, they were somersaulting." Steve Miller saw people jumping from a thousand feet in the air. Kirk Kjeldsen saw people flailing on the way down, people lining up and jumping, "too many people falling." Jane Tedder saw people leaping and the sight haunts her at night. Steve Tamas counted fourteen people jumping and then he stopped counting. Stuart DeHann saw one woman's dress billowing as she fell, and he saw a shirtless man falling end over end, and he too saw the couple leaping hand in hand.

Several pedestrians were killed by people falling from the sky. A fireman was killed by a body falling from the sky.

But he reached for her hand and she reached for his hand and they leaped out of the window holding hands.

The day of the Lord will come as a thief in the night; in which the heavens shall pass away with a great noise, wrote Peter, *and the elements shall melt with fervent heat, the earth also and the works that are therein shall be burned up.*

I try to whisper prayers for the sudden dead and the harrowed families of the dead and the screaming souls of the murderers but I keep coming back to his hand and her hand nestled in each other with such extraordinary ordinary succinct ancient naked stunning perfect simple ferocious love.

There is no fear in love, wrote John, *but perfect love casteth out fear: because fear hath torment.*

Their hands reaching and joining is the most powerful prayer I can imagine, the most eloquent, the most graceful. It is everything that we are capable of against horror and loss and death. It is what makes me believe that we are not craven fools and charlatans to believe in God, to believe that human beings have greatness and holiness within them like seeds that open only under great fires, to believe that some unimaginable essence of who we are persists past the dissolution of what we were, to believe against evil hourly evidence that love is why we are here.

Their passing away was thought an affliction / and their going forth from us, utter destruction, says the book of Wisdom. *But they are in peace.... They shall shine / and shall dart about us as sparks through stubble.*

No one knows who they were: husband and wife, lovers, dear friends, colleagues, strangers thrown together at the window there at the lip of hell. Maybe they didn't even reach for each other consciously, maybe it was instinctive, a reflex, as they both decided at the same time to take two running steps and jump out the shattered window, but they *did* reach for each other, and they held on tight, and leaped, and fell endlessly into the smoking canyon, at two hundred miles an hour, falling so far and so fast that they would have blacked out before they hit the pavement near Liberty Street so hard that there was a pink mist in the air.

I trust I shall shortly see thee, John wrote, *and we shall speak face to face.*

Jennifer Brickhouse saw them holding hands, and Stuart DeHann saw them holding hands, and I hold onto that. [2003]

T.S. Eliot

The Love Song of J. Alfred Prufrock

S'io credesse che mia risposta fosse
A persona che mai tornasse al mondo,
Questa fiamma staria senza piu scosse.
Ma perciocche giammai di questo fondo
Non torno vivo alcun, s'i'odo il vero,
Senza tema d'infamia ti rispondo. —Dante, *Inferno*

Let us go then, you and I,
When the evening is spread out against the sky
Like a patient etherized upon a table;
Let us go, through certain half-deserted streets,

The muttering retreats
Of restless nights in one-night cheap hotels
And sawdust restaurants with oyster-shells:
Streets that follow like a tedious argument
Of insidious intent
To lead you to an overwhelming question....
Oh, do not ask, "What is it?"
Let us go and make our visit.

In the room the women come and go
Talking of Michelangelo.

The yellow fog that rubs its back upon the window-panes,
The yellow smoke that rubs its muzzle on the window-panes
Licked its tongue into the corners of the evening,
Lingered upon the pools that stand in drains,
Let fall upon its back the soot that falls from chimneys,
Slipped by the terrace, made a sudden leap,
And seeing that it was a soft October night,
Curled once about the house, and fell asleep.

And indeed there will be time
For the yellow smoke that slides along the street,
Rubbing its back upon the window panes;
There will be time, there will be time
To prepare a face to meet the faces that you meet;
There will be time to murder and create,
And time for all the works and days of hands
That lift and drop a question on your plate;
Time for you and time for me,
And time yet for a hundred indecisions,
And for a hundred visions and revisions,
Before the taking of a toast and tea.

In the room the women come and go
Talking of Michelangelo.

And indeed there will be time
To wonder, "Do I dare?" and, "Do I dare?"
Time to turn back and descend the stair,
With a bald spot in the middle of my hair—
(They will say: "How his hair is growing thin!")
My morning coat, my collar mounting firmly to the chin,
My necktie rich and modest, but asserted by a simple pin—
(They will say: "But how his arms and legs are thin!")
Do I dare

Disturb the universe?
In a minute there is time
For decisions and revisions which a minute will reverse.

For I have known them all already, known them all:
Have known the evenings, mornings, afternoons,
I have measured out my life with coffee spoons;
I know the voices dying with a dying fall
Beneath the music from a farther room.
    So how should I presume?

And I have known the eyes already, known them all—
The eyes that fix you in a formulated phrase,
And when I am formulated, sprawling on a pin,
When I am pinned and wriggling on the wall,
Then how should I begin
To spit out all the butt-ends of my days and ways?
    And how should I presume?

And I have known the arms already, known them all—
Arms that are braceleted and white and bare
(But in the lamplight, downed with light brown hair!)
Is it perfume from a dress
That makes me so digress?
Arms that lie along a table, or wrap about a shawl.
    And should I then presume?
    And how should I begin?

. . . .

Shall I say, I have gone at dusk through narrow streets
And watched the smoke that rises from the pipes
Of lonely men in shirt-sleeves, leaning out of windows?...

I should have been a pair of ragged claws
Scuttling across the floors of silent seas.

. . . .

And the afternoon, the evening, sleeps so peacefully!
Smoothed by long fingers,
Asleep... tired... or it malingers,
Stretched on the floor, here beside you and me.
Should I, after tea and cakes and ices,
Have the strength to force the moment to its crisis?
But though I have wept and fasted, wept and prayed,

Though I have seen my head (grown slightly bald) brought in upon a platter,
I am no prophet—and here's no great matter;
I have seen the moment of my greatness flicker,
And I have seen the eternal Footman hold my coat, and snicker,
And in short, I was afraid.

And would it have been worth it, after all,
After the cups, the marmalade, the tea,
Among the porcelain, among some talk of you and me,
Would it have been worth while,
To have bitten off the matter with a smile,
To have squeezed the universe into a ball
To roll it toward some overwhelming question,
To say: "I am Lazarus, come from the dead,
Come back to tell you all, I shall tell you all"—
If one, settling a pillow by her head,
    Should say: "That is not what I meant at all;
    That is not it, at all."

And would it have been worth it, after all,
Would it have been worth while,
After the sunsets and the dooryards and the sprinkled streets,
After the novels, after the teacups, after the skirts that trail along the floor—
And this, and so much more?—
It is impossible to say just what I mean!
But as if a magic lantern threw the nerves in patterns on a screen:
Would it have been worth while
If one, settling a pillow or throwing off a shawl,
And turning toward the window, should say:
    "That is not it at all,
    That is not what I meant, at all."

. . . .

No! I am not Prince Hamlet, nor was meant to be;
Am an attendant lord, one that will do
To swell a progress, start a scene or two,
Advise the prince; no doubt, an easy tool,
Deferential, glad to be of use,
Politic, cautious, and meticulous;
Full of high sentence, but a bit obtuse;
At times, indeed, almost ridiculous—
Almost, at times, the Fool.

I grow old . . . I grow old . . .
I shall wear the bottoms of my trousers rolled.

Shall I part my hair behind? Do I dare to eat a peach?
I shall wear white flannel trousers, and walk upon the beach.
I have heard the mermaids singing, each to each.

I do not think that they will sing to me.

I have seen them riding seaward on the waves
Combing the white hair of the waves blown back
When the wind blows the water white and black.

We have lingered in the chambers of the sea
By sea-girls wreathed with seaweed red and brown
Till human voices wake us, and we drown. [1915]

David Foster Wallace

Incarnations of Burned Children

The Daddy was around the side of the house hanging a door for the tenant when he heard the child's screams and the Mommy's voice gone high between them. He could move fast, and the back porch gave onto the kitchen, and before the screen door had banged shut behind him the Daddy had taken the scene in whole, the overturned pot on the floortile before the stove and the burner's blue jet and the floor's pool of water still steaming as its many arms extended, the toddler in his baggy diaper standing rigid with steam coming off his hair and his chest and shoulders scarlet and his eyes rolled up and mouth open very wide and seeming somehow separate from the sounds that issued, the Mommy down on one knee with the dishrag dabbing pointlessly at him and matching the screams with cries of her own, hysterical so she was almost frozen. Her one knee and the bare little soft feet were still in the steaming pool, and the Daddy's first act was to take the child under the arms and lift him away from it and take him to the sink, where he threw out plates and struck the tap to let cold wellwater run over the boy's feet while with his cupped hand he gathered and poured or flung more cold water over his head and shoulders and chest, wanting first to see the steam stop coming off him, the Mommy over his shoulder invoking God until he sent her for towels and gauze if they had it, the Daddy moving quickly and well and his man's mind empty of everything but purpose, not yet aware of how smoothly he moved or that he'd ceased to hear the high screams because to hear them would freeze him and make impossible what had to be done to help his child, whose screams were regular as breath and went on so long they'd become already a thing in the kitchen, something else to move quickly around. The tenant side's door outside hung half off its top hinge and moved slightly in the wind, and a bird in the oak across the driveway appeared to observe the door with a cocked head as the cries still came from inside. The worst scalds seemed to be the right arm and shoulder, the chest and stomach's red was fading to pink under the cold water and his feet's soft soles weren't blistered that the Daddy could see, but the toddler still made little fists and screamed except now merely on reflex from fear the Daddy would know he thought possible later, small face distended and thready veins standing out at the temples and the Daddy kept saying he was here he was here, adrenaline ebbing and an anger at the Mommy for allowing this thing to happen just starting to gather in wisps at his mind's extreme rear still hours from expression. When the Mommy returned he wasn't sure whether to wrap the child in a towel or not but he wet the towel down and did, swaddled him tight and lifted his baby out of the sink and set him on the kitchen table's edge to soothe him while the Mommy tried to check the feet's soles with one hand waving around in the area of her mouth and uttering objectless words while the Daddy bent in and was face to face with the child on the table's checkered edge repeating the fact that he was here and trying to calm the toddler's cries but still the child breathlessly screamed, a high pure shining sound that could stop his heart and his bitty lips and gums now tinged with the light blue of a low flame the Daddy thought, screaming as if almost still under the tilted pot in pain. A minute, two like this that seemed much longer, with the Mommy at the Daddy's side talking sing-song at the child's face and the lark on the limb with its head to the side and the hinge going white in a line from the weight of the canted door until the first wisp of steam came lazy from under the wrapped towel's hem and the parents' eyes met and widened—the diaper, which when they opened the towel and leaned their little boy back on the checkered cloth and unfastened the softened tabs and tried to remove it resisted slightly with new high cries and was hot, their baby's diaper burned their hand and they saw where the real water'd fallen and pooled and been burning their baby all this time while he screamed for them to help him and they hadn't, hadn't thought and when they got it off and saw the state of what was there the Mommy said their God's first name and grabbed the table to keep her feet while the father turned away and threw a haymaker at the air of the kitchen and cursed both himself and the world for not the last time while his child might now have been sleeping if not for the rate of his breathing and the tiny stricken motions of his hands in the air above where he lay, hands the size of a grown man's thumb that had clutched the Daddy's thumb in the crib while he'd watched the Daddy's mouth move in song, his head cocked and seeming to see way past him into something his eyes made the Daddy lonesome for in a strange vague way. If you've never wept and want to, have a child. Break your heart inside and something will a child is the twangy song the Daddy hears again as if the lady was almost there with him looking down at what they've done, though hours later what the Daddy won't most forgive is how badly he wanted a cigarette right then as they diapered the child as best they could in gauze and two crossed handtowels and the Daddy lifted him like a newborn with his skull in one palm and ran him out to the hot truck and burned custom rubber all the way to town and the clinic's ER with the tenant's door hanging open like that all day until the hinge gave but by then it was too late, when it wouldn't stop and they couldn't make it the child had learned to leave himself and watch the whole rest unfold from a point overhead, and whatever was lost never thenceforth mattered, and the child's body expanded and walked about and drew pay and lived its life untenanted, a thing among things, its self's soul so much vapor aloft, falling as rain and then rising, the sun up and down like a yoyo. [2004]

Gabriel García Márquez

The Handsomest Drowned Man in the World

The first children who saw the dark and slinky bulge approaching through the sea let themselves think it was an enemy ship. Then they saw it had no flags or masts and they thought it was a whale. But when it was washed up on the beach, they removed the clumps of seaweed, the jellyfish tentacles, and the remains of fish and flotsam, and only then did they see that it was a drowned man.

They had been playing with him all afternoon, burying him in the sand and digging him up again, when someone chanced to see them and spread the alarm in the village. The men who carried him to the nearest house noticed that he weighed more than any dead man they had ever known, almost as much as a horse, and they said to each other that maybe he'd been floating too long and the water had got into his bones. When they laid him on the floor they said he'd been taller than all other men because there was barely enough room for him in the house, but they thought that maybe the ability to keep on growing after death was part of the nature of certain drowned men. He had the smell of the sea about him and only his shape gave one to suppose that it was the corpse of a human being, because the skin was covered with a crust of mud and scales.

They did not even have to clean off his face to know that the dead man was a stranger. The village was made up of only twenty-odd wooden houses that had stone courtyards with no flowers and which were spread about on the end of a desertlike cape. There was so little land that mothers always went about with the fear that the wind would carry off their children and the few dead that the years had caused among them had to be thrown off the cliffs. But the sea was calm and bountiful and all the men fit into seven boats. So when they found the drowned man they simply had to look at one another to see that they were all there.

That night they did not go out to work at sea. While the men went to find out if anyone was missing in neighboring villages, the women stayed behind to care for the drowned man. They took the mud off with grass swabs, they removed the underwater stones entangled in his hair, and they scraped the crust off with tools used for scaling fish. As they were doing that they noticed that the vegetation on him came from faraway oceans and deep water and that his clothes were in tatters, as if he had sailed through labyrinths of coral. They noticed too that he bore his death with pride, for he did not have the lonely look of other drowned men who came out of the sea or that haggard, needy look of men who drowned in rivers. But only when they finished cleaning him off did they become aware of the kind of man he was and it left them breathless. Not only was he the tallest, strongest, most virile, and best built man they had ever seen, but even though they were looking at him there was no room for him in their imagination.

They could not find a bed in the village large enough to lay him on nor was there a table solid enough to use for his wake. The tallest men's holiday pants would not fit him, not the fattest ones' Sunday shirts, nor the shoes of the one with biggest feet. Fascinated by his huge size and his beauty, the women then decided to make him some pants from a large piece of sail and a shirt from some bridal brabant linen so that he could continue through his death with dignity. As they sewed, sitting in a circle and gazing at the corpse between stitches, it seemed to them that the wind had never been so steady nor the sea so restless as on that night and they supposed that the change had something to do with the dead man. They thought that if that magnificent man had lived in the village, his house would have had the widest doors, the highest ceiling, and the strongest floor, his bedstead would have been made from a midship frame held together by iron bolts, and his wife would have been the happiest woman. They thought that he would have had so much authority that he could have drawn fish out of the sea simply by calling their names and that he would have put so much work into his land that springs would have burst forth from among the rocks so that he would have been able to plant flowers on the cliffs. They secretly compared him to their own men, thinking that for all their lives theirs were incapable of doing what he could do in one night, and they ended up dismissing them deep in their hearts as the weakest, meanest, and most useless creatures on earth. They were wandering through that maze of fantasy when the oldest woman, who as the oldest had looked upon the drowned man with more compassion than passion, sighed:

"He has the face of someone called Esteban."

It was true. Most of them had only to take another look at him to see that he could not have any other name. The more stubborn among them, who were the youngest, still lived for a few hours with the illusion that when they put his clothes on and he lay among the flowers in patent leather shoes his name might be Lautaro. But it was a vain illusion. There had not been enough canvas, the poorly cut and worse sewn pants were too tight, and the hidden strength of his heart popped the buttons on his shirt. After midnight the whistling of the wind died down and the sea fell into its Wednesday drowsiness. The silence put an end to any last doubts: he was Esteban. The women who had dressed him, who had combed his hair, had cut his nails and shaved him were unable to hold back a shudder of pity when they had to resign themselves to his being dragged along the ground. It was then that they understood how unhappy he must have been with that huge body since it bothered him even after death. They could see him in life, condemned to going through doors sideways, cracking his head on crossbeams, remaining on his feet during visits, not knowing what to do with his soft, pink, sea lion hands while the lady of the house looked for her most resistant chair and begged him, frightened to death, sit here, Esteban, please, and he, leaning against the wall, smiling, don't bother, ma'am, I'm fine where I am, his heels raw and his back roasted from having done the same thing so many times whenever he paid a visit, don't bother, ma'am, I'm fine where I am, just to avoid the embarrassment of breaking up the chair, and never knowing perhaps that the ones who said don't go, Esteban, at least wait till the coffee's ready, were the ones who later on would, whisper the big boob finally left, how nice, the handsome fool has gone. That was what the women were thinking beside the body a little before dawn. Later, when they covered his face with a handkerchief so that the light would not bother him, he looked so forever dead, so defenseless, so much like their men that the first furrows of tears opened in their hearts. It was one of the younger ones who began the weeping. The others, coming to, went from sighs to wails, and the more they sobbed the more they felt like weeping, because the drowned man was becoming all the more Esteban for them, and so they wept so much, for he was the most destitute, most peaceful, and most obliging man on earth, poor Esteban. So when the men returned with the news that the drowned man was not from the neighboring villages either, the women felt an opening of jubilation in the midst of their tears.

"Praise the Lord," they sighed, "he's ours!"

The men thought the fuss was only womanish frivolity. Fatigued because of the difficult nighttime inquiries, all they wanted was to get rid of the bother of the newcomer once and for all before the sun grew strong on that arid, windless day. They improvised a litter with the remains of foremasts and gaffs, tying it together with rigging so that it would bear the weight of the body until they reached the cliffs. They wanted to tie the anchor from a cargo ship to him so that he would sink easily into the deepest waves, where fish are blind and divers die of nostalgia, and bad currents would not bring him back to shore, as had happened with other bodies. But the more they hurried, the more the women thought of ways to waste time. They walked about like startled hens, pecking with the sea charms on their breasts, some interfering on one side to put a scapular of the good wind on the drowned man, some on the other side to put a wrist compass on him, and after a great deal of *get away from there, woman, stay out of the way, look, you almost made me fall on top of the dead man*, the men began to feel mistrust in their livers and started grumbling about why so many main-altar decorations for a stranger, because no matter how many nails and holy-water jars he had on him, the sharks would chew him all the same, but the women kept piling on their junk relics, running back and forth, stumbling, while they released in sighs what they did not in tears, so that the men finally exploded with *since when has there ever been such a fuss over a drifting-corpse, a drowned nobody, a piece of cold Wednesday meat.* One of the women, mortified by so much lack of care, then removed the handkerchief from the dead man's face and the men were left breathless too.

He was Esteban. It was not necessary to repeat it for them to recognize him. If they had been told Sir Walter Raleigh, even they might have been impressed with his gringo accent, the macaw on his shoulder, his cannibal-killing blunderbuss, but there could be only one Esteban in the world and there he was, stretched out like a sperm whale, shoeless, wearing the pants of an undersized child, and with those stony nails that had to be cut with a knife. They only had to take the handkerchief off his face to see that he was ashamed, that it was not his fault that he was so big or so heavy or so handsome, and if he had known that this was going to happen, he would have looked for a more discreet place to drown in, seriously, I even would have tied the anchor off a galleon around my neck and staggered off a cliff like someone who doesn't like things in order not to be upsetting people now with this Wednesday dead body, as you people say, in order not to be bothering anyone with this filthy piece of cold meat that doesn't have anything to do with me. There was so much truth in his manner that even the most mistrustful men, the ones who felt the bitterness of endless nights at sea fearing that their women would tire of dreaming about them and begin to dream of drowned men, even they and others who were harder still shuddered in the marrow of their bones at Esteban's sincerity.

That was how they came to hold the most splendid funeral they could conceive of for an abandoned drowned man. Some women who had gone to get flowers in the neighboring villages returned with other women who could not believe what they had been told, and those women went back for more flowers when they saw the dead man, and they brought more and more until there were so many flowers and so many people that it was hard to walk about. At the final moment it pained them to return him to the waters as an orphan and they chose a father and mother from among the best people, and aunts and uncles and cousins, so that through him all the inhabitants of the village became kinsmen. Some sailors who heard the weeping from a distance went off course and people heard of one who had himself tied to the mainmast, remembering ancient fables about sirens. While they fought for the privilege of carrying him on their shoulders along the steep escarpment by the cliffs, men and women became aware for the first time of the desolation of their streets, the dryness of their courtyards, the narrowness of their dreams as they faced the splendor and beauty of their drowned man. They let him go without an anchor so that he could come back if he wished and whenever he wished, and they all held their breath for the fraction of centuries the body took to fall into the abyss. They did not need to look at one another to realize that they were no longer all present, that they would never be. But they also knew that everything would be different from then on, that their houses would have wider doors, higher ceilings, and stronger floors so that Esteban's memory could go everywhere without bumping into beams and so that no one in the future would dare whisper the big boob finally died, too bad, the handsome fool has finally died, because they were going to paint their house fronts gay colors to make Esteban's memory eternal and they were going to break their backs digging for springs among the stones and planting flowers on the cliffs so that in future years at dawn the passengers on great liners would awaken, suffocated by the smell of gardens on the high seas, and the captain would have to come down from the bridge in his dress uniform, with his astrolabe, his pole star, and his row of war medals and, pointing to the promontory of roses on the horizon, he would say in fourteen languages, look there, where the wind is so peaceful now that it's gone to sleep beneath the beds, over there, where the sun's so bright that the sunflowers don't know which way to turn, yes, over there, that's Esteban's village. [1971]

Samuel Green

Some Reasons Why I Became a Poet

Because I wanted to undo each stitch
in time, unravel the nine seams
that inhibit remembering; because I wanted
to roll a stone with such tenderness
that moss would grow & hold light
on all sides at once; because I wanted to teach
every old dog I saw a new set of tricks;
because I wanted to lead a blind horse
to water & make her believe her thirst
mattered; because I wanted to count
the chickens of grief & gain before they hatched;
because I never wanted to let sleeping cats lie
in wait beneath the birdbath; because
I wanted to close the barn door after the last
horse went grazing & know that something
important was left stalled inside; because
I wanted to welcome all Greeks & the desperate
bearing of their gifts; & because I couldn't stop
keeping my poor mouth open in a sort
of continual awe, trusting that flies, like
words, would come & go in their own good time. [2008]

Corrinne Hales

Power

No one we knew had ever stopped a train.
Hardly daring to breathe, I waited
Belly-down with my brother
In a dry ditch
Watching through the green thickness
Of grass and willows.
Stuffed with crumpled newspapers,
The shirt and pants looked real enough
Stretched out across the rails. I felt my heart
Beating against the cool ground,
And the terrible long screech of the train's
Braking began. We had done it.

Then it was in front of us—
A hundred iron wheels tearing like time
Into red flannel and denim, shredding the child
We had made—until it finally stopped.

My brother jabbed at me,
Pointed down the tracks. A man
Had climbed out of the engine, was running
In our direction, waving his arms,
Screaming that he would kill us—
Whoever we were.
Then, very close to the spot
Where we hid, he stomped and cursed
As the rags and papers scattered
Over the gravel from our joke.

I tried to remember which of us
That red shirt belonged to,
But morning seemed too long ago, and the man
Was falling, sobbing, to his knees.
I couldn't stop watching.
My brother lay next to me,
His hands covering his ears,
His face pressed tight to the ground. [1986]

Kathleen Halme

A Study in *O*

Although they felt the chromosomal undertow,
they were prone to follow the old code, and so
no one misspoke.
No one allowed the holy smoke to shroud the throaty episode.
No one moaned an orgy of self-reproach.
The dead bolts on their homes had not corroded.
No one misspoke.

One cold morning on the corner
of Oak and DeSoto, they said hello...
the old vertigo flowed and
overflowed. Even though
they had hoped to postpone
the whole explosion,
no one misspoke. [1998]

Barbara Hamby

Ode to My 1977 Toyota

Engine like a Singer sewing machine, where have you
    not carried me—to dance class, grocery shopping,
into the heart of darkness and back again? O the fruit
    you've transported—cherries, peaches, blueberries,
watermelons, thousands of Fuji apples—books,
    and all my dark thoughts, the giddy ones, too,
like bottles of champagne popped at the wedding of two people
    who will pass each other on the street as strangers
in twenty years. Ronald Reagan was president when I walked
    into Big Chief Motors and saw you glimmering
on the lot like a slice of broiled mahi mahi or sushi
    without its topknot of tuna. Remember the months
I drove you to work singing "Some Enchanted Evening"?
    Those were scary times. All I thought about
was getting on I-10 with you and not stopping. Would you
    have made it to New Orleans? What would our life
have been like there? I'd forgotten about poetry. Thank God,
    I remembered her. She saved us both. We were young
together. Now we're not. College boys stop us at traffic lights

and tell me how cool you are. Like an ice cube, I say,
though you've never had air conditioning. Who needed it?
I would have missed so many smells without you—
confederate jasmine, magnolia blossoms, the briny sigh
of the Gulf of Mexico, rotting 'possums scattered
along 319 between Sopchoppy and Panacea. How many holes
are there in the ballet shoes in your back seat?
How did that pair of men's white loafers end up in your trunk?
Why do I have so many questions, and why
are the answers like the animals that dart in front of your headlights
as we drive home from the coast, the Milky Way
strung across the black velvet bowl of the sky like the tiara
of some impossibly fat empress who rules the universe
but doesn't know if tomorrow is December or Tuesday or June first. [2004]

Patricia Hampl

Red Sky in the Morning

Years ago, in another life, I woke to look out the smeared window of a Greyhound bus I had been riding all night, and in the still-dark morning of a small Missouri river town where the driver had made a scheduled stop at a grimy diner, I saw below me a stout middle-aged woman in a flowered housedress turn and kiss full on the mouth a godlike young man with golden curls. But I've got that wrong: he was kissing her. Passionately, without regard for the world and its incomprehension. He had abandoned himself to his love, and she, stolid, matronly, received this adoration with simple grandeur, like a socialist-realist statue of a woman taking up sheaves of wheat.

Their ages dictated that he must be her son, but I had just come out of the cramped, ruinous half sleep of a night on a Greyhound and I was clairvoyant: This was that thing called love. The morning light cracked blood red along the river.

Of course, when she lumbered onto the bus a moment later, lurching forward with her two bulging bags, she chose the empty aisle seat next to me as her own. She pitched one bag onto the overhead rack, and then heaved herself into the seat as if she were used to hoisting sacks of potatoes onto the flatbed of a pickup. She held the other bag on her lap, and leaned toward the window. The beautiful boy was blowing kisses. He couldn't see where she was in the dark interior, so he blew kisses up and down the side of the bus, gazing ardently at the blank windows. "Pardon me," the woman said without looking at me, and leaned over, bag and all, to rap the glass. Her beautiful boy ran back to our window and kissed and kissed, and finally hugged himself, shutting his eyes in an ecstatic pantomime of love-sweet-love. She smiled and waved back.

Then the bus was moving. She slumped back in her seat, and I turned to her. I suppose I looked transfixed. As our eyes met she said, "Everybody thinks he's my son. But he's not. He's my husband." She let that sink in. She was a farm woman with hands that could have been a man's; I was a university student, hair down to my waist. It was long ago, as I said, in another life. It was even another life for the country. The Vietnam War was the time we were living through, and I was traveling, as I did every three weeks, to visit my boyfriend who was in a federal prison. "Draft dodger," my brother said. "Draft resister," I piously retorted. I had never been kissed the way this woman had been kissed. I was living in a tattered corner of a romantic idyll, the one where the hero is willing to suffer for his beliefs. I was the girlfriend. I lived on pride, not love.

My neighbor patted her short cap of hair, and settled in for the long haul as we pulled onto the highway along the river, heading south. "We been married five years and we're happy," she said with a penetrating satisfaction, the satisfaction that passeth understanding. "Oh," she let out a profound sigh as if she mined her truths from the bountiful, bulky earth, "Oh, I could tell you stories." She put her arms snugly around her bag, gazed off for a moment, apparently made pensive by her remark. Then she closed her eyes and fell asleep.

I looked out the window smudged by my nose which had been pressed against it at the bus stop to see the face of true love reveal itself. Beyond the bus the sky, instead of becoming paler with the dawn, drew itself out of a black line along the Mississippi into an alarming red flare. It was very beautiful. The old caution—Red sky in the morning, sailor take warning—darted through my mind and fell away. Remember this, I remember telling myself, hang on to this. I could feel it all skittering away, whatever conjunction of beauty and improbability I had stumbled upon.

It is hard to describe the indelible bittersweetness of that moment. Which is why, no doubt, it had to be remembered. The very word—Remember!—spiraled up like a snake out of a basket, a magic catch in its sound, the doubling of the m—re mem-memem—setting up a low murmur full of inchoate associations as if a loved voice were speaking into my ear alone, occultly.

Whether it was the unguarded face of love, or the red gash down the middle of the warring country I was traveling through, or this exhausted farm woman's promise of untold tales that bewitched me, I couldn't say. Over it all rose and remains only the injunction to remember. This, the most impossible command we lay upon ourselves, claimed me and then perversely disappeared, trailing an illusive silken tissue of meaning, without giving a story, refusing to leave me in peace.

Because everyone "has" a memoir, we all have a stake in how such stories are told. For we do not, after all, simply have experience; we are entrusted with it. We must do something—make something—with it. A story, we sense, is the only possible habitation for the burden of our witnessing.

The tantalizing formula of my companion on the Greyhound—oh, I could tell you stories—is the memoirist's opening line, but it has none of the delicious promise of the storyteller's "Once upon a time..." In fact, it is a perverse statement. The woman on the bus told me nothing—she fell asleep and escaped to her dreams. For the little sentence inaugurates nothing, and leads nowhere after its dot dot dot of expectation. Whatever experience lies tangled within its seductive promise remains forever balled up in the woolly impossibility of telling the-truth-the-whole-truth of a life, any life.

Memoirists, unlike fiction writers, do not really want to "tell a story." They want to tell it all—the all of personal experience, of consciousness itself. That includes a story, but also the whole expanding universe of sensation and thought that flows beyond the confines of narrative and proves every life to be not only an isolated story line but a bit of the cosmos, spinning and streaming into the great, ungraspable pattern of existence. Memoirists wish to tell their mind, not their story.

The wistfulness implicit in that conditional verb—I could tell—conveys an urge more primitive than a storyteller's search for an audience. It betrays not a loneliness for someone who will listen but a hopelessness about language itself and a sad recognition of its limitations. How much reality can subject-verb-object bear on the frail shoulders of the sentence? The sigh within the statement is more like this: I could tell you stories—if only stories could tell what I have in me to tell.

For this reason, autobiographical writing is bedeviled. It is caught in a self which must become a world—and not, please, a narcissistic world. The memoir, once considered a marginal literary form, has emerged in the past decade as the signature genre of the age. "The triumph of memoir is now established fact," James Atlas trumpeted in a cover story on "The Age of the Literary Memoir" in the *New York Times Magazine*. "Fiction," he claimed, "isn't delivering the news. Memoir is."

With its "triumph," the memoir has, of course, not denied the truth and necessity of fiction. In fact, it leans heavily on novelistic assumptions. But the contemporary memoir has reaffirmed the primacy of the first person voice in American imaginative writing established by Whitman's "Song of Myself." Maybe a reader's love of memoir is less an intrusive lust for confession than a hankering for the intimacy of this first-person voice, the deeply satisfying sense of being spoken to privately. More than a story, we want a voice speaking softly, urgently, in our ear. Which is to say, to our heart. That voice carries its implacable command, the ancient murmur that called out to me in the middle of the country in the middle of a war—remember, remember (I dare you, I tempt you).

Looking out the Greyhound window that red morning all those years ago, I saw the improbable face of love. But even more puzzling was the cryptic remark of the beloved as she sat next to me. I think of her more often than makes sense. Though he was the beauty, she is the one who comes back. How faint his golden curls have become (he also had a smile, crooked and charming, but I can only remember the idea of it—the image is gone). It is she, stout and unbeautiful, wearing her flowery cotton housedress with a zipper down the middle, who has taken up residence with her canny eye and her acceptance of adoration. To be loved like that, loved improbably: of course, she had stories to tell. She took it for granted in some unapologetic way, like being born to wealth. Take the money and run.

But that moment before she fell asleep, when she looked pensive, the red morning rising over the Mississippi, was a wistful moment. I could tell you stories—but she could not. What she had to tell was too big, too much, too something, for her to place in the small shrine that a story is.

When we met—if what happened between us was a meeting—I felt nothing had ever happened to me and nothing ever would. I didn't understand that riding this filthy Greyhound down the middle of bloodied America in the middle of a mutinous war was itself a story and that something was happening to me. I thought if something was happening to anybody around me it was happening to people like my boyfriend: They were the heroes, according to the lights that shined for me then. I was just riding shotgun in my own life. I could not have imagined containing, as the farm woman slumped next to me did, the sheer narrative bulk to say, "I could tell you stories," and then drifting off with the secret heaviness of experience into the silence where stories live their real lives, crumbling into the loss we call remembrance.

The boastful little declaration, pathetically conditional (not "I'll tell you a story" but "I could") wavered wistfully for an instant between us. The stranger's remark, launched in the dark of the Greyhound, floated across the human landscape like the lingering tone of a struck bell from a village church, and joined all the silence that ever was, as I turned my face to the window where the world was rushing by along the slow river. [2000]

Joy Harjo

Suspended

Once I was so small that I could barely peer over the top of the backseat of the black Cadillac my father polished and tuned daily; I wanted to see everything. It was around the time I acquired language, or even before that time, when something happened that changed my relationship to the spin of the world. My concept of language, of what was possible with music was changed by this revelatory moment. It changed even the way I looked at the sun. This suspended integer of time probably escaped ordinary notice in my parents' universe, which informed most of my vision in the ordinary world. They were still omnipresent gods. We were driving somewhere in Tulsa, the northern border of the Creek Nation. I don't know where we were going or where we had been, but I know the sun was boiling the asphalt, the car windows open for any breeze as I stood on tiptoes on the floorboard behind my father, a handsome god who smelled of Old Spice, whose slick black hair was always impeccably groomed, his clothes perfectly creased and ironed. The radio was on. I loved the radio, jukeboxes or any magic thing containing music even then.

I wonder now what signaled this moment, a loop of time that on first glance could be any place in time. I became acutely aware of the line the jazz trumpeter was playing (a sound I later associated with Miles Davis). I didn't know the word jazz or trumpet, or the concepts. I don't know how to say it, with what sounds or words, but in that confluence of hot southern afternoon, in the breeze of aftershave and humidity, I followed that sound to the beginning, to the place of the birth of sound. I was suspended in whirling stars, a moon to which I'd traveled often by then. I grieved my parents' failings, my own life which I saw stretched the length of that rhapsody.

My rite of passage into the world of humanity occurred then, via jazz. The music made a startling bridge between familiar and strange lands, an appropriate vehicle, for though the music is predominantly west African in concept, with European associations, jazz was influenced by the Creek (or Muscogee) people, for we were there when jazz was born. I recognized it, that humid afternoon in my formative years, as a way to speak beyond the confines of ordinary language. I still hear it. [2012]

Terrance Hayes

The Same City

For James L. Hayes

The rain falling on a night
    in mid-December,
I pull to my father's engine
    wondering how long I'll remember
this. His car is dead. He connects
    jumper cables to his battery,
then to mine without looking in
    at me and the child. Water beads
on the windshields, the road sign,
    his thin blue coat. I'd get out now,
prove I can stand with him
    in the cold, but he told me to stay
with the infant. I wrap her
    in the blanket, staring
for what seems like a long time
    into her open, toothless mouth,
and wish she was mine. I feed her
    an orange softened first in my mouth,
chewed gently until the juice runs
    down my fingers as I squeeze it
into hers. What could any of this matter
    to another man passing on his way
to his family, his radio deafening
    the sound of water and breathing
along all the roads bound to his?
    But to rescue a soul is as close
as anyone comes to God.
    Think of Noah lifting a small black bird
from its nest. Think of Joseph,
    raising a son that wasn't his.

Let me begin again.
    I want to be holy. In rain
I pull to my father's car
    with my girlfriend's infant.
She was eight weeks pregnant when we met.
    But we'd make love. We'd make
love below stars and shingles
    while her baby kicked between us.
Perhaps a man whose young child

bears his face, whose wife waits
as he drives home through rain
& darkness, perhaps that man
would call me a fool. So what.
There is one thing I will remember
all my life. It is as small
& holy as the mouth
of an infant. It is speechless.
When his car would not stir,
my father climbed in beside us,
took the orange from my hand,
took the baby in his arms.
In 1974, this man met my mother
for the first time as I cried or slept
in the same city that holds us tonight.
If you ever tell my story,
say that's the year I was born. [2002]

Ernest Hemingway

Hills Like White Elephants

The hills across the valley of the Ebro were long and white. On this side there was no shade and no trees and the station was between two lines of rails in the sun. Close against the side of the station there was the warm shadow of the building and a curtain, made of strings of bamboo beads, hung across the open door into the bar, to keep out flies. The American and the girl with him sat at a table in the shade, outside the building. It was very hot and the express from Barcelona would come in forty minutes. It stopped at this junction for two minutes and went on to Madrid.

"What should we drink?" the girl asked. She had taken off her hat and put it on the table.

"It's pretty hot," the man said.

"Let's drink beer."

"*Dos cervezas*," the man said into the curtain.

"Big ones?" a woman asked from the doorway.

"Yes. Two big ones."

The woman brought two glasses of beer and two felt pads. She put the felt pads and the beer glasses on the table and looked at the man and the girl. The girl was looking off at the line of hills. They were white in the sun and the country was brown and dry.

"They look like white elephants," she said.

"I've never seen one," the man drank his beer.

"No, you wouldn't have."

"I might have," the man said. "Just because you say I wouldn't have doesn't prove anything."

The girl looked at the bead curtain. "They've painted something on it," she said. "What does it say?"

"Anis del Toro. It's a drink."

"Could we try it?"

The man called "Listen" through the curtain. The woman came out from the bar.

"Four reales."

"We want two Anis del Toro."

"With water?"

"Do you want it with water?"

"I don't know," the girl said. "Is it good with water?"

"It's all right."

"You want them with water?" asked the woman.

"Yes, with water."

"It tastes like licorice," the girl said and put the glass down.

"That's the way with everything."

"Yes," said the girl. "Everything tastes of licorice. Especially all the things you've waited so long for, like absinthe."

"Oh, cut it out."

"You started it," the girl said. "I was being amused. I was having a fine time."

"Well, let's try and have a fine time."

"All right. I was trying. I said the mountains looked like white elephants. Wasn't that bright?"

"That was bright."

"I wanted to try this new drink: That's all we do, isn't it—look at things and try new drinks?"

"I guess so."

The girl looked across at the hills.

"They're lovely hills," she said. "They don't really look like white elephants. I just meant the coloring of their skin through the trees."

"Should we have another drink?"

"All right."

The warm wind blew the bead curtain against the table.

"The beer's nice and cool," the man said.

"It's lovely," the girl said.

"It's really an awfully simple operation, Jig," the man said. "It's not really an operation at all."

The girl looked at the ground the table legs rested on.

"I know you wouldn't mind it, Jig. It's really not anything. It's just to let the air in."

The girl did not say anything.

"I'll go with you and I'll stay with you all the time. They just let the air in and then it's all perfectly natural."

"Then what will we do afterward?"

"We'll be fine afterward. Just like we were before."

"What makes you think so?"

"That's the only thing that bothers us. It's the only thing that's made us unhappy."

The girl looked at the bead curtain, put her hand out and took hold of two of the strings of beads.

"And you think then we'll be all right and be happy."

"I know we will. You don't have to be afraid. I've known lots of people that have done it."

"So have I," said the girl. "And afterward they were all so happy."

"Well," the man said, "if you don't want to you don't have to. I wouldn't have you do it if you didn't want to. But I know it's perfectly simple."

"And you really want to?"

"I think it's the best thing to do. But I don't want you to do it if you don't really want to."

"And if I do it you'll be happy and things will be like they were and you'll love me?"

"I love you now. You know I love you."

"I know. But if I do it, then it will be nice again if I say things are like white elephants, and you'll like it?"

"I'll love it. I love it now but I just can't think about it. You know how I get when I worry."

"If I do it you won't ever worry?"

"I won't worry about that because it's perfectly simple."

"Then I'll do it. Because I don't care about me."

"What do you mean?"

"I don't care about me."

"Well, I care about you."

"Oh, yes. But I don't care about me. And I'll do it and then everything will be fine."

"I don't want you to do it if you feel that way."

The girl stood up and walked to the end of the station. Across, on the other side, were fields of grain and trees along the banks of the Ebro. Far away, beyond the river, were mountains. The shadow of a cloud moved across the field of grain and she saw the river through the trees.

"And we could have all this," she said. "And we could have everything and every day we make it more impossible."

"What did you say?"

"I said we could have everything."

"We can have everything."

"No, we can't."

"We can have the whole world."

"No, we can't."

"We can go everywhere."

"No, we can't. It isn't ours any more."

"It's ours."

"No, it isn't. And once they take it away, you never get it back."

"But they haven't taken it away."

"We'll wait and see."

"Come on back in the shade," he said. "You mustn't feel that way."

"I don't feel any way," the girl said. "I just know things."

"I don't want you to do anything that you don't want to do—"

"Nor that isn't good for me," she said. "I know. Could we have another beer?"

"All right. But you've got to realize—"

"I realize," the girl said. "Can't we maybe stop talking?"

They sat down at the table and the girl looked across at the hills on the dry side of the valley and the man looked at her and at the table.

"You've got to realize," he said, "that I don't want you to do it if you don't want to. I'm perfectly willing to go through with it if it means anything to you."

"Doesn't it mean anything to you? We could get along."

"Of course it does. But I don't want anybody but you. I don't want any one else. And I know it's perfectly simple."

"Yes, you know it's perfectly simple."

"It's all right for you to say that, but I do know it."

"Would you do something for me now?"

"I'd do anything for you."

"Would you please please please please please please please stop talking?"

He did not say anything but looked at the bags against the wall of the station. There were labels on them from all the hotels where they had spent nights.

"But I don't want you to," he said, "I don't care anything about it."

"I'll scream," the girl said.

The woman came out through the curtains with two glasses of beer and put them down on the damp felt pads. "The train comes in five minutes," she said.

"What did she say?" asked the girl.

"That the train is coming in five minutes."

The girl smiled brightly at the woman, to thank her.

"I'd better take the bags over to the other side of the station," the man said. She smiled at him.

"All right. Then come back and we'll finish the beer."

He picked up the two heavy bags and carried them around the station to the other tracks. He looked up the tracks but could not see the train. Coming back, he walked through the bar-room, where people waiting for the train were drinking. He drank an Anis at the bar and looked at the people. They were all waiting reasonably for the train. He went out through the bead curtain. She was sitting at the table and smiled at him.

"Do you feel better?" he asked.

"I feel fine," she said. "There's nothing wrong with me. I feel fine." [1927]

Langston Hughes

Harlem (2)

What happens to a dream deferred?

Does it dry up
like a raisin in the sun?
Or fester like a sore—
And then run?
Does it stink like rotten meat?
Or crust and sugar over—
like a syrupy sweet?
Maybe it just sags
like a heavy load.

Or does it explode? [1951]

Maria Hummel

I'm This Many

Are monsters real or not? Is God? Why do
needles hurt people's arms? I don't think
I understand *everything* yet. Red drinks
taste good with straws. When I'm asleep, do
you see my dreams? How did Dinosaur
Land become People Land? Are my legs
longer today? Do stars grow from eggs?
Can I eat like other kids when I turn four?

How many weekends to my birthday?
I want a round cake. I want your hair.
I think the medicine I take for snakes
in-my-stomach is making me cough.
Can you put me to bed now? The air
is dark outside tonight. Who turned it off? [2013]

David Ignatow

The Bagel

I stopped to pick up the bagel
rolling away in the wind,
annoyed with myself
for having dropped it
as if it were a portent.
Faster and faster it rolled,
with me running after it
bent low, gritting my teeth,
and I found myself doubled over
and rolling down the street
head over heels, one complete somersault
after another like a bagel
and strangely happy with myself. [1968]

Denis Johnson

Steady Hands at Seattle General

Inside of two days I was shaving myself, and I even shaved a couple of new arrivals, because the drugs they injected me with had an amazing effect. I call it amazing because only hours before they'd wheeled me through corridors in which I hallucinated a soft, summery rain. In the hospital rooms on either side, objects—vases, ashtrays, beds—had looked wet and scary, hardly bothering to cover up their true meanings.

They ran a few syringesful into me, and I felt like I'd turned from a light, Styrofoam thing into a person. I held up my hands before my eyes. The hands were as still as a sculpture's.

I shaved my roommate, Bill. "Don't get tricky with my mustache," he said.

"Okay so far?"

"So far."

"I'll do the other side."

"That would make sense, partner."

Just below one cheekbone, Bill had a small blemish where a bullet had entered his face, and in the other cheek a slightly larger scar where the slug had gone on its way.

"When you were shot right through your face like that, did the bullet go on to do anything interesting?"

"How would I know? I didn't take notes. Even if it goes on through, you still feel like you just got shot in the head."

"What about this little scar here, through your sideburn?"

"I don't know. Maybe I was born with that one. I never saw it before."

"Someday people are going to read about you in a story or a poem. Will you describe yourself for those people?"

"Oh, I don't know. I'm a fat piece of shit, I guess."

"No. I'm serious."

"You're not going to write about me."

"Hey. I'm a writer."

"Well then, just tell them I'm overweight."

"He's overweight."

"I been shot twice."

"Twice?"

"Once by each wife, for a total of three bullets, making four holes, three ins and one out."

"And you're still alive."

"Are you going to change any of this for your poem?"

"No. It's going in word for word."

"That's too bad, because asking me if I'm alive makes you look kind of stupid. Obviously, I am."

"Well, maybe I mean alive in a deeper sense. You could be talking, and still not be alive in a deeper sense."

"It don't get no deeper than the kind of shit we're in right now."

"What do you mean? It's great here. They even give you cigarettes."

"I didn't get any yet."

"Here you go."

"Hey. Thanks."

"Pay me back when they give you yours."

"Maybe."

"What did you say when she shot you?"

"I said, 'You shot me!'"

"Both times? Both wives?"

"The first time I didn't say anything, because she shot me in the mouth."

"So you couldn't talk."

"I was knocked out cold, is the reason I couldn't talk. And I still remember the dream I had while I was knocked out that time."

"What was the dream?"

"How could I tell you about it? It was a dream. It didn't make any fucking sense, man. But I do remember it."

"You can't describe it even a little bit?"

"I really don't know what the description would be. I'm sorry."

"Anything. Anything at all."

"Well, for one thing, the dream is something that keeps coming back over and over. I mean, when I'm awake. Every time I remember my first wife, I remember that she pulled the trigger on me, and then, here comes that dream...

"And the dream wasn't—there wasn't anything sad about it. But when I remember it, I get like, *Fuck, man, she really, she shot me. And here's that dream.*"

"Did you ever see that Elvis Presley movie, *Follow That Dream*?"

"*Follow That Dream.* Yeah, I did. I was just going to mention that."

"Okay. You're all done. Look in the mirror."

"Right."

"What do you see?"

"How did I get so fat, when I never eat?"

"Is that all?"

"Well, I don't know. I just got here."

"What about your life?"

"Hah! That's a good one."

"What about your past?"

"What about it?"

"When you look back, what do you see?"

"Wrecked cars."

"Any people in them?"

"Yes."

"Who?"

"People who are just meat now, man."

"Is that really how it is?"

"How do I know how it is? I just got here. And it stinks."

"Are you kidding? They're pumping Haldol by the quart. It's a playpen."

"I hope so. Because I been in places where all they do is wrap you in a wet sheet, and let you bite down on a little rubber toy for puppies."

"I could see living here two weeks out of every month."

"Well, I'm older than you are. You can take a couple more rides on this wheel and still get out with all your arms and legs stuck on right. Not me."

"Hey. You're doing fine."

"Talk into here."

"Talk into your bullet hole?"

"Talk into my bullet hole. Tell me I'm fine." [1992]

James Joyce

Eveline

She sat at the window watching the evening invade the avenue. Her head was leaned against the window curtains and in her nostrils was the odour of dusty cretonne. She was tired.

Few people passed. The man out of the last house passed on his way home; she heard his footsteps clacking along the concrete pavement and afterwards crunching on the cinder path before the new red houses. One time there used to be a field there in which they used to play every evening with other people's children. Then a man from Belfast bought the field and built houses in it—not like their little brown houses but bright brick houses with shining roofs. The children of the avenue used to play together in that field—the Devines, the Waters, the Dunns, little Keogh the cripple, she and her brothers and sisters. Ernest, however, never played: he was too grown up. Her father used often to hunt them in out of the field with his blackthorn stick; but usually little Keogh used to keep *nix* and call out when he saw her father coming. Still they seemed to have been rather happy then. Her father was not so bad then; and besides, her mother was alive. That was a long time ago; she and her brothers and sisters were all grown up; her mother was dead. Tizzie Dunn was dead, too, and the Waters had gone back to England. Everything changes. Now she was going to go away like the others, to leave her home.

Home! She looked round the room, reviewing all its familiar objects which she had dusted once a week for so many years, wondering where on earth all the dust came from. Perhaps she would never see again those familiar objects from which she had never dreamed of being divided. And yet during all those years she had never found out the name of the priest whose yellowing photograph hung on the wall above the broken harmonium beside the coloured print of the promises made to Blessed Margaret Mary Alacoque. He had been a school friend of her father. Whenever he showed the photograph to a visitor her father used to pass it with a casual word:

—He is in Melbourne now.

She had consented to go away, to leave her home. Was that wise? She tried to weigh each side of the question. In her home anyway she had shelter and food; she had those whom she had known all her life about her. Of course she had to work hard both in the house and at business. What would they say of her in the Stores when they found out that she had run away with a fellow? Say she was a fool, perhaps; and her place would be filled up by advertisement. Miss Gavan would be glad. She had always had an edge on her, especially whenever there were people listening.

—Miss Hill, don't you see these ladies are waiting?

—Look lively, Miss Hill, please.

She would not cry many tears at leaving the Stores.

But in her new home, in a distant unknown country, it would not be like that. Then she would be married—she, Eveline. People would treat her with respect then. She would not be treated as her mother had been. Even now, though she was over nineteen, she sometimes felt herself in danger of her father's violence. She knew it was that that had given her the palpitations. When they were growing up he had never gone for her, like he used to go for Harry and Ernest, because she was a girl; but latterly he had begun to threaten her and say what he would do to her only for her dead mother's sake. And now she had nobody to protect her. Ernest was dead and Harry, who was in the church decorating business, was nearly always down somewhere in the country. Besides, the invariable squabble for money on Saturday nights had begun to weary her unspeakably. She always gave her entire wages—seven shillings—and Harry always sent up what he could but the trouble was to get any money from her father. He said she used to squander the money, that she had no head, that he wasn't going to give her his hard-earned money to throw about the streets, and much more, for he was usually fairly bad of a Saturday night. In the end he would give her the money and ask her had she any intention of buying Sunday's dinner. Then she had to rush out as quickly as she could and do her marketing, holding her black leather purse tightly in her hand as she elbowed her way through the crowds and returning home late under her load of provisions. She had hard work to keep the house together and to see that the two young children who had been left to her charge went to school regularly and got their meals regularly. It was hard work—a hard life—but now that she was about to leave it she did not find it a wholly undesirable life.

She was about to explore another life with Frank. Frank was very kind, manly, open-hearted. She was to go away with him by the night-boat to be his wife and to live with him in Buenos Ayres where he had a home waiting for her. How well she remembered the first time she had seen him; he was lodging in a house on the main road where she used to visit. It seemed a few weeks ago. He was standing at the gate, his peaked cap pushed back on his head and his hair tumbled forward over a face of bronze. Then they had come to know each other. He used to meet her outside the Stores every evening and see her home. He took her to see *The Bohemian Girl* and she felt elated as she sat in an unaccustomed part of the theatre with him. He was awfully fond of music and sang a little. People knew that they were courting and, when he sang about the lass that loves a sailor, she always felt pleasantly confused. He used to call her Poppens out of fun. First of all it had been an excitement for her to have a fellow and then she had begun to like him. He had tales of distant countries. He had started as a deck boy at a pound a month on a ship of the Allan Line going out to Canada. He told her the names of the ships he had been on and the names of the different services. He had sailed through the Straits of Magellan and he told her stories of the terrible Patagonians. He had fallen on his feet in Buenos Ayres, he said, and had come over to the old country just for a holiday. Of course, her father had found out the affair and had forbidden her to have anything to say to him.

—I know these sailor chaps, he said.

One day he had quarrelled with Frank and after that she had to meet her lover secretly.

The evening deepened in the avenue. The white of two letters in her lap grew indistinct. One was to Harry; the other was to her father. Ernest had been her favourite but she liked Harry too. Her father was becoming old lately, she noticed; he would miss her. Sometimes he could be very nice. Not long before, when she had been laid up for a day, he had read her out a ghost story and made toast for her at the fire. Another day, when their mother was alive, they had all gone for a picnic to the Hill of Howth. She remembered her father putting on her mother's bonnet to make the children laugh.

Her time was running out but she continued to sit by the window, leaning her head against the window curtain, inhaling the odour of dusty cretonne. Down far in the avenue she could hear a street organ playing. She knew the air. Strange that it should come that very night to remind her of the promise to her mother, her promise to keep the home together as long as she could. She remembered the last night of her mother's illness; she was again in the close dark room at the other side of the hall and outside she heard a melancholy air of Italy. The organ-player had been ordered to go away and given sixpence. She remembered her father strutting back into the sickroom saying:

—Damned Italians! coming over here!

As she mused the pitiful vision of her mother's life laid its spell on the very quick of her being—that life of commonplace sacrifices closing in final craziness. She trembled as she heard again her mother's voice saying constantly with foolish insistence:

—Derevaun Seraun! Derevaun Seraun!

She stood up in a sudden impulse of terror. Escape! She must escape! Frank would save her. He would give her life, perhaps love, too. But she wanted to live. Why should she be unhappy? She had a right to happiness. Frank would take her in his arms, fold her in his arms. He would save her.

She stood among the swaying crowd in the station at the North Wall. He held her hand and she knew that he was speaking to her, saying something about the passage over and over again. The station was full of soldiers with brown baggages. Through the wide doors of the sheds she caught a glimpse of the black mass of the boat, lying in beside the quay wall, with illumined portholes. She answered nothing. She felt her cheek pale and cold and, out of a maze of distress, she prayed to God to direct her, to show her what was her duty. The boat blew a long mournful whistle into the mist. If she went, to-morrow she would be on the sea with Frank, steaming towards Buenos Ayres. Their passage had been booked. Could she still draw back after all he had done for her? Her distress awoke a nausea in her body and she kept moving her lips in silent fervent prayer.

A bell clanged upon her heart. She felt him seize her hand:

—Come!

All the seas of the world tumbled about her heart. He was drawing her into them: he would drown her. She gripped with both hands at the iron railing.

—Come!

No! No! No! It was impossible. Her hands clutched the iron in frenzy. Amid the seas she sent a cry of anguish!

—Eveline! Evvy!

He rushed beyond the barrier and called to her to follow. He was shouted at to go on but he still called to her. She set her white face to him, passive, like a helpless animal. Her eyes gave him no sign of love or farewell or recognition. [1914]

Kristiana Kahakauwila

Thirty-Nine Rules for Making a Hawaiian Funeral into a Drinking Game

1) Take a drink each time the haole pastor says "hell."

2) Take a drink each time he asks if anybody in the room wants to go there.

3) Take a drink each time he looks at one of your uncles when he says this.

4) Take a drink because cane was burning next to Kaumuali'i Highway on the drive from Kekaha to Poipu, and the hot scent reminded you of your grandmother's house with its upright piano, rattan furniture, and that deep cement sink in the washroom where laundry was scrubbed, and sometimes babies, too. In the family room you and your older cousins used to jostle each other, each of you hoping to be the one who got to sit on Grandma's lap in her high-backed butterfly chair.

One year ago you moved to Honolulu from Los Angeles, just to be closer to her, and now she's gone.

5) Drink when the pastor claims deeds get us into heaven. Deeds like tithing to the church. Deeds like tithing to *his* church. (Do not comment on how this is unbiblical. Do not comment on how he encouraged your grandmother to give until she had no money left for the upkeep of her house. Do not comment on the Louis Vuitton man-purse you've seen him carry into church.)

6) Sneak a swig when the pastor asks everyone to hold hands and confess the sins in their hearts. Get stuck with his doughy palm in yours. Do not respond when he gives your fingers an encouraging squeeze. Do not interrupt when he prays for your family's wayward souls. Instead, look mournfully at the casket where your grandmother lies, and blame her for his presence.

7) After the sermon, approach the casket for the final viewing. Take a sip for each handmade paper lei and crayon drawing your little cousins have gently placed on top of your grandmother's hands. Do not touch her cheeks, which are full and in the dew of a freshly painted blush. Do not kiss her forehead as your cousins might, nor adjust the sleeve of her Sunday mu'umu'u, the one with the red hibiscus pattern, like your aunties do. You may, however, wrap a fine, gray-white tendril of hair around your finger and remember how you used to comb these same strands as she dozed in the hospital bed.

8) With your degree in English, your aunties expect you to deliver the most grammatically correct homage to your grandmother. Take this responsibility seriously. Your copyediting skills are all you have to offer your family.

After all, you were not born on Kaua'i. You weren't even born in Honolulu. No, you were raised a California girl, like your mother before you. She is haole. White. A foreigner. This makes you hapa haole. Half white. Half foreign.

Your eight-year-old cousin is dancing a hula. She hovers on the balls of her feet, her slender hips swaying like a palm. A neighbor's boy strums "Amazing Grace" on a child-size 'ukulele.

You cannot hula or play the uke. You do not speak pidgin. You never add the right proportion of water to poi. But you can summarize your grandmother's life in a five-paragraph essay, complete with thesis and topic sentences. And for this, you owe yourself a drink.

9) Approach the podium. Look out at your family tucked into neat rows. The mortuary has upholstered the pews in a warm beige color. The walls are sand-hued. You want to disappear into this uniformity. In your nervousness, forget to introduce yourself. During the

eulogy, drink each time you say the words "family," "faith," or "the." Drink for every family member who gets teary during your speech. Drink for reading through the introduction and body paragraphs without taking a breath.

Conclude with a description of your grandmother seated at her kitchen table, the Bible in her hand, her illness not yet evident. Notice your dad wiping his eyes and realize you are seeing him cry for the first time in three years, since his favorite dog passed away. Lose your place in the speech. Forget, momentarily, your grandmother's name. Recall how squeezing her hand in yours felt like holding a fragile bird, and then feel your throat tighten, and tears threaten, and the steadiness of your voice wavering. Emma. Her name was Emma.

Feel angry that your family is making you deliver the eulogy. Rescind this. You are angry they are witnessing your grief. Drink.

10) Ask the family to share their memories of your grandmother. Rush back to your seat and search nervously for your father's hand. Hold it. Hold it as you did when you were eight—desperately, with need and fear. Down the rest of your beer.

11) During the hour of sharing, take a drink each time a family member avoids using the word "Alzheimer's."

12) An eighth cousin four times removed comes to the podium and expresses surprise at having just learned your grandmother was ill. Respond by sneaking a drink for each year your grandmother lived in the dementia wing of Hale Kūpuna (two), the years before that during which your auntie cared for her (three), and the year when the family first noticed your grandmother's memory slipping, her feet unsteady, her weight dropping because she could never remember to eat.

13) Take a drink when this eighth cousin four times removed promises that she, like your grandmother, has denied the sins of the flesh. She does not want to go to hell. She has been saved.

14) Take a drink each time she runs from the podium to the casket, drapes herself over your grandmother, and loudly sobs.

15) Take a drink when she has to be dragged away from the body.

16) Take a drink when both your uncle and dad ask, "Who dat?"

17) Sneak a sip when the cousin who fights MMA takes the podium. He describes how your grandma cared for him after he returned from Desert Storm with shrapnel in his knee, and how she made him attend church with her in hopes of giving him hope. Lean in when your cousin relates how, once, he brought his girlfriend to visit, and Grandma made him sleep in the living room. Late that night, he quietly knocked on the door to his girlfriend's bedroom, and Grandma appeared in the hall to scold him. "Get back to da couch, boy."

Laugh with the rest of the family when your cousin pouts, reliving this moment. When he says his grandmother lived her faith both inside and outside of the home, and she wanted the same of her family, understand that the small mercies your cousin has given in his life, he has given because of her.

18) Take a drink for each male cousin you see cry for the first time:

Kea, who once begged your mom to take him to California with her; who was for so many years your mom's favorite, even if she never admitted to it; of whom your grandmother made a hānai grandson because Kea's dad, her neighbor's son, was a mean alcoholic and Kea's body proved it. During the viewing, he whispers, "Tūtū, my Tūtū," as he gazes down at the body. He sobs when they close the casket. He is a pallbearer, one gloved hand lifting the casket, the other wiping his eyes, hidden behind dark glasses.

Your older cousin, Jason, who was the only person you trusted to teach you to ride a bike. You were seven. He was thirteen and beautiful. A ringer for King Kamehameha. He touches the casket gently, lets his fingers rest on its glossed wood. Like Kea, he is wearing sunglasses. His shoulders tremble with emotion. Later, in the evening, he teases you about buying your first surfboard at twenty-eight, and you tell him that you would have bought one sooner if he gave surf lessons. He laughs at that, and his laughter is a balm.

Finally, your baby cousin Ryan, who is no longer a baby, but a sophomore in high school. He is one of the great-grandchildren. He's lost weight since he was jumped at the end of his freshman year, got mean lickins, his arm broken. He is six foot one and, despite the weight loss, still muscled in a way that belies his teenage scrawniness. You forget how young he is sometimes. He says he doesn't remember how he got home last night. You want to tell him not to end up like some of his friends. You want to tell him he's smarter and better at baseball and masculine in a way no fifteen-year-old boy has any business being. He has that calm rage about him that scares you, that makes you want to hug him, that makes you respect him.

When Ryan helps carry the casket to the bed of the truck where the gravediggers are waiting, he, too, is crying. He, too, is using those clean white gloves to wipe his face. He comes to stand near you, and because you want to cry each time you see a man like that crying, you wrap your arms around his waist and lean into him. You let him be a man. You let yourself be a woman who needs his strength.

19) Take a drink for each cousin who brings his fighting cocks to the burial. Be thankful the birds remain in their cages, left in the shade of so many tarp-covered F-150 truck beds.

20) Return to the mortuary for lunch and notice that the crowd of 200 has dwindled to a more manageable 125. Take a sip each time an auntie urges her homemade dessert on you: sweet potato manju, strawberry layer cake, chocolate mochi, guava Jell-O squares.

21) For the remainder of the day, take a drink every time a distant cousin asks how you're related to the deceased. Why didn't you remember to introduce yourself? Now three-quarters of the guests think you work for the mortuary and keep asking you where extra toilet paper is kept. (Point them to the hall cupboard.)

22) Take a drink when your uncles pull their trucks up to the side of the mortuary and haul out the big plastic coolers filled with beer.

23) Take a drink for each boy cousin who, upon finishing his lunch, drifts out to join the uncles. The men are leaning against the side of a warehouse adjacent to the mortuary, trying to squeeze into the sliver of shadow the building provides. Their wives/girlfriends/baby-mamas are still inside, talking story. Your aunties are cleaning, placing fresh foil over the aluminum trays of k lua pig and laulau, and carefully loading paper plates with food for each neighbor or friend to take home.

Your uncles and aunties have so many friends—from high school, work, the old neighborhood where they grew up—who have come to support them. A few of the friends didn't even know your grandmother, but they are still here for your family. They are hugging your aunties, pressing your uncles' hands, kissing your cousins on the cheek. They are hānai.

Call them uncle, auntie. Kiss them. When they ask whose girl you are, say, "Kanoa's. You know, Emma's eldest boy."

When they say, "Ho, I neva see 'im fo' long time," point your dad out to them. He's with the other men. They leave you, as if in a trance, to go to him, hug him, press his hand in theirs. "Look jus' like you, da daughta," they tell your clad, and he nods proudly.

24) Follow your cousins out to the mortuary parking lot. The sliver of shade from the

neighboring warehouse has widened. The men are louder now, teasing each other. Take a drink for every story that ends with your dad's younger brother, Junior, getting lickins. And for the one that involved a homemade bomb and a telephone booth. "I like get all dat change," your uncle says, defending himself.

Another uncle, the one who will lose his job when the G&R Sugar Mill closes in six months, busts up. "Jus' like you. Find plenny ways fo' get paid." Laugh with all of them.

25) Take a drink for all the stories that compare Junior to his father, your grandfather. Take a drink for every car they restored, every beer they drank together, every football game where your grandpa cheered on Junior.

26) Take a drink when you realize your dad is not part of these stories.

27) Take a drink each time an auntie tells you your dad was not like your uncle. He was not like *any* of your uncles. He was the quiet one. The sweet one. The one who never made pilikia. He was the one who left.

28) Take a drink when they say you take after him.

29) Understand your dad was different from the outset. Hand him a beer. After all, to be a boy and to diverge; to watch football but not play it; to keep the books for your grandpa's market instead of unloading the trucks; to leave the island for boarding school; to want to go to college on the mainland; to want to stay there, on the mainland, with only one child to his name, and a girl at that, is to cease to want what men want. Your father is absent from your uncles' stories not because he left, but because he was never of Kaua'i in the first place. Because he was in his own world. Because he is Hawaiian, but no local.

30) Take a drink because it's dark now and you didn't even notice. You have been awake since before dawn, at the mortuary by 7:30 a.m. You have been in mourning for two weeks, and now the funeral is over. The burial is done. Junior, the son whom everyone knows, has opened up his backyard to the family and extended families, and because it's Kaua'i, this could include more than a third of the island. Rachel, his wife, has put out the plastic card tables in one long row. The uncles sit beside the tables. A second row of chairs provides seating for the adult cousins. Junior's daughter and her husband sit in the outer circle. Auntie Miki, a real tita, like her mom—your grandmother's sister—is there, too. She sits with the men, in that inner circle.

Stay with the rest of the women, hovering around the exterior row of chairs, coming and going through the kitchen. Outside the house, the men have their food. Inside the house, your younger cousins are watching the Tupac biopic.

31) Drink a beer to wash down the raw crab in chili pepper sauce, the dried ahi, the tripe stew, the squid in coconut milk, the sashimi your uncle made from a filet of ono one of his friends gave him. Poi, chicken long rice, mochi, and lilikoi cake from the neighbors are placed in front of the men. One tray of Chinese noodles has spoiled. It doesn't matter. Food covers three dining tables, and these are just the leftovers from lunch.

Junior is holding his Shih Tzu in his lap. Her leather collar has "Baby" printed on it in rhinestones. He is snagging a piece of pork katsu with his chopsticks and feeding bits of fried meat to the dog.

32) Take a shot of Crown Royal because someone found it in Junior's refrigerator and someone else has brought a second bottle and they're starting to run low on Bud Light, though there's still plenty of Heineken left. "Da Napilis, yoa grandma's side, neva drink, dem," your dad tells you. "But da Pakeles. Ho!"

"I know I one Pakele den," Junior says, laughing. He hands your dad a beer.

33) Drink, but do not call your mom. Do not call her even though you know she is missing everyone and wants to know what is happening. Do not call her, all the way in California, even though you said you would. When your auntie calls her, do not ask for the phone, but help pass it around so the other uncles and aunties can say something. Tomorrow you will talk to your mother. Tomorrow you will describe everything. But tonight this is yours. Do not share it. She should have come if she wanted to be a part of it so badly. She would have come if she had been thinking like a Hawaiian and not a haole.

34) Seek out your female cousins, the ones who used to pile onto that rattan chair with you. Squeeze next to Johnell and her husband on the wooden bench, its blue paint peeling on the edges. Accept the beer Johnell hands you. Across from you sits Emmy, the one named for your grandmother, and her husband.

Your cousin Ryan hovers behind the bench. Scoot to make room for him to sit even though he refuses. He busies himself with his phone, but he remains behind you, waiting. Understand he has come to listen to you talk. After all, who knows what you might say? Who knows what someone like you thinks of all this?

Johnell and her husband start to poke fun at the pastor, but Emmy's husband stops them. He says the sermon was good. He liked it. "That sermon was serious," he says, and Ryan nods. His lean face is thoughtful.

But Johnell will have none of it. She's a teacher at Sacred Hearts Academy in Honolulu, so she knows something about sermons, and this one, she says, was crap. "I didn't need to think about hell. I was in it!"

Start to laugh—you couldn't agree more—but then notice Ryan watching you, like he expects an answer from you. Take a sip from your bottle to stall. Try to say something about the goodness of God, about forgiveness, about the pastors you've known who have given their own income to help support their parish. Instead, blurt out: "I don't trust men with manicures."

Everybody laughs, even Emmy and her husband, and Ryan most of all. He looks at you with a hint of admiration. Suspect that you, too, are leading him astray.

35) When your auntie calls you inside to see photos of your grandparents, take a long pull from the beer bottle. You did not know your grandfather. He died almost forty years ago, when your dad was twenty. Your dad kept no photographs of his father. In fact, you have never seen a picture of your grandfather. Now, the black-and-whites reveal a man with broad shoulders, a puffy face. He pulls more Chinese than you expected. In one picture he is laughing, and his eyes are tight and small. This is how your father laughs. This is how you laugh.

36) Take a shot when one of the women gets so drunk she announces her husband is screwing a Korean. Take another shot when the woman calls the mistress a yobo. Find out the drunk woman is a distant cousin. Her husband is a cousin, too, but from the other side of the family. No one claims the yobo.

37) Drink when the fighting cocks start crowing in their truck beds. Hear their cries echo throughout the neighborhood and a dozen dogs howl in sympathy. No one else seems to notice the commotion. The men still talk story, the women still pack plates of food. You are alone in your listening.

38) Take a drink when your cousin Mano, the one whose brother fights MMA, says he'll see you out at Bowls. When he smiles his teeth glint against his deep brown skin. He'll tell the other guys to let you catch some waves. He'll tell the other guys you're his cuz. He'll take care of you, and you know what this means: You are no longer some Honolulu hapa. You are a Napili. You have one more name, another branch of family to whom you belong. One

more from which you can't escape. Perhaps you are not your father after all. "Come see me now, yeah?" Mano says.

39) When you finally make up your mind to depart, do not take a drink. Do not let your dad take a drink. Hand him the keys to the car. He has had only three beers, maybe four, and is at least eight or nine behind the other men. Watch through the window as the resort condos of Poipu give way to Kaua'i's last remaining cane fields. Even in the dark, you can see the tendrils of smoke rising from where cane trash has been burning. The air smells acrid and sweet, like toasted orange rind. Flakes of ash fall and cling to your arms, sticky with a day's worth of sweat. You smell like you've been crying. You smell like beer.

Understand that your grandmother is in heaven now, and heaven has fighting cocks and Heineken, poi and dried ahi, your uncles' teasing and your aunties' cooking and your cousins laughing with you when you talk. Heaven is them acting like this is where you belong, and if that's what haole pastors call hell, then thank God you finally got here. [2013]

Bhanu Kapil

Three Voices

I

The bath heated by pans of water from the stove, the man's glistening mouth when he pours the water over my belly, the oil in my hair, the ice snapping in the tree outside my room, and then, after the green and brown night, I drink hoji-cha, eat toast with black cherry jam, eat a banana, and answer the man's questions. There are phones ringing beyond Beethoven. It is eleven in the morning, and already the day has backed up farther and farther inside me. Today, I cannot shake the lump of coal out of my body. The man wants to go to the supermarket to buy fresh fruit, and some milk. Okay, okay.

A bowl of avocado meat, softened and pressed by the back of a spoon is my pleasure. Beneath the pleasure, the hunger that's made of eggshells, and pieces of cloth. Perhaps it is simply a matter of studying and exercising. Okay, okay. But I am not in the mood to read novels, or spend time with friends, or sing. No. I think I want to sing. But what's this? My voice is a stone in my chest. It doesn't stream. I am filled with music! But I can't swallow.

I am not writing about myself as a rational human being. I'm writing about the substances of an animal and female life: magic, pain, the cracked nails of four feet, and the days like this one, when it is difficult to speak to a good-looking man. He returns with sesame seeds, unleavened bread, ginger and coriander powders, coffee, chives, chocolate, yoghurt, onions, cucumbers, potatoes, and a quart of milk. He thinks I am a woman, because he bathes me, and puts his hands on the sides of my face, and tells me I am beautiful. Yes. Okay. But there is something hard between my lungs. It is the size of a blood orange from northern California.

II

And then, one woman, she cannot breathe from her stomach, tells the man: "I am not in love with you. Next year, I will be twenty-five years old, and perhaps I will panic, and perhaps I will not tell you the truth about my heart. And listen, don't ask me about it unless you want to hear about the piece of stale bread I ate one day, when you were sleeping in my bed. I don't know how this happened. Enough!"

The man is not stupid. He's noticed how, in her own sleep, she rubs her palm between her breasts. He replies: "What the hell do you want from me?"

And the woman starts to speak. There is an orange-colored wave rising up her spine.

III

I am blessed. Even in this loneliness, I am blessed. I open the Spanish dictionary at random to "algun" (someday), and "marriage" (matrimonio). I open a book of symbols to "crane," which is connected to pine trees and the sun. And Neruda, in his memoirs, writes: "She gave up her husband, and she also gave up the soft lighting and the excellent armchairs, for an acrobat in a Russian circus that passed through Santiago."

There are not many Russian acrobats in upstate New York. But here is an orange on the kitchen table. I will learn to juggle it on the tips of my fingers. No. I think I'll place it on the front step. A stranger passing by will, perhaps, noticing it, come into my rooms. He is the coming power of the future.

Anhelo: longing. My life: joven. Joven: young woman. Stranger: Angel. Naranjo: orange. Wonder: milagro. My life: sagrado. Sagrado: sacred. [1996]

Rachel Knudsen

How to Enter the Ocean

Last summer I fell in love with a lifeguard. He said, you can tell everything about a person by how they enter the ocean, so we sat all afternoon and watched fat mothers standing on the hot sand, boys playing water wars, couples strolling along the edge.

The sun made me feel warm and tipsy. I laughed and said, it's funny how everyone is the same. I squinted my eyes and looked toward the other end of the beach, where my father stood in the water up to his stiff, tight calves, watching over my younger sisters.

The lifeguard looked back at me and smiled. No, he said, we're not all the same. Everyone's very different, when you really think about it.

When he turned around to look back at the waves, I could see every mole on his neck. His skin was a perfect olive brown.

Later that night, a rock poked into my back as he kissed me, so we moved. We lay down on the sand. His long, rubbery body held me down and I felt as though I were being opened, as though a boy was being born in my heart.

Now that the summer's over, everything has changed. I can't understand my mother and father at all any more, and my teachers seem unkind. Everything they say about everything is wrong. [2007]

Stephen Kuusisto

Horse

Durham, New Hampshire, 1960

Maybe it was a Saturday. I remember that my parents were still sleeping. I had a plan and dressed quietly. When I was certain that no one was awake I slipped from the house. I loved to walk in the woods and follow the beams of light or depths of shade that fell between trees. I remember that on this particular day I got lost while chasing light and found myself standing in front of the university's horse barn. I knew that somewhere in the cool space before me a horse was breathing. I stood in the door and listened to him breathe. He sounded like water going down a drain. Then I took one step forward into a pyramid of fragrances.

What a thing! To be a young boy smelling hay and leather and turds!
From his place in the dark the horse gurgled like water in the back of a boat.
Mice scurried like beaded curtains disturbed by a hand.
I stood in that magical nowhere and listened to a full range of barn sounds.
I was a blind child approaching a horse!
Behind me a cat mewed.
Who would guess that horses sometimes hold their breath?
The horse was eyeing me from his corner.
Then two cats were talking.
Wind pushed forcefully at the high roof.
Somewhere up high a timber groaned.
My horse was still holding his breath.
When would he breathe again?
Come on boy!
Breathe for me!
Where are you?
I heard him rub his flank against a wall.
Then I heard him breathe again with a great deflation!
He sounded like a fat balloon venting in swift circles.
And then I imitated him with my arm pressed to my mouth.
I made great, flatulent noises by pressing my lips to my forearm.

How do you like that, horse?

He snorted.

I noticed the ringing of silence. An insect traveled between our bursts of forced air.

Sunlight warmed my face. I was standing in a wide sunbeam.

I was in the luminous whereabouts of horse! I was a very small boy and I had wandered about a mile from home. Although I could see colors and shapes in sunlight, in the barn I was completely blind.

But I had made up my mind to touch a horse.

Judging by his breathing, his slow release of air, that sound of a concertina, judging by this I was nearly beside him. And so I reached out and there was the great wet fruit of his nose, the velvet bone of his enormous face. And we stood there together for a little while, all alive and all alone.

At night when I couldn't sleep I thought of this horse. I thought of his glory—his fat sound. I thought of how he pinched the air around him with his breathing. The house and the trees swayed in the night wind. The horse was dry wood talking. He was all nerves and nostrils. He tightened and then unwound like a clock. He groaned like the Finnish women who stood beside the ocean waving their sticks. Strophe and antistrophe. Step. Rhythm. Pulse beat. I'd crossed a threshold, hearing and walking the uncertain space that opened before me… [2006]

Patrick Lane

The Far Field

We drove for more than an hour, my father's hands
on the truck's wheel, taking us farther and farther
into the hills, both of us watching
the sagebrush and spare pines drift
past, both of us silent. He did not know
what to do with me. I think he thought of
my death, as a man will whose son has chosen
to destroy. I think that's why he drove
so long, afraid to stop for fear
of what he'd do. My mother had cried
when we left, her hands over her mouth,
saying through her splayed fingers
my father's name, speaking
that word as if it were a question. I
sat there peaceful with him,
knowing for these hours he was wholly mine.

He stripped me naked in the last hour of day
and made me stand with my back to him, my bare
feet in the dust, my back and buttocks to him,

a naked boy, hands braced upon the hood,
staring across the metal at the hills.

I remember the limb of the tree falling
upon me, the sound of the white wood crying
as it hurt the air, and the flesh of my body
rising to him as I fell to the ground and rose
only to fall again. I don't remember pain,
remember only what a body feels
when it is beaten, the way it resists
and fails, and the sound of my flesh.

I rose a last time, my father dropping
the limb of the tree beside me.
I stood there in my bones wanting it not to be
over, wanting what had happened to continue, to go
on and on forever, my father's hands on me.

It was as if to be broken was love, as if
the beating was a kind of holding, a man
lifting a child in his huge hands and throwing him
high in the air, the child's wild laughter
as he fell a question spoken into both their lives,
the blood they shared pounding in their chests. [1999]

Evelyn Lau

An Insatiable Emptiness

I no longer clearly remember the first time I forced myself to throw up. What I do remember is how inexpert I was and how long it took before I succeeded in actually vomiting instead of just gagging and retching. I began by sticking my finger down my throat and wiggling it around, but this produced few results; it wasn't until articles about bulimia appeared in women's magazines that I finally thought to use the handle of a toothbrush instead of my forefinger. It became easy after that.

In my mid-teens, I was too young to believe I was anything but immortal. It didn't occur to me that what I was doing was dangerous—instead, it seemed a smart and practical way of coping with things. I went through months of throwing up once or twice a day, then brief periods when I did not throw up at all, when I seemed to have broken the pattern. Surely this meant I was in control. But by the time I turned 18, the months of not throwing up had diminished to weeks, and when I *was* vomiting I was doing it four, five, six times a day. I had become addicted to the sensation. It was no longer a penance I had to perform after eating, but the reward at the end of a binge. I loved the feeling I had after purging, of being clean and shiny inside like a scrubbed machine, superhuman. I would rise from the bathroom floor, splash my face with cold water, vigorously brush the acid from my mouth. I would take a wet cloth, wipe off the vomit that had spattered my arms, and feel as energized as someone who had just woken from a nap or returned from an invigorating jog around the block. I felt as if everything disgusting inside me had been displaced so that it was now outside myself. Not only all the food I had eaten, but my entire past.

No one could tell me to stop, not even my friends who eventually knew what I was doing. They could not control this part of my life or any other. This was mine alone—the chemical flower smell of the blue water in the toilet, the vomit that shot out as a burning liquid, drenching the sides of the bowl. After a session in the bathroom, a certain emptiness would sing inside me, a sensation of having become a cage of bones with air rushing through it. I craved this feeling so much I no longer cared what I had to eat in order to vomit—I would cram clusters of bananas into my mouth, or tubs of ice cream that lurched back up my throat in a thin and startlingly sweet projectile.

When I left the bathroom, I felt like someone who had achieved some great thing—climbed a mountain, written a book—and survived. I was overweight by only 10 pounds or so, but when I looked in the mirror all I saw was buttery flesh covering my body. My stomach had become swollen and globular from the gorging and purging; I had earned it the way other women earn washboard stomachs and lean waists from hours of sit-ups and crunches at the gym.

As a child, I had been thin and healthy, with a flat belly and limbs that turned brown in the summer. I had my first period when I was 11, and for the next several years the blood welled out of me in thick, rust-coloured gouts that no tampons or pads could contain. My body had somehow become a vessel filled with secret, terrible workings, and I longed to make it translucent, pared-down, clean as a whistle. But the blood spread in the shapes of clouds on my skirts and pants, for 10 or 12 days each month, and my hips and breasts pressed outwards. I hated what was happening to my body, once so straight and uninflected. I attracted the attention of one of my parents' friends, who stared at the fuzzy-dark crook at the top of my thighs when I sat cross-legged in front of him, who asked me to perform somersaults and splits while his thick lips hung open with desire. My own father grew awkward around me, refusing to touch me or meet my eyes, driven away by this growing body that forced him out like a giant balloon expanding in a small room. I was in despair. I wanted to trick my body back into childhood by starving it, but I was hungry all the time; I craved food during the week prior to my traumatic periods. Sometimes I would consume a whole bag of shortbread cookies or three chocolate bars; the sugar and fat would induce a heavy, mucousy lethargy.

My breasts continued to develop, horrifying my mother, who frequently made me undress in front of her so she could ridicule them. Her actions convinced me there was something wrong with my body. She decided to put the whole family on a diet, serving small portions of steamed fish and vegetables, chicken with the skin removed. During dinner, and in the hungry hours of the evening that followed, she would say over and over again, "It's because of you we didn't get enough to eat, that we're going to bed hungry. Look at the sacrifices we're making for you." I would sit at the dinner table, staring down at my plate with tears in my eyes, grief forming a hot, choking knot in my throat. I would watch my father slowly raise his fork to his mouth while my eagle-eyed mother watched me triumphantly, eating only half of what was on her plate in order to set an example.

My mother was so thin and white that whenever I glimpsed her undressing behind a half-closed door, her thighs looked like those of the Holocaust survivors I examined in photographs in history class at school. Meanwhile, I began to put on weight, growing chubby beneath sweatshirts and loose jeans. I stole chocolates from the drugstore, bought greasy bags of day-old cookies from the bakery, consumed candies in a blind rush on the mile-long walk from school to home. I crammed myself with food, yet I hated food: its veils of grease, its sauces like paste. I hated its fragility beneath my hands, could not bear the delicacy of pastry. But once I started eating, I could not stop, and after I gave in I would again have to cope with the horrible feeling of satiation—a feeling so uncomfortable and guilt-ridden it threatened to annihilate me.

I hated the unaccustomed thickness of my body, yet I took a secret, perverse pride in the space I was filling up, the air I was pushing aside in the family home in order to make room for myself. I looked in scorn upon my mother, who wore tiny pink sweaters with pearl buttons, size XS. Her legs were like bleached sticks, the skin white and crepey; her hipbones jutted visibly beneath her skirts, and she reminded me of a starving cow, its ribs and hips holding up the tent of skin. At 13, I had grown to match my father's weight. But at 130 pounds, he was small for a man, his arms straight, the biceps undefined. He was weak, useless in the battle that had sprung up between my mother and myself. He would not protect me, he took no sides in the daily tug-of-war for power. He merely absented himself, took the coward's way out. For this, I knew, one day I would make him suffer.

I thought that if I were to physically fight my mother I could break her dry arms like twigs. I could twist her skeleton between my hands; I could sit on her and suffocate her. But it never came to that. Instead, with each pound I gained, my mother became more controlling. I felt that in my entire world there was only one thing my mother could not take away from me: my body. She was trying, of course, with her diets and carefully calibrated meals and calorie counters set up around the kitchen. She wanted to watch me day and night, but in this she inevitably encountered frustration and failure: she could not see the junk food I snuck between meals and hid between textbooks and in my locker at school.

And it was driving my mother crazy, I began to realize. She turned to the only thing she could control 24 hours a day: her own body. For every pound I gained, she lost one. In Grade 9, when I came home from school I found her doing jumping jacks and skipping rope in the living room, or following an aerobics show on television. She had virtually stopped eating, complaining that I was doing enough eating for us both. Her eyes grew large in her face, and her hair began to fall out in swirls that clogged up the drain in the sink and the shower. When I stood up from the table and looked down at my mother's skull, I could see the wide, white swathe of the part in her hair.

For a while, my father insisted that she eat, but he soon gave up and came home less and less, always too late for the dinner hour, fraught as it was with its agonizing tensions: my mother staring at me with fascination as I ate, her eyes transfixed with hunger. I thought I could no longer stand it; I was as guilty as a murderer with every bite. At night, I lay in my room contemplating suicide and listening to the footsteps of my father pacing his study, waiting for his wife to fall asleep before daring to enter their bedroom. When I trespassed there, I saw pink walls, pink curtains, a pink throw on the queen-sized bed. The bedroom faced south, and all day the sun shone relentlessly through the gauze curtains, revealing the motes of dust in the air. When I opened the dresser drawers, I found beautiful, tiny clothes, beaded and jewelled, carefully folded and wrapped in plastic, as if their owner had already died. I knew these clothes would never again be worn by my mother, and I would never be small enough to wear them. I knew this was a source of bitterness in my mother's life—she could not pass herself on to me; she could not live her life again through me. In order to survive, I would have to deny my mother this second life and claim my own.

In the en suite bathroom I found orange lipsticks dried to hard, wax nubs, cakes of powder that crumbled at a touch, an old tube of KY Jelly squeezed from the bottom like toothpaste. All of it seemed a shrine to my mother's glamorous past. She had been a beauty in her youth, with thick hair that hung down to her waist, so much hair it was almost impossible to bind into ponytails. She had pale skin and pink cheeks like apple blossoms, and she wore short skirts and high heels to work.

What my mother didn't know was that I was already beginning to incorporate her inside me. She didn't know that she was winning and that for the rest of my life I would contain aspects of her—both the young beauty turning men's heads and the wasted figure doing sit-ups on the living room floor. I would grow up to wear contact lenses and to put a wave in my hair; I would admire myself in mirrors and spend small fortunes on clothes and cosmetics. Beneath this evidence of self-esteem, though, I would learn to cultivate a parallel self-hatred: my thoughts would repeat themselves obsessively; I would become compulsive in my behaviour, desperate for control; I would avoid other women because I was afraid they would be like my mother; and I would live at the mercy of my emotions, the endless stream of hatred that poured out of my mouth when I bent over the toilet.

"You will never succeed at anything," my mother told me day after day. "You're like your father—spineless, weak, good for nothing."

The last time I saw them, when I was 17 and they were in their 50s, he seemed bewildered by what had happened to our family. She had become a confused, agitated woman who plucked ceaselessly at the strap of her purse with an anguished tic. She had become powerless to control me, this piece of herself that had separated from her. She had lost me in her attempt to keep me forever.

I was 20 years old when I began to lose the feeling of immortality. I thought my body would regenerate itself in time, that once again everything would be new and resilient. But it only got worse. My body began showing signs of wear—my throat constantly ached from throwing up, and when I opened my mouth I saw in the mirror a red, inflamed pendulum dangling behind rows of teeth softened and eroded by acid. My own teeth, once so enamel white—the sort of teeth parents thank God for; the sort of teeth a man meeting me for the first time would go away remembering—had, overnight it seemed, turned pitted and yellow, the back ones worn down to shrunken saddles. When I looked in the mirror, they were translucent as X-rays, made, it seemed, of water and putty. I began to brush more vigorously after each purge, not knowing then that I was accelerating the process, scrubbing my teeth with my own stomach acid.

I waited for the day when I would throw up blood. Already I could taste it at the back of my throat, inching farther upward with each heartbeat. Now after vomiting, I would rise shakily from my knees, gripping the edge of the counter for balance, my heart knocking wildly in my chest. A column of flame speared me from my stomach to my throat—my esophagus a two-edged blade in my chest, a tunnel set on fire, a steel pole thrust through me.

Now when I threw up, I reeled from the pain. I was not throwing up half-digested food, as I had for years, but what felt like complete objects—plastic balls, pieces of Lego, nuts and bolts that tore at me as they came out of my body. Afterwards, my stomach would hurt so much that for the rest of the evening any sustenance I sought would have to be the sort given to a convalescent or a starvation victim: thin porridge, vegetable soup, herbal tea.

I no longer thought of myself as a girl or a woman. I no longer felt sexual desire. I was an "it," a conduit for a constant stream of ugliness that had to pass through it in order for me to stay pure.

In some dim part of me, I knew that when I left my apartment to go out into the street, other people did not see me as I saw myself. They did not recoil from me in horror, as I expected. I knew I was a reasonably attractive young woman, like so many young women in the city, neither fat nor thin. But I felt somehow grotesque and abnormal. Strangers knew nothing of my secret; friends were helpless; my dentist would only shake his head over my open mouth and tap his pencil along my teeth to track the path of corrosion the vomit had left in its wake.

Once, in a determined moment, I called the Eating Disorder Clinic at St. Paul's Hospital, but the waiting list meant I would not get in for a year. At that time, a year seemed forever, so I did not add my name to the list. Surely in a year's time everything would change, resolve itself. Twelve months later I called again, but by this time the list was even longer, and again I did not add my name.

I finally stopped being bulimic nearly two years ago, when I was 22. It ended not because of willpower or therapy or something so banal as an increased sense of self-esteem. It ended because the pain from throwing up rendered the pleasure slight by comparison. It ended when my softened teeth cringed at every mouthful and when I woke several times each night with cramps wracking my stomach from one side of my waist to the other. It ended when I arrived at the point where I could no longer feel my feet. Months later, when I went to the doctor, he would diagnose it as an electrolyte imbalance caused by the vomiting up of so many vitamins and minerals. But for a long time, I didn't know what it was, and it frightened me—sometimes when I stood up, I nearly fell over. My feet were like dead fish, cold and clammy, disconnected from the rest of my body. Once in a while they flared suddenly to life, a constellation of pins and needles, so that I could not bear to press my soles to the floor. When I tried to go to the bathroom in the middle of the night, I felt in the underwater light of that hour as if I had transformed into the fairy-tale mermaid who had chosen her lover over the sea: with each step, I landed on knife points.

By then I had also developed a hiatus hernia—a portion of my stomach protruded through my esophagus—and my teeth became so compromised that one day one of them simply disintegrated under pressure.

"Your tooth isn't going to grow back," the dentist said flatly, and it was then I understood for the first time that my body did not possess some secret store of replacement parts, that physical damage, like its psychological counterpart, left marks that could remain a lifetime.

The last time I forced myself to throw up, it felt like internal surgery. Grief, love, rage, pain—it all came pouring out, yet afterwards it was still there inside me. I had been bulimic off and on for eight years, and in all that vomiting I had not purged myself of any of the things that were making me sick. [1995]

Josh Lefkowitz

Saturday Salutation

Saturday Brooklyn Mo(u)rning!
At long last I bid you farewell.
The sun has reached its noontime apex.
Unadorned by clouds, its heat and light spill out across the boroughs of the world.

Women of this past year!
At long last I bid you farewell as well.
You were all the lot of you beautiful individual bookmarks.
You helped us remember where we were.
But now we have a brand new Kindle,
and so we kindle this sharp new spark,
and so we kindly put you back into the desk and close the drawer (we hope) forevermore.

Yet first I am calling you all out by name!
For I am the Elia Kazan of lovers!
Summoned before the committee, I will name all names!
Let me carve those names upon the rock of memory.

Blonde-haired office crush,
She whose finely-drawn cheekbones catch and play off halogen cafeteria lighting,
Farewell!
Your beauty was distracting like the internet.
And pursuing you proved to be as unfulfilling as a day spent surfing that internet.

Ballet dancer, friend of my friend,
How I marveled at your physical flexibility
but you proved to be inflexible in matters of casual lust.
You're swell but not for me. I think on this point we both agree.

Internet start-up girl, friend of my friend,
I spent an awful lot of money on dinners for you.
This was because for me the task of dating was still strange, still new,
and you joined me for those many meals, then said "just friends will do."
Next time I spend that much will be on a craigslist prostitute.

Curly-haired coffee shop barista,
You should have shed that boyfriend months ago.
I chased you like an overweight cop pursues a quick n' lean criminal.
I ran out of longing. I ran out of steam. I ran out of breath. I ran out of hope.
Now I am comfortably seated at some new coffee shop with a poppyseed muffin in my hand and an altogether new woman in my mind.

Red-haired ice cream scooper girl,
You too have a boyfriend,
which you casually mentioned in our first meeting.
Thank you for doing that!
You saved me a lot of time and energy!
I really appreciate that!
And now goodbye forever!

Every random subway longing,
Every momentary crush on a store clerk or secretary or dental hygienist,
Every lillypad of doubt has helped me reach the river's other side.
It is so nice over here.
The grass is dewy and fresh.
Upon arrival they hand you a blanket and a paddleball set.
I want to stay in this place for a good long while.

And everywhere I go I tell my story,
In smiled silence or sometimes even with words.
"I have love!" I tell the Key Food cashiers, who blink back in boredom and don't care
and I don't care that they don't care.

Aboard the subway beggars ask me for change
And I say, "be the change you want to see in the world my good man,"
And they say, "please don't quote Gandhi to me that's really insensitive I'm starving,"
So then I apologize and say "I'm sorry I'm just a little giddy I'm having a really nice life
today" but I regret what I said so I give them like two dollars.

When I close my eyes it is her I see,
and I feel full like a helium balloon that may one day burst.
Hold on, let's try that again:
I feel like a pulsing land mine under a dirt mound, waiting to be found.
Wait, one more:
Y'know how at the state fair there'll be those jets and they're going really fast and almost
out of control and so there's always the chance that they will crash, and, that's
kind of what the spectators are secretly hoping for because it's spectacular and
those words "spectator" and "spectacular" both come from the same root?
Well that's how I feel—like a state fair airplane.
And you my new long-distance love are the corndog—
You are singular and specific and altogether unique.
I want to douse you in mustard and put you in my mouth.
I want to casually hold you in one hand and be the envy of all those walking by who are
dieting from love.
And I will laugh the laugh of immense recognition! For I, too, have dieted—
Have spent the extended winter hunkered below in a bunker of isolation,
Fueled by internet pornography and then half an hour later, some more.

But now I radiate light!
My pheromones are fragrant.
I smell of the salt of summertime ocean—
Unless you prefer the peaks of mountaintops, in which case, I smell like those too!

So long, pining for unrequited love!
Hope you enjoyed May, June, July, August, September, October, November, December

(god damn you December), January, and February—
For now it is March,
And so I do,
In the streets,
Like a mediocre high-school band that's not actually very skilled at wielding its individual instruments but is too excited to be part of the parade to care.
And the band's parents are all there!
As part of the town-wide crowd.
And they're the most proud.
Play on, piccolos!
Trill, you trumpets!
Flag girls, you're all doing a really great job. Keep it up!

Today of this new land I am sovereign, King!
Today I am the Midwest Midas!
Today everything I touch turns to nice, and immediately becomes ten pounds heavier.

Do not wonder why I am being so silly.
That is like asking why a dog chooses to lick its own genitals—
Because it can! Because it feels so goddamn good!

Clouds of the west? Back in the wings!
Death and decay? Just leave a voicemail, I'll call you back later.
Work-related stress? Yes, we know you're still there—nobody cares.

It is noon and I am thirty.
I am making my way in the world.
I close my eyes and wonder what the coffee shop culture is like in Illinois.
I close my eyes and wonder what the job situation is like in Illinois.
I close my eyes and wonder how and if and when I will ever say goodbye to Brooklyn and begin somewhere else somewhere like Illinois.
In my mind I doubt I'll ever leave but on Saturday today I give myself permission to close my eyes and open up some strange new fantasy, where I am in Illinois working as a farm-hand, baling hay, stacking grain inside a silo, tilling the land and telling tales upon a mosquito-repelling-candled porch at night, this imagery is steeped in cartoonish stereotype but I am going with it, I have known this girl for seven days and I am going with it, and now eyes open back here in Brooklyn on a Saturday I count the twenty more days until I will see her again, so get out, doubt, There's no place for you here, not now, not today, not when I am going with it, and I am, O, I am so going with it, I am so going with it, I am so going with it… [2013]

Susan Lester

Belongings

At twenty, he has square feet and wide bones and thick coarse hair; a smile that, while slow, is generous. You want to pet him.

From all the bulk and fur of him you wouldn't expect his hands, magician hands. Quick. He draws caricatures in charcoal, plays Bach on guitar, juggles bean-bags, and folds colored papers into deer and mice, cuts perfect stars with scissors in one snip, hiding, always hiding the effort.

"Ancient Oriental secret," he tells you when you ask. Understand that he drills himself in skills, wrests them painfully from nothingness, trains his hands as if they are wild animals.

Maybe it was night and cold. (According to almanacs, it snows in Seoul.) Concealed by darkness she took him to the orphanage, laid him on a table cunningly designed to revolve, outside to in, accepting infants without revealing mothers. She walked home, still tender from the birthing.

He is seven months old when they send him to us on an airplane. We wait at the terminal to receive him, our son. Thirty babies are carried from the jumbo jet by men and women with dark hair, dark eyes. He is among them, asleep, full head of black hair sticking straight up, skin warm as a fever, voice deep when he murmurs. He doesn't cry. They pass him to me. I cry. I undress him in the airport bathroom like a gift I can't wait to open. His diaper is dry. My hands are shaking.

Maybe it was daylight and, unashamed, she strode to the orphanage to deposit him. She had meant the conception to be a tool with which she would pry open a distinguished place for herself. Too late, she saw it was her censure. She wiped her hands on her clothing going home.

His brother is inside my belly, a quick little fetus seven months old, conceived on the day we decided to adopt. Magic decision. He turns in my womb, taps at me from inside as if curious. I laugh. The Korean men smile for politeness when I laugh, not knowing the joke that is passing between my children.

Maybe she was charmed by a stranger, felt his love like the sun's light and opened herself, morning flower that broke laws with its tenderness. That night when she walked to the orphanage, there were stars above her, stars whose light had begun many hundreds of years before. She knew about stars, she understood that many hundreds of years hence, this moment would be seen by the stars she saw now. Pure light.

They hand him to me, asleep, then bow. Two men. I look at them covertly. This is how my son will look someday, this tall, this dark, this broad of face.

Bewildered, he opens his eyes, dark eyes, so dark I can't see pupils in them. He comes to me nuzzling his forehead in my neck, moving his head back and forth, back and forth, as if saying "No, no, no, no, no." He lays his head against me then sleeps again. Once more, the men bow. They don't know my tongue. We smile. We compare the name-bands on our wrists. Mine. His. Theirs. Yes, they match. We smile.

Maybe this was the punishment she meted out to her lover: to dispose of the object created by his passion and thus make all his passion negligible. Maybe on the way home she ate chocolate.

He is five and in school. He hates school. He says he fears he will fall out of line. On his first day, he asks me to pray to God to see if God can change his eyes. A child told him God could.

I pray a curse on the child who inaugurated this hope in him. I rake leaves in the yard for a week, turn soil, prune branches, master anger. I brush aside pebbles and branches and sticks to discover an ant hill from which emerge a thousand ants. Within seconds they have filed themselves into lines. I shift a stone to divert them. I uncover, with a start, a lemon-colored toy car in a square hole, a small pebbled driveway for its entrance, a pine-cone roof. I kneel and look, intrigued, my heart opened like a flower to the sunlight.

Maybe she was a New Woman, one who stepped away from the governing social order in which, ant-like, individuals served as cells of a greater organism. She was warned that when isolated, one died; when shamed, one lost her place. But she stood brave against it, loved a man despite it, bore a child because of it. In anger she conceived, in triumph gave birth; in hope she gave away her son to live where she believed he would be free.

He is a mewling infant with moist, soft skin, infected navel, self-containment. I do not know him yet. A foster family keeps him. Five sons. They carry him on their backs and feed him rice milk. They sleep with him on their heated floors and tease him so he moves his head back and forth, back and forth, as if saying "No, no, no, no, no." Outdoors, the country smells of minerals and earth, inside, of boiled rice and tea and garlic.

Maybe she hid herself, magician girl, appeared always to be obedient, all the while breaking with the order that sustained her. She bowed as if she obeyed, but broke, then feared the law. She hid the hot fetus within her, the fetus that would cut her, like a sword, from her mother and her father and her husband-to-be. Isolated, she would die. She crept, terrified, to the orphanage's turntable, hoping to abandon there, fear. But fear went home with her, and with it, grief.

He hoards things. I call him a pack rat, though he knows I'm intrigued by the things he keeps. He refuses to cut his thick horse-mane of hair. "Are you saving it for something?" I try to show reason.

"It's only peach fuzz," he answers. "Ancient Oriental peach fuzz."

His room is a labyrinth of beautiful things: guitar, girlfriend's pillow, drawing board, the I Ching, broken clock parts, Holy Bible, plastic jars, blue glass bits, stuffed dogs, burnt-edge corks, wooden boxes, rolls of tape, his baby blanket.

I kneel and look. This, I say, is because, at seven months, he knew that a person could lose everything, his people, his belongings, the smell of his ground, the hot floor where he sleeps, the white robes of ceremony, even the sound of his language. He does not know he remembers these things, or remember that he lost them. I do not remind him, but I let him hoard; I let him explain.

"What happened to your real mother?" asks Clark, blond four-year-old living next door.
"She died," he says.
"So," I say. And maybe she did. I would have. [1994]

Paul Lisicky

Snapshot, Harvey Cedars: 1948

My mother touches her forehead, throwing her green eyes into shade. Her mouth is pink, her hair blond like wheat. She is tanned. She is the best-looking woman on the beach, only she will never recognize it. She wraps her long body in an aqua sarong and winces, believes her hips are a bell. Even now she is counting, waiting for the camera to flicker shut.

My father's arm weights down her shoulder. He is muscular, his stomach flat as a pan. He looks full ahead, pretending he is with my mother, but already he is in Florida, developing new cities, pumping dead mangrove full of sand. He sees himself building, building. He will be healthy. He will have good fortune. And years in the future, after his Army buddies will have grown soft and womanish, all his hard work will pay off: people will remember his name.

Their shoulders touch. Their pose says: this is how young couples are supposed to look—see, aren't we the lucky ones? But my mother's head is tilted. What is she looking at? Is she gazing at the tennis player by the outdoor shower, the one with the gentle hands, the one who will teach her to unlearn things? Or can she already hear the gun which my father will press into his forehead, twenty years away? [1992]

Sonja Livingston

The Ghetto Girls' Guide to Dating and Romance

1. I know how it is. How you turn in the mirror, look here and there for signs of change, look hard for the woman you'll become. Well, look and turn all you want, you won't see it happening—the bends your body will take, the pulling in of, the swelling. You won't see, but they'll inform you. As you walk by, they'll give an "Mm, mmmm, mmm" and "Sure looks fine" and that's when you'll know. Just keep your eyes down. From the time those titties erupt from your chest, point your eyes to the ground and keep on walking. Right on by Lynam's bar, past the fish market on Parsells and Webster where men on break stand outside and call out to girls and women, but mostly girls. Their voices are rainforests at night and you don't mind being called baby all the time. But you must. Forget the smell of them, forget their slippery skin, ignore the slow glow of their cigarettes, the tug of August heat. Just think of all the fish they've handled and keep walking, eyes down.

2. He says come here sweet thing. He wants to talk and only for a minute. Don't be a fool. There's no such thing as a minute. He'll put his mouth on your neck, slip his hand up your

skirt and press small circles into your thighs with the tips of his fingers. He'll say just a minute longer, and though you're smart in every other thing, those fingers will circle their way through your skin and you'll have no choice but to let him move up. And in. A minute becomes an hour, then a lifetime. Just remember to take your watch, since he won't have his and it doesn't matter anyway, because minutes don't exist.

3. He won't be wearing a ring or maybe he will, but can explain it away. One thing's for sure, you can't count on jewelry to tell you anything about a man. If he doesn't take you to his place, he's cheating. If he says he lives with his aunt and her sister and they go to church early in the morning and are all around quiet people so you can't go there late at night, he's lying. If he claims to have two jobs and so can't come around much, and when he does, his wallet's flat, he's lying.

4. Your mother's on the phone with the doctor on call from the Genesee Hospital, trying to get help for the pain in your lower stomach and side. The pain that won't let you sleep. Bits of you pull off and away. The bleeding is heavy. "The doctor wants to know whether you've done it." She tosses the words out like she's asking about the last time you ate, but you know just what she means and you're scared, with your stomach tearing itself up and her sounding so casual. You'll be inclined to tell the truth, but it's much better to lie. You have no idea how disappointed mothers can be. She'll think you haven't listened to one damned thing she's ever said. Your mother won't say this, she'll just return the phone to its cradle and keep her eyes from resting on you the same way after that night.

5. You smell the perfume, find the gold hoop earring in the back seat of his orange pinto, hear from Maria Maldonado that she saw him at the mall with some other girl while she was there buying white satin baptism shoes for her baby. Don't bother asking. You don't need any evidence, because deep down you already know. If you think he is, he is.

6. When he rubs you up and whispers in your ear just how much he likes girls with a little extra flesh on their asses and says that parts of you are like hills he'd like to climb—remember that he told Wanda just last week that he likes girls with high tight asses and that hers is as high and as tight as a button. He tells you there's nothing like a white girl, then tells Stacy from down the street that mocha's his favorite flavor. And while he was talking up her tiny butt, he told small-assed Wanda that he craves the copper of island girls, said he dreamt her ass was a coin in the palm of his hand. Use your sense. He most prefers the ass nearest to his hand.

7. Stay with your girls when you walk to the store. Your mom wants a loaf of bread or a gallon of milk and you have to get it. She can't leave and you don't want to go. You may as well be seed thrown to the birds, the way grown men on porches stare you down and call after you every time you walk to and from the store or to and from anywhere (unless you wake up early and beat them out of bed). Get your friends to walk with you. They won't want to, but they'll go because they'll need you later that same day. Two is safer than one and three is even better. Talk to each other about clothes, shoes, makeup—anything but them. Pretend they don't exist, or if you have to, lie to each other about how much you hate them. Do anything you can to keep from falling.

8. You want to so much it hurts. But don't. Don't spend money from your after-school job on gifts. He's grateful, but receiving becomes an easy habit. Don't let him use your name and phone number to buy the big black sofa from rent-a-center. He won't pay and they'll hound your mother, your sister, and everyone with your last name for payment. Don't lend money. He will not give it back. Or he'll give it back once or twice just to show he can, then follow up his payment with a request for more. Then more. He can't help it, his heart is a sponge. You can't help it either—you are different sides of the same cloth. Your heart is liquid—it would fall through your fingers if you ever tried to touch it. It's better to say you have nothing to give, then hide the bags of stuff you buy at Midtown Plaza at your best friend's mother's house, so he doesn't ask how you paid.

9. The one who gives you roses. The one who says your eyes are better than the stained glass at church, that your skin is like milk. He's the one for you. He wants you to meet his mother, his brother, his Titi Eva in from New York. But it feels all wrong so you push him away. He keeps at you, until you can't take it any longer and give him one last slam. He sees something you don't see and to be wanted like that is a spice you've never tasted. So you spit him out and long for something regular, some taste you recognize. He cries and writes long sad letters. You fold your arms over your chest and laugh. Crow of a girl. You'll never have him, but he's the one for you.

10. He will not take care of you. Even if he wants to, even if he cries in your ear and looks into your eyes while you fuck. He's good deep down, but then so is everyone. He'll walk to your job and meet you there for three days straight, though you look away and pretend to be alone. Though he's five or maybe ten years older and you tell him not to, he's there after work, grabbing at your hand. These are his lies: *She doesn't mean anything. You can drop out of school, quit this job. I'll take care of you.* Listen closely. This is the prettiest of poisons. He's talking crazy, and if you believe him, you're living in la-la land. To be taken care of is not an option. It is for girls on TV and people inside borrowed library books. But for you, it's not an option. It never was.

11. Fool of a girl. You believe he'll meet you on the corner at eleven like he said. Though he did not show last night and was an hour late the night before, you rub oil onto your legs, push yourself into your new white sweater, and wait. He won't show, and even if he does, he'll do nothing but stain up your sweater—but hope is worse than a pebble in the shoe, so you wait and watch, make up counting games with passing cars, and an hour later, walk back home and fold the sweater away for some other night.

12. Avoid boys with warm hands on Halloween night. They smell like falling leaves and overripe cologne and even though they can't dance, one touch on your arm and they melt you. They push you against the fence and groan their way into your long white gown and it's so cold, you don't mind the fog of their breath, the pink of their fingers. The party's over, your friends have all gone home, and his mouth is wet and hard and knows you better than you do. You've been an Egyptian princess all night, snake coiled on your arm, eyes lined in black. Now you're caught between him and a chain-link fence and there's nowhere to go but down.

13. When his woman calls and tells you stay the hell away from her man, you should. You'll be tempted not to—she sounds so broken and he'll explain about how crazy she is, how she won't let go, has their child spy on him during visits, found your number and is making up lies. She'll tell you how it really is. But you won't believe something as ragged as her voice could ever touch those big green eyes or the mouth whose inside tastes of warm beer and coconut. You won't listen, but when his woman calls and tells you to stay the hell away, you should.

14. Run in place. Do jumping jacks. Jog around the park at the end of the street five times. Then five times more. Your period's late and there's only one thing to do. Walk and pray. Jog and pray. Squish your body into sit-ups, push-ups, knee bends. Pray. You hardly believe in God, but this is not the time for questioning. Just pray. When it finally comes, you are happy and grateful and fresh and clean. You help your mother scrub the walls and gather lilacs into jelly jar vases. You'll never take that risk again. Ever.

Until the next time he calls.

15. The health teacher, the parish priest, the public service announcement don't mean to suggest that nothing good can come from you. They don't mean to talk like you're some Humane Society stray. It's just that they know things. Pregnancy equals failure. You see it too. The way your friends drop off one at a time. They let someone into their pants, their bellies swell, then they fade into the gray. They might go to the Young Mothers' Program for a month or two, until the baby comes. Then it's as if they never existed. So be strong, say the health teacher, the priest, the message on TV. Keep your legs safely fastened, or if you absolutely must, be sure to roll the latex on like so. It's the truth and you know it, so don't think so much. Don't be so sensitive. They don't mean to imply that there's something wrong with having more around like you. [2005]

Patricia Lockwood

Rape Joke

The rape joke is that you were 19 years old.

The rape joke is that he was your boyfriend.

The rape joke it wore a goatee. A goatee.

Imagine the rape joke looking in the mirror, perfectly reflecting back itself, and grooming itself to look more like a rape joke. "Ahhhh," it thinks. "Yes. A goatee."

No offense.

The rape joke is that he was seven years older. The rape joke is that you had known him for years, since you were too young to be interesting to him. You liked that use of the word interesting, as if you were a piece of knowledge that someone could be desperate to acquire, to assimilate, and to spit back out in different form through his goateed mouth.

Then suddenly you were older, but not very old at all.

The rape joke is that you had been drinking wine coolers. Wine coolers! Who drinks wine coolers? People who get raped, according to the rape joke.

The rape joke is he was a bouncer, and kept people out for a living.

Not you!

The rape joke is that he carried a knife, and would show it to you, and would turn it over and over in his hands as if it were a book.

He wasn't threatening you, you understood. He just really liked his knife.

The rape joke is he once almost murdered a dude by throwing him through a plate-glass window. The next day he told you and he was trembling, which you took as evidence of his sensitivity.

How can a piece of knowledge be stupid? But of course you were so stupid.

The rape joke is that sometimes he would tell you you were going on a date and then take you over to his best friend Peewee's house and make you watch wrestling while they all got high.

The rape joke is that his best friend was named Peewee.

OK, the rape joke is that he worshiped The Rock.

Like the dude was completely in love with The Rock. He thought it was so great what he could do with his eyebrow.

The rape joke is he called wrestling "a soap opera for men." Men love drama too, he assured you.

The rape joke is that his bookshelf was just a row of paperbacks about serial killers. You mistook this for an interest in history, and laboring under this misapprehension you once gave him a copy of Günter Grass's *My Century*, which he never even tried to read.

It gets funnier.

The rape joke is that he kept a diary. I wonder if he wrote about the rape in it.

The rape joke is that you read it once, and he talked about another girl. He called her Miss Geography, and said "he didn't have those urges when he looked at her anymore," not since he met you. Close call, Miss Geography!

The rape joke is that he was your father's high-school student—your father taught World Religion. You helped him clean out his classroom at the end of the year, and he let you take home the most beat-up textbooks.

The rape joke is that he knew you when you were 12 years old. He once helped your family move two states over, and you drove from Cincinnati to St. Louis with him, all by yourselves, and he was kind to you, and you talked the whole way. He had chaw in his mouth the entire time, and you told him he was disgusting and he laughed, and spat the juice through his goatee into a Mountain Dew bottle.

The rape joke is that come on, you should have seen it coming. This rape joke is practically writing itself.

The rape joke is that you were facedown. The rape joke is you were wearing a pretty green necklace that your sister had made for you. Later you cut that necklace up. The mattress felt a specific way, and your mouth felt a specific way open against it, as if you were speaking, but you know you were not. As if your mouth were open ten years into the future, reciting a poem called Rape Joke.

The rape joke is that time is different, becomes more horrible and more habitable, and accommodates your need to go deeper into it.

Just like the body, which more than a concrete form is a capacity.

You know the body of time is elastic, can take almost anything you give it, and heals quickly.

The rape joke is that of course there was blood, which in human beings is so close to the surface.

The rape joke is you went home like nothing happened, and laughed about it the next day and the day after that, and when you told people you laughed, and that was the rape joke.

It was a year before you told your parents, because he was like a son to them. The rape joke is that when you told your father, he made the sign of the cross over you and said, "I absolve you of your sins, in the name of the Father, and of the Son, and of the Holy Spirit," which even in its total wrongheadedness, was so completely sweet.

The rape joke is that you were crazy for the next five years, and had to move cities, and had to move states, and whole days went down into the sinkhole of thinking about why it happened. Like you went to look at your backyard and suddenly it wasn't there, and you were looking down into the center of the earth, which played the same red event perpetually.

The rape joke is that after a while you weren't crazy anymore, but close call, Miss Geography.

The rape joke is that for the next five years all you did was write, and never about yourself, about anything else, about apples on the tree, about islands, dead poets and the worms that aerated them, and there was no warm body in what you wrote, it was elsewhere.

The rape joke is that this is finally artless. The rape joke is that you do not write artlessly.

The rape joke is if you write a poem called Rape Joke, you're asking for it to become the only thing people remember about you.

The rape joke is that you asked why he did it. The rape joke is he said he didn't know, like what else would a rape joke say? The rape joke said YOU were the one who was drunk, and the rape joke said you remembered it wrong, which made you laugh out loud for one long split-open second. The wine coolers weren't Bartles & Jaymes, but it would be funnier for the rape joke if they were. It was some pussy flavor, like Passionate Mango or Destroyed Strawberry, which you drank down without question and trustingly in the heart of Cincinnati Ohio.

Can rape jokes be funny at all, is the question.

Can any part of the rape joke be funny. The part where it ends—haha, just kidding! Though you did dream of killing the rape joke for years, spilling all of its blood out, and telling it that way.

The rape joke cries out for the right to be told.

The rape joke is that this is just how it happened.

The rape joke is that the next day he gave you *Pet Sounds.* No really. *Pet Sounds.* He said he was sorry and then he gave you *Pet Sounds.* Come on, that's a little bit funny.

Admit it. [2003]

Alistair MacLeod

The Boat

There are times even now, when I awake at four o'clock in the morning with the terrible fear that I have overslept; when I imagine that my father is waiting for me in the room below the darkened stairs or that the shorebound men are tossing pebbles against my window while blowing their hands and stomping their feet impatiently on the frozen steadfast earth. There are times when I am half out of bed and fumbling for socks and mumbling for words before I realize that I am foolishly alone, that no one waits at the base of the stairs and no boat rides restlessly in the waters by the pier.

At such times only the grey corpses on the overflowing ashtray beside my bed bear witness to the extinction of the latest spark and silently await the crushing out of the most recent of their fellows. And then because I am afraid to be alone with death, I dress rapidly, make a great to-do about clearing my throat, turn on both faucets in the sink and proceed to make loud splashing ineffectual noises. Later I go out and walk the mile to the all-night restaurant.

In the winter it is a very cold walk, and there are often tears in my eyes when I arrive. The waitress usually gives a sympathetic little shiver and says, "Boy, it must be really cold out there; you got tears in your eyes."

"Yes," I say, "it sure is; it really is."

And then the three or four of us who are always in such places at such times make uninteresting little protective chit-chat until the dawn reluctantly arrives. Then I swallow the coffee, which is always bitter, and leave with a great busy rush because by that time I have to worry about being late and whether I have a clean shirt and whether my car will start and about all the other countless things one must worry about when one teaches at a great Midwestern university. And I know then that that day will go by as have all the days of the past ten years, for the call and the voices and the shapes and the boat were not really there in the early morning's darkness and I have all kinds of comforting reality to prove it. They are only shadows and echoes, the animals a child's hands make on the wall by lamplight, and the voices from the rain barrel; the cuttings from an old movie made in the black and white of long ago.

I first became conscious of the boat in the same way and at almost the same time that I became aware of the people it supported. My earliest recollection of my father is a view from the floor of gigantic rubber boots and then of being suddenly elevated and having my face pressed against the stubble of his cheek, and of how it tasted of salt and of how he smelled of salt from his red-soled rubber boots to the shaggy whiteness of his hair.

When I was very small, he took me for my first ride in the boat. I rode the half-mile from our house to the wharf on his shoulders and I remember the sound of his rubber boots galumphing along the gravel beach, the tune of the indecent little song he used to sing, and the odour of the salt.

The floor of the boat was permeated with the same odour and in its constancy I was not aware of change. In the harbour we made our little circle and returned. He tied the boat by its painter, fastened the stern to its permanent anchor and lifted me high over his head to the solidity of the wharf. Then he climbed up the little iron ladder that led to the wharf's cap, placed me once more upon his shoulders and galumphed off again.

When we returned to the house everyone made a great fuss over my precocious excursion and asked, "How did you like the boat?" "Were you afraid in the boat?" "Did you cry in the boat?" They repeated "the boat" at the end of all their questions and I knew it must be very important to everyone.

My earliest recollection of my mother is of being alone with her in the mornings while my father was away in the boat. She seemed to be always repairing clothes that were "torn in the boat," preparing food "to be eaten in the boat" or looking for "the boat" through our kitchen window which faced upon the sea. When my father returned about noon, she would ask, "Well, how did things go in the boat today?" It was the first question I remember asking: "Well, how did things go in the boat today?" "Well, how did things go in the boat today?"

The boat in our lives was registered at Port Hawkesbury. She was what Nova Scotians called a Cape Island boat and was designed for the small inshore fishermen who sought the lobsters of the spring and the mackerel of summer and later the cod and haddock and hake. She was thirty-two feet long and nine wide, and was powered by an engine from a Chevrolet truck. She had a marine clutch and a high-speed reverse gear and was painted light green with the name *Jenny Lynn* stencilled in black letters on her bow and painted on an oblong plate across her stern. Jenny Lynn had been my mother's maiden name and the boat was called after her as another link in the chain of tradition. Most of the boats that berthed at the wharf bore the names of some female member of their owner's household.

I say this now as if I knew it all then. All at once, all about boat dimensions and engines, and as if on the day of my first childish voyage I noticed the difference between a stencilled name and a painted name. But of course it was not that way at all, for I learned it all very slowly and there was not time enough.

I learned first about our house, which was one of about fifty that marched around the horseshoe of our harbour and the wharf that was its heart. Some of them were so close to the water that during a storm the sea spray splashed against their windows while others were built farther along the beach, as was the case with ours. The houses and their people, like those of the neighbouring towns and villages, were the result of Ireland's discontent and Scotland's Highland Clearances and America's War of Independence. Impulsive, emotional Catholic Celts who could not bear to live with England and shrewd, determined Protestant Puritans who, in the years after 1776, could not bear to live without.

The most important room in our house was one of those oblong old-fashioned kitchens heated by a wood- and coal-burning stove. Behind the stove was a box of kindlings and beside it a coal scuttle. A heavy wooden table with leaves that expanded or reduced its dimensions stood in the middle of the floor. There were five wooden homemade chairs which had been chipped and hacked by a variety of knives. Against the east wall, opposite the stove, there was a couch which sagged in the middle and had a cushion for a pillow, and above it a shelf which contained matches, tobacco, pencils, odd fish-hooks, bits of twine, and a tin can filled with bills and receipts. The south wall was dominated by a window which faced the sea and on the north there was a five-foot board which bore a variety of clothes hooks and the burdens of each. Beneath the board there was a jumble of odd footwear, mostly of rubber. There was also, on this wall, a barometer, a map of the marine area and a shelf which held a tiny radio. The kitchen was shared by all of us and was a buffer zone between the immaculate order of ten other rooms and the disruptive chaos of the single room that was my father's.

My mother ran her house as her brothers ran their boats. Everything was clean and spotless and in order. She was tall and dark and powerfully energetic. In later years she reminded me of the women of Thomas Hardy, particularly Eustacia Vye, in a physical way. She fed and clothed a family of seven children, making all of the meals and most of the clothes. She grew miraculous gardens and magnificent flowers and raised broods of hens and ducks. She would walk miles on berry-picking expeditions and hoist her skirts to dig for clams when the tide was low. She was fourteen years younger than my father, whom she had married when she was twenty-six and had been a local beauty for a period of ten years. My mother was of the sea, as were all of her people, and her horizons were the very literal ones she scanned with her dark and fearless eyes.

Between the kitchen clothes rack and barometer, a door opened into my father's bedroom. It was a room of disorder and disarray. It was as if the wind which so often clamoured about the house succeeded in entering this single room and after whipping it into turmoil stole quietly away to renew its knowing laughter from without.

My father's bed was against the south wall. It always looked rumpled and unmade because he lay on top of it more than he slept within any folds it might have had. Beside it, there was a little brown table. An archaic goose-necked reading light, a battered table radio, a mound of wooden matches, one or two packages of tobacco, a deck of cigarette papers and an overflowing ashtray cluttered its surface. The brown larvae of tobacco shreds and the grey flecks of ash covered both the table and the floor beneath it. The once-varnished surface of the table was disfigured by numerous black scars and gashes inflicted by the neglected burning cigarettes of many years. They had tumbled from the ashtray unnoticed and branded their statements permanently and quietly into the wood until the odour of their burning caused the snuffing out of their lives. At the bed's foot there was a single window which looked upon the sea.

Against the adjacent wall there was a battered bureau and beside it there was a closet which held his single ill-fitting serge suit, the two or three white shirts that strangled him and the square black shoes that pinched. When he took off his more friendly clothes, the heavy woollen sweaters, mitts and socks which my mother knitted for him and the woollen and doeskin shirts, he dumped them unceremoniously on a single chair. If a visitor entered the room while he was lying on the bed, he would be told to throw the clothes on the floor and take their place upon the chair.

Magazines and books covered the bureau and competed with the clothes for domination of the chair. They further overburdened the heroic little table and lay on top of the radio. They filled a baffling and unknowable cave beneath the bed, and in the corner by the bureau they spilled from the walls and grew up from the floor.

The magazines were the most conventional: *Time*, *Newsweek*, *Life*, *Maclean's*, *The Family Herald*, *The Readers Digest*. They were the result of various cut-rate subscriptions or of the gift subscriptions associated with Christmas, "the two whole years for only $3.50."

The books were more varied. There were a few hardcover magnificents and bygone Book-of-the-Month wonders and some were Christmas or birthday gifts. The majority of them, however, were used paperbacks which came from those second-hand bookstores that advertise in the backs of magazines: "Miscellaneous Used Paperbacks 10¢ Each." At first he sent for them himself, although my mother resented the expense, but in later years they came more and more often from my sisters who had moved to the cities. Especially at first they were very weird and varied. Mickey Spillane and Ernest Haycox vied with Dostoyevsky and Faulkner, and the Penguin Poets edition of Gerard Manley Hopkins arrived in the same box as a little book on sex technique called *Getting the Most Out of Love*. The former had been assiduously annotated by a very fine hand using a very blue-inked fountain pen while the latter had been studied by someone with very large thumbs, the prints of which were still visible in the margins. At the slightest provocation it would open almost automatically to particularly graphic and well-smudged pages.

When he was not in the boat, my father spent most of his time lying on the bed in his socks, the top two buttons of his trousers undone, his discarded shirt on the ever-ready chair and the sleeves of the woollen Stanfield underwear, which he wore both summer and winter, drawn half way up to his elbows. The pillows propped up the whiteness of his head and the goose-necked lamp illuminated the pages in his hands. The cigarettes smoked and smouldered on the ashtray and on the table and the radio played constantly, sometimes low and sometimes loud. At midnight and at one, two, three and four, one could sometimes hear the radio, his occasional cough, the rustling thud of a completed book being tossed to the corner heap, or the movement necessitated by his sitting on the edge of the bed to roll the thousandth cigarette. He seemed never to sleep, only to doze, and the light shone constantly from his window to the sea.

My mother despised the room and all it stood for and she had stopped sleeping in it after I was born. She despised disorder in rooms and in houses and in hours and in lives, and she had not read a book since high school. There she had read *Ivanhoe* and considered it a colossal waste of time. Still the room remained, like a rock of opposition in the sparkling waters of a clear deep harbour, opening off the kitchen where we really lived our lives, with its door always open and its contents visible to all.

The daughters of the room and of the house were very beautiful. They were tall and willowy like my mother and had her fine facial features set off by the reddish copper-coloured hair that had apparently once been my father's before it turned to white. All of them were very clever in school and helped my mother a great deal about the house. When they were young they sang and were very happy and very nice to me because I was the youngest, and the family's only boy.

My father never approved of their playing about the wharf like the other children, and they went there only when my mother sent them on an errand. At such times they almost always overstayed, playing screaming games of tag or hide-and-seek in and about the fishing shanties, the piled traps and tubs of trawl, shouting down to the perch that swam languidly about the wharf's algae-covered piles, or jumping in and out of the boats that tugged gently at their lines. My mother was never uneasy about them at such times, and when her husband criticized her she would say, "Nothing will happen to them there," or "They could be doing worse things in worse places."

By about the ninth or tenth grade my sisters one by one discovered my father's bedroom, and then the change would begin. Each would go into the room one morning when he was out. She would go with the ideal hope of imposing order or with the more practical objective of emptying the ashtray, and later she would be found spellbound by the volume in her hand. My mother's reaction was always abrupt, bordering on the angry. "Take your nose out of that trash and come and do your work," she would say, and once I saw her slap my youngest sister so hard that the print of her hand was scarletly emblazoned upon her daughter's cheek while the broken-spined paperback fluttered uselessly to the floor.

Thereafter my mother would launch a campaign against what she had discovered but could not understand. At times, although she was not overly religious, she would bring in God to bolster her arguments, saying, "In the next world God will see to those who waste their lives reading useless books when they should be about their work." Or without theological aid, "I would like to know how books help anyone to live a life." If my father were in, she would repeat the remarks louder than necessary, and her voice would carry into his room where he lay upon his bed. His usual reaction was to turn up the volume of the radio, although that action in itself betrayed the success of the initial thrust.

Shortly after my sisters began to read the books, they grew restless and lost interest in darning socks and baking bread, and all of them eventually went to work as summer waitresses in the Sea Food Restaurant. The restaurant was run by a big American concern from Boston and catered to the tourists that flooded the area during July and August. My mother despised the whole operation. She said the restaurant was not run by "our people," and "our people" did not eat there, and that it was run by outsiders for outsiders.

"Who are these people anyway?" she would ask, tossing back her dark hair, "and what do they, though they go about with their cameras for a hundred years, know about the way it is here, and what do they care about me and mine, and why should I care about them?"

She was angry that my sisters should even conceive of working in such a place, and more angry when my father made no move to prevent it, and she was worried about herself and about her family and about her life. Sometimes she would say softly to her sisters, "I don't know what's the matter with my girls. It seems none of them are interested in any of the right things." And sometimes there would be bitter savage arguments. One afternoon I was coming in with three mackerel I'd been given at the wharf when I heard her say, "Well, I hope you'll be satisfied when they come home knocked up and you'll have had your way."

It was the most savage thing I'd ever heard my mother say. Not just the words but the way she said them, and I stood there in the porch afraid to breathe for what seemed like the years from ten to fifteen, feeling the damp, moist mackerel with their silver glassy eyes growing clammy against my leg.

Through the angle in the screen door I saw my father, who had been walking into his room, wheel around on one of his rubber-booted heels and look at her with his blue eyes flashing like clearest ice beneath the snow that was his hair. His usually ruddy face was drawn and grey, reflecting the exhaustion of a man of sixty-five who had been working in those rubber boots for eleven hours on an August day, and for a fleeting moment I wondered what I would do if he killed my mother while I stood there in the porch with those three foolish mackerel in my hand. Then he turned and went into his room and the radio blared forth the next day's weather forecast and I retreated under the noise and returned again, stamping my feet and slamming the door too loudly to signal my approach. My mother was busy at the stove when I came in, and did not raise her head when I threw the mackerel in a pan. As I looked into my father's room, I said, "Well, how did things go in the boat today?" and he replied, "Oh, not too badly, all things considered." He was lying on his back and lighting the first cigarette and the radio was talking about the Virginia coast.

All of my sisters made good money on tips. They bought my father an electric razor, which he tried to use for a while, and they took out even more magazine subscriptions. They bought my mother a great many clothes of the type she was very fond of, the wide-brimmed hats and the brocaded dresses, but she locked them all in trunks and refused to wear any of them.

On one August day my sisters prevailed upon my father to take some of their restaurant customers for an afternoon ride in the boat. The tourists with their expensive clothes and cameras and sun glasses awkwardly backed down the iron ladder at the wharf's side to where my father waited below, holding the rocking *Jenny Lynn* in snug against the wharf with one hand on the iron ladder and steadying his descending passengers with the other. They tried to look both prim and wind-blown like the girls in the Pepsi-Cola ads and did the best they could, sitting on the thwarts where the newspapers were spread to cover the splattered blood and fish entrails, crowding to one side so that they were in danger of capsizing the boat, taking the inevitable pictures or merely trailing their fingers through the water of their dreams.

All of them liked my father very much and, after he'd brought them back from their circles in the harbour, they invited him to their rented cabins which were located high on a hill overlooking the village to which they were so alien. He proceeded to get very drunk up there with the beautiful view and the strange company and the abundant liquor, and late in the afternoon he began to sing.

I was just approaching the wharf to deliver my mother's summons when he began, and the familiar yet unfamiliar voice that rolled down from the cabins made me feel as I had never felt before in my young life, or perhaps as I had always felt without really knowing it, and I was ashamed yet proud, young yet old and saved yet forever lost, and there was nothing I could do to control my legs which trembled nor my eyes which wept, for what they could not tell.

The tourists were equipped with tape recorders and my father sang for more than three hours. His voice boomed down the hill and bounced off the surface of the harbour, which was an unearthly blue on that hot August day, and was then reflected to the wharf and the fishing shanties, where it was absorbed amidst the men who were baiting lines for the next day's haul.

He sang all the old sea chanteys that had come across from the old world and by which men like him had pulled ropes for generations, and he sang the East Coast sea songs that celebrated the sealing vessels of Northumberland Strait and the long liners of the Grand Banks, and of Anticosti, Sable Island, Grand Manan, Boston Harbor, Nantucket and Block Island. Gradually he shifted to the seemingly unending Gaelic drinking songs with their twenty or more verses and inevitable refrains, and the men in the shanties smiled at the coarseness of some of the verses and at the thought that the singer's immediate audience did not know what they were applauding nor recording to take back to staid old Boston. Later as the sun was setting he switched to the laments and the wild and haunting Gaelic war songs of those spattered Highland ancestors he had never seen, and when his voice ceased, the savage melancholy of three hundred years seemed to hang over the peaceful harbour and the quiet boats and the men leaning in the doorways of their shanties with their cigarettes glowing in the dusk and the women looking to the sea from their open windows with their children in their arms.

When he came home he threw the money he had earned on the kitchen table as he did with all his earnings but my mother refused to touch it, and the next day he went with the rest of the men to bait his trawl in the shanties. The tourists came to the door that evening and my mother met them there and told them that her husband was not in, although he was lying on the bed only a few feet away, with the radio playing and the cigarette upon his lips. She stood in the doorway until they reluctantly went away.

In the winter they sent him a picture which had been taken on the day of the singing. On the back it said, "To Our Ernest Hemingway" and the "Our" was underlined. There was also an accompanying letter telling how much they had enjoyed themselves, how popular the tape was proving and explaining who Ernest Hemingway was. In a way it almost did look like one of those unshaven, taken-in-Cuba pictures of Hemingway. My father looked both massive and incongruous in the setting. His bulky fisherman's clothes were too big for the green and white lawn chair in which he sat, and his rubber boots seemed to take up all of the well-clipped grass square. The beach umbrella jarred with his sunburned face and because he had already been singing for some time, his lips, which chapped in the winds of spring and burned in the water glare of summer, had already cracked in several places, producing tiny flecks of blood at their corners and on the whiteness of his teeth. The bracelets of brass chain which he wore to protect his wrists from chafing seemed abnormally large and his broad leather belt had been slackened and his heavy shirt and underwear were open at the throat, revealing an uncultivated wilderness of white chest hair bordering on the semi-controlled stubble of his neck and chin. His blue eyes had looked directly into the camera and his hair was whiter than the two tiny clouds that hung over his left shoulder. The sea was behind him and its immense blue flatness stretched out to touch the arching blueness of the sky. It seemed very far away from him or else he was so much in the foreground that he seemed too big for it.

Each year another of my sisters would read the books and work in the restaurant. Sometimes they would stay out quite late on the hot summer nights and when they came up the stairs my mother would ask them many long and involved questions which they resented and tried to avoid. Before ascending the stairs they would go into my father's room, and those of us who waited above could hear them throwing his clothes off the chair before sitting on it, or the squeak of the bed as they sat on its edge. Sometimes they would talk to him a long time, the murmur of their voices blending with the music of the radio into a mysterious vapour-like sound which floated softly up the stairs.

I say this again as if it all happened at once and as if all of my sisters were of identical ages and like so many lemmings going into another sea and, again, it was of course not that way at all. Yet go they did, to Boston, to Montreal, to New York with the young men they met during the summers and later married in those far-away cities. The young men were very articulate and handsome and wore fine clothes and drove expensive cars and my sisters, as I said, were very tall and beautiful with their copper-coloured hair, and were tired of darning socks and baking bread.

One by one they went. My mother had each of her daughters for fifteen years, then lost them for two and finally forever. None married a fisherman. My mother never accepted any of the young men, for in her eyes they seemed always a combination of the lazy, the effeminate, the dishonest and the unknown. They never seemed to do any physical work and she could not comprehend their luxurious vacations and she did not know whence they came nor who they were. And in the end she did not really care, for they were not of her people and they were not of her sea.

I say this now with a sense of wonder at my own stupidity in thinking I was somehow free and would go on doing well in school and playing and helping in the boat and passing into my early teens while streaks of grey began to appear in my mother's dark hair and my father's rubber boots dragged sometimes on the pebbles of the beach as he trudged home from the wharf. And there were but three of us in the house that had at one time been so loud.

Then during the winter that I was fifteen he seemed to grow old and ill all at once. Most of January he lay upon the bed, smoking and reading and listening to the radio while the wind howled about the house and the needle-like snow blistered off the ice-covered harbour and the doors flew out of people's hands if they did not cling to them like death.

In February, when the men began overhauling their lobster traps, he still did not move, and my mother and I began to knit lobster trap headings in the evenings. The twine was as always very sharp and harsh, and blisters formed upon our thumbs and little paths of blood snaked quietly down between our fingers while the seals that had drifted down from distant Labrador wept and moaned like human children on the ice-floes of the Gulf.

In the daytime my mother's brother, who had been my father's partner as long as I could remember, also came to work upon the gear. He was a year older than my mother and was tall and dark and the father of twelve children.

By March we were very far behind and although I began to work very hard in the evenings I knew it was not hard enough and that there were but eight weeks left before the opening of the season on May first. And I knew that my mother worried and my uncle was uneasy and that all of our very lives depended on the boat being ready with her gear and two men, by the date of May the first. And I knew then that *David Copperfield* and *The Tempest* and all of those friends I had dearly come to love must really go forever. So I bade them all good-bye.

The night after my first full day at home and after my mother had gone upstairs he called me into his room, where I sat upon the chair beside his bed. "You will go back tomorrow," he said simply.

I refused then, saying I had made my decision and was satisfied.

"That is no way to make a decision," he said, "and if you are satisfied I am not. It is best that you go back." I was almost angry then and told him as all children do that I wished he would leave me alone and stop telling me what to do.

He looked at me a long time then, lying there on the same bed on which he had fathered me those sixteen years before, fathered me his only son, out of who knew what emotions when he was already fifty-six and his hair had turned to snow. Then he swung his legs over the edge of the squeaking bed and sat facing me and looked into my own dark eyes with his of crystal blue and placed his hand upon my knee. "I am not telling you to do anything," he said softly, "only asking you."

The next morning I returned to school. As I left, my mother followed me to the porch and said, "I never thought a son of mine would choose useless books over the parents that gave him life."

In the weeks that followed he got up rather miraculously, and the gear was ready and the *Jenny Lynn* was freshly painted by the last two weeks of April when the ice began to break up and the lonely screaming gulls returned to haunt the silver herring as they flashed within the sea.

On the first day of May the boats raced out as they had always done, laden down almost to the gunwales with their heavy cargoes of traps. They were almost like living things as they plunged through the waters of the spring and manoeuvred between the still floating icebergs of crystal-white and emerald green on their way to the traditional grounds that they sought out every May. And those of us who sat that day in the high school on the hill, discussing the water imagery of Tennyson, watched them as they passed back and forth beneath us until by afternoon the piles of traps which had been stacked upon the wharf were no longer visible but were spread about the bottoms of the sea. And the *Jenny Lynn* went too, all day, with my uncle tall and dark, like a latter-day Tashtego standing at the tiller with his legs wide apart and guiding her deftly between the floating pans of ice and my father in the stern standing in the same way with his hands upon the ropes that lashed the cargo to the deck. And at night my mother asked, "Well, how did things go in the boat today?"

And the spring wore on and the summer came and school ended in the third week of June and the lobster season on July first and I wished that the two things I loved so dearly did not exclude each other in a manner that was so blunt and too clear.

At the conclusion of the lobster season my uncle said he had been offered a berth on a deep-sea dragger and had decided to accept. We all knew that he was leaving the *Jenny Lynn* forever and that before the next lobster season he would buy a boat of his own. He was expecting another child and would be supporting fifteen people by the next spring and could not chance my father against the family that he loved.

I joined my father then for the trawling season, and he made no protest and my mother was quite happy. Through the summer we baited the tubs of trawl in the afternoon and set them at sunset and revisited them in the darkness of the early morning. The men would come tramping by our house at four a.m. and we would join them and walk with them to the wharf and be on our way before the sun rose out of the ocean where it seemed to spend the night. If I was not up they would toss pebbles to my window and I would be very embarrassed and tumble downstairs to where my father lay fully clothed atop his bed, reading his book and listening to his radio and smoking his cigarette. When I appeared he would swing off his bed and put on his boots and be instantly ready and then we would take the lunches my mother had prepared the night before and walk off toward the sea. He would make no attempt to wake me himself.

It was in many ways a good summer. There were few storms and we were out almost every day and we lost a minimum of gear and seemed to land a maximum of fish and I tanned dark and brown after the manner of my uncles.

My father did not tan—he never tanned—because of his reddish complexion, and the salt water irritated his skin as it had for sixty years. He burned and reburned over and over again and his lips still cracked so that they bled when he smiled, and his arms, especially the left, still broke out into the oozing salt-water boils as they had ever since as a child I had first watched him soaking and bathing them in a variety of ineffectual solutions. The chafe-preventing bracelets of brass linked chain that all the men wore about their wrists in early spring were his the full season and he shaved but painfully and only once a week.

And I saw then, that summer, many things that I had seen all my life as if for the first time and I thought that perhaps my father had never been intended for a fisherman either physically or mentally. At least not in the manner of my uncles; he had never really loved it. And I remembered that, one evening in his room when we were talking about *David Copperfield*, he had said that he had always wanted to go to the university and I had dismissed it then in the way one dismisses one's father saying he would like to be a tight-rope walker, and we had gone on to talk about the Peggottys and how they loved the sea.

And I thought then to myself that there were many things wrong with all of us and all our lives and I wondered why my father, who was himself an only son, had not married before he was forty and then I wondered why he had. I even thought that perhaps he had had to marry my mother and checked the dates on the flyleaf of the Bible where I learned that my oldest sister had been born a prosaic eleven months after the marriage, and I felt myself then very dirty and debased for my lack of faith and for what I had thought and done.

And then there came into my heart a very great love for my father and I thought it was very much braver to spend a life doing what you really do not want rather than selfishly following forever your own dreams and inclinations. And I knew then that I could never leave him alone to suffer the iron-tipped harpoons which my mother would forever hurl into his soul because he was a failure as a husband and a father who had retained none of his own. And I felt that I had been very small in a little secret place within me and that even the completion of high school was for me a silly shallow selfish dream.

So I told him one night very resolutely and very powerfully that I would remain with him as long as he lived and we would fish the sea together. And he made no protest but only smiled through the cigarette smoke that wreathed his bed and replied, "I hope you will remember what you've said."

The room was now so filled with books as to be almost Dickensian, but he would not allow my mother to move or change them and he continued to read them, sometimes two or three a night. They came with great regularity now, and there were more hardcovers, sent by my sisters who had gone so long ago and now seemed so distant and so prosperous, and sent also pictures of small red-haired grandchildren with baseball bats and dolls, which he placed upon his bureau and which my mother gazed at wistfully when she thought no one would see. Red-haired grandchildren with baseball bats and dolls who would never know the sea in hatred or in love.

And so we fished through the heat of August and into the cooler days of September when the water was so clear we could almost see the bottom and the white mists rose like delicate ghosts in the early morning dawn. And one day my mother said to me, "You have given added years to his life."

And we fished on into October when it began to roughen and we could no longer risk night sets but took our gear out each morning and returned at the first sign of the squalls; and on into November when we lost three tubs of trawl and the clear blue water turned to a sullen grey and the trochoidal waves rolled rough and high and washed across our bows and decks as we ran within their troughs. We wore heavy sweaters now and the awkward rubber slickers and the heavy woollen mitts which soaked and froze into masses of ice that hung from our wrists like the limbs of gigantic monsters until we thawed them against the exhaust pipe's heat. And almost every day we would leave for home before noon, driven by the blasts of the northwest wind coating our eyebrows with ice and freezing our eyelids closed as we leaned into a visibility that was hardly there, charting our course from the compass and the sea, running with the waves and between them but never confronting their towering might.

And I stood at the tiller now, on these homeward lunges, stood in the place and in the manner of my uncle, turning to look at my father and to shout over the roar of the engine and the slop of the sea to where he stood in the stern, drenched and dripping with the snow and the salt and the spray and his bushy eyebrows caked in ice. But on November twenty-first, when it seemed we might be making the final run of the season, I turned and he was not there and I knew even in that instant that he would never be again.

On November twenty-first the waves of the grey Atlantic are very high and the waters are very cold and there are no signposts on the surface of the sea. You cannot tell where you have been five minutes before and in the squalls of snow you cannot see. And it takes longer than you would believe to check a boat that has been running before a gale and turn her ever so carefully in a wide and stupid circle, with timbers creaking and straining, back into the face of the storm. And you know that it is useless and that your voice does not carry the length of the boat and that even if you knew the original spot, the relentless waves would carry such a burden perhaps a mile or so by the time you could return. And you know also, the final irony, that your father, like your uncles and all the men that form your past, cannot swim a stroke.

The lobster beds off the Cape Breton coast are still very rich and now, from May to July, their offerings are packed in crates of ice, and thundered by the gigantic transport trucks, day and night, through New Glasgow, Amherst, Saint John and Bangor and Portland and into Boston where they are tossed still living into boiling pots of water, their final home.

And though the prices are higher and the competition tighter, the grounds to which the *Jenny Lynn* once went remain untouched and unfished as they have for the last ten years. For if there are no signposts on the sea in storm, there are certain ones in calm, and the lobster bottoms were distributed in calm before any of us can remember, and the grounds my father fished were those his father fished before him and there were others before and before and before. Twice the big boats have come from forty and fifty miles, lured by the promise of the grounds, and strewn the bottom with their traps, and twice they have returned to find their buoys cut adrift and their gear lost and destroyed. Twice the Fisheries Officer and the Mounted Police have come and asked many long and involved questions, and twice they have received no answers from the men leaning in the doors of their shanties and the women standing at their windows with their children in their arms. Twice they have gone away saying: "There are no legal boundaries in the Marine area"; "No one can own the sea"; "Those grounds don't wait for anyone."

But the men and the women, with my mother dark among them, do not care for what they say, for to them the grounds are sacred and they think they wait for me.

It is not an easy thing to know that your mother lives alone on an inadequate insurance policy and that she is too proud to accept any other aid. And that she looks through her lonely window onto the ice of winter and the hot flat calm of summer and the rolling waves of fall. And that she lies awake in the early morning's darkness when the rubber boots of the men scrunch upon the gravel as they pass beside her house on their way down to the wharf. And she knows that the footsteps never stop, because no man goes from her house, and she alone of all the Lynns has neither son nor son-in-law who walks toward the boat that will take him to the sea. And it is not an easy thing to know that your mother looks upon the sea with love and on you with bitterness because the one has been so constant and the other so untrue.

But neither is it easy to know that your father was found on November twenty-eighth, ten miles to the north and wedged between two boulders at the base of the rock-strewn cliffs where he had been hurled and slammed so many many times. His hands were shredded ribbons, as were his feet which had lost their boots to the suction of the sea, and his shoulders came apart in our hands when we tried to move him from the rocks. And the fish had eaten his testicles and the gulls had pecked out his eyes and the white-green stubble of his whiskers had continued to grow in death, like the grass on graves, upon the purple, bloated mass that was his face. There was not much left of my father, physically, as he lay there with the brass chains on his wrists and the seaweed in his hair.

[1968]

John Marshall

from *Taken With*

22

I was back to help clean out her room when
an old man misaligned in his wheelchair shouted
Young man come here from a corner of the lounge.

No staff visible and again Young man come here.
I went and stood in front of him like we were in the military.
Young man I have a question. I said yes?

Was that man I saw a while ago over there my mother?
I've rarely felt as certain as I did then and I said no.
He said again I want to know if that man I saw a little while ago

was my mother. No panic in his voice just level curiosity.
I said no again like I was a visiting academic. Are you certain?
I'm certain I said and he said Okay. I just wanted to know.

Thank you young man. I went back to her last room.
And what if I had said I'm your mother and still love you?

[2005]

Paul Martínez Pompa

Exclamation Point

Exclamation Point—a punctuation mark that indicates strong feeling in connection with what is being said. It serves as a signpost to a reader that a sentence expresses intense feeling. An exclamation point may end a declaratory statement (Put your fuckin hands up!), a question (Do you want me to put a cap in your mexakin ass!), or a fragment (Now asshole!). It may express an exclamation (Your ass is going to jail!), a wish (If you move, I'll shoot your fuckin ass!), or a cry (Okay, okay, take it easy, officer!). As these examples show, exclamation points are commonest in written dialogue. They should be used carefully in any writing and very seldom in formal writing. [2009]

Marty McConnell

Frida Kahlo to Marty McConnell

leaving is not enough; you must
stay gone. train your heart
like a dog. change the locks
even on the house he's never
visited. you lucky, lucky girl.
you have an apartment
just your size. a bathtub
full of tea. a heart the size
of Arizona, but not nearly
so arid. don't wish away
your cracked past, your
crooked toes, your problems
are papier mache puppets
you made or bought because the vendor
at the market was so compelling you just
had to have them. you had to have him.
and you did. and now you pull down
the bridge between your houses.
you make him call before
he visits. you take a lover
for granted, you take
a lover who looks at you
like maybe you are magic. make
the first bottle you consume
in this place a relic. place it
on whatever altar you fashion

with a knife and five cranberries.
don't lose too much weight.
stupid girls are always trying
to disappear as revenge. and you
are not stupid. you loved a man
with more hands than a parade
of beggars, and here you stand. heart
like a four-poster bed. heart like a canvas.
heart leaking something so strong
they can smell it in the street. [2009]

Edna St. Vincent Millay

[What lips my lips have kissed, and where, and why]

What lips my lips have kissed, and where, and why,
I have forgotten, and what arms have lain
Under my head till morning; but the rain
Is full of ghosts tonight, that tap and sigh
Upon the glass and listen for reply,
And in my heart there stirs a quiet pain
For unremembered lads that not again
Will turn to me at midnight with a cry.
Thus in winter stands the lonely tree,
Nor knows what birds have vanished one by one,
Yet knows its boughs more silent than before:
I cannot say what loves have come and gone,
I only know that summer sang in me
A little while, that in me sings no more. [1923]

Brenda Miller

Getting Yourself Home

You're in the bed of a stranger. Well, not a stranger, really—he's your boyfriend, after all, you agreed to this designation just the other day, both of you content from an afternoon of careful courtship, the binoculars passed from hand to hand as you watched the trumpeter swans and the snow geese sharing a field in the Skagit River plains. But now his face, when you glimpse it sidelong, looks so rigid, the mouth shut tight, the head tilted up and away. Even those creases around his ear, those lines you once found endearing, now seem a deformation. Even if you could see each other clearly, your glances would knock sidelong off each other, deflecting, and you can hardly imagine now the first time you made love: not the sex itself, but the kiss that preceded it—so long, so breathtaking, your head arched back, the body's tendons giving way without a thought.

But now you feel dangerously exposed, your body huddled under the covers: how has it come to this so quickly, so soon? You wrap your arms around your naked chest and long for your flannel pajamas, but they're at your own house, hanging on the hook behind the bathroom door, you can see them so clearly, along with a vision of your new kitten wandering the house by herself, still so bewildered by these rooms, mewling into the dark—did you leave on a light? did you fill her water bowl?—she's frightened, you imagine, and baffled by your absence.

It's three o'clock on a winter morning, foggy, the roads slick with ice. You turn in the bed, away from the man and his thick arms, his muscled chest, the wrists powerful from days spent with hammers and saws. You open your eyes and begin to calculate each of the moves it would take to get you out of here: the flip of the blankets, the swing of your legs onto the floor, the search for your clothes crumpled on the chair by the desk, gathering those clothes in your arms and tiptoeing over the creaking planks to pull them on in the other room—the boyfriend muttering from his side of the bed, or not making a sound, his eyes tightly closed, his head twisted away. And then the search for your purse, your shoes, your keys, your coat, standing with all these things by the doorway, trying to decide whether or not to say good night, and finally just fleeing down the stairs and out the door to your car, the windows covered in a thin sheet of ice. You'd have to scrabble for the lock, nicking the paint, then inside put the defroster on high, jumping out again with scraper in hand, hacking away at the windows, your hands aching with cold. Finally, the creep up the dirt driveway, dipping your head to peer under the scrim of frost, accelerating too hard so the back end swerves as you pull out onto the road. Then the road itself: pitch dark, slick, the air veiled with fog so the high beams do not illuminate so much as blind as you make your clumsy way home.

Just the thought of it exhausts you, and when you contemplate even the first of these moves—the turning back of the covers—you realize the impossibility of even such a simple gesture, one that will lead you out of here and back where you belong. You dare not move a muscle, so you blink back the darkness and try to navigate how you got here in the first place, scrolling in your mind, but all you get is a procession of men from your past—they parade before you, one after the other, all of them turning to smile briefly, forlornly, their foreheads puckered in disappointment.

You shut your eyes. Take a deep breath. You try to remember what your meditation teacher told you about the breath: how you enter your true home with each inhalation, each exhalation, a cadence old and plain as those worn-out concepts of love, of compassion. So you try it: you breathe in, you breathe out, but there's a glitch in your throat, a mass in your chest, and your body feels nothing like home, more like a room in a foreign hotel, the windows greasy, the outlets reversed, the noise of the street rising like soot. The body's no longer an easy abode, not in this bed, not with two strangers lying in the dark and waiting—breath held—for morning to finally arrive. [2005]

Madison Minder

Green

As I was flying through the trees
in my grandpa's '98 Chevy Lumina,
all I saw was green.

Everything from the moment I sleepily drifted off the road,
to the head-on-ceiling, teeth-on-teeth-on-tongue bouncing
was in slow motion.
I remember my keys jangling wildly
against each other.
I remember the bag of Doritos in the back and snacks smacking
across the windows,
my clothes and textbooks smashing
into my seat.

I glanced over at my passenger and watched my driving
paint a look of horror across her face.
She screamed my name over and over,
begging my foot to find the brake.
But I didn't stop;
I couldn't stop.

The maroon beast plowed through
bushes, swam through swamps,
and didn't stop until it was stuck
with its nose in a ditch
and its tail on a slope.
My foot never left the gas.

After crawling out of my car sideways,
I looked at my friends in shock.
My jaw stuck open, my lips rounded dumbly.
I wanted to cry,
but the adrenaline pumping through my blood and brain
made tears impossible.

I was still flying through the trees
in my grandpa's '98 Chevy Lumina,
seeing green.

[2016]

Janice Mirikitani

Recipe

Round Eyes

Ingredients: scissors, Scotch magic transparent tape,
eyeliner—water based, black.
Optional: false eyelashes.

Cleanse face thoroughly.

For best results, powder entire face, including eyelids
(lighter shades suited to total effect desired).

With scissors, cut magic tape 1/16" wide, 3/4"–1/2" long—
depending on length of eyelid.

Stick firmly onto mid-upper eyelid area
(looking down into handmirror facilitates finding
adequate surface).

If using false eyelashes, affix first on lid, folding any
excess lid over the base of eyelash with glue.

Paint black eyeliner on tape and entire lid.

Do not cry. [1987]

Shani Mootoo

Out on Main Street

Janet and me? We does go Main Street to see pretty pretty sari and bangle, and to eat we belly full a burfi and gulub jamoon, but we doh go too often because, yuh see, is dem sweets self what does give people like we a presupposition for untameable hip and thigh.

Another reason we shy to frequent dere is dat we is watered-down Indians—we ain't good grade A Indians. We skin brown, is true, but we doh even think 'bout India unless something happen over dere and it come on de news. Mih family remain Hindu ever since mih ancestors leave India behind, but nowadays dey doh believe in praying unless things real bad, because, as mih father always singing, like if is a mantra: "Do good and good will be bestowed unto you." So he is a veritable saint cause he always doing good by his women friends and dey chilren. I sure some a dem must be mih half sister and brother, oui!

Mostly, back home, we is kitchen Indians: some kind a Indian food every day, at least once a day, but we doh get cardamom and other fancy spice down dere so de food not spicy like Indian food I eat in restaurants up here. But it have one thing we doh make joke 'bout down dere: we like we meethai and sweetrice too much, and it remain overly authentic, like de day Naana and Naani step off de boat in Port of Spain harbour over a hundred and sixty years ago. Check out dese hips here nah, dey is pure sugar and condensed milk, pure sweetness!

But Janet family different. In de ole days when Canadian missionaries land in Trinidad dey used to make a bee-line straight for Indians from down South. And Janet great grandparents is one a de first South families dat exchange over from Indian to Presbyterian. Dat was a long time ago.

When Janet born, she father, one Mr. John Mahase, insist on asking de Reverend MacDougal from Trace Settlement Church, a leftover from de Canadian Mission, to name de baby girl. De good Reverend choose de name Constance cause dat was his mother name. But de mother a de child, Mrs. Savitri Mahase, wanted to name de child sheself. Ever since Savitri was a lil girl she like de yellow hair, fair skin and pretty pretty clothes Janet and John used to wear in de primary school reader—since she lil she want to change she name from Savitiri to Janet but she own father get vex and say how Savitri was his mother name and how she will insult his mother if she gone and change it. So Savitri get she own way once by marrying this fella name John, and she do a encore, by calling she daughter Janet, even doh husband John upset for days at she for insulting de good Reverend by throwing out de name a de Reverend mother.

So dat is how my girlfriend, a darkskin Indian girl with thick black hair (pretty fuh so!) get a name like Janet.

She come from a long line a Presbyterian school teacher, headmaster and headmistress. Savitri still teaching from de same Janet and John reader in a primary school in San Fernando, and John, getting more and more obtuse in his ole age, is headmaster more dan twenty years now in Princes Town Boys' Presbyterian High School. Everybody back home know dat family good good. Dat is why Janet leave in two twos. Soon as A Level finish she pack up and take off like a jet plane so she could live without people only shoo-shooing behind she back... "But A A! Yuh ain't hear de goods 'bout John Mahase daughter, gyul! How yuh mean yuh ain't hear? Is a big thing! Everybody talking 'bout she. Hear dis, riah! Yuh ever see she wear a dress? Yes! Doh look at mih so. Yuh reading mih right!"

Is only recentish I realize Mahase is a Hindu last name. In de ole days every Mahase in de country turn Presbyterian and now de name doh have no association with Hindu or Indian whatsoever. I used to think of it as a Presbyterian Church name until some days ago when we meet a Hindu fella fresh from India name Yogdesh Mahase who never even hear of Presbyterian.

De other day I ask Janet what she know 'bout Divali. She say, "It's the Hindu festival of lights, isn't it?" like a line straight out a dictionary. Yuh think she know anything 'bout how lord Rama get himself exile in a forest for fourteen years, and how when it come time for him to go back home his followers light up a pathway to help him make his way out, and dat is what Divali lights is all about? All Janet know is 'bout going for drive in de country to see light, and she could remember looking forward, around Divali time, to the lil brown paper-bag packages full a burfi and parasad that she father Hindu students used to bring for him.

One time in a Indian restaurant she ask for parasad for dessert. Well! Since den I never go back in dat restaurant, I embarrass fuh so!

I used to think I was a Hindu *par excellence* until I come up here and see real flesh and blood

Indian from India. Up here, I learning 'bout all kind a custom and food and music and clothes dat we never see or hear 'bout in good ole Trinidad. Is de next best thing to going to India, in truth, oui! But Indian store clerk on Main Street doh have no patience with us, specially when we talking English to dem. Yuh ask dem a question in English and dey insist on giving de answer in Hindi or Punjabi or Urdu or Gujarati. How I suppose to know de difference even! And den dey look at yuh disdainful disdainful—like yuh disloyal, like yuh is a traitor.

But yuh know, it have one other reason I real reluctant to go Main Street. Yuh see, Janet pretty fuh so! And I doh like de way men does look at she, as if because she wearing jeans and tee shirt and high-heel shoe and makeup and have long hair loose and flying about like she is a walking-talking shampoo ad, dat she easy. And de women always looking at she beady eye, like she loose and going to thief dey man. Dat kind a thing always make me want to put mih arm round she waist like, she is my woman, take yuh eyes off she! and shock de false teeth right out dey mouth. And den is a whole other story when dey see me with mih crew cut and mih blue jeans tuck inside mih jim-boots. Walking next to Janet, who so femme dat she redundant, tend to make me look like a gender dey forget to classify. Before going Main Street I does parade in front de mirror practising a jiggly-wiggly kind a walk. But if I ain't walking like a strong-man monkey I doh exactly feel right and I always revert back to mih true colours. De men dem does look at me like if dey is exactly what I need a taste of to cure me good and proper. I could see dey eyes watching Janet and me, dey face growing dark as dey imagining all kind a situation and position. And de women dem embarrass fuh so to watch me in mih eye, like dey fraid I will jump up and try to kiss dem, or make pass at dem. Yuh know, sometimes I wonder if I ain't mad enough to do it just for a little bacchanal, nah!

Going for a outing with mih Janet on Main street ain't easy! If only it wasn't for burfi and gulub jamoon! If only I had a learned how to cook dem kind a thing before I leave home and come up here to live!

2

In large deep-orange Sanskrit-style letters, de sign on de saffron-colour awning above de door read "Kush Valley Sweets." Underneath in smaller red letters it had "Desserts Fit for the Gods." It was a corner building. The front and side was one big glass wall. Inside was big. Big like a gymnasium. Yuh could see in through de brown tint windows: dark brown plastic chair, and brown table, each one de length of a door, line up stiff and straight in row after row like if is a school room.

Before entering de restaurant I ask Janet to wait one minute outside with me while I rumfle up mih memory, pulling out all de sweet names I know from home, besides burfi and gulub jamoon: meethai, jilebi, sweetrice (but dey call dat kheer up here), and ladhoo. By now, of course, mih mouth watering fuh so! When I feel confident enough dat I wouldn't make a fool a mih Brown self by asking what dis one name? and what dat one name? we went in de restaurant. In two twos all de spice in de place take a flying leap in our direction and give us one big welcome hug up, tight fuh so! Since den dey take up permanent residence in de jacket I wear dat day!

Mostly it had women customers sitting at de tables, chatting and laughing, eating sweets and sipping masala tea. De only men in de place was de waiters, and all six waiters was men. I figure dat dey was brothers, not too hard to conclude, because all a dem had de same full round chin, round as if de chin stretch tight over a ping-pong ball, and dey had de same big roving eyes. I know better dan to think dey was mere waiters in de employ of owner who chook up in a office in de back. I sure dat dat was dey own family business, dey stomach proudly preceeding dem and dey shoulders throw back in de confidence of dey ownership.

It ain't dat I paranoid, yuh understand, but from de moment we enter de fellas dem get over-animated, even armorously agitated. Janet again! All six pair a eyes land up on she, following she every move and body part. Dat in itself is something dat does madden me, oui! but also a kind a irrational envy have a tendency to manifest in me. It was like I didn't exist. Sometimes it could be a real problem going out with a good-looker, yes! While I ain't remotely interested in having a squeak of a flirtation with a man, it doh hurt a ego to have a man notice yuh once in a very long while. But with Janet at mih side, I doh have de chance of a penny shave-ice in de hot sun. I tuck mih elbows in as close to mih sides as I could so I wouldn't look like a strong man next to she, and over to de l-o-n-g glass case jam up with sweets I jiggle and wiggle in mih best imitation a some a dem gay fellas dat I see downtown Vancouver, de ones who more femme dan even Janet. I tell she not to pay de brothers no attention, because if any a dem flirt with she I could start a fight right dere and den. And I didn't feel to mess up mih crew cut in a fight.

De case had sweets in every nuance of colour in a rainbow. Sweets I never before see and doh know de names of. But dat was alright because I wasn't going to order dose ones anyway.

Since before we leave home Janet have she mind set on a nice thick syrupy curl a jilebi and a piece a plain burfi so I order dose for she and den I ask de waiter-fella, resplendent with thick thick bright-yellow gold chain and ID bracelet, for a stick a meethai for mihself. I stand up waiting by de glass case for it but de waiter/owner lean up on de back wall behind de counter watching me like he ain't hear me. So I say loud enough for him, and every body else in de room to hear, "I would like to have one piece a meethai please," and den he smile and lift up his hands, palms open-out motioning across de vast expanse a glass case, and he say, "Your choice! Whichever you want, Miss." But he still lean up against de back wall grinning. So I stick mih head out and up like a turtle and say louder, and slowly, "One piece a meethai—dis one!" and I point sharp to de stick a flour mix with ghee, deep fry and den roll up in sugar. He say, "That is koorma, Miss. One piece only?"

Mih voice drop low all by itself. "Oh ho! Yes, one piece. Where I come from we does call dat meethai." And den I add, but only loud enough for Janet to hear, "And mih name ain't 'Miss.'"

He open his palms out and indicate de entire panorama a sweets and he say, "These are all meethai, Miss. Meethai is Sweets. Where are you from?"

I ignore his question and to show him I undaunted, I point to a round pink ball and say, "I'll have one a dese sugarcakes too please." He start grinning broad broad like if he half-pitying, half-laughing at dis Indian-in-skin-colour-only, and den he tell me, "That is called chum-chum, Miss." I snap back at him, "Yeh, well back home we does call dat sugarcake, Mr. Chum-chum."

At de table Janet say, "You know, Pud (Pud, short for Pudding; is dat she does call me when she feeling close to me, or sorry for me), it's true that we call that 'meethai' back home. Just like how we call 'siu mai' 'tim sam.' As if 'dim sum' is just one little piece a food. What did he call that sweet again?"

"Cultural bastards, Janet, cultural bastards. Dat is what we is. Yuh know, one time a fella from India who living up here call me a bastardized Indian because I didn't know Hindi. And now look at dis, nah! De thing is: all a we in Trinidad is cultural bastards, Janet, all a we. *Toutes bagailles!* Chinese people. Black people. White people. Syrian. Lebanese. I looking forward to de day I find out dat place inside me where I am nothing else but Trinidadian, whatever dat could turn out to be."

I take a bite a de chum-chum, de texture was like grind-up coconut but it had no coconut, not even a hint a coconut taste in it. De thing was juicy with sweet rose water oozing out a it. De rose water perfume enter mih nose and get trap in mih cranium. Ah drink two cup a masala tea and a lassi and still de rose water perfume was on mih tongue like if I had a overdosed on Butchart Gardens.

Suddenly de door a de restaurant spring open wide with a strong force and two big burly fellas stumble in, almost rolling over on to de ground. Dey get up, eyes red and slow and dey skin burning pink with booze. Dey straighten up so much to overcompensate for falling forward, dat dey find deyself leaning backward. Everybody stop talking and was watching dem. De guy in front put his hand up to his forehead and take a deep Walter Raleigh bow, bringing de hand down to his waist in a rolling circular movement. Out loud he greet everybody with "Alarm o salay koom." A part a me wanted to bust out laughing. Another part make mih jaw drop open in disbelief. De calm in de place get rumfle up. De two fellas dem, feeling chupid now because nobody reply to dey greeting, gone up to de counter to Chum-chum trying to make a little conversation with him. De same booze-pink alarm-o-salay-koom-fella say to Chum-chum, "Hey, howaryah?"

Chum-Chum give a lil nod and de fella carry right on, "Are you Sikh?"

Chum-chum brothers converge near de counter, busying dey-selves in de vicinity. Chum-chum look at his brothers kind a quizzical, and he touch his cheek and feel his forehead with de back a his palm. He say, "No, I think I am fine, thank you. But I am sorry if I look sick, Sir."

De burly fella confuse now, so he try again.

"Where are you from?"

Chum-chum say, "Fiji, Sir."

"Oh! Fiji, eh! Lotsa palm trees and beautiful women, eh! Is it true that you guys can have more than one wife?"

De exchange make mih blood rise up in a boiling froth. De restaurant suddenly get a gruff quietness 'bout it except for a woman I hear whispering angrily to another woman at de table behind us, "I hate this! I just hate it! I can't stand to see our men humiliated by them, right in front of us. He should refuse to serve them, he should throw them out. Who on earth do they think they are? The awful fools!" And de friend whisper back, "If he throws them out all of us will suffer in the long run."

I could discern de hair on de back a de neck a Chum-chum brothers standing up, annoyed, and at de same time de brothers look like dey was shrinking in stature. Chum-chum get serious, and he politely say, "What can I get for you?"

Pinko get de message and he point to a few items in de case and say, "One of each, to go please."

Holding de white take-out box in one hand he extend de other to Chum-chum and say, "How do you say 'Excuse me, I'm sorry' in Fiji?"

Chum-chum shake his head and say, "It's okay. Have a good day."

Pinko insist, "No, tell me please. I think I just behaved badly, and I want to apologize. How do you say 'I'm sorry' in Fiji?"

Chum-chum say, "Your apology is accepted. Everything is okay." And he discreetly turn away to serve a person who had just entered de restaurant. De fellas take de hint dat was broad like daylight, and back out de restaurant like two little mouse.

Everybody was feeling sorry for Chum-chum and Brothers. One a dem come up to de table across from us to take a order from a woman with a giraffe-long neck who say, "Brother, we mustn't accept how these people think they can treat us. You men really put up with too many insults and abuse over here. I really felt for you."

Another woman gone up to de counter to converse with Chum-chum in she language. She reach out and touch his hand, sympathy-like. Chum-chum hold the one hand in his two and make a verbose speech to her as she nod she head in agreement generously. To italicize her support, she buy a take-out box a two burfi, or rather, dat's what I think dey was.

De door a de restaurant open again, and a bevy of Indian-looking women saunter in, dress up to weaken a person's decorum. De Miss Universe pageant traipse across de room to a table. Chum-chum and Brothers start smoothing dey hair back, and pushing de front a dey shirts neatly into dey pants. One brother take out a pack a Dentyne from his shirt pocket and pop one in his mouth. One take out a comb from his back pocket and smooth down his hair. All a dem den converge on dat single table to take orders. Dey begin to behave like young pups in mating season. Only, de women dem wasn't impress by all this tra-la-la at all and ignore dem except to make dey order, straight to de point. Well, it look like Brothers' egos were having a rough day and dey start roving 'bout de room, dey egos and de crotch a dey pants leading far in front dem. One brother gone over to Giraffebai to see if she want anything more. He call she "dear" and put his hand on she back. Giraffebai straighten she back in surprise and reply in a not-too-friendly way. When he gone to write up de bill she see me looking at she and she say to me, "Whoever does he think he is! Calling me dear and touching me like that! Why do these men always think that they have permission to touch whatever and wherever they want! And you can't make a fuss about it in public, because it is exactly what those people out there want to hear about so that they can say how sexist and uncivilized our culture is."

I shake mih head in understanding and say, "Yeah. I know. Yuh right!"

De atmosphere in de room take a hairpin turn, and it was man aggressing on woman, woman warding off a herd a man who just had dey pride publicly cut up a couple a times in just a few minutes.

One brother walk over to Janet and me and he stand up facing me with his hands clasp in front a his crotch, like if he protecting it. Stiff stiff, looking at me, he say, "Will that be all?"

Mih crew cut start to tingle, so I put on mih femmest smile and say, "Yes, that's it, thank you. Just the bill please." De smartass turn to face Janet and he remove his hands from in front a his crotch and slip his thumbs inside his pants like a cowboy 'bout to do a square dance. He smile, looking down at her attentive fuh so, and he say, "Can I do anything for you?"

I didn't give Janet time fuh his intent to even register before I bulldoze in mih most un-femmest manner, "She have everything she need, man, thank you. The bill please." Yuh think he hear me? It was like I was talking to thin air. He remain smiling at Janet, but she, looking at me, not at him, say, "You heard her. The bill please."

Before he could even leave de table proper, I start mih tirade. "But A A! Yuh see dat? Yuh could believe dat! De effing so-and-so! One minute yuh feel sorry fuh dem and next minute dey harassing de heck out a you. Janet, he crazy to mess with my woman, yes!" Janet get vex with me and say I overreacting, and is not fuh me to be vex, but fuh she to be vex. Is she he insult, and she could take good enough care a sheself.

I tell she I don't know why she don't cut off all dat long hair, and stop wearing lipstick and eyeliner. Well, who tell me to say dat! She get real vex and say dat nobody will tell she how to dress and how not to dress, not me and not any man. Well I could see de potential dat dis fight had coming, and when Janet get fighting vex, watch out! It hard to get a word in edgewise, yes! And she does bring up incidents from years back dat have no bearing on de current situation. So I draw back quick quick but she don't waste time; she was already off to a good start. It was best to leave right dere and den.

Just when I stand up to leave, de doors dem open up and in walk Sandy and Lise, coming for dey weekly hit a Indian sweets. Well, with Sandy and Lise is a dead giveaway dat dey not dressing fuh any man, it have no place in dey life fuh man-vibes, and dat in fact dey have a blatant penchant fuh women. Soon as dey enter de room yuh could see de brothers and de couple men customers dat had come in minutes before stare dem down from head to Birkenstocks, dey eyes bulging with disgust. And de women in de room start shoo-shooing, and putting dey hand in front dey mouth to stop dey surprise, and false teeth, too, from falling out. Sandy and Lise spot us instantly and dey call out to us, shameless, loud and affectionate. Dey leap over to us, eager to hug up and kiss like if dey hadn't seen us for years, but it was really only since two nights aback when we went out to dey favourite Indian restaurant for dinner. I figure dat de display was a genuine happiness to be seen wit us in dat place. While we stand up dere chatting, Sandy insist on rubbing she hand up and down Janet back—wit friendly intent, mind you, and same time Lise have she arm round Sandy waist. Well, all cover get blown. If it was even remotely possible dat I wasn't noticeable before, now Janet and I were over-exposed. We could a easily suffer from hypothermia, specially since it suddenly get cold cold in dere. We say goodbye, not soon enough, and as we were leaving I turn to acknowlege Giraffebai, but instead a any recognition of our buddiness against de fresh brothers, I get a face dat look like it was in de presence of a very foul smell.

De good thing, doh, is dat Janet had become so incensed 'bout how we get scorned, dat she forgot I tell she to cut she hair and to ease up on de makeup, and so I get save from hearing 'bout how I too jealous, and how much I inhibit she, and how she would prefer if I would grow my hair, and wear lipstick and put on a dress sometimes. I so glad, oui! dat I didn't have to go through hearing how I too demanding a she, like de time, she say, I prevent she from seeing a ole boyfriend when he was in town for a couple hours *en route* to live in Australia with his new bride (because, she say, I was jealous dat ten years ago dey sleep together). Well, look at mih crosses, nah! Like if I really so possessive and jealous!

So tell me, what yuh think 'bout dis nah, girl? [2000]

Donald Murray

War Stories Untold

Despite such war stories I have told myself and others, I had not thought my war central to my life. It was something to survive and put behind me. During my childhood, I had seen what I called professional veterans, many who had never been under fire, parade on Memorial Day and the Fourth all dressed up in uniforms that never quite fit. I thought them silly, men and women who lived in the past. I would not be one of those barroom heroes telling the same stories over and over again, reliving moments of glory that were not glorious, no bands and banners at the front.

But as I have aged, I have heard myself tell my war stories and I have begun to realize how much the war is still with me. It is not often the topic of conversation with my psychiatrist—my childhood is—but I have come to realize that few of us who fought are ever discharged from our wars.

I unscrew the cap on the carton of ruby red grapefruit juice this morning and find a plastic ring. I put my right index finger in the ring and give a quick tug. My hand remembers a grenade, a ring pulled free with my left index finger, how this right hand held the grenade tight, the arcing toss, more like a shot put than a pitch, the explosion, a scream.

I pour my juice and notice my hand does not tremble as it so often does these days. Perhaps my hand is nineteen and still back in combat.

My time travel began when I woke, still half wound into a dream that fades into brown sepia shapes, then disappears before I can make it out. It must have been of my secret war, the one with the stories untold, because my legs move as if I again crossed a minefield. When I piss in our toilet bowl, steam rises from snow in the Battle of the Bulge; when I wash my face, my hands cup themselves to scoop up the water I have slurped from my canteen into my helmet as I learned to do during those days in the field and still do this morning, so many, so few years later.

When I came home from my war, surprised to be alive, I don't remember joy but a kind of stunned relief, perhaps disbelief. I remember being surprised that a cold glass of milk was always available. I met my father and mother, uncles and cousins as strangers. I opened my closet and found nothing but wire hangers. My mother had sold and given away all my clothes. She had not expected me to return. Well, neither had I. I don't remember anger. When I went to the bank to check on the pay I had sent home to allow Ellen and me to start housekeeping, I was not surprised that Mother, whose name had to be on the account because I was a teenage soldier, had spent it all. I was home. I had changed but home had not.

Within days I married the woman who wore my engagement ring and wrote me every day when I was overseas. Looking back I think Ellen, a literature major who lived an imaginary life in post-World War I Britain, was well prepared to be a fiancée who had lost her lover in battle but not prepared to be the wife of this stranger who did not match the imaginary soldier to whom she had written so many letters.

I started classes at the university where I would later teach, astonished at the innocence of those who had not been to war. I saw them at a distance as if looking through a pair of binoculars turned backwards. They were my age—and so very young. I was determined to race through classes—something my young wife could not understand—and escape the college that was necessary if I was to vault into the middle class, get back the jobs the 4-Fs had stolen while we fought. I would, by golly, live in a single-family house.

Now, half a century and more later, I am still trying to be discharged from my war. I carry my peeled banana, my pills, my juice to the year-round porch we have built on the single-family house I own mortgage free, and study the flat, pale light just before morning when we would attack or were attacked by the enemy that rose out of the early morning shadows.

I escape from memory by flicking on the TV. There I see tanks and soldiers in the old familiar crouch my body remembers, moving against an enemy they cannot yet see. I do not know if I am watching the morning news or a documentary of an earlier war. No matter. Each year that I am further from my war, I remember more.

I have only one war buddy I see regularly; Jim Mortensen, a sergeant for whom I served as jeep driver occasionally in Berlin. But each year I am away from combat, the war grows closer. If I choose a seat in a restaurant, my back will be to the wall and I'll have a view of the door. Sitting on a friend's porch having a drink, I let part of my mind scan the lawn running down to the lake as if a field of fire. I know where I would set up my machine gun, know where the enemy would attack. Walking city streets, I note the doorways and alleys that could hide a German soldier, the windows behind which a sniper might be waiting. I look at the church steeple and scan the openings from which a rifle might suddenly appear. I find my feet making sure to be quiet, and on a walk in the woods with everyone laughing happily I am aware of land mines. Sometimes I realize my body is on patrol, alert to possible ambush.

I begin to understand how much the war marked me, how I have made it one of my most important identities, how I will never resolve the contradictions of pride and shame I will always feel. And now, more than half a century since my war, I am beginning to understand my own content in the surrealism of war and its arctic loneliness.

One day, years ago, I wrote in my daybook, "I had an ordinary war," and I did. But that phrase seemed to turn a key in my memory and unlock what I thought I had put away. In training it became ordinary to crawl toward machine gun fire. The closer the better, because the barrel rises with its firing. It became ordinary, after one of our colonels accidentally ordered his regiment to attack another American regiment, to drive a jeep over the bodies of men I knew, killed by Americans, to get to the colonel's headquarters. He was removed from that command, and sent to England where, we heard, he was promoted to general but kept far from the command of men in battle.

The stories we tell, like the war movies—*A Midnight Clear* or *Saving Private Ryan*—imply a buddy war, young comrades marching toward death together, but my infantry war was one of aloneness. Looking back, I realized my strange, lonely childhood prepared me for the surreal confusion of battle.

In combat, infantrymen keep yards from each other so that one artillery shell, one strafing plane, one grenade, one mortar shell will take only one soldier. In the swirl of combat, I was almost always serving with strangers. We came and went on special assignment.

I was a military policeman and often a messenger and was not surprised that I liked the lonely mission, assigned to deliver or retrieve a message, allowed to find my own way down roads without names, streets that were on no map, towns that had been reduced to rubble, fields and woods made strange by attack and counterattack.

The shame we may feel at our killing—at our being able to kill—is all retrospective. There's no time for philosophy when other human beings are trying to kill you. I don't know if I killed another person. My killing moments were all confusion. Was it my weapon, my hand grenade or someone else's that made a German tumble from a church steeple, scream from behind the wall over which I had tossed a grenade, stagger and stumble into sleep? I will never know, but I know I am brother to all who kill. I cannot stand apart from this shame.

I must also confess the fantasies that come suddenly and are played in the mind of an apparently kind elderly gent with a beard and a belly that precede him into the room. Yet in my mind, I am the one who captures the gunman who bursts into the restaurant and starts to fire. I know how I would chase the robbers as they made their escape from the bank.

Sometimes they have been more than fantasies. When Minnie Mae was carrying our first daughter, we saw a man cash a large check at a grocery store in Massachusetts then leave the groceries. The clerk and I knew what was going on. While he called for help I went after the check casher, tackling him on the roadside and literally sitting on him, feeling increasingly foolish, until the police came.

There is a dark side to my pride and my Walter Mitty fantasies. One summer day, years ago, we were driving back from Ogunquit Beach, my wife beside me, my three daughters in the back of the station wagon, when a New York driver in a Caddy tried once, twice, three times to force me off the road. Suddenly I blocked him off, got out, and pulled him out from behind the wheel and bent him backwards over the hood of his car. I held him with my left arm and body, was ready to chop my right forearm across his neck. I saw the terror in his eyes. In our intimate embrace, he knew and I knew I could kill him. I can still see his eyes, feel his breath. I let him go, and walking back to my car, I realized that a police officer had witnessed all this and done nothing, apparently thinking I was justified.

As we drove away, my hands shaking on the wheel, Minnie Mae looked at me with pride and my daughters cheered, "Daddy, the hero." But I was scared, Daddy the killer. I knew how easy it would have been. My arm knew how simple it would be, how quick.

War is an ultimate and terrible human experience that brings out the best and the worst in us. We reach the limits of exhilaration and terror, exhaustion and fear, live moments of intense feeling and blank numbness. We don't talk about that and we don't talk about the erections we sometimes get in battle. Survivor guilt is real. I do not forget the 6,286 men who were killed or wounded in my division, the 17th Airborne.

It was rarely skill, usually just dumb shit luck that kept us alive. A soldier whose name I do not remember and I went out to take a shit behind a barn high above a snow field in Belgium. We dropped our pants, squatting a couple of feet apart, and were chatting about the beauty of the scene when my companion disappeared. It is true that you do not hear the shell that kills or almost kills you. The German 88 had a shaped charge. It was focused. The soldier disappeared and I was covered with small fragments of bone, blood, skin, dirt, flesh, cloth, shit. No wounds, no Purple Heart, just sudden constipation and the familiar realization that I was lucky, no more, no less.

So much of this seemed normal then. You do what has to be done. Report his death. Go back on duty. No mourning, no memory, at least for decades. I come to realize there is a goodness, a strength in this that I have not appreciated until now, when I live my war and the life that followed in reflection.

Through most of my life, if I thought of my war, I saw my ability to kill as a matter of shame, and yet, I heard in my voice pride. I identified myself as a paratrooper, even during a poetry reading at West Point, enjoyed the respect of faculty and students who treated me as one of them.

Winter makes my body return to duty. We fought the Battle of the Bulge in a wonderland of snow. The Ardennes forest was neater than New Hampshire, but otherwise I fought in the geography of home, the familiar grown strange by war, the beauty of my childhood ominous in combat. On winter nights when I go to the john as old men do, I look out on my woods that stretch down to the riverfront. On the most beautiful nights when moonlight moves the trees apart and the light glistens from snow, I see, in the shadows, Germans advancing toward the house. And the old fear of moonlight when we would be revealed rises in me. I see the scene with double vision, the beautiful woods scene and the war landscape superimposed on it, both real, both immediate.

And then I find myself, in this twice-lived life, admitting what I have known but never before named: I feel a battle-tested strength in me, a feeling of confidence. I know I can do what I did not think I could do. I am a survivor. No guilt now, just pride.

Just going from parked car to supermarket, my feet are on patrol. I know on which foot the weight of my body rests, where it will be a second ahead. I am, even in the staggery years, aware of how I will attempt to move if anyone moves against me. I am alert, ready—perhaps even looking for trouble, for another testing.

Quite simply we learned we could do what had to be done. Trained by forced marches in some heat, by G.I. sergeants who tried to break us, by handling live ammunition, by running obstacle courses, and eventually by doing what had to be done under enemy fire, we explored our endurance and our limits, surprising ourselves that we could measure up.

But we kept quiet about it, even to ourselves. We saw better men than us break. We did not want to tempt the gods by bragging. But when my daughter was dying at twenty years old, which was far worse than anything I experienced in the war, I could call on my combat training and make myself nap on the waiting room floor. As it became clearer that we would have to remove extraordinary means, I had no doubt that I could. I had been tested by combat; I had withdrawn life support from my father and then my mother. I could give the gift of death to my daughter, and I did, drawing on the dark, cold strength I had developed during my years of combat. [2001]

Aimee Nezhukumatathil

The Witching Hour

The Philippine witching hour begins at sundown. While the night is still soft and the rosal blooms fold damp after saying their good-nights, the *aswang* morphs from her day persona as a beautiful young woman with long, silky black hair to a creature of fantastic evil. She discards her lower torso, hiding it in her bedsheets or a dark corner of her house, beside a bookcase, under a rattan table. Anointing her armpits with a musky oil, the aswang smoothes it into the thin skin under her shoulders. Now she can fly at will. Her oil-stiffened hair propels her into the night sky, a terrible helicopter in search of her favorite food: fetus. Claws spring from her fingertips like a Swiss army knife to aid her tongue in its victual catch. If someone happens upon her abandoned lower half and sprinkles any of the following—ashes, salt, vinegar, lemon juice, garlic, or pepper—into the cross-section of the body, reattachment is impossible and the aswang dies fragmented.

For Sunburst Elementary's Endangered Species Week, my teacher, Mrs. Johnson, gave the third graders a list of possible animals to draw in the *"Save the Animals"* poster competition. The blue whale, California condor, American bald eagle, snow leopard, and African rhinoceros—all possible seeds for our blank poster boards. At the very bottom of the list was the phrase, *or any other important animal.* I drew the aswang.

Mrs. Johnson had one of those short, unisex perms of the eighties, very "Conway Twitty." Her large pillow arms swooped over us as she handed out giant posterboard pieces to everyone in the class. As we scribbled furiously on our drawings, she wove in and out of our desks, reminding us of the prizes: first place was a large, one-topping from Pizza Hut, second was to be Line Leader for a whole week, and for third prize, our choice of *one* of her "special" markers—the giant brush pens that she saved for bright and colorful bulletin boards and *Happy Birthday* signs. My knees bobbed up and down as I drew—I couldn't wait for her to walk by my desk. She usually always stopped and remarked on the detail of a face or building that I drew, and sometimes she held my drawing up for the class to see. When Mrs. Johnson came closer, I always looked at my shoes—pink Velcro *'Roos* with a zip-up pocket for my lunch money right there above the arch of my foot. I couldn't tell if she was about to yell or if she just found her slip peeking out from under her dress because her face was always red. Her shadow, lavender in the fluorescent light, paused over my drawing.

"And what animal is that, Aimee?"

I responded quietly as possible, "The aswang."

"Speak up, honey, I can barely hear you."

"It's from the Philippines. It flies only at night though, so no one really sees it." The kids around my desk turned around, craning their necks to see my drawing. Some even walked over, mouths open. On my poster: the witch, tongue extended, long hair sweeping around her in the twilight sky, denoted by the half-circle yellow sun I drew sinking behind the green rectangle of countryside. I had not yet begun to draw a little baby. As I began to explain the nature of the aswang and what it eats, Mrs. Johnson narrowed her eyes to slits.

"Aimee, this is *not* an endangered species. You have to start over. And I don't want you to repeat these lies *ever* again. Do I make myself clear?" I stared at my shoes. "Do I make myself CLEAR?" I think I nodded yes, I don't remember. All I know is the two rips of poster board I heard next. Mrs. Johnson ripped fast, as if faster meant erasing the entire episode. She went back to her desk, depositing the four torn squares of my work into the army green wastebasket. The room was silent—all twenty-five third graders stopped their coloring, their cutting. My best friend, Andrea, walked up to the front of the room to the supplies closet and brought a fresh sheet of poster board to my desk for me, giving me a half-smile. I wiped the mix of snot and tears on my sleeve when the other kids finally went back to their posters. Mrs. Johnson saw me wipe my face with my sleeve, and though a box of billowing Kleenex was on her desk, went back to her grading.

I redrew my poster for Endangered Species Week. I had to miss recess to catch up with the others, but I drew an American bald eagle mother on the left, clutching at a branch that jutted out from the side of a cliff, since that's where the 1983 World Book Encyclopedia said bald eagles lived. The mama eagle I drew had a hat with a daisy on it, wearing a purse across her breast. On the edge of the cliff itself, a giant nest with two baby eagles, one stretching its neck towards the mama eagle, the other with musical notes in a balloon from its mouth. On the bottom of the poster, I carefully lettered, "Save Our Planet" in round bubble letters, each colored like Earth—complete with continents and water within each letter.

I won first place in the whole grade, and third in the school competition. But I still felt invisible. Deep down I didn't *really* believe in the aswang, but in our class's story hour, everyone freely talked about Paul Bunyan and Babe the Blue Ox, or Zeus and the gang, as if they lived right there in Phoenix, so why was the very *mention* of an aswang so dangerous, so naughty? In my mother's wild bedtime stories, the aswang came alive, and was more visceral to me than any giant lumberjack that liked to eat flapjacks and had a blue cow. Her voice softened when she told these stories—I'd have my head in her lap and she never acted rushed, even if she had a stack of paperwork to finish before work the next day. We always rushed—to the dentist, to my sister's violin lessons, to find me toy dinosaurs at ten o'clock at night for a diorama due the next morning in Science class—but never when she told me those stories at night. She took her time during these moments and for me that meant that even if these stories and warnings were not all true, that at the very least I should pay attention. No matter if she was on-call the night before or had to get up early for a meeting at the hospital, or had yelled at me for my messy room—at night, she freely laughed and we giggled together. I loved playing with her long and lovely thick hair as she propped herself up on her elbow next to me in bed. Often, her bedtime "stories" consisted of simply trying to describe a favorite fruit from the islands like the *jackfruit*, or recalling a special bread like *pan de sal*. I always went to bed full of her delicious memories, folktales, and legends. If anyone were to check on me later in the night, they surely would have seen a little girl sleeping with a smile on her face. Maybe clutching her stuffed bunny a bit tighter than usual, but with a smile nonetheless.

I didn't want the pizza for my first place award, much to sister's chagrin. Mrs. Johnson shook my hand at the awards ceremony and even hugged me on stage, as if nothing had happened, grinning for the Principal as if *she* had drawn the winning poster. But when we returned to homeroom, I asked that my prize be her famous colored marker set, the expensive ones—barely even used—and coveted by all the students during art class. She looked at the box, still so glossy and new, paused, and to my surprise—she relented. I skipped recess voluntarily the next day and spent the whole period drawing the aswang over and over again—aswang flying, aswang sleeping, even aswang reading a book under a tree. I smiled as I gathered up my new shiny markers and carefully tucked them each into their special case. When recess was over and the students started filing back in, my classmates shuffled by my desk and marveled over the drawings within earshot of Mrs. Johnson. She came over to see what I was drawing, sighed, and hurried the rest of the class inside to get ready for Science. [2009]

Lewis Nordan

Owls

Once when I was a small boy of ten or eleven I was traveling late at night with my father on a narrow country road. I had been counting the number of beers he drank that night, nine or ten of them, and I was anxious about his driving.

Neither of us had spoken for a long time. What was there to say?—the beers, the narrow road, the stubble fields, a bare bulb shining out in the darkness from a porch far back from the road, the yellow headlights? What was there to talk about? The car held the road on the curves, the heater was making its familiar sound.

Then I saw a road sign, bright yellow and diamond-shaped, and on it I read the word SLOW. My father kept on driving at the same speed and did not slow down, though I knew he had seen the sign. So I was bold. I said, "Did you see that sign?"

Immediately my father let up on the gas and the car began to slow down. He said, "You're right. We should go back."

He pulled his car onto the berm and stopped and looked back over his left shoulder for safety and then pulled out onto the road again and made a U-turn.

I was frightened. I said, "Why are we going back?"

My father shifted the gears and we began driving back in the direction we had come.

"The sign," he said. "I'm going back to see the sign."

I said, "Why? Why are we doing that?"

He said, "Isn't that what you meant? Didn't you want to go back?"

I said, "I wanted you to slow down. I was afraid."

We drove on in the darkness for a minute. My father said, "The sign didn't say SLOW."

I said, "It didn't? I thought it said SLOW."

My father said, "It said OWLS."

So we kept driving and I didn't argue. I listened to the quiet sound of the heater fan. I saw the red eyes of a rabbit on the roadside. I saw the stubble fields. For one second I believed I had lived a very long hard life and that I was all alone in the world.

Then the sign came into view again, the back of the sign, of course. My father slowed the car and pulled over to the right and when he had come to a complete stop he checked over his shoulder for safety and made another U-turn so that we might face the sign again and read its message. The headlights made the sign huge and bright.

My father had been right. The sign said OWLS.

We kept sitting there for a long time. The engine was running, there was a small vibration.

Then my father turned off the engine. The early-spring night air was cold, but he rolled down the windows.

I knew my father wanted me to be quiet. I'm not sure how I knew this. I knew he wanted us to listen. I scarcely breathed I was listening so hard. I did not move at all.

Then I heard the owls overhead. I heard the soft centrifugal buffeting of their feathers on the night air. I heard a sound from their owl-throats so soft that I believed it was their breathing. In my mind I counted them and thought that they were many. The owls were circling and circling and circling in the air above us.

I don't know what I believed would happen. I think I believed I would feel the fingers of my father's hand touch my arm, the sleeve of my shirt. I believed I would turn to him and for the first time in my life I would know what to say. I would tell him all my secrets. I believed my father would say, "I love you." This was what it meant to sit in a car with your father in the middle of the night and listen to a flock of owls while looking at a diamond-shaped sign that said OWLS.

Then he rolled up his window, and so I rolled up mine. In the darkness he said, "You know, your mother is a terrible housekeeper."

We only sat there looking at the OWLS sign. I knew things would not go well after this.

And so then he started up the car and we drove away, back along the dark road, and we did not say anything else to each other that night, and he drank a few more beers.

All I mean to say is this: Many years later I fell in love with a woman, and she was beautiful and strange. One afternoon, after we had made our love, we lay in a band of sunlight that fell across our bed and I told her the story of my father and the dark road and the sign that said OWLS.

I said, "You don't believe me, do you?"

The woman said, "Have you ever told this story to anyone before?"

I said, "I told my mother. That same night, after my father and I got home and my mother came upstairs to tuck me in."

The woman said, "Tell me again about your room, then, with the fake stars on the ceiling."

I told her what she already knew. I said, "It was an attic room, with a slanted ceiling. A desk, and even my clothes drawers were built into the wall to save space. There was a crawl-space in the back of my closet, where I sat sometimes, in the rafters. On the ceiling above my bed were pasted luminous decals of stars and the planets and the moon. Saturn had rings. A comet had a funny tail."

She said, "Tell me again about the real moon."

I said, "The moon outside my window."

She said, "How large was it?"

I said what I had told her many times. I said, "It was a peach-basket-size moon."

She said, "And you were lying in your bed, with the fake stars shining down on you and the peach-basket moon outside your window, and then…"

I said, "I heard my mother coming up the stairs to tuck me in."

She said, "Your mother had been worried about you, out in the car with your father when he had been drinking."

I said, "Yes, she had been worried. She would never say this."

She said, "What did she say?"

I said, "She said, 'Did you have a nice time with Daddy tonight?'"

She said, "What did you say?"

I said, "I told her the story about seeing the sign. About stopping and listening to the owls in the air."

She said, "What did your mother say then?"

I said, "She said, 'That's about like your daddy.'"

She said, "Your mother didn't believe you?"

I said, "She was right. There was no OWLS sign. It's ridiculous. There is no way to hear owls in the air. And, anyway, think about the coincidence of a drunk man and his oversensitive kid stopping at just the moment the owls happen to be flying above a sign."

She said, "Hm."

I said, "And you know that thing my father said. That thing about 'Your mother is a terrible housekeeper'?"

She said, "Mm-hm."

I said, "That's a part of an old joke we used to hear in the South when I was a boy. The punchline is, 'My wife is a terrible housekeeper, every time I go to piss in the sink it's full of dirty dishes.'" I said, "I think I made the whole thing up."

She said, "Where did the owls come from?"

I said, "I'm not sure. Do you remember in Winnie-the-Pooh, the character named Owl?"

She said, "Yes."

I said, "Remember, somewhere, in one of those books, we learn that Owl's name is misspelled on a sign as WOL. Maybe that's where I got the idea. I just happened to think of that book. Jeeziz. It's possible I made this whole thing up."

She said, "Are rabbits' eyes really red?"

I said, "I don't know. I saw a blind dog in my headlights one time, and its eyes looked red. Christ."

The way the sunlight fell across the bed was… Well, I was so much in love.

She said, "Was your father magic?"

I said, "I wanted him to be."

She said, "He might have been."

Now she looked at me, and it was the night of the owls all over again. The car's heater, the vibration of the engine, the red eyes of the rabbit, the stubble fields, the music of the odd birds in flight, the OWLS sign before me. And also the feeling that there was someone beside me to whom I could tell my most terrible secret and that the secret would be heard and received as a gift. I believed my clumsy drunken inexpert father, or my invention of him, had prepared me for this magic. The woman beside me said, "I love you."

In that moment every good thing that I had expected, longed to feel with my father, I felt with her. And I also felt it with my father, and I heard his voice speak those words of love, though he was already a long time dead. He was with me in a way he could not be in life.

For one second the woman and I seemed to become twins, or closer than twins, the same person together. Maybe we said nothing. Maybe we only lay in the band of sunlight that fell across our bed. Or maybe together we said, "There is great pain in all love, but we don't care, it's worth it." [1992]

Howard Norman

from *I Hate to Leave This Beautiful Place*

In late spring of 1981, I went to yet another Eskimo village, Pangnirtung, in the Northwest Territories, to record folktales. Suffice it to say that I was pleased to have the employment, given the fact that I still had no career to speak of and was financially at loose ends. My Pangnirtung notebook was titled "Horizon/Fear," because the stories I worked with there were about threatening entities—horrendous spirits, malevolent weather, terrifyingly strange beasts—appearing on the horizon. Simply put, the repertoire of spirit beings seen on the horizon in those folktales was truly prodigious and disturbing.

What was especially breathtaking in these stories were the currents of anxiety, the intensification of panic, and the acceleration of events that were caused by the first sighting of such harrowing spirits.

In one folktale, when a ten-legged polar bear is seen on the horizon, a number of marriages suddenly take place. In another tale, when it is determined that a giant ice worm is navigating toward a village, a number of murders are committed, all in a single night. In yet another, when the horizon roils up dark clouds that speak in ventriloquial echoes—that is, the clouds seem to be speaking from places other than the ones they are occupying—a number of pregnancies are cut short and children are born months before they otherwise naturally would have been. Healthy children born into a world in extremis. In another folktale, a spirit being with arms that look like awls is reported to be traveling toward a village. In hearing this news, most everyone living there falls victim to a kind of radical arrhythmia—not only do people's heartbeats suddenly accelerate and then just as suddenly become alarmingly slow, but hearts literally "toss people about the village" as if a wind were blowing from inside their bodies.

Eventually I translated eight of these "Horizon/Fear" stories, but as it turned out, I left Pangnirtung before my assigned linguistic work was completed—for two reasons.

First—and such an experience is difficult to describe—the stories got to me. Their plots began to take hold of me beyond all my powers of resistance, to the point where I began consciously to avoid looking at the actual horizon—just while walking between houses, for instance. It takes a great deal of willfulness, or fear, to *not* look at the horizon in an Arctic landscape, especially in a place like Pangnirtung, with its harbor containing flotillas of newly formed ice in all their sculpted shapes and sizes, out where dark birds disappear, where the light shifts its tones hourly, where whale geyser-spumes hang in wavering columns of mist for up to ten minutes after the whales pass by, like signatures composed on the air. One probably should not be in a place like Pangnirtung if one does not wish to take in the horizon, is the conclusion I came to. The horizon, where the rest of the beautiful world resides. Avoid that, and you start to go too far into yourself.

The second and far more compelling reason I fled Pangnirtung was that, during what turned out to be my final week there, I experienced a number of exceedingly unpleasant, often physically violent run-ins with an *angakok*—a shaman. The world of Arctic shamans has enough ethnographic complexities to fill volumes; still, it has to be experienced to be believed. This particular fellow did not have a name, at least I never heard him called by one. He was perhaps fifty or fifty-five, stocky, with a face deeply lined both latitudinally and longitudinally, especially in certain precincts of his forehead. He had a gouged, almost grotesquely cauliflowered left ear and dark reddish-brown skin with splotches of lighter brown, each of which seemed to have been outlined in ash. His right eye was filmed over. To put it directly, he cut an alarming figure.

He had a habit—or a scare tactic—of uttering a phrase first in Inuit, then in broken French, then in English, all more or less sotto voce, as if speaking to two other people who resided inside himself. He wore boots with no laces, frayed thick trousers, two shirts under two sweaters, all beneath a parka. He had lots of snowy-owl feathers haphazardly festooning his hair (as if transforming himself from an owl into a human being, or vice versa), which was filthy and matted. He also wore a kind of necklace that consisted of half a dozen small transistor radios tied together with twine. (I remember thinking back to Edward Shaimaiyuk's vigilance concerning the possibility of radio waves netting his plane. I even—and I realize now this thought contained no small measure of myth-based paranoia—wondered whether this *angakok* was one of Sedna's lackeys.)

This *angakok* hated me from the get-go; it was impossible not to comprehend this. How did I know? Because when we first encountered each other in front of the village's convenience store, he said, "I hate you." I may well have been a surrogate for every Caucasian who ever set foot in Pangnirtung throughout history, and could fully understand that anger. Still, this was our first exchange.

From the moment he had arrived in Pangnirtung ("from somewhere out on the horizon," as one of my hosts put it), he took my presence as a portent of severe weather—and possibly of starvation—in the offing. He immediately began to speak of me in this light. He loudly declared his indictments in front of the convenience store, somewhat in the manner of a crazy person on a city street declaring the end of the world. He smoked cigarette after cigarette (he chewed and spit out the butts) and rattled his transistor radios. I was told by more than one citizen of Pangnirtung not to take his actions personally, but how could I not? Such in-your-face assaults cannot be made less frightening by placing them in the context of historical rage—at least I was not capable of that. It was all expert psychodrama and left me shaken to the core.

"This fellow hates anyone who isn't Inuit," an elderly woman told me. "And he hates most Inuit people, too." Hardly a comfort, but at least it clarified things a bit.

Some people advised me to try to ignore him; others suggested that I leave on the next mail plane out. Both made sense. My host family was kind and generous, and provided me a comfortable room to sleep in, but I definitely understood my outsider status—this wasn't new to me. Generally speaking, after this *angakok* arrived, the village went about its daily business, except that this raving maniac was there. On a number of occasions I saw him standing near the counter of the convenience store, windmilling his arms, shouting incomprehensible things (though maybe not incomprehensible to the spirit world) in a language that only in part consisted of Inuit, or even French or English, words.

On other occasions I would see him standing off to one side of the store, smoking a cigarette or a pipe, scrutinizing me. And one time he shouted, "You have to eat food. I eat weather." This strange locution imposed the same kind of arrhythmia on me that I had heard about in one of the "Horizon/Fear" folktales, or at least that's what it felt like. I had to get out of there fast.

I wanted to fulfill the terms of my employment, though, and had to deal with this fellow in some way, so one day I walked up to him and said, "Leave me alone. I'm not here much longer anyway." His response was to turn on every one of the transistor radios, which seemed in good working order, but because we were in Pangnirtung, far out of all but shortwave radio range, all he could produce was static. Therefore his necklace became an orchestra of hisses and scratches. Then he stubbed his cigarette out against the shoulder of my coat.

"There is another world, but it is in this one," wrote Paul Éluard. With this *angakok*, I definitely was in another world. I could hardly claim any deep knowledge of Pangnirtung, but I did know that throughout the Arctic people believed that shamans were capable of causing illnesses, and in turn were paid to demonstrate their ability to cure those illnesses—a perverse strategy that had apparently worked for centuries. I could see that the *angakok* harassing me was indeed respected, or at least feared, for proven reasons; he scared the hell out of me. One other thing I knew was that *angakoks* often had a direct line of communication to the spirit world. In other Arctic communities I had witnessed elderly people paying shamans to petition certain presiding spirits for luck and good health, and to deliver family news to ancestors in the land of the dead.

I tried another scheme. I approached my nemesis, who was smoking his pipe near the convenience store, and offered to pay him to fly to the moon and stay there until my work was done. I was told by three different people that this particular *angakok* was quite capable of flying to the moon.

He jammed his thumbs up into my nostrils and pushed me so hard that I stumbled backwards. This was shockingly painful. I took this to mean that my request had been denied. He said, "You walk backwards well. Why not walk backwards home now." I told him that my home was thousands of miles away. He said, "Start now before the bad weather." Later I was told by a bystander that I had misinterpreted what the *angakok* had muttered. What he actually said was, "Start now before I bring in bad weather."

In Pangnirtung I worked with storytellers in the morning and spent the afternoons transcribing tapes, getting help with vocabulary, filling notebooks, and walking around town and its outskirts. I especially enjoyed visiting the cemetery, where simple white crosses were bowed daily by wind off the sea. Every time I visited late in the afternoon, I saw an elderly woman dressed in winter bundling who would walk from cross to cross, setting them upright again, tapping them down with a hammer.

Though I never asked, I assumed this was her daily task, perhaps self-appointed. What is more, she was the only Inuit person I had seen being accosted by the *angakok*. I observed him walk up to her in the cemetery, mumble something, and push her down. She rose to her feet and spit at him. This struck me as a scenario borne through the ages—it could have happened a hundred years ago, or two hundred, or a hundred years from that afternoon, a timeless confrontation with no discernible reason behind it, though I did not know what personal history there was between the old woman and the *angakok,* nor whether it had anything to do with her association with the Christian cemetery. No matter. This *angakok* was a nasty piece of work. He had arrived at Pangnirtung a menace and built on that daily. I saw this unfold.

In the few Inuit villages I had worked in before Pangnirtung, recording, transcribing, and translating oral literature had given me insight into the mental culture and mythic history of a community, although that is putting things in too academic a light. But in Pangnirtung it didn't work out that way. Every moment in that village seemed off-kilter somehow; I could not get any real purchase on life there. In Pangnirtung, the stories themselves seemed natural forces to be dealt with. They had put my nerves on edge.

Fairly early in the translation process I began to feel that despite an increasing fluency in the language, I was ill equipped to perform my work with any semblance of poise or competency. Still, I was being paid a decent salary and all of this was a unique experience. I wanted to see it through.

But night after night in my dreams I reprised the Inuit narratives. It got to the point where I imposed insomnia on myself, preferring not to sleep in order to avoid that endless loop of stories. This was my situation; I had to look at it directly. Finally a person has to sleep—but I wasn't sleeping, not really. Brief naps here and there, no more than fifteen minutes at a time, for six, seven, eight days running. It was not so much my drinking too much black coffee as it was that the characters in my dreams—the characters in the Inuit folktales—were constantly drinking black coffee.

Strange but true. Sometimes they ate coffee grounds.

Stenciled in outsize black lettering on the side of the convenience store, in both Inuit phonetics and English, were the words *Blessed Be the Cheerful Buyer.* Accompanying the words was the painted figure of Jesus handing some Canadian dollar bills to a merchant. On closer inspection, this Jesus had an uncanny resemblance to the rock-and-roll legend Jim Morrison (perhaps the sign painter was a fan). The store carried all manner of goods and necessities: winter clothing, canned foods, rifles, ammunition, pharmaceutical products. At the back of the store, on a chair next to the coal-burning stove, I often sat and worked on the stories.

One late afternoon, Michael Pootgoik, who was about forty and who managed the store, showed me some snow globes he had just unpacked from a shipment delivered by mail plane, along a route that originated in Winnipeg and serviced many Arctic villages, including Churchill. The pilot's name was François Denny; he had gone into the store to take a nap on a cot in the supply room. "He snores like a walrus," Michael said. "I have to put the radio on."

There were two dozen glass snow globes in the shipment. Each contained a diorama of an indoor or outdoor scene in miniature. As he dusted each globe with a moistened cloth and inspected it for hairline cracks, Michael also turned it upside down and then right side up so that the fabricated snowflakes inside fell like confetti on the interior tableau. There was a Christmastime village, perhaps somewhere in New England, with a Christmas tree in the town square decorated with angels; children sang carols on the porch of a house. There was a hunter wearing a checked flannel shirt, black trousers, snow boots, and a thick fur hat, aiming his rifle at a buck with its head turned upward to the falling snow. There was a line of three hula dancers wearing grass skirts and no blouses, their breasts hidden by extravagant leis (seeing these Hawaiians in the snow made us both laugh). There was Little Red Riding Hood pursued by the Big Bad Wolf. There was—my favorite—a string quartet sitting in individual chairs on a bandstand in the middle of a tree-lined park. There was a blacksmith shaping a piece of iron in his shop, which was shown in cutaway relief, complete with bellows and hammers and tongs. There were ice-fishing shacks on a pond. There was a cluster of stars and planets on the ground, as if fallen from the heavens in their original array. There was a rural schoolhouse with children on its playground. And there were others I cannot recall.

"Most every family in Pangnirtung has one of these," Michael said.

The next day, I decided to purchase a snow globe as my going-away gift in reverse, for Mary, the five-year-old daughter of my host family. The moment I stepped into the convenience store out of the cold slanting rain that was forming black ice on stretches of road, I saw the *angakok* curled up in the fetal position on the floor near a shelf that contained power tools. I hoped that he was asleep.

Michael was working the counter as usual. I told him I wanted to buy a snow globe for Mary and asked to see the inventory. "I already sold four," he said, "but I'll set out the rest." He lined up the globes on the counter. I took my time looking them over. "Which do you think Mary might like best?" I asked.

"Why not bring her in and have her pick one out?" Michael said.

"Except that would ruin the surprise."

"A surprise is over quick and then you still have to hope you made the right choice, eh?"

"Okay. Good idea."

I left the convenience store purposely avoiding the *angakok*. I found Mary, and as she and I walked into the store she pointed at the shaman and said, "That man stinks. I'm not afraid of him. He can hurt me and he stinks but I don't care."

Mary, a chubby little kid with the sweetest face and the brightest, most stalwart disposition on earth, should have been my teacher in all things having to do with that miserable *angakok*. At the counter, she was delighted to be able to pick out a snow globe. "I think you're giving me a present because I put a lot of sugar in tea when I make it for you," she said. She sat on the counter, dangling her legs, and picked up snow globe after snow globe, studying each one with the utmost seriousness. Finally she said, "I want this one." She held up the snow globe with the hula dancers inside.

I paid for the gift and handed it to Mary, who then walked out of the store. The *angakok* shouted something at her and she burst into tears and fled. She dropped the snow globe just outside the store and kept on running. I picked it up and put it in my coat pocket.

Back in the store now, I glared at the *angakok* and he glared right back. "Okay, got to deliver some boxes to the clinic," Michael said. "Be back in a short time." He lifted two boxes and a somewhat larger one, balanced them in his arms, and left by the back door. If I had been in my right mind, I would have followed him. But I just stood there next to the remaining snow globes.

Then I heard the transistor radios. This creeped me out no end.

I turned and saw that the *angakok*, whom I could smell from across the store, was sitting up and leaning against the wall. He was holding a screwdriver with the sharp end right up against an electric wall socket, as if he were about to jam the screwdriver into it. He was madly grinning, many teeth gone, and bobbing his head back and forth as if he alone could detect a lively tune inside the cacophony of radio static. Perhaps most arresting of all, he was holding a teddy bear. The store carried a variety of stuffed animals: owls, bears, tigers, walruses, seals, ravens.

The *angakok* stood, dropped the screwdriver on the floor, walked over to a shelf, and took up a sewing kit. He retreated to his corner, where he removed his mangy overcoat and began to sew the teddy bear to it by its four legs. Then he turned up the volume of each of the transistor radios. When finally he slid to the floor, a number of radio batteries fell from his coat pockets.

I do not know to this day what reckless impulse compelled me to deepen the antagonism between us, except that I wanted something to happen, something to end it once and for all. I walked to the shelf that held the stuffed animals, found an identical teddy bear, looked at the price tag, and said, "Don't forget to pay the nine dollars for that bear." I pointed to the stuffed bear he had sewn to his overcoat.

"You know how I'll pay for this bear?" he said, as if choking on the English words, as if he had rocks in his throat.

"No."

"I will tell Pootgoik I'm not going to put him inside one of those," he said, pointing to the snow globes. "He will give me as many bears as I want."

I did not know how to respond. He said, "But you choose—*you* choose which one you want to live inside. Right now—choose!"

"Keep the fuck away from me!" I said with all the force I could muster.

I walked along the side of the store opposite him and out the front door. Mary was standing not more than twenty yards away; she had been watching the store. I handed her the snow globe with the hula dancers inside. I attempted a little joke: "I wouldn't mind being in there with those hula dancers." Which of course hardly registered at all with Mary, and she did not laugh or even crack a smile; she ran off toward her house.

Then I saw Michael returning empty-handed from the clinic. He walked up to me and said, "Did he steal anything while I was gone? I know he did. What did he take?"

Humiliated, dispirited, hapless, infantilized—you name it—my catalogue of despondency seemed endless in my interactions with this *angakok*. Maybe this is how it should be, I thought, this is what I deserve, representing as I must centuries of colonial intervention, or something like that, though I was in Pangnirtung only as a kind of stenographer for elderly people who told folktales that I fully understood to be indispensable and sacred to Inuit culture and history.

But this *angakok* couldn't care less what I knew or didn't know, or if I did or did not harbor good intentions. He wanted me to walk backwards two thousand miles south. So far he had followed me from grave marker to grave marker in the cemetery, muttered at me, spat at me, jammed his thumbs up my nostrils, and threatened to imprison me in a snow globe. I had to admire his inventive tenacity even while wanting him to disappear. Even knowing he might kill me. Part of his résumé as an *angakok* was that he had killed people.

He had won. Whatever battle we were having, he had won it. I could already feel myself leaving Pangnirtung. Such a beautiful place, really, but it had become impossible for me. Let's face it, I thought, I have become unhinged. In the convenience store Michael said, "This *angakok* won't leave until you leave."

So I arranged for a flight out. The morning before I left, however, I recorded a story, which when typed out amounted to only a couple of pages. A woman named Jenny Arnateeyk—she was the elderly caretaker of the cemetery—told it, and I gave it the title "The Visitor Put in a Snow Globe," which pretty much sums up the plot.

The Visitor Put in a Snow Globe

A visitor arrived and an angakok arrived at about the same time and things got bad right away. The next day the angakok put the visitor inside a snow globe. He got right to it. He didn't hesitate. Then the angakok dropped the snow globe through the ice.

The snow globe floated up again and could be seen just under the ice if you rubbed the snow away with the side of your hand. A lot of people did this, mostly children.

Some days passed by. The angakok said, "Have you noticed how much better the weather has been since I dropped that snow globe through the ice? Have you noticed how many fish have been caught? How much better everyone is eating these days?"

When children looked at the snow globe, they saw that the visitor was keeping busy. He had a little house in there. He had a fireplace that never ran out of wood, so he kept warm. It didn't seem so bad except he was under the ice. That had to be strange for the visitor. Children visited him every day—that must have been good for him.

One day the angakok said, "I'm going a long way to visit some ravens. Then I'm going even farther to visit some other ravens. When I'm gone, don't take pity on the fellow inside the snow globe. If you let him out, the weather will be terrible and all the fish will swim great distances away."

But when the angakok left to visit the ravens, the people in the village took pity, and they got the snow globe out from under the ice. Then the visitor was his normal size again, and he said, "Thank you. I was only visiting."

"How was it inside a snow globe?" someone asked.

"Unusual."

"Well, then—you'd better leave."

The visitor left on a mail plane. The villagers waited for the weather to turn and for all the fish to leave. But the weather stayed all right, and there were plenty of fish to eat. The villagers hoped the angakok kept visiting ravens for many years to come.

All this happened quite recently. [2014]

B.J. Novak

Julie & the Warlord

"Okay," she laughed after three complicated cocktails. "Now you, sir...."

"Yes."

"You, sir.... Now...I am.... Okay. I feel like we've only talked about me. But I don't know anything about you. Other than that you're very, um, charming and, well, very cute, of course. Ha, don't let that go to your head! Shouldn't have said that."

"Thank you."

"But I feel—okay, if this is my—well. Okay. What do you do?"

"What do I do? You mean what is my job?"

"Sorry, I hate that question too. It's like, is this a date or an interview, right?" He finished his bite of sauce-soaked broccolini and answered, but she didn't hear him clearly. "Hmmmmmmmmmm? All I heard was 'lord.'"

"Yes."

"Ooh! Okay, this is fun. Are you a…landlord? Because I do not have the best history getting along with landlords. My first apartment——"

"I'm not a landlord."

"Are you…a…drug lord?" Julie said, stroke-poking the side of his face with her finger. "'Cause that could be a problem."

"No."

"You're not…the Lord, are you? Because I haven't gone to temple since my bat mitzvah. Ha, don't tell my grandma!"

He laughed politely. She could tell he was laughing just to be nice—and she liked that more than if he had laughed from finding her funny. A nice guy: Now that would be a real change of pace for her.

"Then what kind of lord are you anyways, eh?" she asked with an old-timey what's-the-big-idea accent. God, she was a bit tipsy, wasn't she?

"I'm a warlord."

"In-ter-est-ing! Now, I don't know exactly what this is. But I want to learn. So what exactly…is…a warlord?" Julie asked, her chin now resting playfully on a V of two upturned palms. "Educate meeeee."

"Okay. Can you picture where the Congo is on a map?"

"Kinda," she exaggerated.

"This is Africa," he said, pointing to an imaginary map in the air between them. "This is the Indian Ocean. This is the Democratic Republic of the Congo. This is just regular Congo."

"What? Hold up——"

"I know—that's just how it is. I didn't name them," the warlord laughed. "Anyway. This? All this here? This is what I control."

"So you're, like…the governor of it?"

"No. There are areas of the world where it will show up on your map as a certain country. But in reality, no government is in control of that region, in any real way. They cannot collect taxes. They cannot enforce laws. Do you follow?"

Yes, nodded Julie.

"The people who are in charge are the warlords. They—we—bribe, kidnap, indoctrinate, torture and…what am I forgetting? What's the fifth one? Oh, kill—ha, that's weird that I forgot that one—the population of any region that falls above a certain threshold of natural resources but below a certain threshold of government protection. It's not exactly that simple, Julie, but basically that determines where I'm based. Once those conditions reach that level, me and my team, we show up and terrorize that area until everyone in the entire population is either dead, subdued or, ideally, one of our soldiers. *Ideally* ideally, dream scenario? A child soldier."

"That does not sound legal," said Julie, trying to stall for time so she could object properly and intelligently, which was going to take a second because she had had a few drinks already and had not anticipated having to debate a hot-button topic like this at the top of her intelligence—especially not with someone who did it for a living.

"No, it isn't legal at all—have you been listening?" Julie blushed and rotated her fork on her napkin in a four-point turn so she would have something to focus on besides her embarrassment. "This is a show of force outside the ability of any government to enforce its laws."

He went on and on. The words *rape* and *limbs* came up more than on any other date she could remember.

"What about, like, the international community?" asked Julie, hoping this was a smart question. Usually this was something she was good at on dates, but tonight she was having more trouble. "Don't they ever pressure you to stop? Or," she added, thinking there might be something else there, "or something?"

"Yes," said the warlord. "Sure! For example, there was this thing about me on Twitter a while ago—are you on Twitter?" She said she was but didn't check it often. "Same here!" he laughed. "I have an account, but I can never figure out if it's a thing I do or not. Anyway. I was 'trending.' You know what that is?" She did. "I'll be honest, it weirded me out. I got into this pattern where I was checking my name every two seconds, and there were like 45 new mentions of me. All negative!"

"You can't let yourself fall into that," said Julie.

"Exactly. Anyway, it passed," said the warlord. "You know Twitter—before long everyone's onto the next thing."

"What about," asked Julie, downing the last sip of her cocktail as she felt a premature ripple of seriousness returning, "the ethics of it? How do you feel about that? Doesn't that trouble you?"

The warlord gestured to Julie with his fork. "That top you're wearing. Anthropologie?"

"H&M," said Julie, "but thank you."

"Even better," said the warlord. "Do you know the conditions in the factories that made that top that you're wearing? Do you ever think about that?"

"Yeah, okay, no. That's not—nice try. Just because.... No. And yes, I know, this phone, right here, that I use every day—but no. No! You can't.... It doesn't help anything to equate.... Look," said Julie. "There's no excuse. But that also does not mean——"

"Just in case you're thinking about dessert," whispered the waitress, dropping off two stiff sheets of artisanal paper in front of Julie and the warlord.

"Remember when they used to ask first if you wanted to see a dessert menu?" asked the warlord. "Now everyone just ambushes you with a dessert menu without asking. When did that start?"

"I know!" said Julie. "Everyone started doing that at the same time too! How does stuff like that happen? Everywhere, just"—she snapped her fingers—"changing their policy at the exact same time?"

"Get Malcolm Gladwell on that," said the warlord.

"I know, right?"

They both scanned the menu, each pair of eyes starting in the unhelpful middle of the dessert list for some no-reason, then tipsily circling around and around until most of the important words had been absorbed.

"I have never understood 'flourless chocolate cake,'" stated the warlord finally. "Is flour such a bad thing? I mean, compared to the other things in chocolate cake?"

"You want to split that?" said Julie.

"Flour is probably the least unhealthy thing I can think of in chocolate cake," the warlord continued. "Is that supposed to be the point? That the whole cake is just all eggs and sugar and butter? And anyway, who cares? It's chocolate cake. We know it's not a health food. Use whatever ingredients you want. All it has to do is taste good. We don't need to know how you did it—just make it."

"You want to maybe split that?" said Julie again.

"We will split the flourless chocolate cake," declared the warlord.

"Great!" said the waitress, disappearing again.

"So, do you get to travel a lot?" asked Julie.

"Not as much as I'd like. Now and then we'll reach some cease-fire, after some especially big massacre, and things get quiet for a bit. That's what allowed me to take some time off, travel, meet you, stuff like that. Oh, I meant to say—you look even better in person than in your profile picture."

"Oh.... Thank you."

"Yeah, I've been meaning to tell you that. Nice surprise. Rare it goes in that direction."

"Ha. Well, thanks. Um, same. Don't let that go to your head."

"Thanks. So.... Lost my train of thought."

"Cease-fires?"

"Right! So, you know, cease-fires—they never stick."

"Yes, I think I saw something about that on Jon Stewart. That must be frustrating."

"It is! Thank you, Julie. That's exactly the right word," said the warlord. "It's very frustrating!"

"Flourless chocolate cake," said the waitress.

"Thank you," said Julie and the warlord at the same time.

"Can I get you anything else? Another drink?"

"I really shouldn't," said Julie. "Are you okay to drive, by the way?"

"I have a driver," said the warlord.

Julie ordered a fourth and final cocktail. [2014]

Flannery O'Connor

A Good Man Is Hard to Find

The grandmother didn't want to go to Florida. She wanted to visit some of her connections in east Tennessee and she was seizing at every chance to change Bailey's mind. Bailey was the son she lived with, her only boy. He was sitting on the edge of his chair at the table, bent over the orange sports section of the *Journal.* "Now look here, Bailey," she said, "see here, read this," and she stood with one hand on her thin hip and the other rattling the newspaper at his bald head. "Here this fellow that calls himself The Misfit is aloose from the Federal Pen and headed toward Florida and you read here what it says he did to these people. Just you read it. I wouldn't take my children in any direction with a criminal like that aloose in it. I couldn't answer to my conscience if I did."

Bailey didn't look up from his reading so she wheeled around then and faced the children's mother, a young woman in slacks, whose face was as broad and innocent as a cabbage and was tied around with a green head-kerchief that had two points on the top like rabbit's ears. She was sitting on the sofa, feeding the baby his apricots out of a jar. "The children have been to Florida before," the old lady said. "You all ought to take them somewhere else for a change so they would see different parts of the world and be broad. They never have been to east Tennessee."

The children's mother didn't seem to hear her but the eight-year-old boy, John Wesley, a stocky child with glasses, said, "If you don't want to go to Florida, why dontcha stay at home?" He and the little girl, June Star, were reading the funny papers on the floor.

"She wouldn't stay at home to be queen for a day," June Star said without raising her yellow head.

"Yes and what would you do if this fellow, The Misfit, caught you?" the grandmother asked.

"I'd smack his face," John Wesley said.

"She wouldn't stay at home for a million bucks," June Star said. "Afraid she'd miss something. She has to go everywhere we go."

"All right, Miss," the grandmother said. "Just remember that the next time you want me to curl your hair."

June Star said her hair was naturally curly.

The next morning the grandmother was the first one in the car, ready to go. She had her big black valise that looked like the head of a hippopotamus in one corner, and underneath it she was hiding a basket with Pitty Sing, the cat, in it. She didn't intend for the cat to be left alone in the house for three days because he would miss her too much and she was afraid he might brush against one of the gas burners and accidentally asphyxiate himself. Her son, Bailey, didn't like to arrive at a motel with a cat.

She sat in the middle of the back seat with John Wesley and June Star on either side of her. Bailey and the children's mother and the baby sat in front and they left Atlanta at eight forty-five with the mileage on the car at 55890. The grandmother wrote this down because she thought it would be interesting to say how many miles they had been when they got back. It took them twenty minutes to reach the outskirts of the city.

The old lady settled herself comfortably, removing her white cotton gloves and putting them up with her purse on the shelf in front of the back window. The children's mother still had on slacks and still had her head tied up in a green kerchief, but the grandmother had on a navy blue straw sailor hat with a bunch of white violets on the brim and a navy blue dress with a small white dot in the print. Her collars and cuffs were white organdy trimmed with lace and at her neckline she had pinned a purple spray of cloth violets containing a sachet. In case of an accident, anyone seeing her dead on the highway would know at once that she was a lady.

She said she thought it was going to be a good day for driving, neither too hot nor too cold, and she cautioned Bailey that the speed limit was fifty-five miles an hour and that the patrolmen hid themselves behind billboards and small clumps of trees and sped out after you before you had a chance to slow down. She pointed out interesting details of the scenery: Stone Mountain; the blue granite that in some places came up to both sides of the highway; the brilliant red clay banks slightly streaked with purple; and the various crops that made rows of green lace-work on the ground. The trees were full of silver-white sunlight and the meanest of them sparkled. The children were reading comic magazines and their mother had gone back to sleep.

"Let's go through Georgia fast so we won't have to look at it much," John Wesley said.

"If I were a little boy," said the grandmother, "I wouldn't talk about my native state that way. Tennessee has the mountains and Georgia has the hills."

"Tennessee is just a hillbilly dumping ground," John Wesley said, "and Georgia is a lousy state too."

"You said it," June Star said.

"In my time," said the grandmother, folding her thin veined fingers, "children were more respectful of their native states and their parents and everything else. People did right then.

Oh look at the cute little pickaninny!" she said and pointed to a Negro child standing in the door of a shack. "Wouldn't that make a picture, now?" she asked and they all turned and looked at the little Negro out of the back window. He waved.

"He didn't have any britches on," June Star said.

"He probably didn't have any," the grandmother explained. "Little niggers in the country don't have things like we do. If I could paint, I'd paint that picture," she said.

The children exchanged comic books.

The grandmother offered to hold the baby and the children's mother passed him over the front seat to her. She set him on her knee and bounced him and told him about the things they were passing. She rolled her eyes and screwed up her mouth and stuck her leathery thin face into his smooth bland one. Occasionally he gave her a faraway smile. They passed a large cotton field with five or six graves fenced in the middle of it, like a small island. "Look at the graveyard!" the grandmother said, pointing it out. "That was the old family burying ground. That belonged to the plantation."

"Where's the plantation?" John Wesley asked.

"Gone with the Wind," said the grandmother. "Ha. Ha."

When the children finished all the comic books they had brought, they opened the lunch and ate it. The grandmother ate a peanut butter sandwich and an olive and would not let the children throw the box and the paper napkins out the window. When there was nothing else to do they played a game by choosing a cloud and making the other two guess what shape it suggested. John Wesley took one the shape of a cow and June Star guessed a cow and John Wesley said, no, an automobile, and June Star said he didn't play fair, and they began to slap each other over the grandmother.

The grandmother said she would tell them a story if they would keep quiet. When she told a story, she rolled her eyes and waved her head and was very dramatic. She said once when she was a maiden lady she had been courted by a Mr. Edgar Atkins Teagarden from Jasper, Georgia. She said he was a very good-looking man and a gentleman and that he brought her a watermelon every Saturday afternoon with his initials cut in it, E.A.T. Well, one Saturday, she said, Mr. Teagarden brought the watermelon and there was nobody at home and he left it on the front porch and returned in his buggy to Jasper, but she never got the watermelon, she said, because a nigger boy ate it when he saw the initials, E.A.T.! This story tickled John Wesley's funny bone and he giggled and giggled but June Star didn't think it was any good. She said she wouldn't marry a man that just brought her a watermelon on Saturday. The grandmother said she would have done well to marry Mr. Teagarden because he was a gentleman and had bought Coca-Cola stock when it first came out and that he had died only a few years ago, a very wealthy man.

They stopped at The Tower for barbecued sandwiches. The Tower was a part stucco and part wood filling station and dance hall set in a clearing outside of Timothy. A fat man named Red Sammy Butts ran it and there were signs stuck here and there on the building and for miles up and down the highway saying, TRY RED SAMMY'S FAMOUS BARBECUE. NONE LIKE FAMOUS RED SAMMY'S! RED SAM! THE FAT BOY WITH THE HAPPY LAUGH. A VETERAN! RED SAMMY'S YOUR MAN!

Red Sammy was lying on the bare ground outside The Tower with his head under a truck while a gray monkey about a foot high, chained to a small chinaberry tree, chattered nearby. The monkey sprang back into the tree and got on the highest limb as soon as he saw the children jump out of the car and run toward him.

Inside, The Tower was a long dark room with a counter at one end and tables at the other and dancing space in the middle. They all sat down at a board table next to the nickelodeon and Red Sam's wife, a tall burnt-brown woman with hair and eyes lighter than her skin, came and took their order. The children's mother put a dime in the machine and played "The Tennessee Waltz," and the grandmother said that tune always made her want to dance. She asked Bailey if he would like to dance but he only glared at her. He didn't have a naturally sunny disposition like she did and trips made him nervous. The grandmother's brown eyes were very bright. She swayed her head from side to side and pretended she was dancing in her chair. June Star said play something she could tap to so the children's mother put in another dime and played a fast number and June Star stepped out onto the dance floor and did her tap routine.

"Ain't she cute?" Red Sam's wife said, leaning over the counter. "Would you like to come be my little girl?"

"No I certainly wouldn't," June Star said. "I wouldn't live in a broken-down place like this for a million bucks!" and she ran back to the table.

"Ain't she cute?" the woman repeated, stretching her mouth politely.

"Ain't you ashamed?" hissed the grandmother.

Red Sam came in and told his wife to quit lounging on the counter and hurry up with these people's order. His khaki trousers reached just to his hip bones and his stomach hung over them like a sack of meal swaying under his shirt. He came over and sat down at a table nearby and let out a combination sigh and yodel. "You can't win," he said. "You can't win," and he wiped his sweating red face off with a gray handkerchief. "These days you don't know who to trust," he said. "Ain't that the truth?"

"People are certainly not nice like they used to be," said the grandmother.

"Two fellers come in here last week," Red Sammy said, "driving a Chrysler. It was a old beat-up car but it was a good one and these boys looked all right to me. Said they worked at the mill and you know I let them fellers charge the gas they bought? Now why did I do that?"

"Because you're a good man!" the grandmother said at once.

"Yes'm, I suppose so," Red Sam said as if he were struck with this answer.

His wife brought the orders, carrying the five plates all at once without a tray, two in each hand and one balanced on her arm. "It isn't a soul in this green world of God's that you can trust," she said. "And I don't count nobody out of that, not nobody," she repeated, looking at Red Sammy.

"Did you read about that criminal, The Misfit, that's escaped?" asked the grandmother.

"I wouldn't be a bit surprised if he didn't attact this place right here," said the woman. "If he hears about it being here, I wouldn't be none surprised to see him. If he hears it's two cent in the cash register, I wouldn't be a tall surprised if he..."

"That'll do," Red Sam said. "Go bring these people their Co'-Colas," and the woman went off to get the rest of the order.

"A good man is hard to find," Red Sammy said. "Everything is getting terrible. I remember the day you could go off and leave your screen door unlatched. Not no more."

He and the grandmother discussed better times. The old lady said that in her opinion Europe was entirely to blame for the way things were now. She said the way Europe acted you would think we were made of money and Red Sam said it was no use talking about it, she was exactly right. The children ran outside into the white sunlight and looked at the monkey in the lacy chinaberry tree. He was busy catching fleas on himself and biting each one carefully between his teeth as if it were a delicacy.

They drove off again into the hot afternoon. The grandmother took cat naps and woke up every few minutes with her own snoring. Outside of Toombsboro she woke up and recalled an old plantation that she had visited in this neighborhood once when she was a young lady. She said the house had six white columns across the front and that there was an avenue of oaks leading up to it and two little wooden trellis arbors on either side in front where you sat down with your suitor after a stroll in the garden. She recalled exactly which road to turn off to get to it. She knew that Bailey would not be willing to lose any time looking at an old house, but the more she talked about it, the more she wanted to see it once again and find out if the little twin arbors were still standing. "There was a secret panel in this house," she said craftily, not telling the truth but wishing that she were, "and the story went that all the family silver was hidden in it when Sherman came through but it was never found..."

"Hey!" John Wesley said. "Let's go see it! We'll find it! We'll poke all the woodwork and find it! Who lives there? Where do you turn off at? Hey Pop, can't we turn off there?"

"We never have seen a house with a secret panel!" June Star shrieked. "Let's go to the house with the secret panel! Hey, Pop, can't we go see the house with the secret panel!"

"It's not far from here, I know," the grandmother said. "It wouldn't take over twenty minutes."

Bailey was looking straight ahead. His jaw was as rigid as a horseshoe. "No," he said.

The children began to yell and scream that they wanted to see the house with the secret panel. John Wesley kicked the back of the front seat and June Star hung over her mother's shoulder and whined desperately into her ear that they never had any fun even on their vacation, that they could never do what THEY wanted to do. The baby began to scream and John Wesley kicked the back of the seat so hard that his father could feel the blows in his kidney.

"All right!" he shouted and drew the car to a stop at the side of the road. "Will you all shut up? Will you all just shut up for one second? If you don't shut up, we won't go anywhere."

"It would be very educational for them," the grandmother murmured.

"All right," Bailey said, "but get this: this is the only time we're going to stop for anything like this. This is the one and only time."

"The dirt road that you have to turn down is about a mile back," the grandmother directed. "I marked it when we passed."

"A dirt road," Bailey groaned.

After they had turned around and were headed toward the dirt road, the grandmother recalled other points about the house, the beautiful glass over the front doorway and the candle-lamp in the hall. John Wesley said that the secret panel was probably in the fireplace.

"You can't go inside this house," Bailey said. "You don't know who lives there."

"While you all talk to the people in front, I'll run around behind and get in a window," John Wesley suggested.

"We'll all stay in the car," his mother said.

They turned onto the dirt road and the car raced roughly along in a swirl of pink dust. The grandmother recalled the times when there were no paved roads and thirty miles was a day's journey. The dirt road was hilly and there were sudden washes in it and sharp curves on dangerous embankments. All at once they would be on a hill, looking down over the blue tops of trees for miles around, then the next minute, they would be in a red depression with the dust-coated trees looking down on them.

"This place had better turn up in a minute," Bailey said, "or I'm going to turn around."

The road looked as if no one had travelled on it in months.

"It's not much farther," the grandmother said and just as she said it, a horrible thought came to her. The thought was so embarrassing that she turned red in the face and her eyes dilated and her feet jumped up, upsetting her valise in the corner. The instant the valise moved, the newspaper top she had over the basket under it rose with a snarl and Pitty Sing, the cat, sprang onto Bailey's shoulder.

The children were thrown to the floor and their mother, clutching the baby, was thrown out the door onto the ground; the old lady was thrown into the front seat. The car turned over once and landed right-side-up in a gulch off the side of the road. Bailey remained in the driver's seat with the cat—gray-striped with a broad white face and an orange nose—clinging to his neck like a caterpillar.

As soon as the children saw they could move their arms and legs, they scrambled out of the car, shouting, "We've had an ACCIDENT!" The grandmother was curled up under the dashboard, hoping she was injured so that Bailey's wrath would not come down on her all at once. The horrible thought she had had before the accident was that the house she had remembered so vividly was not in Georgia but in Tennessee.

Bailey removed the cat from his neck with both hands and flung it out the window against the side of a pine tree. Then he got out of the car and started looking for the children's mother. She was sitting against the side of the red gutted ditch, holding the screaming baby, but she only had a cut down her face and a broken shoulder. "We've had an ACCIDENT!" the children screamed in a frenzy of delight.

"But nobody's killed," June Star said with disappointment as the grandmother limped out of the car, her hat still pinned to her head but the broken front brim standing up at a jaunty angle and the violet spray hanging off the side. They all sat down in the ditch, except the children, to recover from the shock. They were all shaking.

"Maybe a car will come along," said the children's mother hoarsely.

"I believe I have injured an organ," said the grandmother, pressing her side, but no one answered her. Bailey's teeth were clattering. He had on a yellow sport shirt with bright blue parrots designed in it and his face was as yellow as the shirt. The grandmother decided that she would not mention that the house was in Tennessee.

The road was about ten feet above and they could see only the tops of the trees on the other side of it. Behind the ditch they were sitting in there were more woods, tall and dark and deep. In a few minutes they saw a car some distance away on top of a hill, coming slowly as if the occupants were watching them. The grandmother stood up and waved both arms dramatically to attract their attention. The car continued to come on slowly, disappeared around a bend and appeared again, moving even slower, on top of the hill they had gone over. It was a big black battered hearse-like automobile. There were three men in it.

It came to a stop just over them and for some minutes, the driver looked down with a steady expressionless gaze to where they were sitting, and didn't speak. Then he turned his head and muttered something to the other two and they got out. One was a fat boy in black trousers and a red sweat shirt with a silver stallion embossed on the front of it. He moved around on the right side of them and stood staring, his mouth partly open in a kind of loose grin. The other had on khaki pants and a blue striped coat and a gray hat pulled down very low, hiding most of his face. He came around slowly on the left side. Neither spoke.

The driver got out of the car and stood by the side of it, looking down at them. He was an older man than the other two. His hair was just beginning to gray and he wore silver-rimmed spectacles that gave him a scholarly look. He had a long creased face and didn't have on any shirt or undershirt. He had on blue jeans that were too tight for him and was holding a black hat and a gun. The two boys also had guns.

"We've had an ACCIDENT!" the children screamed.

The grandmother had the peculiar feeling that the bespectacled man was someone she knew. His face was as familiar to her as if she had known him all her life but she could not recall who he was. He moved away from the car and began to come down the embankment, placing his feet carefully so that he wouldn't slip. He had on tan and white shoes and no socks, and his ankles were red and thin. "Good afternoon," he said. "I see you all had you a little spill."

"We turned over twice!" said the grandmother.

"Oncet," he corrected. "We seen it happen. Try their car and see will it run, Hiram," he said quietly to the boy with the gray hat.

"What you got that gun for?" John Wesley asked. "Whatcha gonna do with that gun?"

"Lady," the man said to the children's mother, "would you mind calling them children to sit down by you? Children make me nervous. I want all you all to sit down right together there where you're at."

"What are you telling US what to do for?" June Star asked.

Behind them the line of woods gaped like a dark open mouth. "Come here," said their mother.

"Look here now," Bailey began suddenly, "we're in a predicament! We're in..."

The grandmother shrieked. She scrambled to her feet and stood staring. "You're The Misfit!" she said. "I recognized you at once!"

"Yes'm," the man said, smiling slightly as if he were pleased in spite of himself to be known, "but it would have been better for all of you, lady, if you hadn't of reckernized me."

Bailey turned his head sharply and said something to his mother that shocked even the children. The old lady began to cry and The Misfit reddened.

"Lady," he said, "don't you get upset. Sometimes a man says things he don't mean. I don't reckon he meant to talk to you thataway."

"You wouldn't shoot a lady, would you?" the grandmother said and removed a clean handkerchief from her cuff and began to slap at her eyes with it.

The Misfit pointed the toe of his shoe into the ground and made a little hole and then covered it up again. "I would hate to have to," he said.

"Listen," the grandmother almost screamed, "I know you're a good man. You don't look a bit like you have common blood. I know you must come from nice people!"

"Yes mam," he said, "finest people in the world." When he smiled he showed a row of strong white teeth. "God never made a finer woman than my mother and my daddy's heart was pure gold," he said. The boy with the red sweat shirt had come around behind them and was standing with his gun at his hip. The Misfit squatted down on the ground. "Watch them children, Bobby Lee," he said. "You know they make me nervous." He looked at the six of them huddled together in front of him and he seemed to be embarrassed as if he couldn't think of anything to say. "Ain't a cloud in the sky," he remarked, looking up at it. "Don't see no sun but don't see no cloud neither."

"Yes, it's a beautiful day," said the grandmother. "Listen," she said, "you shouldn't call yourself The Misfit because I know you're a good man at heart. I can just look at you and tell."

"Hush!" Bailey yelled. "Hush! Everybody shut up and let me handle this!" He was squatting in the position of a runner about to sprint forward but he didn't move.

"I pre-chate that, lady," The Misfit said and drew a little circle in the ground with the butt of his gun.

"It'll take a half a hour to fix this here car," Hiram called, looking over the raised hood of it.

"Well, first you and Bobby Lee get him and that little boy to step over yonder with you," The Misfit said, pointing to Bailey and John Wesley. "The boys want to ast you something," he said to Bailey. "Would you mind stepping back in them woods there with them?"

"Listen," Bailey began, "we're in a terrible predicament! Nobody realizes what this is," and his voice cracked. His eyes were as blue and intense as the parrots in his shirt and he remained perfectly still.

The grandmother reached up to adjust her hat brim as if she were going to the woods with him but it came off in her hand. She stood staring at it and after a second she let it fall on the ground. Hiram pulled Bailey up by the arm as if he were assisting an old man. John Wesley caught hold of his father's hand and Bobby Lee followed. They went off toward the woods and just as they reached the dark edge, Bailey turned and supporting himself against a gray naked pine trunk, he shouted, "I'll be back in a minute, Mamma, wait on me!"

"Come back this instant!" his mother shrilled but they all disappeared into the woods.

"Bailey Boy!" the grandmother called in a tragic voice but she found she was looking at The Misfit squatting on the ground in front of her. "I just know you're a good man," she said desperately. "You're not a bit common!"

"Nome, I ain't a good man," The Misfit said after a second as if he had considered her statement carefully, "but I ain't the worst in the world neither. My daddy said I was a different breed of dog from my brothers and sisters. 'You know,' Daddy said, 'it's some that can live their whole life out without asking about it and it's others has to know why it is, and this boy is one of the latters. He's going to be into everything!'" He put on his black hat and looked up suddenly and then away deep into the woods as if he were embarrassed again. "I'm sorry I don't have on a shirt before you ladies," he said, hunching his shoulders slightly. "We buried our clothes that we had on when we escaped and we're just making do until we can get better. We borrowed these from some folks we met," he explained.

"That's perfectly all right," the grandmother said. "Maybe Bailey has an extra shirt in his suitcase."

"I'll look and see terrectly," The Misfit said.

"Where are they taking him?" the children's mother screamed.

"Daddy was a card himself," The Misfit said. "You couldn't put anything over on him. He never got in trouble with the Authorities though. Just had the knack of handling them."

"You could be honest too if you'd only try," said the grandmother. "Think how wonderful it would be to settle down and live a comfortable life and not have to think about somebody chasing you all the time."

The Misfit kept scratching in the ground with the butt of his gun as if he were thinking about it. "Yes'm, somebody is always after you," he murmured.

The grandmother noticed how thin his shoulder blades were just behind his hat because she was standing up looking down on him. "Do you ever pray?" she asked.

He shook his head. All she saw was the black hat wiggle between his shoulder blades. "Nome," he said.

There was a pistol shot from the woods, followed closely by another. Then silence. The old lady's head jerked around. She could hear the wind move through the tree tops like a long satisfied insuck of breath. "Bailey Boy!" she called.

"I was a gospel singer for a while," The Misfit said. "I been most everything. Been in the arm service, both land and sea, at home and abroad, been twict married, been an undertaker, been with the railroads, plowed Mother Earth, been in a tornado, seen a man burnt alive oncet," and he looked up at the children's mother and the little girl who were sitting close together, their faces white and their eyes glassy; "I even seen a woman flogged," he said.

"Pray, pray," the grandmother began, "pray, pray..."

"I never was a bad boy that I remember of," The Misfit said in an almost dreamy voice, "but somewheres along the line I done something wrong and got sent to the penitentiary. I was buried alive," and he looked up and held her attention to him by a steady stare.

"That's when you should have started to pray," she said. "What did you do to get sent to the penitentiary that first time?"

"Turn to the right, it was a wall," The Misfit said, looking up again at the cloudless sky. "Turn to the left, it was a wall. Look up it was a ceiling, look down it was a floor. I forget what I done, lady. I set there and set there, trying to remember what it was I done and I ain't recalled it to this day. Oncet in a while, I would think it was coming to me, but it never come."

"Maybe they put you in by mistake," the old lady said vaguely.

"Nome," he said. "It wasn't no mistake. They had the papers on me."

"You must have stolen something," she said.

The Misfit sneered slightly. "Nobody had nothing I wanted," he said. "It was a head-doctor at the penitentiary said what I had done was kill my daddy but I known that for a lie. My daddy died in nineteen ought nineteen of the epidemic flu and I never had a thing to do with it. He was buried in the Mount Hopewell Baptist churchyard and you can go there and see for yourself."

"If you would pray," the old lady said, "Jesus would help you."

"That's right," The Misfit said.

"Well then, why don't you pray?" she asked trembling with delight suddenly.

"I don't want no hep," he said. "I'm doing all right by myself."

Bobby Lee and Hiram came ambling back from the woods. Bobby Lee was dragging a yellow shirt with bright blue parrots in it.

"Thow me that shirt, Bobby Lee," The Misfit said. The shirt came flying at him and landed on his shoulder and he put it on. The grandmother couldn't name what the shirt reminded her of. "No, lady," The Misfit said while he was buttoning it up, "I found out the crime don't matter. You can do one thing or you can do another, kill a man or take a tire off his car, because sooner or later you're going to forget what it was you done and just be punished for it."

The children's mother had begun to make heaving noises as if she couldn't get her breath. "Lady," he asked, "would you and that little girl like to step off yonder with Bobby Lee and Hiram and join your husband?"

"Yes, thank you," the mother said faintly. Her left arm dangled helplessly and she was holding the baby, who had gone to sleep, in the other. "Hep that lady up, Hiram," The Misfit said as she struggled to climb out of the ditch, "and Bobby Lee, you hold onto that little girl's hand."

"I don't want to hold hands with him," June Star said. "He reminds me of a pig."

The fat boy blushed and laughed and caught her by the arm and pulled her into the woods after Hiram and her mother.

Alone with The Misfit, the grandmother found that she had lost her voice. There was not a cloud in the sky nor any sun. There was nothing around her but woods. She wanted to tell him that he must pray. She opened and closed her mouth several times before anything came out. Finally she found herself saying, "Jesus. Jesus," meaning, Jesus will help you, but the way she was saying it, it sounded as if she might be cursing.

"Yes'm," The Misfit said as if he agreed. "Jesus thown everything off balance. It was the same case with Him as with me except He hadn't committed any crime and they could prove I had committed one because they had the papers on me. Of course," he said, "they never shown me my papers. That's why I sign myself now. I said long ago, you get you a signature and sign everything you do and keep a copy of it. Then you'll know what you done and you can hold up the crime to the punishment and see do they match and in the end you'll have something to prove you ain't been treated right. I call myself The Misfit," he said, "because I can't make what all I done wrong fit what all I gone through in punishment."

There was a piercing scream from the woods, followed closely by a pistol report. "Does it seem right to you, lady, that one is punished a heap and another ain't punished at all?"

"Jesus!" the old lady cried. "You've got good blood! I know you wouldn't shoot a lady! I know you come from nice people! Pray! Jesus, you ought not to shoot a lady. I'll give you all the money I've got!"

"Lady," The Misfit said, looking beyond her far into the woods, "there never was a body that give the undertaker a tip."

There were two more pistol reports and the grandmother raised her head like a parched old turkey hen crying for water and called, "Bailey Boy, Bailey Boy!" as if her heart would break.

"Jesus was the only One that ever raised the dead," The Misfit continued, "and He shouldn't have done it. He thown everything off balance. If He did what He said, then it's nothing for you to do but thow away everything and follow Him, and if He didn't, then it's nothing for you to do but enjoy the few minutes you got left the best way you can—by killing somebody or burning down his house or doing some other meanness to him. No pleasure but meanness," he said and his voice had become almost a snarl.

"Maybe He didn't raise the dead," the old lady mumbled, not knowing what she was saying and feeling so dizzy that she sank down in the ditch with her legs twisted under her.

"I wasn't there so I can't say He didn't," The Misfit said. "I wisht I had of been there," he said, hitting the ground with his fist. "It ain't right I wasn't there because if I had of been there I would of known. Listen lady," he said in a high voice, "if I had of been there I would of known and I wouldn't be like I am now." His voice seemed about to crack and the grandmother's head cleared for an instant. She saw the man's face twisted close to her own as if he were going to cry and she murmured, "Why you're one of my babies. You're one of my own children!" She reached out and touched him on the shoulder. The Misfit sprang back as if a snake had bitten him and shot her three times through the chest. Then he put his gun down on the ground and took off his glasses and began to clean them.

Hiram and Bobby Lee returned from the woods and stood over the ditch, looking down at the grandmother who half sat and half lay in a puddle of blood with her legs crossed under her like a child's and her face smiling up at the cloudless sky.

Without his glasses, The Misfit's eyes were red-rimmed and pale and defenseless-looking. "Take her off and thow her where you thown the others," he said, picking up the cat that was rubbing itself against his leg.

"She was a talker, wasn't she?" Bobby Lee said, sliding down the ditch with a yodel.

"She would of been a good woman," The Misfit said, "if it had been somebody there to shoot her every minute of her life."

"Some fun!" Bobby Lee said.

"Shut up, Bobby Lee," The Misfit said. "It's no real pleasure in life." [1953]

Michael Ondaatje

The Cinnamon Peeler

If I were a cinnamon peeler
I would ride your bed
and leave the yellow bark dust
on your pillow.

Your breasts and shoulders would reek.
You could never walk through markets
without the profession of my fingers
floating over you. The blind would
stumble certain of whom they approached
though you might bathe
under rain gutters, monsoon.

Here on the upper thigh
at this smooth pasture
neighbour to your hair
or the crease
that cuts your back. This ankle.
You will be known among strangers
as the cinnamon peeler's wife.

I could hardly glance at you
before marriage
never touch you
—your keen-nosed mother, your rough brothers.
I buried my hands
in saffron, disguised them
over smoking tar,
helped the honey gatherers...

*

When we swam once
I touched you in water
and our bodies remained free,
you could hold me and be blind of smell.
You climbed the bank and said

this is how you touch other women
the grass cutter's wife, the lime burner's daughter.
And you searched your arms
for the missing perfume

and knew

what good is it
to be the lime burner's daughter
left with no trace
as if not spoken to in the act of love
as if wounded without the pleasure of a scar.

You touched
your belly to my hands
in the dry air and said
I am the cinnamon
peeler's wife. Smell me. [1989]

Mallory Opel

Among the Blossoms

That is my grandmother
nestled among the gardenia, the rose, the lilac tree,
even the unassuming apple blossom.
Barefoot she would amble about her budding backyard –
the buzz of busy Seattle streets humming
just beyond the borders of the fence –
until she found the perfect flower.

She hated her body.
Never swam.
Still, every summer she would buy a new bathing suit,
busy with floral print,
and stand among the bushes,
among the blooms,
as if she could disappear.
In these photographs
she was careful not to expose her body
or too much of herself –
ensuring the viewer would focus on the blossom,
not the woman.

I would watch my mother gently adjust my grandmother,
taking her shoulders,
positioning them just right,
composing the branches around her tall frame.
In soft wind,

waxy leaves
and feathered petals
would caress the gentle folds of her smiling face.

To document life
meant to capture it amidst a blossoming bush,
heavy with distracting beauty. [2016]

Simon Ortiz

My Father's Song

Wanting to say things,
I miss my father tonight.
His voice, the slight catch,
the depth from his thin chest,
the tremble of emotion
in something he has just said
to his son, his song:
We planted corn one spring at Acu—
we planted several times
but this one particular time
I remember the soft damp sand
in my hand.
My father had stopped at one point
to show me an overturned furrow;
the plowshare had unearthed
the burrow nest of a mouse
in the soft moist sand.
Very gently, he scooped tiny pink animals
into the palm of his hand
and told me to touch them.
We took them to the edge
of the field and put them in the shade
of a sand moist clod.
I remember the very softness
of cool and warm sand and tiny alive mice
and my father saying things. [1985]

Nancy Pagh

Love Song: After T.S. Eliot

Let us go then, you and me,
when the gray clouds rest like scree
poised above the residential lots
and SUVs, the white sedans and minivans
arranged into their stanzas.

Don't ask me why.
Don't ask me why just yet.

And the rain comes.
The rain licks the bumpers and the wiper blades.
The rain rubs itself on oiled pavement and makes
its iridescent sigh, jaywalks on Euclid
toward the A&P, remembers salt
then curls once about the drain hole
and goes to sea.

In apartment complex windows
vague phosphorescent light from TV glows
and infomercial voices that the women disregard
murmur remedies they have no use for;
the small shy cats emerge from furniture
to find the pockets that a body will provide
for them—the shallow bowl of pelvis, soft
seam between half-opened thighs
the fault along one's side
as the arm goes slack.

In the room the men are watching scenes
pornographic on computer screens.

And what if you extend your long
worn self along a length of couch and drop
your gone-gray head into my lap,
unclose your eyes as I
unfix your necktie's simple pin,
draw a blanket, tuck you in;
what if I should dare to touch
the warm bare place you're slightly bald—
a naked pulse of who you are, a current
running corridors toward my sex

(as when my foot soles pressed
against the still-hot metal faucet in a bath)
and I am still, and abluted—
What then?

In the room you're watching **HD** scenes
pornographic on computer screens.

And what if revolution destroyed it
destroyed us all
with obscene gesture, whelming call
toward routine urge and empty pleasure,
apprenticed us to one master
whose only name is Friction.

I know it all already; I know it all.
Know you have chosen lovers
content to play a role—Lolita or a bondage queen
posed upon a straight-back chair;
your cock malingers in her hair
then slips inside the smile she wears.
You disappear.

. . . . .

The rain comes.
The rain lacks some
essential detachment yet falls
so earnest so uncool upon our bodies
upon our vehicles alike.

I should have been a pair
instead.

. . . . .

The virgins are thirty.
The virgins are thirty and forty and going
to the sperm bank.
The medical technician witnesses
immaculate conception every day,
drives a white sedan, parks carefully,
turns on his home computer.
I have seen him heat his dinner in the microwave.
He knows everybody's getting laid
but him. But how should he presume?

In lab coat Monday afternoons
he stirs, dissolves, with sugar spoons
the Sweet'N Low, the saccharine, and then
imagines online sirens giving head
while women ring the waiting room.
I do not think he'll sing to them. [2008]

Elise Partridge

Edwin Partridge

1923-2005

Barely nineteen, volunteered for the war.
On a sweaty Pacific island
monitored radar,
hearing pilots rumble off
into black;

silently noted
which friends didn't come back.
          One August dawn,
          only wind-rattled palms.
He was grateful just to sail home.

Later, with wife and sons, he'd scan the sky
for blips of green—
hummingbirds swooping to his feeder.
Each dusk, for them,
he'd daub it clean.

A grin and a nod meant "Good."
Always the right word, or none.
He read to his sons, dried dishes,
cleared neighbors' drives,
hewed their wood.

At eighty, quavering hands;
teetering on each threshold.
Tenderly he'd loop
his wife's last dahlias with string
so they could stand. [2006]

Sylvia Plath

Mirror

I am silver and exact. I have no preconceptions.
Whatever I see I swallow immediately
Just as it is, unmisted by love or dislike.
I am not cruel, only truthful—
The eye of a little god, four-cornered.
Most of the time I meditate on the opposite wall.
It is pink, with speckles. I have looked at it so long
I think it is a part of my heart. But it flickers.
Faces and darkness separate us over and over.

Now I am a lake. A woman bends over me,
Searching my reaches for what she really is.
Then she turns to those liars, the candles or the moon.
I see her back, and reflect it faithfully.
She rewards me with tears and an agitation of hands.
I am important to her. She comes and goes.
Each morning it is her face that replaces the darkness.
In me she has drowned a young girl, and in me an old woman
Rises toward her day after day, like a terrible fish. [1961]

Sina Queyras

On the Scent, #14

The tummy-flat girls will not embrace feminism. Will not consider ecology or philosophy anything more than a brand name. They are not worried about the environment, a luxury for another generation. A pre-bubble-bursting time. They are so done with all that. They are so over it. They are so *Whatever.* They are so *Yeah, yeah, yeah.* They are so *She's so uptight.* They are so *She's such a nightmare.* They are so *Bummer.* They are so bored. They have so little time for that. They are so done with earnest. They are so *PC is a university credit.* They are so *I wanna sit on his face.* They are so *I want to give head where I want when I want.* They are so *Isn't sexism sexy?* They are so *Boys are just built like that.* They are so *Being gay is passé.* They are so *How could you be so mean?* They are so *What planet are you from?* They are so done with the whiny girls. They are so done with political messages. They are so past any need to protest. They are so *What's your problem?* They are so *We're fine with the way things are.* They are so *That's just the way it is.* They are so *Get over it.* They are so *Accept it.* They are so *Anger is so uncool.* They are so *Move out of our way rigid one, and let the beautiful ones sing.*

[2006]

Simon Rich

Unprotected

I born in factory. They put me in wrapper. They seal me in box. Three of us in box.

In early days, they move us around. From factory to warehouse. From warehouse to truck. From truck to store.

One day in store, boy human sees us on shelf. He grabs us, hides us under shirt. He rushes outside.

He goes to house, runs into bedroom, locks door. He tears open box and takes me out. He puts me in wallet.

I stay in wallet long, long time.

This is story of my life inside wallet.

The first friend I meet in wallet is Student I.D. Jordi Hirschfeld. He is card. He has been around longest, he says. He introduces me to other cards. I meet Learner Permit Jordi Hirschfeld, Blockbuster Video Jordi Hirschfeld, Jamba Juice Value Card, GameStop PowerUp Card Jordi Hirschfeld, Business Card Albert Hirschfeld, D.D.S., Scarsdale Comic Book Explosion Discount Card.

In middle of wallet, there live dollars. I am less close to them, because they are always coming and going. But they are mostly nice. I meet many Ones and Fives, some Tens, a few Twenties. One time, I meet Hundred. He stay for long time. Came from birthday card, he said. Birthday card from an old person.

I also meet photograph of girl human. Very beautiful. Eyes like Blockbuster Video. Blue, blue, blue.

When I first get to wallet, I am "new guy." But time passes. I stay for so long, I become veteran. When I first arrive, Jamba Juice has just two stamps. Next thing I know, he has five stamps—then six, then seven. When he gets ten stamps, he is gone. One day, Learner Permit disappears. In his place, there is new guy, Driver License. I become worried. Things are changing very fast.

Soon after, I am taken out of wallet. It is night. I am scared. I do not know what is happening. Then I see girl human. She is one from photograph. She looks same in real life, except now she wears no shirt. She is smiling, but when she sees me she becomes angry. There is arguing. I go back inside wallet.

A few days later, picture of girl human is gone.

That summer, I meet two new friends. The first is Student I.D. New York University Jordi Hirschfeld. The second is MetroCard.

MetroCard is from New York City and he never lets you forget it. He has real "attitude." He is yellow and black, with Cirque du Soleil advertisement on back.

When MetroCard meets GameStop PowerUp Card Jordi Hirschfeld, he looks at me and says, No wonder Jordi Hirschfeld not yet use you. I become confused. Use me for what?

That night, MetroCard tells me many strange things about myself. At first, I do not believe what he says. But he insists all is true. When I start to panic, he laughs. He says, What did you think you were for? I am too embarrassed to admit truth, which is that I thought I was balloon.

It is around this time that we move. For more than two years, we had lived inside Velcro Batman. It is nice, comfy. One day, though, without warning, we are inside stiff brown leather. I am very upset—especially when I see that so many friends are gone.

No more GameStop PowerUp Card Jordi Hirschfeld. No more Blockbuster Video Jordi Hirschfeld. No more Scarsdale Comic Book Explosion Discount Card.

Only survivors are MetroCard, Driver License, Student I.D., myself, and a creepy new lady named Visa.

I am angry. What was wrong with Velcro Batman? It had many pockets and was warm. I miss my friends and I am lonely.

A few days later, I meet Film Forum Membership Jordan Hirschfeld.

At this point, I am in "panic mode." What is "Film Forum"? Who is "Jordan Hirschfeld"?

Jordan Hirschfeld is same guy as Jordi Hirschfeld, MetroCard explains. He is just trying to "change his image." I am confused. What is wrong with old image? That night, I poke my head out of wallet and look around pocket. It is dark, but I can see we have new neighbor. He says his name is Cigarettes Gauloises. He is very polite, but I get "weird vibe" from him.

It is about this time that I meet strip of notebook paper. On him is written, "rachelfeingold@nyu.edu."

Now we're getting somewhere, MetroCard says. I have never been more frightened in my life.

That Saturday, five crisp Twenties show up. I assume they will stay long time, like most Twenties. But two hours later they are gone, replaced by receipt La Cucina.

MetroCard looks at receipt La Cucina and laughs. She better put out after that, he says. I am confused and worried.

Later on, I am minding my own business, when Jordi (sorry—"Jordan") shoves his finger into me. I am terrified. What was that? I ask. MetroCard grins. He is checking to make sure you're there, he says. For later.

My friends try to calm me down. One of the dollars, a One, tells me about the time he met Vending Machine Pepsi. He was stuffed in and out, in and out, so many times he almost died. I know he is trying to make me feel better, but I am, like, please stop talking about that.

Eventually, the moment comes. It is like other time. I am taken out of wallet and tossed on bed. It is very dark. I can make out shape of girl.

She picks me up and squints at me for a while. Then she turns on lamp. I am confused. So is Jordan Hirschfeld.

"What's wrong?" he asks.

His face is like Jamba Juice Value Card. Red, red, red.

"I think," she says, "that this might actually be expired."

There is long silence. And then, all of a sudden, the humans are laughing! And then the girl is hitting Jordan with pillow! And he is hitting her back with pillow! And they are laughing, laughing, laughing.

The girl reaches into her bag.

"Don't worry," she says. "I've got one."

Part of me kind of wants to watch what happens next. But I am quickly covered in pile of clothes.

When I wake up next day, Jordan is dangling me over trash can. I look down into pit. Inside are Cigarettes Gauloises and Film Forum Schedule. They are talking "philosophy." I sigh. I do not really want to move in with them, but what can I do? I figure this is "end of the line" for me.

Suddenly, though, Jordan carries me away—to other side of room. I am placed inside shoebox under his bed.

At first, I am afraid, because it is dark, but as vision adjusts I see I am not alone. There is strip of notebook paper rachelfeingold@nyu.edu. There is receipt La Cucina, on which is now written, "First Date."

I spend long, long time in shoebox.

When I arrive, I am new guy. But as time passes I become veteran. I welcome many new friends: Birthday card Rachel. Happy Valentine's Day Rachel. And many, many Post-it notes Rachel. I love you, Jordi. Rachel. Good morning, Jordi! Rachel. Everything in here is Rachel.

I do not know how things are in wallet these days. But I am glad to be in shoebox. I feel as if I have "made it." I am happy. I am warm. I am safe. [2012]

Rainer Maria Rilke

Archaic Torso of Apollo

We cannot know his legendary head
with eyes like ripening fruit. And yet his torso
is still suffused with brilliance from inside,
like a lamp, in which his gaze, now turned to low,

gleams in all its power. Otherwise
the curved breast could not dazzle you so, nor could
a smile run through the placid hips and thighs
to that dark center where procreation flared.

Otherwise this stone would seem defaced
beneath the translucent cascade of the shoulders
and would not glisten like a wild beast's fur:

would not, from all the borders of itself,
burst like a star: for here there is no place
that does not see you. You must change your life. [1908]

David Sedaris

The Drama Bug

The man was sent to our class to inspire us, and personally speaking, I thought he did an excellent job. After introducing himself in a relaxed and genial manner, he started toward the back of the room, only to be stopped midway by what we came to know as "the invisible wall," that transparent barrier realized only by psychotics, drug fiends, and other members of the show business community.

I sat enthralled as he righted himself and investigated the imaginary wall with his open palms, running his hands over the seemingly hard surface in hopes of finding a way out. Moments later he was tugging at an invisible rope, then struggling in the face of a violent, fantastic wind.

You know you're living in a small town when you can reach the ninth grade without ever having seen a mime. As far as I was concerned, this man was a prophet, a genius, a pioneer in the field of entertainment—and here he was in Raleigh, North Carolina! It was a riot, the way he imitated the teacher, turning down the corners of his mouth and riffling through his imaginary purse in search of gum and aspirin. Was this guy funny or what!

I went home and demonstrated the invisible wall for my two-year-old brother, who pounded on the very real wall beside his playpen, shrieking and wailing in disgust. When my mother asked what I'd done to provoke him, I threw up my hands in mock innocence before lowering them to retrieve the imaginary baby that lay fussing at my feet. I patted the back of my little ghost to induce gas and was investigating its soiled diaper when I noticed my mother's face assume an expression she reserved for unspeakable horror. I had seen this look only twice before: once when she was caught in the path of a charging, rabid pig and then again when I told her I wanted a peach-colored velveteen blazer with matching slacks.

"I don't know who put you up to this," she said, "but I'll kill you myself before I watch you grow up to be a clown. If you want to paint your face and prance around on street corners, then you'll have to find some other place to live because I sure as hell won't have it in my house." She turned to leave. "*Or in my yard*," she added.

Fearful of her retribution, I did as I was told, ending my career in mime with a whimper rather than the silent bang I had hoped for.

The visiting actor returned to our classroom a few months later, removing his topcoat to reveal a black body stocking worn with a putty-colored neck brace, the result of a recent automobile accident. This afternoon's task was to introduce us to the works of William Shakespeare, and once again I was completely captivated by his charm and skill. When the words became confusing, you needed only to pay attention to the actor's face and hands to understand that this particular character was not just angry, but vengeful. I loved the undercurrent of hostility that lay beneath the surface of this deceptively beautiful language. It seemed a shame that people no longer spoke this way, and I undertook a campaign to reintroduce Elizabethan English to the citizens of North Carolina.

"Perchance, fair lady, thou dost think me unduly vexed by the sorrowful state of thine quarters," I said to my mother as I ran the vacuum cleaner over the living-room carpet she was inherently too lazy to bother with. "These foul specks, the evidence of life itself, have sullied not only thine shag-tempered mat but also thine character. Be ye mad, woman? Were it a punishable crime to neglect thine dwellings, you, my feeble-spirited mistress, would hang from the tallest tree in penitence for your shameful ways. Be there not garments to launder and iron free of turbulence? See ye not the porcelain plates and hearty mugs waiting to be washed clean of evidence? Get thee to thine work, damnable lady, and quickly, before the products of thine very loins raise their collected fists in a spirit born both of rage and indignation, forcibly coaxing the last breath from the foul chamber of thine vain and upright throat. Go now, wastrel, and get to it!"

My mother reacted as if I had whipped her with a short length of yarn. The intent was there, but the weapon was strange and inadequate. I could tell by the state of my room that she spent the next day searching my dresser for drugs. The clothes I took pride in neatly folding were crammed tight into their drawers with no regard for color or category. I smelled the evidence of cigarettes and noticed the coffee rings on my desk. My mother had been granted forgiveness on several previous occasions, but mess with mine drawers and ye have just made thyself an enemy for life. Tying a feather to the shaft of my ballpoint pen, I quilled her a letter. "The thing that ye search for so desperately," I wrote, "resideth not in mine well-ordered chamber, but in the questionable content of thine own character." I slipped the note into her purse, folded twice and sealed with wax from the candles I now used to light my room. I took to brooding, refusing to let up until I received a copy of Shakespeare's collected plays. Once they were acquired, I discovered them dense and difficult to follow. Reading the words made me feel dull and stupid, but speaking them made me feel powerful. I found it best to simply carry the book from room to room, occasionally skimming for fun words I might toss into my ever fragrant vocabulary. The dinner hour became either unbearable or excruciating, depending on my mood.

"Methinks, kind sir, most gentle lady, fellow siblings all, that this barnyard fowl be most tasty and succulent, having simmered in its own sweet juices for such a time as it might take the sun to pass, rosy and full-fingered, across the plum-colored sky for the course of a twilight hour. 'Tis crisp yet juicy, this plump bird, satisfied in the company of such finely roasted neighbors. Hear me out, fine relations, and heed my words, for methinks it adventurous, and fanciful, too, to saddle mine fork with both fowl *and* carrot at the exact same time, the twin juices blending together in a delicate harmony which doth cajole and enliven mine tongue in a spirit of unbridled merriment! What say ye, fine father, sisters, and infant brother, too, that we raise our flagons high in celebration of this hearty feast, prepared lovingly and with utmost grace by this dutiful woman we have the good fortune to address as wife, wench, or mother!"

My enthusiasm knew no limits. Soon my mother was literally begging me to wait in the car while she stepped into the bank or grocery store.

I was at the orthodontist's office, placing a pox upon the practice of dentistry, when the visiting actor returned to our classroom.

"You missed it," my friend Lois said. "The man was so indescribably powerful that I was practically crying, that's how brilliant he was." She positioned her hands as if she were supporting a tray. "I don't know what more I can say. The words, they just don't exist. I could try to explain his realness, but you'd never be able to understand it. Never," she repeated. "Never, never, never."

Lois and I had been friends for six months when our relationship suddenly assumed a competitive edge. I'd never cared who made better grades or had more spending money. We each had our strengths; the important thing was to honor each other for the thing that person did best. Lois held her Chablis better than I, and I respected her for that. Her frightening excess of self-confidence allowed her to march into school wearing a rust-colored Afro wig, and I stood behind her one hundred percent. She owned more records than I did, and because she was nine months older, also knew how to drive a car and did so as if she were rushing to put out a fire. *Fine*, I thought, *good for her.* My superior wisdom and innate generosity allowed me to be truly happy for Lois up until the day she questioned my ability to understand the visiting actor. The first few times he visited, she'd been just like the rest of them, laughing at his neck brace and rolling her eyes at the tangerine-sized lump in his tights. *I* was the one who first identified his brilliance, and now she was saying I couldn't understand him? Methinks not.

"Honestly, woman," I said to my mother on our way to the dry cleaner, "to think that this low-lying worm might speak to me of greatness as though it were a thing invisible to mine eyes is more than I can bear. Her words doth strike mine heart with the force of a punishing blow, leaving me both stunned and highly vexed, too. Hear me, though, for I shall bide my time, quietly, and with cunning, striking back at the very hour she doth least expect it. Such an affront shall not go unchallenged, of that you may rest assured, gentle lady. My vengeance will hold the sweet taste of the ripest berry, and I shall savor it slowly."

"You'll get over it," my mother said. "Give it a week or two and I'm sure everything will be back to normal. I'm going in now to get your father's shirts and I want you to wait here, *in the car.* Trust me, this whole thing will be forgotten about in no time."

This had become her answer to everything. She'd done some asking around and concluded I'd been bitten by what her sister referred to as "the drama bug." My mother was convinced that this was a phase, just like all the others. A few weeks of fanfare and I'd drop show business, just like I had the guitar and my private detective agency. I hated having my life's ambition reduced to the level of a common cold. This wasn't a bug, but a full-fledged virus. It might lay low for a year or two, but this little germ would never go away. It had nothing to do with talent or initiative. Rejection couldn't weaken it, and no amount of success would ever satisfy *it.* Once diagnosed, the prognosis was terminal.

The drama bug seemed to strike hardest with Jews, homosexuals, and portly girls, whose faces were caked with acne medication. These were individuals who, for one reason or another, desperately craved attention. I would later discover it was a bad idea to gather more than two of these people in an enclosed area for any length of time. The stage was not only a physical place but also a state of mind, and the word *audience* was defined as anyone forced to suffer your company. We young actors were a string of lightbulbs left burning twenty-four hours a day, exhausting ourselves and others with our self-proclaimed brilliance.

I had the drama bug and Lois had a car. Weighing the depth of her momentary transgression against the rich rewards of her private chariot, I found it within my bosom to forgive my wayward friend. I called her the moment I learned the visiting actor had scheduled a production of *Hamlet* set to take place in the amphitheater of the Raleigh Rose Garden. He himself would direct and play the title role, but the other parts were up for grabs. We auditioned, and because we were the youngest and least experienced, Lois and I were assigned the roles of the traveling players Hamlet uses to bait his uncle Claudius. It wasn't the part I was hoping for, but I accepted my role with quiet dignity. I had a few decent speeches and planned to work them to the best of my ability.

Our fellow cast members were in their twenties and thirties and had wet their feet in such long-running outdoor dramas as *The Lost Colony* and *Tender Is the Lamb.* These were professionals, and I hoped to benefit from their experience, sitting literally at their feet as the director paced the lip of the stage addressing his clenched fist as "poor Yorick."

I worshiped these people. Lois slept with them. By the second week of rehearsal, she had abandoned Fortinbras in favor of Laertes, who, she claimed, had a "real way with the sword." Unlike me, she was embraced by the older crowd, attending late-night keg parties with Polonius and Ophelia and driving to the lake with the director while Gertrude and Rosencrantz made out in the backseat. The killer was that Lois was nowhere near as committed as I was. Her drama bug was the equivalent of a twenty-four-hour flu, yet there she was, playing bumper pool with Hamlet himself while I practiced lines alone in my room, dreaming up little ways to steal the show.

It was decided that as traveling players, Lois and I would make our entrance tumbling onto the outdoor stage. When she complained that the grass was irritating her skin, the director examined the wee pimples on her back and decided that, from this point on, the players would enter skipping. I had rehearsed my tumble until my brain lost its mooring and could be heard rattling inside my skull, and now, on the basis of one complaint, we were skipping? He'd already cut all my speeches, leaving me with the one line "Aye, my lord." That was it, three lousy syllables. A person could wrench more emotion out of a sneeze than all my dialogue put together. While the other actors strolled the Rose Garden memorizing their vengeful soliloquies, I skipped back and forth across the parking lot repeating, "Aye, my lord," in a voice that increasingly sounded like that of a trained parrot. Lois felt silly skipping and spoke to the director, who praised her instincts and announced that, henceforth, the players would enter walking.

The less I had to do, the more my fellow actors used me as a personal slave. I would have been happy to help them run lines, but instead, they wanted me to polish their crowns or trot over to a car, searching the backseat for a misplaced dagger.

"Looking for something to do? You can help Doogan glow-tape the props," the director said. "You can chase the spiders out of the dressing room, or better yet, why don't you run down to the store and get us some drinks."

For the most part, Lois sat in the shade doing nothing. Not only did she refuse to help out, but she was always the first one to hand me a large bill when placing an order for a thirty-cent diet soda. She'd search through her purse, bypassing the singles in favor of a ten or a twenty. "I need to break this anyway," she'd say. "If they charge you extra for a cup of ice, tell them to fuck themselves." During the rehearsal breaks she huddled in the stands, gossiping with the other actors while I was off anchoring ladders for the technicians.

When it came time for our big scene, Lois recited her line as if she were reading the words from the surface of some distant billboard. She squinted and paused between syllables, punctuating each word with a question mark. "Who this? Has seen with tongue? In venom steeped?"

If the director had a problem with her performance, he kept it to himself. I, on the other hand, was instructed to remove the sweater from around my neck, walk slower, and drop the accent. It might have been easier to accept the criticism had he spread it around a little, but that seemed unlikely. She could enter the scene wearing sunglasses and eating pizza and that was "fine, Lois. Great work, babe."

By this time I was finding my own way home from rehearsal. Lois couldn't give me a ride, as she was always running off to some party or restaurant with what she referred to as "the gang from Elsinore."

"I can't go," I'd say, pretending I had been invited. "I really need to get home and concentrate on my line. You go ahead, though. I'll just call my mother. She'll pick me up."

"Are we vexed?" my mother would ask, pulling her station wagon into the parking lot.

"We are indeed," I answered. "And highly so."

"Let it go," she said. "Ten years from now I guarantee you won't remember any of these people. Time passes, you'll see." She frowned, studying her face in the rearview mirror. "Enough liquor, and people can forget anything. Don't let it get to you. If nothing else, this has taught you to skim money while buying their drinks."

I didn't appreciate her flippant attitude, but the business with the change was insightful.

"Round everything off to the nearest dollar," she said. "Hand them their change along with their drinks so they'll be less likely to count it—and never fold the bills, keep the money in a wad."

My mother had the vengeful part down. It was the craft of acting I thought she knew nothing about.

We were in dress rehearsal when the director approached Lois regarding a new production he hoped to stage that coming fall. It was to be a musical based on the lives of roving Gypsies. "And you," he said, "shall be my lusty bandit queen."

Lois couldn't sing; everyone knew that. Neither could she act or play the tambourine. "Yours is the heart of a Gypsy," he said, kneeling in the grass. "The vibrant soul of a nomad."

When I expressed an interest, he suggested I might enjoy working behind the scenes. He meant for me to hang lights or lug scenery, to become one of those guys with the lowriding pants, their tool belts burdened with heavy wrenches and thick rolls of gaffer tape. Anyone thinking I might be trusted with electrical wiring had to be a complete idiot, and that's what this man was. I looked at him clearly then, noticing the way his tights made a mockery of his slack calves and dumpy little basket. Vibrant soul of a nomad, indeed. If he were such a big stinking deal, what was he doing in Raleigh? His blow-dried hair, the cheap Cuban-heeled shoes, and rainbow-striped suspenders—it was all a sham. Why wear tights with suspenders when their only redeeming feature was that they stayed up on their own—that's how they got their name, tights. And acting? The man performed as if the audience were deaf. He shouted his lines, grinning like a jack-o'-lantern and flailing his arms as if his sleeves were on fire. His was a form of acting that never fails to embarrass me. Watching him was like opening the door to a singing telegram: you know it's supposed to be entertaining, but you can't get beyond the sad fact that this person actually thinks he's bringing some joy into your life. Somewhere he had a mother who sifted through a shoe box of mimeographed playbills, pouring herself another drink and wondering when her son would come to his senses and swallow some drain cleaner.

I finally saw Hamlet for who he really was and recognized myself as the witless Yorick who had blindly followed along behind him.

My mother attended the opening-night performance. Following my leaden "Aye, my lord," I lay upon the grassy stage as Lois poured a false vial of poison into my ear. As I lay dying, I opened my eyes just a crack, catching sight of my mother stretched out on her hard, stone pew, fighting off the moths that, along with a few dozen seniors, had been attracted by the light.

There was a cast party afterward, but I didn't go. I changed my clothes in the dressing room, where the actors stood congratulating one another, repeating the words "brilliant" and "intense" as if they were describing the footlights. Horatio asked me to run to the store for Cigarettes, and I pocketed his money, promising to return "with lightning speed, my lord."

"You were the best in the whole show," my mother said, stopping for frozen pizza on our way home. "I mean it, you walked onto that stage and all eyes went right to you."

It occurred to me then that my mother was a better actor than I could ever hope to be. Acting is different than posing or pretending. When done with precision, it bears a striking resemblance to lying. Stripped of the costumes and grand gestures, it presents itself as an unquestionable truth. I didn't envy my mother's skill, neither did I contradict her. That's how convincing she was. It seemed best, sitting beside her with a frozen pizza thawing on my lap, to simply sit back and learn. [1998]

Richard Selzer

The Knife

One holds the knife as one holds the bow of a cello or a tulip—by the stem. Not palmed nor gripped nor grasped, but lightly, with the tips of the fingers. The knife is not for pressing. It is for drawing across the field of skin. Like a slender fish, it waits, at the ready, then, go! It darts, followed by a fine wake of red. The flesh parts, falling away to yellow globules of fat. Even now, after so many times, I still marvel at its power—cold, gleaming, silent. More, I am still struck with a kind of dread that it is I in whose hand the blade travels, that my hand is its vehicle, that yet again this terrible steel-bellied thing and I have conspired for a most unnatural purpose, the laying open of the body of a human being.

A stillness settles in my heart and is carried to my hand. It is the quietude of resolve layered over fear. And it is this resolve that lowers us, my knife and me, deeper and deeper into the person beneath. It is an entry into the body that is nothing like a caress; still, it is among the gentlest of acts. Then stroke and stroke again, and we are joined by other instruments, hemostats and forceps, until the wound blooms with strange flowers whose looped handles fall to the sides in steely array.

There is sound, the tight click of clamps fixing teeth into severed blood vessels, the snuffle and gargle of the suction machine clearing the field of blood for the next stroke, the litany of monosyllables with which one prays his way down and in: *clamp, sponge, suture, tie, cut.* And there is color. The green of the cloth, the white of the sponges, the red and yellow of the body. Beneath the fat lies the fascia, the tough fibrous sheet encasing the muscles. It must be sliced and the red beef of the muscles separated. Now there are retractors to hold apart the wound. Hands move together, part, weave. We are fully engaged, like children absorbed in a game or the craftsmen of some place like Damascus.

Deeper still. The peritoneum, pink and gleaming and membranous, bulges into the wound. It is grasped with forceps, and opened. For the first time we can see into the cavity of the abdomen. Such a primitive place. One expects to find drawings of buffalo on the walls. The sense of trespassing is keener now, heightened by the world's light illuminating the organs, their secret colors revealed—maroon and salmon and yellow. The vista is sweetly vulnerable at this moment, a kind of welcoming. An arc of the liver shines high and on the right, like a dark sun. It laps over the pink sweep of the stomach, from whose lower border the gauzy omentum is draped, and through which veil one sees, sinuous, slow as just-fed snakes, the indolent coils of the intestine.

You turn aside to wash your gloves. It is a ritual cleansing. One enters this temple doubly washed. Here is man as microcosm, representing in all his parts the earth, perhaps the universe.

I must confess that the priestliness of my profession has ever been impressed on me. In the beginning there are vows, taken with all solemnity. Then there is the endless harsh novitiate of training, much fatigue, much sacrifice. At last one emerges as celebrant, standing close to the truth lying curtained in the Ark of the body. Not surplice and cassock but mask and gown are your regalia. You hold no chalice, but a knife. There is no wine, no wafer. There are only the facts of blood and flesh.

And if the surgeon is like a poet, then the scars you have made on countless bodies are like verses into the fashioning of which you have poured your soul. I think that if years later I were to see the trace from an old incision of mine, I should know it at once, as one recognizes his pet expressions.

But mostly you are a traveler in a dangerous country, advancing into the moist and jungly cleft your hands have made. Eyes and ears are shuttered from the land you left behind; mind empties itself of all other thought. You are the root of groping fingers. It is a fine hour for the fingers, their sense of touch so enhanced. The blind must know this feeling. Oh, there is risk everywhere. One goes lightly. The spleen. No! No! Do not touch the spleen that lurks below the left leaf of the diaphragm, a manta ray in a coral cave, its bloody tongue protruding. One poke and it might rupture, exploding with sudden hemorrhage. The filmy omentum must not be torn, the intestine scraped or denuded. The hand finds the liver, palms it, fingers running along its sharp lower edge, admiring. Here are the twin mounds of the kidneys, the apron of the omentum hanging in front of the intestinal coils. One lifts it aside and the fingers dip among the loops, searching, mapping territory, establishing boundaries. Deeper still, and the womb is touched, then held like a small muscular bottle—the womb and its earlike appendages, the ovaries. How they do nestle in the cup of a man's hand, their power all dormant. They are frailty itself.

There is a hush in the room. Speech stops. The hands of the others, assistants and nurses, are still. Only the voice of the patient's respiration remains. It is the rhythm of a quiet sea, the sound of waiting. Then you speak, slowly, the terse entries of a Himalayan climber reporting back.

"The stomach is okay. Greater curvature clean. No sign of ulcer. Pylorus, duodenum fine. Now comes the gall-bladder. No stones. Right kidney, left, all right. Liver... uh-oh."

Your speech lowers to a whisper, falters, stops for a long, long moment, then picks up again at the end of a sigh that comes through your mask like a last exhalation.

"Three big hard ones in the left lobe, one on the right. Metastatic deposits. Bad, bad. Where's the primary? Got to be coming from somewhere."

The arm shifts direction and the fingers drop lower and lower into the pelvis—the body impaled now upon the arm of the surgeon to the hilt of the elbow.

"Here it is."

The voice goes flat, all business now.

"Tumor in the sigmoid colon, wrapped all around it, pretty tight. We'll take out a sleeve of the bowel. No colostomy. Not that, anyway. But, God, there's a lot of it down there. Here, you take a feel."

You step back from the table, and lean into a sterile basin of water, resting on stiff arms, while the others locate the cancer.

When I was a small boy, I was taken by my father, a general practitioner in Troy, New York, to St. Mary's Hospital, to wait while he made his rounds. The solarium where I sat was all sunlight and large plants. It smelled of soap and starch and clean linen. In the spring, clouds of lilac billowed from the vases; and in the fall, chrysanthemums crowded the magazine tables. At one end of the great high-ceilinged, glass-walled room was a huge cage where colored finches streaked and sang. Even from the first, I sensed the nearness of that other place, the Operating Room, knew that somewhere on these premises was that secret dreadful enclosure where *surgery* was at that moment happening. I sat among the cut flowers, half drunk on the scent, listening to the robes of the nuns brush the walls of the corridor, and felt the awful presence of *surgery*.

Oh, the pageantry! I longed to go there. I feared to go there. I imagined surgeons bent like storks over the body of the patient, a circle of red painted across the abdomen. Silence and dignity and awe enveloped them, these surgeons; it was the bubble in which they bent and straightened. Ah, it was a place I would never see, a place from whose walls the hung and suffering Christ turned his affliction to highest purpose. It is thirty years since I yearned for that old Surgery. And now I merely break the beam of an electric eye, and double doors swing open to let me enter, and as I enter, always, I feel the surging of a force that I feel in no other place. It is as though I am suddenly stronger and larger, heroic. Yes, that's it!

The operating room is called a theatre. One walks onto a set where the cupboards hold tanks of oxygen and other gases. The cabinets store steel cutlery of unimagined versatility, and the refrigerators are filled with bags of blood. Bodies are stroked and penetrated here, but no love is made. Nor is it ever allowed to grow dark, but must always gleam with a grotesque brightness. For the special congress into which patient and surgeon enter, the one must have his senses deadened, the other his sensibilities restrained. One lies naked, blind, offering; the other stands masked and gloved. One yields; the other does his will.

I said no love is made here, but love happens. I have stood aside with lowered gaze while a priest, wearing the purple scarf of office, administers Last Rites to the man I shall operate upon. I try not to listen to those terrible last questions, the answers, but hear, with scorching clarity, the words that formalize the expectation of death. For a moment my resolve falters before the resignation, the *attentiveness*, of the other two. I am like an executioner who hears the cleric comforting the prisoner. For the moment I am excluded from the centrality of the event, a mere technician standing by. But it is only for the moment.

The priest leaves, and we are ready. Let it begin.

Later, I am repairing the strangulated hernia of an old man. Because of his age and frailty, I am using local anesthesia. He is awake. His name is Abe Kaufman, and he is a Russian Jew. A nurse sits by his head, murmuring to him. She wipes his forehead. I know her very well. Her name is Alexandria, and she is the daughter of Ukrainian peasants. She has a flat steppe of a face and slanting eyes. Nurse and patient are speaking of blintzes, borscht, piroshki—Russian food that they both love. I listen, and think that it may have been her grandfather who raided the shtetl where the old man lived long ago, and in his high boots and his blouse and his fury this grandfather pulled Abe by his side curls to the ground and stomped his face and kicked his groin. Perhaps it was that ancient kick that caused the hernia I am fixing. I listen to them whispering behind the screen at the head of the table. I listen with breath held before the prism of history.

"Tovarich," she says, her head bent close to his.

He smiles up at her, and forgets that his body is being laid open.

"You are an angel," the old man says.

One can count on absurdity. There, in the midst of our solemnities, appears, small and black and crawling, an insect: The Ant of the Absurd. The belly is open; one has seen and felt the catastrophe within. It seems the patient is already vaporizing into angelhood in the heat escaping therefrom. One could warm one's hands in that fever. All at once that ant is there, emerging from beneath one of the sterile towels that border the operating field. For a moment one does not really see it, or else denies the sight, so impossible it is, marching precisely, heading briskly toward the open wound.

Drawn from its linen lair, where it snuggled in the steam of the great sterilizer, and survived, it comes. Closer and closer, it hurries toward the incision. Ant, art thou in the grip of some fatal *ivresse*? Wouldst hurtle over these scarlet cliffs into the very boil of the guts? Art mad for the reek we handle? Or in some secret act of formication engaged?

The alarm is sounded. An ant! An ant! And we are unnerved. Our fear of defilement is near to frenzy. It is not the mere physical contamination that we loathe. It is the evil of the interloper, that he scurries across our holy place, and filthies our altar. He *is* disease—that for whose destruction we have gathered. Powerless to destroy the sickness before us, we turn to its incarnation with a vengeance, and pluck it from the lip of the incision in the nick of time. Who would have thought an ant could move so fast?

Between thumb and forefinger, the intruder is crushed. It dies as quietly as it lived. Ah, but now there is death in the room. It is a perversion of our purpose. Albert Schweitzer would have spared it, scooped it tenderly into his hand, and lowered it to the ground.

The corpselet is flicked into the specimen basin. The gloves are changed. New towels and sheets are placed where it walked. We are pleased to have done something, if only a small killing. The operation resumes, and we draw upon ourselves once more the sleeves of office and rank. Is our reverence for life in question?

In the room the instruments lie on trays and tables. They are arranged precisely by the scrub nurse, in an order that never changes, so that you can reach blindly for a forceps or hemostat without looking away from the operating field. The instruments lie *thus*! Even at the beginning, when all is clean and tidy and no blood has been spilled, it is the scalpel that dominates. It has a figure the others do not have, the retractors and the scissors. The scalpel is all grace and line, a fierceness. It grins. It is like a cat—to be respected, deferred to, but which returns no amiability. To hold it above a belly is to know the knife's force—as though were you to give it slightest rein, it would pursue an intent of its own, driving into the flesh, a wild energy.

In a story by Borges, a deadly knife fight between two rivals is depicted. It is not, however, the men who are fighting. It is the knives themselves that are settling their own old score. The men who hold the knives are mere adjuncts to the weapons. The unguarded knife is like the unbridled war-horse that not only carries its helpless rider to his death, but tramples all beneath its hooves. The hand of the surgeon must tame this savage thing. He is a rider reining to capture a pace.

So close is the joining of knife and surgeon that they are like the Centaur—the knife, below, all equine energy, the surgeon, above, with his delicate art. One holds the knife back as much as advances it to purpose. One is master of the scissors. One is partner, sometimes rival, to the knife. In a moment it is like the long red fingernail of the Dragon Lady. Thus does the surgeon curb in order to create, restraining the scalpel, governing it shrewdly, setting the action of the operation into a pattern, giving it form and purpose.

It is the nature of creatures to live within a tight cuirass that is both their constriction and their protection. The carapace of the turtle is his fortress and retreat, yet keeps him writhing on his back in the sand. So is the surgeon rendered impotent by his own empathy and compassion. The surgeon cannot weep. When he cuts the flesh, his own must not bleed. Here it is all work. Like an asthmatic hungering for air, longing to take just one deep breath, the surgeon struggles not to feel. It is suffocating to press the feeling out. It would be easier to weep or mourn—for you know that the lovely precise world of proportion contains, just beneath, *there*, all disaster, all disorder. In a surgical operation, a risk may flash into reality: the patient dies... of *complication*. The patient knows this too, in a more direct and personal way, and he is afraid.

And what of that *other*, the patient, you, who are brought to the operating room on a stretcher, having been washed and purged and dressed in a white gown? Fluid drips from a bottle into your arm, diluting you, leaching your body of its personal brine. As you wait in the corridor, you hear from behind the closed door the angry clang of steel upon steel, as though a battle were being waged. There is the odor of antiseptic and ether, and masked women hurry up and down the halls, in and out of rooms. There is the watery sound of strange machinery, the tinny beeping that is the transmitted heartbeat of yet another *human being*. And all the while the dreadful knowledge that soon you will be taken, laid beneath great lamps that will reveal the secret linings of your body. In the very act of lying down, you have made a declaration of surrender. One lies down gladly for sleep or for love. But to give over one's body and will for surgery, to *lie down* for it, is a yielding of more than we can bear.

Soon a man will stand over you, gowned and hooded. In time the man will take up a knife and crack open your flesh like a ripe melon. Fingers will rummage among your viscera. Parts of you will be cut out. Blood will run free. Your blood. All the night before you have turned with the presentiment of death upon you. You have attended your funeral, wept with your mourners. You think, "I should never have had surgery in the springtime." It is too cruel. Or on a Thursday. It is an unlucky day.

Now it is time. You are wheeled in and moved to the table. An injection is given. "Let yourself go," I say. "It's a pleasant sensation," I say. "Give in," I say.

Let go? Give in? When you know that you are being tricked into the hereafter, that you will end when consciousness ends? As the monstrous silence of anesthesia falls discourteously across your brain, you watch your soul drift off.

Later, in the recovery room, you awaken and gaze through the thickness of drugs at the world returning, and you guess, at first dimly, then surely, that you have not died. In pain and nausea you will know the exultation of death averted, of life restored.

What is it, then, this thing, the knife, whose shape is virtually the same as it was three thousand years ago, but now with its head grown detachable? Before steel, it was bronze. Before bronze, stone—then back into unremembered time. Did man invent it or did the knife precede him here, hidden under ages of vegetation and hoofprints, lying in wait to be discovered, picked up, used?

The scalpel is in two parts, the handle and the blade. Joined, it is six inches from tip to tip. At one end of the handle is a narrow notched prong upon which the blade is slid, then snapped into place. Without the blade, the handle has a blind, decapitated look. It is helpless as a trussed maniac. But slide on the blade, click it home, and the knife springs instantly to life. It is headed now, edgy, leaping to mount the fingers for the gallop to its feast.

Now is the moment from which you have turned aside, from which you have averted your gaze, yet toward which you have been hastened. Now the scalpel sings along the flesh again, its brute run unimpeded by germs or other frictions. It is a slick slide home, a barracuda spurt, a rip of embedded talon. One listens, and almost hears the whine—nasal, high, delivered through that gleaming metallic snout. The flesh splits with its own kind of moan. It is like the penetration of rape.

The breasts of women are cut off, arms and legs sliced to the bone to make ready for the saw, eyes freed from sockets, intestines lopped. The hand of the surgeon rebels. Tension boils through his pores, like sweat. The flesh of the patient retaliates with hemorrhage, and the blood chases the knife wherever it is withdrawn.

Within the belly a tumor squats, toadish, fungoid. A gray mother and her brood. The only thing it does not do is croak. It too is hacked from its bed as the carnivore knife lips the blood, turning in it in a kind of ecstasy of plenty, a gluttony after the long fast. It is just for this that the knife was created, tempered, heated, its violence beaten into paper-thin force.

At last a little thread is passed into the wound and tied. The monstrous booming fury is stilled by a tiny thread. The tempest is silenced. The operation is over. On the table, the knife lies spent; on its side, the bloody meal smear-dried upon its flanks. The knife rests.

And waits. [1996]

Richard Shelton

The Stones

I love to go out on summer nights and watch the stones grow. I think they grow better here in the desert, where it is warm and dry, than almost anywhere else. Or perhaps it is only that the young ones are more active here.

Young stones tend to move about more than their elders consider good for them. Most young stones have a secret desire which their parents had before them but have forgotten ages ago. And because this desire involves water, it is never mentioned. The older stones disapprove of water and say, "Water is a gadfly who never stays in one place long enough to learn anything." But the young stones try to work themselves into a position, slowly and without their elders noticing it, in which a sizable stream of water during a summer storm might catch them broadside and unknowing, so to speak, and push them along over a slope or down an arroyo. In spite of the danger this involves, they want to travel and see something of the world and settle in a new place, far from home, where they can raise their own dynasties away from the domination of their parents.

And although family ties are very strong among stones, many of the more daring young ones have succeeded; and they carry scars to prove to their children that they once went on a journey, helter-skelter and high water, and traveled perhaps fifteen feet, an incredible distance. As they grow older, they cease to brag about such clandestine adventures.

It is true that old stones get to be very conservative. They consider all movement either dangerous or downright sinful. They remain comfortable where they are and often get fat.

Fatness, as a matter of fact, is a mark of distinction.

And on summer nights, after the young stones are asleep, the elders turn to a serious and frightening subject—the moon, which is always spoken of in whispers. "See how it glows and whips across the sky, always changing its shape," one says. And another says, "Feel how it pulls at us, urging us to follow." And a third whispers, "It is a stone gone mad." [1957]

Peggy Shumaker

Moving Water, Tucson

Thunderclouds gathered every afternoon during the monsoons. Warm rain felt good on faces lifted to lick water from the sky. We played outside, having sense enough to go out and revel in the rain. We savored the first cool hours since summer hit.

The arroyo behind our house trickled with moving water. Kids gathered to see what it might bring. Tumbleweed, spears of ocotillo, creosote, a doll's arm, some kid's fort. Broken bottles, a red sweater. Whatever was nailed down, torn loose.

We stood on edges of sand, waiting for brown walls of water. We could hear it, massive water, not far off. The whole desert might come apart at once, might send horny toads and Gila monsters swirling, wet nightmares clawing both banks of the worst they could imagine and then some.

Under sheet lightning cracking the sky, somebody's teenage brother decided to ride the flash flood. He stood on wood in the bottom of the ditch, straddling the puny stream. "Get out, it's coming," kids yelled. "GET OUT," we yelled. The kid bent his knees, held out his arms.

Land turned liquid, that fast, water yanked our feet, stole our thongs, pulled in the edges of the arroyo, dragged whole trees, root wads and all, along, battering rams thrust downstream, anything you left there gone, anything you meant to go back and get history, water so high you couldn't touch bottom, water so fast you couldn't get out of it, water so huge the earth couldn't take it, water... We couldn't step back. We had to be there, to see for ourselves. Water in a place where water's always holy. Water remaking the world.

That kid on plywood, that kid waiting for the flood. He stood and the water lifted him. He stood, his eyes not seeing us. For a moment, we all wanted to be him, to be part of something so wet, so fast, so powerful, so much bigger than ourselves. That kid rode the flash flood inside us, the flash flood outside us. Artist unglued on a scrap of glued wood. For a few drenched seconds, he rode. The water took him, faster than you can believe. He kept his head up. Water you couldn't see through, water half dirt, water whirling hard. Heavy rain weighed down our clothes. We stepped closer to the crumbling shore, saw him downstream smash against the footbridge at the end of the block. Water held him there, rushing on. [2005]

Richard Siken

Scheherazade

Tell me about the dream where we pull the bodies out of the lake
                                        and dress them in warm clothes again.
        How it was late, and no one could sleep, the horses running
until they forget that they are horses.
                    It's not like a tree where the roots have to end somewhere,
    it's more like a song on a policeman's radio,
                    how we rolled up the carpet so we could dance, and the days
were bright red, and every time we kissed there was another apple
                                                            to slice into pieces.
Look at the light through the windowpane. That means it's noon, that means
    we're inconsolable.
                        Tell me how all this, and love too, will ruin us.
These, our bodies, possessed by light.
                                            Tell me we'll never get used to it.   [2008]

Tom Sleigh

Aubade

Lathe of the ocean. Perpetual
Motion machine of the waves. Everything still
Being turned and shaped to a shape nobody
Foresees: Ten years ago, was it, when we

Walked that shore, too earnest and sheepish
To hold hands? The wind cutting through our clothes
Cleansed and burned, the chill off the Atlantic
An ache we courted in our dumbstruck talk:

Callow, expectant, what wouldn't love give?
Cavalcanti's ray from Mars, Dante's wheel that moves
The planets and the stars, how nervous
We were, awkward and shivering: "Like this,

Do you like it like this?" Up all night,
Then waking to the smell of flannel and sweat,
We lay grateful, winded, goosefleshed in the chill,
Our own atmosphere rich and breathable:

We drank round the clock, embracing extremes,
Too hurried and heartsore to think of time ...
Out fishing after midnight, we watched schools of squid
Slide and shimmer, tentacles tight-wrapped

Around our gig's hooks: Yanked from the water,
They spouted jets of ink, then pulsed and quivered
And faded to dead-white, their eyes, resigned and sober,
Opening wider and wider... Ten years more,

And will either of us remember
That ink sticky on our hands, the moon-glare
Rippling as we knelt underneath the pier
And scrubbed and scrubbed our hands in the dark water? [1990]

Patricia Smith

Hip-Hop Ghazal

Gotta love us brown girls, munching on fat, swinging blue hips,
decked out in shells and splashes, Lawdie, bringing them woo hips.

As the jukebox teases, watch my sistas throat the heartbreak,
inhaling bassline, cracking backbone and singing thru hips.

Like something boneless, we glide silent, seeping 'tween floorboards,
wrapping around the hims, and *ooh wee*, clinging like glue hips.

Engines grinding, rotating, smokin', gotta pull back some.
Natural minds are lost at the mere sight of ringing true hips.

Gotta love us girls, just struttin' down Manhattan streets
killing the menfolk with a dose of that stinging view. Hips.

Crying 'bout getting old—Patricia, you need to get up off
what God gave you. Say a prayer and start slinging. Cue hips. [2007]

Mark Spragg

In Wyoming

This place is violent, and it is raw. Wyoming is not a land that lends itself to nakedness, or leniency. There is an edge here, living is accomplished on that edge. Most birds migrate. Hibernation is viewed as necessary, not stolid. The crippled, old, the inattentive perish. And there is the wind.

The wind blows through most every day unchoreographed with the spontaneous inelegance of a brawl. There are tracts where the currents draw so relentlessly that the trees that surround a home, or line an irrigation ditch, all lean east, grown permanently east, as though mere columns of submissive filings bowed toward some fickle pole. Little is decorative. There are few orchards. Fruit enters by interstate, truck-ripened, not tree-ripened. Wyoming boasts coal, oil, gas, uranium, widely scattered herds of sheep and cattle, and once, several million bison. The winds have worked the bison skeletons pink, white, finally to dust. The carboniferous forests rose up and fell and moldered under the winds, layer upon layer, pressed finally into coal. The winds predate the coal. The winds wail a hymn of transience.

On the windward sides of homes, trees are planted in a descending weave of cottonwood, spruce, Russian olive, finished with something thorny, stiff, and fast-growing—a hem of caragana: a windbreak; utilitarian first, ornamental by accident. Shade is a random luxury. There is nearly always at least a breeze. Like death and taxes, it can be counted on. Almost one hundred thousand square miles and a half million residents; there aren't that many homes. Towns grip the banks of watercourses, tenaciously. Ghost towns list, finally tumbling to the east. Gone the way of the buffalo bones. To dust.

There are precious few songbirds. Raptors ride the updrafts. The hares, voles, mice, skunks, squirrels, rats, shrews, and rabbits exist squinting into the sun and wind, their eyes water, their hearts spike in terror when swept by the inevitable shadow of predators. The meadowlark is the state's bird, but I think of them as hors d'oeuvres, their song a dinner bell. Eagle, falcon, hawk, owl live here year-round. The true residents. The natives. The gourmands. Their land-bound relatives work the middle ground. Lynx, lion, fox circle the table. Coyotes make their living where they can: as gypsies do.

Much of the landscape is classified as subarctic steppe. In Laramie a winter's evening entertainment consists of watching the gauges on the local weather channel. Thirty-below-zero, sixty-mile-an-hour winds, are standard fare. From early fall to late spring Wyoming's odor is that of a whetted stone; the tang of mineral slipping endlessly against mineral. There is no tulip festival in Wyoming. The smell of sap risen in cottonwood and pine is remembered, and cherished.

And then the winds quit. It happens on five or six days every season, more often in the summer and autumn. The sky settles as the dome of a perfect bell settles—blue, uninterrupted, moistureless. It is nothing in Wyoming to look twenty miles in every direction, the horizons scribbled in sharp contrast at the peripheries. "No wind," we shout in wonder. We speak too loudly. We are accustomed to screaming over the yowl of air. We quiet to a whisper. "No wind," we whisper. We smile and slump. Think of the slouch that survivors effect at the end of crisis. That is our posture.

We emerge from our shelters. If it is summer we expose our soft bellies to the sun, gaining confidence, we breathe deeply, glut ourselves with the scent of sage, a stimulating and narcotic perfume. We tend our yards. Paint our homes. Wash cars. My neighbor burns back overgrowths of dried weed, heaps of tumbleweed. He mends his fence. "Nice day," he says. I've heard him say as much when it is thirteen degrees above zero. What he means is that the wind is not blowing.

The foolish become bold. They start construction projects that will require more than forty-eight hours to complete. The rest of us work tentatively. We remember we are serfs. We know the lord is only absent, not dethroned. I pass through bouts of giddiness; I cannot help myself, but like the mice and voles, I remain alert. In Wyoming the price of innocence is high. There is a big wind out there, on its way home to our high plains. [2000]

Brent Staples

The Coroner's Photographs

My brother's body lies dead and naked on a stainless steel slab. At his head stands a tall arched spigot that, with tap handles mimicking wings, easily suggests a swan in mourning. His head is squarish and overlarge. (This, when he was a toddler, made him seem top-heavy and unsteady on his feet.) His widow's peak is common among the men in my family, though this one is more dramatic than most. An inverted pyramid, it begins high above the temples and falls steeply to an apex in the boxy forehead, over the heart-shaped face. A triangle into a box over a heart. His eyes (closed here) were big and dark and glittery; they drew you into his sadness when he cried. The lips are ajar as always, but the picture is taken from such an angle that it misses a crucial detail: the left front tooth tucked partly beyond the right one. I need this detail to see my brother full. I paint it in from memory.

A horrendous wound runs the length of the abdomen, from the sternum all the way to the pubic mound. The wound resembles a mouth whose lips are pouting and bloody. Massive staplelike clamps are gouged into these lips at regular intervals along the abdomen. This is a surgeon's incision. The surgeon was presented with a patient shot six times with a large-caliber handgun. Sensing the carnage that lay within, he achieved the largest possible opening and worked frantically trying to save my brother's life. He tied off shattered vessels, resectioned the small intestine, repaired a bullet track on the liver, then backed out. The closing would have required two pairs of hands. An assistant would have gripped the two sides of the wound and drawn them together while a second person cut in the clamps. The pulling together has made my brother's skin into a corset that crushes in on the abdomen from all sides. The pelvic bones jut up through the skin. The back is abnormally arched from the tension. The wound strains at the clamps, threatening to rip itself open. The surgeon worked all night and emerged from surgery gaunt, his greens darkened with sweat. "I tied off everything I could," he said, and then he wept at the savagery and the waste.

This is the body of Blake Melvin Staples, the seventh of my family's nine children, the third of my four brothers, born ten years after me. I know his contours well. I bathed and diapered him when he was a baby and studied his features as he grew. He is the smallest of the brothers, but is built in the same manner: short torso but long arms and legs; a more than ample behind set high on the back; knocking knees; big feet that tend to flat. The second toe is also a signature. It curls softly in an extended arc and rises above the others in a way that's unique to us. His feelings are mine as well. Cold: The sensation moves from my eyes to my shoulder blades to my bare ass as I feel him naked on the steel. I envision the reflex that would run through his body, hear the sharp breath he would draw when steel met his skin. Below the familiar feet a drain awaits the blood that will flow from this autopsy.

The medical examiner took this picture and several on February 13, 1984, at 9:45 a.m. The camera's flash is visible everywhere: on the pale-green tiles of the surrounding walls, on the gleaming neck of the spigot, on the stainless steel of the slab, on the bloody lips of the wound.

The coroner's report begins with a terse narrative summary: "The deceased, twenty-two-year-old Negro male, was allegedly shot by another person on the premises of a night club as a result of a 'long standing quarrel.' He sustained multiple gunshot wounds of the abdomen and legs and expired during surgery."

Blake was a drug dealer; he was known for carrying guns and for using them. His killer, Mark McGeorge, was a former customer and cocaine addict. At the trial Mark's lawyer described the shooting as a gunfight in which Blake was beaten to the draw. This was doubtful. Blake was shot six times: three times in the back. No weapon was found on or near his body. Blake's gunbearer testified that my brother was unarmed when Mark ambushed and gunned him down. But a gunbearer is not a plausible witness. A drug dealer known for shooting a rival in plain public view gets no sympathy from a jury. The jury turned back the prosecution's request for a conviction of murder in the first degree. Mark was found guilty of second-degree murder and sentenced to seven years in jail. Five years for the murder. Two years for using the gun.

Blake is said to have cried out for his life as he lay on the ground. "Please don't shoot me no more. I don't want to die." "*Please don't shoot me no more. I don't want to die.*" His voice had a touch of that dullness one hears from the deaf, a result of ear infections he suffered as a child. The ear openings had narrowed to the size of pinholes. He tilted his head woefully from side to side trying to pour out the pain. His vowels were locked high in his throat, behind his nose. This voice kept him a baby to me. This is the voice in which he would have pleaded for his life.

The coroner dissects the body, organ by organ:

HEART: 300 grams. No valve or chamber lesions. Coronary arteries show no pathologic changes.

LUNGS: 900 grams combined. Moderate congestion. Tracheobronchial and arterial systems are not remarkable.

LIVER: 1950 grams. There is a sutured bullet track at the interlobar sulcus and anterior portion of the right hepatic lobe. There has been moderate subcapsular and intraparenchymal hemorrhage.

SPLEEN: 150 grams. No pathologic changes.

KIDNEYS: 300 grams combined. No pathologic changes.

ADRENALS: No pathologic changes.

PANCREAS: No pathologic changes.

GI TRACT: The stomach is empty. Portions of the small bowel have been resected, along with portions of the omentum. The bowel surface is dusky reddish brown, but does not appear gangrenous.

URINARY BLADDER: Empty.

NECK ORGANS: Intact. No airway obstructions.

BRAIN: 1490 grams. Sagittal and serial coronal sections show no discrete lesions or evidence of injury.

SKULL: Intact.

VERTEBRAE: Intact.

RIBS: Intact.

PELVIS: There is a chip fracture of the left pubic ramus, and there is also fracturing of the right pubic ramus. There is extensive fracturing of the left femur, and there is a through-and-through bullet wound of the right femur just below the hip joint.

The coroner describes the wounds in detail. The surgical incision and its grisly clamps are dismissed in a single sentence. The six bullet holes receive one full paragraph each. The coroner records the angle that each bullet traveled through the body, the organs it passed through along the way, and where it finally came to rest. With all this to occupy him, the coroner fails to note the scar on Blake's left hand. The scar lies in the webbing between the thumb and index finger and is the result of a gun accident. A shotgun recoiled when Blake fired it and drove the hammer deep into the web, opening a wound that took several stitches to close.

I saw the wound when it was fresh, six weeks before Blake was murdered. I was visiting Roanoke from Chicago, where I then lived. I sought Blake out to tell him that it was time to get out of the business and leave Roanoke. The signs of death were everywhere; his name was hot in the street. Blake and I were making small talk when we slapped each other five. Blake clutched his hand at the wrist and cried out in pain. Then he showed me the stitches. This ended the small talk. I told him that he was in danger of being killed if he didn't leave town.

Staples men have been monolinguists for generations. We love our own voices too much. Blake responded to my alarm by telling me stories. He told me about the awesome power of the shotgun that had injured him. He told me about making asses of the police when they raided his apartment looking for drugs. The door of his apartment was steel, he said; they'd sent for a tow truck to pull it from its frame. Inside they found him twiddling his thumbs in the bathroom. He'd flushed the cocaine down the toilet. The night he told me these stories was the last time I saw him alive.

Six weeks later my brother Bruce called me with the news. "Brent, Blake is dead," he said. "Some guy pulled up in a car and emptied out on him with a magnum. Blake is dead." I told myself to feel nothing. I had already mourned Blake and buried him and was determined not to suffer his death a second time. I skipped the funeral and avoided Roanoke for the next three years. The next time I visited my family I went to see the Roanoke Commonwealth Attorney and questioned him about the case. He was polite and impatient. For him, everything about the killing had been said. This, after all, had been an ordinary death.

I asked to see the files. A secretary brought a manila pouch and handed it to the Commonwealth Attorney, who handed it to me and excused himself from the room. The pouch contained a summary of the trial, the medical examiner's report, and a separate inner pouch wrapped in twine and shaped like photographs. I opened the pouch; there was Blake dead and on the slab, photographed from several angles. The floor gave way: and I fell down and down for miles. [1995]

Lawrence Sutin

Father Holding Baby

I say to you that I have been a good father. The one and only time I slipped hard came when Sarah was just a few months old. My wife Mab had gone off one evening to a meeting. Did the young suckling baby miss her mama? Yes, she did. Was Daddy confident with baby alone with him in the house? No. Shortly after Mama left, baby cried and Daddy fed her a bottle and some soft, blended apricots from a glass jar. It was quiet for a while and baby played with colored rings on a blanket spread on the living-room carpet. Then baby started to cry again and Daddy picked her up and held her and walked with her and cooed to her and kissed her lightly on the top of her head and sang to her in the fleeciest voice he could some Grateful Dead ballads that had always sounded to him like lullabies. He had wanted to be a father someday and had thought he would be a good one because he wanted to be. Baby kept crying. Daddy kept walking and rocking baby in his arms and cooing and singing and trying to keep a smile on his face when it came close to hers. Baby kept crying. Baby kept crying. It was nearly an hour and the crying only stopped when baby sobbed, running out of breath. Sleep, baby. No. Baby kept crying. Crying. The sound of a cry is designed by nature to make you unable to stand it and determined to get it to stop. I couldn't. That's why I screamed at her to stop. Thank God at least I did not shake her. Then, shaking all over myself, I laid her on the sofa and sat across the room watching, but saying and doing no more as baby cried and gasped and caught her breath and cried until Mama finally came home. I was yellow and the baby was yellow and we glowed in the dimness of the house from our strain. I have failed to do a good many things in my life. All of those things bother me still, but none so much as that evening alone with a baby for whom a father did and was nothing. [2004]

Amy Tan

Confessions

My mother's thoughts reach back like the winter tide, exposing the wreckage of a former shore. Often she's mired in 1967, 1968, the years my older brother and my father died.

1968 was also the year she took me and my little brother—Didi—across the Atlantic to Switzerland, a place so preposterously different that she knew she had to give up grieving simply to survive. That year, she remembers, she was very, very sad. I too remember. I was sixteen then, and I recall a late-night hour when my mother and I were arguing in the chalet, that tinderbox of emotion where we lived.

She had pushed me into the small bedroom we shared, and as she slapped me about the head, I backed into a corner, by a window that looked out on the lake, the Alps, the beautiful outside world. My mother was furious because I had a boyfriend. She was shouting that he was a drug addict, a bad man who would use me for sex and throw me away like leftover garbage.

"Stop seeing him!" she ordered.

I shook my head. The more she beat me, the more implacable I became, and this in turn fueled her outrage.

"You didn't love you daddy or Peter! When they die you not even sad."

I kept my face to the window, unmoved. What does she know about sad?

She sobbed and beat her chest. "I rather kill myself before see you destroy you life!"

Suicide. How many times had she threatened that before?

"I wish you the one die! Not Peter, not Daddy."

She had just confirmed what I had always suspected. Now she flew at me with her fists.

"I rather kill you! I rather see you die!"

And then, perhaps horrified by what she had just said, she fled the room. Thank God that was over. I wished I had a cigarette to smoke. Suddenly she was back. She slammed the door shut, latched it, then locked it with a key. I saw the flash of a meat cleaver just before she pushed me to the wall and brought the blade's edge to within an inch of my throat. Her eyes were like a wild animal's, shiny, fixated on the kill. In an excited voice she said, "First, I kill you. Then Didi and me, our whole family destroy!" She smiled, her chest heaving. "Why you don't cry?" She pressed the blade closer and I could feel her breath gusting.

Was she bluffing? If she did kill me, so what? Who would care? While she rambled, a voice within me was whimpering, "This is sad, this is so sad."

For ten minutes, fifteen, longer, I straddled these two thoughts—that it didn't matter if I died, that it would be eternally sad if I did—until all at once I felt a snap, then a rush of hope into a vacuum, and I was crying, I was babbling my confession: "I want to live. I want to live."

For twenty-five years I forgot that day, and when the memory of what happened surfaced unexpectedly at a writers' workshop in which we recalled our worst moments, I was shaking, wondering to myself, Did she really mean to kill me? If I had not pleaded with her, would she have pushed down on the cleaver and ended my life?

I wanted to go to my mother and ask. Yet I couldn't, not until much later, when she became forgetful and I learned she had Alzheimer's disease. I knew that if I didn't ask her certain questions now, I would never know the real answers.

So I asked.

"Angry? Slap you?" she said, and laughed. "No, no, no. You always good girl, never even need to spank, not even one time."

How wonderful to hear her say what was never true, yet now would be forever so.

[2003]

Madeleine Thien

Simple Recipes

There is a simple recipe for making rice. My father taught it to me when I was a child. Back then, I used to sit up on the kitchen counter watching him, how he sifted the grains in his hands, sure and quick, removing pieces of dirt or sand, tiny imperfections. He swirled his hands through the water and it turned cloudy. When he scrubbed the grains clean, the sound was as big as a field of insects. Over and over, father rinsed the rice, drained the water, then filled the pot again.

The instructions are simple. Once the washing is done you measure the water this way—by resting the tip of your index finger on the surface of the rice. The water should reach the bend of your first knuckle. My father did not need instructions or measuring cups. He closed his eyes and felt for the waterline.

Sometimes I still dream my father, his bare feet flat against the floor, standing in the middle of the kitchen. He wears old buttoned shirts and faded sweatpants drawn at the waist. Surrounded by the gloss of the kitchen counters, the sharp angles of the stove, the fridge, the shiny sink, he looks out of place. This memory of him is so strong, sometimes it stuns me, the detail with which I can see it.

Every night before dinner, my father would perform this ritual—rinsing and draining, then setting the pot in the cooker. When I was older, he passed this task on to me but I never did it with the same care. I went through the motions, splashing the water around, jabbing my finger down to measure the water level. Some nights the rice was a mushy gruel. I worried that I could not do so simple a task right. "Sorry," I would say to the table, my voice soft and embarrassed. In answer, my father would keep eating, pushing the rice into his mouth as if he never expected anything different, as if he noticed no difference between what he did so well and I so poorly. He would eat every last mouthful, his chopsticks walking quickly across the plate. Then he would rise, whistling, and clear the table, every motion so clean and sure, I would be convinced by him that all was well in the world.

*

My father is standing in the middle of the kitchen. In his right hand he holds a plastic bag filled with water. Caught inside the bag is a live fish.

The fish is barely breathing, though its mouth opens and closes. I reach up and touch it through the plastic bag, trailing my fingers along the gills, the soft, muscled body, pushing my finger overtop the eyeball. The fish looks straight at me, flopping sluggishly from side to side.

My father fills the kitchen sink. In one swift motion he overturns the bag and the fish comes sailing out with the water. It curls and jumps. We watch it closely, me on my tiptoes, chin propped up on the counter. The fish is the length of my arm from wrist to elbow. It floats in place, brushing up against the sides of the sink.

I keep watch over the fish while my father begins the preparations for dinner. The fish folds its body, trying to turn or swim, the water nudging overtop. Though I ripple tiny circles around it with my fingers, the fish stays still, bobbing side-to-side in the cold water.

For many hours at a time, it was just the two of us. While my mother worked and my older brother played outside, my father and I sat on the couch, flipping channels. He loved cooking shows. We watched *Wok with Yan*, my father passing judgement on Yan's methods. I was enthralled when Yan transformed orange peels into swans. My father sniffed. "I can do that," he said. "You don't have to be a genius to do that." He placed a sprig of green onion in water and showed me how it bloomed like a flower. "I know many tricks like this," he said. "Much more than Yan."

Still, my father made careful notes when Yan demonstrated Peking Duck. He chuckled heartily at Yan's punning. "Take a wok on the wild side!" Yan said, pointing his spatula at the camera.

"Ha ha!" my father laughed, his shoulders shaking. "*Wok* on the wild side!"

In the mornings, my father took me to school. At three o'clock, when we came home again, I would rattle off everything I learned that day. "The brachiosaurus," I informed him, "eats only soft vegetables."

My father nodded. "That is like me. Let me see your forehead." We stopped and faced each other in the road. "You have a high forehead," he said, leaning down to take a closer look. "All smart people do."

I walked proudly, stretching my legs to match his steps. I was overjoyed when my feet kept time with his, right, then left, then right, and we walked like a single unit. My father was the man of tricks, who sat for an hour mining a watermelon with a circular spoon, who carved the rind into a castle.

My father was born in Malaysia and he and my mother immigrated to Canada several years before I was born, first settling in Montreal, then finally in Vancouver. While I was born into the persistence of the Vancouver rain, my father was born in the wash of a monsoon country. When I was young, my parents tried to teach me their language but it never came easily to me. My father ran his thumb gently over my mouth, his face kind, as if trying to see what it was that made me different.

My brother was born in Malaysia but when he immigrated with my parents to Canada the language left him. Or he forgot it, or he refused it, which is also common, and this made my father angry. "How can a child forget a language?" he would ask my mother. "It is because the child is lazy. Because the child chooses not to remember." When he was twelve years old, my brother stayed away in the afternoons. He drummed the soccer ball up and down the back alley, returning home only at dinner time. During the day, my mother worked as a sales clerk at the Woodward's store downtown, in the building with the red revolving W on top.

In our house, the ceilings were yellowed with grease. Even the air was heavy with it. I remember that I loved the weight of it, the air that was dense with the smell of countless meals cooked in a tiny kitchen, all those good smells jostling for space.

The fish in the sink is dying slowly. It has a glossy sheen to it, as if its skin is made of shining minerals. I want to prod it with both hands, its body tense against the pressure of my fingers. If I hold it tightly, I imagine I will be able to feel its fluttering heart. Instead, I lock eyes with the fish. *You're feeling verrrry sleepy,* I tell it. *You're getting verrrry tired.*

Beside me, my father chops green onions quickly. He uses a cleaver that he says is older than I am by many years. The blade of the knife rolls forward and backward, loops of green onion gathering in a pyramid beside my father's wrist. When he is done, he rolls his sleeve back from his right hand, reaches in through the water and pulls the plug.

The fish in the sink floats and we watch it in silence. The water level falls beneath its gills, beneath its belly. It drains and leaves the sink dry. The fish is lying on its side, mouth open and its body heaving. It leaps sideways and hits the sink. Then up again. It curls and snaps, lunging for its own tail. The fish sails into the air, dropping hard. It twitches violently.

My father reaches in with his bare hands. He lifts the fish out by the tail and lays it gently on the counter. While holding it steady with one hand, he hits the head with the flat of the cleaver. The fish falls still, and he begins to clean it.

*

In my apartment, I keep the walls scrubbed clean. I open the windows and turn the fan on whenever I prepare a meal. My father bought me a rice cooker when I first moved into my own apartment, but I use it so rarely it stays in the back of the cupboard, the cord wrapped neatly around its belly. I have no longing for the meals themselves, but I miss the way we sat down together, our bodies leaning hungrily forward while my father, the magician, unveiled plate after plate. We laughed and ate, white steam fogging my mother's glasses until she had to take them off and lay them on the table. Eyes closed, she would eat, crunchy vegetables gripped in her chopsticks, the most vivid green.

*

My brother comes into the kitchen and his body is covered with dirt. He leaves a thin trail of it behind as he walks. The soccer ball, muddy from outside, is encircled in one arm. Brushing past my father, his face is tense.

Beside me, my mother sprinkles garlic onto the fish. She lets me slide one hand underneath the fish's head, cradling it, then bending it backwards so that she can fill the fish's insides with ginger. Very carefully, I turn the fish over. It is firm and slippery, and beaded with tiny, sharp scales.

At the stove, my father picks up an old teapot. It is full of oil and he pours the oil into the wok. It falls in a thin ribbon. After a moment, when the oil begins crackling, he lifts the fish up and drops it down into the wok. He adds water and the smoke billows up. The sound of the fish frying is like tires on gravel, a sound so loud it drowns out all other noises. Then my father steps out from the smoke. "Spoon out the rice," he says as he lifts me down from the counter.

My brother comes back into the room, his hands muddy and his knees the colour of dusty brick. His soccer shorts flutter against the backs of his legs. Sitting down, he makes an angry face. My father ignores him.

Inside the cooker, the rice is flat like a pie. I push the spoon in, turning the rice over, and the steam shoots up in a hot mist and condenses on my skin. While my father moves his arms delicately over the stove, I begin dishing the rice out: first for my father, then my mother, then my brother, then myself. Behind me the fish is cooking quickly. In a crockery pot, my father steams cauliflower, stirring it round and round.

My brother kicks at a table leg. "What's the matter?" my father asks.

He is quiet for a moment, then he says, "Why do we have to eat fish?"

"You don't like it?"

My brother crosses his arms against his chest. I see the dirt lining his arms, dark and hardened. I imagine chipping it off his body with a small spoon.

"I don't like the eyeball there. It looks sick."

My mother tuts. Her nametag is still clipped to her blouse. It says *Woodward's*, and then, *Sales Clerk*. "Enough," she says, hanging her purse on the back of the chair. "Go wash your hands and get ready for supper."

My brother glares, just for a moment. Then he begins picking at the dirt on his arms. I bring plates of rice to the table. The dirt flies off his skin, speckling the tablecloth. "Stop it," I say crossly.

"*Stop it*," he says, mimicking me.

"Hey!" My father hits his spoon against the counter. It *pings*, high-pitched. He points at my brother. "No fighting in this house."

My brother looks at the floor, mumbles something, and then shuffles away from the table. As he moves farther away, he begins to stamp his feet.

Shaking her head, my mother takes her jacket off. It slides from her shoulders. She says something to my father in the language I can't understand. He merely shrugs his shoulders. And then he replies, and I think his words are so familiar, as if they are words I should know, as if maybe I did know them once but then I forgot them. The language that they speak is full of soft vowels, words running together so that I can't make out the gaps where they pause for breath.

My mother told me once about guilt. Her own guilt she held in the palm of her hands, like an offering. But your guilt is different, she said. You do not need to hold on to it. Imagine this, she said, her hands running along my forehead, then up into my hair. Imagine, she said. Picture it, and what do you see?

A bruise on the skin, wide and black.

A bruise, she said. Concentrate on it. Right now, it's a bruise. But if you concentrate, you can shrink it, compress it to the size of a pinpoint. And then, if you want to, if you see it, you can blow it off your body like a speck of dirt.

She moved her hands along my forehead.

I tried to picture what she said. I pictured blowing it away like so much nothing, just these little pieces that didn't mean anything, this complicity that I could magically walk away from. She made me believe in the strength of my own thoughts, as if I could make appear what had never existed. Or turn it around. Flip it over so many times you just lose sight of it, you lose the tail end and the whole thing disappears into smoke.

My father pushes at the fish with the edge of his spoon. Underneath, the meat is white and the juice runs down along the side. He lifts a piece and lowers it carefully onto my plate.

Once more, his spoon breaks skin. Gingerly, my father lifts another piece and moves it towards my brother.

"I don't want it," my brother says.

My father's hand wavers. "Try it," he says, smiling. "Take a wok on the wild side."

"No."

My father sighs and places the piece on my mother's plate. We eat in silence, scraping our spoons across the dishes. My parents use chopsticks, lifting their bowls and motioning the food into their mouths. The smell of food fills the room.

Savouring each mouthful, my father eats slowly, head tuned to the flavours in his mouth. My mother takes her glasses off, the lenses fogged, and lays them on the table. She eats with her head bowed down, as if in prayer.

Lifting a stem of cauliflower to his lips, my brother sighs deeply. He chews, and then his face changes. I have a sudden picture of him drowning, his hair waving like grass. He coughs, spitting the mouthful back onto his plate. Another cough. He reaches for his throat, choking.

My father slams his chopsticks down on the table. In a single movement, he reaches across, grabbing my brother by the shoulder. "I have tried," he is saying. "I don't know what kind of son you are. To be so ungrateful." His other hand sweeps by me and bruises into my brother's face.

My mother flinches. My brother's face is red and his mouth is open. His eyes are wet.

Still coughing, he grabs a fork, tines aimed at my father, and then in an unthinking moment, he heaves it at him. It strikes my father in the chest and drops. "I hate you! You're just an asshole, you're just a fucking asshole chink!" My brother holds his plate in his hands. He smashes it down and his food scatters across the table. He is coughing and spitting. "I wish you weren't my father! I wish you were dead."

My father's hand falls again. This time pounding downwards. I close my eyes. All I can hear is someone screaming. There is a loud voice. I stand awkwardly, my hands covering my eyes.

"Go to your room," my father says, his voice shaking.

And I think he is talking to me so I remove my hands.

But he is looking at my brother. And my brother is looking at him, his small chest heaving.

A few minutes later, my mother begins clearing the table, face weary as she scrapes the dishes one by one over the garbage.

I move away from my chair, past my mother, onto the carpet and up the stairs.

Outside my brother's bedroom, I crouch against the wall. When I step forward and look, I see my father holding the bamboo pole between his hands. The pole is smooth. The long grains, fine as hair, are pulled together, at intervals, jointed. My brother is lying on the floor, as if thrown down and dragged there. My father raises the pole into the air.

I want to cry out. I want to move into the room between them, but I can't.

It is like a tree falling, beginning to move, a slow arc through the air.

The bamboo drops silently. It rips the skin on my brother's back. I cannot hear any sound. A line of blood edges quickly across his body.

The pole rises and again comes down. I am afraid of bones breaking.

My father lifts his arms once more.

On the floor, my brother cries into the carpet, pawing at the ground. His knees folded into his chest, the crown of his head burrowing down. His back is hunched over and I can see his spine, little bumps on his skin.

The bamboo smashes into bone and the scene in my mind bursts into a million white pieces.

My mother picks me up off the floor, pulling me across the hall, into my bedroom, into bed. Everything is wet, the sheets, my hands, her body, my face, and she soothes me with words I cannot understand because all I can hear is screaming. She rubs her cool hands against my forehead. "Stop," she says. "Please stop," but I feel loose, deranged, as if everything in the known world is ending right here.

In the morning, I wake up to the sound of oil in the pan and the smell of French toast. I can hear my mother bustling around, putting dishes in the cupboards.

No one says anything when my brother doesn't come down for breakfast. My father piles French toast and syrup onto a plate and my mother pours a glass of milk. She takes everything upstairs to my brother's bedroom.

As always, I follow my father around the kitchen. I track his footprints, follow behind him and hide in the shadow of his body. Every so often, he reaches down and ruffles my hair with his hands. We cast a spell, I think. The way we move in circles, how he cooks without thinking because this is the task that comes to him effortlessly. He smiles down at me, but when he does this, it somehow breaks the spell. My father stands in place, hands dropping to his sides as if he has forgotten what he was doing mid-motion. On the walls, the paint is peeling and the floor, unswept in days, leaves little pieces of dirt stuck to our feet.

My persistence, I think, my unadulterated love, confuse him. With each passing day, he knows I will find it harder to ignore what I can't comprehend, that I will be unable to separate one part of him from another. The unconditional quality of my love for him will not last forever, just as my brother's did not. My father stands in the middle of the kitchen, unsure. Eventually, my mother comes downstairs again and puts her arms around him and holds him, whispering something to him, words that to me are meaningless and incomprehensible. But she offers them to him, sound after sound, in a language that was stolen from some other place, until he drops his head and remembers where he is.

Later on, I lean against the door frame upstairs and listen to the sound of a metal fork scraping against a dish. My mother is already there, her voice rising and falling. She is moving the fork across the plate, offering my brother pieces of French toast.

I move towards the bed, the carpet scratchy, until I can touch the wooden bed-frame with my hands. My mother is seated there, and I go to her, reaching my fingers out to the buttons on her cuff and twisting them over to catch the light.

"Are you eating?" I ask my brother.

He starts to cry. I look at him, his face half hidden in the blankets.

"Try and eat," my mother says softly.

He only cries harder but there isn't any sound. The pattern of sunlight on his blanket moves with his body. His hair is pasted down with sweat and his head moves forward and backward like an old man's.

At some point I know my father is standing at the entrance of the room but I cannot turn to look at him. I want to stay where I am, facing the wall. I'm afraid that if I turn around and go to him, I will be complicit, accepting a portion of guilt, no matter how small that piece. I do not know how to prevent this from happening again, though now I know, in the end, it will break us apart. This violence will turn all my love to shame and grief. So I stand there, not looking at him or my brother. Even my father, the magician, who can make something beautiful out of nothing, he just stands and watches.

A face changes over time, it becomes clearer. In my father's face, I have seen everything pass. Anger that has stripped it of anything recognizable, so that it is only a face of bones and skin. And then, at other times, so much pain that it is unbearable, his face so full of grief it might dissolve. How to reconcile all that I know of him and still love him? For a long time, I thought it was not possible. When I was a child, I did not love my father because he was complicated, because he was human, because he needed me to. A child does not know yet how to love a person that way.

How simple it should be. Warm water running over, the feel of the grains between my hands, the sound of it like stones running along the pavement. My father would rinse the rice over and over, sifting it between his fingertips, searching for the impurities, pulling them out. A speck, barely visible, resting on the tip of his finger.

If there were some recourse, I would take it. A cupful of grains in my open hand, a smoothing out, finding the impurities, then removing them piece by piece. And then, to be satisfied with what remains.

Somewhere in my memory, a fish in the sink is dying slowly. My father and I watch as the water runs down. [2003]

James Tyner

At a Barbecue for R.C. One Week after He Is Out of Iraq

He laughs and tosses back
another shot of whiskey.
There are questions about cousins,
how is Lisa doing, she still drinking,
did Eddy finally marry that big
bitch, heard Monica is in L.A. now.
I fill him in, crack open another beer
chaser, and tell what stories I can.
I am light here, keeping things brief,
smiling, avoiding the heat from his skin,
the pocks and purple circles
that tighten his face, mar it.
A curl of scarred flesh lifts up
from the collar of his shirt,
hanging like a question

I can't ask. And suddenly the food
is done, barbeque finished,
mom calls out to get the kids
ready to eat, and his face fills
with an emptiness, jaw loosens
and he is muttering now, about kids
something about so many goddamn
kids. He asks me if I know what
the color of brains really is,
and I answer that the ribs
are getting cold. [2009]

Priscila Uppal

Sorry, I Forgot to Clean Up After Myself

Sorry, Sirs and Madams, I forgot to clean up after myself
after the unfortunate incidents of the previous century.

How embarrassing; my apologies. I wouldn't advise you
to stroll around here without safety goggles, and I must insist
that you enter at your own risk. You may, however, leave
your umbrella at the door. Just keep your ticket.

We expected, of course, to have this all cleared away by the time
you arrived. The goal was to present you
with blue and green screens, whitewashed counters.

Unforeseen expenses.
Red tape.
So hard to find good help these days.

But, alas, excuses. Perhaps you will appreciate
the difficulties I've faced in providing you a clean slate.
If you step into a hole, Sirs and Madams, accept the loss
of a shoe or two. Stay the course.

Progress is the mother of invention. Here: take my hand.
Yes, that's right. You can return it on the way back. [2006]

Luisa Valenzuela

Vision Out of the Corner of One Eye[i]

It's true, he put his hand on my ass and I was about to scream bloody murder when the bus passed by a church and he crossed himself. He's a good sort after all, I said to myself. Maybe he didn't do it on purpose or maybe his right hand didn't know what his left hand was up to. I tried to move farther back in the bus—searching for explanations is one thing and letting yourself be pawed is another—but more passengers got on and there was no way I could do it. My wiggling to get out of his reach only let him get a better hold on me and even fondle me. I was nervous and finally moved over. He moved over, too. We passed by another church but he didn't notice it and when he raised his hand to his face it was to wipe the sweat off his forehead. I watched him out of the corner of one eye, pretending that nothing was happening, or at any rate not making him think I liked it. It was impossible to move a step farther and he began jiggling me. I decided to get even and put my hand on his behind. A few blocks later I got separated from him. Then I was swept along by the passengers getting off the bus and now I'm sorry I lost him so suddenly because there were only 7,400 pesos in his wallet and I'd have gotten more out of him if we'd been alone. He seemed affectionate. And very generous. [1979]

Thomas S. Whitecloud III

Blue Winds Dancing

There is a moon out tonight. Moons and stars and cloud tipped with moonlight. And there is a fall wind blowing in my heart. Ever since this evening, when against a fading sky I saw geese wedge southward. They were going home.... Now I try to study, but against the pages I see them again, driving southward. Going home.

Across the valley there are heavy mountains holding up the sky, and beyond the mountains there is home. Home, and peace, and the beat of drums, and blue winds dancing over snowfields. The Indian lodge will fill with my people, and our gods will come and sit among them.

But home is beyond the mountains, and I am here. Here where fall hides in the valleys, and winter never comes down from the mountains. Here where all the trees grow in rows; the palms stand stiffly by the roadsides and in the groves the orange trees line in military rows, and endlessly bear fruit. Beautiful, yes; there is always beauty in order, in rows of growing things! But it is the beauty of captivity. A pine fighting for existence on a windy knoll is much more beautiful.

In my Wisconsin, the leaves change before the snows come. In the air is the smell of wild rice and venison cooking; and when the winds come whispering through the forests, they carry the smell of rotting leaves. In the evenings, the loon calls, lonely; and birds sing their

i Translated by Helen Lane.

last songs before leaving. Bears dig roots and eat late fall berries, fattening for their long winter sleep. Later, when the first snows fall, one awakens in the morning to find the world white and beautiful and clean. Then one can look back over his trail and see the tracks following. In the woods there are tracks of deer and snowshoe rabbits, and long streaks where partridges slide to alight. Chipmunks make tiny footprints on the limbs and one can hear squirrels busy in hollow trees, sorting acorns. Soft lake waves wash the shores, and sunsets burst each evening over the lakes, and make them look as if they were afire.

That land which is my home! Beautiful, calm—where there is no hurry to get anywhere, no driving to keep up in a race that knows no ending and no goal. No classes where men talk and talk and then stop now and then to hear their own words come back to them from the students. No constant peering into the maelstrom of one's mind; no worries about grades and honors; no hysterical preparing for life until that life is half over; no anxiety about one's place in the thing they call Society.

I hear again the ring of axes in deep woods, the crunch of snow beneath my feet. I feel again the smooth velvet of ghost-birch bark. I hear the rhythm of the drums.... I am tired. I am weary of trying to keep up this bluff of being civilized. Being civilized means trying to do everything you don't want to, never doing everything you want to. It means dancing to the strings of custom and tradition; it means living in houses and never knowing or caring who is next door. These civilized white men want us to be like them—always dissatisfied—getting a hill and wanting a mountain.

Then again, maybe I am not tired. Maybe I'm licked. Maybe I am just not smart enough to grasp these things that go to make up civilization. Maybe I am just too lazy to think hard enough to keep up.

Still, I know my people have many things that civilization has taken from the whites. They know how to give; how to tear one's piece of meat in two and share it with one's brother. They know how to sing—how to make each man his song and sing them; for their music they do not need to listen to other man singing over a radio. They know how to make things with their hands, how to shape beads into design and make a thing of beauty from a piece of birch bark.

But we are inferior. It is terrible to have to feel inferior; to have to read reports of intelligence tests, and learn that one's race is behind. It is terrible to sit in class and hear men tell you that your people worship sticks of wood—that your gods are all false, that the Manitou forgot your people and did not write them a book.

I am tired. I want to walk again among the ghost-birches. I want to see the leaves turn in autumn, the smoke rise from the lodgehouses, and to feel the blue winds, and to feel the blue winds. I want to hear the drums; I want to hear the drums and feel the blue whispering winds.

There is a train wailing into the night. The trains go across the mountains. It would be easy to catch a freight. They will say he has gone back to the blanket; I don't care. The dance at Christmas....

A bunch of bums warming at a tiny fire talk politics and women and joke about the Relief and the WPA and smoke cigarettes. These men in caps and overcoats and dirty overalls living on the outskirts of civilization are free, but they pay the price of being free in civilization. They are outcasts. I remember a sociology professor lecturing on adjustment to society; hobos and prostitutes and criminals are individuals who never adjusted, he said. He could learn a lot if he came and listened to a bunch of bums talk. He would learn that work and a woman and a place to hang his hat are all the ordinary man wants. These are all he wants, but other men are not content to let him want only these. He must be taught to want radios and automobiles and a new suit every spring. Progress will stop if he did not want these things. I listen to hear if there is any talk of communism or socialism in the hobo jungles. There is none. At best there is a sort of disgusted philosophy about life. They seem to think there should be a better distribution of wealth, or more work, or something. But they are not rabid about it. The radicals live in the cities.

I find a fellow headed for Albuquerque, and talk road-talk with him. "It is hard to ride fruit carts. Bums break in. Better to wait for a cattle car going back to the Middle West, and ride that." We catch the next east-bound and walk the tops until we find a cattle cart. Inside, we crouch near the forward wall, huddle, and try to sleep. I feel peaceful and content at last. I am going home. The cattle cart rocks. I sleep.

Morning and the desert. Noon and the Salton Sea, lying more lifeless than a mirage under a somber sun in a pale sky. Skeleton mountains rearing on the skyline, thrusting out of the desert floor, all rocks and shadow and edges. Desert. Good country for an Indian reservation....

Yuma and the muddy Colorado. Night again, and I wait shivering for the dawn.

Phoenix. Pima country. Mountains that look like cardboard sets on a forgotten stage. Tucson, Papago country. Giant cacti that look like petrified hitchhikers along the highways. Apache country. At El Paso my road-buddy decides to go on to Houston. I leave him, and head north to see mesa country. Las Cruces and the terrible Organ Mountains, jagged peaks that instill fear and wondering. Albuquerque. Pueblos along the Rio Grande. On the boardwalk there are some Indian women in colored sashes selling bits of pottery. The stone age offering its art to the twentieth century. They hold up a piece and fix the tourist with black eyes until, embarrassed, he buys or turns away. I feel suddenly angry that my people should have to do such thing for a living....

Santa Fe trains are fast, and they keep them pretty clean of bums. I decide to hurry and ride passenger coaltenders. Hide in the dark, judge the speed of the train as it leaves, and then dash out, and catch it. I hug the cold steel wall of the tender and think of the roaring fire in the engine ahead, and of the passengers back in the dining car reading their papers over hot coffee. Beneath me there is a blur of rails. Death would come quick if my hands should freeze and fall. Up over the Sangre De Cristo range, around cliffs and through canyons to Denver. Bitter cold there, and I must watch out for Denver Bob. He is a railroad bull who has thrown bums from fast freights. I miss him. It is too cold, I suppose. On north to the Sioux Country.

Small towns lit for the coming Christmas. On the streets of one I see a beam-shouldered young farmer gazing into a window filled with shining silver toasters. He is tall and wears a blue shirt buttoned, with no tie. His young wife by his side looks at him hopefully. He wants decorations for his place to hang his hat and please his woman....

Northward again. Minnesota, and great white fields of snow; frozen lakes, and dawn running into dusk without noon. Long forests wearing white. Bitter cold, and one night the northern lights. I am nearing home.

I reach Woodruff at midnight. Suddenly I am afraid, now that I am but twenty miles from home. Afraid of what my father will say, afraid of being looked on as a stranger by my own people. I sit by a fire and think about myself and all other young Indians. We just don't seem to fit anywhere—certainly not among the whites, and not among the older people. I think again about the learned sociology professor and his professing. So many things seem to be clear now that I am away from school and do not have to worry about some man's opinion of my ideas. It is easy to think while looking at dancing flames.

Morning, I spend the day cleaning up, and buying some presents for my family with what is left of my money. Nothing much, but a gift is a gift, if a man buys it with his last quarter. I wait until evening, then start up the track toward home.

Christmas Eve comes in on a north wind. Snow clouds hang over the pines, and the night comes early. Walking along the railroad bed, I feel the calm peace of snowbound forests on either side of me. I take my time; I am back in a world where time does not mean that much now. I am alone; alone but not nearly so lonely as I was back at the campus at school. Those are never lonely who love the snow and the pines; never lonely when pines are wearing white shawls and snow crunches coldly underfoot. In the woods I know there are the tracks of deer and rabbit; I know that if I leave the trails and go into the woods I shall find them. I walk along feeling glad because my legs are light and my feet seem to know that they are home. A deer comes out of the woods ahead of me, and stands silhouetted on the rails. The North, I feel, has welcomed me home. I watch him and am glad that I do not wish for a gun. He goes into the woods quietly, leaving only the design of his tracks in the snow. I walk on. Now and then I pass a field, white under the night sky, with houses at the far end. Smoke comes from the chimneys of the houses, and I try to tell what sort of wood each is burning by the smoke; some burn pine, others aspen, others tamarack. There is one from which comes black coal smoke that rises lazily and drifts out over the tops of the trees. I like to watch houses and try to imagine what might be happening in them.

Just as a light snow begins to fall I cross the reservation boundary; somehow it seems as though I have stepped into another world. Deep woods in a white-and-black winter night. A faint trail leading to the village.

The railroad on which I stand comes from a city sprawled by a lake—a city with a million people who walk around without seeing one another; a city sucking the life from all the country around; a city with stores and police and intellectuals and criminals and movies and apartment houses; a city with its politics and libraries and zoos.

Laughing, I go into the woods. As I cross a frozen lake I begin to hear the drums. Soft in the night the drums beat. It is like the pulse beat of the world. The white line of the lake ends at a black forest, and above the trees the blue winds are dancing.

I come to the outlaying houses of the village. Simple box houses, etched black in the night. From one or two windows soft lamplight falls on the snow. Christmas here, too, but it does not mean much; not much in the way of parties and presents. Joe Sky will get drunk. Alex Bodidash will buy his children red mittens and a new sled. Alex is a Carlisle man, and tries to keep his home up to white men standards. White standards. Funny that my people should be ever falling farther behind. The more they try to imitate whites the more tragic the result. Yet they want us to be imitation white men. About all we imitate well are their vices.

The village is not a sight to instill pride, yet I am not ashamed; one can never be ashamed of his own people when he knows they have dreams as beautiful as white snow on a tall pine.

Father and my brother and sister are seated around the table as I walk in. Father stares at me for a moment, then I am in his arms, crying on his shoulder. I give them the presents I have brought, and my throat tightens as I watch my sister save carefully bits of red string from the packages. I hide my feelings by wrestling with my brother when he strikes my shoulder in token of affection. Father looks at me, and I know he has many questions, but he seems to know why I have come. He tells me to go alone to the lodge, and he will follow.

I walk along the trail to the lodge, watching the northern lights forming in the heavens. White waving ribbons that seem to pulsate with the rhythm of the drums. Clean snow creaks beneath my feet, and a soft wind sighs through the trees, winging to me. Everything seems to say, "Be happy! You are home now—you are free. You are among friends—we are your friends; we, the trees, and the snow, and the lights." I follow the trail to the lodge. My feet are light, my heart seems to sing to the music, and I hold my head high. Across white snow fields blue winds are dancing.

Before the lodge door I stop, afraid, I wonder if my people will remember me. I wonder—"Am I Indian, or am I white?" I stand before the door a long time. I hear the ice groan on the lake, and remember the story of the old woman under the ice, trying to get out, so she can punish some runaway lovers. I think to myself, "If I am white I will not believe that story; If I am Indian, I will know that there is an old woman under the ice." I listen for a while, and I know that there is an old woman under the ice. I look again at the lights, and go in.

Inside the lodge there are many Indians. Some sit on benches around the walls, other dance in the center of the floor around a drum. Nobody seems to notice me. It seems as though I were among a people I have never seen before. Heavy women with long hair. Women with children on their knees—small children that watch with intent black eyes the movements of the dancers, whose small faces are solemn and serene. The faces of the old people are serene, too, and their eyes are merry and bright. I look at the old men. Straight, dressed in dark trousers and beaded velvet vests, wearing soft moccasins. Dark, lined faces intent on the music. I wonder if I am at all like them. They dance on, lifting their feet to the rhythm of the drums swaying lightly, looking upward. I look at their eyes, and am startled at the rapt attention to the rhythm of the music.

The dance stops. The men walk back to the walks, and talk in low tones or with their hands. There is little conversation, yet everyone seems to be sharing some secret. A woman looks at a small boy wandering away, and he comes back to her.

Strange, I think and then remember. These people are not sharing words—they are sharing a mood. Everyone is happy. I am so used to white people that it seems strange so many people could be together without someone talking. These Indians are happy because they are together, and because the night is beautiful outside, and the music is beautiful. I try hard to forget school and white people, and be one of these—my people. I try to forget everything but the night, and it is a part of me that I am one with my people and we are all a part of something universal. I watch eyes, and see now that the old people are speaking to me. They nod slightly, imperceptibly, and their eyes laugh into mine. I look around the room. All the eyes are friendly; they all laugh. No one questions my being here. The drums begin to beat again, and I catch to invitation in the eyes of the old men. My feet begin to lift to the rhythm, and I looked out beyond the walls into the night and see the lights. I am happy. It is beautiful. I am home. [1938]

Walt Whitman

When I Heard the Learn'd Astronomer

When I heard the learn'd astronomer,
When the proofs, the figures, were ranged in columns before me,
When I was shown the charts and diagrams, to add, divide, and measure them,

When I sitting heard the astronomer where he lectured with much applause in the
lecture-room,
How soon unaccountable I became tired and sick,
Till rising and gliding out I wander'd off by myself,
In the mystical moist night-air, and from time to time,
Look'd up in perfect silence at the stars.

[1865]

Theresa Williams

Urgent Note for My Son Langston

***to be pinned to his collar upon age eleven*

This is Langston.
He likes mutant turtles and the ghost grey
power ranger please
do not
shoot him he
is your new friend he
will jump in your arms
and ask
to be swung
in circles not
in news spin please he
is scared of very loud
noises and he would not
respond to a shot he
might just fall in dirt
infra red and not move at

all like when we play ninjas and he is the blackest
because he say that's the baddest

and I say no but
he say yes so
I'm the blackest

so how to make easy
topic better get meta
and none of this race shit really matters so
lowbrow I talk hawking but he waffles
and I don't give a fuck 'bout
machines stretched in time

I would just like Langston man boy
demon home
in time please don't

kill him he likes pancakes not waffles
like on Sundays when he asks for extra syrup
I pour on so much syrup
yes please
don't fire we hymn strange hold
hands I put him on hips even
alters big
ger black
er and scary

arms scarecrow my neck brow clammy
while he mouths the word god then mom
round his tongue, spun like a fat marble.

And I know this note is a little long, but I just thought you should know that
this is Langston
and I love him he absorbs all the light
and so can you I mean yes
he's not an angel stole once maybe twice
you learned his lesson well he

is or might be volatile please
return home safe so I can see the blue white
light from top peaks of his covers pulled tight
round his door bends blackbodies soft
sweet pulse a blue night [2015]

Jeanette Winterson

The Three Friends

Once upon a time there were two friends who found a third. Liking no one better in the whole world, they vowed to live in one palace, sail in one ship, and fight one fight with equal arms.

After three months they decided to go on a quest.

"What shall we seek?" they asked each other. The first said "Gold."

The second said "Wives."

The third said "That which cannot be found."

They all agreed that this last was best and so they set off in fine array.

After a while they came to a house that celebrated ceilings and denied floors. As they marched through the front door they were only just in time to save themselves from dropping into a deep pit. While they clung in terror to the wainscotting, they looked up and saw chandeliers, bright as swords, that hung and glittered and lit the huge room where the guests came to and fro. The room was arranged for dinner, tables and chairs suspended from great chains. An armoury of knives and forks laid out in case the eaters knocked one into the abyss.

There was a trumpet sound and the guests began to enter the room through a trap door in the ceiling. Some were suspended on wires, others walked across ropes slender as youth. In this way they were all able to join their place setting. When all were assembled, the trumpet blew again, and the head of the table looked down and said to the three friends, "What is it you seek?"

"That which cannot be found."

"It is not here" she answered, "but take some gold," and each of the diners threw down a solid gold plate, rather in the manner that the Doge of Venice used to throw his dinnerware into the canal to show how much he despised worldly things.

Our three friends did not despise worldly things, and caught as many of the plates as they could. Loaded down with treasure they continued on their way, though more slowly than before.

Eventually they came to Turkey, and to the harem of Mustapha the Blessed CIXX. Blessed he was, so piled with ladies, that only his index finger could be seen. Crooking it he bade the friends come forward, and asked in a muffled voice, "What is it you seek?"

"That which cannot be found."

"It is not here," he said in a ghostly smother, "but take some wives."

The friends were delighted, but observing the fate of Mustapha, they did not take too many. Each took six and made them carry the gold plate.

Helter skelter down the years the friends continued their journey, crossing continents of history and geography, gathering by chance the sum of the world, so that nothing was missing that could be had.

At last they came to a tower in the middle of the sea. A man with the face of centuries and the voice of the wind opened a narrow window and called,

"What is it you seek?"

"That which cannot be found... found... found" and the wind twisted their voices into the air.

"It has found you" said the man.

They heard a noise behind them like a scythe cutting the water and when they looked they saw a ship thin as a blade gaining towards them. The figure rowed it standing up, with one oar that was not an oar. They saw the curve of the metal flashing, first this side and then that. They saw the rower throw back his hood. They saw him beckon to them and the world tilted. The sea poured away.

Who are they with fish and starfish in their hair? [2013]

James Wright

A Blessing

Just off the highway to Rochester, Minnesota,
Twilight bounds softly forth on the grass.
And the eyes of those two Indian ponies
Darken with kindness.
They have come gladly out of the willows
To welcome my friend and me.
We step over the barbed wire into the pasture
Where they have been grazing all day, alone.
They ripple tensely, they can hardly contain their happiness
That we have come.
They bow shyly as wet swans. They love each other.
There is no loneliness like theirs.
At home once more,
They begin munching the young tufts of spring in the darkness.
I would like to hold the slenderer one in my arms,
For she has walked over to me
And nuzzled my left hand.
She is black and white,
Her mane falls wild on her forehead,
And the light breeze moves me to caress her long ear
That is delicate as the skin over a girl's wrist.
Suddenly I realize
That if I stepped out of my body I would break
Into blossom.

[1992]

Bethany Yeager

Divorce

Father bought the wrong kind of fertilizer. He's in the kitchen with mother now, shouting about it and *how different can it be, anyway?* Mother is shouting counterpoint, her voice softening dangerously when father gets too loud, then revving up once he pauses for a breath. My father is shouting a lot of calming words: *it doesn't matter, it will work out just fine, there's nothing to worry about.* Mother's not buying it.

In the garden, I hear but don't listen to the battle echoing inside the house. My attention is fixed on the dark purple vines that are creeping out into the yard. Like any good sneaking soldier, each tendril hugs the ground as it spreads, thorns tasting their way through grass and mud and the wrong kind of fertilizer. The soil churns as they spread. As I watch it, I wonder what the word "soil" really means. To my father—an engineer—soil is any unconsolidated sediment. To my mother—a gardener—soil is dirt that can sustain life. Soil contains carbon, the word that still tastes funny in my mouth. The element in our body that survives fire, freezing, burial. The element that supports life.

Now the vines wrap about my ankles, tickling the soles of my feet. They grind through my skin like soil, red iron dripping from my toes and ankles. Behind me, the rhythm continues. *It's not that hard, you just never listen.* Rain mimics the cadence of mother's voice, tapping on my face with *you're never here anymore, you're never engaged.* Roses are blooming, weaving in and out of the vine and piercing my skin. I fall apart like clumps of dirt while flowers tumble out of my eyes.

You're crazy! You're just crazy. I can't take this anymore. Grass tastes like mint leaves, rain sparkles as it falls harder, and I remember the words my mom told me so many years before. *Life is a garden. You must nurture it, prune away the parts of yourself that are selfish and ungiving, water your talents with rich nutrients. Cherish them. Never let your life stagnate and fester without trying to grow it a little. What is a garden without a gardener? And what is a life lived without self-discipline and care? Chaos.*

Chaos, chaos like the thunder and lightning raining down overhead, like a hundred vines with roses overrun by thorns. Like a yawning earth shaking homes down to their foundations, like a wildfire lunging over foaming rivers by clasping the trees on each bank.

I take my time, I sneak forward. My skin is soil, moist from the humidity and darkened by the churning of the vines. Worms and seeds and petals huddle inside me for warmth, grass follows my path like a bridesmaid with a veil. There waits an entire world of pavement and cars and houses, serene lies slumbering between *man* and *wife*. I will creep outward, encircling and crushing and rolling them all into soil. Lightning flashes as a door slams. There's an engine revving back from the house. Or is it thunder? [2016]

Permissions Acknowledgments

Agodon, Kelli Russell. "Geography," from *Geography*. Floating Bridges Press, 2003. Reprinted with the permission of Kelli Russell Agodon.

Ak'Abal, Humberto. "The Dance," from *The FSG Book of Twentieth-Century Latin American Poetry*, translated by Ilan Stavans. Farrar, Straus and Giroux, 2011. Copyright © 2011 by Ilan Stavans. Used by permission of Ilan Stavans.

Alexie, Sherman. "Totem Sonnet One" and "Totem Sonnet Seven," from *The Summer of Black Widows*. Copyright © 1996 by Sherman Alexie. Hanging Loose Press, 1996. Reprinted with the permission of Hanging Loose Press.

Alfred, Taiaiake. "What I Think of When I Think of Skin," from *In the Flesh: Twenty Writers Explore the Body*, edited by Kathy Page and Lynne Van Luven. Brindle and Glass, 2012. Reprinted with the permission of Taiaiake Alfred.

Allison, Dorothy. Excerpt from *Two or Three Things I Know for Sure*. Copyright © 1995 by Dorothy Allison. Used by permission of Dutton, an imprint of Penguin Publishing Group, a division of Penguin Random House LLC.

Anderson, Sherwood. "Death in the Woods," from *Death in the Woods and Other Stories*, first published in *The American Mercury*. Copyright © 1926 by American Mercury Inc. Copyright renewed 1953 by Eleanor Copenhaver Anderson. Reprinted with the permission of Harold Ober Associates Incorporated.

Arenas, Reinaldo. "The Downpour," from *Before Night Falls: A Memoir*, translated by Dolores M. Koch. Copyright © 1992 by the Estate of Reinaldo Arenas; translation copyright © 1993 by the Estate of Reinaldo Arenas and Dolores M. Koch. Used by permission of Viking Books, an imprint of Penguin Publishing Group, a division of Penguin Random House LLC.

Bachinsky, Elizabeth. "For the Pageant Girls," from *Home of Sudden Service*. Nightwood Editions, 2006; www.nightwoodeditions.com. Reprinted with the permission of Nightwood Editions.

Bashō, Matsuo. Untitled Haiku, from *Narrow Road to the Interior and Other Writings*, translated by Sam Hamill. Copyright © 1998 by Sam Hamill. Reprinted by arrangement with The Permissions Company, Inc., on behalf of Shambhala Publications Inc., Boulder, CO. www.shambhala.com.

Bauby, Jean-Dominique. "Bathtime," from *The Diving Bell and the Butterfly: A Memoir of Life in Death*, translated by Jeremy Leggatt. Translation © 1997 by Alfred A. Knopf, a division of Penguin Random House LLC. Reprinted in the United States by permission of Alfred A. Knopf, an imprint of the Knopf Doubleday Publishing Group, a division of Penguin Random House LLC. All rights reserved. Any third party use of this material, outside of this publication, is prohibited. Interested parties must apply directly to Penguin Random House LLC for permission.

Beard, Jo Ann. "The Fourth State of Matter," from *The Boys of My Youth*. Copyright © 1998 by Jo Ann Beard. Reprinted with the permission of Little, Brown and Company. All rights reserved.

Bloom, Barbara. "Making Things Right," from *On the Water Meridian*. Hummingbird Press, 2007. Reprinted with the permission of Barbara Bloom.

Bolster, Stephanie. "Many Have Written Poems about Blackberries," from *Two Bowls of Milk*. Toronto: McClelland & Stewart, 1999. Reprinted with the permission of Stephanie Bolster.

Broughton, T. Alan. "Song for Sampson," from *A World Remembered*. Copyright © 2010 by T. Alan Broughton. Reprinted with the permission of The Permissions Company, Inc., on behalf of Carnegie Mellon University Press.

Carr, Emily. "The Cow Yard," from *The Book of Small*. Douglas and McIntyre, 2004.

Carver, Raymond. "Chef's House," from *Cathedral*. Copyright © 1981, 1982, 1983 by Tess Gallagher. Reprinted with the permission of Alfred A. Knopf, an imprint of the Knopf Doubleday Publishing Group, a division of Penguin Random House LLC. All rights reserved. Any third party use of this material, outside of this publication, is prohibited. Interested parties must apply directly to Penguin Random House LLC for permission.

Cashier, Arlan. "Lost Sweater," reprinted with the permission of Arlan Cashier.

Choi, Ann. "The Shower," from *Premonitions: The Kaya Anthology of New Asian North American Poetry*, edited by Walter K. Lew. Kaya/Muae, 1995. Originally published in *The Asian American Literary Realm*, No. 4, 1991.

Cisneros, Sandra. "My Wicked Wicked Ways," from *My Wicked Wicked Ways*. Copyright © 1987 by Sandra Cisneros. By special arrangement with Third Woman Press. Published by Vintage Books in paperback and ebook, in hardcover by Alfred A. Knopf, and originally by Third Woman Press. By permission of Susan Bergholz Literary Services, New York, NY and Lamy, NM. All rights reserved.

Coyote, Ivan E. "This, That, and the Other Thing," from *Close to Spider Man*. Arsenal Pulp Press, 2000. Reprinted with the permission of Arsenal Pulp Press.

Crace, Jim. Untitled #17, from *The Devil's Larder*. Viking/Penguin Group, 2001. Copyright © 2001 by Jim Crace. Reprinted in Canada with the permission of Penguin Books Ltd. Reprinted in the United States by permission of Farrar, Straus and Giroux, LLC.

Crews, James. "Lover Boys," from *One Hundred Small Yellow Envelopes*. Parallel Press, University of Wisconsin-Madison Libraries, 2009. Reprinted with the permission of James Crews.

Crozier, Lorna. "first cause: light," from *small beneath the sky: A Prairie Memoir*. Greystone Books, 2010. Reprinted with the permission of Greystone Books, Ltd.

Crummey, Michael. "Bread," from *Hard Light: Brick Books Classics 5*. Brick Books, 2015. Reprinted with the permission of Brick Books.

Dao, James. Excerpt from "Families of Military Suicides Seek White House Condolences," in *The New York Times*, November 25, 2009. Copyright © 2009 The New York Times. All rights reserved. Used by permission and protected by the Copyright Laws of the United States. The printing, copying, redistribution, or retransmission of this content without express written permission is prohibited.

Diaz, Natalie. "My Brother at 3 A.M.," from *When My Brother Was an Aztec*. Copyright © 2012 by Natalie Diaz. Reprinted with the permission of The Permissions Company, Inc., on behalf of Copper Canyon Press, www.coppercanyonpress.org.

Dillard, Annie. "Signals at Sea," from *Mornings Like This: Found Poems*. Copyright © 1995 by Annie Dillard. Reprinted by permission of HarperCollins Publishers.

Doyle, Brian. "Leap," from *Leaping: Revelations and Epiphanies*. Loyola Press, 2013. Reprinted with the permission of Loyola Press, www.loyolabooks.org.

Dumont, Marilyn. "Still Unsaved Soul," from *A Really Good Brown Girl: Brick Books Classics 4*. Brick Books, 2015. Reprinted with the permission of Brick Books.

Flenniken, Kathleen. "What I Saw," from *Famous*. Copyright © 2006 by the Board of Regents of the University of Nebraska Press. Reprinted with the permission of the University of Nebraska Press.

Forché, Carolyn. "The Colonel," from *The Country Between Us*. Copyright © 1981 by Carolyn Forché. Originally appeared in *Women's International Resource Exchange*. Reprinted by permission of HarperCollins Publishers.

García Márquez, Gabriel. "The Handsomest Drowned Man in the World," from *Leaf Storm & Other Stories*. Copyright © 1971 by Gabriel García Márquez. Reprinted by permission of HarperCollins Publishers.

Green, Samuel. "Some Reasons Why I Became a Poet," from *The Grace of Necessity*. Copyright © 2008 by Samuel Green. "Stroke," from *All That Might Be Done*. Copyright © 2014 by Samuel Green. Both reprinted with the Permission of The Permissions Company, Inc., on behalf of Carnegie Mellon University Press.

Hales, Corrine. "Power," from *Underground*. Copyright © 1986 Corrine Hales. Reprinted with the permission of The Permissions Company, Inc., on behalf of Asahta Press, http://ahsahtapress.boisestate.edu.

Halme, Kathleen. "A Study in *O*," from *Equipoise*. Copyright © 1998 by Kathleen Halme. Reprinted with the permission of The Permissions Company, Inc., on behalf of Sarabande Books, www.sarabandebooks.org.

Hamby, Barbara. "Ode to My 1977 Toyota," from *Babel*. Copyright © 2004 by Barbara Hamby. Reprinted by permission of the University of Pittsburgh Press.

Hampl, Patricia. "Red Sky in the Morning," from *I Could Tell You Stories: Sojourns in the Land of Memory*. Copyright © 1999 by Patricia Hampl. Used by permission of W.W. Norton & Company, Inc.

Harjo, Joy. "Suspended," from *Crazy Brave: A Memoir*. Copyright © 2012 by Joy Harjo. Used by permission of W.W. Norton & Company, Inc.

Hayes, Terrance. "The Same City," from *Hip Logic*. Copyright © 2002 by Terrance Hayes. Used by permission of Penguin Books, an imprint of Penguin Publishing Group, a division of Penguin Random House LLC.

Hemingway, Ernest. "Hills Like White Elephants," from *The Short Stories of Ernest Hemingway*. Copyright © 1927 by Charles Scribner's Sons. Copyright © renewed 1955 by Ernest Hemingway. Reprinted with the permission of Scribner, a division of Simon & Schuster, Inc. All rights reserved.

Hughes, Langston. "Harlem (2)," from *The Collected Poems of Langston Hughes*. Editor, A. Rampersad; Associate Editor, David Roessel. Copyright © 1994 by the Estate of Langston Hughes. Used by permission of Alfred A. Knopf, an imprint of the Knopf Doubleday Publishing Group, a division of Penguin Random House LLC. All rights reserved. Any third party use of this material, outside of this publication, is prohibited. Interested parties must apply directly to Penguin Random House LLC for permission.

Hummel, Maria. "I'm This Many," from *House and Fire*. *American Poetry Review*, November/December 2013. Reprinted with the permission of Maria Hummel.

Ignatow, David. "The Bagel," from *Against the Evidence: Selected Poems 1934–1994*. Copyright © 1993 by David Ignatow. Reprinted with the permission of Wesleyan University Press.

Johnson, Denis. "Steady Hands at Seattle General," from *Jesus' Son*. Copyright © 1992 by Denis Johnson. Reprinted by permission of Farrar, Straus and Giroux, LLC.

Kahakauwila, Kristiana. "Thirty-Nine Rules for Making a Hawaiian Funeral into a Drinking Game," from *This Is Paradise: Stories*. Copyright © 2013 by Kristiana Kahakauwila. Reprinted by permission of Crown Books, an imprint of the Crown Publishing Group, a division of Penguin Random House LLC. All rights reserved. Any third party use of this material, outside of this publication, is prohibited. Interested parties must apply directly to Penguin Random House LLC for permission.

Kapil, Bhanu. "Three Voices," from *In Short: A Collection of Brief Creative Nonfiction*. Norton, 1996. Reprinted with the permission of Bhanu Kapil.

Knudsen, Rachel. "How to Enter the Ocean," from *Geist 64*, 2007.

Kurono, Yasuko. Haiku, untitled ["Winter and summer solstice ..."]. Reprinted with the permission of Yasuko Kurono.

Kuusisto, Stephen. "Horse," from *Eavesdropping: A Life by Ear*. Copyright © 2006 by Stephen Kuusisto. Used by permission of W.W. Norton & Company, Inc.

Lane, Patrick. "The Far Field," from *Mortal Remains*. Exile Editions, 1999. Reprinted with the permission of Patrick Lane.

Lau, Evelyn. "An Insatiable Emptiness," from *Inside Out: Reflections of a Life So Far*. Doubleday, 2001. Reprinted with the permission of Evelyn Lau.

Lefkowitz, Josh. "Saturday Salutation," as seen at https://winningwriters.com/past-winning-entries/saturday-salutation. Reprinted with the permission of Josh Lefkowitz.

Lester, Susan. "Belongings," from *Ploughshares*, Fall 1994; as seen at http://susanlynnlester.com/stories/Belongings.pdf. Reprinted with the permission of Susan Lester.

Lisicky, Paul. "Snapshot, Harvey Cedars: 1948," from *Flash Fiction: 72 Very Short Stories*. Norton, 1992. Reprinted with the permission of Paul Lisicky.

Livingston, Sonja. "The Ghetto Girls' Guide to Dating and Romance," from *Short Takes: Brief Encounters with Contemporary Nonfiction*, edited by Judith Kitchen. W.W. Norton & Company, 2005. Reprinted with the permission of Sonja Livingston.

Lockwood, Patricia. "Rape Joke," from *Motherland Fatherland Homelandsexuals*. Copyright © 2014 by Patricia Lockwood. Used by permission of Penguin Books, an imprint of Penguin Publishing Group, a division of Penguin Random House LLC.

MacLeod, Alistair. "The Boat," excerpted from *Island: The Complete Stories* (US). Reprinted in the United States by permission of W.W. Norton & Company, Inc. Excerpted from *Island: The Collected Stories* (Canada). Reprinted in Canada by permission of McClelland & Stewart, a division of Penguin Random House Canada Limited. Copyright © 2000 Alistair MacLeod.

Marshall, John W. Part 22, "Taken With," ["I was back to help clean out her room"], from *Meaning a Cloud*. Oberlin College Press, 2008. Reprinted with the permission of Oberlin College Press.

Martínez Pompa, Paul. "Exclamation Point," from *My Kill Adore Him*. Notre Dame University Press, 2009.

McConnell, Marty. "Frida Kahlo to Marty McConnell," published in *Salt Hill Journal*, Issue 23; as seen at http://www.martyoutloud.com/frida-kahlo-to-marty-mcconnell/. Reprinted with the permission of Marty McConnell.

Mendoza, Carlos. "Young Don Juan," reprinted with the permission of Carlos Mendoza.

Millay, Edna St. Vincent. "[What lips my lips have kissed, and where, and why]," from *Collected Poems*. Copyright © 1923, 1951 by Edna St. Vincent Millay and Norma Millay Ellis. Reprinted with the permission of The Permissions Company, Inc., on behalf of Holly Peppe, Literary Executor, The Edna St. Vincent Millay Society, www.millay.org.

Miller, Brenda. "Getting Yourself Home," from *Blessing of the Animals*. Eastern Washington University Press, 2009. Reprinted with the permission of Brenda Miller.

Minder, Madison. "Green," reprinted with the permission of Madison Minder.

Mirikitani, Janice. "Recipe," from *Shedding Silence*. Copyright © 1987 by Janice Mirikitani. Reprinted with the permission of Celestial Arts, an imprint of the Crown Publishing Group, a division of Penguin Random House LLC. All rights reserved. Any third party use of this material, outside of this publication, is prohibited. Interested parties must apply directly to Penguin Random House LLC for permission.

Mootoo, Shani. "Out on Main Street," from *Out on Main Street*. Copyright © 1993 by Shani Mootoo. Reprinted with the permission of Shani Mootoo.

Murray, Donald M. "Chapter 13: War Stories Untold," from *My Twice-Lived Life: A Memoir*. Copyright © 2001 by Donald M. Murray. Used by permission of Ballantine Books, an imprint of Random House, a division of Penguin Random House LLC. All rights reserved.

Nezhukumatathil, Aimee. "The Witching Hour," from *Creative Writing: Four Genres in Brief*, edited by David Starkey. Bedford/St. Martin's, 2008. Reprinted with the permission of Aimee Nezhukumatathil.

Nordan, Lewis. "Owls," from *Music of the Swamp*. Copyright © 1992 by Lewis Nordan. Reprinted with the permission of Algonquin Books of Chapel Hill. All rights reserved.
Norman, Howard. Excerpt from "I Hate to Leave This Beautiful Place," from *I Hate to Leave This Beautiful Place*. Copyright © 2013 by Howard Norman. Reprinted with the permission of Houghton Mifflin Harcourt Publishing Company. All rights reserved.

Novak, B.J. "Julie & the Warlord," from *One More Thing: Stories and Other Stories*. Copyright © 2014 by B.J. Novak. Used by permission of Alfred A. Knopf, an imprint of the Knopf Doubleday Publishing Group, a division of Penguin Random House LLC. All rights reserved. Any third party use of this material, outside of this publication, is prohibited. Interested parties must apply directly to Penguin Random House LLC for permission.

O'Connor, Flannery. "A Good Man Is Hard to Find," from *A Good Man Is Hard to Find and Other Stories*. Copyright © 1953 by Flannery O'Connor. Copyright © renewed 1981 by Regina O'Connor. Reprinted with the permission of Houghton Mifflin Harcourt Publishing Company. All rights reserved.

Oliver, Mary. "The Summer Day," from *House of Light*. Boston: Beacon Press. Copyright © 1990 by Mary Oliver. Reprinted with the permission of The Charlotte Sheedy Literary Agency Inc.

Ondaatje, Michael. "The Cinnamon Peeler," from *The Cinnamon Peeler*. Copyright © 1989 by Michael Ondaatje. Reprinted in Canada with the permission of Michael Ondaatje. Reprinted in the United States by permission of Alfred A. Knopf, an imprint of the Knopf Doubleday Publishing Group, a division of Penguin Random House LLC. All rights reserved. Any third party use of this material, outside of this publication, is prohibited. Interested parties must apply directly to Penguin Random House LLC for permission.

Opel, Mallory. "Among the Blossoms," reprinted with the permission of Mallory Opel.

Ortiz, Simon J. "My Father's Song," from *A Good Journey*. University of Arizona Press, 1985. Copyright © Simon J. Ortiz. Reprinted with the permission of Simon J. Ortiz.

Pagh, Nancy. "After I Die," from *No Sweeter Fat*. Copyright © 2007 by Nancy Pagh. Reprinted with the permission of The Permissions Company, Inc., on behalf of Autumn House Press, www.autumnhousepress.org. "Love Song: After T.S. Eliot" reprinted with the permission of Nancy Pagh.

Partridge, Elise. "Edwin Partridge," from *Chameleon Hours*. House of Anansi Press, 2008. Reprinted in Canada with the permission of House of Anansi Press. Copyright © 2008 by The University of Chicago. Reprinted in the United States with the permission of The University of Chicago Press.

Plath, Sylvia. "Mirror," from *Crossing the Water*. Copyright © 1963 by Ted Hughes. Originally appeared in *The New Yorker*. Reprinted by permission of HarperCollins Publishers.

Purpura, Lia. "September 9," from *Increase*. Copyright © 2000 by Lia Purpura. The University of Georgia Press, 2000. Reprinted with the permission of The University of Georgia Press.
Queyras, Sina. "On the Scent, #14," from Lemon Hound. Copyright © 2006 by Sina Queyras. Coach House Books, 2006. Reprinted with the permission of Coach House Books.

Rich, Simon. "Unprotected," from *The Last Girlfriend on Earth and Other Stories*. Copyright © 2013 by Simon Rich. Reprinted with the permission of Little, Brown and Company.

Rilke, Rainer Maria. "Archaic Torso of Apollo," from *Ahead of All Parting: The Selected Poetry and Prose of Rainer Maria Rilke*, edited and translated by Stephen Mitchell. Translation copyright © 1982 by Stephen Mitchell. Reprinted with the permission of Random House, an imprint and division of Penguin Random House LLC. All rights reserved. Any third party use of this material, outside of this publication, is prohibited. Interested parties must apply directly to Penguin Random House LLC for permission.

Sedaris, David. "The Drama Bug," from *Naked*. Copyright © 1997 by David Sedaris. Reprinted with the permission of Little, Brown and Company. All rights reserved.

Seibles, Tim. "Treatise," from *Hurdy Gurdy*. Copyright © 1992 by Tim Seibles. Reprinted with the permission of The Permissions Company, Inc., on behalf of the Cleveland State University Poetry Center.

Selzer, Richard. "The Knife," from *Mortal Lessons: Notes on the Art of Surgery*. Copyright © 1974, 1975, 1976, 1987 by Richard Selzer. Reprinted by permission of Georges Borchardt, Inc., on behalf of the author.

Shelton, Richard. "The Stones," from *Selected Poems 1969–1981*. Copyright © 1982. Reprinted with the permission of the University of Pittsburgh Press.

Shumaker, Peggy. "Moving Water, Tucson," from *Just Breathe Normally*. Copyright © 2007 by the Board of Regents of the University of Nebraska. Reprinted with the permission of the University of Nebraska Press.

Siken, Richard. "Scheherezade," from *Crush*. Copyright © 2005 by Yale University. Reprinted with the permission of the publisher, Yale University Press.

Sleigh, Tom. "Aubade," from *Waking*. University of Chicago Press, 1990. Copyright © 1990 by the University of Chicago. Reprinted with the permission of the University of Chicago Press.

Smith, Patricia. "Hip-Hop Ghazal," from *Poetry Magazine*, July/August 2007. Reprinted with the permission of Patricia Smith.

Spragg, Mark. "In Wyoming," from "Wind," in *Where Rivers Change Direction*. Riverhead Books, 2000. Reprinted with the permission of Nancy Stauffer Associates.

Staples, Brent. "The Coroner's Photographs," from *Parallel Time: Growing Up in Black and White*. Copyright © 1994 by Brent Staples. Reprinted with the permission of Pantheon Books, an imprint of the Knopf Doubleday Publishing Group, a division of Penguin Random House LLC. All rights reserved.

Sutin, Lawrence. "Father Holding Baby," from *Postcard Memoir*. Copyright © 2003 by Lawrence Sutin. Reprinted with the permission of The Permissions Company, Inc., on behalf of Graywolf Press, Minneapolis, Minnesota; www.graywolfpress.org.

Tan, Amy. "Confessions," copyright © 1997 by Amy Tan. Reprinted with the permission of the author and the Sandra Dijkstra Literary Agency.

Thien, Madeleine. "Simple Recipes," from *Simple Recipes*. Copyright © 2001 by Madeleine Thien. Reprinted in the United States with the permission of The Wylie Agency LLC. Reprinted in Canada by permission of McClelland & Stewart, a division of Penguin Random House Canada Limited.

Turner, Brian. "Eulogy," from *Here, Bullet*. Copyright © 2005. Reprinted with the permission of The Permissions Company, Inc., on behalf of Alice James Books, www.alicejamesbooks.org.

Tyner, James. "At a Barbecue for R.C. One Week after He Is Out of Iraq," from *The Ghetto Exorcist*. Copyright © 2009 by James Tyner. Reprinted with the permission of The Permissions Company Inc., on behalf of Autumn House Press, www.autumnhouse.org.

Uppal, Priscila. "Sorry, I Forgot to Clean Up After Myself," from *Ontological Necessities*. Exile Editions, 2006. Reprinted with the permission of Priscila Uppal.

Valenzuela, Luisa. "Vision Out of the Corner of One Eye," from *Strange Things Happen Here: Twenty-Six Short Stories and a Novel*, translated by Helen Lane. English translation copyright © 1979 by Houghton Mifflin Harcourt Publishing Company. Reprinted with the permission of Luisa Valenzuela and Houghton Mifflin Harcourt Publishing Company. All rights reserved.

Wallace, David Foster. "Incarnations of Burned Children," from *Oblivion*. Copyright © 2004 by David Foster Wallace. Used by permission of Little, Brown and Company.

Whitecloud III, Thomas S. "Blue Winds Dancing," 1938. Reprinted with the permission of the Estate of Thomas Whitecloud III.

Wilbur, Richard. "Sleepless at Crown Point," from *The Mind-Reader*. Copyright © 1971 and renewed 1999 by Richard Wilbur. Reprinted with the permission of Houghton Mifflin Harcourt Publishing Company. All rights reserved.

Williams, Theresa. "Urgent Note for My Son Langston," published in *Jeopardy*, Issue 51, 2015. Reprinted with the permission of Theresa Williams.

Winterson, Jeanette. "The Three Friends," from *The World and Other Places: Stories*. Copyright © 1998 by Jeanette Winterson. Reprinted in Canada with the permisson of Alfred A. Knopf Canada, a division of Penguin Random House Canada Limited. Reprinted in the United States by permission of Alfred A. Knopf, an imprint of the Knopf Doubleday Publishing Group, a division of Penguin Random House LLC. All rights reserved. Any third party use of this material, outside of this publication, is prohibited. Interested parties must apply directly to Penguin Random House LLC for permission.

Wright, James. "A Blessing," from *The Branch Will Not Break*, copyright © 1963 by James Wright. Published by Wesleyan University Press; reprinted with permission.

Yeager, Bethany. "Divorce," reprinted with the permission of Bethany Yeager.

Young, Kevin. Excerpt from "Ode to the Midwest," from *Dear Darkness: Poems*. Copyright © 2008 by Kevin Young. Used by permission of Alfred A. Knopf, an imprint of the Knopf Doubleday Publishing Group, a division of Penguin Random House LLC. All rights reserved. Any third party use of this material, outside of this publication, is prohibited. Interested parties must apply directly to Penguin Random House LLC for permission.

The publisher has endeavored to contact rights holders for all copyrighted material, and would appreciate receiving any information as to errors or omissions.

Index

From the Publisher

A name never says it all, but the word "Broadview" expresses a good deal of the philosophy behind our company. We are open to a broad range of academic approaches and political viewpoints. We pay attention to the broad impact book publishing and book printing has in the wider world; for some years now we have used 100% recycled paper for most titles. Our publishing program is internationally oriented and broad-ranging. Our individual titles often appeal to a broad readership too; many are of interest as much to general readers as to academics and students.

Founded in 1985, Broadview remains a fully independent company owned by its shareholders—not an imprint or subsidiary of a larger multinational.

For the most accurate information on our books (including information on pricing, editions, and formats) please visit our website at www.broadviewpress.com. Our print books and ebooks are also available for sale on our site.

broadview press
www.broadviewpress.com

This book is made of paper from well-managed FSC® - certified forests, recycled materials, and other controlled sources.

Arm Knitting

Arm Knitting

30 no-needle projects for you and your home

Contents

Introduction

Arm knitting—it's exactly what it sounds like. Instead of working with knitting needles, you knit on your arms. If you don't know how to knit, this is the perfect way to get acquainted with the craft. That's because it's easier than learning to manage cumbersome needles, but you still create the same stitches. If you're new to arm knitting, be warned: It's incredibly addictive—and fun for everyone.

Four reasons to arm knit

It's fast

Traditional knitting involves multiple stitches and different sizes of needles. But in arm knitting, your arms are like giant needles, and you typically use multiple strands of really thick yarn held together. Pairing big "needles" and big yarns means you can create several inches of knitting with just one row. You'll be amazed at how quickly you can knit scarves, home décor, and many other objects.

It's easy

You don't need to have any previous knitting experience to arm knit. In fact, you can get away with learning just a single stitch: the knit stitch. You can make many of the projects in this book with just that technique. If you become addicted—and you will—then you can try other stitches, like purling, cabling, and shaping.

It's fun

Arm knitting is enjoyable because you can almost effortlessly make a project in less than an hour, but it's also fun because you can experiment with many different fibers and stitches. You'll love choosing yarns and then seeing how they work up when you use a different number of strands. Success with arm knitting might even inspire you to design your own projects.

It's beautiful

Arm knitting is a great way to show off stunning chunky yarns. Because the stitches are large, they perfectly set off interesting textures. Your arm knitted accessories will look like they've been plucked right off the runway, while your arm knitted home décor will look cozy and stylish.

Arm knitting is something
you'll definitely want to
share with friends,
discussing ideas
and techniques
as well as knitting together.
And because you can
do this almost anywhere,
it's conducive to socializing.

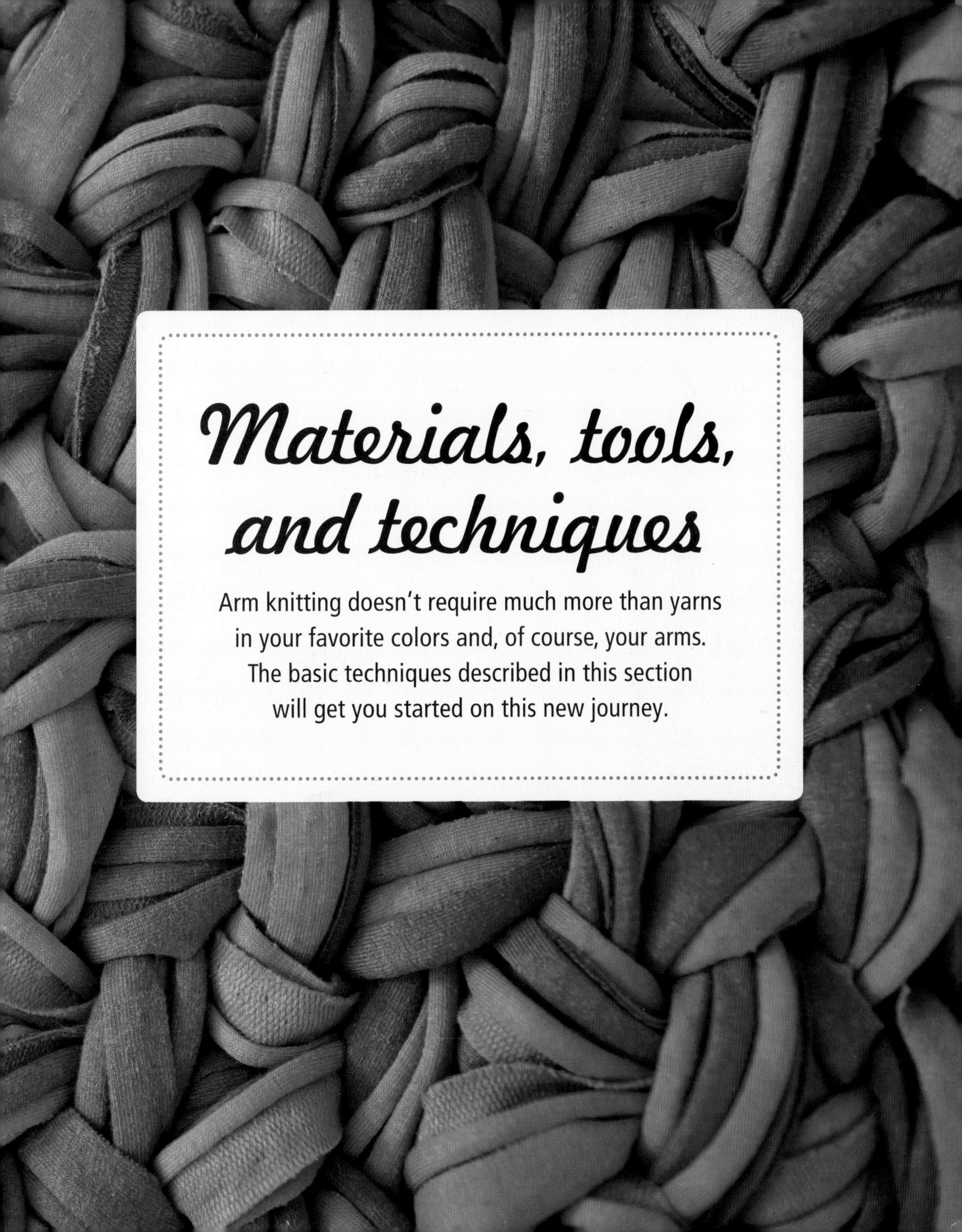

Materials, tools, and techniques

Arm knitting doesn't require much more than yarns in your favorite colors and, of course, your arms. The basic techniques described in this section will get you started on this new journey.

Yarns

Learning about the yarns that will work best for arm knitting will make this activity enjoyable. You'll have a chance to work with yarns of varying weights, including heavier yarns that are hard to use with needles but are ideal for arms.

Fibers

The fiber you choose for a project depends on a couple different factors. If you're arm knitting an item that needs frequent laundering, choose a superwash wool or a washable cotton or acrylic. If you're on a budget, choose a low-cost synthetic yarn so you can get more bulk at a lower cost.

Animal fiber

Animal fiber can include anything from wool to alpaca to mohair. Animal fiber is perfect for winter accessories and garments. While such fibers are warm and luxurious, remember to diligently follow the care instructions.

You should wash most animal fibers in cold water and by hand. Otherwise, the fibers will felt together and ruin your beautiful stitches. If you want an animal fiber that's easier to care for, look for the word *superwash* on the label.

Plant fiber

Plant fibers include cotton, linen, or bamboo yarns. Because these fibers are strong and ideal for warmer temperatures, consider using them for such projects as home décor and summer accessories. Plant fibers are also a good yarn substitution for arm knitters who have an allergy to animal fibers.

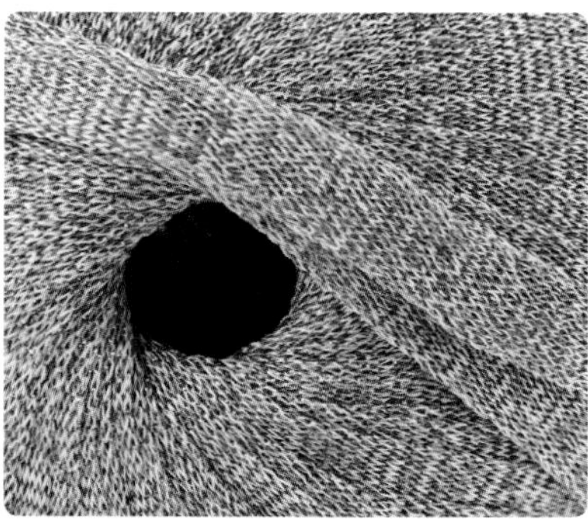

Synthetic fibers and blends

Synthetic fibers, like acrylic and nylon, are generally the easiest to care for. Synthetic yarn is a good choice if you're looking for a specific property. For example, if you want your project to have some elasticity, then a synthetic yarn with nylon in it is a good choice.

Synthetic yarns are also more budget-friendly. Novelty yarns, like ribbon yarn, are slippery and can be difficult to work with, so gain some experience before arm knitting projects that use these fibers.

Unusual yarns

Several projects in this book give you a chance to arm knit with other kinds of yarns. Experiment with these materials, especially with projects that don't take long to make.

T-shirt yarn

T-shirt yarn is a stretchy material that's made from cotton or a cotton blend. You can purchase T-shirt yarn from a fabric store or you can make your own T-shirt yarn at home by using T-shirt fabric you purchase from a bolt at a fabric store or using a T-shirt (or several) you no longer want. Do-it-yourself T-shirt yarn is a great choice for budget-conscious arm knitters.

Rope

Rope may seem like an unlikely candidate for arm knitting. However, thanks to its thickness and durability, it's a great choice for arm knitting projects, particularly home décor. You can use any type of rope you'd like, but the most common rope fibers are cotton and synthetics, like nylon.

Roving

Roving is a bulky fiber that's fuzzy and lofty. Because roving isn't plied, it doesn't have a twist to join the fibers like most yarns. You can find roving in a yarn store packaged just like other types of yarn, but you can also purchase roving by the pound. You can separate roving by gently pulling the fibers apart to create a tapered edge that's easier to weave in. If the roving is difficult to pull apart, try holding your hands farther apart when you pull.

Nomenclature

Yarn is packaged in different types of bundles. If you purchase your yarn as a ball, skein, cake, or bump, no prep is necessary before knitting. Some projects in this book will give you specific instructions about how to prepare your yarn for arm knitting.

Tools

Arm knitting doesn't require much more than your arms. Every pattern for the projects in this book lists any special tools needed. Collect all the tools and materials listed for a project before starting to knit so you don't have to interrupt your work and figure out what to do with the stitches on your arms.

Essentials

Because this is arm knitting, you don't need knitting needles. But you'll always need scissors to trim yarn and rulers to measure.

Rulers

For all projects, you'll need to do some measuring. A standard ruler lets you check sizes or trim fringe to uniform lengths. A quilting ruler is especially useful for checking your gauge, but you can use a standard ruler for that too.

Quilting ruler

Standard ruler

Keep a Toolkit Handy

Store all your arm knitting tools together in a pouch or a bag so they're readily available when you begin an arm knitting project. If you have experience with conventional knitting and already own tools you like to use for any specific technique, feel free to use them for arm knitting if they're useful. And pop them in your arm knitting kit for future use.

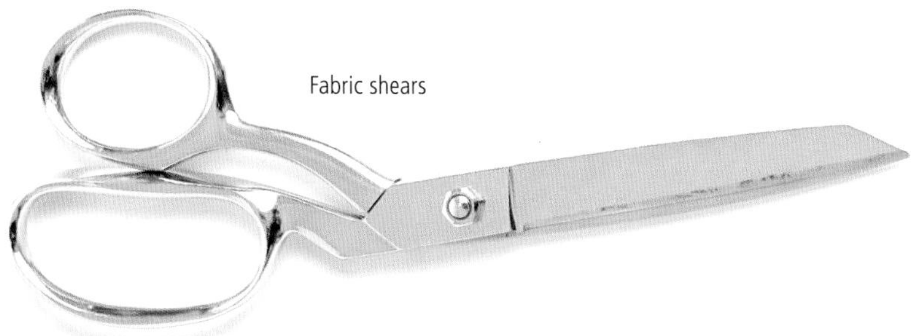

Fabric shears

Scissors

Any size scissors will do for snipping yarn. Only use your scissors to cut yarn and fabric, and have them sharpened regularly. Scissors used on paper become dull and will cut yarn or fabric in a ragged fashion.

Useful extras

Some projects, like those made from roving or those with seams, may require additional tools, but they aren't necessary for all the patterns.

Stitch markers

If you're familiar with stitch markers for conventional knitting, note that you won't use them in the same way for arm knitting. Locking stitch markers can hold two pieces of knitted fabric that you need to seam together. You can also lock a marker around strands as a reminder to weave in the ends in that spot. Pipe cleaners or scrap yarn wrapped around strands can serve the same purpose.

Stitch holders

Stitch holders come in a variety of lengths. Use one to secure your work if you stop in the middle of a project; just open the holder, slip the stitches off your arm and onto it, and close it. In lieu of a stitch holder, just slide your arm knitting onto a broomstick or dowel.

Tapestry needles

This heavy, blunt needle has a large eye for threading thick yarns. It's useful for seaming two pieces of arm knitting together. You can also use it to weave in loose ends. It's optional—you can use your fingers to seam or weave instead—but it can make some tasks easier.

Felting needles

This very sharp needle has a barbed surface that compresses wool fibers together to join them. You'll use this tool to secure the cast-on and bind-off tails of roving to knitted work or to join balls of roving.

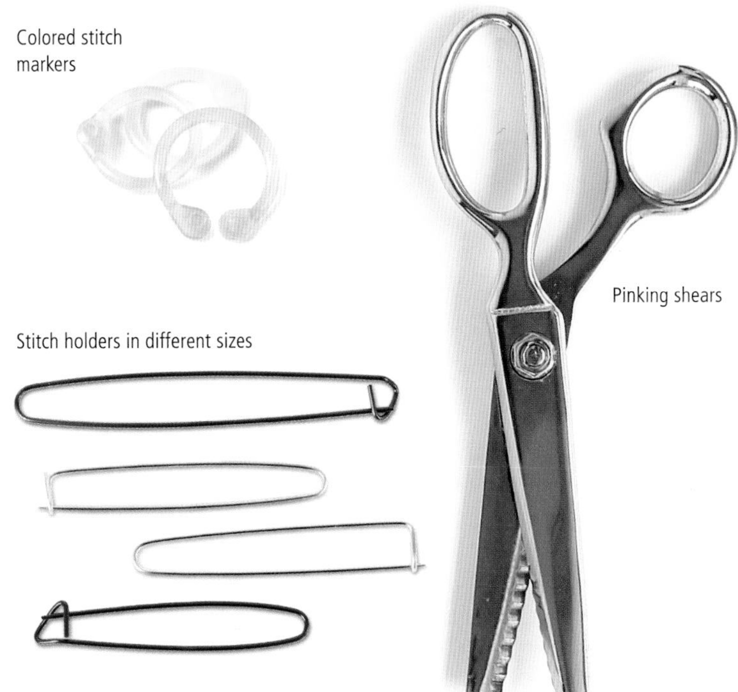

Tapestry needles

Pinking shears

These scissors produce a zigzag cut on fabric, which prevents unraveling. In this book, you'll only need them for projects that have a fabric lining.

Felting needles

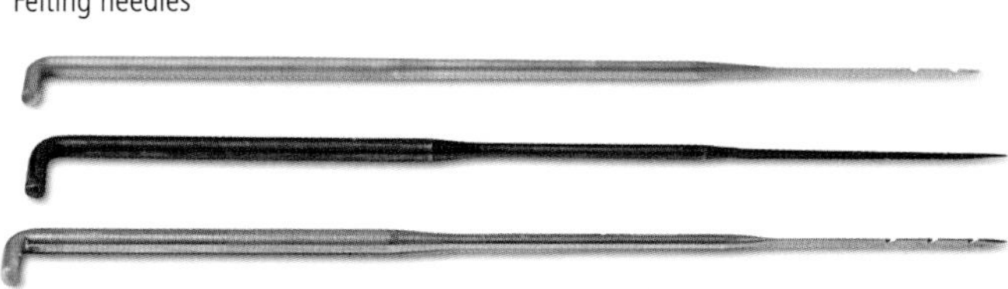

Yarn gauge and weight

Yarn gauge is the number of stitches and rows per inch of your knitting. Your knitting must match the gauge listed for each project to ensure you make the right size. If you know how to use a ruler, you can measure gauge.

Yarn weight chart

Yarn labels usually give information about thickness and weight. Many include a drawing of a skein with a number on it. You should match your yarn weight to the specific weight listed for your project.

Symbol	Weight
0	**Lace** Fingering
1	**Superfine** Fingering, Sock, Baby
2	**Fine** Sport, Baby
3	**Light** Double Knit, Light Worsted
4	**Medium** Worsted, Afghan, Aran
5	**Bulky** Chunky, Craft, Rug
6	**Super bulky** Super Bulky, Roving
7	**Jumbo** Jumbo, Roving

Understanding gauge

Gauge depends on three things: the diameter of the knitter's arms, the thickness of each strand, and the number of strands held together. To control the finished size, you need to understand how to make adjustments. You don't generally need to worry too much about yarn gauge for something like a scarf or a necklace. However, it's critical for garments, where size is important to get the right fit.

The thickness of each yarn strand as well as how many strands you hold together will also play a role in determining the gauge. The thicker the yarn and the more strands of yarn you use, the fuller the arm knitting will be. For example, a project that uses 4 strands of super bulky yarn needs 8 strands of bulky yarn to achieve the same gauge.

Engage your gauge

The diameter of every knitter's arms is different, so every knitter's stitches will be different. Each pattern specifies the number of stitches and rows per inch. If your gauge is larger than this, your finished project will be larger than the finished measurements given. If your gauge is smaller, your finished project will be smaller than the finished measurements. You may have to make adjustments to get the right size.

Roving Jumbo Super bulky Bulky Medium

Creating and using a gauge swatch

Always create a gauge swatch before knitting up your project to measure your gauge with the yarn you selected and determine how to make modifications.

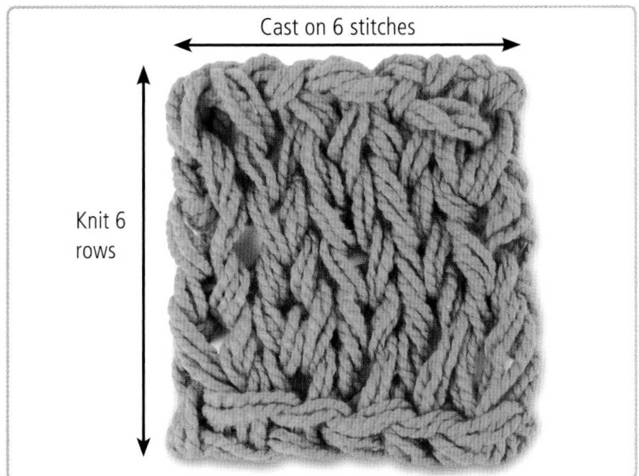
Cast on 6 stitches
Knit 6 rows

1 Cast on 6 stitches. Arm knit about 6 rows in the stitch the pattern uses. For example, if your project uses a knit stitch, then knit each row. Bind off all the stitches.

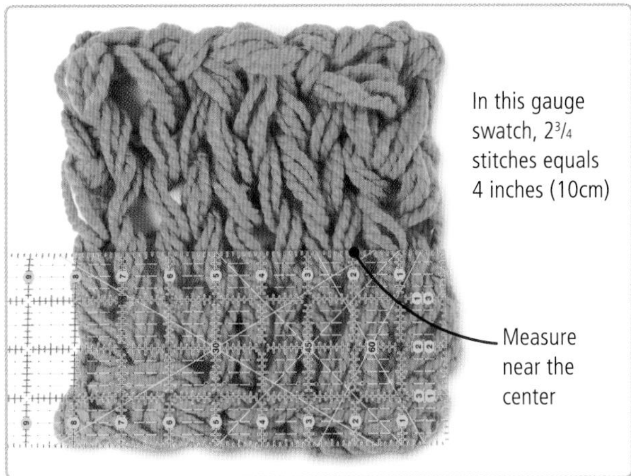
In this gauge swatch, 2¾ stitches equals 4 inches (10cm)
Measure near the center

2 Place a ruler across the width of the swatch and then count the number of stitches for 4 inches (10cm). It's best to measure near the center of the swatch to find the most accurate measurement.

In this gauge swatch, 2½ rows equals 4 inches (10cm)

3 Along the length of the swatch, count the number of rows in 4 inches (10cm). Compare your gauge to the one listed in the project you want to make. Too many stitches and rows? Knit a new swatch with one less strand of yarn and measure the gauge again. Too few stitches? Add a strand. Adjust until your gauge matches.

Adjusting stitch size

You can't change the size of your arms, but one other trick can adjust your gauge: knitting stitches that are either looser or tighter. If your gauge is too big, tighten the stitches on your arms as you knit. The smaller stitches this creates result in a smaller gauge. If your gauge is too small, do the opposite: Loosen the stitches as you knit, giving the loops a little more wiggle room on your arm and making each stitch bigger.

Substituting yarn

You might sometimes need or want to use a different yarn than the one a project calls for. Knowing how to substitute yarn will help you select the appropriate replacement fiber.

Same weight, different yarn

Every project in this book lists the specific materials used so you can replicate it exactly. You'll find this information at the very bottom of the "Essential information" column. Each project also offers generic information so you can substitute the yarns you want. It's simplest to substitute a yarn in the same weight category as the designer's yarn. For example, if a project uses a super bulky yarn and you also use a super bulky yarn, you likely won't have to adjust your gauge.

Different yarn weights

If you want to use a yarn in a different weight category, all you need to do is alter the number of strands. For example, if the project uses 4 strands of super bulky yarn, it might equal 10 strands of a lighter bulky yarn. For this kind of substitution, you'll definitely need to make a swatch to check your gauge The more strands you add to your project, the fuller and thicker the stitches will be and the bigger your gauge; if you use fewer strands, then the project will feel and look lighter and have a smaller gauge.

12 strands of bulky yarn

8 strands of bulky yarn

5 strands of super bulky yarn

These swatches have the same number of stitches and rows but different weights and strands. They're the same finished size and thus have the same gauge.

10 strands
of bulky yarn

6 strands
of super bulky
yarn

4 strands
of super bulky
yarn

Adding loft to yarn

Some fibers, like alpaca and mohair, have beautiful airy lofts that are perfect for soft, dreamy projects. Give a yarn that's not fuzzy some loft by gently untwisting several of the strands. This gives the fiber a thicker look without substituting the yarn.

When substituting yarn, always knit up a gauge swatch before you begin working on the actual project to make sure the gauge of the new yarn matches the gauge of the pattern.

Starting techniques

Every arm knitting project begins with a slipknot and cast-on stitches. But before you start any project, gather all the materials and tools for it, and read the instructions completely through to familiarize yourself with all its techniques.

Making a slipknot

Creating a slipknot is how you'll start any arm knitting project. A slipknot secures the knitting to your arm, and it's also your first cast-on stitch.

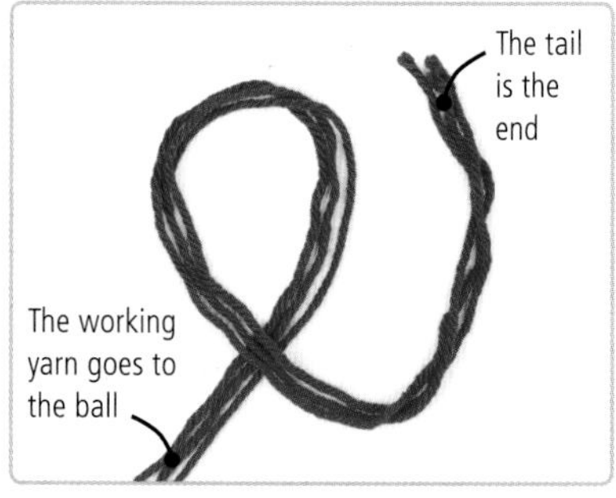
The tail is the end
The working yarn goes to the ball

1 Leaving a long tail for casting on (about 1¼ yards [1.2m] for every 10 stitches), cross the tail over the working yarn to create a circle.

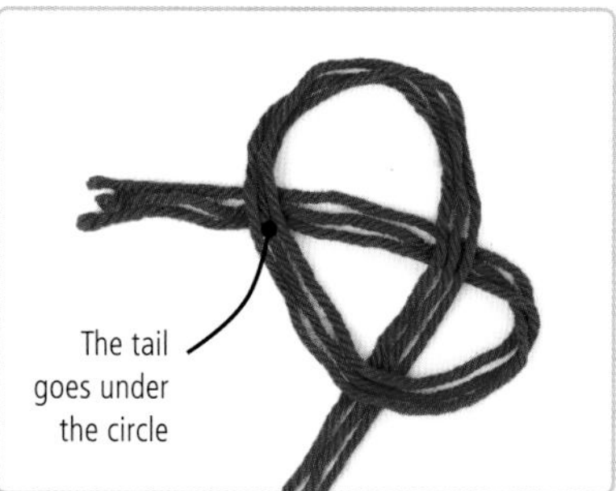
The tail goes under the circle

2 Place the tail under the circle, extending it across the center.

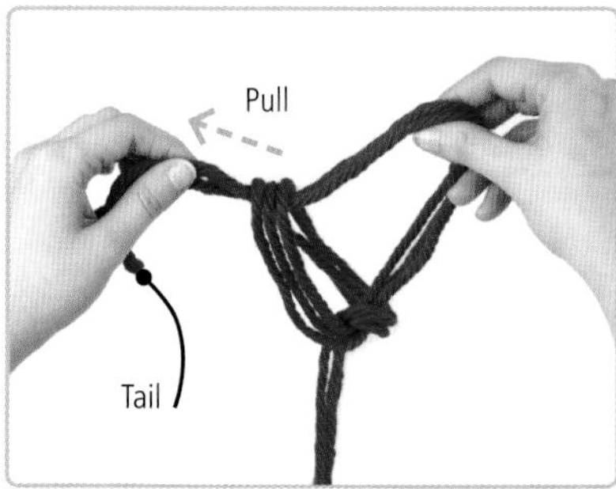
Pull
Tail

3 Hold the yarn tail with one hand and pull it taut, creating a loop at the center of the circle.

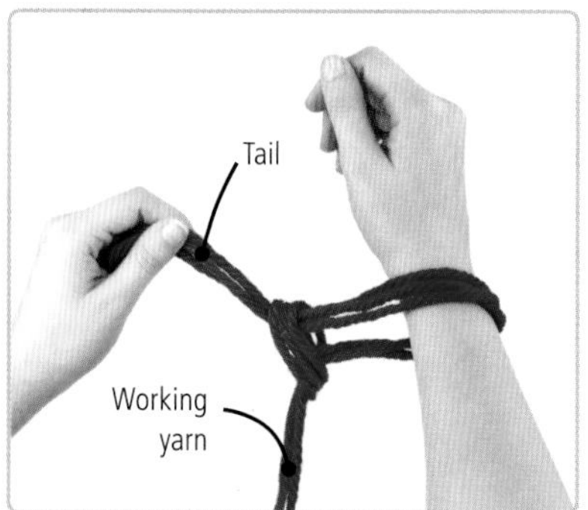
Tail
Working yarn

4 Place the loop on your right wrist, with the yarn tail in front facing you and the working yarn extending from the back.

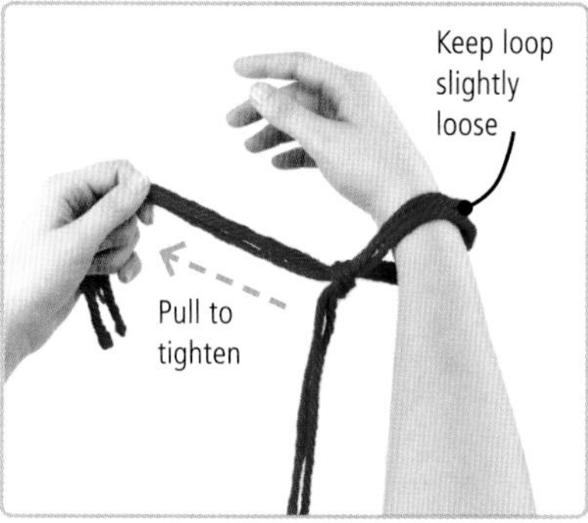
Keep loop slightly loose
Pull to tighten

5 Tighten the slipknot, but leave the loop on your wrist slightly loose. This counts as your first cast-on stitch.

Using Multiple Skeins and Strands

When knitting with several strands together, you might need to use several skeins. A scale that measures ounces is a great way to divide one skein into multiple equal balls. Divide the weight of the skein into the number of strands you need and then weigh the ball as you wind it.

Long-tail cast on

Once you've placed the slipknot—which serves as your first stitch—on your arm, you'll need to cast on additional stitches. Make sure the cast-on tail extends from the side of the wrist closest to you and the working yarn extends from the back.

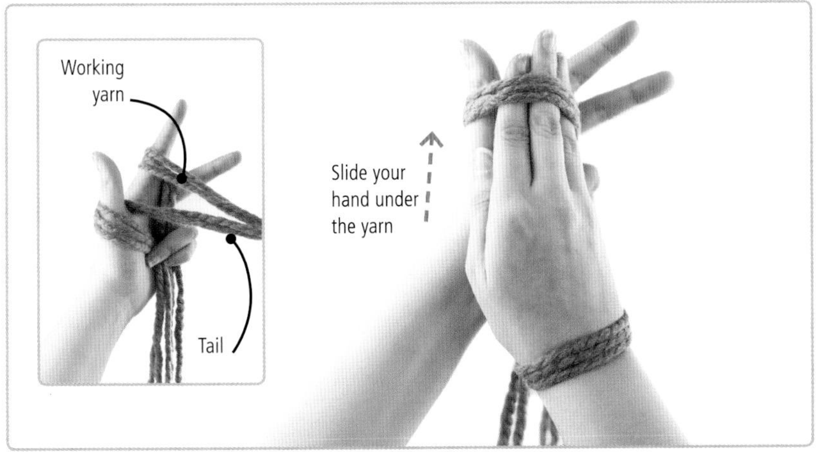

1 Place the yarn tail behind your left thumb, and place the working yarn behind your left index finger. Spread your fingers apart to create a "slingshot" of yarn. Slide your right hand under the slingshot, entering from the side of your left thumb.

2 With your right hand, grab the working yarn that's wrapped around the front of your index finger.

3 Pull the loop through and onto your right hand.

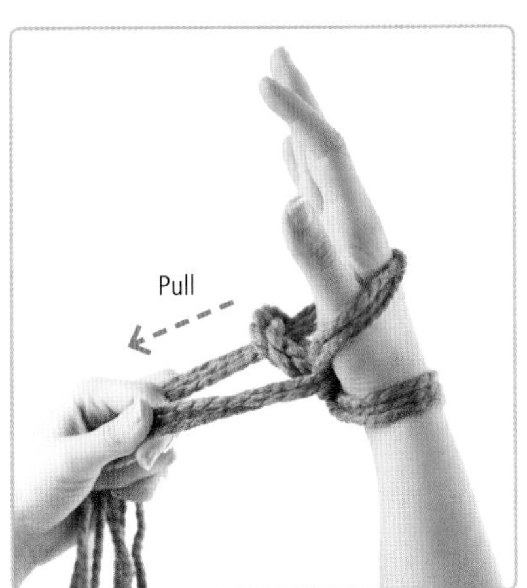

4 Pull the working yarn and tail to tighten the loop, being careful to leave enough room to pull the loop off your hand when you begin stitching.

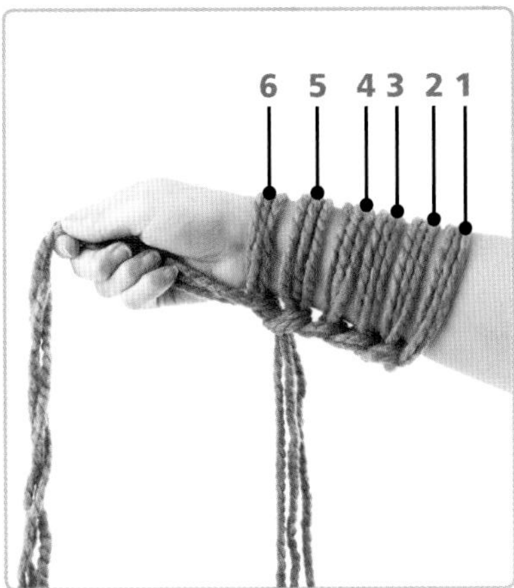

5 Repeat these steps to cast on the number of stitches required by the pattern, keeping in mind that your slipknot counts as the first cast-on stitch.

Stitches

The two foundation stitches of knitting are the knit stitch and the purl stitch. These two basic stitches can be combined to create different stitches and textures. For some projects, you'll only knit. For others, you might only purl or mix them up in various ways.

Knit stitch

Arm knitting's most basic stitch is the knit stitch. With this stitch, you can create practically any project in this book.

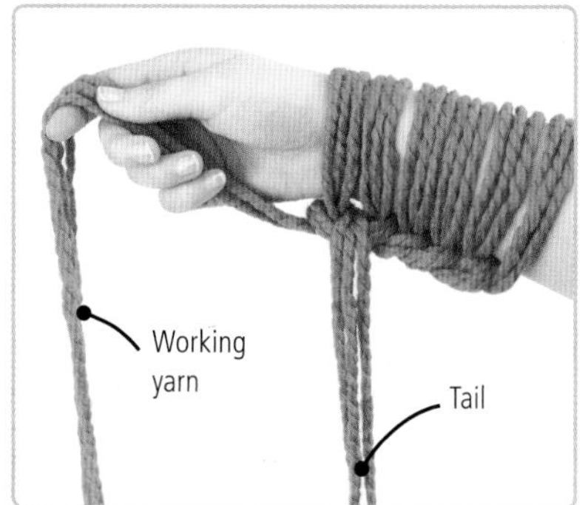

1 Cast on the number of stitches you need.

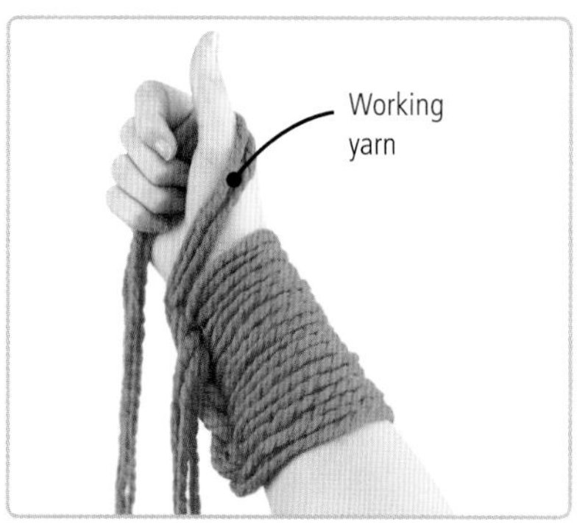

2 Place the working yarn over your right thumb from front to back, with the tail moving away from you, and close your fingers over the yarn.

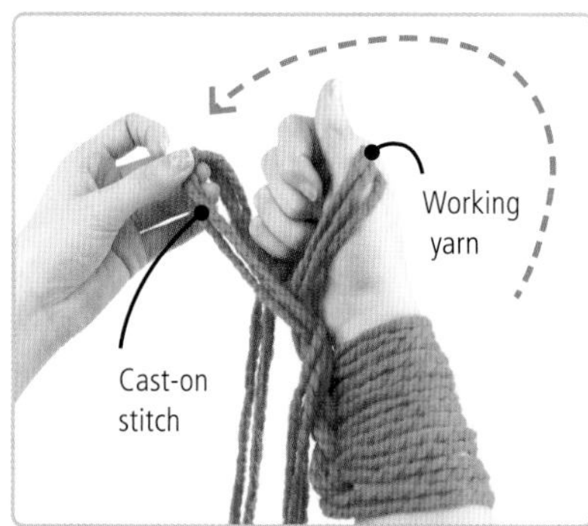

3 Drop the cast-on stitch closest to the thumb off your arm and over your hand.

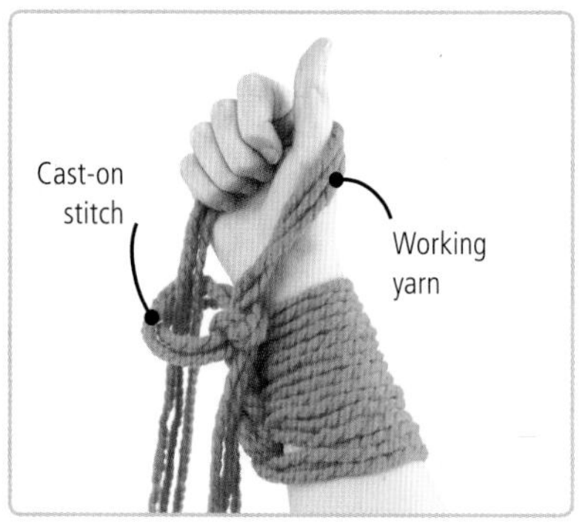

4 Drop the cast-on stitch while still grasping the working yarn.

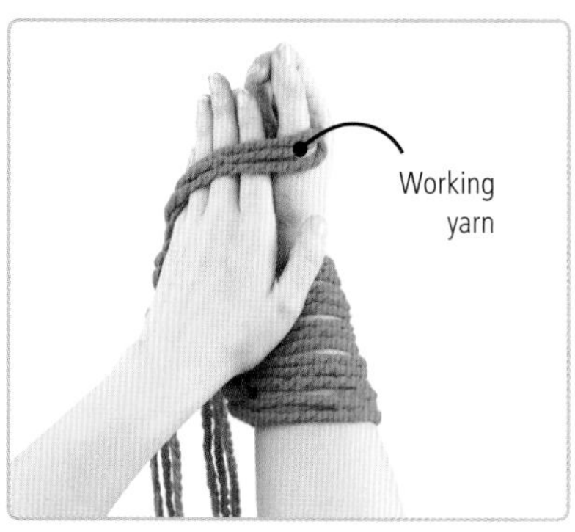

5 Slide your left hand under the loop on your right hand.

6 Slide this loop onto your left wrist. This twists the loop so the working yarn is in front.

Pull
taut

7 Pull taut on the working yarn to tighten the stitch around your left arm.

The right side
faces you

8 Repeat steps 2 through 7 until you've moved all the stitches from one arm to the other.

Carry on...

To knit the next row, repeat these steps, but this time, move the stitches from your left arm to your right arm. The rows of knitting will continue like this, moving back and forth from arm to arm. The right side of the work will always face you.

Front leg vs. back leg

The side of the stitch that faces you is called the *front leg* of the stitch. When the knitted stitches are on your left arm, the right side of the loop will be the front leg. When the stitches are on your right arm, the left side of the loop should always be the front leg. If you reverse this, your knit stitches will create a twist at the bottom.

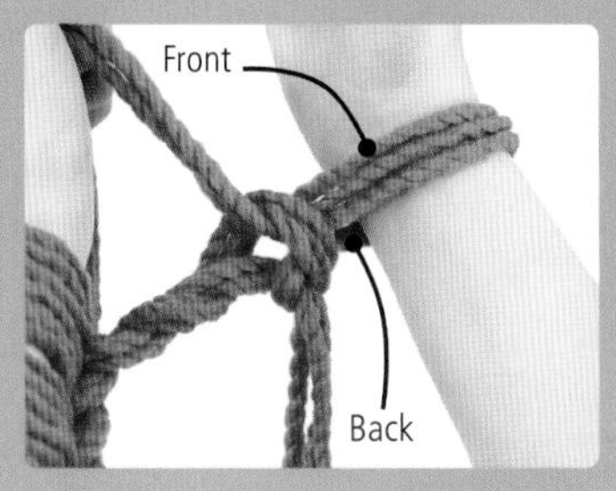
Front
Back

Stockinette stitch

When you're arm knitting, the right side of the work always faces you. If you knit every row, you'll knit what's called a *stockinette stitch.* This creates a piece with V stitches on the right side and bumps on the wrong side.

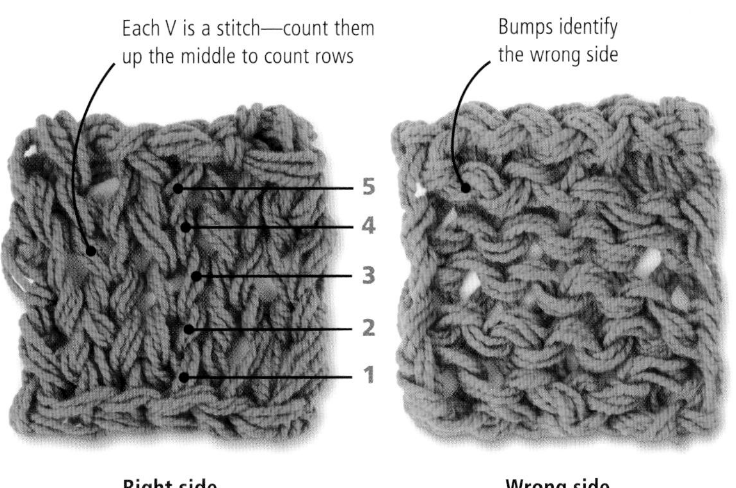
Each V is a stitch—count them up the middle to count rows
Bumps identify the wrong side
5
4
3
2
1
Right side
Wrong side

Purl stitch

The purl stitch is the sister stitch to the knit stitch. Adding it to your repertoire opens up the opportunity for special stitches with interesting textures, like seed stitch and rib stitch. You should become as familiar with this stitch as with knit stitch.

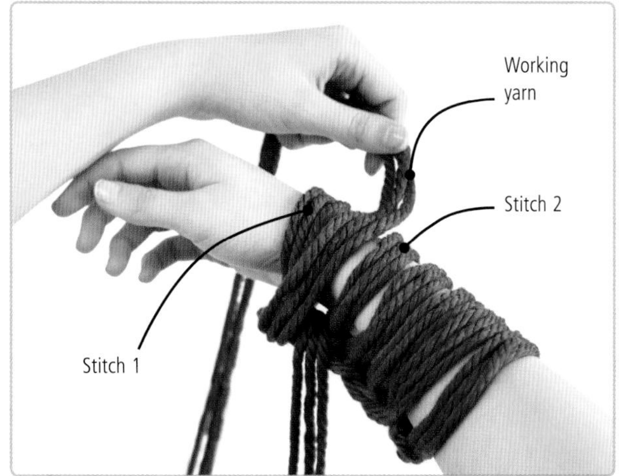

1 Place the working yarn from front to back across your arm in the space between the first two stitches closest to your hand and then let go of the working yarn.

2 Reach through the first stitch, grabbing the working yarn with your left hand and pulling the working yarn through to create a new stitch.

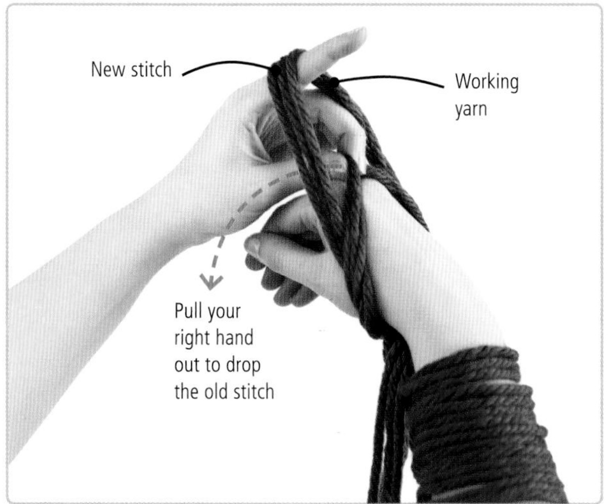

3 Drop the old stitch off your right arm.

4 Place the new stitch onto your opposite arm.

5 Pull on the working yarn to tighten the loop.

6 Repeat steps 1 through 5 until you've moved all the stitches from one arm to the other.

Carry on...

To purl the next row, repeat these steps, but this time, move the stitches from your left arm to your right arm. Continue the rows of purling in this manner, moving back and forth from arm to arm, with the right side of the work always facing you.

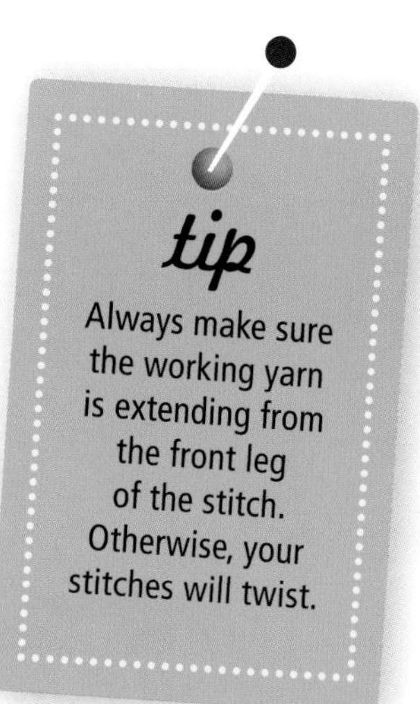

tip
Always make sure the working yarn is extending from the front leg of the stitch. Otherwise, your stitches will twist.

Garter stitch

Once you learn the purl stitch, you can create the garter stitch. A garter stitch alternates knit and purl rows, creating a knitted piece with a different texture from the stockinette stitch you create by knitting all the rows.

Finishing

When you've finished arm knitting, you'll need to close the stitches and remove them from your arms so they don't unravel. After that, you'll also need to secure the ends by either weaving them in or needle felting them.

Binding off

Binding off closes the stitches so they don't come apart. It's similar to knitting, except you'll remove the stitches from your arm as you work across the row.

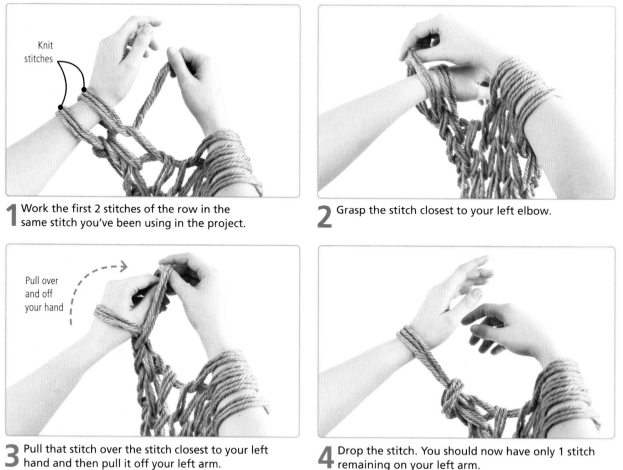

1 Work the first 2 stitches of the row in the same stitch you've been using in the project.

2 Grasp the stitch closest to your left elbow.

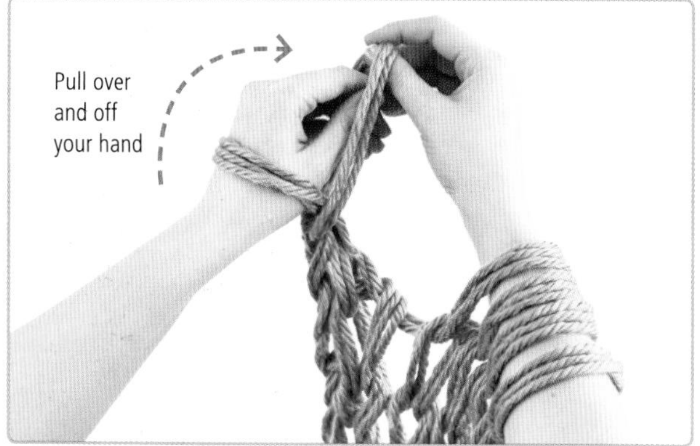

3 Pull that stitch over the stitch closest to your left hand and then pull it off your left arm.

4 Drop the stitch. You should now have only 1 stitch remaining on your left arm.

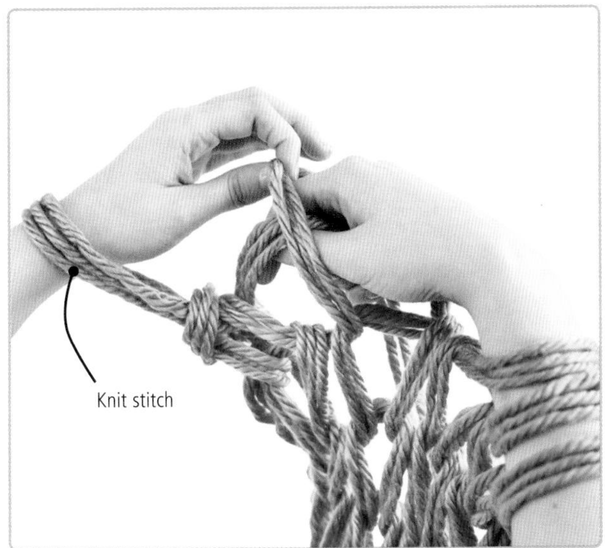

5 Work another stitch on your right arm. You'll have 2 stitches on your arm.

6 Grasp the stitch closest to your left elbow and pull it over the stitch closest to your left hand and then pull it off your left arm. Keep repeating step 5 and this one until only 1 stitch remains on your left arm. Cut the working yarn, leaving a long tail for weaving.

A bind-off end looks like a braid at the edge of the knitting

7 Remove the stitch from your left wrist and then pull the yarn tail through the loop of the last stitch. Pull the yarn taut to secure it.

tip
Make sure the bind-off row matches the project's stitches. For example, if you knitted the project in seed stitch, then your bind-off row also needs to be in seed stitch.

Weaving in ends

You'll need to weave any tails—from casting on, binding off, or adding new yarns—into the project to hide and secure them. If you have a project with seams, use your cast-on or bind-off tail to seam first and then weave in the ends. If your project calls for multiple strands of yarn held together while knitting, weave them in as a single unit.

1 Working on the wrong side of the work, weave the tail (shown in orange) through the nearest stitch.

2 Following the shape of the adjacent stitches, weave the tail through the stitches.

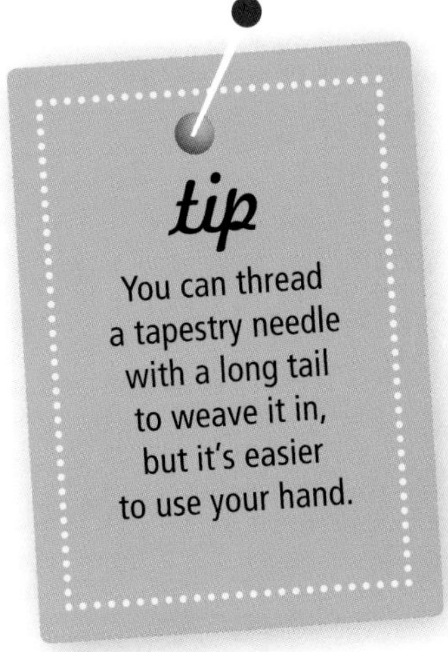

tip
You can thread a tapestry needle with a long tail to weave it in, but it's easier to use your hand.

3 Keep weaving until you've weaved in the entire tail and then tuck the end into one of the nearest stitches to secure it.

Variation

Weave the yarn tail in and out of the bind-off edge, cast-on edge, or, if your project has one, through the seam where the work is tightest and most durable.

Needle felting roving

Roving benefits from a special finishing method to ensure the tail ends don't come loose. The technique of felting interlocks the roving fibers together. You can use it to join any yarn tails to the stitches near them so they'll permanently stay in place.

What you'll need

- Thick foam pad or needle felting mat
- Felting needle

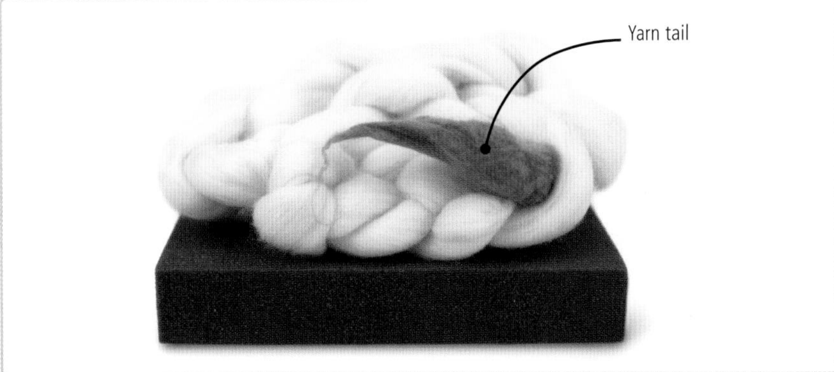

1 Place the knitted piece right side down on a thick foam pad (or on a needle felting mat). Place the yarn tail (shown in blue) to be needle felted on top of adjacent stitches, allowing an overlap of about 3 inches (8cm).

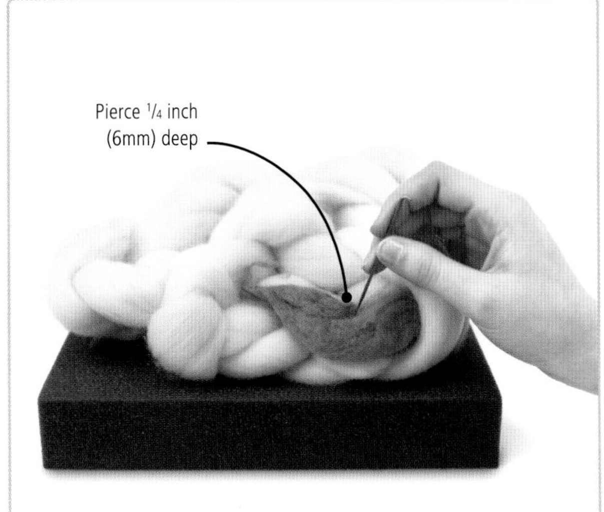

2 Lightly pierce the felting needle straight up and down through both layers of roving, piercing about 1/4 inch (6mm) deep into the stitches.

3 Continue to pierce the yarn tail with the needle until the tail is compressed firmly and securely into the stitches.

Seaming

Seaming is how you connect two pieces of arm knitting. There are two methods used in this book. The project instructions will tell you which to employ.

Whip stitch

This seaming technique creates a stitch that's sturdy and functional but not stretchy. It's visible because it wraps around the edges of two pieces—even when using the same color yarn as the knitting—and it looks decorative when you use a different color.

Wrong sides together

1 Place two knitted pieces on top of each other, with the wrong sides together and the edge stitches lined up evenly. The seaming yarn will be the tail of the bottom piece.

Seaming yarn

2 Insert the seaming yarn (shown in orange) from the bottom to the top through the bottom-right corner stitch of both pieces. (If you're using separate yarn rather than an existing tail, leave a long tail for weaving in later.)

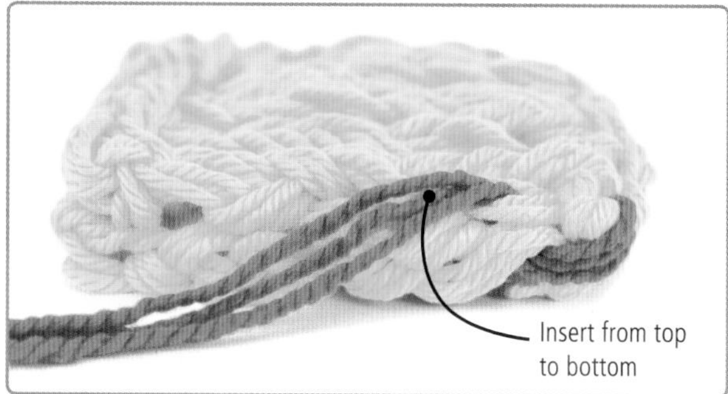
Insert from top to bottom

3 Insert the seaming yarn from the bottom to the top of the next set of stitches. The seaming yarn will wrap around the outside of the work.

Line up the top and bottom pieces evenly

4 Repeat step 3, working your way up the seam and lining up the stitches as evenly as possible, until you've seamed the entire edge.

Mattress stitch

This stretchy stitch creates a barely visible seam on the right side of the work when you use the same color yarn as for the knitting. Take care to line up the pieces side by side.

1 Place the two knitted pieces side by side, with the right sides up (unless the project instructions say to arrange them differently).

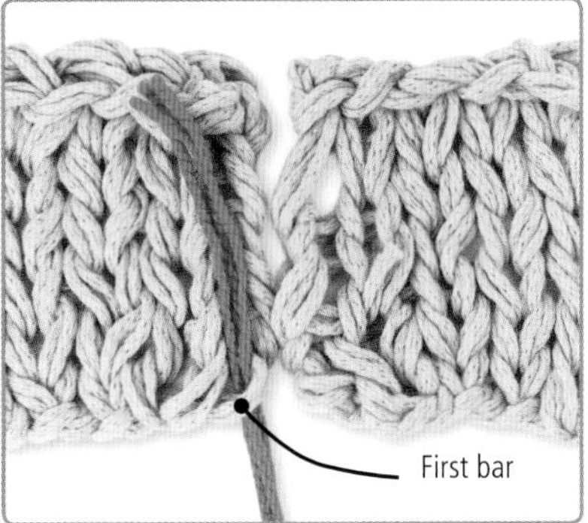

2 Stretch the side edges of both pieces to reveal the small "bars" that run side to side. Insert the seaming tail (shown in orange) under the first bar on the left piece.

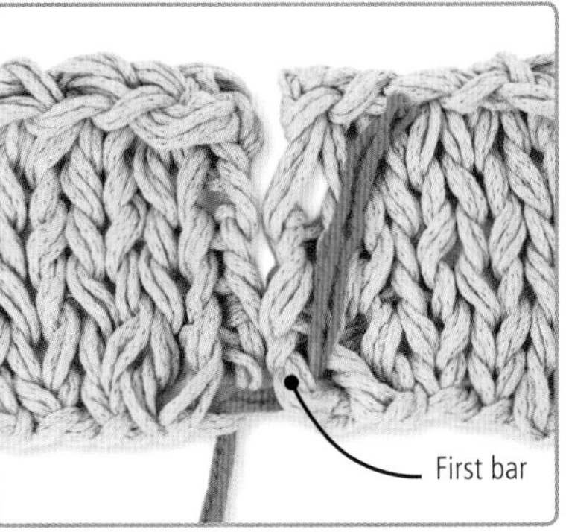

3 Insert the seaming tail under the first bar on the right piece.

4 Insert the seaming tail under the second bar on the left piece.

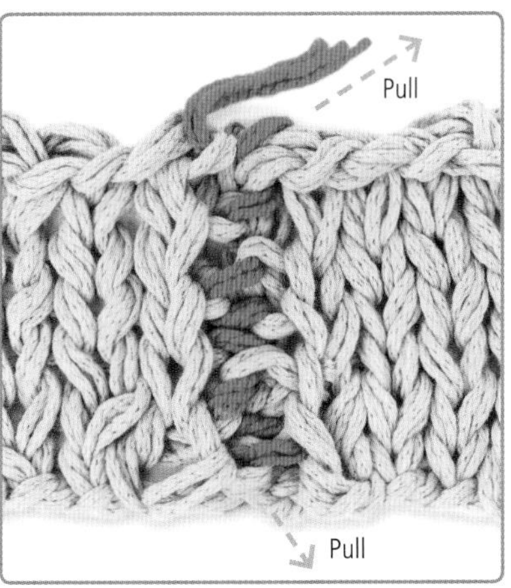

5 Continue weaving the seaming tail under the next bar, moving from side to side. When you finish seaming the entire edge, pull on each end of the seam to hide the seaming yarn and then weave in any loose ends.

tip

To avoid the hassle of weaving in lots of ends, leave longer tails when you cast on and bind off. Use those tails for seaming. This also makes the seams more secure because the seaming yarn is securely attached to one end of the work.

Adding more yarn

What do you do if you find that your ball has run out of yarn or that you'd like to change the color you're using to knit some rows in another shade? You can use the spit splice and changing colors techniques.

Spit splice

If you're knitting with 100% animal fibers, like 100% wool or alpaca, you can literally join both of the yarn ends into a single strand using a spit splice. Note that this technique works best for joining together yarns in the same color.

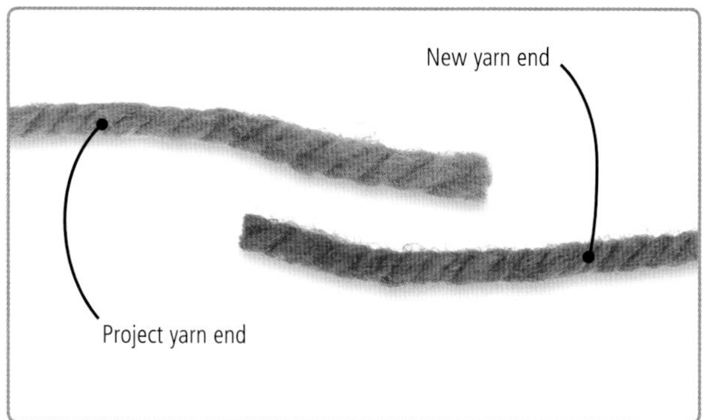

1 To join new yarn of the same color as your worked yarn, start with the end from your project and one from the new yarn.

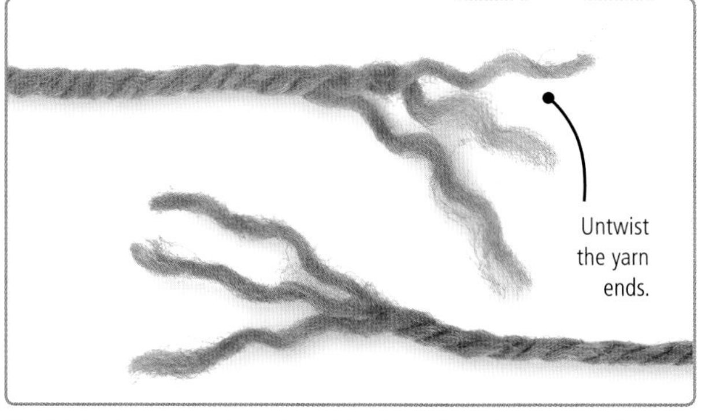

2 Untwist about 3 inches (8cm) of the plies on each yarn end and then overlap them, with the tails going in opposite directions.

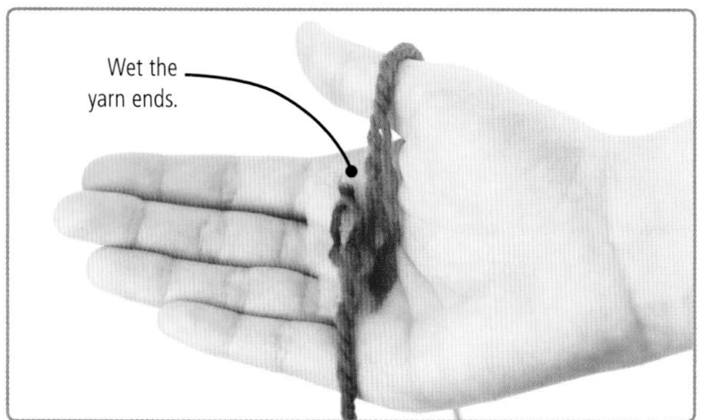

3 Soak the ends with water. Place the ends on one hand and then rub both palms together vigorously to agitate the ends.

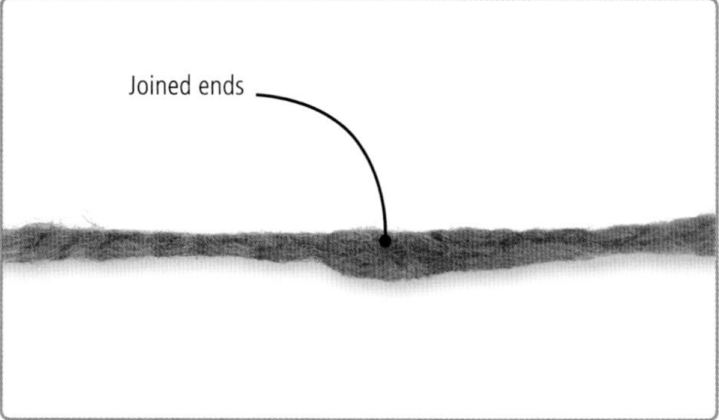

4 You can stop rubbing your hands together when the two ends look like a single strand of yarn, indicating that they've felted together.

Joining yarns or changing colors

If you're working with a synthetic yarn or a blend and the ball runs out or if you want to alternate colors to create stripes, you'll need to properly join the yarns so your stitches don't come unraveled. It's best to join yarns or change colors when you're ready to start a new row.

Gray yarn is being added to knitted pink yarn

1 At the beginning of a new row, hold the new yarn with your left hand, leaving a tail about 10 inches (25cm) long, and then knot the new yarn loosely around the working yarn to secure it.

Pull the first stitch over your right hand.

2 While grasping the new yarn in your right hand, pull the first stitch of the row over your hand.

tip
When you finish arm knitting your project, weave the tails of the new and old yarns into the wrong side.

3 Pull the first stitch of the row over your hand.

4 Place the new stitch on your left arm. Continue knitting as usual using the new yarn.

Decreasing

Decreasing combines two stitches into one to shape the work. (Increases are also used for shaping but not in this book.) The two decreasing methods result in stitches that lean in different directions, which depends which arm the stitch is on.

Knit 2 together

This decrease is almost identical to a knit stitch, except you'll grab and drop 2 stitches instead of 1.

1 Knit until you reach the place where you want to decrease. End with the working yarn over your right thumb—just as if you were going to knit the next stitch.

Pull both stitches over at the same time

2 Pull 2 stitches over your hand (rather than 1 stitch, which is what you would do for a knit stitch).

3 Put the new loop on your arm. You've decreased 1 stitch. Continue knitting as usual.

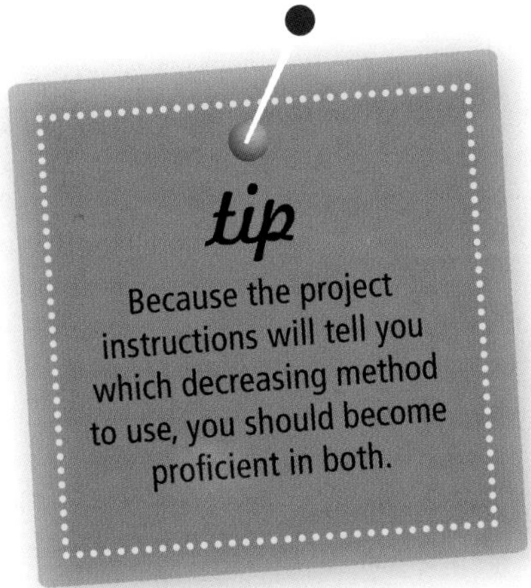

tip
Because the project instructions will tell you which decreasing method to use, you should become proficient in both.

Slip, slip, knit

Slip, slip, knit results in a decrease that leans in the opposite direction as a knit 2 together.

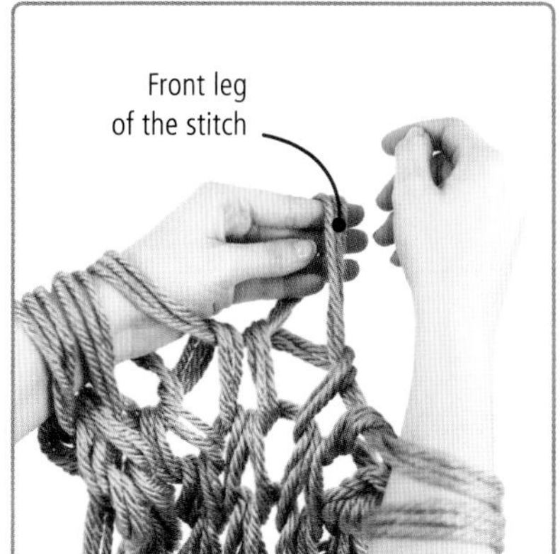

1 Knit until you reach the place where you want to decrease and then slip the next 2 stitches one at a time from one arm to the other, twisting the loops so the right side of the loop becomes the front leg.

2 Lay the working yarn from front to back over your left thumb.

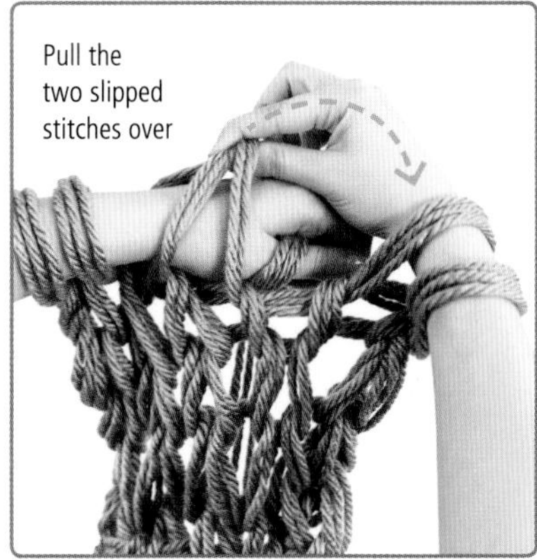

3 Pull the 2 slipped stitches over your hand and drop them. You have decreased 1 stitch.

Leaning stitches: Comparing knit 2 together to slip, slip, knit

Knit 2 together slants to the right when you're working from your left arm to your right and to the left if you're working from your right arm to your left.

Slip, slip, knit slants to the left when you're working from your left arm to your right and to the right when you're working from your right arm to your left.

When decreasing, the stitches on the left edge should lean right into the center, while the stitches on the right edge should lean left into the center.

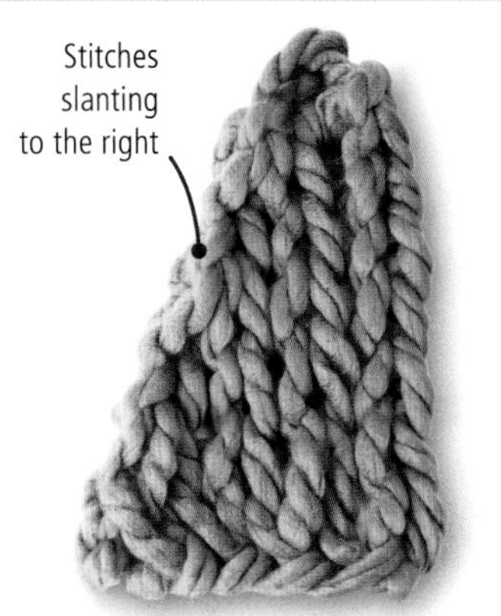

Figure 1 Knit 2 together worked from the left arm to the right.

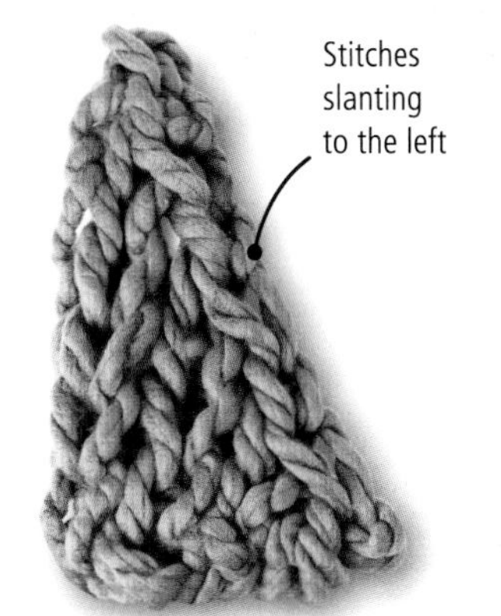

Figure 2 Slip, slip, knit worked from the left arm to the right.

Additional techniques

Despite being easy, arm knitting does have a couple tricks you can use to further simplify some techniques. These two methods are used in only a handful of projects in this book, but for those few, they're indispensable.

Navajo plying technique

This technique—sometimes called *chain plying*—allows you to create 3 strands from one skein. You'll avoid having to knit with multiple balls, which can result in tangled strands.

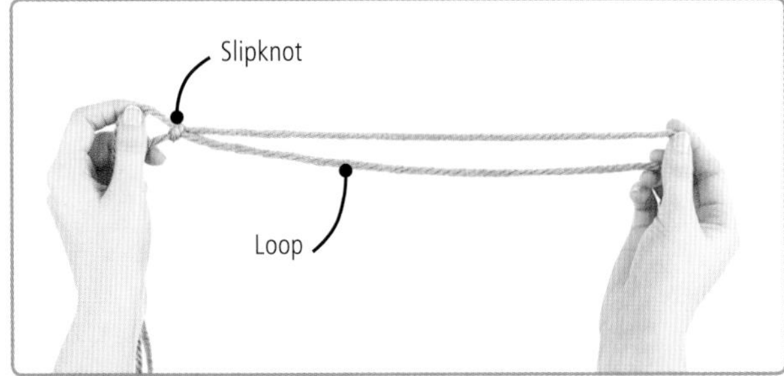

1 Make a slipknot, pulling the yarn loop until it's about 12 inches (30cm) long.

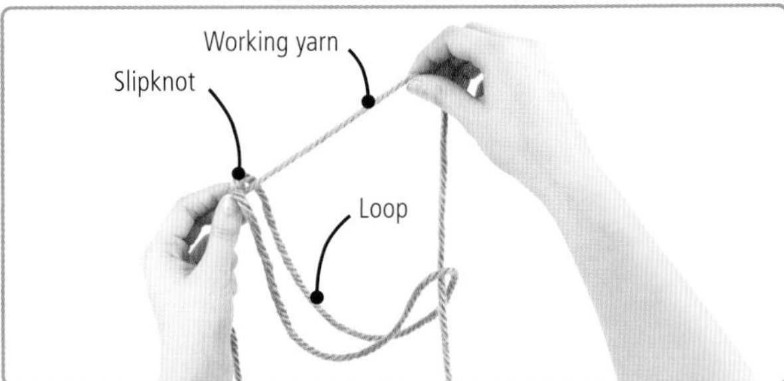

2 Holding the slipknot and tail in your left hand, reach through the loop with your right hand to pull up on the working yarn, drawing it through the loop to create a second loop about 12 inches (30cm) long.

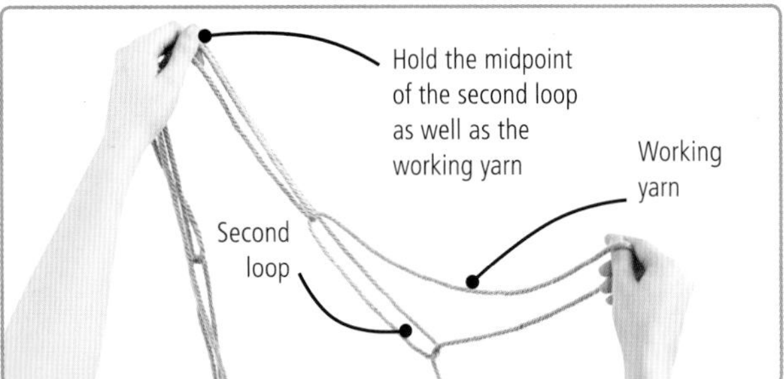

3 Drop the slipknot, and use your left hand to hold all 3 strands midway along the length of the second loop. Reach through the right end of the loop to draw out the working yarn to create a third loop 12 inches (30 cm) long. Repeat this step to Navajo ply the entire skein.

Concealed loops

Knitting made with this plying technique looks the same as if you had held 3 strands together from 3 different balls of yarn. The loops created during the plying process aren't noticeable because the many strands and stitches in the knitting camouflage their presence.

Picking up stitches

Picking up stitches allows you to create new loops on the edges of a knitted piece. It's great for creating shape and definition or adding additional length.

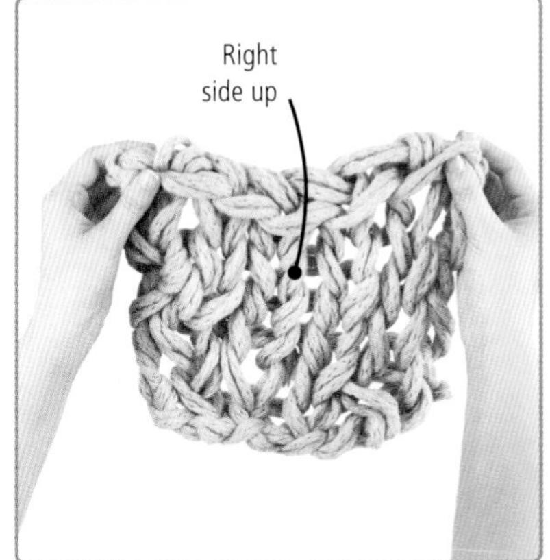

1 Hold the knitted piece right side up, with the edge you want to pick up stitches from at the top.

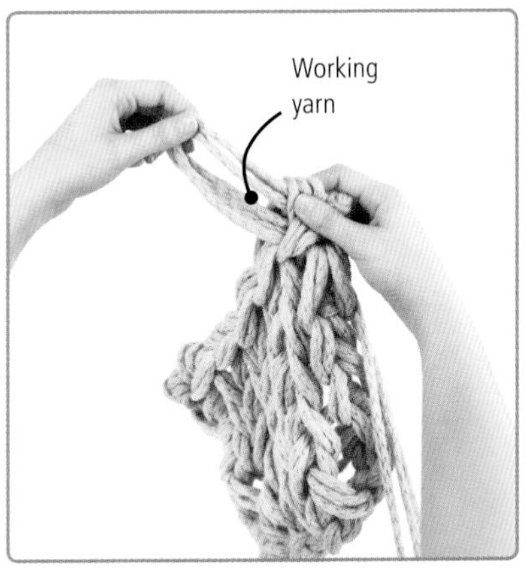

2 Place your hand through the center of the first V-shaped stitch and grab your working yarn. Leaving a long tail for weaving in later, pull the working yarn through the stitch, creating a loop.

3 Place the loop on your right arm, with the working yarn extending from the stitch's front leg.

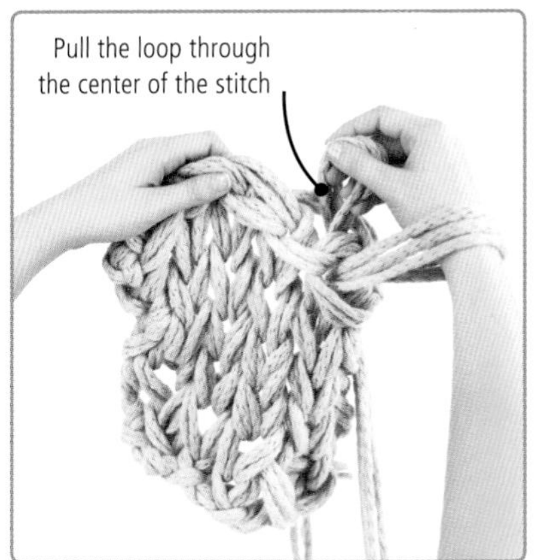

4 Place your right hand through the center of the next V-shaped stitch and then pull up another loop.

5 Place the loop on your right arm once again, with the working yarn extending from the stitch's front leg.

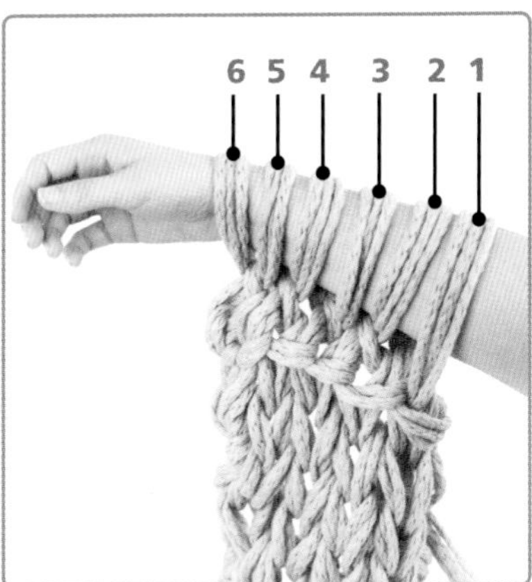

6 Repeat steps 4 and 5 across the edge, pulling up a loop from each V-shaped stitch until you've picked up the number of stitches instructed in the pattern.

Head to toe

From hats and scarves to bags and boot cuffs, these projects offer various accessories to complement your everyday look. You'll also learn to make fringe and pompoms.

Twisted scarf

Rather than being knitted from plied yarn, this scarf uses a yarn knitted as a netted tube. This gives the fiber more loft and bulk, making it perfect for arm knitting.

Essential information

Difficulty level
Easy

Time to make
20 minutes

Finished size
48 inches (122cm) long

Materials
26 yards (24m) of super bulky netted acrylic-blend yarn

Tools
Scissors

Gauge
2 stitches and 2 rows equals 4 inches (10cm).

This project was made with 2 skeins of Premier Yarns Couture Jazz in Pumpkin Pie, 13 yards (11m).

Wear this scarf by running one end through a knit stitch a third of the way along the scarf's length.

How to make

Magic knot

The purpose of this nearly invisible knot is to connect the 2 skeins of yarn into one single piece of yarn before you start knitting. That way, you'll have fewer ends to weave in later.

1 Pull one end out from each skein and then place them on your work surface, with the tails going in opposite directions.

2 Tie one tail around the other and then tie the loose tail around the other working yarn, as shown in Figure 1, and then loosely tighten the knots.

3 Holding the working yarns, pull gently in opposite directions until the knots slide together.

4 Pull the knots tight and then trim the ends close to the knot.

Scarf

1 Cast on 4 stitches.

2 Arm knit until you have approximately 1 yard (1m) of working yarn left.

3 Bind off all the stitches, leaving a 10-inch-long (25cm) tail.

Finish

At each end of the scarf, tie the long tail into a loop on the inside of the scarf and then cut the remaining yarn or weave it into the scarf.

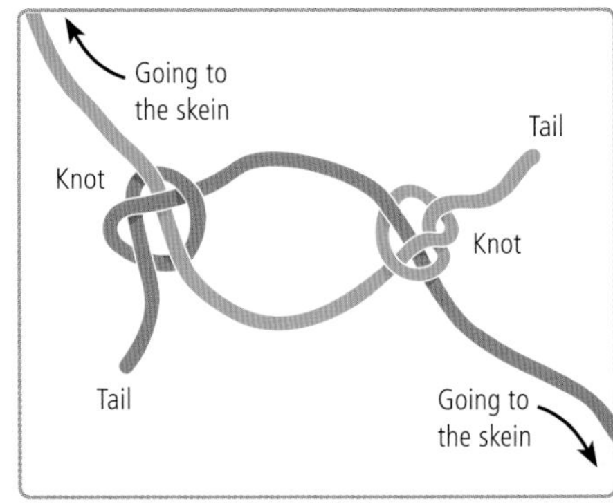

Figure 1 In the second step of making a magic knot, tie each tail around the other.

Keep the stitches consistently tight on your arms to ensure even stitches that aren't too large.

tip
You can create a striped effect with two colors by using multiple magic knots to attach several colors of yarn together.

tip
Try on the boot cuffs as you arm knit them—and before you add the buttons—to ensure a snug fit around your calf.

Essential information

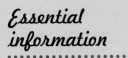

Difficulty level
Easy

Time to make
45 minutes

Finished size
5 x 18 inches (13 x 46cm)

Materials
55 yards (50m) of super bulky T-shirt yarn, with 3 strands held together

Four 1⅜-inch (3.5cm) decorative buttons

Sewing thread in any color

Tools
Sewing needle

Scissors

Gauge
3 stitches and 2.5 rows equals 4 inches (10cm) before stretching.

This project was made with 1 skein of Lion Brand Yarns Fettuccini in Solid, 55 yards (50m).

Boot cuffs

Choose plant-based or synthetic yarn to make these funky accessories. Animal fibers will felt together if they rub against your boots, causing the cuffs to form pills.

How to make

Cuffs (make 2)

1 Cast on 6 stitches.

2 Arm knit in stockinette stitch until the cuff measures 18 inches (46cm) long when stretched or the desired length plus 1 inch (2.5cm). Before you measure the length, stretch out the cuff lengthwise.

3 Bind off all the stitches, and weave in all the ends.

Assemble

Sew 2 buttons to the short edge of the stockinette side of each boot cuff. To hide the thread, use your fingers to unroll the T-shirt yarn and then sew the button there. When you finish, the yarn will roll back up, hiding the sewing. Trim the button threads.

Choose buttons that either stand out against the yarn you use or ones that blend into the cuffs.

You can use a different yarn or a different number of strands, but make sure the cuff isn't too bulky. A bulky cuff might cause an uncomfortable fit when your boot goes over it.

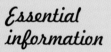

Essential information

Difficulty level
Easy

Time to make
30 minutes

Finished size
4.5 x 72 inches
(11 x 182cm)

Materials
125 yards (114m) of super bulky yarn, with 3 strands held together

Tools
Scissors

Gauge
2 stitches and 3.75 rows equals 4 inches (10cm).

This project was made with 1 bump of BagSmith Big Stitch Merino in Multi Fawn, 125 yards (114m).

Infinity scarf

A yarn that resembles dreadlocks gives this infinity scarf its unique appearance. Wrap it twice around your neck for a casual look or three times for a super snug cowl.

How to make

Scarf

1 Cast on 4 stitches.

2 Arm knit until the piece measures approximately 72 inches (183cm).

3 Bind off all the stitches.

4 Seam the cast-on and bind-off edges together.

5 Weave in and trim all the ends.

Creating a scarf is a great introduction to arm knitting: It doesn't take long to make; it's inexpensive; and you'll quickly enjoy knitting with your arms.

This scarf looks like it includes three different yarns in several different colors, but the designer actually achieved it by using a single multicolored yarn.

tip

Making this scarf with a light-colored yarn allows you to wear it with myriad shades of clothing.

tip
Placing the piece flat on a table to seam it will result in a neater and less bulky seam because you can more easily line up the stitches.

Essential information

Difficulty level
Easy

Time to make
20 minutes

Finished size
28 x 12 inches (71 x 31cm)

Materials
42 yards (38m) of super bulky yarn, with 2 strands held together

Tools
Scissors

Gauge
2 stitches and 1 row equals 4 inches (10cm).

This project was made with 2 balls of Loops & Threads Biggie in Dark Gray, 21 yards (19m).

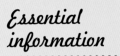

Keeping the stitches tight as you arm knit will give this cowl more durability.

Mega cowl

You'll arm knit this soft, cozy cowl in no time flat! Made with a luxurious roving-like yarn, this delightful accessory will keep the compliments coming—and the chill away.

How to make

Cowl

1 Cast on 6 stitches.

2 Arm knit until the piece measures 28 inches (71cm) long.

3 Bind off all the stitches, leaving an 18-inch-long (46cm) tail.

4 Place the piece on your work surface wrong side up and then seam the edges by using a whip stitch.

5 Weave in all the ends.

Whip stitch the seam carefully so it's barely visible no matter how you wear this cowl.

Try leaving the cowl unseamed. Instead, sew a large decorative button to one of the edge corners. You don't need to make a buttonhole—slide the button through any open stitch.

Essential information

Difficulty level
Easy

Time to make
10 minutes

Finished size
17 x 5 inches (43 x 13cm)

Materials
318 yards (291m) of super bulky yarn, with 3 strands held together

Tools
Scissors

Gauge
4 stitches and 2 rows equals 4 inches (10cm).

This project was made with 3 balls of Lion Brand Yarns Wool-Ease Thick & Quick in Blossom, 106 yards (97m).

Choose colors for this ear warmer that match your seasonal outfits.

Ear warmer

Need a last-minute gift? One that's not only fast and easy to arm knit but is also fun to wear? Made with a soft, cozy yarn, this pretty accessory meets all those desires.

How to make

Ear warmer

1 Cast on 6 stitches.

2 Arm knit until the piece measures approximately 17 inches (43cm) long.

3 Bind off all the stitches.

4 Seam the short ends together with a whip stitch.

5 Weave in all the ends.

Before you seam the short edges together, make sure the piece isn't twisted.

After you finish arm knitting to the noted length, try this on your head before binding off all the stitches.

tip
To make this
ear warmer
extra thick
and extra cozy,
hold together
4 or 5 strands of
a super bulky yarn.

tip

You can make the fringe as long or as short as you like—just make incremental cuts until you feel it's the perfect length.

Cable scarf

If you're eager to use a luxury yarn, this is the project for it. This scarf is easy to make, and it's versatile because you can drape it over your shoulders or wrap it.

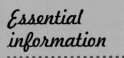

Essential information

Difficulty level
Moderate

Time to make
90 minutes

Finished size
8 x 91 inches (20 x 231cm)

Materials
382 yards (349m) of super bulky yarn, with 3 strands held together

Tools
Stitch holder

Scissors

Measuring tape

Gauge
3 stitches and 2 rows equals 4 inches (10cm).

This project was made with 7 balls of Plymouth Yarn Baby Alpaca Magna in 3317 Tiffany, 54.5 yards (50m).

How to make

Scarf

1 Cast on 8 stitches.

2 Stitch row: Purl the first 2 stitches, knit the next 4 stitches, and purl the last 2 stitches.

3 Cable row: Purl the first 2 stitches and then slip the next 2 stitches onto the stitch holder, as shown in Figure 1.

Figure 1 This is how you slip 2 stitches onto your stitch holder.

Slip the stitches on the stitch holder off your arm and place them behind the piece. Arm knit the next 2 stitches. Place the stitches from the stitch holder back onto your arm, as shown in Figure 2, and then knit these 2 stitches.

Purl the last 2 stitches of the row.

Figure 2 This is how you slip the 2 stitches on the stitch holder back onto your arm.

4 Continue knitting, alternating between the stitch and cable rows, until the scarf measures 91 inches (231cm) or your desired length.

5 Bind off all the stitches, and weave in all the ends.

Continued

Fringe

1 Cut forty-eight 20-inch-long (51cm) strands of yarn.

2 Form the fringe by holding 3 strands of yarn together and folding the strands in half, forming a loop at the top.

3 Slide the loop through the first stitch of the cast-on edge.

4 Slip the fringe tails through the loop.

5 Pull taut on the fringe tails to secure the fringe.

6 Repeat this fringe process across the cast-on and bind-off edges. Trim the fringe evenly.

See the Making Fringe section for more specific instructions.

This long scarf could easily be knit as a cowl or an infinity scarf. Knit to the length you'd like and then seam the cast-on and bind-off edges together—and, of course, leave off the fringe.

Choose a light color for this scarf to help spotlight and define the cable that runs down the center.

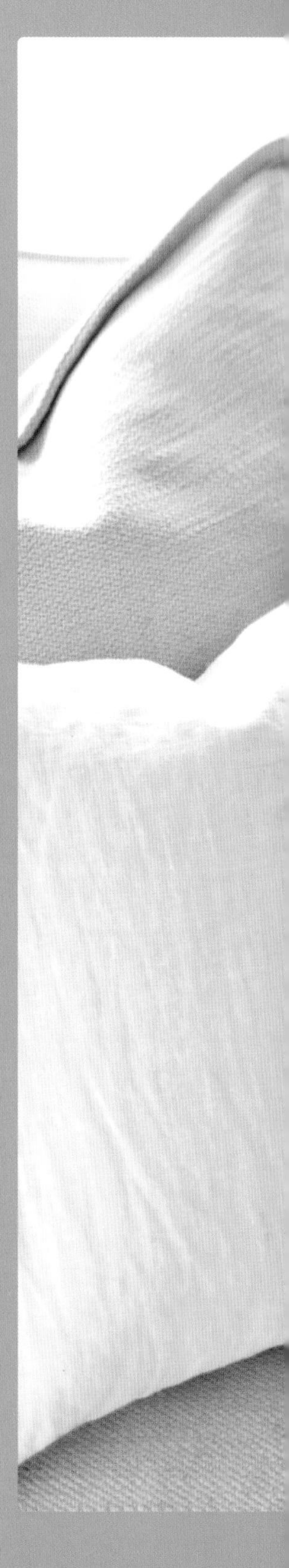

tip
This scarf can feel heavy as you arm knit.
Use a tabletop to hold it as you work.
This will take some of the weight off your arms.

Making fringe

Fringe is a great embellishment for scarves and rugs. Customize it as thick, long, and luxurious as you like. You can also select a different color than the one used for the main part of the project, attach fringes in alternating colors, or mix several hues.

What you'll need

- Scissors
- Yarn specified by the project instructions
- Ruler

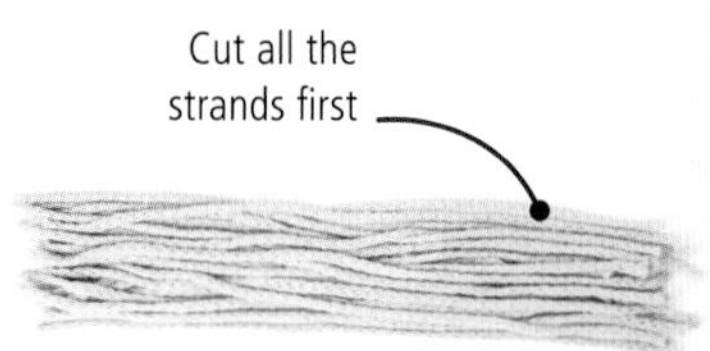

1 Cut the strands of yarn as instructed by the pattern. (The instructions will tell you how many strands and how long each strand should be.)

3 Slide the loop under the first stitch closest to the edge.

6 Repeat steps 2 through 5 across the edges where you want fringe.

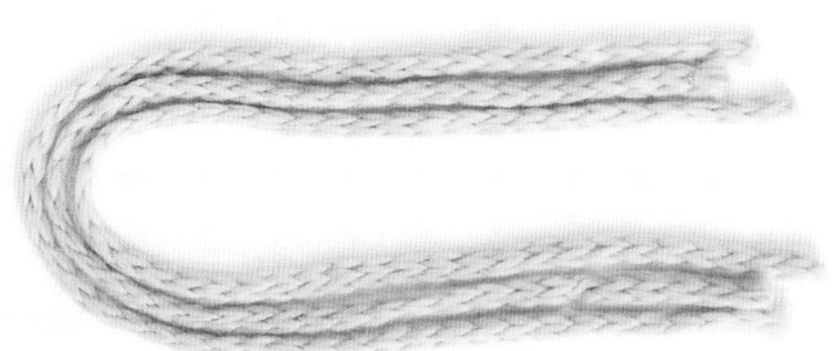

2 Hold together the number of strands mentioned in the project instructions and then fold the strands in half, forming a loop on one side.

Fringe Modifications

To make your fringe look and feel thicker than the one shown for a project, just cut more strands of yarn in step 1 and then add additional strands to each stitch in steps 2 to 6. For longer fringe, in step 1, cut the yarn twice as long as the desired finished length, plus 1 inch (2.5cm) for waste.

4 Pull the fringe tails through the loop.

Pull the tails to tighten them

5 Pull the fringe tails taut to secure them.

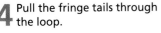

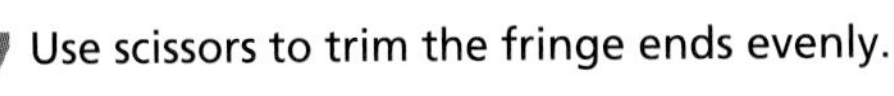

Make brisk cuts

7 Use scissors to trim the fringe ends evenly.

tip
To keep the fringe ends even, place a ruler across the entire fringe to use as a guide as you cut.

Essential information

Difficulty level
Moderate

Time to make
90 minutes

Finished size
16 x 15 inches (41 x 38cm)

Materials
176 yards (161m) of super bulky yarn, with 6 strands held together (or 2 strands held together if using the Navajo plying technique)
Thread

Tools
Scissors
Sewing needle

Gauge
2 stitches and 3.75 rows equals 4 inches (10cm).

This project was made with 2 skeins of Premier Craft-Tee Yarn in Light Grey Shades, 88 yards (81m).

Bento bag

Based loosely on a Japanese design, this bag has an asymmetrical structure that looks symmetrical once assembled. It folds flat but actually holds a lot.

How to make

Bag

1 Cast on 8 stitches, leaving a 15-inch-long (38cm) tail for seaming.

2 Arm knit 23 rows or until the piece measures approximately 32 inches (81cm).

3 Bind off all the stitches. Cut the yarn, leaving a 15-inch-long (38cm) tail.

You can line your bag by tacking fabric to the knit piece before seaming the bag together and then sew the fabric permanently to the edges after assembling the bag.

This isn't your usual handbag. But that's what will make a statement, especially when you tell people you made it with your arms.

Continued

tip

Use the Navajo plying technique to turn 1 strand into 3 strands so you don't have to hold 6 strands simultaneously.

You can give your bag a different personality by making your own yarn from stretchy fabric.

Assemble

1 Place the piece wrong side up and horizontally on your work surface. Fold the left edge across the piece so a section 7 inches (18cm) wide overlaps the rest of the piece, as shown in Figure 1. Using a mattress stitch, seam only the bottom edges together along the 7-inch (18cm) overlap.

2 Unfold corner A down as far as possible toward the bottom-left corner to get it out of the way, as shown in Figure 2. Now fold the right edge across the piece so a 7-inch-wide (18cm) section overlaps the rest of the piece, as shown in Figure 3. (It might look messy, but forge on!) Using a mattress stitch, seam only the upper edges together along the 7 inches (18cm).

3 Sew corners A and B to each other to make the handle.

See the Making T-Shirt Yarn and Navajo Plying Technique sections for more specific instructions.

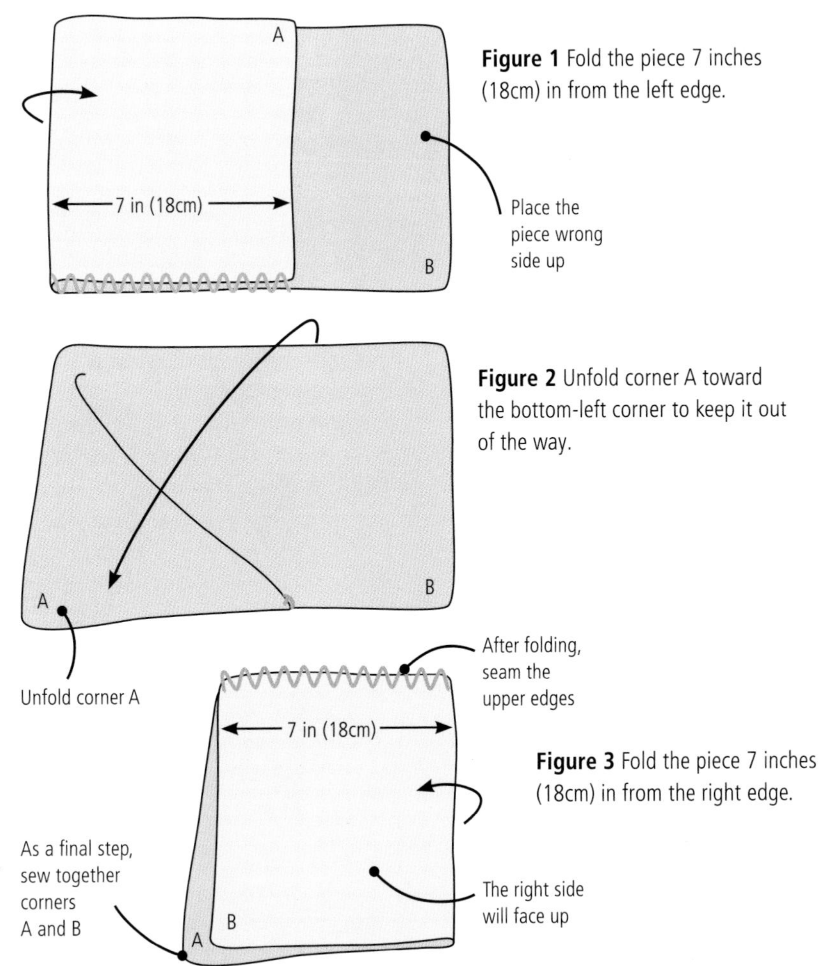
A
7 in (18cm)
B
Place the piece wrong side up
A
B
Unfold corner A
After folding, seam the upper edges
7 in (18cm)
As a final step, sew together corners A and B
A
B
The right side will face up

Figure 1 Fold the piece 7 inches (18cm) in from the left edge.

Figure 2 Unfold corner A toward the bottom-left corner to keep it out of the way.

Figure 3 Fold the piece 7 inches (18cm) in from the right edge.

Boho vest

This chunky cropped vest is made as a single piece—except for two small seams at the shoulders. And it's also reversible, making it even more irresistible.

Essential information

Difficulty level
Moderate

Time to make
45 minutes

Finished size
Chest: 28 (32, 36, 40) inches [71 (81, 91, 102) cm]

Materials
30 to 60 yards (27 to 55m) or 1.5 to 3 pounds (680 to 1360g) of raw, unspun merino wool roving with a 23-micron count (or use giant yarn in the same amount)

Tools
Felting needle

Scissors

Gauge
2 stitches and 3 rows equals 4 inches (10cm).

This project was made with 1 ball of Intreccio Giant Merino roving in Natural, 30 yd (27m).

How to make

Vest

Measure your bust. Referring to the finished size in the column at left, when following the instructions, use the number in the same position as your chest size.

1 Cast on 14 (16, 18, 20) stitches.

2 Arm knit 4 (5, 6, 7) rows of stockinette stitch.

Right-front lapel

1 Knit 1, knit 2 together. This is the beginning of the front-right lapel, which now consists of 2 stitches. For now, work only with the 2 stitches you just knitted and leave the other 11 (13, 15, 17) stitches unworked.

2 Arm knit 7 (8, 9, 10) more rows of your 2-stitch right-front lapel and then bind off all the stitches on the front-right lapel.

3 Cut the roving/yarn to begin working on the center-back section of the vest, leaving a 15-inch-long (38cm) tail to stitch the lapel to the back section at the shoulders once you've completed the knitting.

Keep your stitches as tight as you can in order to create a solid texture for your vest.

Because you have so few stitches to knit, you won't need to push them all the way up your arm.

Continued

Center-back section

1 Return to the 11 (13, 15, 17) unworked stitches. Slip, slip, knit to decrease 1 stitch, knit 4 (6, 8, 10) stitches, knit 2 together. Leave the final 3 stitches unworked for the left-front lapel. Continue working with the 6 (8, 10, 12) remaining stitches for the center-back section.

2 Arm knit 5 (6, 7, 8) rows of the center-back section and then bind off. Cut the roving/yarn to begin working on the second lapel. You don't need to leave a tail.

Front-left lapel

1 Return to the 3 remaining stitches. Slip, slip, knit to decrease 1 stitch, knit 1. The left-front lapel now has 2 stitches.

2 Arm knit 7 (8, 9, 10) more rows of the 2-stitch front-left lapel and then bind off. Cut the roving/yarn, leaving a 15-inch-long (38cm) tail to stitch the front and back pieces together at the shoulders later.

Join the shoulders

Use your fingers and the tails to stitch the lapel tops to the 2 outside stitches on either side of the center-back section, as shown in Figure 1. You'll join A to A, B to B, C to C, and D to D.

Finish

Trim all the ends of the roving/yarn to about 8 inches (20cm) long and then weave or needle felt the ends of the yarn/roving into the vest to ensure they permanently stay in place.

See the Needle Felting Roving section for more specific instructions.

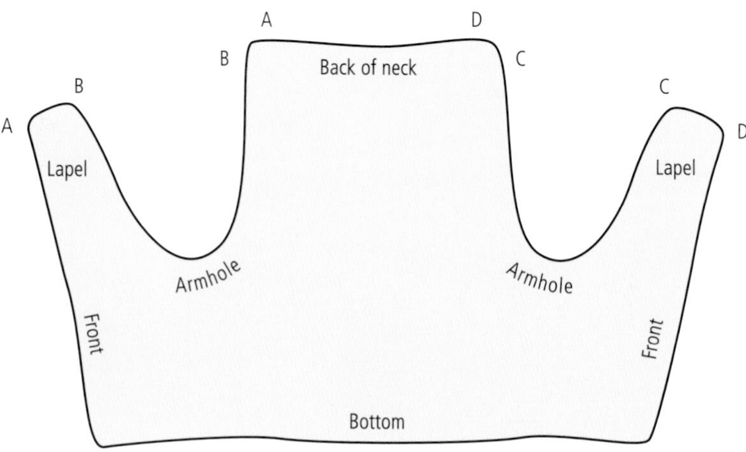

Figure 1 Join A and B on the lapel to A and B on the back of the neck and then join C and D on the lapel to C and D on the back of the neck.

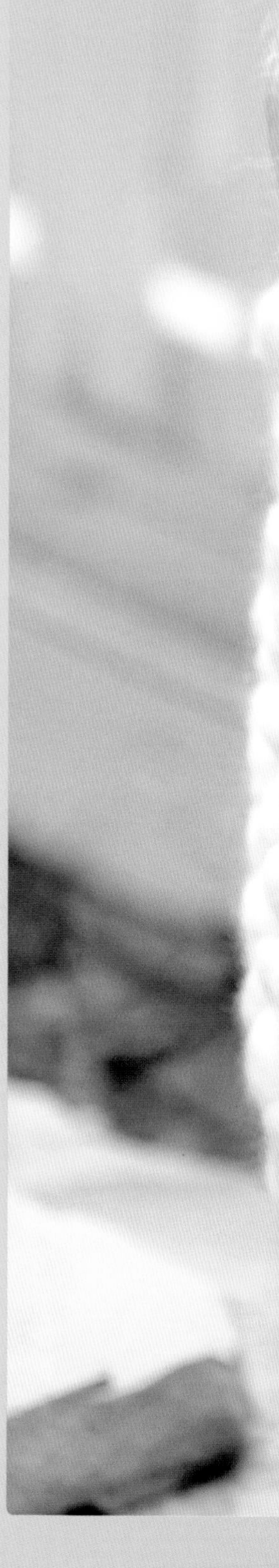

tip

You'll use the tails left after making the lapels to join the shoulders. You don't need a needle—just use your fingers.

Essential information

Difficulty level
Moderate

Time to make
20 minutes

Finished size
20-inch (51cm) circumference

Materials
15 yards (14m) or .75 pounds (340g) of raw, unspun merino wool roving with a 23-micron count (or use giant yarn in the same amount)

Tools
Felting needle

Scissors

Gauge
2 stitches and 3 rows equals 4 inches (10cm).

This project was made with 1 ball of Intreccio Giant Merino roving in Dusty Rose, 20 yards (18m).

Quirky hat

This hat is the perfect beginner project because it knits up fast and lets you practice a new skill: decreases. Making this hat in roving results in a structured shape.

How to make

Hat

1 Cast on 12 stitches.

2 Arm knit 1 row.

Row 2: Knit 2 together, knit 8, slip, slip, knit (2 decreases made).

Row 3: Knit 2 together, knit 6, slip, slip, knit (2 decreases made).

Row 4: Knit 2 together, knit 4, slip, slip, knit (2 decreases made).

Row 5: Knit 2 together, knit 2, slip, slip, knit (2 decreases made).

3 Draw yarn through the 4 remaining stitches. To avoid a bump at the top of your hat, consider tightening the tension on those last 4 stitches before pulling the tail through them. Cut the roving/yarn, leaving a 24-inch-long (61cm) tail, and pull it all the way through, cinching the top by pulling the tail firmly through the remaining 4 stitches.

4 Use your fingers to thread the roving/yarn tail through the edge stitches of either side, creating a back seam.

You can adjust this hat's shape after knitting. Roving is easy to work with, but treat it gently.

Finish

Weave in both ends of the roving/yarn. If you're using roving, you may also choose to secure your ends after weaving them by needle felting them into the underside of a stitch. This will create an invisible and permanent connection.

See the Needle Felting Roving section for more specific instructions.

Roving can remain durable if you keep your stitches tight and secure any loose ends.

tip

To create a more relaxed fit, try using multiple strands of yarn rather than roving.

tip

Because ribbon yarn is slippery, make sure you aren't dropping any loops off your arm as you knit.

Essential information

Difficulty level
Moderate

Time to make
20 minutes

Finished size
34 x 2.5 inches (86 x 6cm)

Materials
69 yards (63m) of bulky ribbon yarn, with 6 strands held together

17 inches (43cm) of chain in your preferred color

Lobster clasp

Four 10mm jump rings

Tools
2 pairs of flat-nose jewelry pliers

Wire cutters

Scissors

Gauge
2 stitches and 2 rows equals 4 inches (10cm).

This project was made with 1 ball of Lion Brand Yarns Martha Stewart Crafts Glitter Ribbon in Verdalite, 69 yards (63m).

Knitted necklace

Try the rope-like I-cord stitch with this quick and easy necklace. You don't need any jewelry-making experience—assembly requires just basic techniques.

How to make

Necklace

1 Divide the yarn into 6 equal lengths and then rewind it into balls.

2 Cast on 3 stitches.

3 Transfer the stitches to your opposite arm by slipping them one at a time. When you finish, the working yarn should be on the same side as your elbow rather than on the same side as your hand.

4 Arm knit these 3 stitches, pulling the working yarn across the back of the piece before you knit the first stitch. This helps create the rope-like I-cord look.

5 Transfer the stitches back to your other arm. Note that you're only knitting the stitches off one arm—always beginning with the working yarn on the same side as your elbow.

6 Repeat the knitting and transferring steps, working in I-cord until the piece measures 16 inches (41cm) or your desired length, and then bind off.

7 Weave in all the ends.

Use a synthetic but bright ribbon yarn for this necklace, allowing the color to stand out no matter what you wear with it.

Don't panic if you weave in your ends and they poke out a bit. You can use a needle and thread to secure them in the center of the I-cord.

Continued

Jewelry findings

1 Grasp one side of a jump ring with your jewelry pliers and then grasp the other side with the second pair of pliers. Turn one wrist away from you, opening the jump ring, as shown in Figure 1. Don't open the jump ring by pulling the ends apart from each other, as this can weaken and deform the ring.

2 Repeat the previous step to open the other 3 jump rings.

3 Using the wire cutters, cut the chain into 2 equal lengths.

Assemble

1 Attach the chain to the I-cord by slipping 1 jump ring into either end of the I-cord, working the jump ring through as many strands of ribbon yarn as possible.

2 Slip one end of a piece of chain onto that jump ring. Grasp one side of the jump ring with your pliers and then grasp the opposite side of the jump ring with the second pliers. Turn one wrist toward you, allowing the jump ring ends to meet and thus closing the jump ring.

3 Attach the clasp to the chain by catching the loose end of the chain and one half of the lobster clasp in another jump ring. Close this jump ring.

4 Repeat the previous three steps to attach the chain and the clasp on the other end of the I-cord.

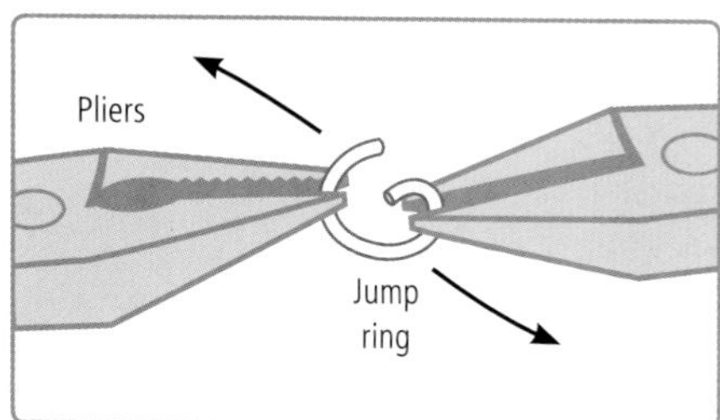

Figure 1 Open the ring by twisting the ends away from each other, not by pulling them apart.

You can use a different length of chain. Make sure it feels comfortable around your neck before you attach it to the necklace.

Essential information

Difficulty level
Moderate

Time to make
45 minutes

Finished size
Adult: Circumference equals 20 inches (51cm)

Child: Circumference equals 16 inches (41cm)

Materials
33 yards (30m) of jumbo netted acrylic-blend yarn for each hat

Tools
Scissors

Gauge
2 stitches and 3.75 rows equals 4 inches (10cm).

Each project was made with 2 skeins of Premier Yarns Couture Jazz in Denim, 16.5 yards (15m).

These bonnets are easy to assemble and fun to wear.

Ski bonnet

Who doesn't love a hat topped with a sprightly pompom? Braided ties also add to this bonnet's charm. This pattern comes in two sizes: adult and child.

How to make

Adult size

1 Cast on 5 stitches.

2 Arm knit 15 rows.

3 Bind off all the stitches, leaving a 10-inch-long (25cm) tail.

Child size

1 Cast on 4 stitches.

2 Arm knit 13 rows.

3 Bind off all the stitches, leaving a 10-inch-long (25cm) tail.

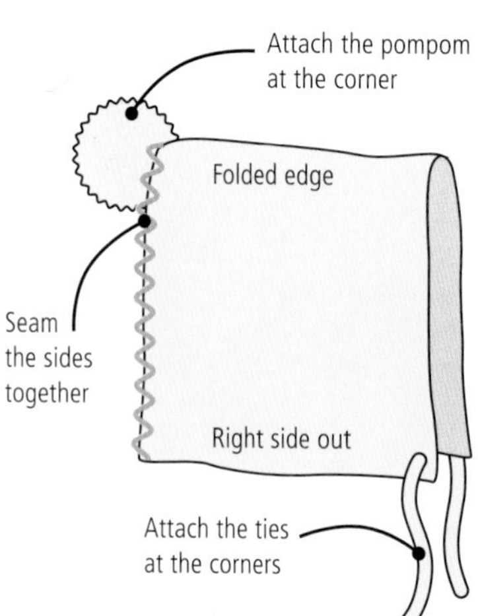
Attach the pompom at the corner
Folded edge
Seam the sides together
Right side out
Attach the ties at the corners

Figure 1 Seam the sides before adding the ties and the pompom.

Finish

1 Fold the fabric in half—right side out. Place the fold at the top and the cast-on and bind-off edges at the bottom. Use a mattress stitch to seam one side—the hat's back when it's unfolded.

2 Weave in and trim all the ends.

Ties (make 2)

Cut three 18-inch (46cm) strands of yarn. Knot them to the hat's front corners. Braid the strands and then tie a knot.

Pompom

Make a 2-inch (5cm) pompom and then tie it to the crown of the hat with a thinner piece of yarn. Figure 1 shows how to seam the hat, attach the ties, and add the pompom.

See the Making Pompoms section for more specific instructions.

tip
Make the pompom in a contrasting color for a completely different look.

Making pompoms

If your project needs a little something extra, consider adding a pompom. You can make one in less than 15 minutes. The more you wrap in step 4, the better your finished pompom will look. To attach it to your project, pass a needle threaded with yarn through the center tie holding the pompom together.

What you'll need

- Small cardboard scrap
- Scissors
- Yarn
- Tapestry needle

1 Decide how wide you'd like your pompom. Cut a piece of cardboard 6 inches (15cm) wide by the desired diameter of the pompom. Cut an opening from one short edge to the center, reaching about three quarters of the way down the length.

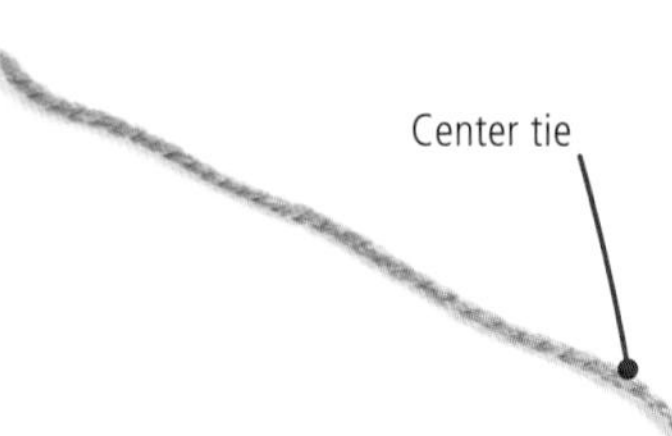

2 Cut a 10-inch (25cm) length of yarn and set it aside. You'll use this center tie in step 5.

5 Insert the center tie from step 2 through the space in the cardboard and then tie it tightly around the wrapped yarn.

Size considerations

For a pompom 2 inches (5cm) in diameter, cut the cardboard 6 inches (15cm) wide and 2 inches (5cm) tall. The taller the cardboard, the larger the pompom will be. If you want to make a smaller pompom, you can substitute a fork for the cardboard.

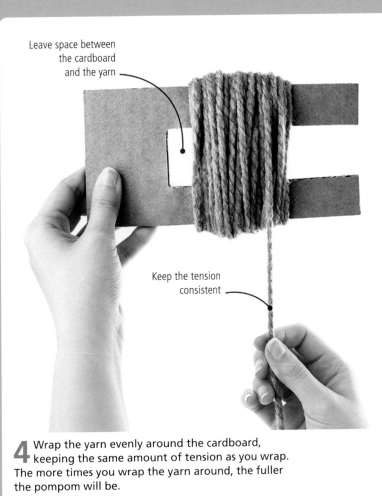

Hold the tail with your thumb

3 Place the yarn tail on the cardboard, lining up the end with the edge of the rectangle.

Leave space between the cardboard and the yarn
Keep the tension consistent

4 Wrap the yarn evenly around the cardboard, keeping the same amount of tension as you wrap. The more times you wrap the yarn around, the fuller the pompom will be.

Use heavy shears

6 Use your scissors to cut the loops on one side of the wrapping. Cut as evenly as possible to ensure all the strands are the same length.

Trim it round

7 Repeat step 6 on the opposite side. Fluff the pompom and then trim around it to make the edges even.

Essential information

Difficulty level
Moderate

Time to make
90 minutes

Finished size
Bag: 17.5 x 11.5 inches (45 x 29cm)
Handle: 29 inches (74cm)

Materials
100 yards (91m) of 3mm faux suede lacing
18 inches (46cm) of a 45-inch-wide (114cm) unstretched fabric for lining
Thread

Tools
Sewing machine
Sewing needle
Pinking shears
Scissors
Pen or pencil
Ruler
Disappearing ink fabric marker
Cardboard: 17.5 x 11.5 inches (45 x 29cm)
Iron
Craft knife

Gauge
3 stitches and 2 rows equals 4 inches (10cm).

This project was made with faux suede lacing in green, 100 yards (92m), 3mm wide.

Open-weave bag

Knitting in garter stitch is easy, but suede lacing is challenging to work with and will expand your skill set. Buy it in bulk to avoid having to connect short yardages.

How to make

Bag

1 Cast on 9 stitches, leaving a 30-inch-long (76cm) tail for seaming.

2 Beginning with a knit row, arm knit in garter stitch until the bag measures 35 inches (89cm) long, ending after completing a purl row. Bind off on a knit row, leaving another 30-inch-long (76cm) tail for seaming.

3 Fold the knitting in half lengthwise so the cast-on and bind-off edges meet. You should have a long tail on each top edge. Seam each side by using the long tails left from the cast on and the bind off.

Handle

1 Cut 3 strands of suede lacing that are each 3 yards (2.75m) long.

2 Hold the 3 strands with their ends lined up and then fold them in half, creating a loop. Slip the loop through one of the top edges of the bag where you seamed one of the sides. Slide the tails of the strands through the loop, securing one side of the handle to the bag.

Use a clothespin to hold the unfastened end in place before firmly knotting it. This allows you to make the handle any length you prefer.

3 Braid the tails until the handle measures approximately 29 inches (74cm) long. You should then have a length of fringe remaining.

4 Being careful not to twist the braid, knot it to the opposite side seam.

5 Trim the handle fringe evenly.

Continued ➡

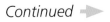

Make the lining

1 Place the bag on top of the piece of cardboard. Grasp the top and bottom edges, pulling the bag to stretch it. Using a pen or pencil, trace around the outside of the bag. Using a ruler, draw straight lines for seam allowance along the lines you sketched, creating a uniform lining template for cutting.

Cut out the template and then insert it into the bag, making sure it fits. If it doesn't, redraw the template, adding or subtracting width or length as necessary.

2 Fold the fabric in half, with the right sides together, keeping the selvages together. Place the template on top of the fabric, lining up the bottom edge of the template with the fold of the fabric.

Using a fabric marker or tailor's chalk, add seam allowances of 1 inch (3cm) to one side of the fabric and also to the top. Trace right against the edge of the other side of the template.

Cut out the fabric on the ruler you drew.

3 Sew the side seams of the lining using a ½-inch (1.3cm) seam allowance, as shown in Figure 1. Finish the seams with pinking shears to prevent unraveling.

4 Fold the top of the lining over ½ inch (1.3cm). Press with an iron. Fold over ½ inch (1.3cm) again. Press again with an iron.

5 Stitch around the top edge of the lining a bit less than ½ inch (1.3cm) from the edge.

Attach the lining

1 Turn the lining right side out, inserting it inside the bag and pinning it in place.

2 Use a sewing machine to sew around the top of the lining, catching as much of the suede as possible under the needle while securing the lining to the bag.

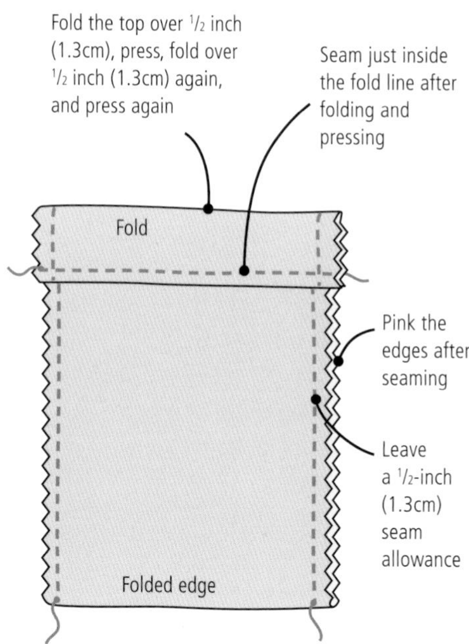
Fold the top over ½ inch (1.3cm), press, fold over ½ inch (1.3cm) again, and press again
Seam just inside the fold line after folding and pressing
Fold
Pink the edges after seaming
Leave a ½-inch (1.3cm) seam allowance
Folded edge

Figure 1 This is how the lining should look before you turn it right side out and put it inside the bag.

If you want to make the bag sturdier, you can use a more durable material, like rope, or even hold multiple strands of yarn together.

tip

This bag isn't designed to hold heavy items. Check the label for how much weight the suede can support.

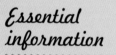

Essential information

Difficulty level
Moderate

Time to make
2 hours

Finished size
36- to 40-inch
(91 to 102cm) chest

Materials
140 yards (128m) or
8 pounds (3.6kg) of
hand-dyed merino wool
roving for arm knitting

120 yards (110m) or
4 ounces (113g) of 1 skein
of bulky 100% merino
wool yarn for sewing

Tools
Felting needle

Scissors

Gauge
1.5 stitches and 2 rows
equals 4 inches (10cm).

This project was made with:
4 balls of UrbanGypZ hand-dyed roving in Wild Raspberry, 35 yards (32m).

1 skein of UrbanGypZ Bulky 3-ply yarn in Wild Raspberry, 120 yards (110m).

Plush sweater

Roving creates mega stitches for this cropped top. It can take weeks to knit a sweater with needles. That's not the case with this design—guaranteed!

How to make

Front and back (work both the same)

1 Cast on 8 stitches.

2 Arm knit 9 rows.

3 Bind off all the stitches.

Sleeves (make 2)

1 Cast on 7 stitches.

2 Arm knit 6 rows.

3 Bind off all the stitches.

This sweater might look challenging, but it's quite easy: You knit four rectangular pieces and then assemble them using mattress stitches.

Although roving is delicate, you'll be struck by how sturdy this sweater looks and feels.

Continued

tip

Because roving can develop entangled fibers called *neps*, keep your sweater looking tidy by shaving them off with a sweater shaver.

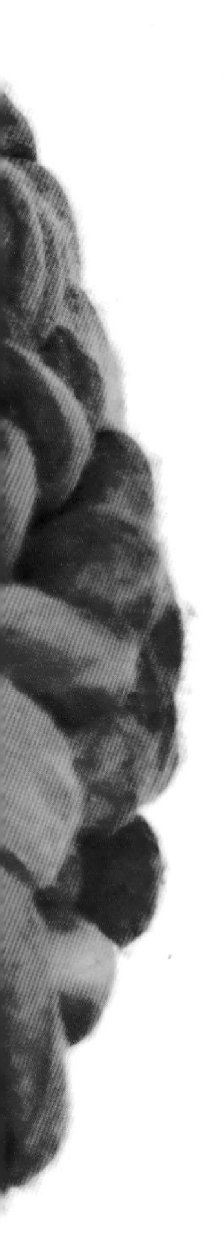

Assemble

1 With the right sides of the back and front facing up, as shown in Figure 1, use a mattress stitch and the bulky yarn to seam 4 inches (10cm) in from each shoulder corner, leaving a 12-inch-wide (30cm) opening for the neck.

2 Find the center stitch at the top of each sleeve, and use yarn to tie each sleeve to the shoulder seam through the center stitch, as shown in Figure 2.

3 Stitch each sleeve to the body by using a mattress stitch. Fold the piece as shown in Figure 3 and then use a mattress stitch to sew the sleeve and side seams.

4 Weave in all the ends.

See the Needle Felting Roving section for more specific instructions.

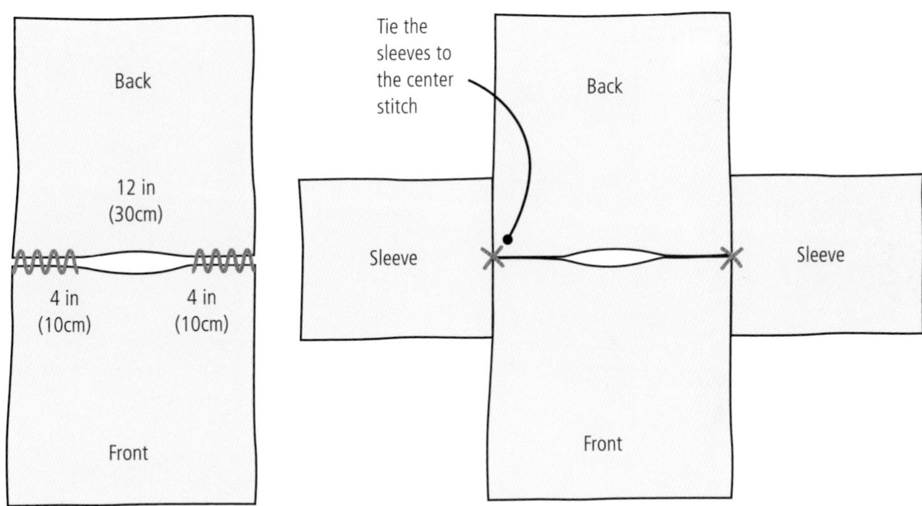

Figure 1 Use a mattress stitch to seam the shoulders, leaving an opening for your neck.

Figure 2 Make sure all the pieces are right side up before tying a sleeve to each shoulder seam.

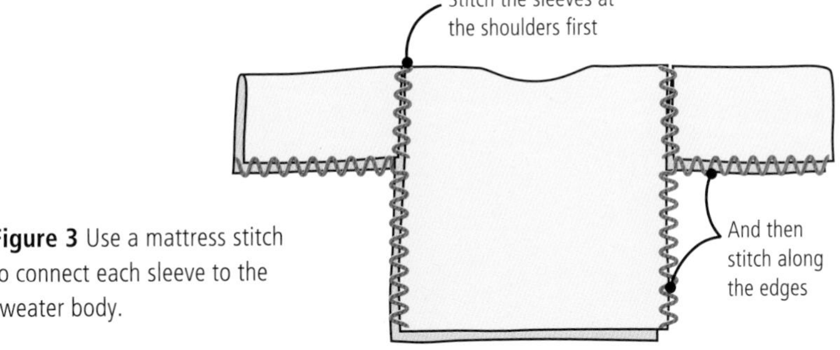

Figure 3 Use a mattress stitch to connect each sleeve to the sweater body.

Home sweet home

From a bed for your four-legged friends and blankets to wrap yourself in on cold days to covers for pillows and lampshades, these projects will be focal points for any room.

Essential information

Difficulty level
Easy

Time to make
1 hour

Finished size
20 x 30 inches (51 x 76cm)

Materials
352 yards (322m) of super bulky yarn, with 6 strands held together (or 2 strands held together if using the Navajo plying technique)

Tools
Scissors

Gauge
2 stitches and 3.75 rows equals 4 inches (10cm).

This project was made with 4 skeins of Premier Craft-Tee Yarn in Blue Shades, 88 yards (81m).

Doormat

Super stretchy T-shirt yarn yields a hardy doormat that feels extra plush. Create your own T-shirt yarn to almost completely make this doormat with your own hands.

How to make

Doormat

1 Cast on 13 stitches.

First row: *Knit 1, slip 1 stitch with the yarn held in front. Repeat from * to the last stitch, knit 1.

Second row: Knit 1, *knit 1, slip 1 stitch with the yarn held in front. Repeat from * to the last 2 stitches, knit 2.

2 Repeat the first and second rows until your rug measures approximately 18 inches (46cm) or your desired length.

3 Bind off all the stitches.

4 Weave in and trim all the ends.

See the Making T-Shirt Yarn and Navajo Plying Technique sections for more specific instructions.

Linen stitches give this doormat a woven look, and you can even change colors every other row to create a different visual effect.

Reserve this doormat for indoor use. Because it's so thick, it won't dry quickly if it becomes wet outside.

tip

Knitting with 6 strands of T-shirt yarn held together will result in a doormat that can withstand heavy use.

Making T-shirt yarn

Making your own T-shirt yarn is fun. Different variables, like how much stretch the fabric has and how wide you cut the strips, will determine how much fabric you need to start with to get the amount of yarn required for your project. The wider you cut the strips, the heavier the yarn weight.

What you'll need

- Several yards (meters) of stretch-knit fabric
- Ruler
- Rotary cutter
- Self-healing cutting mat
- Fabric scissors

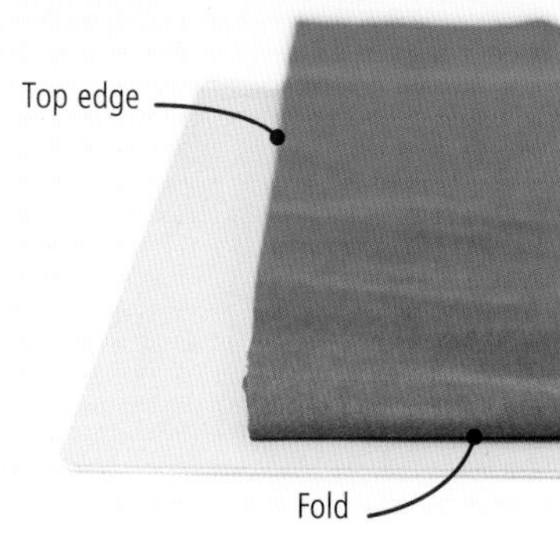

1 Fold the fabric in half on the self-healing cutting mat, with the selvages meeting.

Cut in from the fold

3 Roll the rotary cutter along the edge of the ruler and across the fabric, starting at the fold and stopping about 2 inches (5cm) from the selvages. The cut should be parallel to the fabric's top edge.

Cut off the fold

Leave the first fold unclipped

6 At the folds and on the edges, use scissors to clip the corners of the cuts into "curves," clipping across all but the first fold. These cuts don't have to look perfect because you won't see them once you stretch out the fabric later.

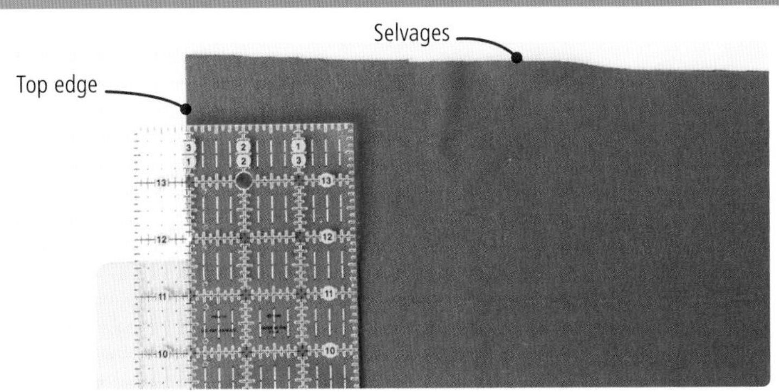

2 Place the edge of your ruler along the width of the fabric—3 inches (8cm) from the top edge of the fabric and parallel to it.

tip
Stretch-knit fabric is also known as jersey. Use a poly-cotton blend; the polyester will make your T-shirt yarn more durable.

4 Cut the fabric again—3 inches (8cm) from the first cut and parallel to it—but this time starting at the selvages and stopping 2 inches (5cm) from the fold.

5 Repeat steps 3 and 4 to cut what will look something like zigzags (as the cuts open up) across the entire length of the fabric.

7 You should now have one continuous strand of T-shirt yarn. Gently pull it to stretch it.

8 Roll the entire length of fabric into a ball and then use it as directed for any given T-shirt yarn pattern.

Using actual T-shirts

You can upcycle T-shirts into yarn, but the technique is different from the one described here because T-shirts are tubes of fabric, whereas fabric is a sheet. The advantage of using fabric to make yarn is that depending on how much fabric you start with, it yields far more yarn than an actual T-shirt.

Essential information

Difficulty level
Easy

Time to make
1 hour

Finished size
12 feet (3.7m) long

Materials
310 yards (283m) each of two different colors of bulky yarn, with 4 strands held together

Tools
Scissors

Gauge
4 stitches and 2 rows equals 4 inches (10cm).

This project was made with: 2 balls of Bernat Softee Baby Chunky in Cream Puff, 155 yards (142m).

2 balls of Bernat Softee Baby Chunky in Buttercup, 155 yards (142m).

Pompom garland

Playful décor for a kid's room or a festive accent for parties, this garland spells F-U-N. Make it as long as you like—striped or solid—and include cheerful pompoms.

How to make

Garland

Divide and rewind both yarn colors into 4 equal balls of each color.

1 Cast on 5 stitches of either color.

2 Arm knit all the stitches for 12 inches (31cm). Change color and then knit for another 12 inches (31cm). Continue until the garland is your desired length, changing colors every 12 inches (31cm).

3 Bind off all the stitches.

4 Leave the tails at both ends intact to use them for hanging the garland. Weave in the rest of the ends or you can snip the ends short.

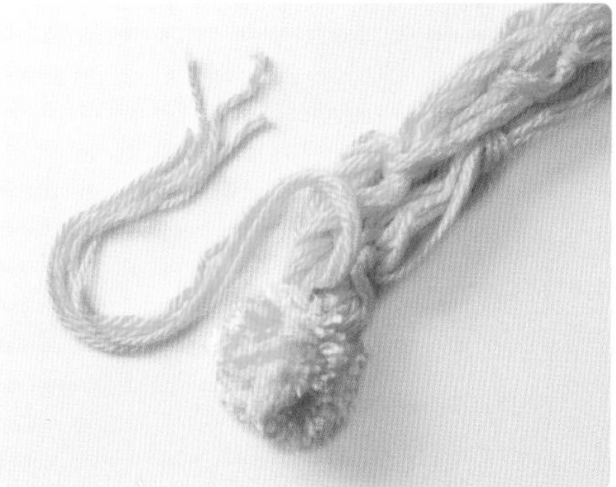

Leaving tails at the ends will give you ways to hang the garland.

Pompoms

Make 2 pompoms (either in one color or two colors) and then tie a pompom to each end of the garland with separate strands of yarn.

See the Making Pompoms section for more specific instructions.

For an even more festive garland, weave a string of party lights into the strands to create a decoration that sparkles and glows!

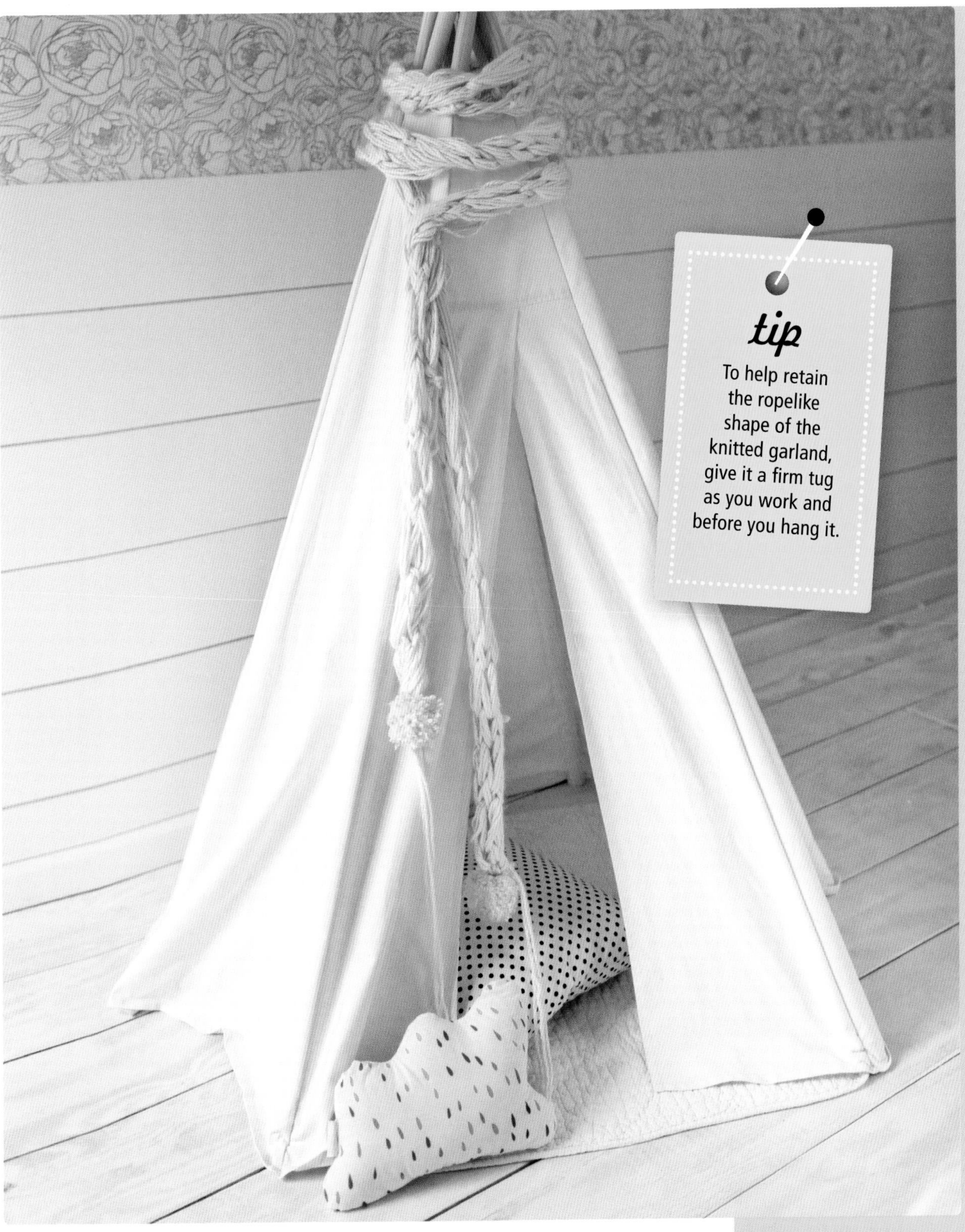

tip

To help retain the ropelike shape of the knitted garland, give it a firm tug as you work and before you hang it.

tip

You can make the pillow cover with yarn, but you might find that roving provides a more sturdy and elegant look.

When seaming the edges together, pull them taut to close the seam, but don't pull so tightly that the edges bunch up.

Essential information

Difficulty level
Easy

Time to make
1 hour

Finished size
16 x 16 inches (41 x 41cm)

Materials
Color A: 90 yards (82m) of roving (or use super bulky yarn, with 4 strands held together)

Color B: 90 yards (82m) of roving (or use super bulky yarn, with 4 strands held together)

16-inch (41cm) pillow form or throw pillow

Tools
Scissors

Felting needle

Gauge
2 stitches and 2 rows equals 4 inches (10cm).

This project was made with: 1 ball of Cloudborn Fibers Highland Roving in Stormy Skies, 90 yards (82m).

1 ball of Cloudborn Fibers Highland Roving in Dolphin Blue, 90 yards (82m).

Two-toned pillow cover

This pillow cover offers practice with seaming. Using roving means a soft texture. Make a pair, choosing roving or yarn colors that coordinate with your décor.

How to make

Divide each roving/yarn color into 4 balls.

First piece

1 Cast on 8 stitches with color A.

2 Arm knit 7 rows.

3 Bind off, leaving a 20-inch-long (51cm) tail for seaming.

Second piece

1 Cast on 8 stitches with color B.

2 Arm knit 7 rows.

3 Bind off, leaving a 20-inch-long (51cm) tail for seaming.

Assemble

1 Place the two pieces side by side, with the right sides up.

2 Using one of the long tails you left earlier, seam one side of the pieces together with a mattress stitch.

3 Place the two pieces' wrong sides together and then sew the top and bottom edges together.

4 Weave in all the loose ends, except for the remaining seaming tail.

5 Turn the piece right side out and then slip the pillow form inside.

6 Seam the final edge of the two pieces together using the remaining seaming tail and a mattress stitch. You might have to pull on the edges a little to get them to come together.

7 Weave in or needle felt any remaining roving/yarn.

See the Needle Felting Roving section for more specific instructions.

You can customize this pattern to fit any square or rectangular pillow.

Essential information

Difficulty level
Easy

Time to make
30 minutes

Finished size
13 x 25 inches (33 x 64cm)

Materials
100 feet (31m) of 3/16 -inch (.5cm) nylon rope

Tools
Scissors

Gauge
2 stitches and 3.75 rows equals 4 inches (10cm).

This project was made with nylon rope in white, 100 feet (30m), 3/16-inch (.5cm) in diameter.

Mini hammock

Looking for a way to showcase a stuffed animal collection? This hammock can fit in corners or along walls, offering ways to keep toys off the floor but still within reach.

How to make

Hammock

1 Cast on 10 stitches, leaving a 15-inch-long (38cm) tail.

2 Arm knit until the piece measures approximately 25 inches (64cm).

3 Bind off all the stitches, and trim the ends to approximately 15 inches (38cm).

Hanging mechanism

Loop the end through the opposite side of the hammock from where the rope is currently attached so the rope is doubled. Tie the end of the rope to the spot where the yarn is coming from. This section of doubled rope creates "handles" you can attach to the walls or the ceiling for hanging the hammock.

This hammock is best used for light toys—despite being made with nylon rope—and it's definitely not sturdy enough to hold people.

If you'd like a less open look to your hammock, use a thicker rope. This will also make the hammock stronger and able to hold larger toys or items.

tip

You can make this hammock larger by casting on more stitches and then arm knitting for a little while longer.

tip
Use a bolster pillow slightly smaller than the cover's finished size to help make the cover look more plump.

Bolster pillow cover

Combining complementary yarns adds visual texture to this quick knit project. You'll love how such a vibrant pillow cover can have a huge impact on any room design.

Essential information

Difficulty level
Easy

Time to make
30 minutes

Finished size
15 x 7 inches (38 x 18cm)

Materials
36 yards (33m) each of at least five different yarns, with all strands held together

Bolster pillow:
14.75 x 6 inches (38 x 15cm)

Tools
Tapestry needle
Scissors

Gauge
1.75 stitches and 1.5 rows equals 4 inches (10cm).

This project was made with:

2 balls of Big Twist Yarns Natural Blend in Aged Brass, 98 yards (90m).

1 ball of Lion Brand Yarns Wool-Ease Thick & Quick in Butterscotch, 106 yards (97m).

1 ball of Lion Brand Yarns Heartland in Yellowstone, 251 yards (230m).

1 ball of Lion Brand Yarns Heartland in Bryce Canyon, 251 yards (230m).

1 skein of Lion Brand Yarns Homespun in Golden, 185 yards (169m).

1 skein of Buttercream Luxe Craft Rainbow Boucle in Mardi Gras, 621 yards (568m).

How to make

Pillow cover

1 Cast on 12 stitches.

2 Arm knit 12 rows.

3 Bind off all the stitches.

Assemble

1 With 1 strand of sturdy but plain yarn for seaming, use a mattress stitch to seam the two sides together—with the knit side of the piece on the inside and the purl side on the outside.

2 Thread a double length of the seaming yarn through all the cast-on stitches.

3 Close the cast-on end by using a double length of the seaming yarn and threading that yarn through all the cast-on stitches.

4 Insert the bolster pillow completely into the knitted piece via the bind-off end.

When you hold the different yarns together before arm knitting, they should feel as thick or thicker than a super bulky yarn.

5 Cinch the cast-on edge opening closed by pulling the yarn and securing it to hold the stitches tightly.

6 Repeat closing the cast-on end and cinching the cast-on edge opening closed for the bind-off end.

7 Weave in all the ends.

Using thinner yarns or fewer strands will allow more of the bolster pillow to show.

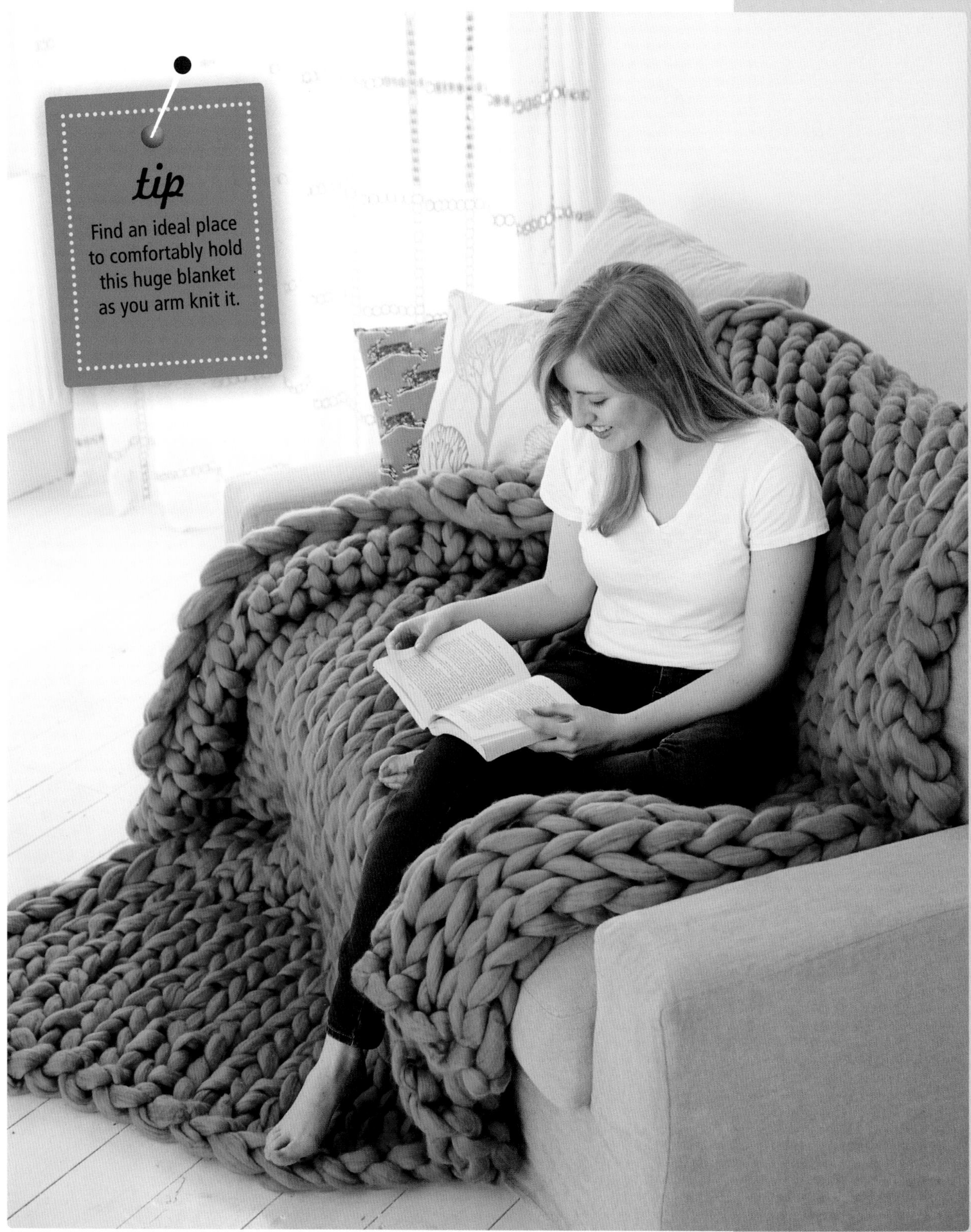
tip
Find an ideal place to comfortably hold this huge blanket as you arm knit it.

Essential information

Difficulty level
Easy

Time to make
2 hours

Finished size
Double blanket:
76 x 80 inches
(193 x 203cm)

Materials
Double blanket:
300 yards (274m) or
15 pounds (7kg) of raw, unspun merino wool roving with a 23-micron count (or use giant yarn in the same amount)

Tools
Scissors

Gauge
1⅓ stitches and 1⅓ rows equals 4 inches (10cm) or 3 inches (8cm) per stitch.

This project was made with 1 ball of Intreccio Giant Merino roving in Sea Foam, 300 yards (274m).

Snuggly blanket

This is no ordinary blanket! You have the option to make it really large—as a double blanket—but if that feels too big, make a smaller size: twin or lap.

How to make

Double blanket (shown)

1 Cast on 25 stitches.

2 Arm knit in stockinette stitch for 26 rows, until your desired length is reached, or until you run out of yarn, making sure to unravel your last row to prevent having a partial row.

3 Bind off all the stitches.

4 Weave in all the ends. For extra security, consider needle felting the ends.

See the Needle Felting Roving section for more specific instructions.

Even the back side of this huge blanket showcases an attractive stitch pattern.

Twin blanket

Finished size: 40 x 76 inches (102 x 193cm)

Materials: 225 yards (206m) or 11 pounds (5kg) of roving (or giant yarn)

Knit count: 14 stitches x 25 rows

Lap blanket

Finished size: 36 x 45 inches (91 x 114cm)

Materials: 150 yards (137m) or 7.5 pounds (3.4kg) of roving (or giant yarn)

Knit count: 12 stitches x 14 rows

tip

T-shirt fabric (or T-shirt yarn) with polyester in it will give this pillow cover more durability.

Essential information

Difficulty level
Easy

Time to make
2 hours

Finished size
24 x 24 x 10 inches
(61 x 61 x 25cm)

Materials (makes 1)
95 yards (87m) of super bulky polyester/cotton blend T-shirt yarn or polyester blend T-shirt yarn for one pillow cover

Floor pillow: 24 inches (60cm) square

Tools
Tapestry needle
Scissors

Gauge
1.5 stitches and 1.75 rows equals 4 inches (10cm).

This project was made with: Handmade T-shirt yarn in heather gray, 5.5 yards (5m).

Handmade T-shirt yarn in teal, 5.5 yards (5m).

Pillow cover with tassels

Arm knitting is all about scale. And T-shirt yarn produces enormous stitches—ideal for sturdy covers for giant pillows. Immense tassels emphasize the corners.

How to make

Front and back (make 2)

1 Cast on 15 stitches.

Rib stitch row: Slip the first stitch, *purl 1, knit 1, then repeat from * to the end of the row to form a 1 x 1 rib stitch pattern.

2 Repeat the rib stitch for 10 more rows.

3 Bind off all 15 stitches in the 1 x 1 rib stitch pattern.

Assemble

1 Place the wrong sides of the back and front together, matching all the edges. Using a mattress stitch, seam together three sides of the cover: one set of sides, then the cast-on edges, and finally the other set of sides.

2 Insert the pillow into the cover.

3 Using a mattress stitch, sew the pillow cover closed at the bind-off edges.

4 Weave in all the ends.

Tassels help the pillow cover and its corners look more polished.

Tassels

Make 4 tassels, with each being 6 inches (15cm) long. Tie or knot a tassel to each of the pillow corners with a separate piece of yarn.

See the Making Tassels section for more specific instructions.

Making tassels

Tassels are simple adornments you can add to anything—from home décor (like pillows) to accessories (like scarves). They look great at the corners of a project but are equally sharp when attached along the length of a side. A tassel takes less than 15 minutes to make.

What you'll need

- A book as tall as the desired length of the finished tassel
- Scissors
- At least 3 yards (2.75m) of yarn

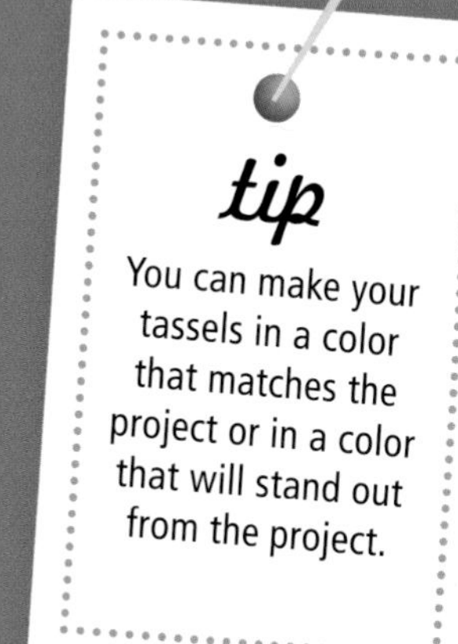

tip

You can make your tassels in a color that matches the project or in a color that will stand out from the project.

3 Cut a 24-inch (61cm) piece of yarn, looping one end and holding it vertically against the tassel's tied end with your thumb.

1 Wrap the yarn around the book 12 times. Cut a piece of yarn 6 inches (15cm) long, and tie it around the wrapped yarn.

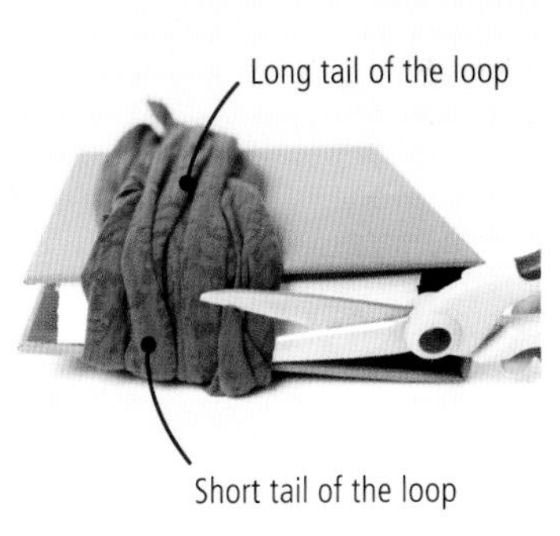

2 Cut through the wrapped yarn opposite the tied end.

4 Wrap the long tail of the loop tightly around all the strands three times and then thread the end of the long tail through the loop.

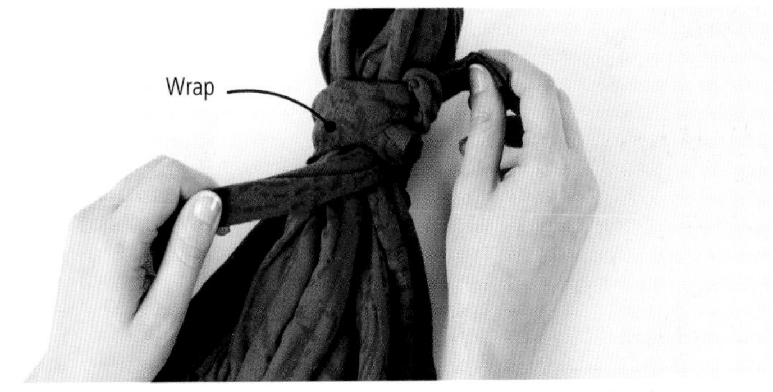

5 Pull the end of the short tail end of the loop to tighten the loop. It should be tucked just beneath the wraps, locking the ends in place. (Tuck the end in if it's not completely camouflaged.)

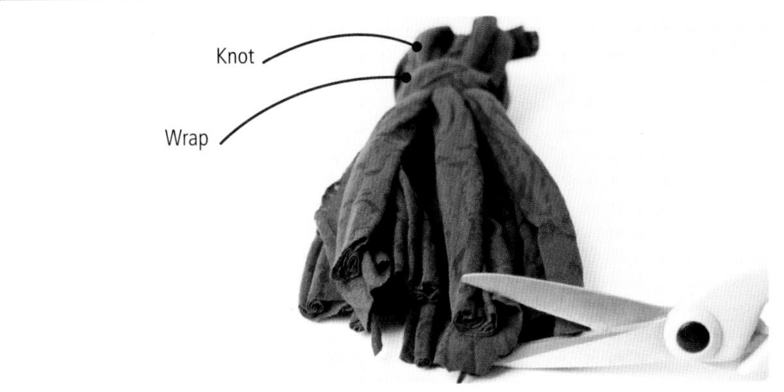

6 Trim the tassel ends so they're all the same length.

Essential information

Difficulty level
Easy

Time to make
45 minutes

Finished size
45 x 15 inches
(114 x 38cm)

Materials
210 yards (192m) of super bulky yarn, with 3 strands held together

Pot or planter: 17.5 inches (45cm) tall and 62 inches (158cm) in circumference

Tools
Scissors

Plastic clips for assembly

Gauge
4 stitches and 2 rows equals 4 inches (10cm).

This project was made with 3 balls of Red Heart Mixology in Ivory, 70 yards (64m).

Planter cover

Chunky seed stitches give this highly textured piece a woven appearance. Not only does this cover liven up any plain pot, but it also adds a subtle focus to a room.

How to make

Cover

1 Cast on 10 stitches.

First row: Knit the first stitch. Purl the next stitch. Repeat this knit–purl sequence for the remainder of the row.

Second row: Create the seed stitch by purling the knit stitches and knitting the purl stitches.

2 Repeat the first and second rows until the piece measures approximately 45 inches (114cm).

3 Bind off all the stitches, leaving an 18-inch-long (46cm) tail.

4 Seam the cast-on and bind-off edges together by using a whip stitch.

Drawstrings

1 Cut two strands of matching yarn—each one measuring twice the pot's circumference.

2 Along one edge of the cover, beginning at the seam, weave one of the strands around that entire edge of the piece to create a drawstring for the top edge.

3 Along the other edge, beginning at the seam, weave the other strand around that entire edge of the piece to create a drawstring for the bottom edge.

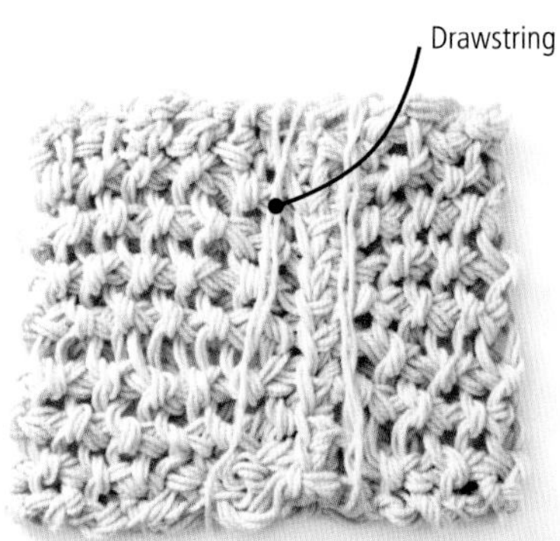

Drawstrings allow you to adjust the cover size for planters with different circumferences.

Assemble

1 Stretch the cover around the pot, using plastic clips as needed to help hold the cover in place.

2 Pull the top drawstring tightly and then tie a strong knot to secure the cover in place. Firmly pull and stretch the cover downward and then pull the bottom drawstring tightly to secure the bottom part. If the plant pot has a tapered bottom, the bottom can be pulled tighter than the top to fit. Knot tightly.

3 Weave in all the ends.

tip
You can match the yarn color to your planter or to the flowering plant's color. Or be bold and use a contrasting color.

tip
Flip the throw over to reveal the completely different texture of the reverse stockinette side.

Essential information

Difficulty level
Easy

Time to make
90 minutes

Finished size
60 x 65 inches (152 x 165cm)

Materials
954 yards (872m) of super bulky yarn, with 2 strands held together

Tools
Scissors

Gauge
4 stitches and 2 rows equals 4 inches (10cm).

This project was made with 9 balls of Lion Brand Yarns Wool-Ease Thick & Quick in Glacier, 106 yards (97m).

Soft fringed throw

Loose stitches make this throw easy to create—perfect for a super quick gift. Each side has a different stitch texture—knit on one and reverse stockinette on the other.

How to make

Throw

1 Cast on 50 stitches.

2 Arm knit all the stitches until the throw measures 55 inches (140cm).

3 Bind off all the stitches.

4 Weave in all the ends.

Fringe

Cut 2 strands of yarn—each approximately 10 inches (25cm) long—and then make a 5-inch (13cm) fringe evenly along the throw's top and bottom edges.

See the Making Fringe section for more specific instructions.

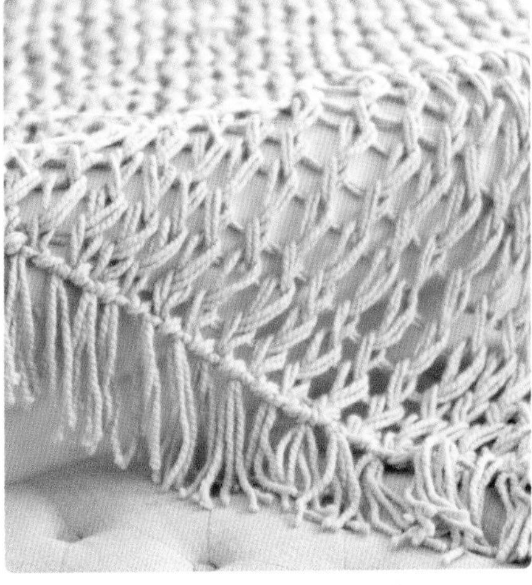

To make the fringe look neater, knit it a little longer than needed. After the fringe has been attached, trim across it in a straight line with a pair of sharp scissors.

Try **knitting half** the throw in one color and the other half in **another color** for an on-trend color block look.

Essential information

Difficulty level
Easy

Time to make
40 minutes

Finished size
17 inches (43cm) tall and 88 inches (224cm) in circumference

Materials
210 yards (192m) of super bulky yarn, with 3 strands held together

Lampshade: 14 inches (36cm) tall and 28 inches (71cm) in diameter

Tools
Scissors

Large plastic clips

Gauge
4 stitches and 2 rows equals 4 inches (10cm).

This project was made with 3 balls of Red Heart Mixology in Grey, 70 yards (64m).

Lampshade cover

Clean lines in neutral tones make this cover bold and modern. Mount it wrong side out on an oversized lampshade to showcase the reverse stockinette stitch.

How to make

Cover

1 Cast on 9 stitches.

2 Arm knit all the stitches until the piece measures approximately 80 inches (203cm). It will be a little smaller than the lampshade's circumference and height because the cover will be stretched open when it's attached. To change the cover's circumference, knit fewer or more rows according to the gauge.

3 Bind off all the stitches, leaving an 18-inch-long (46cm) tail.

4 Seam the cast-on and bind-off edges together by using a whip stitch.

5 Weave in all the ends.

Drawstrings

1 Cut two pieces of matching yarn, making each one measure twice the shade's circumference.

2 Along one edge of the cover and beginning at the seam, weave one of the strands around that entire edge. This becomes the top edge.

3 Repeat that weaving process for the opposite edge. This becomes the cover's bottom edge.

4 Place the cover onto the shade, with the back of the piece facing out, stretching it so it completely covers the lampshade. (Showing the reverse stockinette side gives the cover a grid-like texture.) Use clips as needed to help hold the cover in place as it's fitted.

5 Pull the top drawstring tightly and then tie a strong knot to secure the cover in place. The drawstring should be hidden from sight inside the top of the shade, so you may need to shift the clips a bit to keep the cover from slipping as it's worked into place.

Pull and stretch the cover firmly downward and then pull the bottom drawstring tightly to secure the bottom part of the lampshade cover, making sure the drawstring is hidden from sight inside the bottom of the shade. Knot tightly.

tip

Use large plastic clips to hold the cover in place while attaching it to the lampshade. This will help as you secure the drawstrings.

A drawstring ensures the cover remains securely in place.

tip
A ruler makes measuring your fringe easier. Changing the length of the fringe gives the rug a different vibe.

Essential information

Difficulty level
Easy

Time to make
1 hour

Finished size
32 x 36 inches (81 x 91cm)

Materials
Color A: 296 yards (271m) of super bulky yarn, with 6 strands held together

Color B: 296 yards (271m) of super bulky yarn, with 6 strands held together

Tools
Scissors

Gauge
2 stitches and 3.75 rows equals 4 inches (10cm).

This project was made with: 4 skeins of Premier Mega Tweed in Gray, 74 yards (68m).

4 skeins of Premier Mega Tweed in Mint, 74 yards (68m).

Striped rug with fringe

Making this project gives you a chance to practice adding fringe as well as changing colors after knitting several rows. Pick colors that complement your décor.

How to make

Rug

1 Cast on 17 stitches in color A.

2 Arm knit 4 rows in color A.

3 Switch to color B and then knit 4 rows.

4 Repeat steps 2 and 3 two more times.

5 Bind off all the stitches.

Fringe

Attach fringe along the top and bottom of the rug. For each fringe, cut a 9-inch-long (23cm) strand of each color. Hold both strands together while attaching the fringe. Trim the fringe evenly to 4 inches (10cm) long.

See the Making Fringe section for more specific instructions.

You can add fringe that incorporates both colors you used for the rug, just one color from the project, or even another color entirely.

Create your own design for this accent rug by varying the length of the stripes or making it a longer runner.

Essential information

Difficulty level
Moderate

Time to make
30 minutes

Finished size
18 x 14 x 5 inches
(46 x 36 x 13cm)

Materials
35 yards (32m) or
2 pounds (907g) of
hand-dyed merino
wool roving

Tools
Scissors

Felting needle

Gauge
1.5 stitches and 2 rows equals 4 inches (10cm).

This project was made with 1 ball of UrbanGypZ hand-dyed roving in Periwinkle Grey, 35 yards (32m).

Pet bed

After knitting a rectangle, you'll pick up and bind off stitches to make the bed's sides. Loop the tails through the corners and then tighten them to form a basket.

How to make

Base

1 Cast on 6 stitches.

2 Arm knit 6 rows.

3 Bind off all the stitches.

Sides

Edgings are worked one at a time along each edge of the bed base.

1 To make the first edging, pick up 4 center stitches along the bind-off edge of the knitted base, skipping the first and last stitches. Bind off these 4 stitches, leaving at least an 8-inch-long (20cm) tail from the last bind-off stitch.

2 To make the next edging, pick up 4 center stitches along the cast-on edge of the knitted base, skipping the first and last stitches. Bind off these 4 stitches, leaving at least an 8-inch-long (20cm) tail.

3 To make the side edgings, pick up 3 stitches centered along one side of the base. Bind off these 3 stitches, leaving at least an 8-inch-long (20cm) tail.

Don't worry about shaping this bed—your pet will stretch it to his or her liking.

4 Pick up 3 stitches along the other side edge of the base. Bind off these 3 stitches, leaving at least an 8-inch-long (20cm) tail from the last bind-off stitch.

Continued

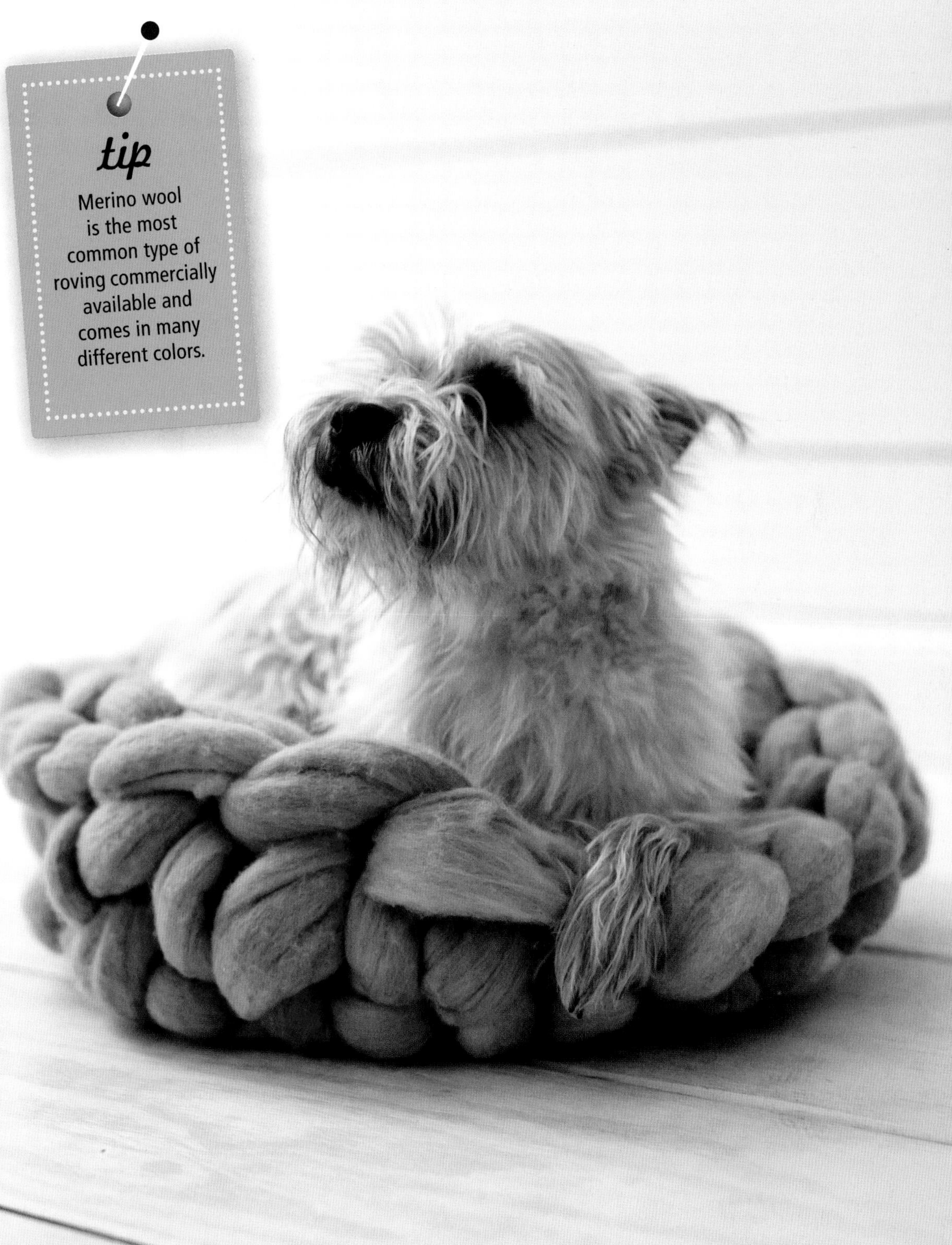

tip

Merino wool is the most common type of roving commercially available and comes in many different colors.

Finish

Refer to Figure 1 as you work. (It doesn't matter whether the stockinette side faces up.) Using the 8-inch-long (21cm) bind-off tails, connect the two sides of each corner together by looping the tail through the first stitch of the connecting side piece and then tucking the tail back into the last bind-off stitch on the tail side. This creates a seamless edge to the bind off.

Weave in all the ends. Shape the bed so the stockinette side is what's visible inside the bed. If desired, needle felt the ends of the roving for a more secure connection.

See the Needle Felting Roving section for more specific instructions.

Merino roving is exceptionally comfy and snuggly—upon discovering this bed, your pet will claim it immediately.

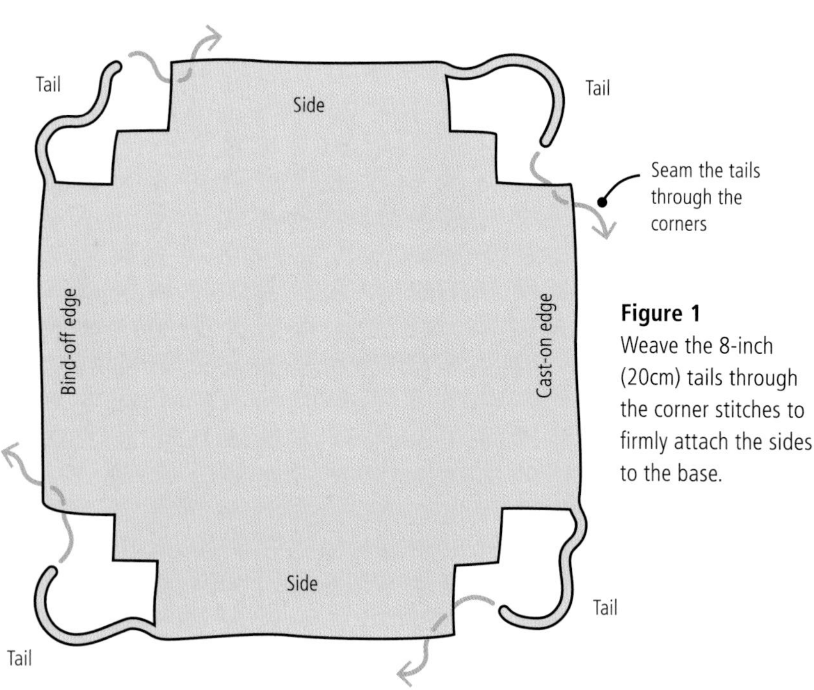

Figure 1
Weave the 8-inch (20cm) tails through the corner stitches to firmly attach the sides to the base.

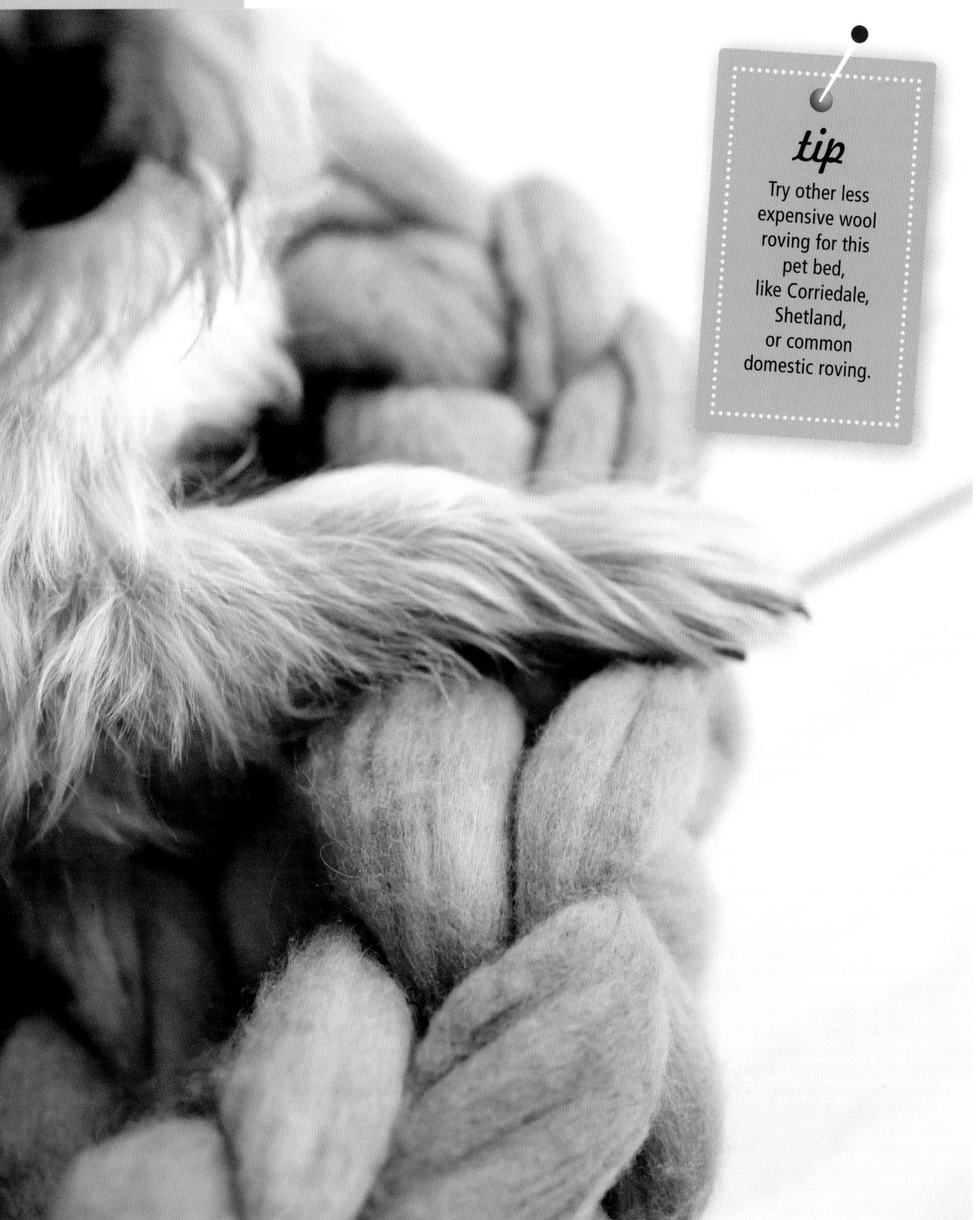

tip

Try other less expensive wool roving for this pet bed, like Corriedale, Shetland, or common domestic roving.

tip
Because this beanbag has several different components, you don't need to make it in one sitting.
5

Essential information

Difficulty level
Moderate

Time to make
5 hours

Finished size
24 x 24 x 44 inches
(61 x 61 x 110cm)

Materials
657 yards (601m) of 5mm polyester cord, with 3 strands held together

Three buttons: 1.5-inch (4cm) in diameter

One lighter

Two rectangles of fabric for the inner bag: 45 x 25 inches (114 x 64cm) each

Sewing thread to match the inner casing fabric

One 24-inch (61cm) zipper

Filling: 2.5 to 5 cubic feet (.07 to .14cbm) of feathers, polyester fiber, beanbag balls, etc.

Tools
Scissors

Pinking shears

Sewing needle

Sewing machine

Gauge
3 stitches and 5 rows equals 4 inches (10cm).

This project was made with 3 balls of polyester cord in gray, 219 yards (200m).

Beanbag

This beanbag has an unusual shape—the closed ends are perpendicular to each other, not parallel. Hypoallergenic polyester cord is ideal for this project.

How to make

Beanbag

1 Prepare 3 separate balls of cord—each 219 yards (200m) long. Cut 3 yards (3m) of cord from each ball. Set them aside to use to seam the beanbag sides together.

2 Cast on 18 stitches.

3 Arm knit until you run out of cord, ending with a full row. The piece should measure approximately 48 inches (122cm) long.

4 Fold the bind-off edge to meet the cast-on edge, with the right side facing out. (The fold will be the bottom edge of the finished cover.) Use a whip stitch to seam both sides of the beanbag while holding together all three of the 3-yard (3m) cords set aside earlier. Make sure the ends of the cords are properly knotted to the piece so they don't slip loose later.

5 Sew buttons to the right side of the open top edge. Fold the piece so the side seams are one above the other and run along the middle of the work instead of the edges. Evenly space the buttons before attaching them. Sew on the first one along one seam line, with the others about 4 inches (10cm) from it.

6 Weave in any loose ends. Carefully run the tips of each cord through the flame of the lighter to prevent fraying.

Attach the buttons evenly spaced along the opening after arranging the side seams so they're in the middle of the work and one atop the other.

Continued 

Inner casing

1 As shown in Figure 1, join the short ends of the pieces of fabric with the zipper. Make sure to center the zipper along the seam, leaving the fabric at either end unsewn.

2 Open the zipper. Turn the pieces of fabric inside out. Pin the long sides and then stitch them, as shown in Figure 2. Finish the seams with pinking shears to prevent unraveling.

3 Fold the fabric as shown in Figure 3, making sure the seams sewn in the previous step are no longer on the sides but are along the center. Stitch closed the short open end. Finish the seams with pinking shears and then turn the casing right side out.

4 Stuff the casing with your chosen filling and then zip the casing closed, as shown in Figure 4.

Finish

Place the filled casing into the knitted beanbag and then button the beanbag to close it. The buttons can go through any corresponding stitch.

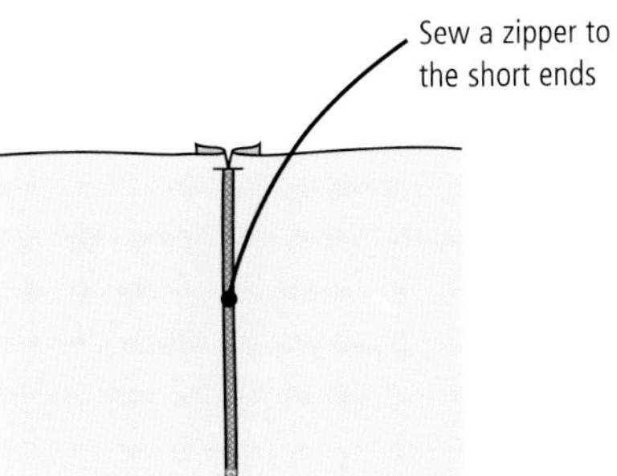

Figure 1 Use a ruler to ensure you center the zipper along the seam.

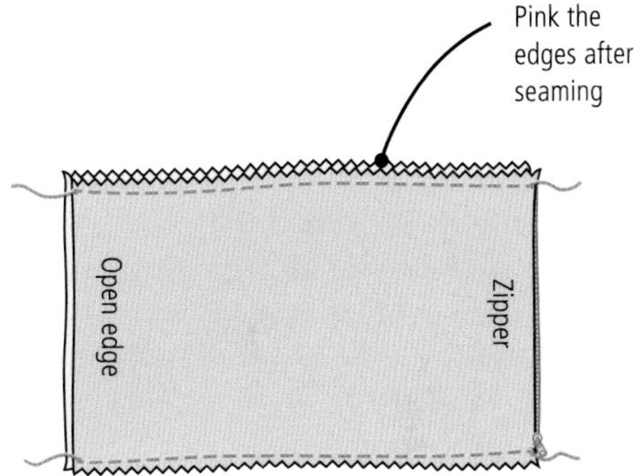

Figure 2 Make sure to open the zipper before seaming the side edges.

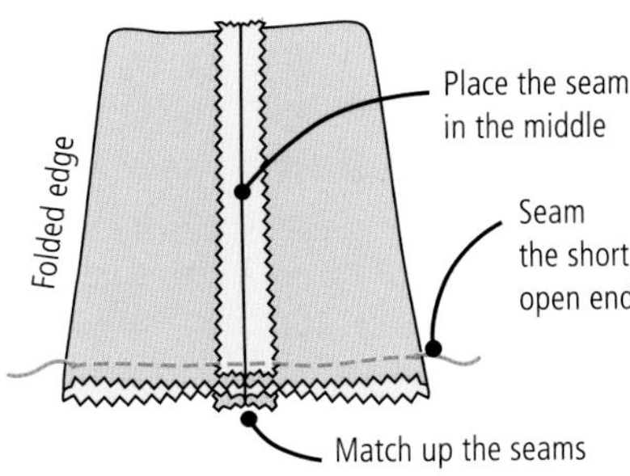

Figure 3 Fold the fabric so the side seams meet in the middle.

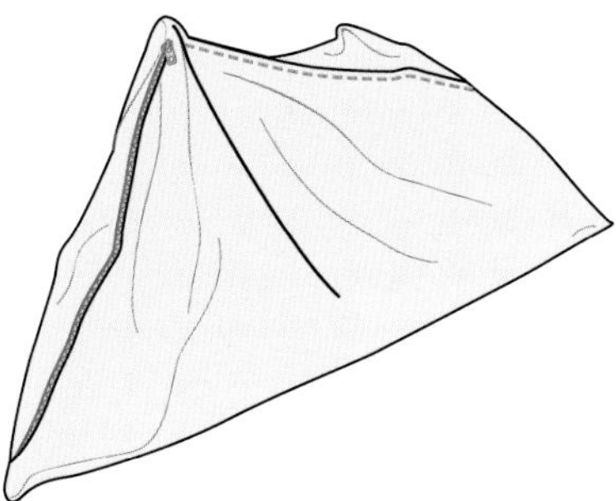

Figure 4 Turn the casing inside out, filling it with your chosen material before putting the casing inside the beanbag.

Essential information

Difficulty level
Moderate

Time to make
3 hours

Finished size
44 x 44 inches
(112 x 112cm)

Materials
Color A: 88 yards (81m) of super bulky yarn, with 3 strands held together

Color B: 176 yards (161m) of super bulky yarn, with 3 strands held together

Color C: 176 yards (161m) of super bulky yarn, with 3 strands held together

Tools
Scissors

Gauge
2 stitches and 3.75 rows equals 4 inches (10cm).

This project was made with:
2 skeins of Premier Craft-Tee Yarn in Dark Grey Shades, 88 yards (81m).

2 skeins of Premier Craft-Tee Yarn in Light Blue Shades, 88 yards (81m).

1 skein of Premier Craft-Tee Yarn in Dark Blue Shades, 88 yards (81m).

Concentric squares rug

This project has you knitting in all directions. After making a central square in one color, you'll rotate the piece several times to add stitches in a different color.

How to make

Color A: Center square

1 Cast on 5 stitches with color A.

2 Arm knit 6 rows.

3 Bind off all the stitches.

Color B: Middle square

1 Pick up the stitches for Side 1 as follows: Turn the piece 90°. Using color B, pick up and arm knit 6 stitches along the edge of the color A square.

2 Arm knit 6 rows.

3 Bind off all the stitches.

4 Pick up the stitches for Side 2 as follows: Turn the piece 90°. Using color B, pick up and arm knit 8 stitches along the color B section just worked and along the edge of the color A square.

5 Arm knit 6 rows.

6 Bind off all the stitches.

7 Pick up the stitches for Side 3 as follows: Turn the piece 90°. Using color B, pick up and arm knit 8 stitches along the edge of the color B section and the color A square.

8 Arm knit 6 rows.

9 Bind off all the stitches.

10 Pick up the stitches for Side 4 as follows: Using color B, pick up and arm knit 18 stitches along the color B strip, the color A square, and the color B strip.

11 Arm knit 6 rows.

12 Bind off all the stitches.

The log cabin knitting technique builds on a central square, allowing you to add flourishes once you construct that center square.

Continued

This project will give you ample opportunity to practice several arm knitting techniques, including changing colors.

Color C: Outer square

1 Pick up the stitches for Side 1 as follows: Turn the piece 90°. Using color C, pick up and arm knit 18 stitches along the edge of the color B square.

2 Arm knit 6 rows.

3 Bind off all the stitches.

4 Pick up the stitches for Side 2 as follows: Turn the piece 90°. Using color C, pick up and arm knit 6 stitches along the edge of the color C section and 18 stitches along the edge of the color B square.

5 Arm knit 6 rows.

6 Bind off all the stitches.

7 Pick up the stitches for Side 3 as follows: Turn the piece 90°. Using color C, pick up and arm knit 6 stitches along the edge of the color C section and 18 stitches along the edge of the color B square.

8 Pick up the stitches for Side 4 as follows. Using color C, pick up and arm knit 30 stitches along the color C strip, the color B square, and the color C strip.

9 Arm knit 6 rows.

10 Bind off all the stitches.

11 Weave in and trim all the ends.

tip
You can always experiment with other yarns and fewer or more colors depending on your confidence and ability level.

tip

Orient all the side panels in the same direction so they'll stretch at the same rate and stay the same size once they're assembled.

Essential information

Difficulty level
Moderate

Time to make
1 hour

Finished size
14.5 x 14.5 x 14.5 inches (37 x 37 x 37cm)

Materials
99 yards (91m) of super bulky netted acrylic-blend yarn

Cube-shaped footstool: 14 x 14 x 14 inches (36 x 36 x 36cm)

Tools
Scissors

Gauge
1.75 stitches and 1.5 rows equals 4 inches (10cm).

This project was made with 6 balls of Premier Yarns Couture Jazz in Slate, 16 yards (15m).

The footstool fabric should show through the stitches of this top panel more than the side panels.

Footstool cover

This cover can quickly add texture to humdrum furniture. Its large stitches serve as the attachments—hook a corner stitch under the corresponding footstool leg.

How to make

Top panel

1 Cast on 8 stitches.

2 Starting with a knit stitch, alternate 1 knit stitch and 1 purl stitch, working all the stitches across.

3 Repeat step 2 seven times (for a total of 8 rows).

4 Bind off all the stitches.

Side panels

Repeat the steps for the top panel four more times to make 4 side panels.

Assemble

1 Working on a flat surface, arrange the panels as shown in Figure 1, with the right sides facing up.

Be sure all the side panels face in the right direction (the bind-off edge is the top edge) to ensure the side seams remain the same size when stitched.

Attach the side panels to the top panel by using a mattress stitch.

2 Position the cover on the stool. Stitch the side seams along the stool's corners by using a mattress stitch.

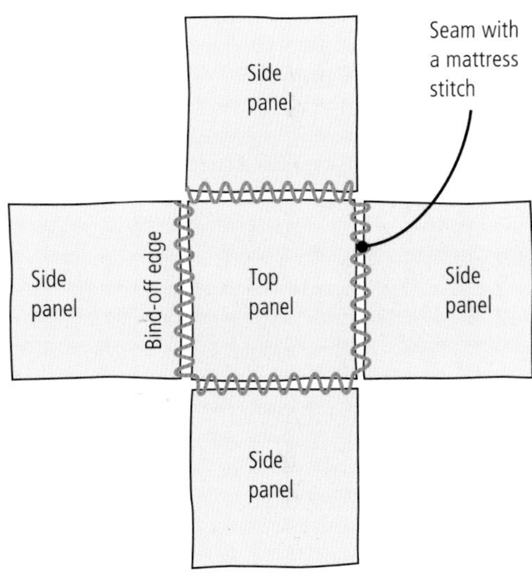

Figure 1 Arrange the panels with their right sides facing up, as shown here.

Add a whimsical touch by working each panel in a different color—making this a perfect accent piece.

Essential information

Difficulty level
Moderate

Time to make
3 hours

Finished size
42 x 60 inches (107 x 152cm)

Materials
165 yards (151m) of jumbo netted acrylic-blend yarn

Tools
Scissors

Gauge
2 stitches and 3.75 rows equals 4 inches (10cm).

This project was made with 10 skeins of Premier Yarns Couture Jazz in Olive, 16.5 yards (15m).

Textured throw

You'll alternate knit rows with a few purl rows to create a reversible throw that looks almost horizontally ribbed. Netted yarn lends more loft—and more warmth.

How to make

Throw

1 Cast on 24 stitches.

2 Arm knit 4 rows.

3 Purl 2 rows.

4 Repeat steps 2 and 3 five more times.

5 Arm knit 4 rows.

6 Bind off all the stitches.

7 Weave in and trim all the ends.

Alternating knit and purl stitches creates a throw that's not only beautiful and warm but also durable.

Probably the hardest aspect to this project is choosing which room or piece of furniture you'll accent with this throw. Move it around your living space as needed—you'll find it can fit anywhere.

tip

Knit this throw in two different colors for a great color block scheme.

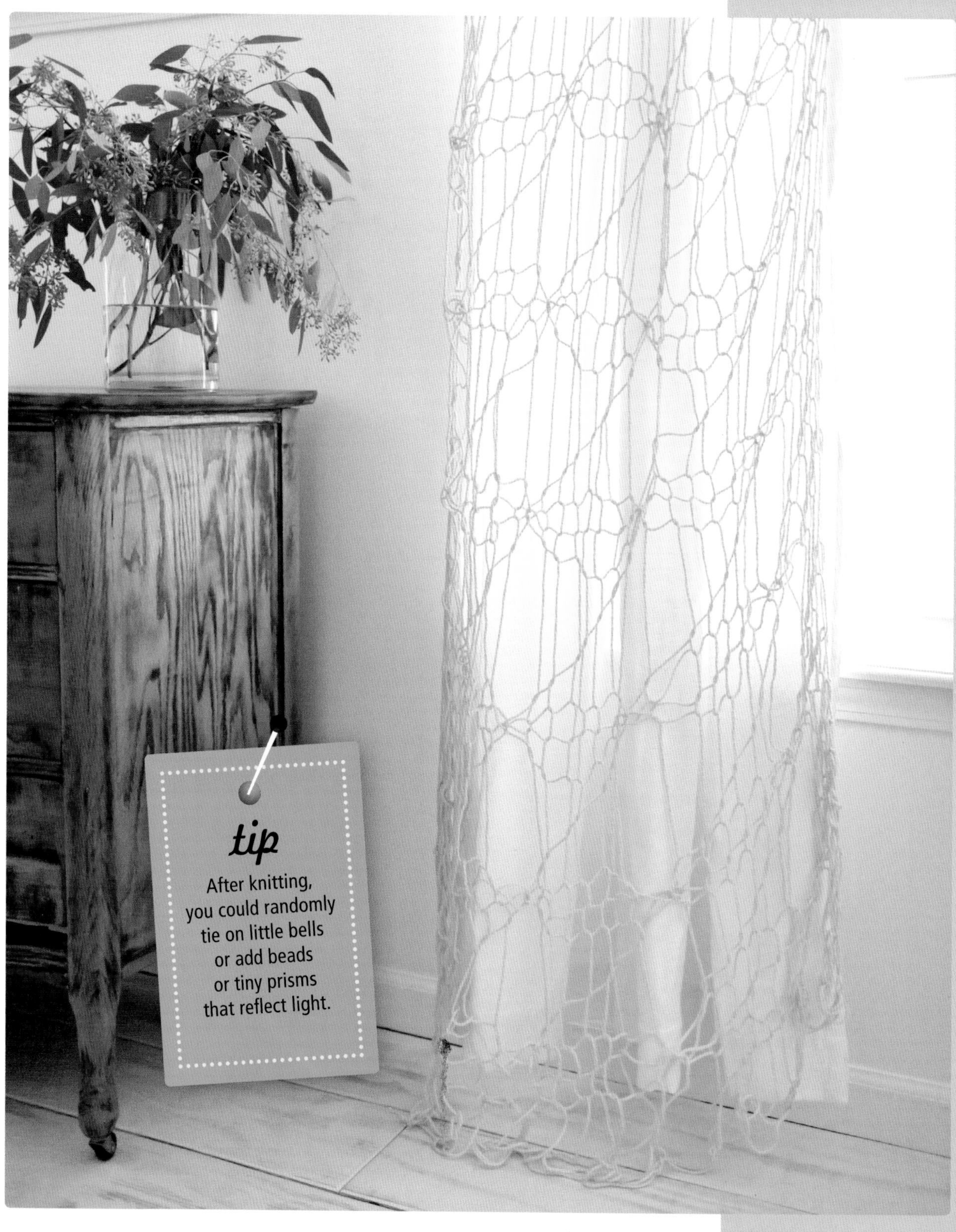
tip
After knitting, you could randomly tie on little bells or add beads or tiny prisms that reflect light.

Essential information

Difficulty level
Moderate

Time to make
2½ hours

Finished size
36 x 84 inches
(91 x 213cm)

Materials
150 yards (137m) of 100% worsted weight cotton yarn

Thread to match the chosen yarn color

Solid-colored sheer curtain to match the yarn color: 50 x 84 inches
(127 x 213cm)

Tools
Sewing needle

Straight pins

Scissors

Gauge
2 stitches and 2 rows equals 4 inches (10cm).

This project was made with 1 skein of Blue Sky Alpacas Worsted Cotton in Bone, 150 yards (137m).

Lacy curtain

Inspired by 1970s macramé, this airy curtain has a delicate pattern. Putting a solid-colored sheer curtain behind the knitting allows its lacy effect to stand out visually.

How to make

Curtain

1 Cast on 23 stitches loosely.

2 Arm knit for 4 rows.

3 Purl 1 row.

4 *Knit 2 stitches together, yarn over; repeat from * to the last stitch and then knit the last stitch.

(To perform a yarn over, place the working yarn behind the arm holding the stitches and then immediately bring the yarn up, over, and around to the front.

This wraps it partially around your wrist from back to front.

You can then simply continue working as described in these instructions.)

5 Arm knit 1 row.

6 Purl 1 row.

7 Repeat the previous 8 rows three more times for a total of 24 rows.

8 Bind off all the stitches.

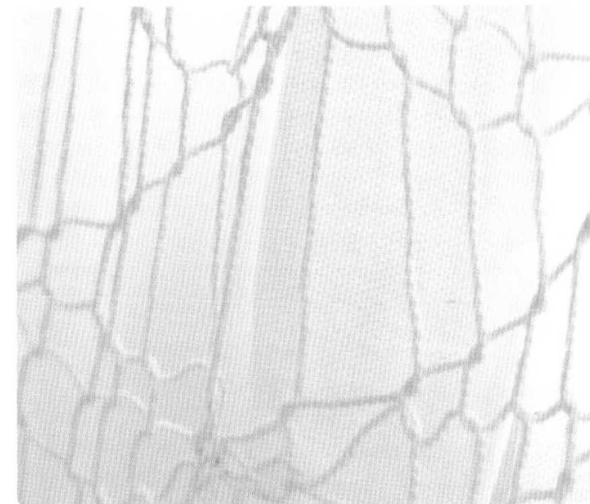

The yarn over technique creates an extra loop on your arm and results in a deliberate hole in the knitting. That creates the larger stitches.

Assemble

Spread the cast-on end of the piece flat on your work surface. Put the sheer panel face down on the curtain, arranging it evenly and aligning the top and side edges of both curtains. Pin them together, and working with each cast-on stitch, use the needle and thread to tack the cast-on end to the curtain.

Contributors

Stacey Budge-Kamison

Stacey Budge-Kamison is a fiber artist with a hand-crafted yarn business (UrbanGypZ.com) that specializes in edgy yarns and fibers for knitters, crocheters, weavers, and handspinners—with a focus on sustainable fibers and unexpected colorways. Stacey's studio is located in Raleigh, North Carolina, where she lives with her husband, two cats, and two dogs.

Mari Chiba

Mari Chiba started knitting while serving in Armenia as a Peace Corps volunteer. During the long, cold winters, she'd knit herself a blanket to keep warm. This led her to start designing knitting patterns. Mari has had designs published in *Twist Collective*, *Knitscene*, *Interweave Knits*, *Knitty*, and many other publications. You can follow her adventures in knitting and designing on her blog at mariknits.com.

Jennifer Dickerson

Jennifer Dickerson is a freelance writer, knitting and crochet pattern designer, and all-around craft enthusiast. She authors the popular Fiber Flux blog (FiberFluxBlog.com), sharing patterns, articles, book and yarn reviews, and tutorials. Jennifer also teaches crochet and knitting techniques on her growing YouTube channel. Jennifer is the author of *Mini Flower Loom Crafts: 18 Super Simple Projects* and contributed designs to *American Gift Knitting* and *Knitting 2014 Day-to-Day Calendar*. She designs regularly for *I Like Crochet* magazine, and she was named a top blogger by Prime Publishing in 2012, 2013, 2014, and 2015.

Haven Evans

Haven Evans lives in Pennsylvania and is a busy mother of three who works from home full time. She recently discovered that arm knitting is a fun and easy way to de-stress at the end of the day, and she has since pursued this hobby with enthusiasm.

Ashley Little

Ashley Little is a craft writer and editor by day and a serial crafter by night. Her blog TheFeistyRedhead.com explores knitting, crocheting, sewing, and crafting, and it includes her own original patterns and reviews. Ashley's also a regular contributing writer for *Craftsy* (craftsy.com), and she authored *Chunky Knits*.

Rugilė Mickevičiūtė

Rugilė Mickevičiūtė hails from Lithuania and has always been driven by the desire to create attractive things. She has found that her true calling is to craft items that make people's homes cozy and comfortable. She likes objects that are exclusive, unique, and authentic, and she wants her own designs to reflect this attitude. Rugilė loves soft shapes and materials, large spaces, and low furniture, so it's no surprise she makes chunky Scandinavian-style poufs, beanbags, and pillowcases in various colors, as showcased on her website puffchic.com. She sells her creations on Etsy at etsy.com/shop/Puffchic.

Emilie Odeile and Ken Chapin

Emilie Odeile and Ken Chapin are the team behind a business called Intreccio. This Italian word means to weave together, interlace, or intertwine, and it perfectly describes the work Emilie and Ken are doing at their design studio located at the base of one of Colorado's highest peaks. Emilie loves to knit, and Ken's pretty happy in the wood shop. They've combined her many years of designing unique knitwear for private and celebrity clients with his artistic vision and masterful use of tools to create a full collection of giant knitting needles, a growing selection of patterns, and a vibrant community of giant knitters. You can see more of their work at etsy.com/shop/Intreccio.

Acknowledgments

The publisher is grateful to the following companies for contributing yarns for some of the projects in this book: Cloudborn Fibers, Lion Brand Yarns, Plymouth Yarn, and Red Heart.

Thanks to Ashley Little, the consultant who wrote the "Materials, tools, and techniques" section.

Special thanks to Grayson Davis, Philippa Nash, Gina Rodgers, Lexy Scheele, Anissa Zajac, and Everly Zajac for modeling the projects as well as Lindsay Dobbs for modeling the techniques.

And a big round of applause (and a few yummy treats and gentle caresses) for Rocky—that little pooch who turned into a supermodel when the camera pointed at him.

Publisher Mike Sanders
Associate Publisher Billy Fields
Acquisitions Editor Nathalie Mornu
Development Editor Christopher Stolle
Technical Editor Rita Greenfeder
Cover Designer Harriet Yeomans
Book Designer Hannah Moore
Art Director Becky Batchelor
Photographers Katherine Scheele (projects)
and Becky Batchelor (techniques)
Stylist Anissa Zajac
Illustrator Philippa Nash
Prepress Technician Brian Massey
Proofreader Monica Stone

First American Edition, 2016
Published in the United States by DK Publishing
6081 E. 82nd Street, Indianapolis, Indiana 46250

16 17 18 19 10 9 8 7 6 5 4 3 2 1
001–295789–November/2016

Published in the United States by Dorling Kindersley Limited.
ISBN: 978-1-4654-5438-6
Library of Congress Catalog Card Number: 2016938283

Printed in China